marketing communications

marketing communications

AN INTEGRATED APPROACH

third edition

P R Smith with **Jonathan Taylor**

KOGAN PAGE

P R Smith:
To my mother, Una
'... to free the breath from its restless tides...'
(Kahlil Gibran)

First edition published in 1993, reprinted 1993, reprinted 1994 (twice), reprinted with revisions 1995, reprinted 1996, reprinted 1997. Second edition published in 1998, reprinted 1999. Third edition published in 2002

Kogan Page Limited
120 Pentonville Road
London N1 9JN
UK

Kogan Page US
22 Broad Street
Milford CT 06460
USA

British Library Cataloguing in Publication Data

A CIP record for this book is available from the British Library.

ISBN 0 7494 3669 7

Typeset by Saxon Graphics Ltd, Derby
Printed and bound in Great Britain by Bell & Bain Ltd, Glasgow

Contents

vi ▍ Contents

Foreword

Marketing communications is becoming more integrated! Whether you are a businessperson determined to obtain the maximum effectiveness from a limited promotional budget or a student coming to grips with all the different promotional elements in a marketing mix, it is important to make sense of the total process. It will only be possible to do so if marketing communications is seen as an integrated process.

The publisher of this best-selling book is launching a third edition with the introduction of a new author, Jonathan Taylor, who has joined with P R Smith to bring a fresh and practical insight to the development of marketing communications thinking and planning.

Jonathan's wealth of experience of working with blue-chip clients in leading advertising agencies such as Leo Burnett, Gold Greelees Trott and Young & Rubicam provides great support to Paul's knowledge and insight of marketing communications planning.

The joint authors bring to the writing of this book a valuable blend of their wide-ranging and up-to-date client experience, and the ability to deliver teaching and learning that is fun and insightful for their students at Guildhall University and the University of North London.

Although the logic of an integrated approach is obvious, it is not easy to achieve, either theoretically or practically. Despite this inherent difficulty, Smith and Taylors' third edition demonstrates the potential of an integrated approach to marketing communications in a very clear and enjoyable manner.

Advertising has up until now dominated much promotional thinking and teaching, partly because it is the promotional form that is most obvious to us every day and partly because it often accounts for the largest proportion of the promotional budget. Increasingly, however, below-the-line activities have become more important. Sales promotion and point of sale have vigorous roles to play; direct marketing has grown strongly and public relations has increasingly become a separate discipline with its own agencies and academic courses. The Internet and e-marketing are making a dramatic impact on the world of marketing communications planning. Internal marketing, the art of persuading an organization's own employees to adopt a marketing orientation, is still in its infancy. All these separate elements must be integrated together.

However, the academic world has not yet provided a sufficiently strong theoretical framework either to support a totally integrated approach to the study of marketing communications or to assist practitioners' valuable work already carried out in the field of consumer behaviour and organizational behaviour, which rightly underpins promotional decisions.

The term 'marketing communications' is neither well known nor widely understood. The number of people with the title 'Marketing Communications Manager', although growing, is still very limited. In my experience as Chairman of Ogilvy Group, one of the UK's leading integrated communication agencies, it is academics who are more comfortable with the term, but in the United States 'marketing communications' is a preferred term among marketing practitioners.

Whatever the precise market situation, this lack of clarity only adds weight to the proposition that marketing communications must become more integrated and better understood both academically and in business. By 'integrated', I mean that all the various elements of promotion devoted to informing, persuading or inducing action from a range of target audiences must be studied, analyzed, planned and implemented in a coordinated and effective manner. This is an extremely difficult process. It presupposes that all the elements are individually understood and that their effects can be reasonably predicted.

I warmly endorse the third edition of this best-selling book by European authors. It provides a comprehensive framework to enable the reader to better understand the individual contribution and the collective combination of the elements involved. There is a new and varied range of excellent case studies, from Lucozade to Gatwick Express to Talisker whisky! All readers should be able to learn a lot from reading how these consumer and business-to-business companies developed integrated marketing communications that have worked in the market.

In my various senior management roles within the world of communications over many years, I have encouraged such integration. I therefore commend to the reader this approach to marketing communications, whether they be a student getting to grips with the subject or a practitioner with a limited promotional budget.

Paul Simons
Chairman & Chief Executive, Ogilvy & Mather UK

Acknowledgements

Many friends, colleagues, business partners and students have helped in the development of the material in this third edition. Our thanks are extended to:

Jim Addison, CPM Sales Promotion
Joe Agius, McGregor Cory
Will Arnold-Baker, Duckworth Finn Grubb Waters
Patricia Bacon, Henley Centre
Melissa Bacuzzi, Bristows
Louise Barfield, Tutssels
Ross Barr, BMP DDB
Martin Bartle, Direct Marketing Association
Sally Anne Bennett, Pretty Polly
Quentin Bell, QBO
Michael Blakstad, Workhouse
Alan Briefel, Stratcom
Hugh Cameron, Duckworth Finn Grubb Waters
Vicky Carrell, Ogilvy & Mather
Kevin Clarke, BBH
John Cooper, Institute of Sales Promotion
Caroline Crawford, ASA
Julian Cummins, Avista
Phil Danter, Media Planning

Anna Davies, Nomadic displays
Geoff Dawson, Lykes Lines
Catherine Derbyshire, Admap
Jane Dickinson, Bamber Forsyth
John Farrell, DMB&B
Lisa Foster, MORI
Clare Fuller, Bamber Forsyth
Les Geary, Nissan Motor (GB)
Steve Grime, Mitchell Patterson Grime Mitchell
Robin Hall, CPM Field Marketing
Margery Hancock, BJM
Emma Hanson, Media Planning
Neil Hegarty, BMP Optimum
Nick Hewison, Nestlé
Susan Holder, Future Featuring
Shirley Horn, Hewlett-Packard
Craig Houston, NRS
Alan Hyde, Harrison Cowley
Roger Hyslop, The Triangle Group
Michael Ingram, The Ingram Company
Kirsten Jenson, RSCG Conran Group
Allison Jones, Miller Shandwick
Margaret-Anne Lawlor, Dublin Institute of Technology
Simon Mahoney, SMP
Audrey Mandela, Consultant
David Marshall, Shell UK
Steve Martin, Adidas
James Mathewson, Shrinking Earth
Ian Maynard, RSCG Euro
Harry McDermott, Exhibition Surveys
Paul McFarland, Goldhawk
Gerry McGovern, NCLA
Mike McGuire, Procter & Gamble
Claire Mitchell, Natural History Museum
Ian Mortimer, Happy Tuesday
John Nolan, The Collage Shop
Bob Offen, Media Planning
Paul O'Sullivan, Dublin Institute of Technology
David Poole, DP&A
Alan Pulford, Manchester Metropolitan University

Bill Reed, Canning International Management Development
Dennis Sandler, Pace University
Amy Silverston, Grey Direct
Clodagh Smith, Beiersdorf
Conor Smith, Snap Printing
Rory Smith, We Serve Homes
Ross Sleight, BMP Interaction
Dave Stewart, DVA
Rex Sweetman, Muscatt Sweetman
Alan Topalian, Alto Design
Glenn Tutssel, Tutssels
Jon Vocal, craik Jones
Linda Wallace, Colgate Palmolive
Mike West, Be Strategic
Gerald Whiting, Waitrose
Geoff Wicken, TGI
Andy Wilson, ITC

Thanks also to our marketing colleagues, both past and present, at the London Guildhall University and the Universities of North London and Strathclyde.

Paul's particular thanks to Jeremy Baker, Andy Inglis, Owen Palmer, Mark Wronski and Chris Berry. Constant inspiration from my brother, Rory, and the brother Mullarkey, not to mention the lovely Beverley, whose patient support never ceases to amaze me.

Jonathan's particular thanks to Keith Crosier, Jack Bureau, Prosper Riley-Smith, Michael Yorke, Emmanuel Ohehe, Annette Mencke and the students of MT 206. Thanks also to Gill, Katharine and Sophie for giving me the space to add this string to my bow and to Joe Sample and other Jazz FM artistes for inspiration.

How to use this book

This book should not be read from cover to cover but rather it should be used as a reference when addressing a particular aspect of marketing communications. The integrated nature of the subject does, however, refer the reader to other chapters and sections which are relevant to the particular area of interest. The anecdotal style, examples, cases, questions, key points and sections have been carefully structured so that the reader can dip into an area of interest, absorb the information and cross-refer if required. This allows the reader to extract specific answers quickly and easily. This book is designed to entertain as well as inform and so it is hoped that when dipping into a particular area, the reader will be lured into reading more.

Part I gives a general introduction to marketing, the marketing communications mix, theories of communication and buyer behaviour, and shows how to write a marketing communications plan using the now refined system called SOSTAC®. This first part of the book continues to build a background to marketing communications by looking at what marketing research can and cannot provide, how to work with agencies and consultancies of all types, understanding the media, moving with the changing business environment and, finally, international marketing communications. Part 2 covers specific marketing communication tools which marketing professionals have to manage at some time or other. These include selling and sales management; advertising; sales promotion; direct marketing; publicity and public relations; sponsorship; exhibitions; packaging; merchandising; word of mouth; e-marketing; and, finally, corporate identity and image.

The case studies at the end of each chapter in Part 2 (and also chapters 2, 5, 7 and 9 in Part 1) have been carefully selected to show a range of different types and sizes of organizations

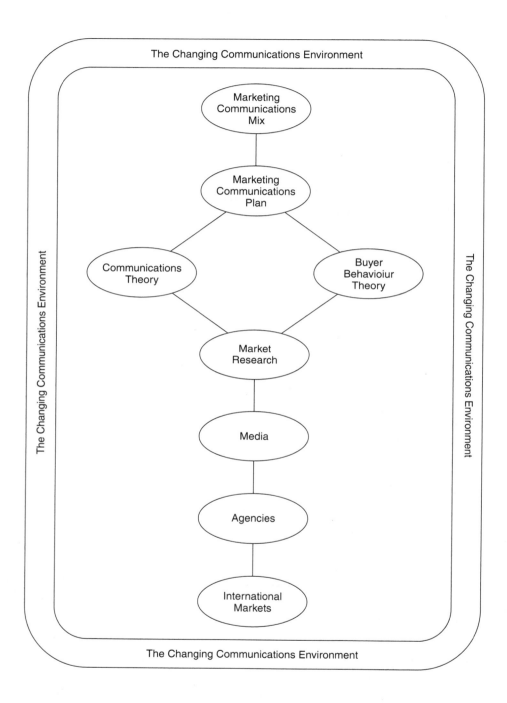

Figure 0.1   Part One: Background to the communications process

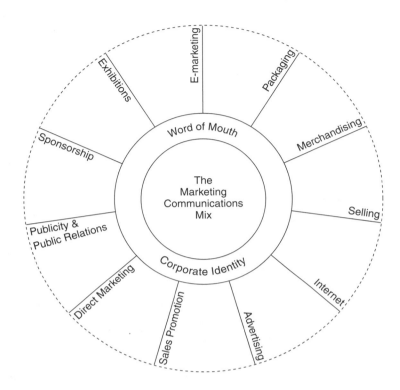

Figure 0.2 Part Two: The marketing communications tools

using various communications tools across a range of different industries and markets. Materials are drawn from both individuals (with marketing communications budgets of only £500) and organizations (with budgets of £2 billion). In this way, the book should prove useful to anyone interested, or working, in marketing.

The reader will discover that all of the communication tools can and should integrate with each other, as shown in Figure 0.2 and explained at the end of Chapter 1.

It is therefore sometimes difficult to separate and categorize an activity as being one type of tool or another. For example, direct marketing and sales promotions should probably be called 'direct promotions' since they both more than likely involve each other. The chapters are not listed in order of importance. Selling and sales management is not always included in a marketing communications budget but the salesforce is a potent form of communication and generally they (or the sales manager) report to the marketing manager. In fact it has been put to the top of the list because all the other chapters thereafter tend to lead into each other.

The successful application of the marketing communications mix is helped by an understanding of communication theory and buyer behaviour theory. Marketing research can provide some practical and specific answers to the questions that the theories generate. This provides the building blocks for the marketing communications plan, which draws upon an understanding of how agencies operate and how different media work. The details of the plan are worked out within the sometimes complex, but always integrated, web of the marketing communications mix (see Figure 0.2). The changing marketing communications environment and international opportunities/threats constantly affect the whole marketing communications mix. The world has moved on since the second edition. Different organizations allocate the same communication tools to different departments/budgets, eg exhibitions may be seen to be part of public relations, although the sales team will man the stand and benefit from extra sales. Sponsorship is considered by some to be an extension of advertising, while others consider it to be part of PR. And no one is too sure about whose budget covers the Web site. Regardless of classifications, ownership and responsibilities, each tool must integrate with many others. The end of the opening chapter provides some guidance for those that are keen to integrate their communications.

We are always looking to update the material within the book and our readers are invited to contact us with any ideas, suggestions and contributions to the next edition. As our subject of marketing communications is ever changing, we are keen to keep the content fresh and lively.

Please e-mail the authors via Jonathan@mktgcomms.com and make regular visits to our Web site, on which we will develop supplementary materials and resources – an area for you to add your comments about how the book can be developed – you will find it at www.mktgcomms.com.

All lecturers who use this third edition can obtain a free CD ROM, which contains detailed PowerPoint slides on a chapter-by-chapter basis. Please e-mail amurphy@kogan-page.co.uk for your free CD ROM.

Part 1

The background to the communications process

1

Marketing and the integrated communications mix

The changing nature of marketing 3; The marketing mix 6; The communications mix 7; Mixing the communications mix 9; Integrating the communications mix – initial steps 13; Integrated marketing communications – the benefits 15; Integrated marketing communications – the barriers 16; Integrated marketing communications – the golden rules 18; Intensive marketing communications 19; Marketing mix must also be balanced and integrated 20; Appendix 1.1 21; Appendix 1.2: *Above the line and below the line 22*; Appendix 1.3: *Market structure (share, growth and concentration) 22*; *Resources available 25*; Appendix 1.4: *Integrated marketing communications – the cost-saving benefits 26*; Further reading 27; Further contacts 28

THE CHANGING NATURE OF MARKETING

Marketing and the marketing communications mix are changing. New insights, new tools, new opportunities and new challenges are emerging as we step into the 21st century. The world's six billion consumers and almost four hundred million business customers are becoming increasingly accessible. And so too are your customers… ready targets for new global competitors. New pressures also emerge as managers operate in delayered organizations, stripped of supporting services and yet freed from the quagmire of tier upon tier of management. This means more managers need to understand marketing which, itself, is changing.

Marketing has moved from 'customer acquisition' (winning new customers) through 'customer retention' (keeping customers for life) towards 'customer deselection' (dumping unprofitable customers while selectively seeking and keeping the more profitable ones). This is sometimes called 'adverse selection'. It is becoming obvious that some customers are promiscuous, non-loyal bargain hunters who exploit any sales promotion and move on to the next supplier as and when the next special offer appears. These customers cost a lot for very little return; in fact, most of them are unprofitable. Given that some estimates suggest that new customers cost five times more than existing customers or, put another way, selling to existing customers can be five times more profitable than winning new customers, you can see how it pays to know and love your customers, particularly the loyal and profitable ones. Some customers become loyal because they prefer your product or service, others want a stable relationship with one supplier, others spend more, pay more quickly, require less service. Although recovery strategies (for lost customers) are important, some defectors are not worth saving. Carefully designed customer selection strategies can leave the competition with nothing but undesirable customer segments to fight over.

Marketing is changing. New tools, such as data-mining (see page 379) and the much misunderstood on-line world, offer a host of dynamic opportunities beyond selling (see Chapter 20). Change is rampant, particularly in marketing. Even the traditional suppliers, or agencies, are changing. Apart from changing the services they offer, they are changing their names to reflect changes in the marketing services marketplace. Burson Marstellar, the world's biggest PR agency, has dropped 'Public Relations' from its name, and Saatchi and Saatchi has dropped 'advertising' from its name. Managers too have to change – to accept the need for 'lifelong learning', and continually update and improve themselves with new skills, new insights, new tools.

New insights – wired Barbies

By the year 2010, there will be more wired up Barbie dolls than Americans.

Nicholas Negroponte, Massachusetts Institute of Technology

Before looking at the marketing communications mix and the marketing mix, consider briefly marketing. A simple dictionary definition of marketing reveals: **Marketing**, *n., the business of moving goods from the producer to the consumer.* 'Goods' can be taken to mean goods or services. The Chartered Institute of Marketing in the UK defines marketing as: 'The management process responsible for identifying, anticipating and satisfying customer requirements profitably.' Some years ago the American Marketing Association spent time and effort considering the appropriateness and accuracy of their definition of marketing. Their new definition incorporated one major change – they took 'profit' out, possibly because it excluded the vast armies of marketing professionals who work for charities and other non-profit-making organizations. Perhaps the UK definition could replace 'profitably' with 'efficiently', or 'in a way that meets the organization's goals'? A simpler definition is 'marketing is the selling of goods that don't come back to people who do'. 'Goods that don't come back' emphasizes the importance of matching the promise (made by, say, the advertising or the packaging) with the reality of the product's or service's quality, ie the level of quality should match that which is advertised. In the long term it does not pay to cheat the customer.

Real marketing success depends on repeat business, and that is where 'people who do come back' embraces the customer's 'lifetime value' concept (see Chapter 13). Customers do not buy just one can of beans, one car, or one photocopying machine. They buy thousands of cans of beans, dozens of cars and dozens of photocopiers during their 'lifetime'. There the marketing challenge lies in attracting and retaining profitable customers efficiently. A move away from the 'one-off sales syndrome' allows marketing horizons to broaden to lifetime customers and lifetime strategies. And today marketers are really interested in separating unprofitable from profitable customers, so that those customers who really do contribute to the bottom line can be nurtured. Lifetime customers are built through strong relationships which, in turn, require relationship marketing skills. Another set of relationship skills is also emerging in the form of marketing marriages. Marketing marriages such as joint promotions, shared databases, shared distribution networks and strategic alliances offer new opportunities for existing markets but also offer new routes into global markets previously inaccessible because of an organization's limited resources.

Foul-smelling mountain – small portion of life

The tinned cat food market in the UK is huge. To put it in perspective imagine, if you can, the entire Albert Hall filled from floor to ceiling with cat food. Remove the shell of the building, like a giant jelly mould, to leave a quivering mountain of foul-smelling, jellied meat and you have a vivid picture of the amount of food that cats in the UK munch their way through every two months – amazing when you consider that only 23 per cent of homes in the UK have a cat.

Source: Ivan Pollard, Media Planning Director, BMP DDB Needham

Marketers must view customers as lifetime customers with lifetime values beyond short-term horizons.

THE MARKETING MIX

The marketing mix is essentially a conceptual framework which helps to structure the approach to each marketing challenge. There are many different approaches to the marketing mix, eg 4Ps, 5Ps and 7Ps. Canadian author Jerome McCarthy first called the 4Ps the marketing mix. Criticized by some as oversimplified and by others as outdated, the 4Ps nevertheless do provide a basic framework. These four ingredients (product, price, place/distribution and promotion/communication) can be mixed together in an infinite number of ways. Some argue that the most important P – people – is missing. This can be interpreted as customers or as staff. Although originally used by FMCG (fast-moving consumer goods) marketers, the 4Ps were also borrowed and used by service marketers (eg restaurants) until they developed the 7Ps. The additional Ps covered people (staff), physical evidence (eg buildings and uniforms) and processes (methods of producing, delivering and consuming the service). It is interesting to see how the FMCG marketers can now borrow the 7Ps.

In 1961, Albert Frey suggested that all the marketing mix variables could be categorized into just two groups: The Offering (product, packaging, service, brand and price) and The Methods/Tools (distribution channels, personal selling, advertising and sales promotion). Whichever approach you take, it is the combination of these components, and a fifth P, people (customers and competition), which are the basic building blocks of a marketing programme. The marketing mix variables are usually considered as internal variables over which a manager has control and makes decisions (albeit influenced by customers, competition and other external uncontrollable factors).

It is worth remembering that all of the marketing mix communicates. A poor-quality product or service generally says more to the user than any amount of advertising (see Chapter 19). Price communicates, eg high price sends a different message to low price, and price is used by many buyers as an indicator of quality. The place of purchase also communicates, eg an item purchased in Harrods has a different perceived value to an item purchased from a street stall. The fourth P, promotion, has its own mix of communication tools, which are sometimes called the promotions mix or the communications mix. This mix includes every communications tool that is available to the organization (see list in next section). The relation of the communications mix to the marketing mix is shown in Figure 1.1.

The fifth P, people, or staff, communicate, in fact create, a good or bad experience through the quality of service delivered at any particular time (see NatWest's 900 million brand moments on page 20). Physical evidence communicates as demonstrated by the physical presence, style, location and decoration of the Temple of Convenience Bar shown on page 8. It grabs attention, interest and, to some, creates the desire to enter and explore. Process, the final P, also communicates. If McDonald's process was slow, sloppy or dirty, it would send out negative messages to their customers and sales would suffer.

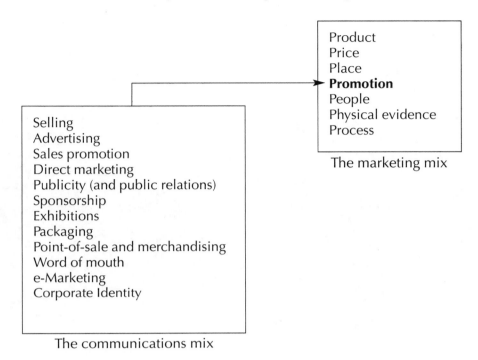

Figure 1.1 How the communication mix feeds into the marketing mix

THE COMMUNICATIONS MIX

Sometimes referred to as the promotional mix, the communications mix lists all of the communications tools available to a marketer:

1. Selling
2. Advertising
3. Sales promotion
4. Direct marketing
5. Publicity (and public relations)
6. Sponsorship
7. Exhibitions
8. Packaging
9. Point-of-sale and merchandising
10. Word of mouth
11. E-marketing
12. Corporate identity

Manchester's Temple of Convenience Bar – physical presence, style and location all communicate.

This list is not in any order of priority, since different industries lay different emphasis on certain communication tools, eg an FMCG (such as a tin of beans) manufacturer may consider advertising, packaging, sales promotion and point-of-sale to be the most important tools, while a heavy industrial machine manufacturer may lay emphasis on selling, exhibitions and word of mouth. The second part of this book devotes a chapter to each of the communication tools listed in the communications mix. The next couple of paragraphs clarify and explain the interpretation and categorization of the marketing communications mix, since many marketing professionals interpret or categorize them differently.

Direct marketing draws on, and integrates with, advertising and sales promotion, and includes direct response advertisements, direct mail and telemarketing/telesales. Chapter 13 focuses on direct mail and telemarketing/telesales. Publicity means positive editorial coverage in the media; it is not meant to include 'bad press'. It does include stunts, or events, as well as certain other techniques included in Chapter 14.

The marketing communications mix should, in one way, include employees and customers since 'word of mouth' can be extremely effective among their own networks. Their salaries and wages are not part of the communications budget but they are worth including in some of the communications activities that enhance the word-of-mouth process (see Chapter 19). Although selling is all about communicating, some companies choose to leave selling and sales management out of the communications budget and put the salesforce into their distribution plan instead. This makes sense, since one of the salesforce's main responsibilities is to service existing distribution channels and penetrate new ones. However, since face-to-face selling is a potent marketing communications tool (and expensive on a cost per thousand contacts basis), it is clearly included in the marketing communications mix.

It is worth remembering that customers and distributors are not the only target audience. There are other 'stakeholders' such as shareholders and employees who have a keen interest in the business. See the diverse range of audiences (stakeholders) with which wind-farm company Future Wind Partnership must communicate in order to grow clean energy (in Appendix 1.1).

MIXING THE COMMUNICATIONS MIX

Should more be spent on sales promotions than on advertising? What would happen if a company (like Heinz) switched all press, print and TV advertising over to direct mail? Or perhaps it should spend half on advertising and half on sales promotion and exclude publicity? Almost every promotional activity involves sacrificing something else. Advertising is still seen by many in the UK as the most effective way to nurture a brand's image over the long haul, whereas sales promotions tend to be seen as shorter-term, tactical, temporary sales boosters (although there are exceptions, where some companies actually try to develop strategic promotions that build on each other while strengthening brand values and customer loyalty). Professor Ehrenberg's Pan-European sales promotion research claimed that sales promotions had basically no positive effect on brand building, brand loyalty and repeat purchase patterns. This is not surprising, since the research focused mostly on price promotions (money-off discounts, etc). Price discounts dilute the brand franchise or the quality images of the brand. Endorsing this obvious logic, *International News* reported a change in the communications mix chosen by American companies:

> Many giant consumer good companies are saddled with huge levels of debt so, in category after category, brand managers are scrambling to boost quarterly sales instead of investing in image advertising to nurture brands for the long haul. To increase sales they are shifting marketing dollars from ads to promotions such as coupons, contests, sweepstakes and, because most promotions are placed locally, companies are shifting dollars from national to local media. Many experts believe that such strategies – carried to an extreme – run the risk of damaging valuable brand franchises that enable marketers to price their products at a premium.

A lot depends on the objectives and the specific response required. Building awareness requires advertising and PR, while brand switching requires some kind of integrated sales promotion initially supported by advertising or direct mail. There are always exceptions;

	Unawareness	Awareness	Acceptance	Preference	Insistence	Reassurance
Television	███████████▶					◆
Radio	███████████▶					◆
Posters	███████████▶					◆
National Press	███████	┈┈┈▶				◆
Business Press	████████████▶					◆
PR Editorials	███████		┈┈┈┈▶			◆
Company Magazines	┈┈┈	████████████▶				◆
Direct Mail	┈┈┈	████████████▶				◆
Database Marketing	┈┈┈	██████████	┈┈┈▶			◆
Literature		██████████	┈┈┈▶			◆
New Media (Internet)		██████████	┈┈┈▶			◆
Exhibitions & Seminars	┈┈┈	██████████	┈┈┈▶			◆
Sales Promotions	┈┈┈	██████████	┈┈┈▶			◆
Others			███████████▶			◆
Face-to-Face		┈┈┈	███████████▶			◆
After-Sales Support					██████████▶	◆
	Attention	Interest	Desire	Conviction	Action	Repeat Purchase

███████▶ Major contribution   ┈┈┈┈┈▶ Minor contribution

Source: Spira; reproduced with kind permission of Admap NTC Publications

Figure 1.2   The power of integration in business marcoms

some advertising and sales promotions are designed to create a database which in turn allows a dynamic dialogue and relationships to be nurtured. Communications need to flow to all the the stages through which a customer moves on his or her route towards making a purchase and subsequent repeat purchases. Figure 1.2 shows how certain communications tools (and specific media, eg TV versus press), within a category of communications tool (eg advertising) can be used to move customers through various stages of their buying process.

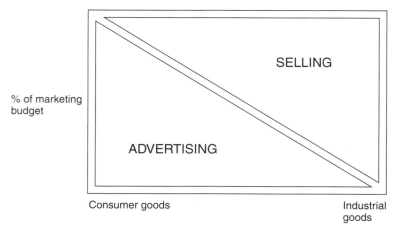

Figure 1.3   Type of product or service and the communications mix

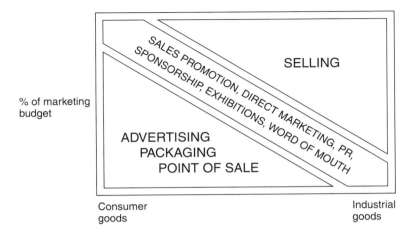

Figure 1.4   Type of product or service and the communications mix

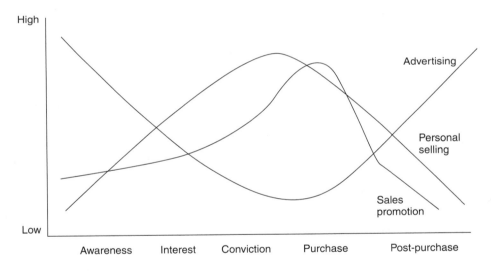

Figure 1.5   The relative effectiveness of communications tools

This is an oversimplification, as sales promotion, PR, direct mail, exhibitions and much more should be added in.

The problem is that all of the market does not move simultaneously through each stage; some customers move more slowly than others. This makes the marketing challenge a little bit more interesting. Another way of looking at it is through the purchaser's decision process. One model suggests that a purchaser first becomes aware, then interested, then is convinced, buys and eventually engages in post-purchase feelings and/or behaviour (see Figure 1.5). Different communications tools have varying levels of effectiveness at each stage of the buying process, eg advertising and PR (generating publicity) are very effective at raising awareness but not nearly as effective as personal selling when it comes to actually moving the customer towards making a purchase. Advertising does, however, provide reassurance after the purchase and thereby increases the likelihood of positive post-purchase behaviour such as repeat purchases. Sales promotions, on their own, are an expensive and less effective way of generating awareness but they can be highly effective in moving a customer from conviction to purchase.

Another dimension to be considered when choosing communications tools is the type of purchase, ie whether it is a high-involvement purchase or a low-involvement purchase. Chapter 4 deals with these in more detail, so suffice it to say here that high-involvement purchases are important purchases that are expensive, risky and require careful analysis before any purchase decision is made, eg a new computer system. Low-involvement purchases, on the other hand, are low-risk, frequently bought inexpensive purchases like a can of cola. This requires a mix of primarily heavy advertising and point-of-sale, as opposed to the purchase of a high-involvement item such as a house, which requires a mix primarily of personal selling and limited advertising.

Different blends (or mixes) of the marketing communications mix are required for different marketing strategies. Take 'push' and 'pull' strategies. A 'push strategy' is dependent on a strong salesforce supported by trade promotions which serve to 'push' the product hard into the distribution channels and on to the distributors' shelves. It is all about distribution penetration. A 'pull strategy' is more concerned with pulling the customers into the store/distributor and motivating them to 'pull' the product off the shelf. This requires an investment in advertising to create customer demand. Many retailers today want to be assured that a brand has comprehensive marketing support, eg advertising. In effect the 'pull' helps the 'push', since the advertising reassures the retailer that the stocks will move and this, in turn, makes the salesperson's 'push' that bit easier. Two of the biggest and most successful FMCG companies, Lever Brothers and Procter and Gamble, have different basic strategies here. Philip Kotler has reported that Lever Brothers emphasize a push strategy, while Procter and Gamble prefer a pull strategy. However, in the past two to three years both companies appear to have adopted a strategy that integrates a mix of both push and pull.

So type of product (industrial or consumer), specific objectives, type of buying situation, push and pull, all affect the shape of the communications mix. There are additional variables to consider. Some years ago research suggested that the optimum communications mix could be determined according to position in the market (market share), market growth and market concentration. Research by PIMS suggested that market leaders should spend 70 per cent of the total A&P budget (advertising and promotions – which included all communications tools other than salesforce costs) on advertising, while the numbers two and three brands should only spend somewhere between 50 per cent and 60 per cent on advertising. PIMS also suggested that the proportion of advertising spend should increase in declining markets and in high-growth markets the proportion spent on promotions (below the line – see Appendix 1.2) should increase. Advertise in declining markets, promote in growth markets. Finally, PIMS suggested that as markets concentrate, the proportion of advertising spend should reduce, while optimum profits are found in fragmented markets when the proportion of advertising takes almost 85 per cent of the total communications spend. Some marketing managers challenge these findings. Appendix 1. 3 explains them in more detail.

Ignoring the internal strategies, the actual proportion of real money spent on different elements of the communications mix (communications tools) appears to be changing. There seems to be a shift away from 'above the line' towards 'below the line' spending. Table 1.1 shows some recent UK estimates of how marketing budgets are being spent across the communications mix.

INTEGRATING THE COMMUNICATIONS MIX – INITIAL STEPS

Each element of the communications mix should integrate with other tools of the communications mix so that a unified message is consistently reinforced. Some major advertising campaigns are supported by PR activity, and many advertisements have press launches not for the product but for the advertisement itself. Thus publicity and advertising work together to create a bigger impact in a cost-effective way. Press launches and photo opportunities were seized on by the political parties when they released new advertisements during the 2001 UK general election. Many poster advertisements were officially unveiled by celebrities or senior politicians. The free media (editorial) coverage that followed was often greater than the coverage generated by advertising. Here, below the line (PR) supports above the line (advertising) activity.

Sales promotion, another below-the-line communications tool, is often tied in with, or supported by, advertising or PR or both. It is no use having a great sales promotion campaign if no one hears about it in the first place; so, instead of the product being advertised, it is the sales promotion that is advertised. Here, above the line supports the below-

Table 1.1 Estimates of the communications mix spend in the UK for 2000

Advertising	Selling	Sales promotion
£12B	£19B	£15B
PR and exhibitions	Direct marketing	
£3.5B	£9B	

Source: Advertising Association and industry estimates (NB Industry estimates have wide variations)

the-line activity. There are publicity opportunities that public relations professionals can exploit if they are briefed and integrated into the overall programme at an early enough stage. Some sales promotions get national coverage without any above-the-line support. A few years ago British Airways launched a sensational sales promotion when they announced free flights to anywhere in the world. The sales promotion was so newsworthy it hardly needed any advertising by the time the public relations people had maximized the editorial opportunities. The sales promotion also helped to build a database for future direct mail activities.

Many direct-response advertisements (with coupons or free-phone numbers) offer an incentive, premium, gift or sales promotion. The term 'direct promotion' succinctly combines direct marketing with sales promotion. Fully integrated hybrid marketing systems are looked at in more detail in Chapter 13. Many FMCG (such as groceries) sales promotions are also promoted on the product itself (on-pack promotion). A new pack or new sales promotion usually has to be brought to the attention of the retailer by the sales-force. They need to be fully briefed and may need new literature to leave with the retail buyers. In addition, new point-of-sale materials may be required to display and promote the sales promotion inside a retail outlet. A modified pack (carrying the on-pack promotion) has to be designed and produced. This means new stocks and so a properly coordinated team has to be briefed and ready to move into sometimes several hundred outlets within, say, 24 hours. This is generally too big a job for the regular salesforce, so it is sometimes supplemented by a team of merchandisers or field marketing team.

Pepsi page customers

Mountain Dew, a soft drink made by Pepsi, ran a promotion: in exchange for ten pack tops plus $20, consumers were sent a pager which has real street cachet in the US. Pepsi sent out thousands of these pagers to eager participants of the scheme and then proceeded to page them directly every week with special offers and promotions. As their consumers tended to be teenagers and young adults, they were sent offers on snowboarding equipment, track shoes and sports holidays.

Precision Marketing

Communications tools must integrate with each other. Integrating marketing communications requires people skills. Other managers have to be convinced. To do this, a full understanding of the benefits of integrated marketing communications (IMC) is required.

INTEGRATED MARKETING COMMUNICATIONS – THE BENEFITS

Although IMC requires a lot of effort, it delivers many benefits. It can create competitive advantage, and boost sales and profits, while saving time, money and stress.

IMC can wrap communications around customers and help them move through the various stages of their buying process. The organization simultaneously consolidates its image, develops a dialogue and nurtures its relationship with its customers. This 'relationship marketing' cements a bond of loyalty with customers that can protect them from the inevitable onslaught of competition. The ability to keep a customer for life is a powerful competitive advantage.

IMC also increases profits through increased effectiveness. At its most basic level, a unified message has more impact than a disjointed myriad of messages. In a busy world a consistent, consolidated and crystal-clear message has a better chance of cutting through the 'noise' of over 1,000 commercial messages that bombard customers each and every day. At another level, initial research suggests that images shared in advertising and direct mail boost both advertising awareness and mailshot responses. So IMC can boost sales by stretching messages across several communications tools to create more avenues for customers to become aware, aroused and, ultimately, make a purchase. Carefully linked messages also help buyers by giving timely reminders, updated information and special offers which, when presented in a planned sequence, help them move comfortably through the stages of their buying process – and this reduces their 'misery of choice' generated by the wide range of competitive offerings. IMC also makes messages more consistent and therefore more credible. This reduces risk in the mind of the buyer and, in turn, shortens the search process and helps to dictate the outcome of brand comparisons.

Unintegrated communications send disjointed messages that dilute the impact of the message. This may also confuse, frustrate and arouse anxiety in customers. Integrated communications present a reassuring sense of order. Consistent images and relevant, useful messages help nurture long-term relationships with customers. Here, customer databases can identify precisely which customers need what information when, and throughout their whole buying life.

Finally, IMC saves money, as it eliminates duplication in areas such as graphics and photography since they can be shared and used in, say, advertising, exhibitions and sales literature. Agency fees are reduced by using a single agency for all communications. And even if there are several agencies, time is saved when meetings bring all the agencies together – for briefings, creative sessions, or tactical or strategic planning. This reduces workload and subsequent stress levels.

INTEGRATED MARKETING COMMUNICATIONS – THE BARRIERS

Despite its many benefits IMC has many barriers. In addition to the usual resistance to change and the special problems of communicating with a wide variety of target audiences, there are many other obstacles which restrict IMC. These include: functional silos; stifled creativity; timescale conflicts and a lack of management know-how.

Take functional silos. Rigid organizational structures are infested with managers who protect both their budgets and their power base. 'Why should they share their budgets and allow someone else to make decisions which previously were theirs?'

Sadly, some organizational structures isolate communications, data, and even managers from each other; for example the PR department often doesn't report to marketing, the sales-force rarely meet the advertising or sales promotion people, and so on. Imagine what can happen when sales reps are not told about a new promotional offer! And all of this can be aggravated by turf wars or internal power battles where specific managers resist having some of their decisions (and budgets) determined or even influenced by someone from another department.

Here are two difficult questions – What should a truly integrated marketing department look like? And how will it affect creativity? It shouldn't matter whose creative idea it is, but often it does.

Keeping budgets = keeping power?
Reproduced from *On-line Marketing Course 10: Integrated Marketing Communications* with kind permission from Multimedia Marketing.com. Photograph: Hugh Lacey

It shouldn't matter whose idea it is, but often it does
Reproduced from *On-line Marketing Course 10: Integrated Marketing Communications* with kind permission from Multimedia Marketing.com. Photograph: Hugh Lacey

An advertising agency may not be so enthusiastic about developing a creative idea generated by, say, a PR or a direct marketing consultant. IMC can restrict creativity. No more wild and wacky sales promotions unless they fit into the overall marketing communications strategy. The joy of rampant creativity may be stifled, but the creative challenge may be greater and ultimately more satisfying when operating within a tighter, integrated, creative brief.

Add different timescales into a creative brief and you'll see time horizons provide one more barrier to IMC. For example, image advertising, designed to nurture the brand over the longer term, may conflict with shorter-term advertising or sales promotions designed to boost quarterly sales. The two objectives can be accommodated within an overall IMC if carefully planned, but this kind of planning is not common. A survey in the mid-1990s revealed that most American managers lack expertise in IMC. But it's not just managers, it's also agencies and there is a proliferation of single-discipline agencies. There appear to be very few people who have real experience of all the marketing communications disciplines. This lack of know-how is then compounded by a lack of commitment. The following section, on the Golden Rules for IMC, examines this in more detail.

Identify the problem and the solution will follow

Understanding the barriers is the first step in successfully implementing IMC.

INTEGRATED MARKETING COMMUNICATIONS – THE GOLDEN RULES

Here's how you can ensure you become integrated and stay integrated, with the ten Golden Rules of Integration.

1. Get senior management support for the initiative by ensuring they understand the benefits of IMC. IMC fits with ISO 9001: 2000 as it requires companies to continually monitor all their processes and procedures (including marketing) and continually seek ways to improve them. With senior management support the IMC concept can move downwards and across the organization, provided the internal marketing of the idea is properly executed.

2. Integrate at different levels of management. Put 'integration' on the agenda for various types of management meetings – whether annual reviews or creative sessions. Horizontally, ensure that all managers, not just marketing managers, understand the importance of a consistent message – whether on delivery trucks or product quality. Also ensure that Advertising, PR and Sales promotions staff are integrating their messages. To do this you must have carefully planned internal communications, that is, good internal marketing.

3. Ensure the design manual or even a brand book is used to maintain common visual standards for the use of logos, typefaces, colours and so on.

4. Focus on a clear marketing communications strategy. Have crystal-clear communications objectives; clear positioning statements; link core values into every communication. Ensure all communications add value to (instead of dilute) the brand or organization. Exploit areas of sustainable competitive advantage.

5. Start with a zero budget. Start from scratch. Build a new communications plan. Specify what you need to do in order to achieve your objectives. In reality, the budget you get is often less than you ideally need, so you may have to prioritize communications activities accordingly.

6. Think customers first. Wrap communications around the customers' buying process. Identify the stages they go through before, during and after a purchase. Select communication tools that are right for each stage. Develop a sequence of communications activities which help the customer to move easily through each stage. One car company identified 17 points of customer contact. Marketers have to think through the detailed stages of the mental, emotional and behavioural processes through which customers move when they buy different products and services.

7. Build relationships and brand values. All communications should help to develop stronger and stronger relationships with customers. Ask how each communication tool helps to do this. Remember customer retention is as important as customer acquisition.

8. Develop a good marketing information system which defines who needs what information when. A customer database, for example, can help the telesales, direct marketing and salesforce. IMC can help to define co-vital information. Does the database have a field for customer complaints and suggestions?
9. Share artwork and other media. Consider how, say, advertising imagery can be used in mailshots, exhibition stands, Christmas cards, news releases and Web sites. Some jeans companies are considering putting their Web addresses on the jeans labels.
10. Be prepared to change it all. Learn from experience. Constantly search for the optimum communications mix. Test. Test. Test. Improve each year. 'Kaizen'.

Ambient shoe imprint

9 West Shoes now have their Web address on the soles of their shoes, so any mud prints will display their Web address.

INTENSIVE MARKETING COMMUNICATIONS

Buying models (see page 94) are helpful when considering how to plug all the communication gaps or channels that lead to a buyer's mind. By identifying the stages a buyer goes through, and all the possible communication channels, it is possible to force a product or service into the mind of a buyer (if the resources are available). Hopefully, what is forced in is accepted and perceived to be pleasant rather than resented and rejected.

A major soft-drinks manufacturer once tested this idea in a European town. There was blanket local advertising supported by street bands, free samples, free gifts, new point-of-sale material in every CTN (confectioner, tobacconist and newsagent). Even extra vending machines and street stalls were placed strategically to maximize the consumer's opportunity to sample and buy the brand. The consumer could not avoid the brand. Every route to the consumer's mind was filled.

The term 'share of mind' is an awesome piece of marketing jargon. It effectively means how many minds you can get a brand or an organization into. Share of mind can be bought by increasing the marketing communications spend. Many companies obviously want to keep their brands in the front of the buyer's mind ('front of mind awareness'). This obviously depends on the quality and frequency of advertising and other marketing communication tools compared to a competitor's communications. 'Share of voice' refers to the share of advertising spend against the total market spend on advertising. Of course it isn't all plain sailing since, first, most companies have limited resources and, second, there is a phenomenon called 'competition'. They may be trying to use the same communication channels.

Integrated banana skins

Dole bananas all have a sticker with the Web address to Internet search engine 'Ask Jeeves', all about bananas.

MARKETING MIX MUST ALSO BE BALANCED AND INTEGRATED

A well-planned and carefully executed marketing communications programme cannot, on its own, guarantee success. This is dependent on a balanced marketing mix. A great advertisement may succeed in getting people to go out and ask for a particular product, but the overall plan fails if, say, the place is wrong. Too much 'pull' and not enough 'push'. Perhaps less investment in advertising ('pull') and more investment in sales training ('push') or simply more direct investment in distribution (new delivery vehicles, more drivers, better serviced vans, bigger stocks, smaller minimum orders, quicker deliveries, etc) might enable the right goods to get to the right place at the right time. If the goods are not there when they are needed, then 'the success of advertising' fails. Similarly, the promotion and the place might work to bring a potential customer close to buying a particular product but the price might just put the product out of reach. Finally, the product (or service) must match the promise made through the communications mix if long-term success (repeat sales) is to be achieved. A customer only buys a bad product once. This means that difficult investment decisions have to be made in areas often outside the marketing manager's control, eg product quality programme, product design programme, new product development programme, production equipment, staff motivation, customer care programmes and so on. Today's businesses are leaner and flatter and run by multifunctional (and therefore multiskilled) managers. Even those managers who are not directly involved in marketing will require an overall integrated marketing perspective, as they will have to balance financial decisions along with production, quality, human resources and marketing decisions. Perhaps we will at last see more boardrooms displaying proud pictures of the organization's products, services and employees?

900 million brand moments

What is our product (financial services)? I say it is our staff. The product is the experience, the brand moment. NatWest calculate they have 900 million such moments a year. That's 900 million chances to get it right or wrong.

Raoul Pinnell, former director of Marketing and Communications, NatWest

APPENDIX 1.1

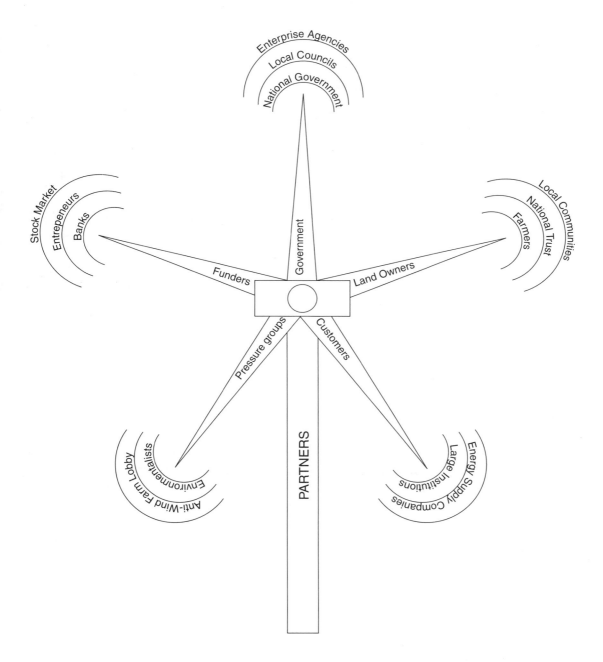

Figure A1.1 Wind Farm Company, Future Wind Partnership, must communicate with many stakeholders and audiences

APPENDIX 1.2

Above the line and below the line

'Above the line' refers to advertising. 'Below the line' basically refers to any other communications tool other than the salesforce (which does not fall into either category). Traditionally, below the line refers to sales promotion and public relations. Above-the-line advertising means any advertising that has to pay for the space it uses, eg TV, press, print, cinema or radio space, all of which cost money.

Advertising agencies used to separate activities to above and below the line because the agencies earned commission on above-the-line advertising and fees only on below-the-line activities.

The line is eroding as many agencies are moving away from commission-based earnings to fee-based earnings. The line is somewhat vague since some professionals see direct marketing as 'through the line'. In addition, advertorial (advertising that looks like editorial) is sometimes paid for out of a PR budget (below the line) since it is written through the eyes of a journalist as opposed to an advertising copywriter, yet it is paid-for space that is bought like advertising space (above the line).

APPENDIX 1.3

Market structure (share, growth and concentration)

Some years ago PIMS international business consultancy collated and analysed worldwide FMCG marketing communications mixes across North America and Europe. This research led them to conclude that a company's profits are affected by, among other things, how it mixes its communications mix. It is not so much the size of the budget but more the allocation of that budget among different communications tools (ie the mixing of the mix) that affects profits.

The optimum communications mix can be determined by an individual company's relative market share, the growth of the market itself and whether the market is concentrated in the hands of a few key players or fragmented among many players. Here are five specific findings:

1. Good profitability depends on the mix of advertising and promotion. It does not depend on the total marketing spend, either in absolute terms or relative to competitors.
2. Gaining market share depends on the sum of the two amounts – advertising and promotion.

3. Market share rank determines the optimum mix of advertising and promotion. For example, the market leader should spend 70 per cent or more of its marketing budget above the line (on advertising). The optimum amount of advertising for number two and three brands lies between 50 and 70 per cent of the marketing budget (with the balance being spent below the line). The fourth place brand, by contrast, would actually lose money by employing the same strategy. *Low share businesses with high advertising, on average, lose money* in their attempt to play the big boy's turf. The optimum above-the-line allocation here is between 30 and 50 per cent of the marketing budget.

The PIMS figures use one measure of profit known as ROCE (return on capital employed) or profit expressed as a percentage of everything tied up in (or invested in) the business. In the long term the percentage of profit returned from the business (and its investment) should be more than the bank rate. Otherwise the business might consider selling itself (realize its assets) and invest the funds realized in a bank so that it could earn a higher percentage return.

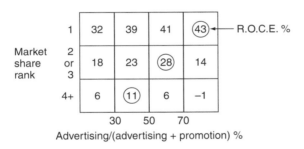

Source: PIMS FMCG database

Figure A1.3.1 Maximizing profits by matching the mix with market share

Figure A1.3.1 shows average profitability / return on capital employed (over a four-year period) resulting from different mixes and brand ranks (1 = market leader, 4 = 4th place, etc). The highest ROCE is circled in each row. The bottom row shows how tough life is for the smaller brands (with smaller market share). The best they can do is earn 11 per cent ROCE, probably less than their cost of capital. They can even lose money (–1 per cent ROCE) if they use the worst mix (eg advertising gets 70 per cent of the communications mix). The best mix for these low-market-share brands is around 40:60 (advertising:advertising + promotion). As mentioned, the optimum mix for the number one brand shows advertising taking 75 per cent or more of the mix.

4. Advertise in declining markets, promote in growth markets. This suggests that heavy advertising can wait until a market is bigger and the consumer matures. In the interim

(during the growth stages), sales promotions can stimulate consumer trial. During the decline stages, the survivors will be the well-advertised brands.

As you can see from Figure A1.3.2, maximum profits during the decline stage appear where the advertising proportion of the mix is increased. Sluggish and declining markets need brand maintenance (advertising). As Keith Roberts of PIMS says:

> Advertise in declining markets, promote in growth markets... The underlying explanation seems to be that competition is very different in a boom. Dozens of entrants jostle for leadership, and brand franchises don't count for much with inexperienced consumers. Marketers must be single-minded about getting their product on the shelf and stimulating consumer trial: they do not need to advertise. Advertising can wait until the market is bigger and consumers more mature.

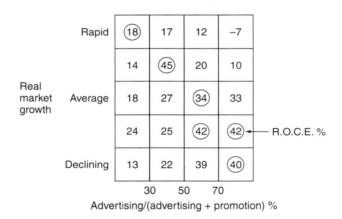

Source: PIMS FMCG database

Figure A1.3.2   Maximizing profits by matching the mix with market growth

5. As markets concentrate, reduce the proportion of advertising expenditure. Many markets today are concentrating as buyers get bigger and gain more buying power. Inevitably concentrated markets with a few powerful buyers means lower profits as the buyers exert their buying power.

    As Figure A1.3.3 shows, optimum profits in fragmented markets emerge when advertising takes almost 85 per cent of the marketing communications budget.

    Optimum profits in more concentrated markets emerge when less emphasis is placed on advertising, ie around 45 per cent.

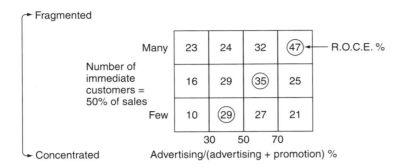

Source: PIMS FMCG database

Figure A1.3.3 Maximizing profits by matching the mix with market concentration

Resources available

Products in organizations with a portfolio of different products or services may have to compete internally for a limited supply of resources. Specific allocation of resources to products may depend on the overall balance of the product range or portfolio, with some products requiring more money proportionately (high-growth markets) than other products (say, low-growth brand-dominant markets).

The three key resources, the three Ms, men/women, money (budgets) and minutes (time) are limited in supply. Money is invariably a limited resource. Time is also a limited resource. The management of time affects the organization's overall performance since, first, time management is vital in any kind of project management and, second, good time management improves an individual's performance. Stress, health, time management and job performance are generally linked.

Minutes and men are linked. How much management time can be allocated to each communications tool? Some departments say that they don't have the time to start researching, testing and learning about alternative marketing communications tools. How many organizations that do not use direct marketing have reviewed the feasibility of introducing database marketing (see 'Database marketing', page 376)? How many staff can be delegated to various tasks? Are some tasks more time consuming than others? Can some be handled by junior staff? Who has to be involved at every stage?

As Dan O'Donoghue, Strategic Planner Worldwide of Publicis, says:

... some marketing directors started to believe the Thatcherite theory that ads could solve everything... some people would be spending 50 per cent of their time with creative directors rather than sticking to their knitting... it's the more cautious marketers, who kept to more classical marketing strategies, who have emerged strongly. Advertising shouldn't really occupy more than about 5 per cent of a marketing director's time.

Some of the larger FMCG companies do see advertising as the key element, so much so that they call brand managers, 'advertising managers'. These kinds of companies would like the managers to devote half of their time to the constant monitoring, refining and developing of advertising campaigns, but time pressures prevail and therefore often restrict their total devotion to the advertising process. In reality, less than 50 per cent of the time is spent on advertising campaigns.

A large FMCG company with agencies, consultants and experts has a different approach to a medium- or small-sized company with only a secretary to help the sales and marketing manager. There is no simple answer here.

Time and money can be saved and the impact of marketing communications increased if the various activities are planned and integrated in advance. Planning or scheduling various activities allows time to build a better picture, and gain a better understanding by putting the jigsaw of communications tools together to seize any overlapping opportunities which may emerge (eg a video news release can be produced along with a TV or cinema advertisement – see page 443). The planning process helps to give a clearer vision of where the organization is going. Good plans take the stress out of work. Planning also saves money since it is possible to get alternative quotes and shop around for the best deal when buying services. Expensive rush rates or overnight rates can be avoided by planning and scheduling. Advance order discounts can sometimes be taken if, say, a printer is given a couple of months' notice.

There is no one, single, exact, perfect communications mix. Several guidelines have been discussed, but there is no substitute for experience, particularly when it is enriched by constant 'testing and measuring' in the continual search for better performance from the marketing communications mix.

Equipped with these communications mix guidelines, how should a marketing communications plan be written? What must it include? The next chapter builds a framework for a marketing communications plan so that the reader can start to develop his or her own plan.

APPENDIX 1.4

Integrated marketing communications – the cost-saving benefits

Any communications tool should integrate with and draw on as many other communications tools as possible in order to maximize cost effectiveness and reinforce a consistent image. Photography, design and printing of advertisements, sales promotion leaflets, new packs, point-of-sale, press packs, direct mail leaflets, sales literature, etc can all, for example, be coordinated by choosing and briefing the same service supplier, whether a photographer, designer or printer. This can save time and money and simultaneously keep the communications mix integrated. This may not always be possible, eg some photographs may be suitable for inclusion in the pack design but not suitable for inclusion in a press pack, although the photographer can of course be briefed to cover both requirements. Even this is not always possible since, for example, some designers may specialize in (or only be experts in), say, packaging or direct mail leaflets. Alternatively, sometimes different people handle different aspects; an in-house marketing or advertising department may prefer an à la carte approach by working with several agencies or consultants on different promotional aspects. In fact, some organizations avoid giving one agency all their promotional work for fear of it all having the same 'look'. That is fine as long as, first, an integrated approach is considered and, second, a bigger budget (and more time) is available, since many potential cost savings are lost (eg pack photography that could have been used in a mailshot or blown up for a backdrop to an exhibition stand). Careful planning creates marketing communications synergy which reinforces a consistent message or image in a cost-effective manner.

Key points from Chapter 1:

1. Integrate all elements.
2. Make time to plan ahead.

FURTHER READING

Arnold, W (1992) Meet the brand man, *Media and Marketing Europe*, October

Bird, Julie (1997) How to keep them faithful the world over, *Precision Marketing*, 26 May

Brannan, T (1998) *A Practical Guide to Integrated Marketing Communications*, Kogan Page, London

Ehrenberg, A, Hammond, K and Goodhardt, G (1991) *The After Effects of Large Consumer Promotions*, London Business School

Fitzpatrick, Michael (1997) Made in Japan, *Creative Review*, November

Kotler, P (2000) *Marketing Management Analysis, Planning, Implementation and Control*, The Millennium Edition, Prentice-Hall, Englewood Cliffs, New Jersey

McDonald, M (1992) *The Marketing Planner*, Butterworth-Heinemann, Oxford

Moore, M (1997), Improving customer retention by analyzing defection, *Integrated Marketing Communications Research Journal*, Spring, pp 23–39

Pickton, D and Broderick, A (2001) *Integrated Marketing Communications*, Financial Times, London

Smith, P R (1999) *Great Answers to Tough Marketing Questions*, Kogan Page, London

Smith, P R (1996) *On-line Marketing Course 10: Integrated Marketing Communications*, Multimedia Marketing.com, London

FURTHER CONTACTS

Chartered Institute of Marketing, Moor Hall, Cookham, Maidenhead, Berkshire SL6 9QH (tel: 01628 427500; Web site: www.cim.co.uk)

Communications Advertising and Marketing Education Foundation (CAM Foundation), Moor Hall, Cookham, Maidenhead, Berkshire SL6 9QH (tel: 01628 427192; Web site: www.camfoundation.com)

Incorporated Society of British Advertisers, 44 Hertford Street, London W1J 7AE (tel: 020 7499 7502; Web site: www.isba.org.uk)

Institute of Public Relations, The Old Trading House, 15 Northburgh Street, London EC1V 0PR (tel: 020 7253 5151; Web site: www.ipr.org.uk)

Institute of Sales and Marketing Management, Romeland House, Romeland Hill, St Albans, Herts AL3 4ET (tel: 01727 812500; Web site: www.ismm.co.uk)

Institute of Sales Promotion, Arena House, 66–68 Pentonville Road, London N1 9HS (tel: 020 7837 5340; Web site: www.isp.org.uk

Marketing Society, St George's House, 3–5 Pepys Road, London SW20 8NJ (tel: 020 8879 3464; Web site: www.marketing-society.org.uk)

Public Relations Consultants Association, Willow House, Willow Place, London SW1P 1JH (tel: 020 7233 6026; Web site: www.prca.org.uk)

2

The marketing communications plan

OUTLINE MARKETING COMMUNICATIONS PLAN – THE SOSTAC® PLANNING SYSTEM

There are many different approaches to building a marketing plan or, more specifically, a marketing communications plan. There is no single common approach, but there are essential elements that every plan must have. SOSTAC® is a simple *aide mémoire* that helps managers to recall the key components of a marketing communications plan. SOSTAC® can in fact be applied to any kind of plan – corporate, marketing, marketing communications, direct mail or even a personal plan.

> **S** – Situation Analysis (where are we now?).
> **O** – Objectives (where do we want to go?).
> **S** – Strategy (how do we get there?).
> **T** – Tactics (the details of strategy).
> **A** – Action (or implementation – putting the plans to work).
> **C** – Control (measurement, monitoring, reviewing and modifying).

SOSTAC®'s simple structure is applicable at different levels and in different situations, as shown in the short cases at the end of this chapter. At the end of each chapter in Part II of this book, SOSTAC® is applied at a lower level for each of the communications tools, an advertising plan, a direct mail plan, etc. SOSTAC® can also be used to check other plans to see if they are comprehensive and cover the key items that every plan needs. You don't have to use the same terminology, or even the same sequence, but SOSTAC® should help the development of a logical structure combined with the key elements of a plan.

SOSTAC® has been adopted as a planning system by over 1,000 marketing managers worldwide.

The 3Ms

Every plan must include resources required. The three key resources, the 3Ms, cover:

1. Men/women (the human resources).
2. Money (budgets).
3. Minutes (time).

Men means men and women – the human resources: who is required to do what? Men means professional men and women skilled and capable of handling specific activities. Some can be drawn from within the organization, others have to be brought in from an agency or consultancy or recruited as full-time members of staff. Many organizations may not have this calibre of person or, if they do, they may be kept so busy that they cannot do any additional tasks. Is it worth asking over-busy people to give half their attention to a project or asking under-qualified and under-utilized people to have a go? Perhaps the marketing communications task is too important to be casual? There is no doubt about the importance and limited supply of the human resource.

Money means budgets and most managers' eyes scan budgets first and foremost. There are many different ways of setting marketing communications budgets and there is not a generally agreed methodology but rather a whole range of approaches that can be described as either *scientific* or *heuristic*.

Managers tasked with setting a budget ask themselves a series of 'what if' questions about what will happen if a particular strategy and series of tactics are pursued. A combination of judgement, experience and rational evaluation is applied to develop an appropriate budgeting method for your business.

Outlined below are the most common forms of *scientific* and *heuristic* budget setting approaches that are used in marketing communication planning today.

Scientific

1. Objective and tactics   reviews the objectives, then summarizes the strategy and subsequent tactics (and costs/budget) required to achieve them. This is sometimes called the 'ideal' or 'task' approach.
2. Modelling   uses a variety of econometric and simulation techniques to model how various budget levels may affect performance (such as sales levels, awareness and profit). An example of this would be Unilever's AMTES area market-testing model.
3. Payback period   is the time taken for an integrated campaign to pay back the costs (or budget) of the marketing communications.
4. Profit optimization   argues that investment in marketing communications is continued as long as the marginal revenue from the revenue exceeds the marginal cost.

Heuristic

1. Percentage of sales   uses a simple calculation of a fixed percentage of either past or anticipated sales.
2. Competitive parity   uses competition and its relative marketing spend as a yardstick.
3. Affordable   is based upon using all available monies after costs are deducted from required profits.
4. Arbitrary   uses a senior manager to arbitrate between different views of the marketing team.

You may have to justify to the financial director the actual return on investment of the marketing communications investment. Return on investment calculates the profit (created from the extra sales generated from the integrated marketing communications campaigns) as a percentage of the investment. This can be done for the whole mix or, more easily, for a specific marketing communications tool such as exhibitions (see page 486).

In reality several approaches are used. Although a manager might use the ideal task approach, the review panel (of senior management) will immediately convert it into a percentage figure, compare it with the competition's spend and ask 'can we really afford it?', 'does it deliver the required level of profits?' It is not unusual to find the initial budget request cut back by senior management as other divisions and departments compete internally for limited funds for the following year's marketing. Few companies have sophisticated optimum profit models that attempt to identify the optimum spend.

Minutes – the third M – is the most limited resource – time. Is there enough time to do the job, to carry out the research, to develop a new pack, to prepare properly for a good mailshot, etc? Timescales are fundamental. Without them any plan becomes uncontrollable because there are no time-related milestones. Timescales for objectives, and deadlines for each activity (eg proposals, concept development, concept testing, regional testing, national roll-out, European launch) are required. How much lead time do you need if you want to launch a new toy at Christmas? When should the product be ready? In February, if it is going to make the New York Toy Show, when major US retailers place their orders. How long would a new pack take to create? Six to nine months. So even if you allow four months to develop a mailshot and simultaneously four months for a TV advertisement, you still need a total of 18 months for the pack and exhibitions. Managers have to manage teams of people who have different attitudes to deadlines. Time is a precious commodity and deserves careful attention. Some consider it now to be the currency of competitive advantage.

Whooshing deadlines

'I love deadlines. I like the whooshing sound they make as they fly by.'

The late Douglas Adams

SOSTAC® provides an outline or a structure upon which a comprehensive plan can be built. A real plan requires much more detail, and the first component, the situation analysis, is often considered so important that it can take up half of the total plan. Objectives and strategies should be written in a concise manner, while the tactics and action plans can require a lot of detailed planning. Control, feedback and monitoring mechanisms should be built into the plan so that managers know if the plan is succeeding or failing early on rather than at the end of the year when it is too late to change. So SOSTAC® and the 3Ms provide a simple approach for building a marketing plan (and marketing communications plans in particular).

Here is what some experts feel about SOSTAC®:

Professor Philip Kotler: 'SOSTAC® is a system for going through the steps and building a marketing plan.'

Sam Howe, Director of CATV Marketing, Southwestern Bell: 'SOSTAC® is a great approach for anyone going ahead and building a marketing plan.'

David Solomon, Marketing Director, TVX: 'It appears that we are following the principles of SOSTAC®.'

John Leftwick, Marketing Director, Microsoft UK: 'We use SOSTAC® within our own marketing planning.'

Peter Liney, Concorde Marketing Manager: 'I think SOSTAC® is very good in terms of identifying, if you like, major component parts of what you're doing in marketing.'

You can see how easily SOSTAC® works for any type of product or service in both consumer and business-to-business markets in the short cases at the end of this chapter. Although they only provide an outline plan, they demonstrate how easily SOSTAC® can be applied to either planning the overall marketing communications (Gold Heart case) or just planning a campaign for a single communications tool such as direct mail (St James Church). In reality, a proper plan would cover a lot more detail.

Consider now each SOSTAC® component in more detail.

SITUATION ANALYSIS

The situation analysis needs to be comprehensive. Over 2,000 years ago Sun Tzu wrote the *Art Of War*, which has become a classic read, particularly for some enlightened marketing managers. Here is an excerpt:

Those who triumph,
Compute at their headquarters
A great number of factors
Prior to a challenge.

Those who are defeated,
Compute at their headquarters
A small number of factors
Prior to a challenge.

Much computation brings triumph.
Little computation brings defeat.
How much more so with no computation at all.

By observing only this,
I can see triumph or defeat.

The analysis should include a review of the performance (sales, market share, profitability) during the most recent period. Comparisons with previous years reveal any trends and comparisons against competitors reveal relative performance. The analysis should include a summary review of the overall marketing performance, the marketplace, competition, and strengths and weaknesses. The marketing communications plan does not require a full SWOT analysis, which is usually found in the full marketing plan. The situation analysis in the marketing communications plan must keep the focus on communications aspects such as (a) performance (identifying which elements of the communications mix work best), (b) target markets, and (c) positioning. It should certainly include an explanation of the product or service's positioning – how the product is perceived in the minds of the target market. Lucozade was positioned as a sick child's drink until the marketing people saw a bigger opportunity and repositioned it as a healthy adults' drink. Perceptual maps plot where different brands and product types are positioned on certain criteria, as shown in Figure 2.1.

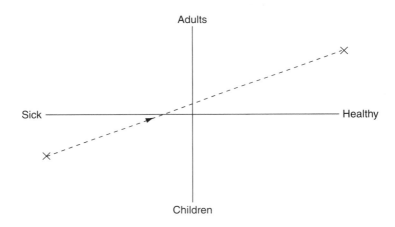

Figure 2.1 A perceptual map showing Lucozade's image repositioning (see case study in Chapter 11)

The situation analysis can include a PEST Analysis specifically relevant to communications, eg political – what new laws or regulations affect communications; how economic fluctuations might affect media and messages; social trends and changes in attitudes and media usage; technology's fast changing impact on communications.

A vital part of any analysis is the market and its structure. How is it segmented? What are the most suitable segments that can become target markets? Are the target markets big enough? Profitable enough? Vulnerable to competition? Do the existing distribution and communications channels serve them properly? Are customers satisfied in each target market? Do they intend to repurchase? Who is involved in the decision-making unit (DMU)? Do the key opinion leaders and opinion formers support the brand?

Segmentation and target marketing

Segmentation and target marketing are so important that they appear almost everywhere in a marketing plan: in the situation analysis in detail, in the objectives briefly, in the strategy (as a fundamental component) and obviously they are referred to in all tactical campaigns and events.

Target marketing involves the division of a large market into smaller market segments. Each segment has its own distinct needs and/or its patterns of response to varying marketing mixes. The most attractive segments are targeted according to the organization's resources. Attractive target markets are those that will generally be more profitable, eg segments located closer to the organization, or loyal customer groups, or heavy users of a particular product or service. Targeting reduces wastage of resources (eg money spent on mass advertising) and, ultimately, it increases sales since better prospect customers are contacted. Segmentation and target marketing are absolutely fundamental approaches to marketing. Some communication channels are more wasteful than others, eg TV, but the Target Group Index (TGI) (see Chapter 5) helps to identify what kind of brands people buy, papers they read, programmes they watch, etc. As mass markets fragment and splinter into mini-markets or segments, and technology provides more tailored communications, there is less requirement for mass marketing and mass communications. Chapter 13 explains how product differentiation and market fragmentation occur, while Chapter 20 examines the Internet and its potential for a dynamic dialogue with customers. The ability to segment a market accurately is a key skill that marketers need to spend time on again and again, revisiting their marketplace and thinking about how it can be broken into segments.

Segment criteria

Ideally, segments should satisfy the following criteria:

1. **Measurable**   Is it quantifiable? Can buyers who fall into this category or segment be identified?
2. **Substantial**   How many buyers fall into this segment? Is there a sufficient number of buyers in the segment to warrant special attention and targeting?
3. **Accessible**   Can this group be contacted? Can they be isolated or separated from other non-targeted markets? Are there specific media and distribution channels that provide access to them?

4. **Relevant**   The benefits of the product or service being offered must be relevant to the target. There is no point picking measurable, accessible and substantial segments if they have no interest in what is being offered in the first place. Know your own customers. Knowing the ideal customer's profile is fundamental to success. Some database companies actually carry out 'profiling' or an analysis of an organization's own customers into groups with distinctive profiles. This helps target the appropriate message through the appropriate medium.

£50 Rembrandt

A Rembrandt probably would not sell (even for £50) in the wrong target market, whereas in the right target market it would fetch several million pounds.

Some segments are obvious. Cat food is bought by cat owners. Petrol is bought by motorists and heavy-duty cranes are bought by both large construction companies and leasing companies. Other segments are less obvious. Expensive cars are bought by high-income groups, while cheaper cars are bought by both high-income groups (as a second or third car) and low-income groups. Who are the heavy users, eg who are the 9 per cent of the UK adult population who drink 65 per cent of the lager consumed? Who are the buyers? Gift boxes of chocolates are bought for women by men. Who are the deciders? Cola drinkers may tend to be young, but who does the buying, who makes the decision, who influences, and who pays? This is where segmentation focuses on the decision-making unit.

Decision-making units

The DMU is made up of influencers, advisers, deciders, users, buyers and payers. It applies to all types of markets (industrial, consumer, products and services). A baby's pram may be used by mother and child, bought by the mother and father, influenced by the mother-in-law, and decided on by the whole family. Similarly, the purchase of a new photocopier may have been instigated by the secretary who keeps complaining to her boss about the old machine breaking down. The end-user may be several secretaries, the decider may be the financial director, the buyer may be the organization's professional buyer or the managing director. In some organizations the DMU may be a committee. In other organizations there is a central decision maker or there may be a decentralized approach with each branch/region making their own decisions. The acronym SPADE (Starter Payer Adviser Decider End-user) helps to identify some of the different members of the decision-making unit.

The DMU can consist of several people or committees, or it can sometimes be just one person. There is one other influential member of a business-to-business or industrial DMU, and that is the 'gatekeeper' who acts as a screen and sorts out unsolicited sales pitches from more important incoming communications. The gatekeeper is often a secretary or personal assistant who may decide whether to interrupt a manager with a phone call or allow a direct mailshot to land on the manager's desk.

Global segments

Global convergence

So tastes are converging and to discover that all you have to do is talk to my teenage son. I have taken him with me on trips all over the world and I keep introducing him to a local boy who he can spend the day with to learn something about the life in those countries. And in every country he's visited, whether it is Jakarta, Indonesia; São Paulo, Brazil; Manila in the Philippines or a small town in The Netherlands, he has spent the day exactly the same way. They have gone to a local shopping mall, played video games and eaten a McDonald's hamburger.

Professor Rosabeth Moss Kanter (2001) *On-line Marketing Course 2: Segmentation, Positioning and the Marketing Mix*, Multimedia Marketing.com, London

Segments do not always have to be localized or defined on a geographic basis. Values, attitudes and lifestyles (VALS) can be used to identify cross-cultural common characteristics. For example, the advertising agency Euro RSCG Wnek Gosper identified the four main European psychographic segments as follows:

1. Modern materialists: 117 million.
2. New radicals: 50 million (concerned with change and reform).
3. Get what you deserve: 110 million (more conservative and resistant to change).
4. Bygones: 83 million (oldest, most moralistic group threatened by consumerism).

Global idiosyncrasies complicate the supposedly simple global segments. Chapter 9 looks at the international arena in more detail.

Consumer segments

Segmenting markets into groups of buyers and targeting those groups that are more likely to be the best customers is absolutely vital if marketing communications are to be both effective and efficient. Markets can be broken into segments using many different criteria. Here are some typical consumer criteria:

- demographics:
  - age: see figures in Appendix 2.1,
  - job type: see socio-economic grouping in Appendix 2.1;
- geodemographics:
  geographical location, type of neighbourhood and demographic data: see ACORN types in Appendix 2.2 and on page 133;
- psychographics;
- lifestyle: see TGI data on page 132;
- attitudes, beliefs and intentions (as above);
- benefits sought: see 'The toothpaste test' on page 91.

Floating targets

Other markets have a floating percentage who move in and out of the market. For example, less than 1 per cent of the population buy any financial service in any one month. And to the remaining 99 per cent financial services, particularly insurance, are dull and off-putting subjects they would rather not think about. With such a small number of consumers in the market at any one time there is clearly little point talking about specific product benefits. Instead the role of advertising is to ensure the Prudential is on the candidate list when people do have a need for a particular service.

A *Media Week* Awards winner

Industrial segments

In industrial markets and business-to-business markets segmentation criteria are different but nonetheless vital. The Hewlett Packard short case at the end of Chapter 16 shows that their target market (for a particular promotional activity) was 'executive directors responsible for long-term investments and the management of change'. This was further refined into two target markets: (a) directors and board-level management in companies with £10–50 million turnover; (b) directors, board-level managers plus information technology management plus financial management in companies with over £50 million turnover.

Here are some commonly used segmentation criteria for industrial markets:

- type of company (Standard Industrial Code (SIC));
- size of company;
- structure of company (autocratic vs centralized);
- location/geographical area;
- heavy or light users;
- existing suppliers;
- benefits sought;
- title or position of key decision makers.

Most airlines target at least two different segments on each plane: the business traveller and the leisure traveller. These segments can be further segmented, eg the business traveller may be divided into Club Class, Executive Class and so on. These can be further divided into different benefit segments, eg those who want a fast check-in, those who want frequent flights, those who want top-class in-flight service, those who want a reasonable price, those who want 'seamless travel' (connections for the next flight, cars and hotels all booked for them). Most travellers want all of these benefits, but usually consider some more important than others, so much so that they choose one airline over another because of a particular key benefit. If this type of flier proves to be significant in number, then it is a valid segment (see other criteria for valid segments below). The organization then decides if it has the resources and sustainable advantages suitable to target this segment.

To continue the airline example, Transavia Airlines segmented various companies who might have had some connection with Holland (and therefore might have had a need for their services) into five different target groups of business fliers and travel agents. As shown in Figure 2.2, a different communications strategy was developed for each segment. A

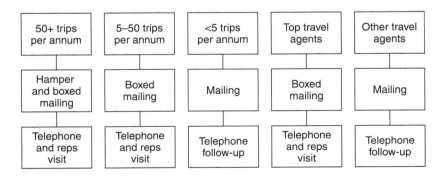

Source: Stevens, M (1991)

Figure 2.2 Business traveller segments and communication mixes

gift/food hamper and a boxed presentation were delivered personally by the sales manager to those accounts (customers) that warranted this kind of attention (resources). Lighter users had a smaller mailing. Top travel agents got a boxed mailing, while other travel agents just got a mailing.

Segmentation requires careful analysis

In reality, all the target customers rarely fall neatly into one single segment, eg 67 per cent of the *Sun*'s customers might be C2DEs and 33 per cent ABC1s (see Appendix 2.3 for a full explanation of the ABC1 C2DE social grades). As mentioned, not all buyers of small cars are in lower- to middle-income groups. Many small cars are bought by mid- to higher-income groups as a second or third car in the family. There is, however, usually a core target made up of heavy users or easily convertible prospects, eg Lyons Tetley's Quickbrew tea is targeted at women aged 35+ (core C1C2D). Some markets have several people involved in the decision making (DMUs). For example, the advertising campaign promoting Shell's free miniature classic sports car collection was aimed at ABC1 fathers aged between 25 and 64 with children aged 3–9; within this they also had to ensure high coverage of high-mileage drivers (heavy users). Other markets have customers who drift into the marketplace and then out again, as in the case of financial services (see below).

Who knows who they are or why they buy from us?

A few years ago a comparative study of British and foreign-owned companies revealed that 47 per cent of British and 40 per cent of American companies (vs 13 per cent of Japanese) acknowledged that they were unclear about the type of customers in the market and what their needs were.

Doyle, Saunders and Wright

OBJECTIVES

After analysing the situation through secondary and primary sources (see Chapter 5) a clear picture of 'where we are now' emerges. The next step is to define as specifically as possible 'where do we want to go?' Ideally objectives should be quantified in terms of success or failure criteria. Timescales should also be set. Clearly defined objectives make the management task of 'control' much easier. Drawing up objectives for the first time is a difficult task. In future years, the previous year's objectives and corresponding results will help to make the planning job a little easier, as everyone has a better idea of what is realistic and what is not. Establishing clear objectives is necessary to give a focus to the organization or division. Clear objectives also give direction to subsequent creative efforts. Some marketing managers and agencies break objectives into many different types; other marketers use just one set of objectives (and sometimes without quantification or numbers attached). As a discipline it is useful to break up objectives so that performance can be measured more accurately. Objectives should be SMART:

S – Specific.
M – Measurable.
A – Actionable.
R – Realistic.
T – Time specific.

Two types of objectives are examined here: marketing objectives and communications objectives.

Marketing objectives

Typical marketing objectives refer to sales, market share, distribution penetration, launching a number of new products and so on. For example, marketing objectives might be to:

- increase unit sales of product/brand X by 10 per cent over the next 12 months;
- increase market share by 5 per cent over the next 12 months;
- generate 500 new enquiries each month;
- increase distribution penetration from 25 per cent to 50 per cent within 12 months;
- establish a network of distributors covering Germany, France, Holland and Italy during the first six months, followed by Switzerland, Austria, Belgium and Luxembourg in the second six months.

It is worth noting that not all marketing objectives are growth oriented. In Denmark electricity boards no longer pride themselves on how much electricity they sell, but on how little. Product withdrawals are another example where objectives are not attached to year-on-year growth. In very competitive mature markets, with new entrants appearing on the market, maintaining market share and consolidating sales might be more appropriate than expecting big growth. Given that marketing is shifting towards retention of profitable customers and deselection of unprofitable customers (see page 4), the emphasis in some companies has moved from growth in turnover or sales to growth in profit or ROI (return on investment).

Communications objectives

These typically refer to how the communications should affect the mind of the target audience, eg generate awareness, attitudes, interest or trial. Again, these tend to be most useful when quantified. DAGMAR (defining advertising goals for measuring advertising responses) and AIDA (attention, interest, desire and action) provide yardsticks for communications objectives by trying to separate the various mental stages a buyer goes through before buying. These response hierarchy models are discussed in Chapter 4.

The mental stages suggested by DAGMAR and AIDA are as follows:

DAGMAR	AIDA
Unawareness	–
Awareness	Attention
Comprehension	Interest
Conviction	Desire
Action	Action

Here are some examples of communications objectives:

- To increase awareness from 35 per cent to 50 per cent within eight weeks of the campaign launch among 25- to 45-year-old ABC1 women.
- To position the service as the friendliest on the market within a 12-month period among 70 per cent of heavy chocolate users.
- To reposition Guinness from an old, unfashionable, older man's drink to a fashionable younger person's drink over two years among all 25- to 45-year-old male drinkers.
- To maintain brand X as the preferred brand (or number one brand) of photo-copiers among at least 50 per cent of current UK buyers in companies with 1000+ employees.
- To include Bulgarian wines in the repertoire of possible wine purchases among 20 per cent of ABC1 wine buyers within 12 months.
- To support the launch of a new shop by generating 50 per cent awareness in the immediate community one week before the launch.
- To announce a sale and create 70 per cent awareness one day before the sale starts.
- To reposition *The European* as an up-market business paper (from a general mid-market newspaper) (see Figure 2.3).

The European positioned itself in new market space, where the management saw a better gap in the market. But was there a market in the gap? Was there a real need for a weekly European newspaper at that time? *The European* has now ceased publication.

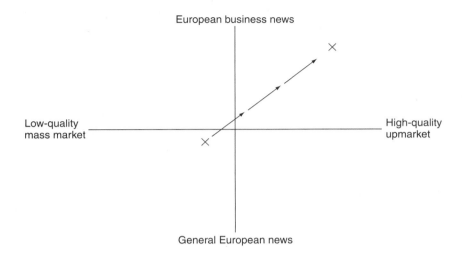

Figure 2.3   Objective: To reposition *The European* newspaper

The European *attempted to reposition itself from mass-market, general European news to upmarket European business news – a gap in the market, but no market in the gap?*

Objectives can cover a variety of goals. It is useful to separate marketing objectives from marketing communications objectives. Detailed, specific objectives ensure that the subsequent choice of strategy is clearly focused.

STRATEGY

Strategy summarizes 'how we get there' – how the objectives will be achieved. Strategy drives tactics in the same direction. Strategy summarises tactics. Communications strategy helps to harmonize and integrate all of the tactical communications tools. Communications strategy can include selection of target markets, positioning, selection of communications tools, sequence of communications tools (are different tools used at different stages?), and more.

Marketing communications strategies are hard to find. Often the strategy is retrospective in so far as the tactics are planned and then a strategy is created to make sense of the tactics. This is far from ideal.

One *aide-mémoire* for the components of marketing communications strategy is: **STOP & SIT**.

Segmentation (how is the market broken up?)
Target markets (what target markets are chosen plus who is the 'ideal customer'?)
Objectives (strategy must fulfil objectives)
Positioning (of the product or service and also what is the overall proposition)
&
Stages (is there a sequence or series of stages?)
Integration (does it all integrate smoothly?)
Tools (are we going on TV, or just opt-in e-mail?)

Ideally the communications strategy can succinctly answer all of these questions. Objectives, by the way, don't have to be regurgitated, but do keep an eye on them, as strategy that ignores objectives is a waste of time. As Kenichi Ohmae says: 'There's no point rowing harder, if you're rowing in the wrong direction.'

Developing good marketing communications strategies requires careful consideration. Although occasionally frustrating, it is worthwhile:

developing marketing communications strategies delivers many benefits. It is important to remember this because developing and agreeing strategic decisions costs time, money and energy. Many marketers have an inner urge to get on with the job, get creative, develop wonderful advertising campaigns, wacky sales promotions, delightful new sales literature, sensational exhibition stands and more. Other marketers are under pressure to get out and talk to customers, bring in some sales, generate revenues and justify their existence. So seemingly self-indulgent navel gazing such as strategic contemplation may not always appear worthwhile – in the immediate term. But, beyond the immediate term, a good strategy will reap many benefits.

Smith, Berry and Pulford (1999)

Here are five examples of marketing communications strategy taken from Smith, Berry and Pulford's *Strategic Marketing Communications*, each demonstrating a very different approach.

Tupperware marketing communications strategy

… a multimillion-dollar direct-response campaign… the company maintained its personal selling approach but modified its party format to accommodate the increasing limitations for working women… installed a toll-free number to link customers to a local dealer… catalogues were originally available only for dealers, hosts and hostesses, they were made accessible to everyone and reached 30 million people.

Adapted from Engel, Warshaw & Kinnear (1994)

IBM insurance marketing communications strategy

Position the business as a solution provider who fully understands client needs and is easily able to provide complete and successful solutions. All communications reinforce our unique capability which combines marketing and IT in an integrated manner. The key target group is 'European insurers with medium to large customer bases (usually over 1 million)'. All communications are below the line, editorially driven, and drawn from sound research into leading-edge solutions. The published papers are used across a series of public conferences, own conferences and training awareness days, along with a constant media relations campaign.

ETC human resource company's marketing communications strategy

A client relationship strategy focusing on a few key sectors (industry, health, local government and financial services) instead of the previous machine gun (broad advertising) approach. Direct mailings and seminar events aimed at key opinion formers developed through targeted mailings create a tightly focused database for future presentations and high-value mailings.

Daewoo marketing communications strategy

Position Daewoo as the most customer-focused car company in the UK. Car buyers are happy with cars but unhappy with dealers. Daewoo must own customer service. This differentiates Daewoo.

Stage 1: Build corporate credibility through TV and motoring press.
Stage 2: Develop Daewoo dialogue, collecting information about likes and dislikes about car ownership.
Stage 3: Launch brand.

This necessitates integration throughout the marketing communications and operational implementation. Advertising will build brand awareness and direct people into Daewoo's telemarketing database. The complete mix includes retail design, interactive point of sale, sales promotion, direct marketing, database construction and management, PR and advertising. (For more information on Daewoo, see short case study in Chapter 11.)

Telewest communications strategy

Create/educate the market (get consumers to a point where they are predisposed to consider cable from Telewest Communication); build the brand (by teaching customers to value most what Telewest does best); stimulate acquisition (through three big sales promotion ideas); build and manage relationships (through good service and constant database dialogue).

There is no one single approach to building marketing communications strategies. In fact many companies do not put them together at all. A good communications strategy helps to keep all the subsequent tactical communications tools integrated and moving in the same direction, delivering bigger impacts and reducing costs. A simple way to practice writing marketing communications strategies is to generate several alternative strategies, so that strategic options can be considered. Try generating a bad strategic option so that you can begin to see, first, that there is always more than one strategy available to choose from and, second, that some strategies are better than others.

TACTICS

Tactics are the details of strategy. In marketing, communications tactics are the communications tools such as advertising, PR, direct mail, etc. The tactics in the marketing communications plan list what happens when and for how much. It is often best expressed as a Gantt chart as shown in Table 2.1.

Table 2.1 Tactical timings of different communication tools

	Jan	Feb	Mar	Apr	May	Jun	Jul	Aug	£
Advertising – TV – Press									
Sales Promotion – Sample drop – Competition – Collection									
Direct marketing – Mailshot – Telesales									
Publicity (and public relations)									
Sponsorship									
Exhibitions									
Packaging									
Point-of-sale and Merchandising									
Internet									
Word of mouth									
Corporate identity									

ACTION

The action stage reveals the details of tactics. Detailed project plans are required in order to implement the tactics. Detailed action plans bring the tactics to life. Actions implement the tactics. This is the not-so-glossy side of marketing which requires attention to detail, good project planning skills, time management, prioritizing, people management skills, and an ability to handle pressure and to get things done. In reality the action/implementation of the marketing communications tactics requires an ability to get other people (staff, agencies, printers, etc) to deliver on time and within budget. It also requires an ability to plan for contingencies because things do go wrong (eg advertisements fall down).

Any kind of project planning can be used here, whether critical path or just a Gantt chart. A detailed project plan is required for each tactical communications tool. For example, the production of a mailshot can be as shown in Figure 2.4.

This is just for one mailing. More detailed planning is required if there are a series of mailings. The response handling also needs to be planned carefully. With hybrid marketing systems (see page 374), the responses can be routed to an inbound telesales team who filter respondents, rank them in terms of urgency, size and location, and pass the enquiry to a relevant sales person, or dispatch further information and update the database for future activities. All of this requires careful planning to ensure sufficient resources are available to make the strategies and tactics actually happen.

CONTROL

Plans should identify how they will be monitored, measured and controlled. Managers need to know at an early stage (rather than when it's too late) how a campaign is running, whether it is an advertising campaign or a mailshot. If it is not working, it should be stopped. Control systems need to be in place to help monitor any campaigns or activities (see Table 2.2). This is where clear objectives can once again help, since the objectives can usually be broken down into more detailed objectives covering shorter periods of time. Armed with clearly defined, precise objectives, money can be spent on measuring performance (whether defined as sales, enquiries, awareness, etc) against the objectives.

Control includes various areas of market research and testing, so measurement systems need to be built into the plan.

	Wk 1	Wk 2	Wk 3	Wk 4	Wk 5	Wk 6	Wk 7	Wk 8	Wk 9	Wk 10	Wk 11	Wk 12
Creative brief	X											
List brief		X										
List proposal			X									
Visual concepts			X									
Visuals approved				X								
List order				X								
Final copy/design					X							
Artwork brief					X							
Print quotes					X							
Set artwork proofs						X						
Receive lists						X						
Data preparation						X						
Finished artwork							X					
Printer brief							X					
Printer proofs								X				
Merge purge lists								X				
Print									X			
Computer bureau output files									X			
Live laser proofs									X			
Mail house brief									X			
Print delivery										X		
Laser print letter										X		
Mail house delivery											X	
Mail house sort/ enclose											X	
Mail												X

Figure 2.4 An action plan for one communication tool – a mailshot

Table 2.2 Control systems

Quantified objectives State each quantified objective and its time period	Means of measuring Sales analysis; number of responses; surveys	Frequency of measurement Daily; weekly; monthly; quarterly; annually?	Accountability Who does it?	Cost How much does it cost to measure?	Action? Who needs to be alerted if significant variances are found?

Planning is really an iterative process. A manager puts together a plan and a budget. Senior management agree it or reduce it by way of budgets. The manager revises the plan in the light of the resources available. The plan is then rolled out, results watched carefully and action taken to change the plan if necessary (ie if it is not working). If something is not right, it is better to find out why, make corrections and move on, hence the importance of control mechanisms. They provide a manager with useful feedback as to whether the plan is working or not. Everything a manager does is a learning process since, assuming the desire for constant improvement, a manager is monitoring what works best and what doesn't. Each year, as experience is gained, improvements can be made through this longer-term iterative process. Procter and Gamble ask their managers to build on their 'learnings' (what they have learned from the marketplace). They constantly learn from the marketplace and then incorporate those 'learnings' in their next marketing plan.

Here are two short case studies showing how SOSTAC® can be applied to different levels of marketing communications – first, a full marketing communications plan (in outline form) for the Gold Heart charity and, second, for a specific communications tool – a direct mail campaign for the Friends of St James Church.

CASE STUDY 2.1

Gold Heart Appeal

Gold Heart

Situation

The Variety Club of Great Britain is a conduit charity and prides itself on raising funds for disadvantaged children regardless of race, colour or creed. Unlike some other charities, overheads are kept to a minimum and well over 90p in every £1 raised goes directly to help the children. The Variety Club of Great Britain has run the Gold Heart Appeal annually since 1991. Over the past 10 years the Appeal has raised over £35 million through the sale of Gold Heart 'badges' and associated merchandise. The Gold Hearts sell for a minimum donation of £1 and are available to the public via a network of retail outlets (Gold Heart Appeal partners). The Appeal culminates on 14 February – Valentine's Day – which the charity claims as 'Gold Heart Day'. Money raised from the Appeal goes directly to benefit sick, disabled and disadvantaged children throughout the UK.

The 1998 campaign embraced a totally new approach in order to fight more aggressively in an increasingly competitive marketplace, particularly against a twice-weekly National Lottery.

The Ingram Agency was commissioned to run the Gold Heart Appeal and was charged with creating a fully integrated marketing programme, incorporating sales promotion, national TV advertising, national broadcast and print PR.

However You Say I Love You

Objectives

- To raise the profile of the Variety Club of Great Britain and in turn their annual fund-raising Gold Heart Appeal.
- Achieve year-on-year growth, enjoyed since 1991.
- To raise in excess of £4 million for sick, disabled and disadvantaged children.
- To maximize awareness among the core target audience (25- to 45-year-old ABC1 housewives with children), and extend the Appeal to reach new audiences.
- To create a Gold Heart Appeal 'brand' that can attain a commercial value and explore new avenues to sell Gold Hearts and the Gold Heart proposition.

Strategy

- To take ownership of Gold Heart's natural 'provenance' of love, by creating a motivating and relevant balance between romantic and benevolent love.
- To generate an integrated advertising, sales promotion and PR campaign focusing on the love theme.
- To communicate the love theme to potential new partners, retailers, brands and media owners, to generate increased distribution of Gold Hearts and increase the awareness of the Gold Heart Appeal.

Tactics

- Development of a strong 'upbeat' creative treatment to demonstrate the core proposition of romantic and benevolent love – 'However you say I love you, a Gold Heart says you care' (visual of in-store point-of-sale).

- Television campaign – 3 × 30″ and 1 × 10″ commercials, including classic romantic film footage. The ads drive the public into partners' outlets to buy Gold Hearts – Cilla Black provides the voice-over.
- Create powerful styling adaptable to a crowded in-store environment but also suitable for a television campaign (visual of still from commercial or storyboard).
- Point of sale – to create a family of materials to flag the Appeal wherever Gold Hearts are on sale.
- Utilization of campaign theming to generate integrated publicity.
- PR/media – external agency SPA Partnership recruited to raise the profile of the Gold Heart Appeal and gain coverage in national and regional press, radio and television.
- Include human-interest stories – children helped by the Variety Club and fund-raising activities.
- Mailing packs sent to prospective partners, including manufacturers, brands and retailers, outlining Appeal objectives, background on the charity and information on the number of ways that partners can become involved – from sponsorship through to third-party affinity deals. Follow-up calls made. Presentations to warm leads.
- Rental of a number of databases to mail to new revenue generators, including petrol retail outlets, schools and trade unions.

Further fund-raising initiatives include:

- Littlewoods Lotteries producing Gold Heart-themed scratchcards.
- Merchandise leaflet featuring Gold Heart jewellery, clothing and gifts, as well as previous years' Gold Hearts. Print run of 500,000. Distributed via February insertion into Gold Heart-themed issue of *OK!* magazine, as well as via a mailing to the Gold Heart supporters database.

Action/production

In line with the agency's ISO requirements, the objectives, recommended strategy and initial creative concepts based on the love theme were presented and subsequently approved by the client. The theme line, 'However you say I love you, a Gold Heart says you care', was researched among Gold Heart partners and a sample of 150 consumers from the Gold Heart database. Included within this research was a selection of romantic film titles to rank, in order to gauge the most popular film clips to feature in the TV campaign.

Starting with the TV concept, the agency then produced a TV storyboard featuring the visual and audio elements of the proposed commercials. Permission for the usage of the film clips was sought and generously donated by the film distributors.

Layouts were then prepared for the supporting point-of-sale elements of the campaign and for key imagery to be featured within the integrated PR activity. The linking device of the rainbow, as featured on the 1998 Gold Heart, was utilized on all materials and provided the bright and 'upbeat' imagery needed in an aggressive and cluttered in-store environment. The point-of-sale was then presented to each of the partners to gain their approval. Quantities, sizes and special requirements were checked with each retailer, proofs approved and finally all materials printed and delivered in advance of the campaign launch to each of the partners with their consignment of Gold Hearts.

The overall budget for the marketing support for the Gold Heart campaign was £500,000, although much of this funding was maximized by the agency, PR company, media owners and partner-added value.

Control

1. Measure the number of Gold Hearts sold.
2. Amount of extra revenue from alternative fund-raising/promotional activities.

A total is counted at the end of the campaign period, giving a calculated measurement of success. However, the campaign is controlled throughout, by assessing various factors, including partner acquisitions, the value of secured promotions and level of awareness via media coverage, both paid for and via the Variety Club's integrated PR.

Results to date:

- New retail partner outlets secured, including Courts, Comet and Hamleys – selling Gold Hearts.
- Additional promotions run with existing partners, creating new avenues to increase funds.
- New 'partners' recruited, therefore greater distribution of Gold Hearts: schools, petrol retail outlets, theatres, hospitals, trade unions.
- Extensive PR/media stories throughout national/regional press plus selected women's titles.
- Television campaign on air for a two-week period in the lead up to Gold Heart Day. Will be seen on terrestrial and cable channels.
- New relationships established guaranteeing brand awareness, including links with TNT cable channel and Talk Radio.

Case study Table 2.1.1 Tactical timings of summary action plan

	1997							1998		
	J	J	A	S	O	N	D	J	F	M
Concept designs			X	X						
Concept development					X	X				
Partner planning		X	X	X	X	X	X			
Heart production		X	X	X	X	X	X			
Launch								x		
Heart distribution								X	xx	
Merchandise leaflet production			X	X	X	X	X			
Merchandise leaflet distribution								xx	xx	
Point-of-sale production				X	X	X	X			
Point-of-sale in-store								X	X	
TV production					X	X	X			
TV airtime									xx	
PR planning			X	X	X	X	X			
PR coverage								X	X	X
Partner promotions								X	X	

CASE STUDY 2.2

Friends of St James Church

St James Church

Situation

The financial crisis that affected the Church of England meant that individual churches had to be self-supporting or close. The Grade II listed church of St James Norlands was under threat because it operated at an annual deficit. Although the Church is situated in Holland Park, a wealthy part of London, most of the residents spend their weekends in the country and therefore the church-goers among them did not attend St James. Since the building was only used for religious purposes on Sundays, it was hired out as a performance space to generate additional revenue, but due to the appalling state of St James Norlands' existing facilities, fees were low. However, many recognized the great potential the building had if it were to be improved. It desperately needed a heating system, toilet facilities, wheelchair access, a meeting room, lighting and a kitchen. Moreover the church's magnificent pipe organ, built by Auguste Gern in 1879, was in need of major renovation. The Friends of St James was formed by concerned people within the community. The organization's objectives were to improve the facilities of the church in order to create space for a day nursery and a financially viable centre for the performing arts. A fund-raising appeal was launched, targeting households within the community as well as grant-giving organizations. There was little money to launch a campaign (the resources were several boxes of letterhead, the church's rudimentary database and some time from the talented team at the agency Craik Jones).

Objectives

The fund-raising campaign's objectives were to raise awareness of the plight of the church and the plans to make it self-supporting, and to raise £170,000 for much-needed renovation.

Strategy

There were three key steps to the strategy:

1. To find out as much as possible about those who lived in the parish, or who used the church.
2. To build a database.
3. To use this knowledge to write strong, highly relevant and emotive letters tailored to each group's greatest point of leverage.

The database was compiled from a range of sources and segmented by wealth (house value), location (proximity to the church) and by each individual's use of the church. A manual search identified celebrities.

Key segments were: extremely wealthy people who lived on the church square, people who had previously donated to the church, celebrities, couples who had married in the church, parents of children baptised in the church, parents of children who attend the private Norland Place School (which used the church's facilities), well-off people in the parish, church attendees (both well off and those who lived in local council estates).

Tactics

Those with modest means were asked for small donations, the wealthy were asked for more (range £5 to £25,000). The extremely wealthy and celebrities were followed up by telephone and an invitation to a reception at the House of Lords. Table 2.2 (page 58) shows how each segment was targeted, with a tailored 'hook' or reason why they should donate.

Case study Table 2.2.1 Targeted segments and their motivations

Audience/segment	Hook: the issue of greater interest/concern
Anyone living in the Norlands conservation area	We will lose a valuable and vibrant part of the community if the church closes.
Living in houses worth £3m plus	Your property value will plummet – if the church closes.
Norland Conservation Society members	Maintain the fabric of the community and keep the church as the proper focal point of the Norlands Conservation Area.
Parents of children baptised in the church	The church has steadfastly supported your children – please support us in our hour of need.
Parents of children in West 11 Children's Opera Company or the North Ken Chorale – both used the church for their concerts	For your child's sake, please keep this venue open (and with improved facilities you'll enjoy it better).
Parents of children who attend Norland Place School	The church provides valuable facilities to the school. Losing them would be a disaster for your child.

Action

A lot of work was required to develop this campaign. Taking just one aspect, the database, here is a list of actions required to create it:

1. Loaded or data-captured names and addresses from the following sources: the electoral roll (parish postcodes only), the church's database of attendees (plus handwritten lists of those baptised or married in church), members of the Norland Conservation Society, the patrons and previous donors to the Friends of St James.
2. Add postcodes and correct addressing errors.
3. De-duplicate names (there was massive duplication), taking care to flag on the resulting database the list sources for each name and address.
4. Manual search to verify results, identify celebrities and flag those who were known to be wealthy.
5. Add approximate house value. There were three house value bands, based on: street/postcode (a complex set-up based on local knowledge), single house vs multiple flats in same building, and council estate addresses.

6. Segmentation into key target groups. Where a household appeared in several segments it was placed in the segment that it was felt gave the greatest amount of emotional leverage.
7. Print personalized letters and labels. (For parents of children attending Norland Place School, packs were given to the school to mail out as it was, of course, inappropriate for them to give out their list.)

Control

This simple but effective campaign was able to get people who had never donated to the church before to do so in unprecedented numbers. Of those mailed, 95 per cent had not previously donated, but 8.9 per cent made a donation. The campaign cost £195 and raised over £145,000. For every £1 spent on the campaign £744 was received.

The campaign team also received a sackful of warm letters of appreciation which praised the approach, and some even volunteered their assistance with the campaign.

Postscript

As a result of winning both the fund-raising and database categories of the DMA awards, Craik Jones were able to convince the National Lottery that the church's plan to make itself self-supporting was professionally managed. Although they had previously rejected the application, these awards tipped the balance and the church was given an additional £45,000.

APPENDIX 2.1

UK population segmented by age and sex

RESIDENT POPULATION

	1991 '000s	%	1994 '000s	%	1999 '000s	%
England	48,208	83.4	48,707	83.4	49,800	83.3
Scotland	5,107	8.8	5,132	8.8	5,120	8.6
Wales	2,891	5.0	2,913	5.0	2,937	4.9
Northern Ireland	1,601	2.8	1,642	2.8	1,892	3.2
United Kingdom	**57,807**	**100.0**	**58,394**	**100.0**	**59,749**	**100.0**

Note: Latest available figures at the time of publication. Figures may not add up to the totals, due to rounding
Sources: OPCS; General Register Offices for Scotland and Northern Ireland

RESIDENT POPULATION OF THE UK BY SEX AND AGE: 2000

Age	Total '000s	%	Male '000s	%	Female '000s	%
0–14	11,339	19.0	5,814	19.7	5,525	18.2
15–29	11,439	19.1	5,868	19.9	5,571	18.4
30–44	13,710	22.9	6,970	23.7	6,740	22.2
45–59	11,070	18.5	5,513	18.7	5,557	18.3
60–74	7,794	13.1	3,700	12.6	4,095	13.5
75 & over	4,398	7.4	1,587	5.4	2,811	9.3
Total	**59,750**	**100.0**	**29,451**	**100.0**	**30,299**	**100.0**
Mean age	38.8		37.4		40.2	
Median age	37.4		36.2		38.6	

Note: Figures may not add up to the totals, due to rounding

PROJECTED POPULATION OF THE UK: MID-YEAR

Thousands	Projections					
	2005	2010	2015	2020	2026	2038
Total	60,681	61,587	62,537	63,470	64,355	64,869
Males	30,036	30,586	31,129	31,628	32,072	32,281
Females	30,645	31,001	31,408	31,842	32,283	32,588
0–14	10,993	10,617	10,541	10,585	10,649	10,305
15–29	11,499	11,949	11,882	11,539	11,146	11,189
30–44	13,720	12,651	11,937	11,989	12,424	11,777
45–59	11,811	12,518	13,443	13,449	12,256	12,194
60–74	8,116	9,167	9,761	10,466	11,419	11,471
75+	4,542	4,685	4,972	5,440	6,461	7,933

Note: 1998-based projections. Figures may not add up to the totals, due to rounding
Source: Government Actuaries Department

POPULATION DISTRIBUTION BY SOCIAL GRADE OF CHIEF INCOME EARNER

Social grade	All adults 15+		Men		Women		(Total)	
	'000s	%	'000s	%	'000s	%	'000s	%
A	1,407	3.0	778	3.4	629	2.6	884	2.9
B	9,508	20.4	4,987	21.9	4,521	18.9	6,208	20.4
C1	12,706	27.2	5,847	25.7	6,859	28.7	8,564	28.1
C2	10,152	21.8	5,438	23.9	4,714	19.7	6,138	20.1
D	8,110	17.4	3,929	17.3	4,181	17.5	5,129	16.8
E	4,758	10.2	1,746	7.8	3,011	12.6	3,579	11.7
Total	46,641	100.0	22,725	100.0	23,916	100.0	30,501	100.0

Notes: Figures are based on the social grade of the chief wage earner. Figures may not add up to the totals, due to rounding
Source: National Readership Survey (NRS Ltd), January–December 2000

NRS SOCIAL GRADE DEFINITIONS*

Social grade	Social status	Occupation
A	Upper middle class	Higher managerial, administrative or professional.
B	Middle class	Intermediate managerial, administrative or professional.
C1	Lower middle class	Supervisory or clerical, and junior managerial administrative or professional.
C2	Skilled working class	Skilled manual workers.
D	Working class	Semi- and unskilled manual workers.
E	Those at lowest level of subsistence	State pensioners or widows (no other earner), casual or lowest-grade workers.

*These are the standard social grade classifications using definitions agreed between Research Services Ltd and NRS

Source: National Readership Survey (NRS Ltd)
Reproduced by kind permission of the *1998 Marketing Pocket Book*, NTC Publications

APPENDIX 2.2

Geodemographic segments

Group		Type		% of GB population
1	Wealthy achievers, suburban areas	1	Wealthy Suburbs, Large Detached Houses	3.0
		2	Villages with Wealthy Commuters	2.7
		3	Mature Affluent Home-Owning Areas	2.8
		4	Affluent Suburbs, Older Families	3.8
		5	Mature, Well-Off Suburbs	2.7
2	Affluent, greys, rural communities	6	Agricultural Villages, Home-Based Workers	1.5
		7	Holiday Retreats, Older People, Home-Based Workers	0.6
3	Prosperous pensioners, retirement areas	8	Home-Owning Areas, Well-Off Older Residents	1.4
		9	Private Flats, Elderly People	1.1
4	Affluent executives, family areas	10	Affluent Working Families with Mortgages	2.8
		11	Affluent Working Couples with Mortgages, New Homes	1.1
		12	Transient Workforces, Living at their Place of Work	0.4
5	Well-off workers, family areas	13	Home-Owning Family Areas	2.1
		14	Home-Owning Family Areas, Older Children	3.2
		15	Families with Mortgages, Younger Children	2.0
6	Affluent urbanites, town and city areas	16	Well-off Town & City Areas	1.2
		17	Flats & Mortgages, Singles & Young Working Couples	0.9
		18	Furnished Flats & Bedsits, Younger Single People	0.4
7	Prosperous professionals, metropolitan areas	19	Apartments, Young Professional Singles & Couples	1.0
		20	Gentrified Multi-Ethnic Areas	1.0
8	Better-off executives, inner-city areas	21	Prosperous Enclaves, Highly Qualified Executives	0.8
		22	Academic Centres, Students & Young Professionals	0.7
		23	Affluent City Centre Areas, Tenements & Flats	0.9
		24	Partially Gentrified Multi-Ethnic Areas	0.7
		25	Converted Flats & Bedsits, Single People	0.9
9	Comfortable middle agers, mature home-owning areas	26	Mature Established Home-Owning Areas	3.0
		27	Rural Areas, Mixed Occupations	3.4
		28	Established Home-Owning Areas	4.4
		29	Home-Owning Areas, Council Tenants, Retired People	2.3
10	Skilled workers, home-owning areas	30	Established Home-Owning Areas, Skilled Workers	4.1
		31	Home-Owners in Older Properties, Younger Workers	4.0
		32	Home-Owning Areas with Skilled Workers	4.7
11	New home owners, mature communities	33	Council Areas, Some New Home Owners	2.8
		34	Mature Home-Owning Areas, Skilled Workers	2.6
		35	Low-Rise Estates, Older Workers, New Home Owners	2.7
12	White-collar workers, better-off multi-ethnic areas	36	Home-Owning Multi-Ethnic Areas, Young Families	0.9
		37	Multi-Occupied Town Centres, Mixed Occupations	1.8
		38	Multi-Ethnic Areas, White-Collar Workers	1.3
13	Older people, less prosperous areas	39	Home Owners, Small Council Flats, Single Pensioners	1.9
		40	Council Areas, Older People, Health Problems	1.3
14	Council estate residents, better-off homes	41	Better-Off Council Areas, New Home Owners	2.6
		42	Council Areas, Young Families, Some New Home Owners	2.7
		43	Council Areas, Young Families, Many Lone Parents	1.7
		44	Multi-Occupied Terraces, Multi-Ethnic Areas	0.8
		45	Low-Rise Council Housing, Less-Well-Off Families	2.0
		46	Council Areas, Residents with Health Problems	1.5
15	Council estate residents, high unemployment	47	Estates with High Unemployment	0.9
		48	Council Flats, Very High Unemployment, Singles	1.1
16	Council estate residents, greatest hardship	50	Council Areas, High Unemployment, Lone Parents	1.8
		51	Council Flats, Greatest Hardship, Many Lone Parents	0.7
17	People in multi-ethnic, low-income areas	52	Multi-Ethnic, Large Families, Overcrowding	0.5
		53	Multi-Ethnic, Severe Unemployment, Lone Parents	1.1
		54	Multi-Ethnic, High Unemployment, Overcrowding	0.5

APPENDIX 2.2, cont'd

Type 1 Wealthy Suburbs, Large Detached Houses

This ACORN Type contains the most affluent neighbourhoods in Great Britain. They are wealthy, high status areas on the suburban/rural fringe which are found predominantly in the Home Counties, although there are enclaves in other parts of the country such as Bearsden, Milngavie and Eastwood in Glasgow and Solihull in the West Midlands.

DEMOGRAPHICS
The age profile of ACORN Type 1 peaks in the 45-64 age group. There are relatively few young children, though the proportion of older children is roughly 10% above average. These are predominantly family areas, though in many households the children have left home.

SOCIO-ECONOMIC PROFILE
ACORN Type 1 comprises a highly educated population - almost 3 times the national level of residents have degrees. In terms of employment, these are largely professional and managerial people. Unemployment is around a third of the national level.

HOUSING
Over 90% of homes are owner occupied, 32% being owned outright and the remainder being purchased by mortgage. Homes are large - almost 60% having 7 or more rooms - and nearly three quarters are detached. Virtually all homes have central heating.

FOOD AND DRINK
Nearly all grocery shopping is done by car weekly or less regularly. The consumption pattern is biased towards expensive, quality, healthy items such as ground coffee, mineral water, fresh fish

and fresh fruit. The usage of frozen ready meals is twice the national average. The consumption profile of alcoholic drinks is low in draught beers but high in wines and spirits, in particular port and gin.

DURABLES
Levels of car ownership are very high: there are 3.5 times the national level of households with 3 or more cars. Cars are likely to be new, large and very expensive. The proportion of cars costing over £20,000 is nearly 10 times higher than average and the proportion of 2500cc+ cars is nearly 4 times higher than average. The incidence of company cars is also above average - at 13%, this is 3 times higher than the national rate. There is not a great deal of home improvement activity in these areas. Purchase rates of white and brown goods are average. Installation rates for new central heating and double glazing are well below average.

FINANCIAL
These are extremely high income areas - the proportion of households earning more than £40,000 per annum is 5.4 times higher than average.

Ownership of National Savings Certificates is 2.8 times higher than average, and there are also well above average holdings of stocks and shares, all plastic cards and personal pensions.

MEDIA
By far the most popular daily newspaper is The Telegraph, which has a readership level 3.5 times higher than average. The Times is read by almost 5 times more people in these neighbourhoods than nationally, and readership of The Financial Times is also over 3 times higher than average. The most widely read Sunday newspaper is The Sunday Times, which is read by 3.3 times more people in this ACORN Type than nationally. The readership of The Sunday Telegraph is 4.2 times higher than average and both The Observer and The Independent on Sunday are more than twice as popular as nationally. ITV viewing levels are very low, with 57% of people classified as light viewers. Commercial radio listening levels, however, are average.

LEISURE
Winter holidays and long holidays are very popular, and the proportion of people holidaying in their own holiday home or timeshare is over 3 times higher than average. Gardening is a popular activity. People are less likely than average to go to pubs, clubs and wine bars, but much more likely than average to eat out, with French, Italian and Greek cuisines all being highly favoured. People in these neighbourhoods are very active, with above average participation rates in many sports. Tennis, skiing, sailing, windsurfing and ten-pin bowling are particularly popular. Theatre attendance is over twice the national rate and people are much more likely than average to visit stately homes.

ATTITUDES
These are people who are generally very happy with their standard of living. They are concerned about their health, and this is reflected in their preference for a low-fat diet and in their frequent exercise. They like to go somewhere different for each holiday, and are very keen to keep up to date with developments in technology. They do not tend to like television and radio commercials, but they are more likely than average to notice press advertisements and to respond to direct mail. On the whole, they would be prepared to pay more for environmentally friendly products.

APPENDIX 2.2, cont'd

Type 54 Multi-Ethnic, High Unemployment, Overcrowding

F
17
54

These are low income communities with residents from Indian, Pakistani and Bangladeshi ethnic groups. There are many very large families living in owner-occupied or privately rented homes, and the level of over-crowding is extremely high. Unemployment is also very high. In London this very small ACORN Type is only found in Tower Hamlets. Outside London it occurs in many manufacturing towns in the Midlands and the North such as Birmingham, Bradford, Blackburn and Oldham.

DEMOGRAPHICS
These neighbourhoods have extremely high levels of under-25 year olds. 36% of the population is aged under 15, compared with only 19% nationally. 70% of people are from Indian, Pakistani or Bangladeshi ethnic groups. The household profile is dominated by very high propor-tions of big households with large numbers of children.

SOCIO-ECONOMIC PROFILE
The unemployment rate is 3.1 times higher than average. The profile of those in employment shows high levels of manufac-turing workers and above average concentrations of semi-skilled and unskilled workers. These areas also contain above average proportions of students. The proportion of people using bus as a mode of transport to work is more than twice the average.

HOUSING
A striking feature of these neighbourhoods is the fact that the level of overcrowding is nearly 14 times higher than average. Since the proportion of small (1-2 room) homes is below average, the overcrowding is due to household size. 75% of homes are terraced houses. The proportion of homes owned outright is 18% higher than average. The level of furnished, private rented accommodation is 2.4 times higher than average.

FOOD AND DRINK
People here are over 4 times more likely than average to do their grocery shopping daily, and 2.7 times more likely to do this shopping on foot. Both freezer ownership and usage of freezer centres are very low, but consumption of some frozen foods such as fish fingers is extremely high. People here are heavy users of brown sauce and ketchup, fruit juice, crisps, fresh meat and sausages. Consumption of beers and wines is low, but consumption of spirits is, on the whole, average and vodka consumption is fairly high.

DURABLES
Car ownership levels are very low, with 57% of households having no car. People are much more likely than average to have owned their car for more than 5 years. Purchase rates for consumer durables are, in general, well below average. There are a few exceptions to this however - washer dryers are bought by 95% more people here than average and video cameras by 30% more people.

FINANCIAL
2.8 times more people than average have an income of less than £5,000 per annum in these neighbourhoods. With the exception of current accounts, ownership of financial products is extremely low. Current account ownership is slightly above average and 3.4 times more people are opening new current accounts.

MEDIA
Very few people have satellite television, but almost twice the average number have cable television. An extremely wide range of daily newspapers are read here from The Financial Times and The Telegraph to The Sun. The most widely read daily paper is The Mirror.

Similarly, the most widely read Sunday paper is The Sunday Mirror, but The Observer and The Independent on Sunday are also widely read here. ITV viewing is light, but commercial radio listening is medium.

LEISURE
Although 54% of people take no holiday at all, those who do go on holiday are more likely than average to take a long holiday. People here are over 3 times more likely than average to go to wine bars regularly. Sports which are particularly popular here are tennis and bowls. Other popular activities are dancing and going to the cinema.

ATTITUDES
People here are not keen on DIY at all. They are much more likely than average to be vegetarian, and they love buying new gadgets and appli-ances. They tend to prefer well known brands to own label products and are very often tempted to buy new brands when they see them.

APPENDIX 2.3

GB population distribution by socio-economic group

DISTRIBUTION OF THE POPULATION BY SOCIAL GRADE

Social grade	All adults15+		Men		Women		Main shopper (female)	
	'000s	%	'000s	%	'000s	%	'000s	%
A	1,415	3.1	755	3.37	660	2.78	576	2.84
B	8,348	18.1	4,344	19.38	4,004	16.87	3,423	16.90
C1	12,837	27.8	6,002	26.77	6,834	28.80	5,885	29.06
C2	10,350	22.4	5,503	24.55	4,847	20.43	4,117	20.33
D	7,843	17.0	3,786	16.89	4,056	17.09	3,379	16.70
E	5,357	11.6	2,029	9.04	23,729	100.00	20,250	100.00

Note: These social grades are based on the occupation of chief income earners

Main shoppers are identified as those who personally select half or more of the items bought from supermarkets and food shops.

	'000s	%
Female main shopper	20,251	68.78
Male main shopper	9,192	31.22
Total	**29,443**	**100.00**

Source: National Readership Survey (NRS Ltd), July 1996–June 1997

Key points from Chapter 2:

1. Always carry out a careful analysis of the situation. Do your homework. Know your customers (and competitors).
2. Objectives can be quantified and used to measure performance.
3. More than one strategy should be considered.

FURTHER READING

Doyle, P (1998) *Marketing Management Strategy*, 2nd edn, Prentice-Hall, Hemel Hempstead

Doyle, P, Saunders, J and Wright, L (1987) 'A comparative study of US and Japanese marketing strategies in the British market', Warwick University Report

Engel, J, Warshaw, M and Kinnear, T (1994) *Promotional Strategy: Managing the Marketing Communications Process*, Irwin, Boston, MA

Kanter, Rosabeth Moss (2000) *On-line Marketing Course 2: Segmentation Positioning and the Marketing Mix*, Multimedia Marketing.com, London

Kotler, P *et al*, (2001) *On-line Marketing Course 3: Marketing Planning*, Multimedia Marketing.com, London

Smith, P, Berry, C and Pulford, A (1999) *Strategic Marketing Communications*, Kogan Page, London

Wing, R L (1989) *The Art Of Strategy* (translation of Sun Tzu, c 480–221 BC, *The Art of War*), Aquarian Press, Wellingborough, Northants

3

Communications theory

COMMUNICATIONS THEORY

A dictionary definition of 'communications' is as follows:

communication n. 1. a transmitting 2. a) giving or *exchange of information,* etc. by talk, writing b) the information so given 3. a means of communicating 4. the science of transmitting information.

What is interesting is the exchange of information. Communication is not a one-way flow of information. Talking at or to someone does not imply successful communication. This only occurs when the receiver actually receives the message that the sender intended to send. Message rejection, misinterpretation and misunderstanding are the opposite of effective communication.

Millions die from ineffective communications

There is evidence that a mistake in translating a message sent by the Japanese government near the end of World War II may have triggered the bombing of Hiroshima, and thus ushered in atomic warfare. The word 'mokusatsu' used by Japan in response to the US surrender ultimatum was translated by Domei as 'ignore', instead of its correct meaning, 'withhold comment until a decision has been made'.

Cutlip, Center and Broom (1985)

The above is an extreme and tragic example of communications gone wrong. *Communication errors* in marketing generally do not cost lives but can, if allowed to continue unchecked, *cost market share*, company survival and jobs. On the other hand, good marketing communications help an organization to thrive by getting its messages across in a focused and cost-effective way.

Good marketing communications is *not as simple as it may appear*. Even David Ogilvy, the advertising guru, was once reported to have used the word 'obsolete' in an advertisement only to discover that (at the time) 43 per cent of US women had no idea what it meant. The delicacy and difficulty of creating effective communications to target audiences can be explained by Douglas Smallbone's analogy of radio communication.

The human radio

'Given good transmitting conditions and receiver and transmitter tuned to the same wavelength, perfect reception can be effected.'

Smallbone (1969)

Perfect transmitting conditions might exist if there was no noise (extraneous factors that distract or distort the message, such as other advertisements, poor reception, a flashing light, a door bell, an ambulance). Without noise perfect transmitting conditions would exist. In reality there is almost always noise, so perfect transmitting conditions do not exist. Cinemas may be the exception, where a captive audience is in an attentive state and receptive to, say, a well-produced X-rated advertisement. But even when the target audience is seemingly tuned in (watching, listening or looking at a particular organization's package, promotion, advertisement, etc) they may not be on the same wavelength because of the hidden internal psychological processes that may be reshaping or distorting the message to suit the audience's own method of interpretation.

The human receiver is in fact equipped with five distinct means of receiving messages or information or marketing communications – the five senses of hearing, sight, touch, taste and smell. Marketing communications tools can address many senses simultaneously (eg packaging).

Non-verbal and non-symbolic communications

Although verbal and visual communications gain a lot of conscious attention, there are *non-verbal* and *non-symbolic* ways of communicating, such as space, time and kinetics. Crowded areas, or lack of *space*, send messages to the brain which, in turn, can stimulate a different set of thoughts and a different behavioural response. The opposite is also true: a spacious office or living room conveys different images. In Western cultures the use of *time* creates images, eg a busy but organized person gives an impression of authority. 'Thanks for your time' immediately conveys a respect for and an appreciation of a seemingly important person's time. A busy diary can project an image of importance. 'I can squeeze you in on Friday at…' implies seniority in the relationship. In the UK, the term 'window' is starting to be used for free time or space in a busy diary. Some advertisements sell products and services primarily on time-saving / convenience benefits. In fact, banks are really time machines that allow an individual to move forward in time by buying, say, a house that would not normally be affordable for 30 years. Finally, *kinetics* communicate. Gestures and movements send messages. Even the simple, swift clicking of a briefcase, entering or leaving a room or closing or not closing a door can communicate. Most of all, body language and facial gestures are powerful communicators. An understanding of body language allows an individual to learn more about what another person is really feeling. A smile, for example, communicates immediately, effectively and directly.

Semiotics

The field of semiotics (or semiology) opens up a rich discussion of how symbols and signs are used in communications, particularly advertising. Audiences often unconsciously perceive images stimulated by certain symbols.

Engel, Warshaw and Kinnear (1991) demonstrated how Lever Brothers' fabric softener, Snuggles, uses a cuddly teddy bear in its advertising.

Carol Moog, advertising consultant and psychologist, says that:

> the bear is an ancient symbol of aggression, but when you create a teddy bear, you provide a softer, nurturant side to that aggression. As a symbol of tamed aggression, the teddy bear is the perfect image for a fabric softener that tames the rough of clothing.

Engel, Warshaw and Kinnear comment:

> The key point here is that if marketing communicators are not aware of the subtle meanings of symbols, then they are liable to communicate the wrong message.

Miss Moog's advice to Pierre Cardin on their men's fragrance advertisement, which was designed to show men who are 'aggressive and in control' splashing fragrance, was accepted but rejected! Miss Moog saw 'cologne gushing out of a phallic shaped bottle' creating a conflict of images, since it 'symbolised male ejaculation and lack of control'. Pierre Cardin acknowledged that she was probably right but decided to keep the shot as it was 'a beautiful product shot plus it encourages men to use our fragrance liberally'.

Closer to home, Guinness used Rutger Hauer's black clothes and blonde hair in the now classic Guinness Genius advertisements to symbolize the pint of Guinness itself.

The user symbolizes the product

COMMUNICATIONS MODELS

No simple diagram can reflect all the nuances and complexities of the communication process. This section considers some basic theories and models.

A single-step communications model

There are three fundamental elements in communication, the sender (or source), the message and the receiver, as shown in Figure 3.1.

Figure 3.1 A simple communications model

This basic model assumes that the sender is active, the receiver is inactive or passive and the message is comprehended properly. In reality this is rarely the case. Chapter 4 demonstrates how we see what we want to see and not necessarily what is sent. An understanding of the target receiver or audience helps to identify what is important to the audience and how symbols, signs and language are interpreted. The message is 'dressed up' or coded in an appropriate way, sent through a media channel and, if it gets through all the other noise, finally decoded by the receiver. Guinness advertisements basically ask their target audience to drink Guinness, but they are very carefully coded. For example, 'It's not easy being a dolphin' were the only words uttered in one of their television advertisements. The audience decodes the message (correctly or incorrectly) and ultimately rejects, accepts, stores or decides whether to drink Guinness or not. Amidst the careful coding and decoding there is noise, the extraneous factors that distract or distort the coded messages; Figure 3.2 demonstrates this.

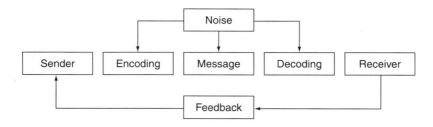

Figure 3.2 The communication process (based on Schramm's 1955 model)

The sender monitors feedback (eg whether the receiver changes his or her behaviour, facial expression, beliefs or attitudes) so that the message (and/or the channel in which it is sent) can be modified or changed. With so many other advertisements out there it is easy to understand why so little communication actually gets through and works on the target market.

Mass communications

Despite the attractions of one-to-one marketing (see Chapter 13), mass communications such as television advertising is still considered attractive because it can reach a large audience quickly and cheaply (when comparing the cost per thousand individuals contacted – see page 387). Much of this kind of mass advertising is ignored or distorted by an individual's information processing system. However, there is usually, within the mass audience, a percentage who are either actively looking for the particular product type or who are in a receptive state for this type of message (see the financial services example on page 38). Mass communication is therefore of interest to many marketing communicators. It is not the single-step process it was considered to be in the early mass communications model shown in Figure 3.3.

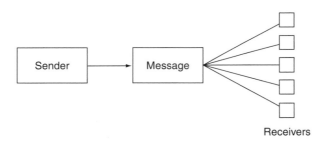

Figure 3.3 One-step communications model

This kind of inaccurate model of mass communication suggests that the sender has the potential to influence an unthinking and non-interacting crowd. Audiences (receivers) are active in that they process information selectively and often in a distorted manner (we see what we want to see). Receivers (the audience) also talk to each other. Opinion formers and opinion leaders also influence the communications process.

Two-step communications model

Katz and Lazarsfeld's two-step hypothesis (1955) helped to reduce fears of mass indoctrination by an all-powerful media. It assumed mass messages filtered through opinion leaders to the mass audience. Figure 3.4 shows how messages are filtered through opinion leaders (or) as well as going directly to some members of the target audience.

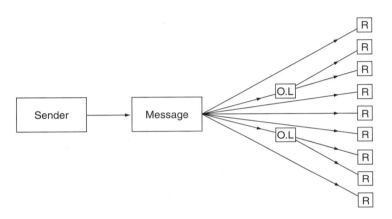

Figure 3.4   Two-step communications with opinion leaders

When opinion formers (OF) are added in, the communications model becomes a little bit more interesting. Opinion formers can be separated from opinion leaders as shown in Figure 3.5 (page 76). Opinion formers are formal experts whose opinion has influence, eg journalists, analysts, critics, judges, members of a governing body. People seek their opinions and they provide advice. Opinion leaders, on the other hand, are harder to identify – they are not formal experts, they do not necessarily provide advice but other buyers are influenced by them. Other customers look towards them. Opinion leaders often enjoy higher social status (than their immediate peer group), are more gregarious and have more confidence to try new products and services. Endorsements from both opinion formers and opinion leaders are valuable. The opinion formers are often quoted in promotional literature and advertisements, while the style leaders are often seen with the brand through clever editorial exposure engineered by public relations professionals. This can be generated by collecting third party endorsements, creating events around celebrities and 'placing' products alongside celebrities (eg branded mineral water on the top table at press conferences or actual product placement in films). In business-to-business markets blue-chip customers are opinion leaders and are much sought after, as their presence on a customer list influences other customers. Both opinion formers and opinion leaders can contribute towards credibility. 'Credibility before visibility' means that a solid platform of credibility should be developed before raising visibility with any high-profile activities.

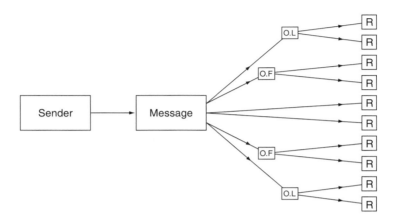

Figure 3.5   Two-step communications model with opinion leaders and opinion formers

Multi-step communications model (a)

Communication is in fact a multifaceted, multi-step and multi-directional process. Opinion leaders talk to each other. Opinion leaders talk to their listeners. Listeners talk to each other (increasingly with discussion groups/Internet groups) and subsequently feed back to opinion leaders, as shown in Figure 3.6. Some listeners/readers receive the message directly.

Multi-step communications model (b)

Noise, channels and feedback can be added to the multi-step model to make it more realistic, as shown in Figure 3.7.

The process of communicating with groups is fascinating. Group roles (leaders, opinion formers/leaders and followers), group norms and group attitudes are considered in 'Group influence' (page 110) and 'Social change' (page 218). In fact, all the intervening psychological variables can be added into the communications models to show how perception, selection, motivation, learning, attitudes and group roles all affect the communication process. The intervening variables and some more complex models of buyer behaviour are considered in more detail in Chapter 4.

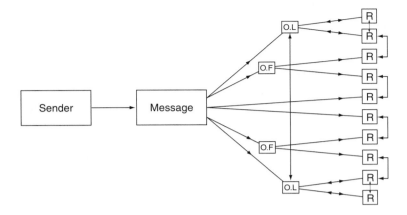

Figure 3.6   Multi-step communications model (a)

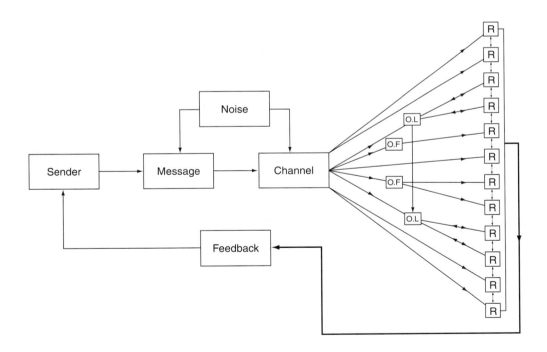

Figure 3.7   Multi-step communications model (b)

James Bond – opinion leader

Product placement does not always have to be expensive. European Telecom touted their new piece of mobile technology (a car fax) to all the major product placement agencies that act on behalf of the film company giants. They had no budget for any deals or link-ups with any film but they had a visually interesting piece of technology. To their surprise and delight, the placement agency handling the James Bond film, *Tomorrow Never Dies*, requested two working prototypes, which were duly delivered and demonstrated at Pinewood Studios. The product was shown as Moneypenny receives a fax from the clearly branded prototype, and hands it to Bond, who is sitting alongside M in the back of the Daimler. An additional car fax is also clearly seen alongside Bond in the back of the car. Now the PR team can really milk the opportunity. After all, 'a portable fax that is approved by James Bond surely has more cachet than one that isn't' – Jeff Lucas, Marketing Director.

Web communications models

Let's take this a stage further and consider today's new Web communications models which revolve around the brand instead of simply being sent to the masses by the brand owner. Markets are conversations. Word of mouth works much more quickly online than offline. With the Internet came the easier facilitation of customer communities, where customers can talk, first, to each other (C2C) and, secondly, back to the company (C2B). The flow of communications eventually becomes like a web of communications between customers and opinion leaders – all built around the brand.

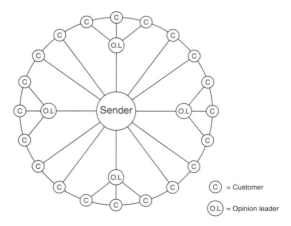

Figure 3.8 Simple Web communications model

The company facilitates these conversations. In doing so, it keeps close to customers, as it can look and listen to what's being said. It can also communicate easily with the customers and ultimately develop strong relations with them. Newsgroups and discussion rooms hosted by the brand discuss the brand, its applications, problems, issues, ideas, improvements and a broader array of topics linked with some of the brand values. In a sense, a web of conversations is spinning around the brand. Customers talk to each other. For example, more than half of eBay's customers come from referrals (Reichfield *et al*, 2000).

The e-marketing team should also monitor user group sites it does not host; some of the truths may be painful but extremely useful. C2C communications can be negative. Remember the Pentium chip problem? It spread like wildfire as the worry spread online. C2C communications can also be fuelled by some customer groups who set up fake sites and hate sites that are devoted to spreading negative messages about brands. One type of C2C that is positive – and in fact generates a lot of business – is referrals, where happy customers become advocates and recommend other customers. Another positive form of C2C and P2P is viral, where customers pass the message on. This is accelerated word of mouth. Clever, creative messages with interesting ideas, amazing ideas, special offers, announcements and invitations are good for viral marketing.

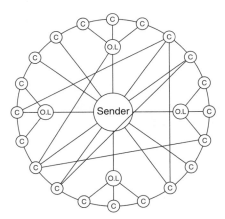

Figure 3.9   Advanced Web communications model

Affiliate marketing also spreads awareness of a brand amongst a community of relevant customers, who in turn talk to each other and can spread ordinary or clever viral messages among their own communities. Implicit in all of these communications models is permission-based marketing. In this time-compressed, information-cluttered world, customers resent unsolicited spam. Excellent e-marketers win permission to send future messages. If the customer agrees, a message is finally sent.

Individuals do talk to each other (at least 400 million on the Internet and billions on the phone), particularly when sharing personal product experiences. In fact, dissatisfied customers tell up to another 11 people about their bad experience, whereas satisfied customers tell only three or four. As marketing guru Philip Kotler says, 'Bad news travels faster than good news'. Although this is not in the realm of mass communications, it does demonstrate how everything an organization does communicates something to someone somewhere. Chapter 19 looks at this whole process in a lot more detail. Suffice to say, at this stage, that many advertisers use teaser, surreal and puzzle advertising (by sending incomplete or obscure messages) to arouse involvement and discussion among target audiences.

Understanding multi-phase communication

Whether online, offline or integrated, here is how an understanding of multi-phase communication helps many advertisers to communicate directly to the mass (through the mass media) and indirectly through opinion leaders, style leaders, innovators, early adopters, influential individuals and opinion formers.

Advertisers recognize that in each market there are smaller target markets of opinion leaders who influence other members in the marketplace. Major brands can maintain their credibility by talking (advertising) specifically to these leaders as well as talking to the mass through other media channels (sometimes with messages tailored for the two groups). Whether advertising hi-fis, fashion, tennis rackets or social issues, multi-step communications can be employed.

In the world of fashion, the leaders are called 'style leaders'. Even cult fashion products can be mass marketed by carefully splitting the messages between style leaders and the mass. While the leaders want to set themselves apart from the rest, the mass market consciously and/or unconsciously looks to the leaders for suggestions about what to buy. The difficulty lies with success – as the mass market buys more, the leaders lose interest unless they are reinforced with brand values that preserve the brand's credibility among the cognoscenti. This is important because if the leaders move away today, the mass sales will eventually start falling away next year or the year after. So, in addition to the mass advertising, some brands use small-audience, targeted, opinion-leader media to send the 'right' messages to reinforce the leaders' relationship with the brand.

Hi-fi trendsetters need a different kind of advertising than just colour supplements with glossy brand images. These 'innovators and early adopters' read additional magazines and look for more detailed technical information in music magazines or specialist hi-fi magazines, buyers' guides, etc. Less knowledgeable buyers often refer to a friend who is a bit of a music buff (innovator or adopter) for an opinion on a brand of hi-fi before deciding to buy. Just getting the product into the hands of the opinion leaders can help a brand competing in a large market. American marketing guru Philip Kotler suggests that special offers to opinion formers can work wonders:

A new tennis racquet may be offered initially to members of the high-school tennis teams at a special low price. The company would hope that these star high-school tennis players (or *influential individuals*) would 'talk up' their new racquet to other high schoolers.

An understanding of multi-phase communication processes can contribute something to the development of social issue campaigns like that concerning AIDS. The initial stages of the campaign were temporarily restricted by inaccurate editorial coverage. Some tabloid *journalists* were feeding conflicting messages to the same mass which the advertising was addressing. The factual advertising was switched into the press so that *opinion formers* (journalists) could not write any more conflicting and inaccurate reports.

The power of *influential individuals* and *influential organizations* can also be seen in industrial markets. An entire industry may follow a well-respected and highly successful company that makes an early decision to buy. Expert sales teams focus on these kinds of companies initially. Marketers in consumer markets can also focus on the people who are the first to buy new ideas. Better information today can provide a focused approach through database marketing (see page 376), while the imagery used can reflect the lifestyles, attitudes and aspirations of these 'innovators/early adopters' of fresh ideas.

Who are these 'early adopters' of new products and services? Are they different from the other potential customers in the same market? How do they 'adopt' new products or services? Is there a particular type of process through which they pass? The final section of this chapter provides some answers.

Word of mouth

Word of mouth is the most potent of all the communications tools. Product/service quality and customer care greatly influence word of mouth (see Chapter 19). Millions of people have seen the British film *The Full Monty* without any major advertising support; the Body Shop avoid advertising yet have also succeeded through word of mouth. Word has spread about the new Web company, Nua. Although they are physically based in Ireland, word of mouth has encouraged over 100,000 business executives to subscribe to their free electronic web surveys (see Chapter 20). Many Internet campaigns are designed to encourage the most potent tool, word of mouth. Regardless of source, and often regardless of fact, people do talk. Rumours can spread like wildfire without any mass advertising. People do talk to each other, whether opinion formers, opinion leaders or just groups of people talking on the Internet, on chat shows or on street corners. Chapter 19 looks at how word of mouth can be influenced.

Chewing gum hysteria

Rumours spread in Egyptian university town Al-Mansura that after chewing certain brands of gum female students experience uncontrollable passion for their male peers. *Time* magazine reported that 'in a society where girls are expected to remain virgins until marriage the news has generated considerable anxiety. Suspicion of who might be spiking the gum with aphrodisiacs fell on the usual suspect, Israel, frequently accused of supplying the Egyptian black market with pornography. However laboratory analysis showed that some gum samples actually lowered the libido.' Scientific fact may not be relevant. For once a rumour gets going, 'the suggestibility factor can be so strong that it can greatly affect one's mind and actions without there being a scientific explanation' says sociologist Madiha El Safty.

Time magazine

Adoption model

Several different hierarchical message models are considered in Chapter 4. The adoption model (Rogers, 1962) is one of these. As shown in Figure 3.8, it attempts to map the mental process through which an individual passes on his or her journey towards purchasing, and ultimately adopting (or regularly purchasing) a new product or service.

This somewhat simplistic hierarchical model is nevertheless useful for identifying, first, communication objectives and, second, the appropriate communications tools.

For example, television advertising may create awareness, while a well-trained salesman or expertly designed brochure may help the individual in the evaluation stage. In reality, the process is not simply hierarchical. Some individuals move directly from awareness to trial, while others loop backwards from the later stages by never actually getting around to trying the new idea, subsequently forgetting it and then having to go through being made aware of it again.

Rogers was also interested in how a new idea spreads or diffuses through a social system or market. He defined diffusion as 'the spread of a new idea from its source of invention or creation to its ultimate users or adopters'. Several groups who moved towards adoption – at different rates – were identified. The first group to try a new product were called 'innovators'. They represent approximately 2.5 per cent of all of the buyers who will eventually adopt the new product. Their profile was different from those who were last to try a new idea (the 'laggards'). Opinion leader characteristics were part of the innovators. The key to the market is to identify, isolate and target resources at the innovators rather than everyone (84 per cent will not buy the product until they see the innovators and early adopters with it first). The 'early adopters' are the second group to adopt a new idea (they represent

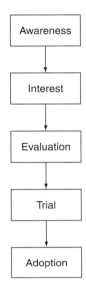

Figure 3.10 Adoption model

13.5 per cent of the total market), followed by the 'early majority' (34 per cent), the 'late majority' (34 per cent) and the 'laggards' (16 per cent).

Treat early adopters differently

Burton's Web site is careful to try to match the products on offer to those that would appeal to the early adopters.

Eva Pascoe, Burton Group Online Manager

Each group has a different profile, encompassing income, attitudes, social integration, etc. Innovators are venturesome, socially mobile and they like to try things that are new. The early adopters tend to be opinion leaders who carefully adopt new ideas early. The early majority adopt earlier than the majority of the market and they are even more careful, almost deliberate, in their buying process. The late majority only adopt after they have seen the majority of people try it. They tend to be sceptical. The laggards are self-explanatory – tradition-bound and the last to adopt.

Adapting the adoption process

Although it is not a new product, Guinness have adapted the adoption process. They researched the 'adoption process' for a pint of Guinness because high increases in consumption among young session drinkers resulting from the previous Guinness campaign were not sustained. This prompted the question: 'How does one adopt a pint of Guinness?' How many pints, sessions or weeks does it take before becoming a regular, fully converted, loyal Guinness drinker? The answers to these questions were carefully collected before the commencement of the Genius campaign.

Many of the previously discussed models offer some insight into the communication process but, almost invariably, they distort or oversimplify the process of communication. Chapter 4 draws on some of the communication models discussed here and looks at buying models, the buying process and the intervening psychological variables. How do we buy? Why do we buy? What influences our choices? Are there unconscious motives playing havoc with our day-to-day shopping behaviour? The next chapter attempts to look inside the customer's mind and answer some of these questions.

Key points from Chapter 3:

1. Communication involves a two-way flow of information.
2. Communication theories can be applied to practical marketing situations.

FURTHER READING

Cutlip, S, Center, A and Broom, G (1985), *Effective Public Relations*, 6th edn, Prentice-Hall International, Englewood Cliffs, NJ

Engel, J, Warshaw, M and Kinnear, T (1991), *Promotional Strategy: Managing the Marketing Communications Process*, 7th edn, Irwin, Homewood, IL

Floch, J-M (2001) *Semiotics, Marketing and Communication*, Palgrave, Basingstoke

Godin, S (1999) *Permission Marketing*, Simon & Schuster, Hemel Hempstead

Guirdham, M (1999) *Communicating Across Cultures*, Palgrave, Basingstoke

Katz, E and Lazarfeld, P (1955) *Personal Influence: The Part Played by People in the Flow of Mass Communications*, New York Free Press, New York

Kotler, P (2000) *Marketing Management Analysis, Planning, Implementation and Control*, The Millennium edn, Prentice-Hall, Englewood Cliffs, NJ

Lucas, Jeff (1997), License to sell, *Marketing Director International*, October

Reichfield, F and Schefter, P (2000) Eloyalty: your secret weapon on the Web, *Harvard Business Review*, July–August

Rogers, E (1962) *Diffusions of Innovations*, New York Free Press, New York

Schramm, Wilbur (1955), *The Process and Effects of Mass Communications*, University of Illinois Press, Urbana, IL

Smallbone, D (1969) *The Practice of Marketing*, Staples Press, London

Smith, P R (2001) *Online eMarketing Course: eCustomers*, Multimedia Marketing.com, London

Smith, P R and Chaffey, D (2001) *eMarketing Excellence*, Butterworth-Heinemann, Oxford

Time magazine (1996) 'Chewing Gum Hysteria', 22 July

Tuck, M (1976) *How Do We Choose: A Study in Consumer Behaviour*, Methuen, London

4

Buying behaviour

INTRODUCTION

The first step in formulating a marketing communications strategy is to identify, analyse and ultimately understand the target market and its buying behaviour. This chapter considers some of the theories and models which the marketing professional can use to help to communicate with and influence the buyer at various stages before, during and after purchasing. Buying behaviour is often more complex than it appears. Individuals are generally not very predictable, but, in the aggregate, groups of customers (or percentages of markets) can be more predictable.

Whether in the industrial or consumer market, or whether they are buying products or services, buyers respond in different ways to the barrage of marketing communications that are constantly aimed at them. Theoretical frameworks borrowed from psychology, sociology, social psychology, cultural anthropology and economics are now added to by both commercial and academic market research into consumer and industrial buyer behaviour. All of this contributes to a better understanding of buyer behaviour. It is this understanding that helps to reveal what kind of marketing communications work best.

This chapter can only provide an outline of the vast amount of work written in this area. The complex burger buyer example is used to open up some of the types of question that need to be considered. The chapter then looks at types of purchases, the buying process (including some buying models) and eventually briefly considers how the 'intervening variables' of perception, motivation, learning, memory, attitudes, beliefs, personality and group influence can influence the communication process and, ultimately, buying behaviour.

THREE KEY QUESTIONS

There are three key groups of questions that have to be answered before any marketing communications can be carried out:

1. Who is the buyer (target market/s and decision-making units)?
2. Why do they buy (or not buy) a particular brand or product?
3. How, when and where do they buy?

The second question, 'Why do they buy?', is the most difficult to answer. It requires *qualitative* rather than *quantitative* data (which generally answers the other questions). Products and services are bought for a range of different reasons or benefits, some conscious, others unconscious, some rational, others emotional. Many buyers buy for a mixture of reasons. Consider a simple hamburger.

THE COMPLEX BURGER BUYER

Why buy a burger? The answer might be as simple as 'because I was hungry – so I bought a Big Mac'. The real reason, however, may be quite different. Perhaps the buyer was in a receptive state for food because of the time of the day. In the same way that a stimulus such as a bell for Pavlov's dog (see 'Learning', page 104) can cause a dog to salivate, the highly visible yellow McDonald's logo can act as a stimulus to the customer to remind him of food and arouse feelings of hunger – even salivation. Perhaps the yellow logo also acts as a *cue* by triggering memories of the happy advertising images which are learned and stored in memory banks?

A teenage burger buyer may prefer McDonald's because friends hang out there and it feels nice to be in with the in-crowd (Maslow's need to be accepted or loved, see 'Motivation' on page 107). Maybe the friendly image and the quick service simultaneously satisfy two basic needs – love and hunger? Many convenience purchases today are, in fact, purchasing time, ie buying a time-saving product or service releases free time to do something else, to satisfy another need. It is likely that buyers have many different reasons with different orders of importance. Different segments can seek many different reasons with different orders of importance. But why don't they go into a Wimpy restaurant or a fish and chip shop instead of a McDonald's?

Choice is often influenced by familiarity with the brand, or sometimes the level of trust in a brand name. Familiarity can be generated by actual experience and/or increased awareness boosted by advertising. If one brand can get into the front of an individual's mind ('*front of mind awareness*') through advertising, etc, then it will stand a better chance of being chosen in a simple buying situation like this, unless, of course, the buyer has a *preferred set* of fast-food restaurants that specifically exclude a particular brand. In this case the buyer is usually prepared to search a little harder (even cross the road) before satisfying the aroused need.

The choice of another group of burger buyers can be determined simply by location – offering the right goods or services in the right place at the right time at the right prices. Assuming this is all supported by the right image (eg clean and friendly, nutritious, fast service, socially responsible), then the marketing mix has succeeded in capturing this segment of non-loyal burger buyers who have no strong preferred set of fast-food outlets.

More health-conscious buyers may prefer a nice warm cup of soup. Why? What motivates them? Health? A desire to live longer? A fear of death? A desire to be fit, stay slim, look good (esteem) or just feel healthy/feel good (self-actualization, see Figure 4.7, page 109)? Or perhaps it's cheaper than a burger? Or is it because everyone else in the office recommends the local delicatessen's soup (pressure to conform to group norms, desire to be accepted by a group – again, the need to be loved)?

There are other possibilities that lie in the dark depths of our vast information storage chambers, otherwise known as our unconscious. For example, in the 1950s Vance Packard suggested that:

> the deepest roots of our liking for warm, nutritious and plentiful soup may lie in the comfortable and secure unconscious prenatal sensations of being surrounded by the amniotic fluid in our mother's womb.

Impulse buying and repeat purchasing of low-cost fast food obviously differs from the buying behaviour involved in the purchase of, say, a new compact disc system, a house, a holiday or a fleet of new cars for the company. It is likely that more 'information search' will occur than in the simple stimulus–response buying model (McDonald's yellow logo stimulates the senses and arouses hunger, which generates the response – buy a Big Mac). Regular low-cost purchases are known as '*routinised response behaviour*' and therefore have a different buying process than a high-cost, high-risk, irregular purchase, which is known as a '*high-involvement purchase*'. Some basic buying models help to explain the different types of purchases and the types of buying process involved. These will be considered later in this chapter, but first let us consider why buyers buy.

Some people behave differently online than offline. They assume different pseudonyms and personalities. Sometimes it's hard to know who's who online. As they say, 'Who knows you're a dog online?'

Complex personalities

A 25-year-old New York stockbroker had an online fling with a 21-year-old blue-eyed blonde Miami beauty. They arranged to meet at JFK airport with red roses at a meeting point. The young New Yorker was horrified to see a 70-year-old man sitting in a wheelchair, wearing a red rose and roaring with laughter at him.

WHY DO THEY BUY?

Marketing people really do need to know the reasons why buyers buy. There appears to be a host of conscious and unconscious reasons underlying why people buy what they buy. Some reasons are more important than others to a particular segment. Some reasons are rational and some are emotional. The split between the two is called the '*emotional/rational dichotomy*'. Ex-CEO Robert Gouezeta said, 'We sell on image. We don't know how to sell on performance. Everything we sell, we sell on image.'

Rational shoppers?

Typically, shoppers give the correct price of only 50 per cent of what they have just put in their trolley.
Consumers remain loyal to brands even when better products are available.
Consumers rarely complain to suppliers when dissatisfied about a product.
Is this a time-efficient way of dealing with repetitive purchases, or emotional madness?

Professor Robert East

This rational and emotional quagmire is not restricted to consumer purchasing but applies also to supposedly hard-nosed rational professional buying behaviour. The bottom line is that marketing managers have constantly to ask the question: 'Why are they buying or not buying my products or services?' The answers are not static, one-off pieces of research findings but a constant flow of information. Reasons change, people change, markets change, competition and technology change. A valid reason for buying a particular product yesterday may become obsolete tomorrow. Likewise, an apparently irrelevant feature yesterday may become a key reason for buying tomorrow.

A company executive might buy one brand of a computer rather than another simply because of a distant fear of being fired. Even an apparently simple product like toothpaste presents a complex web of reasons for buying. The toothpaste manufacturers respond by supplying different images of different benefits of different types of toothpaste to different segments who have different reasons (needs or motives) for brushing their teeth. The following toothpaste test explains.

The toothpaste test

Why do you buy toothpaste? 'To keep teeth clean.' 'To stop cavities and visits to dentist.' 'To keep a full set of beautiful shining teeth.' Some people will admit that 'it is habit' or that 'my parents taught me always to…' All of these answers suggest different benefits that different groups or segments want from their toothpaste and so the toothpaste suppliers oblige by positioning certain brands as those that deliver a particular benefit. But when do you brush your teeth? First thing in the morning? If people were serious about seeking the above benefits they would carry a small portable brush and use it after each meal. Why do most people brush first thing in the morning? To avoid bad breath (which destroys one's confidence). Yet many people do not like admitting it. The real reason is often hidden beneath the surface reasons.

The Colgate 'ring of confidence' was one of the UK's best-known toothpaste advertisements. It was basically selling a tube of social confidence. This need to be accepted is relatively obvious although not always admitted initially. There are, however, deeper feelings, emotions, memories, moods, thoughts, beliefs and attitudes locked up inside the dark depths of our unconscious. Sigmund Freud suggested that the mind was like an iceberg in so far as the tip represents the conscious part of the mind while the greater submerged part is the unconscious. Even long-forgotten childhood experiences can affect buying behaviour, including hard-nosed American industrial buyers (see 'Mommy's never coming back', page 127). Some theories of motivation are discussed further in this chapter (page 107).

In the UK many organizations use in-depth research, eg Guinness carry out in-depth research to tap into drinkers' deeply ingrained feelings about the product. Individuals are asked to express their (often unconscious) feelings through clay modelling, picture completion and cartoon completion techniques. This kind of research has revealed that people associate natural goodness and quasi-mystical qualities with the brand. The section on motivation (page 107) looks at in-depth feelings.

Bloatware

Forty-five per cent of software features are never used, 19 per cent rarely used, 16 per cent sometimes used... So some software suppliers launched 'lite ware' with less functions and lower prices. It flopped. Why? Because people didn't want to be without features that other people had – so bloatware prevails.

TYPES OF BUYING SITUATION

The amount of time and effort that a buyer is prepared to put into any particular purchase depends on the level of expenditure, the frequency of purchase and the perceived risk involved. Relatively larger expenditure usually warrants greater deliberation during search and evaluation phases. In consumer markets this buying process is classified as '*extensive problem solving*' (EPS) if the buyer has no previous product experience and the purchase is infrequent, expensive and/or risky. The situation is different where the buyer has some knowledge and experience of, and familiarity with, a particular product or service. This is called '*limited problem solving*' (LPS). In the case of strong brand loyalty for an habitually purchased product, '*routinized response behaviour*' (RRB) can be identified by the repeat brand purchasing of convenience products like baked beans. The buyer chooses quickly and has a *low involvement* with the purchase. EPS requires *high involvement* from the buyer, which means that the buyer spends time and effort before actually deciding to buy a particular product or brand. This can be complicated by further advisers and influencers who form part of the '*decision-making unit*' or DMU (see below). LPS obviously requires lower levels of involvement than EPS but more than RRB.

Industrial buying is even more clearly influenced by decision-making units, particularly when the purchase is considered large, infrequent or risky. Like consumer buying, types of purchase situation also vary in industrial markets. A '*new task*' buying situation means what it says – the organization has no experience of the product or service and is buying it for the first time. A '*modified rebuy*' situation is where the industrial buyer has some experience of the product or service, while a '*straight rebuy*' is where the buyer, or purchasing department, buys on a regular basis.

DECISION-MAKING UNITS

As mentioned previously, there are often several individuals involved in any one person's decision to purchase either consumer or industrial products and services. The choice of a family car may be influenced by parents, children, aunts, uncles, neighbours, friends, the Automobile Association and so on. Each may play a different role in the buying process. Similarly, the purchase of a new factory machine may have been instigated by a safety inspector, selected by a team of engineers, supervisors, shop steward, production manager, agreed by the board, bought or ordered by the purchasing director and paid for by the financial director or company secretary.

PAGES is a simple acronym that helps to build a marketing communications DMU checklist:

Purchaser   (orders the goods or services)
Adviser   (those that are knowledgeable in the field)
Gatekeeper (secretaries, receptionists and assistants who want to protect their bosses from being besieged by marketing messages)
End user   (sometimes called 'the customer')
Starter   (instigator or initiator)

The actual decision maker and the payer (cheque authorizer) may be added to the above *PAGES*.

MODELS OF BUYER BEHAVIOUR

There are many different models that attempt to model the buyer's behaviour. Figure 4.1 (page 94) shows how a buyer in either an EPS (extensive problem-solving) or LPS (limited problem-solving) situation moves through the purchasing cycle or purchasing continuum. The basic model can be borrowed and used in industrial markets also. It highlights some of the stages through which a potential buyer passes. Sources and channels of information plus buying criteria can also be identified, which, in turn, provide a checklist for the marketing plan.

The buying process

We can demonstrate this simple buying model by considering, say, the purchase of a new compact disc player. Somewhere, somebody or something tells you that you need a CD.

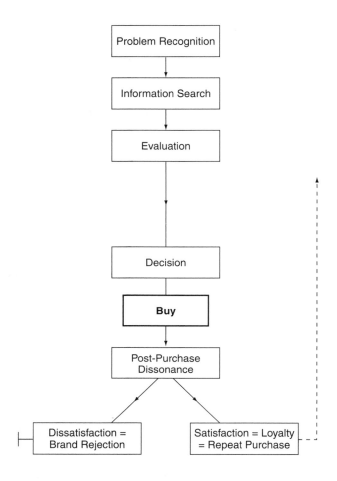

Figure 4.1 A simple model of the buying process

This is known as problem recognition, which is followed by 'information search'. This may involve ads and editorial in magazines, visits to stores, discussion among friends, etc. Next comes evaluation. Leaflets, catalogues, ads and discussions are amassed and a set of criteria is further refined. This may include size, shape, colour, delivery, guarantee, etc. Performance is really difficult to assess, since few of us can read sound graphs, let alone decipher a good sound in a shop full of other speakers. Finally, a decision is made to choose a particular model. It isn't over yet. The chosen brand may be out of stock (in which case the communications mix has worked but the marketing mix has failed, since distribution has not got the product on the shelf). Another brand is eventually purchased. This is when waves of worry, doubt or '*post-purchase dissonance*' arise. This may be addressed by reassuring the buyer (with a congratulatory note, additional advertising, after-sales service and, most of all, a product or service that lives up to the promise made in the advertising). And if the product matches the promise, then both repeat business and word-of-mouth referrals are more likely to occur over the longer run.

The simple buying model shown in Figure 4.1 serves as a useful checklist to see whether you are filling in all the communication gaps in the buying process. Interestingly, many Web sites now use this as a checklist to ensure that the site helps different customers to move through different stages of their buying process. The model should not be hierarchical since in reality there are loops, eg between information and evaluation as the buyer learns about new criteria not previously considered.

This model is more relevant for a high-involvement purchase whether extensive problem solving (consumer) or new task (industrial). A routinized response situation, like buying a beer, would not involve this lengthy deliberation.

Low-involvement purchases can sometimes appear to be thoughtless (impulsive) responses (purchases) to stimuli (point-of-sale displays or well-designed packs). If attention can be grabbed, then some brands can be bought, apparently, without much considered thought processing. Basically, if you see the brand, you try it, and if you like it, you rebuy it. Some advertising aims to remind customers and reinforce the benefits of the brand.

Advertising can also reassure existing customers that they have bought the right brand. This defensive advertising (defending market share) reduces any post-purchase dissonance (or worries) and also keeps the brand on the buyer's shopping list (or repertoire of brands).

In contrast with high-involvement purchases, attitudes towards low-involvement brands can be formed after the brand experience and not before. In the more considered, high-involvement purchases attitudes are formed after awareness but before any purchasing behaviour actually occurs. The attitude may subsequently be reinforced by, first, the real experience of buying and using the brand and, second, any subsequent advertising or word-of-mouth communications.

Professor Ehrenberg's 1974 ATR model (Awareness Trial Reinforcement) suggested that consumers become aware of a brand, try it (buy it) and then are exposed to reinforcement by advertising (or even the actual brand experience).

Trial can occur many months after an advertisement has created awareness. Advertising here is also seen as defensive, in so far as it reassures existing buyers that they have made the right choice, as opposed to advertising that might make them run out and buy the advertised brand immediately. Ehrenberg acknowledges that some advertising actually does prompt (or 'nudge') buyers to buy, as demonstrated with his more explicit 1997 ATR + N (Awareness Trial Reinforcement plus occasional Nudging) model. Ehrenberg's specific views differ from many other approaches highlighted in this chapter, yet his research findings are used by top blue-chip companies around the world.

Many other academics believe that different buying situations (high and low involvement) require different thought processes and timescales. Even within the same product sector different processes can occur. Take grocery shopping. Australian academics Rossiter and Percy have identified differences in thought processes within the grocery sector. They suggest that most grocery brands (65 per cent) need recognition at the point of purchase, since buyers tend to see the brand first and then realise they want it. Less than 10 seconds elapse between recognition and putting the product into the trolley. The other 35 per cent of groceries are chosen in advance, so brand awareness (before purchase) is important for these.

It does not stop there. There are more differences depending on whether the purchase is a relief purchase (to solve a problem such as dirty clothes) or a reward purchase (to provide gratification, like ice cream). The relief purchases require a more rational approach and the reward purchases a more emotional approach. So each market and each brand needs to be carefully analysed. Professor Robert Shaw (1997) points out 'many different measures such as brand knowledge, esteem, relevance or perceived quality may need to be monitored'. Any marketing manager, whether industrial or consumer, product or service has constantly to watch the market, its segments and how it is fragmenting.

Response hierarchy models

Although the ultimate objective for most marketing managers is to build repeat purchases from profitable customers, there are many stages between creating problem recognition or need arousal and purchase (as shown in Figure 4.1). The communication models in Figure 4.2 show what are thought to be the sequence of mental stages through which a buyer passes on his or her journey towards a purchase.

These models are sometimes called '*message models*' or '*response hierarchy models*', since they help to prioritize the communication objectives by determining whether a cognitive, affective or behavioural response is required, ie whether the organization wants to create awareness in the target audience's mind, or to change an attitude, or to act in some way (buy, vote, participate, etc). (See 'Attitudes' on page 110 for a more detailed explanation of the cognitive, affective and behavioural/conative elements of an attitude.) Message models are

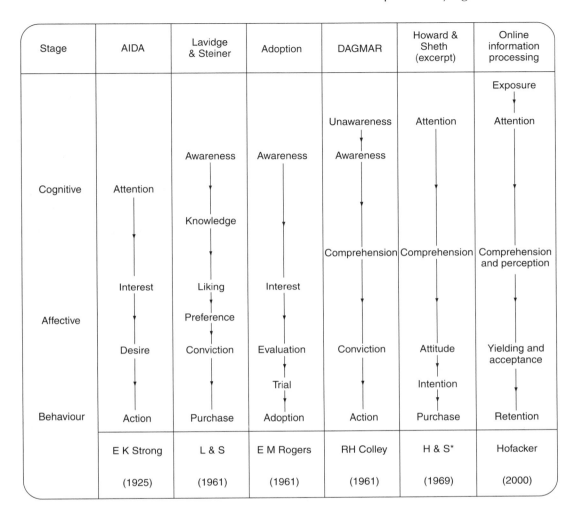

Stage	AIDA	Lavidge & Steiner	Adoption	DAGMAR	Howard & Sheth (excerpt)	Online information processing
						Exposure
				Unawareness	Attention	Attention
		Awareness	Awareness	Awareness		
Cognitive	Attention					
		Knowledge				
				Comprehension	Comprehension	Comprehension and perception
	Interest	Liking	Interest			
Affective		Preference				
	Desire	Conviction	Evaluation	Conviction	Attitude	Yielding and acceptance
			Trial		Intention	
Behaviour	Action	Purchase	Adoption	Action	Purchase	Retention
	E K Strong	L & S	E M Rogers	RH Colley	H & S*	Hofacker
	(1925)	(1961)	(1961)	(1961)	(1969)	(2000)

*The Howard and Sheth excerpt is taken from the full model shown on page 101

Figure 4.2 Response hierarchy models

helpful but not conclusive since (1) not all buyers go through all stages, (2) the stages do not necessarily occur in a hierarchical sequence and (3) impulse purchases contract the process.

Although expanding repeat purchase (loyal behaviour) from profitable customers is the ultimate marketing goal, a PR campaign, advertisement or sales promotion may have a tactical objective focusing on a particular stage in the above models, eg increasing awareness, changing an attitude or generating trial. In fact, Hofacker's online information processing model shows how online messages from banner ads and Web sites are processed (see Appendix 4.1 for more detail).

These hierarchical communication models identify the stages through which buyers generally pass. An understanding of these stages helps to plan appropriate marketing communications. DAGMAR (defining advertising goals for measuring advertising results) was created to encourage measurable objectives for each stage of the communications continuum.

Some of the stages can sometimes occur simultaneously and/or instantaneously, as in the case of an impulse purchase. Buyers can also avoid moving in a straight line or hierarchy of stages when making a more considered purchase (extended problem solving). For example, during the evaluation stage a potential buyer may go back to the information stage to obtain more information before making a decision to buy. Each hierarchical model really requires a loop from the 'last' stage up to the first stage – to show that the sale (action) is not the end stage, but rather the beginning of an ongoing dialogue that nurtures a relationship and a report buying process.

Ideally, these models should allow for these and other loops caused by '*message decay*' (or forgetting), changes in attitudes, competitive distractions, etc. The models also ignore the mind's 'intervening variables', some of which are identified in both the '*personal-variable models*' of Fishbein *et al* (page 99) and the '*complex models*' of Howard and Sheth, and Engel, Blackwell and Kollatt (1978). The complex models, do, in fact, allow for both loops and the complexities of the intervening variables (see page 102).

Three types of model, 'black-box', 'personal-variable' and 'complex', will now be considered briefly. Black-box models consider external variables that act as stimuli (such as price, shops, merchandise, advertisements, promotions and the social environment including families and friends) and responses such as sales. Personal-variable models focus on some of the internal psychological variables such as attitudes and beliefs. The complex models attempt to include both the internal and external variables in one grand model. To some this proves impossible. As Gordon Foxall (1992) pointed out: 'No one model can capture human nature in its entirety; nor can a handful of theoretical perspectives embrace the scope of human interaction.'

Black-box models

The behaviourist school of psychology concentrates on how people respond to stimuli. It is not concerned with the complex range of internal and external factors that affect the behaviour. The complexities of the mind are left locked up in a '*black box*'. The resulting *stimulus–response models* ignore the complexities of the mind (including the intervening variables such as perception, motivation, attitudes, etc) and focus on the input or stimulus, eg advertising, and the output, eg purchase behaviour. A classical approach to stimulus-response models is considered in 'Learning' on page 104. Figure 4.3 shows a black-box model.

Figure 4.3 Black-box model

As Williams (1989) says: 'Black box models treat the individual and his physiological and psychological make-up as an impenetrable black box.' Only the inputs and outputs are measured. Any internal mental processes (the intervening processes) that cannot be measured are ignored. The model below shows some examples of 'input' and 'output'.

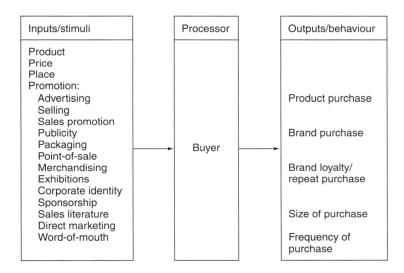

Figure 4.4 An enlarged black-box model

The black-box approach considers only the inputs and outputs. Careful analysis under controlled tests (using reasonably sophisticated computer models) can reveal the optimum price, the optimum level of advertising and so on.

Personal-variable models

These models take a glimpse inside the black box of the mind. The models only involve a few personal variables such as beliefs, attitudes and intentions. These kinds of model are sometimes used within more complex models. Three types of personal-variable models, 'linear additive', 'threshold' and 'trade-off' are briefly considered below.

Linear additive models

Linear additive models like that of Fishbein are based on the number of attributes a particular product or service has, multiplied by the score each attribute is perceived to have, multiplied by the weighting which each attribute is deemed to have. This model opens up attitudes by indicating which attributes are considered to be important to the customer and how each attribute is scored by the customer. Attitudes are not always translated into purchasing behaviour. Even intentions are not always translated into action. Nevertheless, marketing strategies can be built around changing beliefs about attributes, and altering their evaluation or scores.

Threshold models

Most purchases have cut-off points or thresholds beyond which the buyer will not venture. It may be price or some particular feature that a product or service must have (or must not have in the case of some environmentally damaging ingredients) if it is to be considered at all. Here, the buyer has a selection process that screens and accepts those products or services within the threshold for either further analysis or immediate purchase. Those beyond the threshold are rejected and will not be considered any further.

Trade-off models

Buyers generally have a wide array of choices, many with different types and amounts of attributes. A trade-off occurs when the buyer accepts a product that is lacking in one attribute but strong in another. A sort of compensatory mechanism emerges. When buying a car, engine size and price can be traded off against each other, eg a bigger engine means a worse price (higher price). A number of combinations of price and engine size can be researched to find the value or 'utility' for different prices and engine sizes.

Complex models

The *cognitive school* attempts to open the lid and look inside the mind's black box. Here more complex buying models, like that of Howard and Sheth (1969), try to incorporate into the hierarchical communication models the intervening variables of perception, motivation, learning, memory, attitudes, beliefs, group influence, etc; in fact, almost everything inside the mind.

Howard and Sheth

A simplified version of Howard and Sheth's complex model divides the black box into perceptual constructs and learning constructs, as shown in Figure 4.5. The exogenous variables are external to this model and include personality traits, social class, financial status, the social/organizational setting and even the importance of the purchase to the individual.

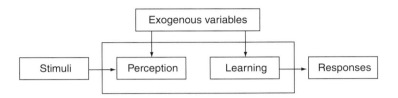

Figure 4.5 A simplified version of Howard and Sheth's model

The complete complex model in Figure 4.6 includes perception, learning, attitudes and motivation. Stimulus ambiguity implies inadequate information to make a decision. Perceptual bias (see Perception, below) basically means that there is a certain amount of distortion in the way that an individual perceives a stimulus.

This complex model has been criticized for lacking a clear definition of the relationships between some of the variables and for a lack of distinction between the endogenous variables (within the model) and exogenous variables (external to the model). The model is, for many readers, difficult to understand and, for many practitioners, impossible to use. Nevertheless it does provide a useful insight into the possible workings of the mind.

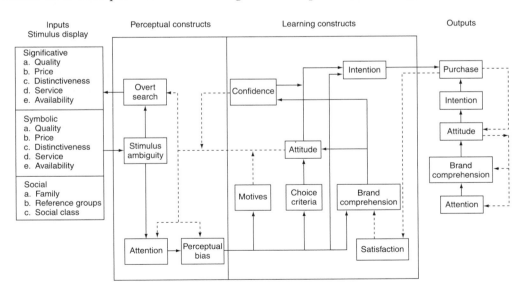

Source: Howard, J and Sheth, J N (1969)
© Copyright (1969) John Wiley & Sons. Reprinted by permission of John Wiley & Sons Inc

Figure 4.6 The complete Howard and Sheth model

The remainder of this chapter looks at some of the influencing variables such as perception, learning, motivation, values, attitudes and lifestyles, and considers how an understanding of them helps to make more effective marketing communications.

THE INTERVENING VARIABLES

Perception

Perception means the way stimuli, such as commercial messages, advertisements, packaging, shops, uniforms, etc are interpreted. Messages and images are not always perceived in the manner intended by the advertiser. As Chisnall (1984) says: 'Our perceptual system has a tendency to organise, modify and distort information reaching it.' Perception is selective. We see what we want to see.

The smoker

Here's a simple test. Ask a smoker to recall exactly what the health warning says on the side of their packet of cigarettes. Few will be able to tell you the exact words. This is because we all selectively screen out messages or stimuli that may cause discomfort, tension or 'cognitive dissonance'. Imagine that the smoker allows the message (warning) to be perceived. This will cause discomfort every time a cigarette is taken, since the box will give the smoker an unpleasant message. In order to reduce this tension, the smoker has two options: (a) change behaviour (stop smoking) or (b) screen out the message and continue the behaviour (smoking).

Many stimuli are *screened out* by the perceptual system, which, it is estimated, is hit by between 500 and 1,500 different advertisements a day. The next example shows how preferences and motivations affect perception.

Many smokers screen out negative messages

The football match

A striker is clean through with only the goalkeeper to beat when out of nowhere a defender slides in and makes a tackle. Fifteen thousand people applaud the 'great tackle', while the opposing 15,000 fans, having received exactly the same information (the tackle), scream at the referee and demand that he gives a penalty to the attacking side. We see what we want to see. We like to organize, modify and distort the information or messages that come to us.

So perceptions are biased by our underlying motivations. Take this example from Hong Kong, where in 1997 China regained control over this former British colony. The committee responsible for celebrating the resumption of Chinese sovereignty chose the white dolphin as its symbol. A British newspaper, the *Independent*, pointed out that this was a species threatened with extinction in Chinese waters by the end of this century. The committee also chose to place it alongside the new symbol for the future Special Administrative Region of Hong Kong, the Bauhina flower, which, reported the newspaper, was a sterile hybrid that produces no seed. The newspaper perceived Hong Kong to be marching into the future under the symbols of an endangered species and sterility. The Hong Kong committee saw the friendly dolphin as appealing to everybody, especially children: 'Its leaping movement symbolises Hong Kong's vibrancy.' They differ vastly even over the same symbol or stimulus. Perceptions can vary even within the same region. A UK TV advertisement for Unilever's Persil washing powder showed a Dalmatian shaking off its black spots, a white horse breaking away from black horses and a skater dressed in white beating other skaters dressed in black. The advertisement was perceived by some as being racist. Despite the advertisements having been tested with Afro-Caribbean women before going on air, the ITC (Independent Television Commission) received 32 complaints.

Before perception occurs, attention has to be gained by, say, the advertiser. As Williams (1989) says, interests, needs and motives determine 'not only what will arouse attention, but also what will hold it'. For example, advertisements for a new house are ignored by the mass population. But there is a sector of the population that is actively looking for a house. This sector has a need for a new house and it is therefore receptive to any of these advertisements. Individuals from this sector positively select information relevant to their needs. This is known as '*selective attention*'.

There are also certain physical properties that increase the likelihood of a message gaining attention: intensity and size; position; sound; colour; contrast; and movement (eyes are involuntarily attracted to movement because of the body's instinctive defence mechanism). Given that an individual's attention is constantly called upon by new stimuli, repetition can enhance the likelihood of a message getting through. Novelty can also be used to jar expectations and grab attention.

Perceived differences in brands are not necessarily dependent on real product differences (in either function or form). As Chisnall (1984) says: 'Consumers evaluate products against the background of their experiences, expectations and associations. Perception is seldom an objective, scientific assessment of the comparative values of competing brands.'

An understanding of the way our perceptual system organizes information has helped some brand advertisers to exploit perceptual systems through an understanding of gestalt psychology. Gestalt means 'total figuration'. One of the four basic perceptual organizing techniques from the gestalt school is '*closure*'. An individual strives to make sense of incomplete messages by filling in the gaps or shaping the image so that it can fit comfortably into his or her cognitive set (or set of knowledge). Marlboro's 'MARL' advertisements and Kit-Kat's 'Kit' advertisements play on the need to fill in these gaps. This may happen so fast that the viewer is not aware of what is going on inside his or her head. Effectively, the mind momentarily becomes the medium, since the complete image is visible only inside our head, while the external advertisement shows the incomplete image. In a sense, a giant billboard inside our forehead is switched on by an incomplete stimulus. The natural perceptual tendency towards 'closure' completes the advertisement's image inside the audience's mind.

Perception is also inextricably linked with past experiences, motivation, beliefs, attitudes and the ability to learn.

Learning

Marketers obviously want customers to learn about, first, the existence of their brand or company and, second, its merits. A knowledge of the learning process is therefore useful in understanding how customers acquire, store, and retrieve messages about products, brands and companies. How are attitudes about companies, products and brands developed (or learned)? Advertising and sales promotions can help customers learn in different ways (see '*classical*' and '*operant*' *conditioning* below). In addition, how many times (*frequency*) should an advertisement be shown before it is remembered or, alternatively, before it causes irritation? Should it be repeated regularly once a week for a year ('drip' strategy) or concentrated into 12 times a week for four weeks only ('burst' strategy)? Differing levels of

---

The party

When introduced to someone at a party, do you ever forget their name? An inability to learn and remember names can create embarrassment. Perhaps the host should increase the frequency of the branding process by repeating the individual's name three times during the introduction? Or would this be irritating? Perhaps it would be better if the individual's name was inserted in a 'drip' strategy rather than a 'burst' strategy, ie occasionally the host will pass by, casually drop the individual's name into the conversation and move on.

intelligence, memory capacity, motivations, perceptual systems, associations and rewards (reinforcement) affect the learning process.

Connectionist learning theories

Simple '*connectionist theory*' suggests that associations can be made between messages, or stimuli, and responses. Hence the term 'stimulus–response' model. In the late 1890s the Russian physiologist Ivan Pavlov demonstrated how '*classical conditioning*', or involuntary conditioning, worked on dogs. By regularly ringing a bell before presenting food to a dog, the dog learned to associate (or connect) the bell with food. After a period of conditioning the dog would salivate (respond) upon hearing the bell (stimulus) without any food arriving. As Williams (1989) says: 'It is the idea of association that underlines the concept of branding in modern marketing.' Constant repetition can build associations between needs, products and brands, eg if you are thinking of beans, think Heinz: 'Beanz Meanz Heinz'.

'*Operant conditioning*', on the other hand, is voluntary in so far as the participant actively searches for solutions. The '*Skinner box*' was devised by the United States' Dr Skinner during the 1930s. By placing a hungry rat in a box where food only arrived once the rat pressed a lever, Skinner observed that the rat would search, investigate and, eventually, press the lever accidentally. Food then arrived. Over a period of time the rat, when aroused by the hunger motive, learned to press the lever for food. An association or connection was made between the lever pressing and the drive to satisfy the hunger need. This approach to building associations through voluntary participation suggests that sales promotions can actively invite the buyer to participate, be rewarded, and eventually connect a particular product or service with a particular stimulated need.

Stimulus–response

Connectionist theories of learning highlight the importance of, first, timing and, second, frequency of marketing communications. The establishment of a connection or association between a stimulus and a response is fundamental to the conditioning process. Advertising jingles, pictures and even smells are some of the stimuli that can arouse emotional or behavioural responses. Some people still feel good when they hear the Coca-Cola jingle 'I'd like to teach the world to sing…', others are aroused and excited when they hear the sound of a sports commentator's voice with crowd sound effects in the background. Ice cream van jingles arouse children. McDonald's large, highly visible yellow 'M' logo can trigger a response, particularly if an individual is involved in goal-oriented behaviour (is hungry and is ready to consider eating food). Could this yellow logo be the equivalent of Pavlov's bell? Do some humans salivate just at the sight of the logo?

Cyber logo salivates customers

'Seeing your logo on the Net made me hungry' (feedback from a McDonald's Web site visitor, demonstrating classical conditioning?)

Smith, Berry and Pulford (1999)

Certainly the release of certain aromas can stimulate immediate responses. For example, as customers leave a pub and walk down the street they are often greeted by the wafting smell of frying chips, which can stimulate or arouse the need for food, and lead to an immediate purchase.

A UK travel operator, Next Island, is using perfume impregnation in its packaged holiday brochure. 'What does a holiday smell like?' Their brochures have the smell of coconut suntan oil to help to conjure up associations, connections, memories and feelings of sun, sea and holiday time.

Reinforcement and *reward* enhance the learning process. In other words, good-quality products and services reward the buyer every time. This consistent level of quality reinforces the brand's positive relationship with the buyer. On the other hand, if the quality is poor, there is no reward (response does not satisfy the need) and the response (to buy a particular brand or visit a particular shop) will not be repeated.

Positive reinforcement helps the learning process (or helps the buyer to remember the brand or shop). It is possible to 'unlearn' or forget ('message decay'), so many advertisers seek to remind customers of their products, their names and their benefits. Some advertisements seek to remind the buyer what a good choice they have already made by frequently repeating their messages. The connectionist approach ignores all the other complex and influential variables involved in learning and, ultimately, buying. Arguably, it oversimplifies a complex process.

Packaging design can also act as a cue to arouse momentarily the happy images conveyed in the previously seen and unconsciously stored advertising images. This is where a 'pack shot' of the product/pack in the advertisement (usually at the end) aids recall of the brand, the advertisement and its image when the consumer is shopping or just browsing along shelves full of different brands.

Every brand's manager would like to have their brand chosen automatically every time. Some brands achieve this through an unconsciously learned response. How? By building a presence through frequency of advertising and maximum shelf facings (amount of units displayed on shelves – see Chapter 18) and, most importantly, by supplying an appropriate level of *reinforcement* (an appropriate level of *quality* in the product or service itself). Chapter 19 emphasizes the importance of quality in the long-term repeat-buying success strategies of today and tomorrow.

Cognitive learning

Cognitive learning focuses on what happens in between the stimulus and the response. It embraces the intervening mental processes.

Insight, meaning, perception, knowledge and problem solving are all considered relevant concepts. Cognitive learning is not dependent on 'trial and error'. It depends on an ability to think, sometimes conceptually, and to perceive relationships and 'what if' scenarios. It is not dependent on an immediate reward to reinforce the learning process; in fact, *'latent learning'* occurs in the absence of reward and without any immediate action. Of course, an individual has to be suitably motivated to achieve this kind of learning. The next intervening variable – motivation – will now be considered.

Motivation

Motivation is defined as the drive to satisfy a need. Some motives are socially learned (eg wanting to get married) and others are instinctive (eg wanting to eat when hungry). Sigmund Freud suggested that an individual is motivated by conscious and unconscious forces. Many motives are unconscious but active in that they influence everyday buying behaviour. Brands carry covert messages that are fleetingly understood at a subconscious level. As the Market Research Society said in its 1986 conference paper, 'It is often this deeper meaning which is what is exchanged for money. These deep underlying feelings are often the real reason why people buy products or services.'

Freud's psychoanalytical approach broke the personality into the id (instinctive drives and urges, eg eat food, grab food), the ego (the social learning process that allows the individual to interact with the environment (eg ask politely for food or pay for food) and the super-ego, which provides a conscience or ethical/moral referee between the id and the ego. Freud suggested that 'all actions are the results of antecedent conditions' (see how childhood experiences might affect industrial buying behaviour some 30 or 40 years later in 'Mommy's never coming back', page 127). Occasionally these unconscious stirrings manifest themselves in dreams, responses to ambiguous stimuli and slips of the tongue (Freudian slips).

Clinical psychology uses thematic apperception tests, Rorschach tests and word association tests to help them to analyse the underlying and sometimes unconscious personality traits and motivations of an individual. In-depth market researchers (*qualitative researchers*) use metaphors, picture completion and montages in an attempt to throw the interviewee's ego off guard and dip into the real underlying feelings that interviewees find difficult both to become aware of and to express in an articulate manner.

In the 1950s Vance Packard was concerned about how *in-depth researchers* like Dr Ernest Dichter were attempting to extract buyers' unconscious feelings, aspirations and motivations, which were then subtly reflected through advertising imagery, which in turn manipulated buyers unconsciously. Although discredited by some and criticized by others, Dichter's *Handbook of Consumer Motivations* (1964) is an extremely thought-provoking and entertaining read.

Here are some other well-known, in-depth research findings from the 1950s that supposedly reveal the deep underlying motivations that drive certain forms of behaviour, including buying behaviour:

- A woman is very serious when she bakes a cake because unconsciously she is going through the act of birth.
- Soon after the trial period housewives who used a new improved cake mix (no egg needed, just add water) stopped buying it. The new improved cake mix provoked a sense of guilt as the cooking role of the housewife was reduced.
- A man buys a convertible car as a substitute mistress.
- Smoking represents an infantile pleasure of sucking.
- Men want their cigars to be odoriferous in order to prove that they (the men) are masculine.
- Shaving for some men is the daily act of cutting off this symbol of manliness (stubble). It is therefore a kind of daily castration.

This all appears to be too American and is arguably outdated now. Man is a rational animal and is not concerned with such psychoanalytic interpretations of everyday, ordinary and, supposedly, common-sense behaviour. Consider the close shave below.

A close shave?

I have a simple test that I use in lectures with different groups. I pose a question and ask for male respondents only. The question is 'How many of you find shaving a hassle?' Usually a unanimous show of hands emerges. 'How many of you would like to be able to dispense with the aggravation of shaving?' Slightly fewer hands emerge. 'Well, here is a cream that will solve your problem. This cream closes your hair follicles so that hair will never grow there again. It is medically approved and cleared for a market launch next year. Who would like to try some right now?' All the hands are gone. The question 'Why not?' is usually answered faintly with 'Freedom to choose to have a beard later in life' and so on. Or is there something deeper here? Dichter would have said 'Yes'.

Abraham Maslow's *hierarchy of needs* (1954) provides a simple but useful explanation of the way an individual's needs work. Essentially he showed that one is driven or motivated initially to satisfy the lower level needs and then, when satisfied, move up to the next level of need. This theory also implies that motivation can be cyclical, in so far as buying a house may be motivated initially by the lower level survival needs and subsequently by the higher level need of esteem. Figure 4.7 shows Maslow's hierarchy of needs.

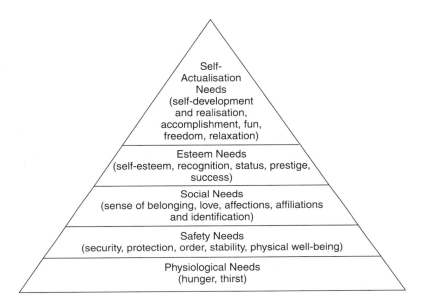

Figure 4.7   Maslow's hierarchy of needs

Cars transport people from A to B. Sometimes the need to buy a car is a basic survival need (eg to get to work, to earn money to buy food). Sometimes it can provide a cocoon (or shelter) from the mass of bodies scrambling for the public transport system. Sometimes it can provide freedom to explore the countryside, visit friends, do what you want (self-actualize). Cars can also act as status symbols (esteem). Some cars position their benefits (power, speed, safety, environmental, etc) so that they dominate the ad and appeal to the predominant need of a particular segment. Page 108 refers to Dichter's 'substitute mistress car'.

Different people (or groups of people) extract different benefits from the same product. Some people want to drive a Porsche because it gives them power; others because they see it as a symbol of success (good for the ego and esteem); others just want the thrill of driving very fast (self-actualization), as in the case of the driver's last wish in Nevil Shute's *On the Beach*; others again may simply want a very fast, reliable car that allows them to get from A to B (around Europe) without delay. Markets can be broken up into '*benefit segments*' so that communications can be tailored to develop the ideal positioning for a particular segment. In some cases benefit segmentation demands different products for different segments, as in the case of the toothpaste market (page 91).

Attitudes

Attitudes affect buying behaviour. Attitudes are learned and they tend to stick; they *can* be changed, but not very quickly.

As Williams (1989) says: 'If a marketer is able to identify the attitudes held by different market segments towards his product, and also to measure changes in those attitudes, he will be well placed to plan his marketing strategy.' An attitude is a predisposition towards a person, a brand, a product, a company or a place.

An interesting question is 'which came first, the attitude or the behaviour?' Are attitudes formed prior to purchase or post purchase? Can attitudes be formed without any experience?

The answer is 'yes' to both. Attitudes are sometimes formed without direct experience and, equally, products are often bought without any prior attitude. In the latter case, however, it is likely that an attitude will form as a result of the good or bad experience the buyer has with the product. Advertising, in this case, serves to reinforce attitudes rather than create awareness.

Attitudes can be broken down into three components, which are often explained as 'think, feel, do' or '*cognitive*', '*affective*' and '*conative*'. The cognitive element is the awareness or knowledge of, say, a brand. The affective element is the positive or negative feeling associated with the brand. The conative element is the intention to purchase. It can be important to measure all three components, since an isolated element can be misleading. For example, Rolls-Royce score highly on the cognitive and affective elements of the attitude, but few of those who express awareness of and liking towards a Rolls-Royce will actually buy one. Identifying the levels of each attitudinal element helps to set tighter communication objectives. For example, the creative strategy for increasing brand awareness would be different from the strategy required to change the target market's feelings (or reposition the brand). A different communications strategy (perhaps an emphasis on sales promotions) would be required if the objective was to convert high awareness and positive feelings into trial purchases.

Group influence

Much of human behaviour, and buyer behaviour in particular, is shaped by group influence. Whether cultural, religious, political, socio-economic, lifestyle, special interest groups or just family, social groups affect an individual's behaviour patterns. Watch explicit group influence occur as thousands of people perform a 'Mexican wave' at football matches, the Olympics, etc.

Most individuals are members of some kind of group, whether *formal* (eg committees) or *informal* (eg friends), *primary* (where face-to-face communications can occur, eg family) or *secondary* (eg the Chartered Institute of Marketing). Groups develop their own *norms* or

The effects of group influence are often seen in a queue or waiting area where charity collectors are attempting to collect money. Success or failure is often determined by the reaction of the first encounter, ie if the first person acknowledges the collector and makes a contribution, the next person is more likely to do so too. I have often seen a whole platform generously giving money after a successful start. Equally, I have seen almost total rejection by a whole queue once the initial contact has refused to donate. This is a bizarre or perverse form of charity giving and seems to be about *peer group pressure*. In a sense a donation buys some relief from guilt or embarrassment.

standards that become acceptable within a particular group. For example, normal dress among a group of yacht club members differs considerably from the norm or type of clothes worn by a group of clubbers. Yet both groups adhere to the rules (mostly unwritten) of their own group. Both groups also go through some sort of purchasing process.

Roles are played by different members within a group. An individual may also have to play different roles at different stages of the same day, eg a loving mother, tough manager, loyal employee, client entertainer and, when returning home, a happy wife and, perhaps later, a sensuous lover. In the online world the same person can adopt different roles and even multiple personalities (see 'Complex personalities' on page 90).

Activities, interests and opinions can form useful segmentation criteria. Roles within groups help to target decision makers and influencers in the *decision-making units*. Roles are also identifiable from the *family life cycle*, which shows how an individual moves from bachelor to newly wed to Full Nest 1 (youngest child under six) to Full Nest 2 (youngest child is six or over) to Full Nest 3 (dependent children) to Empty Nest 1 (children moved out) to Empty Nest 2 (retirement) or Solitary Survivor 1 (still working) to Solitary Survivor 2 (retired). The income levels, needs and spending patterns are often predictable as the income earner moves through various family life cycle roles. Spending patterns, influenced by changing roles, can be monitored and forecast before communicating any marketing messages. For example, direct mail companies often mail new mothers within a few days of the arrival of their baby.

SUMMARY AND CONCLUSION

The marketing professional must understand the target market's buying behaviour before, during and after the actual purchase. Even the apparently simple act of purchasing a hamburger can reveal a host of hidden motives. In-depth research reveals some deep and unconscious reasons that demonstrate some of the complexities of buying behaviour. The time and effort spent in the buying process depends on the type of buying situation. Decision-making units affect the process. Buying models highlight some of the stages through which the buyer passes, offering a kind of checklist for marketing communications to ensure that they carry the buyer through each stage successfully. The behaviourist school differs from the cognitive school of more complex buying models. Motivation, perception, learning, values, attitudes and lifestyles all interact and influence the buying process.

Equipped with a clearer understanding of both the motives for buying and the buying process itself, a marketing communications strategy can be developed to ensure that it covers as many avenues to the mind of the buyer as resources allow.

Reasons and motives range from the rational to the bizarre. Motives are, however, only one variable among many other intervening variables that integrate and influence buying behaviour. For example, beliefs and attitudes affect motives, which, in turn, affect the way an individual sees or perceives things (images, ads, products, shops, etc). We learn these opinions, attitudes and beliefs partly from groups (such as friends, colleagues), partly from commercial messages carefully aimed at us through advertising, sales promotion, etc and partly from real experiences of products or services.

All these influences interact with commercial stimuli such as advertisements. The effects are ultimately reflected in our behaviour (or lack of behaviour in some circumstances).

In consumer markets buying behaviour is affected by the complex web of mostly internal intervening variables (motivation, perception, attitudes, learning, memory, lifestyle, personality and groups). Sex, age, income and even an individual's face or body affect their behaviour. Other external variables such as laws and regulations, the weather, opening hours, an out-of-stock situation or an emergency can all change buying behaviour.

An industrial buyer is also influenced by internal variables, including the organization's objectives, policies, procedures, structure and systems, and variables external to the organization such as the state of the economy, level of demand and competition, the cost of money, etc.

Some argue that it is impossible, as Foxall (1992) says, to 'capture human nature in its entirety' because of the complexity of the decision-making process. This complexity is created by the web of rational and emotional factors that are generated from internal processes and guided by external influences.

> Perhaps Oscar Wilde was too generous when he said that 'man is a rational animal except when asked to act within the dictates of reason'.

Marketing communications do affect aggregate buying behaviour, as evidenced by changed behaviour patterns after the National Lottery integrated campaign, which stimulates some 65 per cent of the British adult population into shops to buy Lottery tickets on a regular (monthly) basis. Everything changes, including the buying processes. See Appendix 4.2 for an insight into how radically different the buying process of the future might be.

Figure 4.8 Factors influencing buyer behaviour

Key points for Chapter 4:

1. A clear understanding of both the motives for buying and the buying process itself is vital if an effective marketing communications strategy is to be developed.
2. An effective communications strategy then covers as many avenues or channels to the mind of the buyer as resources allow.

APPENDIX 4.1

Hofacker's online information processing

(Taken from *Online eMarketing Course: eCustomers*, by kind permission of Multimedia Marketing.com.)

One approach to online information processing is Charles Hofacker's five stages of on-site information processing.

1. Exposure.
2. Attention.
3. Comprehension and perception.
4. Yielding and acceptance.
5. Retention.

Each stage acts as a hurdle, since if the site design or content is too difficult to process, the customer cannot progress to the next stage. The e-marketer fails. The best Web site designs take into account how customers process information. Good e-marketers are aware of how the messages are processed by the customer and of corresponding steps we can take to ensure that the correct message is received.

The first stage is *exposure*. This is straightforward. If the content is not present for long enough, customers will not be able to process it. Think of splash pages, banner ads or Shockwave animations: if these change too rapidly the message will not be received.

The second stage is *attention*. The human mind has limited capacity to pick out the main messages from a screen full of single-column format text without headings or graphics. Movement, text size and colour help to gain attention for key messages. Note though that studies show that the eye is immediately drawn to content, not the headings in the navigation systems. Of course, we need to be careful about using garish colours and animations, as these can look amateurish and distract from the main message.

Comprehension and perception are the third of Hofacker's stages. They refer to how the customer interprets the combination of graphics, text and multimedia on a Web site. If the design uses familiar standards or metaphors, it will be most effective, since the customer will interpret them based on previous experience and memory. Once relevant information is found, visitors sometimes want to dig deeper for more information.

Changing the layout of a Web site will be as popular with customers as a supermarket changing its store layout every six months! Metaphors are another approach to aid comprehension of e-commerce sites, a shopping basket metaphor is used to help comprehension.

Fourthly, *yielding and acceptance* refers to whether the information you present is accepted by the customer. Different tactics need to be used to convince different types of people.

Classically a US audience is more convinced by features rather than benefits, while the reverse is true for a European audience. Some customers will respond to emotive appeals, perhaps reinforced by images, while others will make a more clinical evaluation based on the text. This gives us the difficult task of combining text, graphics and copy to convince each customer segment.

Finally, *retention* – how well the customer can recall their experience. A clear, distinctive site design will be retained in the customer's mind, perhaps prompting a repeat visit when the customer thinks, 'Where did I see that information?' and then recalls the layout of the site. A clear site design will also be implanted in the customer's memory as a mental map and they will be able to draw on it when returning to the site, increasing their flow experience.

To summarize, understanding how customers process information through the stages of exposure, attention, comprehension and perception, yielding and acceptance, and retention can help us design sites that really help us get our message across and deliver memorable messages and superior customer service.

APPENDIX 4.2

Post-PC customer

(Reproduced from *Online eMarketing Course: eCustomers*, by kind permission of Multimedia Marketing.com.)

The post-PC customer may occasionally accept payment to view some ads. The rest are screened out by both sophisticated browser software and little 'TiVo-type' boxes attached to wall-to-wall screen TVs. Neither governments nor society permit old-style intrusive advertising any more. No more intrusive evening telephone calls from script-reading intelligent agents. It is also illegal to litter anyone's doorstep or house with mailshots and inserts. Heavy fines stopped all that a long time ago. The only ads that do get inside are carried by the many millions of private media owners who rent out their cars, bikes and bodies as billboards.

The tedious task of shopping for distress purchases like petrol, electricity or memory storage is delegated completely to embedded shopping bots.

Non-embedded bots spun out of control some years ago when they first appeared in three-dimensional hovering holograms – always at your side, always double-checking the best price for hire cars, hotels, even drinks at the bar. Some are programmed to be polite, aggressive or even abusive. All are programmed to be intrusive whenever anything is being bought. Delays on buses and traffic jams regularly occurred when argumentative bots engaged in lengthy negotiations. Frustration broke out. Bots attacked bots, people attacked bots and bot owners. Eventually bots were banned from buses, planes, trains and several 'peaceful supermarkets'.

Next came the great worm wars: programming bots so they only buy your brand – for life. But, unlike humans, bots can be reprogrammed by a competitor. The advertising agent worm was born. Agent eaters soon followed. Despite being information fatigued and time compressed, the post-PC customer lives a lot longer than many bots. And certainly longer than most of the new brands that seem to come and go. The 150-year-old person has already been born.

Live longer

Humans may develop smaller ears (from constant use of headphones) and better body organs replaced as a result of early-warning systems carried by miniature submarines constantly patrolling in the bloodstream. These wireless database-driven devices identify wearing parts and organs, check cloned stock availability, reserve beds and preferred surgeons and estimate time before breakdown replacement is required. Discounts for early bookings into leisure hospitals are also negotiated automatically.

Meanwhile, back at the ranch, microwaves insist on offering suggestions of ideal wines to go with your meal, offering instant delivery from the neighbourhood's wired-up 24-hour roving delivery van. Your fridge offers special incentives to buy Pepsi when you run out of Coke (or whichever brand owns or hires the fridge-linked database). Children happily play chess and interact with their opponents on the giant vertical screens, called refrigerators. Voice-operated computers are considered noisy and old fashioned as discrete, upmarket, thought-operated computers operate silently, but extremely effectively.

And all the time blue-tooth type technology facilitates ubiquitous communications, which allows constant interaction between machines. Man and machine integrate into a vast database. We have more IT power in today's average luxury car than the rocket that went to the moon. Yes, Moore's law suggests the tectonic shift will continue. Yes, marketing will continue in a new guise (probably not even called marketing but just common sense).

Time-compressed, information-fatigued and disloyal, the post-PC customer seeks relationships not from brands themselves but from databases that know, understand and seemingly care about them. Witness the virtual girlfriend relationships in Japan, relationships with shops and vending machines, oh, and relationships with people, real, quaint, touchy, feely, physical people.

And all the time the technology, if truly mastered, can free up time to do the important things in life, to give the post-PC customer a genuinely higher quality of life both at work and at home with family and friends.

FURTHER READING

Chisnall, P (1984) *Marketing: A behavioural analysis*, McGraw-Hill, Maidenhead

Colley, R H (1961) *Defining Advertising Goals and Measuring Advertising Results*, Association of National Advertisers, New York

Dichter, E (1964) *Handbook of Consumer Motivations: The psychology of the world of objects*, McGraw-Hill, New York

Ehrenberg, A (1974) Repetitive advertising and consumer awareness, *Journal of Advertising Research*, **14**, pp 25–34

Ehrenberg, A (1977) How can consumers buy a new brand?, *Admap*, March, pp 20–27

Engel, J F, Blackwell, R D and Kollatt, D T (1978) *Consumer Behaviour*, 3rd edn, Dryden Press, Hinsdale, IL

Engel, J F, Kinnear, T C and Warshaw, M R (1991) *Promotional Strategy: Managing the marketing communications process*, 7th edn, Irwin Shaw, Homewood, IL

Fishbein, M (1975) Attitude, attitude change and behaviour: A theoretical overview, in Levine, P (ed) *Attitude Research Bridges the Atlantic*, American Marketing Association, Chicago

Foxall, G (1992) *Consumer Psychology in Behavioural Perspective*, Routledge, London

Hofacker, C (2001) *Internet Marketing*, 3rd edn, Wiley, New York

Howard, J A and Sheth, J N (1969) *The Theory of Buyer Behaviour*, Wiley, New York

Kotler, P (1998) *Practice of Marketing*, Prentice-Hall, Englewood Cliffs, NJ

Lavidge, R and Steiner, G (1961) A model for predictive measurements of advertising effectiveness, *Journal of Marketing*, October, p 61

Market Research Society Conference Papers (1986) Research is good for you – the contribution of research to Guinness advertising, MRS, London

Maslow, A (1954), *Motivation & Personality*, Harper & Row, New York

Packard, V (1957), *The Hidden Persuaders*, Penguin, Harmondsworth

Rogers, E M (1961) *Diffusion of Innovations*, 1st edn, Free Press, New York

Shaw, R (1997) Appreciating assets, *Marketing Business*, Dec 1997/Jan 1998

Smith, P, Berry, C and Pulford, A (1999) *Strategic Marketing Communications*, Kogan Page, London

Smith, P R (2001) *Online eMarketing Course: eCustomers*, Multimedia Marketing.com, London

Strong, E K (1925) *The Psychology of Selling*, McGraw-Hill, New York

Williams, K C (1989) *Behavioural Aspects of Marketing*, Heinemann, Oxford

Williams, T G (1982) *Consumer Behaviour*, West Publishing, St Paul, MN

5

Understanding markets – market research

MARKET RESEARCH

The card trick

An Oxford Street card-trick man places four cards face down on a portable table. As the crowd gathers, he shouts, '£10 to anyone who picks the ace.' Embarrassment, scepticism, even mistrust run through the crowd. No one responds to the offer of a simple £1 bet to win £10. As the card man leans forward to show the crowd a crisp £10 note, a grinning young man leans behind the card man and sneaks a look at the outside card. It's a jack of diamonds. Word quickly spreads through the crowd that the outside card is not the ace. Prompted by the fund (and the improving odds) someone shouts, 'That's not a real tenner.' The card man responds by stepping into the crowd to allow a closer inspection of the £10 note. A second stranger boldly leans across and briefly turns the other outside card over. It's a two of hearts. The card man returns. 'Come on now. Who wants to win £10?' A well-spoken young woman replies, 'If you show me one of the two middle cards, I will place a £2 bet against your £10.' The card man accepts. What has happened here?

Information reduces risk

As more and more relevant information became available, the risk was eventually reduced to zero and a certainty emerged. The young women could pick the ace as soon as she knew what the other three cards were. Market research (information) also reduces risk. So why not use research to reduce all risks? There are three reasons – it costs *men, money and minutes* – the three key resources (the 3Ms) (see pages 30–32). First, knowing exactly what information you want and how to gather it (whether commissioning a research agency or handling the research in-house) is a relatively rare management skill. Second, research costs money; and third, it takes time to define and write a brief, carry out the fieldwork, analyse the data, read a report and, ultimately, act upon the information. The *fieldwork* (asking the questions and collecting the answers) can also give competitors an early warning of intended activities. In a sense, it can give them time to respond.

Information is power

In both military and marketing strategies information creates power. If an organization knows what its customers really want, and its competitors do not, then it has a powerful advantage. If the organization knows what a competitor's next move is before they make it, then the organization is in a stronger position to react or even pre-empt it. In negotiations, if one party knows more about the other party, then the information holder carries a hidden advantage. The classic salesman versus buyer situation emphasizes how sales and profits can be increased as a direct result of information: the salesman desperately wants an order and is prepared to cut prices to get the business. The buyer desperately needs to buy the salesman's product because all their existing stocks were destroyed the night before in a fire in one of their factories and the salesman's company is the only company that can supply the goods immediately. If the buyer knows how desperate the salesman is, then a low price will be negotiated by the buyer. On the other hand, the salesman seizes control over the negotiations (power) if he has been informed about the buyer's desperate situation. In addition, the salesman takes total control if the buyer does not know how desperate the salesman is for the order. In this situation the salesman will make the sale, probably at a higher price. Information is power.

World Chess Championship

To avoid giving his competitor too much information, Bobby Fischer wore a green visor to stop Spassky, the challenger, from looking into his eyes during an alternative world chess championship.

Notice how senior managers always seem to ask questions that are potentially embarrassing (because sometimes you don't know the answers). When they ask the question, you might think, 'I wish I'd thought of that.' Questions are indicators of ability and seniority, or potential seniority. The ability to ask the right question is a precious skill that usually takes time and practice to develop. The ability to ask the right question is the precursor to providing the right answer. This is becoming increasingly important as more and more information becomes more easily available and the potential for information overload and information fatigue grows.

Information overload

A Reuters report which links information overload with analysis paralysis and poor quality of life reveals that 'one in four people admit to suffering ill health as a result of the amount of information they now handle'. Out of 1,300 managers, two-thirds said that their social life was affected by having too much information to process at work.

   Not often mentioned, however, is one simple way of dealing with stress. All you have to do is laugh. Laughing cures stress, experts say. It pumps adrenaline and endorphins into the bloodstream. It reduces muscular tension, improves breathing and regulates the heartbeat.

Robert Nurden, ex-*The European*

Prioritize information

There is an unlimited amount of information available to all marketing managers. There is more information available and obtainable than any manager can absorb, let alone pay for, in any one period. So the key is to *define what the problem is and outline the kind of information that might help*. An experienced market researcher (whether in-house or from an agency) can guide the marketing manager towards defining specifically what kind of information is needed. Since the research budget is usually limited, the manager may then have to *prioritize* which kinds of information are more important than others. Ask for ambiguous information and a lot of ambiguous answers will be delivered.

Information junkies

Another Reuters survey revealed that a growing proportion of Internet users find themselves addicted to information on the Internet. Over 50 per cent of managers were accumulating information they didn't have the capacity to assimilate; rather they were overwhelmed by it. Over half the respondents pronounced themselves information junkies who got 'cravings' for new information, especially from the Internet.

Information overload, overload

A weekday edition of the *New York Times* contains more information than the average person was likely to come across in a lifetime in 17th-century England.

Time magazine

A certain amount of discipline is needed to focus on relevant issues and not become side-tracked by indulging in 'interesting' bits of information. When briefing a market researcher as to the kind of information that is required, it is often tempting to add extra, 'interesting' questions. Before adding extra information requests, check that the following questions are answered satisfactorily:

What will I do with this information?
How will it affect my strategy or tactics?
What action or withdrawal may result from this information?
How much is the information worth?
How much will it cost?
Can I afford it?
When do I need it?
Have I checked all secondary sources? (See Table 5.1 on pages 125–26.)

Too much information can be bad for you
Reproduced from *Online Marketing Course: Marketing Research*, with kind permission from Multimedia Marketing.com, London. Photograph: Martin Lello

Decision-making aid

Research is an *aid to decision making* and not a decision in itself. As Torin Douglas (1984) said: 'In practice, most organisations have a continuous programme of research, often stretching back many years, which is designed not solely for advertising purposes, but also to help them run their businesses properly.'

Statistical abuse of the first order – correlation is not causation!

Thirty-seven per cent of people who have a coffee mug with their company logo on it have been promoted within the last six months, compared to just eight per cent of those people who did not have a coffee mug with their company logo on it.

www.iswag.com

TYPES OF RESEARCH

There are basically two types of research sources: primary and secondary. *Primary data* are gathered specifically for and commissioned by an organization for a particular purpose (eg a research survey to find out about attitudes towards a company's brand). *Secondary data*, on the other hand, already exist and have been gathered by someone else for some other reason (eg government statistics, newspaper features, published reports, etc). *Desk research* can be carried out in a library or office, since it requires researching secondary sources. It is worthwhile doing some desk research before embarking on the more expensive primary research.

There are essentially two types of research: quantitative and qualitative. *Quantitative* research uses surveys based on a representative sample of the population or target group. *Qualitative* research involves an in-depth, unstructured exploration with either small groups of individuals (group discussions or focus groups) or with individuals on a one-to-one basis (depth interviews).

Research can provide the marketing professional with *information on just about anything* from markets to distributors, to customers, to competition, to new products, new packs, new promotions, new advertisements, new prices and so on. Different types of research can reveal information about customers, where they are located, what they buy, read, watch on TV, how they spend their holiday time, which competitors they prefer and so on.

Ideas on new or modified products, packs, brand names or advertisements can be discussed initially in *focus groups* (six to eight people), which generate information explaining how people feel about a concept. This kind of '*concept testing*' can be used to reduce a number of ideas to only one or two for further testing, or can be used to give feedback to the creative people so that they can refine a particular concept. These qualitative interviews open up and identify areas that may need further investigation on a larger scale (quantitative survey) to find out how important certain aspects are among a statistically valid sample (minimum 400 in the sample). In the case of a new advertising concept, or a new pack or brand name concept, the refined concept can then be shown in a *'hall test'* (where respondents are invited into a hall to make comments). The packs and brand name concepts can be shown as mock-up artwork and the advertisements might be shown either as a storyboard or an animatic. A new product (concept) can be tested by using *in-home trials* or hall tests. Some data sources such as the *Target Group Index* (see pages 132–33) are often used in the early research stages of consumer campaigns to identify buying behaviour, socio-economic groups, lifestyles, locations and appropriate media channels.

After all this, a new pack or brand name (or product) can be *test marketed*. This reduces the risk by holding back from national or international roll-out until the advertising campaign (or pack or name or product) can be tested within a representative test area. Owing to the high cost of test marketing, and the increasing difficulty in the UK of truly isolating the test market area (especially in terms of distribution, where the national retail chains do not want to limit stocks to certain parts of the country), companies often prefer to conduct a *simulated market test* instead of carrying out a test marketing exercise. The main research companies in the field are Burke (BASES test), Nielsen (QUARTZ model) and Research International (MICROTEST). These models use information from the concept test or product test, simulate an expected level of distribution penetration (percentage of stores that will stock the product), assume a certain level of advertising spend required to generate certain levels of awareness, and then assume competitive activity, prices and other factors to predict the likely sales of a new product with an accuracy of +/–20 per cent.

Since television advertisements are so expensive, many companies prefer to do all the careful checking and testing through focus groups and hall tests instead of testing the advertisement in a specific test region. They can, and do, however, test the weight of advertising in different regions and measure the incremental sales to help them to find the most cost-effective levels (frequency and timing) of advertising expenditure.

If a product is launched nationally or regionally, its launch can be monitored in several ways. Its usage (user profiles, frequency of purchase, etc) can then be monitored through *consumer panels*. *Retail audits* provide information about distribution penetration and how the product is moving off which shop shelves. It is also likely that *tracking studies* will monitor the immediate reactions and effects of the launch advertising. *Pre-* and *post-quantitative surveys* can monitor the levels of branded awareness before and after a new campaign breaks, and then be used again to measure the effect of the advertising and the product's development in the marketplace.

Summary table

Table 5.1 summarizes some of the many different types of research information that are readily available. The cost figures give only a very rough indication of the budget requirements. They have been included so that the reader can get some idea of the costs involved. Costs will increase over time, but these figures can be used as a 2001 basis.

Table 5.1   Types of research/information available

Information on	Type of research/information	Sources	Approximate costs
Markets	Market reports (analysing market size, structure, market shares and trends, prices, key players, etc)	Mintel Jordans Keynotes Syndicated FT & trade magazines	£750 to £2,000 £1,000–15,000 £1
Distributors	Retail audit (analysing a brand's penetration into various retailer store categories, average stocks bought, held and sold per period, retail prices)	Nielsen	£15,000–50,000*
Customers' attitudes and awareness	Surveys – recommended minimum of 200 interviews; preferably a minimum of 500 interviews. £10–30 per person interviewed plus set-up plus analysis costs	Quantitative market research agencies	£7,500–30,000
		Omnibus surveys	£750 per question
Customers' motivations and perceptions	In-depth research, sometimes using projective techniques	Qualitative market research agencies	£650 per individual, £1,950 per group of eight
Customers' future lifestyles	Social forecasting, futurology, etc	Future Forecasting	£1,500–3,000 annual subscription
Customers' buying behaviour and trends over time	Who's buying what, when and from where; how buyers respond over time to various marketing activities, eg special offers, new ads and competitor activities	Consumer panels, eg AGB's Super	£15,000–40,000

Table 5.1 *continued*

Information on	Type of research/information	Sources	Approximate costs
Customers' penetration	Penetration of production into % of homes and frequency of usage	Omnibus survey	£750 per question
Competition	As for markets, distribution and customers, if the budgets are available. The sales force and marketing departments' 'ear to the market' can also provide much competitive information	As before	As already indicated
Simulated test market	Total mix test of product, brand name, price, positioning	Nielsen Research International RSGB	£25,000–100,000
Test market	Running a new product or variation of its mix in a test area	Sales analysis plus above options	–
Product	New product concepts can be researched ('concept research')	Focus groups	£1,950 per group of eight
Packs	New pack design concepts can be discussed	Focus groups Hall tests	£1,950 per group of eight £5,000+
Advertisements	New advertisement concepts can be researched before going to expensive production Pre and post-advertising research measures levels of awareness before and after a campaign (tracking studies)	Focus groups Hall tests Quantitative survey	£1,950 per group of eight £1,000+ £20–40 per person
Exhibitions	Stand design, memorability, number of passers-by, number that stopped and looked, number that visited. % of total exhibition visitors	Exhibition surveys	

* Prices can vary enormously, eg a single brand retail price check might be carried out for as little as £750, while a full-blown retail audit for multiple products can run into hundreds of thousands of pounds.

Anything can be researched and tested, including sales promotion ideas (concepts), mail-shots and even press releases and journalists' attitudes to particular companies and brands. A new and exciting area of research is that of Web sites, which can be tested before, during and after development. (See Appendix 5.1 for more information.) Media research and planning is discussed in Chapter 7.

Qualitative research

An in-depth interview with an individual provides a lot of qualitative information. There are usually a series of individuals interviewed on a one-to-one basis. This type of research attempts to reveal what customers sometimes don't even know about themselves by delving deep into their unconscious motivations. As Wendy Gordon (1991) says: 'Consumers are often unaware as to why they do or don't use/buy/choose a particular brand. Asking for this kind of information in a direct way is like shouting at a foreigner in the belief that he will then understand English more easily.' In-depth researchers employ a range of techniques (including psycho drawings, word associations, metaphors, collages, picture completion, clay modelling and role playing) that throw the ego off guard and allow the subconscious feelings to be expressed. Chapter 4 considers the underlying motivations and complex information processes through which buyers pass on their journey towards a purchase.

Mommy's never coming back

In-depth research for an American manufacturer of security doors revealed deeply ingrained unconscious fears of being trapped inside, or abandoned, when doors are closed. The report suggested that a young child's first experience of a door is when its mother puts it to bed and closes the door behind her as she leaves. The child fears that it may never see its mother again. Many years later, the adult's unconscious mind can react to the sight of a closed door with an 'underlying feeling of discomfort and anxiety'. The Simpson Timber Company was reported as having gained a significant increase in its market share when they changed their advertise-ments to show partly open security doors rather than their traditional images of securely closed doors.

Marketing Breakthroughs

Focus groups

Group discussions can be a more cost-effective way of collecting information that is perhaps less in depth but never the less useful in understanding why and how people (in the target market) feel about certain brands, advertisements or just new ideas (concepts).

A variety of creative stimuli materials are used within these groups, including cartoons, pictures, words and brand maps. One of the most common types is the collage or mood board which is made up from scrap art taken from a wide variety of magazines and newspapers. It is used to explore a variety of themes, such as user lifestyles, occasion usage and abstract concepts such as freshness or vitality. Two examples of collage boards are featured here and have been developed by The Collage Shop for use in focus groups. One is a simple mood board showing different eating experiences or occasions and the other is more complex, exploring concept pack themes for a shower gel.

Some companies, like MTV, use online discussions and discussion groups as online focus groups – 'a year-long focus group'. But all of this resource is wasted if the right questions are not asked (see 'If Yeltsin were a tree' opposite).

Eating experiences and occasions
Source: Collage provided by the The Collage Shop

Concepts for shower gel packs
Source: Collage provided by The Collage Shop

If Yeltsin were a tree

During the final stages of the 1996 Russian election campaign focus-group operators were asking respondents, 'If Yeltsin were a tree what kind of tree would he be?' in a standard approach to throw the respondents' egos off-guard and extract real answers. American consultants came in and cancelled these questions since they urgently 'needed to know whether voters would move to Yeltsin if he adopted a particular policy', and not whether he was a tree or not.

Time magazine

Concept research

Concept testing helps every element of the communications mix. Whether it is an advertisement, new sales promotion, new piece of packaging, new direct-mail leaflet or even a product or service, the concept should be researched and discussed at least among colleagues and customers and, ideally, among unattached / unbiased focus groups that are representative of the target audience / customer.

| *Bear concept 1* | *Bear concept 2* | *Bear concept 3* |

'Sartorial Elegance' was created to convey Hofmeister as the best lager. Comments picked up through focus group discussions included: 'He looks like he's never been in a pub' and 'The advert's aimed at the higher class, but they drink wine –it's us yobs that drink lager – he's a snob!'
Result: Rejected

'Sporting Bear' was perceived to be 'quite old'. Other comments from the discussion groups revealed: 'He's got a beer gut' and 'He looks grumpy, like a bear with a sore head – it should be a young bear to appeal to youngsters.'
Result: Rejected

'George the Bear' pretested the best. Group feedback included comments like: 'It's the Fonz, a bit like Flash Harry', 'a cool dude' and, perhaps most importantly, he was perceived to be 'streetwise'.
Result: Developed

Advertising *concept testing* measures responses to advertisements before they are fully produced (see the now classic Hofmeister example above). Storyboards, and key frames (see the milkman campaign concept, page 308) or animatics (video cartoons) are made up and shown to focus groups. This kind of group discussion is used to identify the best idea from a range of different concepts, to iron out any glaring problems with a chosen concept or simply to help to refine the concept itself, as shown with the Hofmeister bear concepts opposite.

The fully developed George the Bear (concept 3) in one of the finished advertisements used in the classic Hofmeister campaign by BMP DDB Needham

Qualitative research is also used to define parameters or types of questions that should be asked in future quantitative research. For example, focus group / qualitative research into newspapers may have revealed that some readers feel mentally uncomfortable if they don't read all of their newspaper before throwing it out. This is obviously a problem if part of the paper's advertising proposition is 'the newspaper you can digest on the way to work'. So quantitative research will seek to substantiate the variables or issues revealed during the initial qualitative stage. The quantitative stage may be carried out by surveying several hundred or a thousand respondents. The interviewer's questionnaire might ask, 'Which papers on this list do you find a quick and easy read / long / difficult?' etc.

Target Group Index

The Target Group Index (TGI) collects and compiles information on consumer brands and the profiles of heavy, medium and light users, and non-users, in a vast range of product categories and sub-categories. This is all cross-referenced to types of papers read, TV programmes viewed, and lifestyle/attitude statements. It can even classify 'light users' according to whether they buy a brand exclusively ('solus users'), whether they prefer it to another brand also used ('most often users') or whether they are more casual in their use ('minor users'), again cross-referenced to demographic data, lifestyles and media used. Advertisers use the TGI to find out who the users of a particular brand are and what they read, watch and listen to. The same information is available on competitors and their brands.

The excerpt shown in Figure 5.1 demonstrates how the index might be used by a company marketing cold and flu remedies. It identifies the heavy users, their age and the percentage of the total age group who are actually heavy users, and provides an index which compares the percentage of heavy users in this age group to the national average percentage of heavy users in all age groups. The excerpt analyses which papers and magazines the heavy users use.

Elsewhere the index also gives lifestyle data, eg 'heavy drinkers of low-alcohol lager'. This gives an insight into what motivates them. The excerpt in Figure 5.2 shows that they are

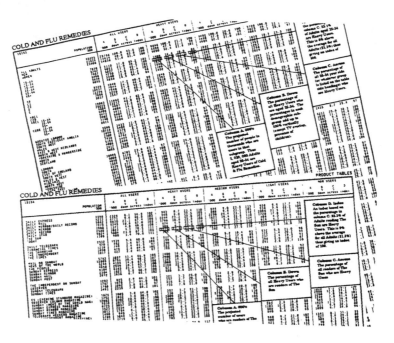

Figure 5.1   An example of the Target Group Index in use

```
Base: NEW 18+
Pop: 20699
Private Eye Target: HEAVY DRINKERS OF LOW ALCOHOL BEER AND LAGER
Pop: 1155(000)    X of Base: 5.57
```

		INDEX	UNWTD RESP	PRJ (000)	VERT (%)	HORZ (%)
1	D8 DRINK LAGER RATHER THAN BEER THESE DAYS	176	183	366	31.68	9.83
2	PA9 I LIKE TO KEEP UP WITH LATEST FASHION	165	53	121	10.47	9.20
3	T7 HOLIDAY-ONLY WANT TO EAT, DRINK, SUNBATHE	165	75	158	13.67	9.18
4	PA15 MEN'S FASHION MORE EXCITING NOWADAYS	161	105	238	20.60	8.96
5	F7 I TEND TO SPEND MONEY WITHOUT THINKING	160	65	141	12.20	8.96
6	SP3 CO'S/PRESTIGE SPONSOR ART/SPORT	157	88	190	16.45	8.76
7	DH6 HEALTH FOODS ONLY BOUGHT BY FANATICS	155	78	179	15.49	8.65
8	D9 I LIKE TO TRY NEW DRINKS	155	70	143	12.38	8.65
9	D12 I REALLY ENJOY A NIGHT OUT AT THE PUB	146	164	345	29.87	8.12
10	P4 I WOULD LIKE TO BUY A HOME COMPUTER	142	58	148	12.81	7.92
11	F4 I AM NO GOOD AT SAVING MONEY	138	87	190	16.45	7.72
12	F15 USUALLY CONSULT FINANCIAL ADVISOR	138	62	114	9.87	7.68
13	PA2 IT'S IMPORTANT TO LOOK WELL DRESSED	137	104	247	21.38	7.65
14	T11 TRY TO TAKE ONE+ HOLIDAY ABROAD A YEAR	135	60	116	10.04	7.55
15	PA13 I REALLY ENJOY SHOPPING FOR CLOTHES	134	70	130	11.25	7.50

Figure 5.2   An example of lifestyle data from the TGI

keen pub-goers and have a propensity to try new drinks. They are highly image conscious, aiming to keep abreast of new fashions. They appear to be fairly 'flash with the cash' and admit to being no good at saving money. In spite of, or maybe because of, this, they show a strong tendency to seek the advice of a financial consultant. They see their holidays as a way of achieving total relaxation, not wishing to do anything but eat, drink and lie in the sun.

Just about anything can be cross-referenced with any other variable. For example, the index can identify Heinz beans users and what kind of cars they drive. Another package, called 'trender', can be used to track product, brand, attitudinal, demographic or media trends. The index can also link into various on-line geodemographic packages.

Geodemographics

Geodemographics mixes geographical population data together with basic demographic data. It uses neighbourhood types to predict the kind of people who live within them and thus their behaviour as consumers. If a brand is found to appeal to certain geodemographic groups, their locations can be mapped and the subsequent communications can be targeted at the geographical areas that offer the greatest potential (see page 373 for examples of how precise geodemographic data is becoming).

ACORN (a classification of residential neighbourhoods) uses postcodes to identify different types of houses and generally gives useful indications about buying behaviour. Other UK on-line demographic analyses can be cross-referenced, eg *PINPOINT*, which uses 60 different neighbourhood classifications. *MOSAIC* has 58 neighbourhood categories linked with financial information. *SUPER PROFILES* uses 150 neighbourhood types.

Test marketing

Test marketing refers to new packs, new brands and new products that are only marketed in a limited test region or geographical area, eg the Yorkshire TV area. A full marketing drive (distribution and advertising, etc) is released in the test area only. This gives the company a chance to spot any last-minute problems which previous research has not identified. If the test market proves to be positive, then the marketing campaign can be extended nationally.

As mentioned, everything can be tested. A new advertising campaign, a new sales promotion or even a direct-mail campaign can be tested among a few thousand names on a mailing list (in direct mail some companies test right down to whether different coloured signatures affect direct-mail response levels). Some organizations do not, however, test market because of the associated problems of security, timing, costs and seasonality.

Some tests are considered to create *security* problems since they can alert competition with an early warning about, say, an intended new brand. Testing also costs *time* and *money*, which may not be available as launch deadlines loom closer. The limited time period of a test often restricts the accuracy of the measured results, since additional time may be required to monitor whether repeat purchases continue beyond the 'trial period'. That is, do customers keep buying, or still remember a particular advertisement after the impact of the initial launch has died down? *Seasonal* products and services are further complicated since they may need to be tested 12 months in advance. Testing, of course, costs money, which needs to be budgeted for at the beginning of the planning period. Both freak results and results manipulated by competitors can also invalidate certain tests. If this kind of inaccurate information is used to decide whether to launch or not, or how much advertising spend is required nationally, etc, then the results could be disastrous.

Tracking studies

Advertising tracking involves *pre-* and *post-*advertising research which aims to measure levels of awareness and brand recognition before and after an advertising campaign. It can also be used to measure the series of mental stages through which a customer moves: unawareness, awareness, comprehension, conviction and action. These are the stages identified in *DAGMAR* (defining advertising goals for measuring advertising results – see page 42). It is worth remembering that some elements of the communications mix, such as sales promotions, packaging and point of sale, can be more effective than advertising when pushing the customer through the final stage of 'action' or buying.

An analysis of the sales figures can identify an advertising campaign's effect on overall sales. Home audit panel data like SuperPanel can reveal information on what is happening within the total sales figures, such as who is switching brands, who are the heavy users, etc. Quantitative techniques involving street surveys, in-home interviews or telephone surveys (obviously not used if prompting respondents with visual prompt material, eg storyboard, press or poster ad) can measure the other DAGMAR stages listed above.

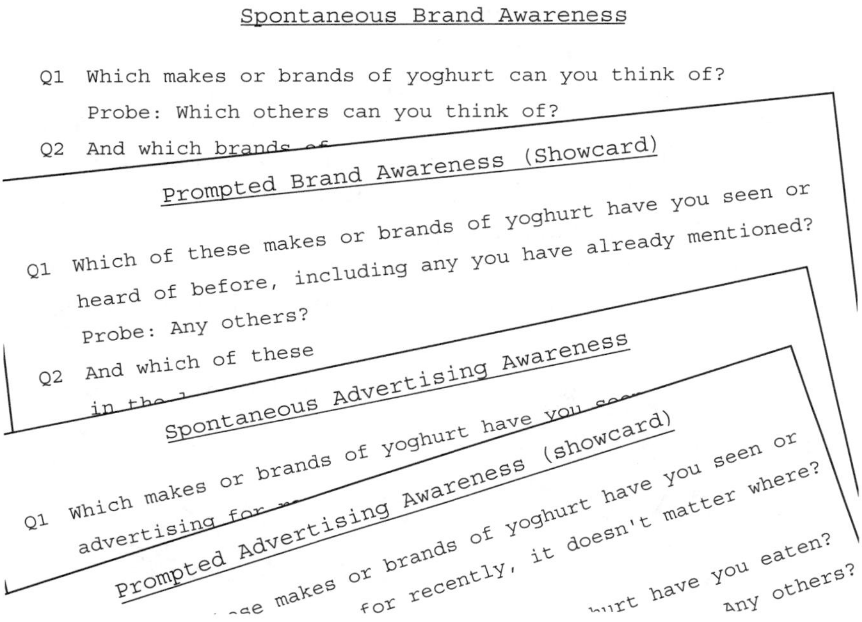

Spontaneous Brand Awareness

Q1 Which makes or brands of yoghurt can you think of?
    Probe: Which others can you think of?
Q2 And which brands of

Prompted Brand Awareness (Showcard)

Q1 Which of these makes or brands of yoghurt have you seen or
    heard of before, including any you have already mentioned?
    Probe: Any others?
Q2 And which of these

Spontaneous Advertising Awareness

Q1 Which makes or brands of yoghurt have you seen
    advertising for

Prompted Advertising Awareness (showcard)

...se makes or brands of yoghurt have you seen or
    for recently, it doesn't matter where?

...urt have you eaten?
    Any others?

Figure 5.3 Awareness questionnaire

The percentage of respondents with *spontaneous awareness* (which brands of beer can you remember seeing an advertisement for this week?) is always lower than those with *prompted awareness* (since the interviewer prompts the respondent by showing a list of brand names or a storyboard of the ad). See *Marketing Magazine*'s weekly brand awareness results for an example of who is leading the awareness tables. Incidentally, telephone surveys cannot currently be used for measuring prompted awareness of a TV campaign (they can be used to research a radio campaign) since prompt materials such as storyboards, press advertisements or lists of brands can only be shown to a misrepresentative sample (homes with videophones). Verbal prompts can be made, but this is obviously not the ideal situation. This situation may change as more homes begin to use videophones (ie, as penetration increases and 'the diffusion of innovations' occurs).

Although awareness is of interest, '*salience*' is, as Wendy Gordon (1991) points out, 'a far more valuable tool for understanding what a brand means than brand awareness'.

Retail audits

Retail audits monitor share of shelf space, prices and turnover of particular brands (including competitors') in a large and representative sample of retailers. It is worth noting that Boots, Sainsbury's and Marks & Spencer do not allow auditors to come in to their stores. This means that the audit results have to be weighted and adjusted. Where auditors are allowed access, they check shelves, facings, prices and stock levels. Most FMCG companies buy these audits, since they provide a picture of what is happening at the retail level (average price of a product, stock levels in each outlet, and each product/brand's market share (see Figure 5.4)). *Bar codes* and laser scanning can provide much of this information online directly to the user. Sales out of shops do not necessarily reflect actual customer usage. Home audits (see below) can provide customer purchase information.

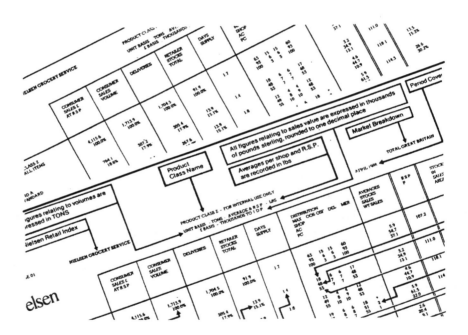

Figure 5.4 Sample extract from a Nielsen retail audit containing details of sales broken down by brand, regions, types of shops and national figures

Home audits

Instead of, or in addition to, researching the retail store, home audits research the customer directly. The retail audit data can be backed up with customer usage data. Representative families (sample size: 8,500) are recruited and asked to log all their purchases using a bar code recorder. The device asks for the name of the store and the price paid per brand, etc. All of this data is transferred to the central computer via a modem and telephone lines. Non-bar coded items are recorded on paper. Analysis of this wealth of data over time shows consumers' repertoire of brands, the effects of sales promotions on purchases, frequency of purchase, etc. This is automatically cross-referenced with the household's demographic data already held. Diaries and dedicated dustbins used to be used to collect this type of information. Today the automated on-line bar code system is preferred. The table excerpt in Figure 5.5 shows a small part of the monthly audit, including the amount bought (by price and volume/weight), market share, and average price paid for any particular brand and its competitors.

Think 'secondary' first

All communications plans should be based on sound research. Expensive primary data should only be used when all possible secondary data sources have been checked. Why pay £25,000 for a market research report analysing your industry when it may be possible to subscribe for less to a *syndicated survey* carried out specifically for a group of companies in an industry sector (eg air travel or car manufacturers)? Alternatively, some markets are researched regularly by market report companies such as Mintel, Keynotes and Jordans. These reports can be purchased by anyone for a few hundred pounds. Academic institutes often publish reports on various markets or aspects of the marketing process within a particular industry. Sometimes these are available at not much more than the cost of duplication and dispatch. A newspaper like the *Financial Times* may have done its own analysis or survey which costs less than £1. Other research reports are available free of charge as the commissioning companies see published surveys as a useful marketing tool to generate free media coverage. It also gives them something to talk to clients and prospective clients about. On the other hand, some free survey results may be biased in favour of the organization that commissioned the research in the first place, particularly if they have a vested interest in revealing certain positive results or trends.

THE MARKET RESEARCH PROCESS

The key to using information efficiently lies in the ability to *define exactly what information* is required. This is a valuable management skill. Defining the problem or defining the research objectives is the first step in the market research process shown overleaf.

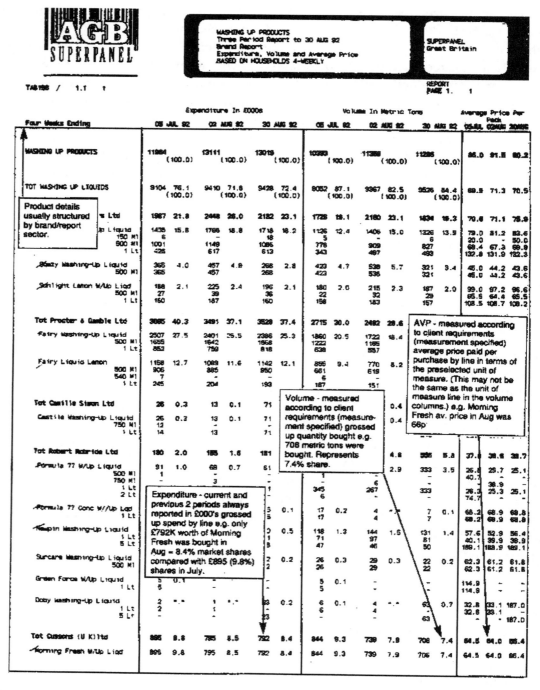

Figure 5.5 Sample extract from an AGB home audit containing details of amount bought by price and volume, market share, average prices, etc

1.	**Problem definition**	Decide clearly what information is needed and why it is needed. Is it qualitative and/or quantitative? What will be done with it?
2.	**Research plan**	Data sources: secondary/primary. Research techniques: observation, survey, experiment, focus group. Sample: size and type. Degree of confidence. Fieldwork: face to face, phone or post. Questionnaire design. Cost and timing.
3.	**Fieldwork**	Actual interviews/data collection and supervision.
4.	**Data analysis**	Coding, editing, weighting, summing, consistency/check questions, extracting trends and correlations, if any.
5.	**Report presentation**	The interpretation of the figures, summary, and sometimes conclusions.
6.	**Action taken/ not taken**	If the information is not used, then perhaps it wasn't worth collecting in the first place.

BRIEFS, PROPOSALS AND AGENCY SELECTION

Research brief

Depending on the type of research, the brief can include SOS from SOSTAC® plus 3Ms (see pages 29–33):

- Summary.
- Situation analysis (including target and marketing mix).
- Objectives of the research (problem definition – what information is required and what decisions should be made as a result of the research finding?).
- Strategy* (why the information is required/how the research findings may affect the communications strategies).
- Men/women (who will liaise with the agency?).
- Money (how much is the research budget?).
- Minutes (timing – when is the information needed?).

*Some clients prefer not to divulge too much strategic or tactical information for security reasons. On the other hand, the more the research agency knows, the more useful their contribution to the success of the project will be.

Research proposal

If an external research agency has been briefed, their research proposal should incorporate a research plan (point 2 above). You will also want to look at the agency's credentials.

Subcontract research but not understanding

There are certain research functions, marketing research functions, that are sometimes provided by outside firms that are specialists in doing nothing but research. But the core aspect of marketing, which is understanding our customer and having a close bond with the customer, that should never be turned over to anybody else.

Professor Rosabeth Moss Kanter

Agency selection

If the organization is not handling the research in-house, a market research agency will be chosen. Some of the usual agency selection procedure will apply (see 'Agency selection process', page 164).

A shortlist of agencies can be developed from personal recommendations from colleagues and advertising agencies, and from the organization's own observation of research agencies and their advertisements or editorial coverage. Agency size, specialism/expertise, reputation, location and whether the agency works for any competitors can be used as shortlisting criteria. The agencies that 'pitch' or make a presentation will then be judged by the quality of their research proposal, security of data, cost, and spin-offs (like free training). Even small details can make an impression – for example, the number of bound reports that will be delivered when the research findings are eventually presented or e-mailing presentations and providing client access to extranets, so that clients can monitor project progress. The personal chemistry or relationship between the client and the agency presenter is often the key variable that swings the choice of agency one way or another. It is also important to find out who will be handling the project and, if it is a junior member of staff, the degree of supervision that will be offered. The *IQCS* (interviewer quality control scheme) follows rigid procedures to supervise and check the quality of the information.

Some agencies demonstrate great care about the security of the data they hold. Computer hackers pose a problem to any computer-stored data. Product test samples need to be controlled carefully and securely. All samples, mock-ups and concept boards need to be returned by the interviewers, and logged as returned once they are received by the research agency. Samples, mock-ups and concept boards can then be kept under lock and key.

My girlfriend

About 10 years ago my girlfriend used to work for a well-known market research agency in London. On Fridays, I would go in and collect her before going to the pub. Whenever I was late I would dash through the main front door, past the security guard and go up in the lift. Occasionally I jumped out at the wrong floor and found myself wandering through empty offices full of live, unattended, expensive (and competitor-sensitive) research projects. Such a situation would not be allowed to happen today, and the particular agency has since changed its security procedures.

Anonymous

MARKETING INTELLIGENCE AND INFORMATION SYSTEM

Every organization should have a marketing intelligence and information system (MIIS) which lists secondary data sources. The system can be a useful starting point. The basic checklist at the end can be refined as new and better sources are identified. Essentially an MIIS should be built and constantly refined as new sources become available and old ones become redundant.

Internal figures such as sales, percentage of sales expenditures (of say, advertising), response levels, cost per order/enquiry, etc can and should be compared with external industry averages or competitor activities. Not all the information is readily available immediately, but competitors' sales figures (of grocery products and some other large markets) are available from companies such as *Nielsen Retail Audits*. Information on levels of advertising is available from MMS (Media Monitoring Services Ltd).

In an ideal marketing department, competitors' products, leaflets and advertisements should be filed, monitored and counted (so as to estimate the competitors' advertising spend), but busy marketing departments sometimes find this too time consuming. Certain monitoring companies offer to collect competitors' press clippings and published advertisements. They will also estimate a competitor's advertising spend, if this is not available from MMS. Again, this costs money and therefore it may be deemed to be 'outside the budget', particularly if it was never included in the annual marketing budget in the first place. Estimating a competitor's advertising spend can also be done by collecting all the competitor's press ads and calculating the spend from rate card costs less bulk discounts.

A marketing log filing previous marketing activities, advertisements, mailshots, editorial clippings, etc should be tagged with 'cost, objective and result'.

Comparing internal sales figures with external figures (eg total market size) gives you *market share* figures, which can also be used to calculate your competitors' market share and, more importantly, whether it is growing. Figures in isolation are relatively useless. *Figures have to be pushed backwards and across.* Backwards gives you the trend over, say, the past five-year period, and across gives you a comparison across your market (including your competitors).

The *sales force* can, if trained, provide the most up-to-date and relevant information from the MIIS. They are closest to the marketplace and in touch with what is happening. They need to be encouraged to collect relevant information.

The intelligent rep

In the United States one particular chain of stores that sold Christmas crackers held buying days when their buyers would see visiting sales representatives. Appointments were not accepted and once they had registered with the receptionist for the appropriate buyer, 'reps' proceeded to queue in a waiting room on a first-come, first-served basis. The room had rows of desks with telephones where the reps sat down quietly filling in order forms, drafting letters, completing call sheets and making phone calls. Although it was only 7.30 am a dozen registered reps were already busily working away. By 8.05 am the room was packed. The large chap beside me was on the phone at 8.00 am reporting some hot information he had come across during another breakfast appointment earlier that day. He told his boss how the competition had offered the other buyer a new buyer-incentive scheme which would commence next month, followed by a new consumer-incentive programme scheduled four months down the road. They had now four months to react or pre-empt the competition!

Staff members throughout an organization can be trained or briefed as to what type of information is considered important. Different members of the team can identify their choice of newspapers and/or trade journals. They can then scan them for anything relevant. Alternatively, a *press clipping agency* (eg Romeike and Curtice) can be hired to do this work. An *on-line database* like Textline accepts key words, companies, products, people or issues. Once you have keyed in what period of time (three/six/twelve months, etc), what area (US, UK, Europe, etc) and what types of journals or magazines, the screen will register how many references there are and ask you if you would like to read/print the headlines, read/print all the abstracts, or refine the definition/choice of keyword if too many references are recorded. Some of this information can then be used in a *SWOT analysis* (strengths, weaknesses, opportunities and threats). This is particularly useful in monitoring uncontrollable external 'OT' (opportunities and threats) variables such as political, economic, social and technical (PEST) factors. PEST developments can be difficult to forecast but the portents cannot be ignored (see Chapter 8). Many forecasting companies specialize in certain aspects such as social forecasting, and they will also carry out *econometric forecasting*, which correlates the likely sales effect resulting from a change in pricing or advertising expenditures (price elasticity or advertising elasticity).

THE DIFFICULTY WITH RESEARCH

Researching new ideas

How can answers to questions about anything that is new, unseen or previously untried be valid? The first commercially produced electric car, the Sinclair C5, had the benefit of some product research, but how can research ask people about something they cannot experience? Driving a C5 in a hall is very different to driving one along a coast road or a busy, wet and windy dual carriageway with a 40-foot truck trying to overtake. Here lies one of the difficulties with researching a new idea: how can the reality of some markets and product usage be simulated? Another problem lies with the difficulty in taking the novelty factor out. When presented with something new, buyers may be prepared to give it a try, but can the marketing people sustain the marketing effort after the excitement of the initial launch?

No one asked for a burger... until they were invented

Consumers can't be expected to embrace previously unseen solutions. Let us not forget that no one had asked for a hamburger until they were invented.

Richard Murray

The same applies to advertising. Most advertisements try to be new, different and refreshing. So how can research help produce something that is radically different to people's existing levels of expectancy? One of the UK's most successful advertising campaigns, 'Heineken refreshes the parts other beers cannot...', had the normal focus groups/concept research carried out. It 'researched poorly', ie the results said, 'This is rubbish. We don't understand this type of ad. Don't do it.' Sir Frank Lowe (chairman of the advertising agency Lowe Group) tells the story of how he had to tell the client (Heineken) about the negative concept research findings on their radically different advertising concept. 'He [the client] took a very brave decision and placed the research report document in the bin. He said "we had best leave that alone and get on with the ad!"' Expensive and carefully prepared market research findings are sometimes ignored.

Expensive research also gets it wrong if it fails to ask the right question. Even world-class companies can ask the wrong question and make huge mistakes. Take Coca-Cola – although they researched the taste of the new Coke, their 1985 flop occurred because they failed to research how consumers felt about dropping the old Coke. Here is Philip Kotler:

> Blind comparisons which took no account of the total product... name, history, packaging, cultural heritage, image – a rich mix of the tangible and the intangible. To many people Coke stands beside baseball, hotdogs and apple pie as an American institution. It represents the fabric of America. The company failed to measure these deep emotional ties, but Coke's symbolic meaning was more important to many consumers than its taste. More complete concept testing would have detected these strong emotions.

Coke flop

Sometimes research gets it wrong because it fails to understand that people can only buy a complete brand. People don't buy products, they don't buy packages, they don't buy brand names. They most certainly don't buy advertising. They buy the sum total of all those things. At one point the Coca-Cola company thought they could improve Coke and invented a new Coke. They had thousands of consumers in the US blind test new Coke vs old Coke without telling them what it was. New Coke won. So the Coca-Cola Company launched new Coke. It failed miserably. When the company researched new Coke versus old Coke they missed the understanding that the brand Coca-Cola was far more than just a product. It's the sum total of all elements of the brand.

George Bradt

Dangers to guard against

Here are some of the areas where problems can occur in market research.

1. Ambiguous definition of problem.
2. Ambiguous questions.
3. Misinterpretation (of the written question by the interviewer).
4. Misinterpretation (of the question by the interviewee).
5. Misinterpretation (of the answer by the interviewer).

6. Interviewer bias (street interviewers may select only attractive-looking respondents and exclude anyone else from the sample).
7. Interviewee inaccuracies (trying to be rational, pleasant, offensive, disruptive, knowledgeable when ignorant, etc).
8. Interviewer fraud (falsely filling in questionnaires).
9. Non-response (a refusal to answer questions).
10. Wrong sample frame, type or size.
11. Incorrect analysis.
12. Freak clustering/result (an inherent danger of sampling).
13. Timing (researching seasonal products out of season).

Research is valuable but, as can be seen, it does require experienced advice and strict control if the data are to be usefully applied. 'Dodgy data is worse than no data!' Having said that, good data can make the difference between winning and losing. Asking good questions is a great skill. It is important to know what you need to know, as demonstrated by the following poem.

There is something I don't know
that I am supposed to know.
I don't know what it is I don't know,
and yet am supposed to know,
and I feel I look stupid
if I seem both not to know it
and not know what it is I don't know.
Therefore I pretend to know it.
This is nerve racking
since I don't know what I must pretend to know.
Therefore I pretend to know everything.

I feel you know what I am supposed to know
but you can't tell me what it is
because you don't know that I don't know what it is.

You may know what I don't know, but not
that I don't know it,
and I can't tell you. So you will have to tell me everything.

A poem about information from R D Laing's *Knots*. Reproduced by kind permission of Tavistock Publications

CASE STUDY 5.1

Why not let the consumer do the thinking for you?

Situation

A global white-goods manufacturer was designing a new dishwasher for the European market. Lead time was 18–24 months, R & D had produced prototypes and manufacturing trials were due to begin. Some consumer input was desirable, but was it feasible?

Conventional wisdom on the value of consumer research at this critical product development stage says that:

- consumers cannot see the future, they can only see the present through a rear-view mirror of their own past experiences – which is not very helpful to the R & D team who are designing for a future marketplace;
- consumers tend to lack creativity and are usually critical of new ideas until they become familiar with them in the mainstream marketplace – which again is not helpful to developers looking for reassurance about their business plans.

Some would say this a scenario that requires the use of 'early adopters', but as they rarely account for more than 15 per cent of a market, and as dishwasher penetration itself was only at 18 per cent of households, where do you find them, and where do you begin looking?

With so many questions and unknowns, many companies would choose to ignore the consumer and use their own judgement when making decisions, but in this instance they chose to think differently.

Objectives

They decided to try to find a different solution by using a new methodology developed by Future Featuring Ltd which invites consumers with something to say to join the company team and express their views as experts from the 'real world'. These people have an in-depth knowledge of the market to be explored.

Strategy

Insert an invitation (*Interested in dishwashers?*) in media/a medium (in this instance, large-circulation newspapers in four major cities) that reach/es a significantly large audience in the marketplace. By responding to this invitation, people recruit themselves.

INTERESTED IN DISHWASHERS **?**

If you would like the opportunity to participate in market research discussions to develop your ideal dishwashing system please fill in and return the questionnaire below

Send to: *FUTURE Featuring (Market Research)1 Winders Road London SW11 3HE*

My personal details are:

Name: Mr/Mrs/Ms _____ Age _____

Address: _____

_____ Post Code _____

Tel No: (Home) _____ (Work) _____

Q1 Do you have a dishwasher now?
  YES → ☐ How many machines have you owned ? (write in) ☐
      How often do you use your machine each week ? (write in) ☐
  NO → ☐ Are you planning to get one? (✓) Yes ☐ No ☐
Q2 Which of the following features are you <u>very</u> interested in seeing improved in dishwashing machines? (✓)
Q3 Amongst these which are your top 3 required improvements? (1,2,3,)
Q4 Which features are you satisfied with currently? (✓)

	Q2 Very interested in improving	Q3 My top 3 improvements	Q4 Currently satisfied
Loading	☐	☐	☐
Durability	☐	☐	☐
Speed	☐	☐	☐
Size	☐	☐	☐
Servicing	☐	☐	☐
Fine china/cutlery care	☐	☐	☐
Cleaning pots, pans, large items	☐	☐	☐
Rinsing	☐	☐	☐
Drying	☐	☐	☐
Economy	☐	☐	☐
Environmental friendliness	☐	☐	☐
Style/design	☐	☐	☐
Filtering waste	☐	☐	☐
Noisy/vibration	☐	☐	☐
Cleaning performance	☐	☐	☐
Storage	☐	☐	☐

Advertisement placed in the London Evening Standard *to recruit research group contributors*

The results in this project matched those experienced before:

- people were recruited with both practical knowledge and a genuine interest in the subject matter (dishwashers);
- most were, in fact, experienced users of dishwashers, many having owned more than one and thus were very *active* consumers in the marketplace, always on the lookout for something *better* that could meet their unsatisfied needs.

Advertisements that appeared in the local press in (a) Italy, (b) France and (c) Germany

Tactics/action

A series of two focus group workshops were undertaken in each of the four cities, with each session lasting for 2–3 hours. This allowed the respondents to download their own information and insights about the market before engaging in the client-developed agenda.

This experience, coupled with their interest and commitment to category improvement, led them to make both practical and insightful suggestions to the company R & D team.

The wide range of ideas and initiatives developed at the sessions were distilled by the research team before conclusions and recommendations were made to the client.

Control

- The company R & D team had predetermined that the consumer was most concerned about having a large choice of wash cycles and the design and function of the control panel (the most costly and sensitive aspect of the product development).
- The consumer team, however, was most concerned with the machine's ability to wash better *and*, in particular, the internal configuration of the machine.
- Each country researched used crockery that matched their national eating habits and their personal cooking styles, yet all dishwashers were currently provided with the same internal basket layout – why?

As a result of listening to what these expert consumers had to say, the company discovered they currently outsourced the production of the baskets and that the cost of production was low. They could customize the dishwasher baskets to precisely meet the needs of each country, region, or even specific consumer segments, and so be the first manufacturer to produce 'bespoke' dishwashers *and* to create an actual difference in a marketplace that was typified by white boxes that all look alike!

Customization of the internal fittings went a long way to providing customer delight, added positively to the company's corporate image of being consumer-led and saved a considerable amount of time and money through cutting out the unnecessary production of expensive control mechanisms that were not required even by these expert consumers.

Conclusion

People *do* have genuinely useful, innovative ideas to contribute if you provide them with the opportunity to express themselves and you listen to *their* agenda.

In future we must be more prepared to consider new or different research methodologies that allow active consumers (the experts in the marketplace) to work *with* active companies (the experts in the production of goods and services) – together, as a team. The process is not complex and a small team of 4–5 can operate the workshop programme.

One of the key advantages of a methodology such as that described above is its simplicity and the fact that a programme can be set up, undertaken and debriefed very speedily. A typical timescale would be 4–6 weeks, but it could be completed in a week!

The costs of this project were in the region of £20,000–25,000, which included eight focus group workshops, small (20 centimetres by 2 columns) black-and-white advertisements in newspapers and the executive time required to manage the project. It should be noted that the usual incentive that is normally given to respondents was not necessary as they were keen to take part because of their ability to contribute, so they received only travel expenses.

And the new team-effort dishwasher? Economic changes and currency movements meant the company had to shelve all new product launches – welcome to the real world!

Key points from Chapter 5:

1. Budgets allowing, research can reveal anything required.
2. Consider carefully exactly what information is required, because there is too much information out there.
3. Always check secondary sources before commissioning expensive primary research.
4. Set up a marketing intelligence and information system.

APPENDIX 5.1

Web sites and research

Web sites can help with marketing research by:

- asking customers questions;
- offering on-site search engines (to find out what customers are looking for);
- using questionnaires but only sparingly, as they can cause people to leave a site, particularly if the questionnaire is on the home page;
- monitoring Web logs to see which are the most popular pages.

Every click potentially captures data, building a better profile about the visitor and his or her interest.

Chat rooms offer a wonderful opportunity to listen, free of charge, to customers discussing your product or service. And more sophisticated data-mining software can drill down into data mines and build profiles that help companies to understand their customers better.

FURTHER READING

Birn, R, Hague, P and Vangelder, P (1990) *A Handbook of Market Research Techniques*, Kogan Page, London

Bradt, G (1996, 2000) *Online Marketing Course 5: Marketing Research*, Multimedia Marketing.com, London

Cerha, Jarko (1970) *Inventing Products to Fit the Future Market*, paper given at ESOMAR, Neu Isenburg, November

Crimp, M (1990) *The Marketing Research Process*, 3rd edn, Prentice-Hall, Englewood Cliffs, NJ

Crouch, S (1984) *Marketing Research for Managers*, Heinemann, Oxford

Douglas, T (1984) *The Complete Guide to Advertising*, PaperMac, London

Gordon, W (1991) Accessing the brand through research, in *Understanding Brands*, ed D Cowley, Kogan Page, London, pp 31–56

Gordon, W (1999) *Goodthinking*, Admap, Oxford

Holder (1999) Talking to the right consumer, *Design Week*, May

Holder and Gray (2001) *Design or Die!*, paper given at MRS conference, Brighton, March

Holder and Young (1995a) *A Journey Beyond Imagination*, paper given at ESOMAR, Berlin, February

Holder and Young (1995b) *Managing Change: Moving towards a leaner future*, paper given at Business Industry Group, May

Holder and Young (1997) *Researching the Future in the Present*, paper given at ESOMAR, Edinburgh, September

Holder and Young (2000) *Getting to the Future First*, paper given at AEMRI, Paris, June

Kanter, R (1996, 2000) *Online Marketing Research Course 5: Marketing Research*, Multimedia Marketing. com, London

Knave, M (1996) Rescuing Boris, *Time* magazine, 15 July

Knave, M (1996) Unlocking deep-seated reactions makes ads more sympathetic, in *Marketing Breakthroughs*, ed Bruce Whitehall, December 1991, p 9

Kotler, P (2000) *Marketing Management, Analysis, Planning, Implementation and Control*, The Millennium edn, Prentice-Hall International, London

Market Research Society Conference Papers (1986) Research is good for you – The contribution of research to Guinness advertising, MRS, London

Marketing Guide 6: Market Research (1989) *Marketing Magazine*, Haymarket Publishing Limited, 13 April

Murray, R (1997) Clone zone, *Creative Review*, November

Nurden, R (1997) Managers pay price for office pressures, *The European*, 27 November

Wurman, R (1996) Information Anxiety, system overload, *Time* magazine, 9 December

Young (2001) *Innovation Networking*, paper given at AEMRI, Berlin, June

FURTHER CONTACTS

Association of British Market Research Companies (ABMRC), Devonshire House, 60 Goswell Road, London EC1M 7AD (tel: 020 7566 3636; Web site: www.bmra.org.uk)

European Society for Opinion and Market Research (ESOMAR) Central Secretariat, Vionvelstraat 172, 1054 GV Amsterdam, the Netherlands (tel: 00 31 20 6642141; Web site: www.esomar.nl)

The Market Research Society, The Old Trading House, 15 Northburgh Street, London EC1V 0JR (tel: 020 7490 4911; Web site: www.mrs.org.uk)

Media Monitoring Services (formerly known as Media Expenditure Advertising Ltd (MEAL)), Nielsen House, London Road, Headington, Oxford OX3 9RX (tel: 01865 742742; Web site: www.mediamonitoring.com)

Millward Brown, Olympus Avenue, Tachbrook Park, Warwickshire CV34 6RJ (tel: 01926 452233; Web site: www.millwardbrown.com)

6

Understanding agencies – agency relationships

This chapter covers agencies, types of agencies, their structure, fees and working relationships, from shortlisting to briefing, selecting, hiring and firing.

There are many types of agencies, including advertising, sales promotion, direct mail, PR, corporate identity design, Web design and more. Some call themselves agencies and others, consultancies. Regardless of title, the barriers created by the separate disciplines are falling. Corporate identity design consultants' services are spreading into advertising campaigns (to launch the new identities); sales promotion consultants are tempted into direct mail as this communications tool requires a constant flow of incentives, premiums and sales promotions; advertising agencies are dropping the word advertising and PR consultants dropping PR (see page 4) as these terms restrict them from developing and delivering the integrated services their clients require. The overall approach by, and structures of, advertising agencies are changing. Some agencies are moving their focus beyond the one-way 'tell medium' of traditional broadcasting with its limited levels of interactive responsiveness. These agencies integrate more closely with the 'responsive disciplines', such as direct mail, sales promotions and Web marketing. Moving from 'tell campaigns' to 'listening campaigns' requires a constant customer dialogue nurtured and integrated across many media (see page 15).

2001 – Have things changed?

I do not find today's advertising agencies much of a match for tomorrow's marketing opportunities.

Niall Fitzgerald, Chairman, Unilever, 1997

Unless Madison Avenue agencies get their interactive act together, companies like P&G will find other ways to tell consumers about their products.

Edwin Artz, Chairman, Procter and Gamble, 1995

Some agencies see new structures as an exciting challenge for the agency world. 'At the very least, the shaking up of structures and processes that pre-date the new technology by about 100 years can't fail to have a liberating effect that should be greatly to the benefit of clients,' says Martin Sorrell, Chairman, WPP Group. Other agencies feel that the required changes in agency structure require not just new structures but new language. UK agency HHCL suggest that 'impact' should be replaced by 'dialogue', 'poster advertising' by 'street dialogue', that 'direct mail and radio' should change to 'kitchen dialogue', and 'customer base' be replaced by 'customer community', while 'response' should become 'interaction' and 'knowledge' replace 'awareness'. The process of change among agencies is being driven partly by unsettled clients, visionary agency directors, the media explosion and new types of competition emerging.

Agencies under siege?

Many brands today are dying. Not the natural death of absence but the slow, painful death of sales and margin erosion. The managers of these brands are not complacent – in fact, they are constantly tweaking the advertising, pricing and cost of their brands. At the heart of the problem is a more fundamental issue: can the original promise of the brand be recreated and a new spark lit with today's consumers? We believe it can. Most brands can be reinvented through brand renaissance.

Excerpt from a Boston Consulting Group brochure

Although advertising agencies are under siege from aggressive management consultants, young, hungry integrated agencies and disgruntled heavyweight marketing clients, the advertising agency's structure is still used here as it offers a broad base upon which other agencies and consultancies often develop their structures.

AGENCY STRUCTURE

Different types and sizes of agencies have different structures. The structure of a large advertising agency shown in Figure 6.1 illustrates the many different departments, people and skills that have to work together to create an advertisement. Companies that have their own in-house advertising departments, and smaller, external agencies, will subcontract in (or hire) any of the departments they do not have. Many of the bigger agencies also hire or subcontract directors, producers, cameramen, photographers, film companies, print and production facilities. Any other agent, agency, consultant or consultancy – whether public relations, direct mail, sales promotion or corporate identity – also relies on many of the different skills/departments shown in Figure 6.1.

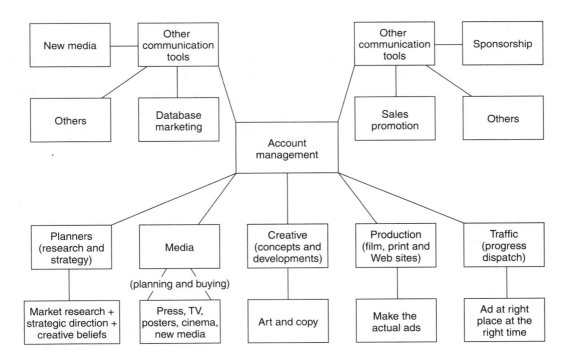

Figure 6.1 Structure of a large advertising agency

The account executive

Sometimes also called an account representative, the account executive is dedicated to a particular client. The account executive wears two hats – the client's when talking to the agency and the agency's when talking to the client. Responsibilities include: attendance at all client meetings, writing up 'contact reports' and general liaising between the many different members of the agency's team and the client. Many agencies write up *contact reports* (after each meeting) because they confirm and clarify all key points discussed, conclusions reached and any actions to be taken. This cuts out the opportunity for any misinterpretation further down the road when the client says 'I never said that' or 'I never asked for that'. When agreed by the client, vital documents, such as a summary of the agency's interpretation of the client's brief, or concept proposals, are sometimes required to be signed by the client as 'approved'. This keeps communication clear, reduces ambiguities and, if a row does break out over a particular strategic direction or over the details of copy (the words in the advertisement), the agency can pull out a signed 'approved by'. This is particularly helpful when a manager leaves a client company, because it confirms the stage-by-stage approval of the development of a campaign.

Planning department

Planners are more than glorified researchers. They have to know the right kind of questions to ask in the research, commission the research and interpret the results at two different levels. First, they have to absorb, summarize and translate large market research reports into simple layman's terms for inclusion in the creative brief that they, in conjunction with the account manager, give to the creative team. Second, the information has to be interpreted at a strategic and tactical level for discussion with the account executive, account manager, account director and often the client. Planners provide an objective voice, unhindered by both the account executive, who sometimes wants to 'sell' an advertising concept to the client simply because the creative director wants to get on with it, and by clients who sometimes want to get on with it by quickly running some advertisements to satisfy the sales-force, who are anxiously waiting for news on the new campaign.

Creative department

It is unfair to stereotype creative people as unshaven, wearing faded jeans and silk shirts, who come in late, lie around and dream up the big ideas and concepts that drive all advertising campaigns. They can work long hours under extreme pressure to deliver unique, creative ideas that grab attention, build brands and win customers. They constantly search for the big idea that has to fit the single-minded strategy presented in the creative brief that is developed by the planning department. Creative people usually work in pairs, covering words and pictures, ie a copywriter (or wordsmith) and an art director.

Media department

The media department basically plans and buys the space where the advertisements are eventually placed (press, posters, TV, radio, cinema, etc). Media planners/schedulers are sometimes separate from media buyers, who negotiate and ultimately buy the space from the media owners. Both media planners and media buyers can be further separated into those who specialize in TV, press, or new media, etc. The emergence of cable and satellite TV, low-cost print technology and thousands of new Web sites increases the range of media available to media buyers. As markets fragment and media explode into many more magazines, TV stations and Web sites, large audiences become more difficult to buy. Despite this, the media explosion presents new opportunities for schedulers and buyers as these new media vehicles have access to more tightly defined target markets. The media department now analyses the appropriateness and cost effectiveness of much more media than ever before. This is quite a responsibility as the bulk of the advertising spend is in media and not production (eg a £20 million campaign might have a £19 million media budget and a £1 million production budget). On top of this, media departments can deliver highly creative media strategies which find new ways of delivering advertisements to target audiences. See pages 312–13, for examples.

Production department

The production department actually makes the advertisement. Many agencies subcontract various parts of the production, eg hiring a studio, camera crew/photographer, director, editing suites, etc. This can involve long pre-production meetings finalizing all the minute details, flying around the world to shoot some film and the less glamorous, lonely post-production – working around the clock in a dark and dingy editing suite.

Traffic department

Dispatch, or traffic, is responsible for getting the right artwork or film to the right magazine or TV network at the right time. This becomes complicated where posters, cinema, radio and magazine inserts are included in the media strategy. Multiply this by several different campaigns for a range of different clients and the need for a traffic manager becomes self-evident.

In addition to marathon pre-production meetings and lonely post-production editing, the actual production, although often long and tedious, can sometimes involve exciting location shoots

The account management team

In a large agency this can involve an account director, account manager, account executive, planner, creative director, copy-writer, art director, TV producer, media director, TV media scheduler, TV airtime buyer, press planner and press buyer.

The three key components

The three key components of the agency are:

1. Planning/strategy.
2. Creative.
3. Media.

AGENCY TYPES

The larger agencies offer a *full service*, including creative, research and planning, media planning and buying, and production. Some full-service agencies also have departments specializing in forecasting, market intelligence and business planning, together with support services for the advertising campaign, including point-of-sale design, sales literature, sales conferences and other below-the-line activities such as sales promotion, PR or direct mail. The agency, like any other business, also has other departments that are of little interest to the client, such as accounting and finance, personnel, administration, etc (see Table 6.1).

Advertisers can choose to use only their own in-house staff to run a campaign. Do-it-yourself or *in-house advertising* also varies, as some advertisers prefer to contract out some of their requirements to specialist services such as a specialist media scheduling and buying agency known as a *'media independent'*. Similarly, the creative work can be put out to a *'hot shop'*, or *'creative shop'*. Saatchi and Saatchi started as a creative shop. Alternatively, the advertiser can go à la carte by picking and choosing separate agencies with specialist services for different parts of the process, eg using four different agencies for the research, creative, production and media planning/buying stages. There are other types of specialist agencies that focus on a particular industry sector.

A recent discrete development in the à la carte option is the agreement of a large, well-known, full-service advertising agency to sub-contract the large agency's creative services to a small communications consultancy on an ad hoc basis. This may last only as long as the agency has spare capacity or is searching for extra revenue. Some clients demand that their full-service agencies work alongside the client's separate choice of media independents. Some full-service agencies only get a portion of the full job. A recession can force some clients to cut back their own in-house advertising department and operate a less costly and more flexible ad hoc project arrangement with various agencies.

Different working relationships

At the end of the day the coordination of campaign development, launch and measurements requires time and management skills. Powerful personalities in agencies need to be controlled. *The ability to ask the right question* is a valuable management skill. The fatigue factor in negotiations or discussions can also cause rash decisions to be made. Marketing people tend to be energetic, enthusiastic, action-oriented achievers. Sometimes steely patience needs to be exercised. Perhaps a decision has to be delayed until further research can answer some emerging questions. Painstaking attention to detail may sometimes seem irksome to the advertising agency, but it is often the mark of a true professional. On the other hand a key resource, time, may be running out. More research reduces the risk but costs time and money. Can deadlines be moved? Is there money left for more research? A decision made in haste is rarely the best one.

Table 6.1 The pros and cons of different working relationships

Aspect	Full services (under one roof)	Specialist services	In-house
Management and control	Easier since it is all under one roof	More work (coordinating)	Total control but more work involved
Security	Limited risk – sensitive information is shared with agency	More risk – more people have access to information	Minimal risk – no outsiders
Speed/response	Reasonably good	Possible problems if à la carte = more coordination	Fast, since all decision makers are available
Cost	Expensive, high overheads, but lower media costs with agency buying power	Cheaper, fewer overheads	Cheaper but less media buying power
Fresh views	Yes	Yes	No
Expertise	Yes (Jack of all trades, master of none?)	Yes (fill in gaps in client's skills)	No (lack of specialized knowledge)
Stress	Less pressure/workload	Delegate some workload	More stress – more work

How to ensure good agency relationships

1. Agree a system of remuneration – fees, commissions, mark-ups, time, expenses and method of billing – in writing. Remember, it is better to argue over a quote than an invoice.
2. Trust the agency team (share research and information with them, involve them).
3. Make them become part of the marketing team. Use their expertise. See how suppliers (eg agencies) become extensions of the client's team through 'partnership sourcing' in the McGregor Cory short case at the end of Chapter 19.

4. Ask relevant questions. Listen carefully to the answers. Do not be intimidated by strong agency characters. All propositions should be justifiable. The final decision is the client's.
5. Explain to the agency who makes what decisions, ie who has authority for which decisions.
6. Sign/approve in writing each stage from brief to concepts – finished artwork, running proofs and so on.
7. Keep briefs short and unambiguous.
8. Regular reviews help to plug any gaps in performance, whether creative, strategic or personal.
9. Write an occasional 'thank you' note to the team.
10. A stable relationship builds a real team since the agency gets to know the client, the team, the company and the market inside out. In addition, the client does not have to worry about unfriendly, discarded agencies who have previously had access to sensitive information.

AGENCY REMUNERATION

Agencies have three basic methods of calculating their remuneration: commission, fees and pay-by-results.

Commission

Historically, media owners have given recognized agencies a 15 per cent discount off the rate card price. Thus, in the case of a £10 million TV advertising campaign, the agency gets invoiced by the TV station at rate card £10 million less 15 per cent, ie £8.5 million. The client then gets invoiced by the agency at the full rate card price, ie £10 million (this can be checked with British Rate and Data (BRAD) or the media owner's published rate card). The 15 per cent commission really represents 17.65 per cent mark-up, ie the £1.5 million commission is the mark-up which the agency adds on to their media cost of £8.5 million.

£10 million ad campaign

Agency invoiced by TV station less 15%	=	£8.5 million
Agency invoices client at full rate card	=	£10.0 million
Agency mark-up		1.5 million
Agency mark-up	=	17.65%

The agency will also apply its agreed mark-up to other services which it subcontracts, such as market research and so on. Thus a piece of research that costs the agency £10,000 would be charged to the client (+17.65 per cent) at £11,765. One of the problems with the commission system is that it can tempt agencies to get clients to spend, spend, spend. Incidentally, the commission system does not necessarily cover all production costs, so production costs are often separately invoiced directly to the client by the agency. Over the past 10 years the number of clients using this method has declined significantly, in favour of a combination of the payment methods outlined below.

Commission rebating

Specialist media-buying companies – with much lower overheads – can work with commissions as low as 2 or 3 per cent. Some clients insist that the full-service agency only takes a smaller commission, say 10 per cent, with the balancing 5 per cent going back to the client. Commission rebating occurs when an agency passes on some of its commission to the client. There is no actual refund or rebate. The agencies simply invoice the client at rate card costs less the level of rebate, in this case 5 per cent. Commission rebating opens the door to agencies competing on price instead of, as they have done traditionally, on quality of service. Most industries dislike price wars and advertising is no exception. Way back in 1984 Allen Brady and Marsh (ABM) once resigned its £3.5 million B & Q account after a request for rebates. It also took a large advertisement in the advertising trade press explaining that the 15 per cent commission left most agencies with 2 per cent profits after tax and any reduction would affect the quality of advertising. It fought against the tide of change, and refused to become involved in commission rebating. ABM was a fantastic agency generating some classic advertising campaigns, but, sadly, it no longer exists.

Many clients today are moving towards fees instead of solely commission-based remuneration.

Fees

Smaller clients with smaller media spends do not generate sufficient commission, so a fee will generally be agreed. Larger clients are also moving towards fees – an annual, quarterly or monthly retainer or, alternatively, a project fee. No commission means *no media bias*, since the agency is then free to recommend, say, direct mail, without losing any of its income (which would have been generated through commissions).

Many agencies receive a fee along with some level of commission. The agency's remuneration essentially depends on how much work is involved and how much the client is likely to spend (on media). The trend, particularly with larger clients, appears to be moving towards a fee basis or a mixture of fees, commissions and results.

Frowned upon by some agencies, pay-by-results can be mutually beneficial. It is sometimes disliked because of the lack of control that the agency has over its own destiny.

Pay-by-results

Some agencies, often young and new agencies, are prepared to put their heads on the block and offer their services on a pay-by-results basis. The problem is that some results are beyond the agency's influence, eg poor product quality control, late delivery or inadequate distribution, a price change, a strike at the factory or competitor activities such as doubling their advertising and cutting their prices. So if sales form the main criterion for payment, then the agencies are vulnerable by the very nature of their dependency on so many uncontrollable variables.

If, on the other hand, the payment is linked to results directly influenced by advertising, say level of awareness or a shift in image or positioning, then the agency has more control over its own destiny. These, of course, have to be measured through market research. One area where results are easily measured and are directly related to the agency's input is media buying. If an agency achieves media buying at a price that is better than average, then the saving is shared between client and agency. For example, if the average advertising cost per thousand to reach, say, housewives with children is £3.50, and if the agency gets this for 10 per cent less, then the saving might be split 8 per cent to the client and 2 per cent to the agency. (Note: quality of the media is also taken into account.) Some agencies, like BBH, prefer a fixed bid system with shared risk system. For example, if an advertisement is produced under budget, the production company keeps a percentage and the client receives a percentage. If the advertisement is 10 per cent over budget, the client pays; over that and the production company pays.

Pay-by-results extends beyond advertising into other disciplines as far away as design. This can apply to new product design (as a royalty) or even packaging design, when the packaging design consultancy bases its fee (or a portion of its fees) on the client's increase in sales occurring after the launch of the newly designed pack. Although payment-by-results appears attractive to the client, it can generate extra administrative work, as exact results have to be measured, royalties/contributions calculated, invoices requested and cheques raised for each agreed accounting period.

The method of agency reimbursement is fundamental to the client/agency relationship (both working and contractual). An agency's range of reimbursement packages can influence the client's selection process.

AGENCY SELECTION PROCESS

Defining exactly what is required is the first stage of agency selection. This is because an appropriate choice is partly determined by a specific requirement. Some furniture retail chains may consider the strength of the media department the key criterion when choosing an agency, particularly if the store primarily wants maximum media coverage for its relatively straightforward black-and-white product information advertisements. Another client may be looking for a radically fresh approach and have a bias towards agencies with abundant creative talent. Either way, a clear brief should be prepared to identify exactly what – in marketing and advertising terms – the new advertising campaign is trying to achieve (see 'The brief' on page 166).

The agency selection procedure can be as follows:

1. Define requirements.
2. Develop a pool list of attractive agencies.
3. Credentials pitch (by the agencies).
4. Issue brief to shortlisted agencies.
5. Full agency presentation or pitch.
6. Analysis of pitch.
7. Select winner.
8. Agree contract details.
9. Announce winner.

Some clients prefer to get on with it by issuing a full brief to the shortlist of, say, six agencies without going through the agency credentials presentation. Other clients prefer to restrict the valuable research findings and strategic thinking to as few agencies as possible because the unsuccessful agencies are free to work for the competition at any time in the future.

Chapter 12 has a mock agency selection game that is somewhat biased towards the agency that made the advertisement (see page 352).

Pool list

Most advertising managers and marketing managers *observe* various campaigns by watching advertising and noting any particularly attractive campaigns. Agencies working for the competition need to be excluded or treated with extreme caution. Some desk research, both online and offline, can reveal the agencies behind the brands by reference to organizations such as Media Monitoring Services (MMS) or Adforum.com, which allow advertisers to look for agencies using sensible criteria. Advertisers can create shortlists, preview creative work and explore an agency's profile, online and for free. Many marketing managers have a fair idea of who is doing what advertising in their sector by constantly reading the *trade press*. Other managers simply increase their advertising dosage by spending a few weeks watching more advertising than normal. Some clients sift through the agency *portfolio videos* which can be bought from Campaign Portfolio or Marketing Week Portfolio for a few hundred pounds (the agencies pay a lot more to acquire this advertising space in the first place). In these videos agency after agency present themselves in a sometimes surprisingly tedious fashion. Some clients prefer to do their own screening and request an *agency reel* (video) or an agency information pack directly from a particular agency so that they can view the agency's best work. Advertisements can also be sourced and viewed online through AdChannel from AMX Digital. Grey Direct's ad, below, gets them on to pool lists.

Another way of building a pool list is through the *professional associations*. Upon receipt of information about a potential client's basic requirements, professional bodies or trade associations such as the IPA (Institute of Practitioners in Advertising), the ISBA (Incorporated Society of British Advertisers) and the AA (Advertising Association) all offer to provide lists of agencies which they feel are suitable to handle a specific type and size of business. Similar services are offered by the relevant professional institutes of other service sectors such as public relations, sales promotion, design, direct mail, etc (see 'Further contacts' at the end of each chapter). This service is normally free and the associations are extremely helpful to the uninitiated.

Grey Direct's ad gets them on to pool lists
Source: Photograph by Roger Eaton

There are also *agency assessors*, such as the Advertising Agency Register, whose business is agency selection. They can handle the development of the pool list, pitch list, pitch analysis, agency selection and even performance assessment of the agency when it starts working for the client. The assessor services are popular with international clients who need help in all aspects of their quest for the right agency. Similar services are available for PR, direct mail, sales promotion and corporate identity.

Credentials

Some clients, before issuing a full brief, prefer to ask the pool of agencies to present their *credentials*. This includes examples of current and previous work, team members' profiles, and company history, structure and facilities. It is worth visiting the agency, and sometimes at short notice, as this gives the client a 'feel' for the potential agency, and its atmosphere, organization, professionalism, etc. From this a final *shortlist* is selected and issued with a detailed brief.

Long shortlist

Some years ago Westminster City Council invited 10 agencies to pitch for their communications work. A long shortlist creates an unnecessary amount of unpaid work for everyone concerned.

Briefing, pitching and selecting take time and skills. Apart from creating a lot of work, a large pitch list sometimes leaves sensitive marketing information with many different people. Some cynics see it as an opportunity to get free strategic and tactical ideas from the best brains in each agency.

The brief

Briefs vary in size, structure and level of detail. Some clients may summarize on to a single A4 sheet of paper, others issue a much more detailed briefing document (a recent Guinness brief was 100 pages). Essentially, the brief should incorporate at least the SOS (situation, objectives and strategy) and 3Ms (men/women, money and minutes) part of the SOSTAC® planning system explained in Chapter 2. The brief tends to be brief, while a marketing communications plan has much more detail. Since the brief usually goes out to several agencies pitching for the business (only one of whom will get the business) a difficult dilemma emerges. How much confidential and strategic information should be revealed in the brief, given that the majority of the recipients will not work for you and may one day work for your competition? Food for thought. At the bare minimum, the brief will usually include the following.

1. Situation – where you are now – including the market, channels, segments, target markets, trends, competition, market share, position, current and previous campaigns, strengths and weaknesses, USPs (unique selling propositions), features and benefits of the brand and the organization.
2. Objectives – where you want to go – marketing objectives and communications objectives (see page 41 for examples).
3. Strategy – how you are going to get there (including all elements of the marketing mix and target markets).
4. 3Ms:
    Men/women – who makes the final decision, members of the team, who reports to whom, contacts for additional questions.
    Money – key question for the agency – what is the budget?
    Minutes – timescale and deadlines for pitch, agency selection and eventual campaign launch.

Control is sometimes included as it outlines how the campaign will be measured, which in turn motivates the team to get it right. A smaller client may prefer to replace the advertising and/or marketing objectives with a statement of the problem and subsequently ask the agency to present a complete promotional plan. It is likely that the agency's first question will be: 'How much do you have to spend?' As mentioned, there are obvious dangers of releasing strategic information to several agencies, the majority of whom will never work for you (since there is usually only one winner or single agency selected). The corollary is that too little information reduces the quality (and possibly strategic direction) of the proposals.

Pre-pitch agency efforts

The shortlisted agencies are invited to make a full presentation or sales pitch. This usually involves several members of the agency staff and is viewed by several members of the client company. The cost of a major pitch varies from £10,000 to £50,000 (up to six agency people involved for six weeks, £36k, plus £10k for materials plus £4k research). Preparation for a pitch is usually an intensive affair and can include researching the client's market, media, company structure and individual personalities (prior knowledge of who will attend the pitch and hopefully some background information on their personalities and interests), strategic planning, brainstorming, concept development (advertising ideas), slide shows, videos, rehearsals and even mediation. Without doubt, new business pitches increase the adrenalin flow inside agencies.

US-owned McCann-Erickson are reported to draft in a professional teacher of meditation and relaxation techniques before every pitch. JWT practise their pressure presentation techniques with bizarre scenarios like asking their teams to imagine that they discover one of their art directors pushing cocaine and that, as they prepare to fire him, they discover his wife is dying of cancer and in need of private medical treatment.

Real empathy, sound strategy, exciting creative work and reasonable costs are often considered to be the key factors during a pitch, but some agencies take initiatives before the actual pitch, as Table 6.2 shows.

Table 6.2 Pre-pitch agency initiatives

Client	Agency	Stunt
Kiss FM Radio	BBDO	Delivered a framed poster to the Kiss MD bearing the legend 'We'll put your name on everyone's lips'*
Kiss FM Radio	Saatchi	Covered Kiss HQ with pink balloons on Valentine's Day
Guardian	Publicis	Booked a 96-sheet (40' × 10' poster) site opposite the newspaper's offices during the week of the pitch and ran flattering ads that changed each day*
Financial services company	Publicis	Sent a safe containing the agency's credentials
Toyota	Saatchi	Three Toyota cars suspended above Charlotte Street, hanging out of the agency's offices.*

* Won the account

Pre-pitch feelings – a client's view?

Will they love me?

'Our research has shown that, generally speaking, clients are not happy about changing agencies. Such events are usually a signal that they are unable to sustain a productive relationship with other people, which is something that none of us is pleased to accept, however difficult the other people might be... the prospect (potential client) is under pressure from his boss to get it right quickly... so when he steps from the bustle and stress of his own trade into the palm-fringed oasis of Berkeley Square or Charlotte Street or Covent Garden it is possible that he has two questions in his mind: "Will they love me?" and "Can they save my neck?" '

Brian Johnson, new business director, JWT

Other potential or prospective clients would deny any such self-imposed pressure. They may see the pitch as an exciting and stimulating process full of fresh ideas and strategic thinking presented by clever, articulate (and sometimes entertaining) people. Client egos are massaged and generally the prospect is treated as a revered guest. Other prospective clients see pitches as a more tedious affair, since they have to repeat their brief in detail several times over and then sit through the inevitable credentials bit before they get to the heart of the matter – the agency proposals.

Most selling situations, including pitches, are about the removal of uncertainty. So understanding the problem, and identifying clear solutions with enthusiasm and conviction, is a winning formula.

The pitch

After weeks of intensive preparation of exciting creative ideas, ingenious media plans and pitch rehearsals, copies of the proposal or pitch document are laser printed, bound and made ready for client distribution after the main presentation. The pitch itself is where an advertising agency has the opportunity to advertise or sell itself. Given that most campaigns try to be different, to grab attention and make an impression, it is understandable that some agencies should regard a pitch as a creative opportunity also. There are many stories of daring pitch techniques, some of which work and some of which do not. Here are a few.

Legendary 1980s agency, ABM, created the classic British Rail pitch which purposely created client tension when the top executives from British Rail were kept waiting in a smoke-filled reception area while the receptionist ignored them throughout her gossip-filled telephone conversation. Eventually a space was cleared among the empty cans and orange peels, and the executives were invited to wait as the agency people were 'busy'. After some minutes the British Rail executives had had enough. As they got up to leave, the agency chairman, Peter Marsh, clad in full BR uniform (complete with cap, whistle and flag), burst in and said, 'You don't like it, why should your passengers?' He then invited them to listen to how he and his colleagues were going to solve their problems.

Don White of Benton and Bowles is reported to have dressed up as a Butlins redcoat for a Butlins pitch. The client took one look, said, 'Anyone dressed like that isn't suitable for my business' and left. David Abbott of Abbott Mead Vickers is reported to have greeted Metropolitan Police Commissioner Sir Robert Mark with a high-pitched nasal 'Hello, hello, hello' as he arrived to hear the agency pitch. Not amused, Sir Robert left the building and was never heard of again.

Agencies pitching for the Weetabix breakfast cereal account were invited to make their pitches in a hotel. As ABM was the last agency to pitch on the final morning, they decided to redecorate the function room in the ABM colours. This required an overnight painting and carpeting exercise. A stage was built and a special chair was delivered to the function room for

Mr Robinson, the arthritic and ageing Weetabix chairman. As the Weetabix panel seated themselves the next morning, the lights dimmed until they were all immersed in an enthralling darkness. A spotlight burst a stream of light on to the stage, where Peter Marsh kneeled as he opened his pitch with: 'As one of Britain's few remaining wholly owned independent advertising agencies, it gives me great pleasure to present to you, Mr Robinson, as chairman of one of Britain's few wholly owned cereal manufacturers…' ABM won the account.

One final ABM classic pitch was for Honda. ABM hired the 60-piece Scots Guards bagpipe band to play the Honda jingle 'Believe in freedom, believe in Honda', while marching up and down London's Norwich Street (where ABM were making their pitch). Again, ABM picked up the account. Another agency, AMV, had Hollywood hero Bob Hoskins at their pitch for BT (which they won).

Strict adherence to the time and type of presentation (specified by the client) is essential. When Burkitt Weinreich Bryant was pitching for Littlewoods it was asked to make a 'short and sweet' final pitch since the then 92-year-old chairman, Sir John Moores, would be in attendance. The trade press reported that 'after over 30 minutes managing director Hugh Burkitt was asked to finish as it became obvious that Sir John's interest and attention was waning'. A row broke out as Hugh Burkitt persisted and a senior Littlewoods executive tried to stop the pitch.

In 1992, when British Airways moved from Saatchi and Saatchi to Maurice and Charles's new outfit, M&C Saatchi, all the agencies involved threw everything at this prestigious £30 million account. In an attempt to dramatize BA's global reach S&S did the pitch in different rooms for different stages. Each room had been completely redecorated in the styles, natural habitat and climate of particular parts of the world – tropical rain forests, etc. When Bartle Bogle Hegarty got its chance it reassured BA about BBH's ability to create extremely satisfied clients by providing ready-made testimonials after the presentation – a wall went back and BA were surrounded by the key decision makers of every one of BBH's clients, who then had lunch with them. When M&C Saatchi got their chance, Maurice stood up and talked about the importance of music to the BA brand, explaining that they had commissioned their own composer to create a unique blend of popular classical music that BA could own. A growing murmur of approval was heard. He went on to say that they would like the client to meet the composer, at which point in walked Andrew Lloyd Webber.

Dropping your guard

During an intense high-profile, multi-million pound pitch, the client called for a 10-minute break. Unfortunately for the agency (who will remain unnamed), a senior agency member had forgotten to remove his scribbled notes, which the client accidentally read. 'Watch out for the xxxxxx in the glasses' it said at one point.

Not surprisingly, the agency lost the pitch. Some time later, the same agency was pitching for another piece of the business and as the agency opened their pitch all of the client team simultaneously donned pairs of glasses! The agency coped and went on to win this separate piece of business.

Pitches, like presentations for major campaigns, are now an ongoing process where effort is concentrated on developing a relationship (relationship marketing) with the client before the final presentation. This can sometimes involve client exposure to the strategy and even the advertisements before D-Day. One UK agency, Howell Henry Chaldecott Lury, has tried to appropriate this process on its own with what they call 'tissue groups', ie a series of build-up meetings with the client. In the US the most notable exponent, Chiat Day, has been doing this for a long time. Without doubt there is a cultural shift to ongoing pitches rather than a big finale.

Analysing the agency

As Nigel Bogle, chairman of Bartle Bogle Hegarty, says: 'The key questions today are less about an agency's ability to execute brilliantly and more about visionary strategic thinking, razor-sharp positioning, pinpoint targeting and ingenious media solutions.'

The order of importance of the following questions can vary, depending on what the prospective client really wants. Some clients may consider the agency's location and car parking facilities relevant, whereas other clients would discount this as trivial and irrelevant to good advertising. Here are some of the questions to help choose the right agency.

1. Does the agency really have a feel for my product and market? Do they really understand my brand's situation and potential?
2. Have they got strong research and planning capability?
3. Do they know the best media to use? Will their media-buying skills make my budget go a long way?
4. Have they got creative flair? Do they win awards? Do they suggest new ideas?
5. Are they full service or does everything get subcontracted out? Can they handle a pack redesign, public relations, sales promotion and direct mail if called upon?
6. How much integration experience with above, through and below the line as well as online do they have?
7. Are they international? Can their headquarters force them to resign the account should they decide to seek business in the same industry overseas? Alternatively, can they take on a lot of our coordination work through their own international management network?
8. What will they charge? And on what basis? How much time will they spend on the account?
9. How do they allocate resources in the planning, testing and evaluation process?
10. Do they display cost consciousness?
11. How will they measure their effectiveness?
12. Are we a small fish in a big pond? Are they too small or too big for us? Do we have

contact with the principal partners? Will they fire us if a competitor offers them a bigger account (should we insist on a five-year contract)?

13. Who will work on the account? Are we likely to get on together (chemistry)?* Will the pitch team be involved? How stable will our account team be? Are the people who worked on the case histories still with the agency? *Crucial Question.

14. Do they have a good track record? Do clients stick with them and place repeat business with the agency? If not, why not?

15. Check their references. References of past clients can also be requested.

Choosing an agency – an assessment form

The assessment form shown in Figure 6.2 can be weighted and scored as appropriate for each client's needs. A rating scale of 1–6 can be used. Agencies should be assessed using the *same criteria*. Few agencies perform so outstandingly that they remove all doubt in the client's mind as to whom he or she should choose. The criteria should be agreed in advance by the team involved in the selection process. The sample agency selection score sheet in Figure 6.2 shows one approach that attempts to formalize the selection by using consistent criteria. Each company obviously tailors its own approach.

The pitch is never over…

After making a good pitch a well-known agency kindly offered a chauffeur-driven car to take the clients to the next agency on the pitch list. During the journey the client team analysed the previous pitch and commented that the media strategy appeared 'off brief'. The next day the agency found a way of representing the media strategy… and they won the business.

The limo driver was an account man at the agency. Ethical or not, it's reality.

After the pitch – the agency awaits the decision

Post-pitch tension is agonizing. Awaiting the outcome of a pitch is a tense and worrying time. When the phone eventually rings and it turns out to be the prospect, everyone holds their breath. Rejection means total failure. All the brilliant ideas, the careful research, the buzz of excitement, the long hours – all down the drain. Selection means total success. The post-pitch wait makes the mind wander. Were there any clues as to what the client thought of the pitch? Len Weinreich, now an advertising guru, tells a story called 'Scratching an indecent living' (see page 174).

AGENCY	Understand our product and company?	Commitment to our project?	Research, planning & strategic thinking	Media planning and buying	Creative	Size, in-house resources, full service	International	Location	Fee/cost	Will we get on?	Opinion of existing clients
1											
2											
3											
4											
5											

Figure 6.2 Choosing an agency – an assessment form

Scratching an indecent living

My ferrety acquaintance, Crispin Neat, intrepid slogan detective, telephoned recently. "Hello, Lenny," he burbled. "I thought you might like to know that I'm branching out. Diversifying."

"Excellent news, Crispin," I replied, feigning enthusiasm. "What other services will you offer the hard-pressed advertiser?"

"Scratch pad deciphering."

"What's that?"

"Simple, Lenny, old chum. You gather and despatch the scratch pads after a crucial meeting and we'll decipher the scribbles and the doodles. We'll interpret the curious, dubious squiggles that clients leave behind."

"Crispin, that is the most ridiculous scam I've ever encountered."

He paused to draw breath on the other end of the 'phone. "Lenny, Lenny," he admonished. "If cynicism is your only reaction to my new sca . . . I mean, venture, then I have to tell you that you've been ignoring one of the most invaluable sources of high-grade intelligence in the business."

"Talk me through it." I was compelled to listen.

"Well, look at it this way. You've got this captive audience. You're either presenting for the account, or pleading to retain the business. Either way, it's hypertension ad biz max stressworld for all participants and the anxious clients need to combust mega-kilojoules of excess nervous energy."

"Hence the doodling?"

"Correct. But (and here's the brilliance of the idea) it's their *sub-*

Len Weinreich

conscious that's doing the doodling. So, whatever materialises on the pad is an action diagram of the client's thought processes. See?"

"I see. But how do you decipher their darkest thoughts if they're only scribbly doodles? And anyway," I added, "some clients actually tear their encrypted messages off the pad and tuck them into pockets. What's your action then?"

"The rub, Lenny. The old brass rubbing lark. We massage the undersheet delicately with a 9B pencil and a palimpsest of the jotting appears, by magic. From then on, interpretation is everything."

"OK. I How do you interpret?"

"You mean you've missed my new book: *Corporate Doodling: The Direct Line To Your Clients' Intentions*. It reveals all."

"I missed the book. Supply the topline, please."

"Well, many symbols are clear. Sketches of knives, revolvers, bludgeons, barbed wire and strategic nukes mean that he or she

might be firing the agency."

"Crispin, what about clients who can't draw? Can you explain *their* scratch pads?"

"All in my book, old chap, £9.50 at leading booksellers. Since you ask, anything resembling a maze represents confusion on their part. Blurred shading or scratchy hatching means they think you're a shifty bunch of crooks."

"Crispin, in my experience, they generally scribble down a few low key phrases from the presentation or make a few critical comments for subsequent reference."

"Of course, Lenny, of course. But each one can be a telling pointer. In order to cope with that eventuality, we've cobbled together a computer program called SNOOP which correlates their scratch notes with the agency slides and overheads in order to present you with an Attention Rating Admiration Factor and Purchase Property Index on a scale of one to ten."

"What happens if they've only scribbled a 'phone number or an enigmatic address in SW10?"

Crispin was wounded. "Haven't you read *any* of my books?"

"Er . . . which of your *oeuvre* have I missed now, Crispin?"

"*Corporate Blackmail for Profit and Pleasure* one of my all-time chart-toppers and money spinners. A right little cash cow."

"Thanks, Crispin. Don't call us . . ." *Clickbrrrrrr*

Len Weinreich is a vice-chairman of Burkitt Weinreich Bryant Clients and Company

---

Reproduced by kind permission of Haymarket Marketing Publications Ltd and Len Weinreich
Source: Marketing

When no news is bad news

"Why don't they ring? It's been four, no, three, days since they were in for the presentation. Didn't they say they'd make their minds up the next day? God. No news is bad news. Or is it good news? I can never quite remember.

"Anyway, I don't think we won it. I mean, we would have heard, wouldn't we? That guy, the one down the end of the table with the woolly khaki tie, he never liked us. He asked the worst questions. Like that one about putting all their press money in TV. That was a stinker, maliciously inserted to distract me. Quite arrested my flow, log-jammed my drift. No sense of unfolding drama, silly sod.

"The woman liked us though. I had a feeling she'd marked us down because we had too few women in the presentation team. But I could tell she warmed to me. Smiled a lot when I projected in her direction. God! Why haven't they rung yet? It's not as if we really need their lousy business, after all it's only an account. Ad agencies are like revolving doors: one account leaves and another one follows, I mean, enters. Have you seen this year's free-fall figures? The income from their billing would make good the loss of those bastards from . . .

"We won't get it. They hated the

Len Weinreich

creative work. Detested it. They sneered at the ads. You would've thought they'd never seen a real commercial before. On the other hand, they'd asked us to be radical. Their brief advised ignoring all restraints. Still, I think it might have been wiser to check the script with the ITVA before the presentation. The naked couple and the golden retriever might be a little rich for today's audience.

"We spent a month assembling this presentation and now, a week, okay, maybe three days later, not a dicky bird. Not a peep. Not even a whimper. Not even one of those mysterious calls to the media department dishing them undercover dirt. Nothing.

"Perhaps we should have bribed them. Maybe we should have taped a few large denomination notes to the inside covers of their documents. Perhaps I really should have nobbled the top man when he dashed out for a pee.

"Quite frankly, I think they loathed the work. And my suit. And our media director. It didn't help that our creative (ho, ho) director completely cocked up the order of the storyboards. Or that our dizzy planner addressed their company by the wrong name, twice. This instant they obviously are appointing someone else because they have no wit, taste, imagination, discernment or balls.

"I'm not so sure we'd be happy handling their business. They'd be terrible clients. Endless trips to their remote offices to niggle over a charity ad mechanical.

"Stuff their lousy business. Probably seriously unprofitable. In fact, I shouldn't be surprised if they went belly up. I've heard some interesting City whispers concerning the bizarre hotel bedroom habits of their chairman. Apparently . . . ***, is that the phone?"

Len Weinreich is a vice chairman of Burkitt Weinreich Bryant Clients and Company

Reproduced by kind permission of Haymarket Marketing Publications Ltd and Len Weinreich
Source: Marketing

Agency rejection

A rejected agency's managing director has the difficult job of picking the shattered team up and building up the agency morale again. The rejected agencies usually ask the prospect for some feedback for future reference. Here are some answers which rejected agencies have recorded upon asking why they had failed:

- I just didn't like you.
- I'm afraid you are not European.
- You're too small.
- They (the other agency) have more experience of this sector.
- You have too much experience in this sector. We're looking for a fresh approach.

- If it wasn't for the other agency you would have come first.
- The final decision was evenly split and you lost 8–7.
- Although we preferred your creative work, the other agency does have a place to park in London on Saturdays – and it's terribly handy for the shops.

As managing directors are never told that their pitches are terrible and come last having always been narrowly beaten into second place, there is a plea from the advertising industry to clients that they should tell it like it really is!

After the pitch – the agency still awaits

Occasionally the prospect client actually helps the agency by giving an answer which identifies where they saw a real weakness. The agency can then eradicate the weakness before the next pitch. Similarly, a successful agency will be interested to find out why they were chosen, so that they can capitalize on their strengths.

Firing the agency

Although over a decade old, *Campaign* magazine's '13 Ways to be a Loser' article identifies many recurring reasons why agencies still get fired.

A more recent *Campaign* survey identified the following reasons in order of clients' importance:

1. Receiving no fresh input.
2. Account conflict at the agency.
3. New marketing director arrives.
4. Change of client's policy.
5. Other accounts leaving the agency.

Firing the client

Agencies sometimes resign accounts, particularly if a larger competing account is offered to them. Occasionally, they are obliged to resign if an agency takeover or merger brings in some competing accounts and thereby creates a conflict of interest. New demands by a client sometimes become so difficult that the account becomes unprofitable or, as in the case of ABM, a reduced commission is considered unsatisfactory.

1 Control of brand's advertising switches to rival of client: Gold Greenlees Trott lost Fosters when Elders IXL and its Courage division took over control of marketing Fosters from Watneys, a GGT client.

2 Agency produces irrelevant or inappropriate advertising: Lowe Howard-Spink lost some of its prized Mobil account after its "breakthrough" Dan Dare campaign failed. Insufficient planing was cited as a reason behind the fiasco.

3. Client is unsettled over too many changes at agency: Foote Cone and Belding lost £22 million worth of business – including Heinz and Cadbury – because of management upheaval.

4 Client unhappy over excess negative publicity surrounding its agency: IBM is uncomfortable over the widely reported lawsuits involving its agency and breakaway Lord Einstein O'Neill and Partners. Could result in IBM choosing neither and picking a new shop.

5 Takeover of agency infuriates client: Goodyear, Philips, Pilsbury said goodbye to JWT after it was taken over by WPP. Most cite "disruption" as a reason for leaving.

6 Client rationalises its agency roster: Toyota chose its dealer agency Brunnings over its main agency Lintas London after a creative shoot-out. British Telecom reviewed its entire account and picked three main agencies — BBH, Abbott Mead and JWT.

7 Total breakdown in agency-client relationship: GGT resigns the *Daily Express* after repeated clashes an inability to work with title's marketing staff.

8 Agency fails to come to terms with account: BMP got the sack by Comet, its first major retail client. Former vice-chairman Paul Leeves said BMP won the business "one year too soon".

9 Lack of solution creatively: Abbot Mead couldn't crack the *Daily Telegraph*. Later the agency admitted to producing tasteless series of press ads which aroused the ire of women, among others.

10 New client arrives: Allen Brady and Marsh's long-standing Milk account was reviewed after new NDC chief Richard Pears joined.

11 Agency can't master the client's politics: JWT lost British Rail. Agency was allied to the central advertising body while the chairman, Bob Reid, was committed to devolution. Network SouthEast chief Chris Green was not keen on JWT after it produced two poor ads, one in which it was in legal hot water with the *Monty Python* people.

12 Agency merges with another, producing conflict and massive disruption: Difficulties surrounding the merger of Reeves Robertshaw Needham and Doyle Dane Bernbach resulted in massive client fall-out.

13 Client is subject of a merger or takeover: Fast becoming a major reason for account moves. Expect major international agency fall-out after the conclusion of the Nestlé/Rowntree/Suchard negotiations.

Reproduced by kind permission of Haymarket Marketing Publications Limited and Laurie Ludwick

Arrogance and egos

Some years ago, a continually critical senior marketing manager commented at the end of yet another long, unsatisfactory meeting: 'If this were my company [which it wasn't, he was an employee], I would fire the agency.' The long-suffering creative director responded 'If this were my agency, which it is, I would fire the client, which I am.'

He left the room, with the client knowing he had to now face colleagues and break the news that there was still no campaign ready to roll out, no agency and an agonizing new pitch process was now required.

Key points from Chapter 6:

1. Clear communications between client and agency are important if the right messages are going to be successfully communicated to target audiences.
2. Agencies, consultancies and consultants can become more than just suppliers of marketing services; they can become strategic partners of the client.
3. Careful selection is crucial to ensure the development of a mutually beneficial long-term relationship.

FURTHER READING

Cowley, D (ed) (1987) *How to Plan Advertising*, Cassell, London

Fitzgerald, N (1997) excerpt from an article entitled 'Is the ad agency all washed up?' *Marketing* magazine, October 23

Rijkens, R (1992) *European Advertising Strategies*, Cassell, London

Sorrell, M (1996) Beans and Pearls, D&AD President's Lecture

Weinreich, L (2000) *Seven Steps to Brand Heaven*, Kogan Page, London

ADMAP, NTC Publications, Henley-on-Thames

Campaign, Haymarket Marketing Publications Ltd, London

Marketing, Haymarket Marketing Publications Ltd, London

Marketing Business, Chartered Institute of Marketing and Maxwell Publications, London

Marketing Week, Centaur Communications, London

Media Week, EMAP Business Publications, London

FURTHER CONTACTS

Adforum, www.adforumcom

Advertising Agency Registrar Services, 26 Market Place, London W1W 8AN (tel: 020 7612 1200; Web site: www.aargroup.co.uk)

The Advertising Association, Abford House, 15 Wilford Road, London SW1V 1NJ (tel: 020 7828 2771; Web site: www.adassoc.org.uk)

Agency Assessments, 19 Buckingham Street, London WC2N 6EF (tel: 020 7976 1300; Web site: www.agencyassessments.co.uk (under construction))

British Rate and Data (BRAD), EMAP Business Communications, 33–39 Bowling Green Lane, London EC1 (tel: 020 7505 8273; Web site: www.brad.co.uk)

The Incorporated Society of British Advertisers (ISBA), 44 Hertford Street, London W1J 7AE (tel: 020 7499 7502; Web site: www.isba.org.uk)

The Institute of Practitioners in Advertising (IPA), 44 Belgrave Square, London SW1X 8QS (tel: 020 7235 7020; Web site: www.ipa.co.uk)

PR Consultancy Registrar Services, comes under Advertising Agency Registrar Services (see above), which also covers sales promotion, media, design, digital, direct marketing, sponsorship and strategic consultancy

The addresses of other professional institutes are listed at the end of the appropriate chapters.

7

Understanding the media

INTRODUCTION – THE CHALLENGE OF THE MEDIA MIX

Some marketing managers and agency media people consider that 'media' includes communications tools such as sponsorship, direct mail and point-of-sale as well as the mainstream media such as TV, cinema, radio and the press. Buildings, they would say, are permanent media which, planning permission allowing, can be used to carry a message. For the purposes of this chapter media means the more traditional media as well as new media such as Web radio, interactive television and mobile messaging. Although good media planners consider media outside of the traditional advertising realm, this chapter focuses on the mainstream advertising media, while other communications tools are addressed separately in their respective chapters in Part 2 of this book.

Deciding to include advertising in the communications mix is a relatively easy decision compared to deciding which media and which media vehicles (eg the specific magazine title) to use. Should the press, TV, radio, cinema and/or posters be used? If so, how much of each? Should they be mixed together (the media mix)? If press advertising is chosen, which publications should be used – national dailies, Sunday newspapers, evening newspapers, daily or weekly regional papers, or magazines? How many times should the audience see or hear the ad (*optimum frequency*)? When should it happen? On which page? Even a great advertisement will not work if (a) it is in the wrong place, (b) it is placed at the wrong time or (c) it is in the right place at the right time but not seen enough times (insufficient frequency).

Most of the advertising budget gets spent on the media (and not the creative or production side). This is why careful attention to detailed media planning, knowledge and negotiating skills are so important. Expert media planners and buyers get the best out of advertising by finding the right spaces or places for an ad campaign at the lowest cost.

Media planning is both a science and an art. Traditionally it has been based on 'number crunching' media analysis and the application of complex computer models. Today media planners are also interested in the qualitative side, which tells them how audiences actually use (and feel about) different media. Before looking at media research and analysis, or media planning, scheduling and buying, it is useful to be familiar with the media vocabulary or jargon that is commonly used.

New media opportunities abound

MEDIA JARGON/VOCABULARY

Cover and reach

'Coverage' is the percentage of the target audience reached by the advertising. If, for example, *News at Ten* reaches 5 million viewers, 16 per cent of whom are ABC1 male, then an ad placed during the break will reach 0.8 million ABC1 males (16 per cent of 5 million viewers). If ABC1 men are the target audience and there are, in fact, 10.6 million ABC1 men in the UK, then although the advertisement reaches 0.8 million ABC1 men the coverage is only 8 per cent (0.8 million as a percentage of the total target market of 10.6 million).

Frequency

This is the number of times an ad is shown / placed in a particular period of time. How many times should an ad be shown and seen? Between four and six times? The *optimum frequency* is often really unknown. Should it be concentrated over a short period ('*burst strategy*') or spread steadily over a longer period ('*drip strategy*')? For example, an advertising frequency of 60 can be built up by either (a) having the same advertisement shown before, during and after *News at Ten* every weekday for four weeks, or (b) having one advertisement every six days throughout the year.

Opportunities to see (OTS)

OTSs are the number of exposures or opportunities that a particular audience has to see a particular advertisement. In the previous example there would have been 5 million OTSs for adults and 0.8 million for ABC1 men. If the ad went out every night for five nights during the *News at Ten* break, the total number of ABC1 men OTSs would be 5 × 0.8 million = 4m OTSs.

Cost per thousand (CPT)

CPT calculates the average cost of reaching 1,000 of the population. If it costs, say, £100,000 to place a 30-second spot (advertisement) on national TV with a peak time audience of, say, 10 million, then the cost per thousand or the cost of reaching each or any group of 1,000 people within the audience is £100,000 divided by 10,000 (10 million = 10,000 groups of 1,000 people). The cost per thousand here is £10. CPT allows cross-comparisons across different media types and media vehicles (although quality of media must also be analysed). For example, if a full-page advertisement in the *Sun* reaches, say, 9.5 million (bought by 3.5 million but read by 9.5 million) and costs, say, £45,000, then the CPT is £45,000 divided by

9,500 (9.5 million = 9,500 lots of 1,000 people), which gives a cost of £4.74 per thousand. Pages 202–03 show a wide range of media vehicles and their CPT examples. The term 'CPM' (cost per mille/thousand) is the same as CPT and is commonly used in the United States.

Ideally, cost per enquiry/order generated gives a truer picture, but this can only be measured after the advertisement has run (and if the advertisement was designed to achieve these kinds of responses rather than, say, increase awareness or change attitudes). Experience and knowledge provide useful insights into media scheduling and buying.

TV rating points (TVRs)

TV rating points are referred to as Gross rating points (GRPs) in the US and overseas. GRPs can be used across different media, whereas TVRs obviously refer to TV in the UK. One TV rating point is 1 per cent of the target audience. The percentage of the target audience viewing a spot ('reach') multiplied by the average number of opportunities to see gives the TVR. Television companies will sell packages of guaranteed TVRs. For example, a target of 240 TVRs means that 60 per cent of the target audience will have, on average, 4 OTSs. It could also mean that 40 per cent have seen it six times. Reference to the media schedule quickly identifies the frequency. Four hundred TVRs (80 per cent seeing the message five times) is considered an average-sized one-month campaign. Eight hundred TVRs in one month is a big campaign. It has been suggested that some confectionery and record companies run a lightweight campaign and buy 100 TVRs so that they can tell the retail trade that they are running a television advertising campaign (the 'pull' helps the 'push' – see page 12).

Impacts

Impacts refer more to TV than the press. Impacts measure the total number of people who saw the ad multiplied by the number of times they saw it. In the *News at Ten* case it would be 0.8 million × 5 = 4 million impacts (for ABC1 men). To make more sense of impacts, divide them by the universe (number of people within the target market) to get TVRs (television rating). Impacts are more useful when converted to TVRs.

Position

Position refers to the place where the ad is shown. Back pages, inside cover pages, right-hand pages, TV pages and so on have greater readership and more impact than other pages (eg the third right-hand page has a bigger impact than the first left-hand page). Similarly, some positions on a page are more effective than others. Media buyers are aware of this and so are the media owners, since their rate cards (prices) reflect the value of, and demand for, certain positions. Boddington's beer media strategy was built around position, ie they concentrated their advertisements on the back page of glossy magazines to the extent that they 'owned' the back pages for a period of time.

Environment

The environment or context in which an ad is exposed affects the message itself. The type of feature or editorial, and other advertisements, that run alongside an advertisement affect the likely effectiveness of that advertisement. An advertiser can lose credibility if the programme is a parody of the product being advertised, for example the film *Airplane* with an *airline* ad in the break.

WHICH MEDIUM?

Should the press and/or radio be used? How should a client or an agency choose which medium to use? Which TV stations and/or publications should be used? Which vehicles within a particular medium (eg the *Guardian* or *The Times*)? The press includes national dailies, Sunday newspapers, evening newspapers, daily and weekly regional papers, and magazines. Television, radio, cinema and posters are considered. Table 7.1 on pages 190–92 summarizes the key points that help to decide which medium and vehicle is the most suitable. The key points are as follows:

1. Audience size (reach or penetration). Some media cannot carry national brands because they cannot offer national coverage. Media such as the regional press are generally considered to be local media since they talk to the community. Television can get to large audiences quickly.
2. Audience type (eg 15- to 24-year-olds don't watch much TV but do go to the cinema; on the other hand, not many over 45+ year olds watch the music station MTV).
3. Budget (production cost, media cost and CPT).
4. Message objective:
   (a) Response required – is action required after the ad (eg filling in a coupon or phoning an 0800 number)?
   (b) Creative scope: colour, sound and movement needed (eg TV's movement can show impulsive purchases)?
   (c) Demonstration (product usage often best shown on TV, but all media can show product benefits).
   (d) Technical detail – TV no good, press is better.
   (e) Urgency (TV, radio and national papers can be topical and announce urgent commercial news).

(f) Compatibility, 'rub-off' or image effect of media and vehicle on product itself. For example, would Harrods advertise in the *Sun*? TV puts a product or company alongside the big boys and therefore enhances the image, since many viewers think 'they can't be cowboys if they're on national TV'.

(g) TV adds credibility – 'as seen on TV'.

5. Ease of booking:

(a) Lead times for space (magazines, TV and cinema have long lead times or notice of booking).

(b) Lead times for production (some press can be knocked out overnight, whereas a cinema production takes months).

6. Restrictions. Some products are excluded from certain media, eg cigarettes on TV and alcohol in children's magazines.

7. Competitive activity. Advertisers watch, copy and sometimes avoid the places where their competitors advertise.

MEDIA SELECTION

Audience size

TV allows commercial messages to 'reach' large numbers of people on a national or regional level. TV used to be known as a mass medium, but as the number of stations increases, more niche channels are emerging on cable, satellite and mainstream terrestrial TV, which means that TV is becoming less of a mass medium. Radio attracts smaller regional audiences, although it can offer national coverage. Cinema attracts small audiences and can offer slow national coverage among younger audiences, but can be great for 35- to 45-year-olds. National and regional press deliver what they say – national and regional audiences respectively. Because posters can prove difficult to coordinate on a national scale, there are poster-buying specialists. Direct mail can address large national and international audiences, but because of its high cost per thousand the target audiences are likely to be tightly defined and targeted. Finally, TV's audience size is seasonally influenced, with the audience increasing in winter and reducing in the summer.

Audience type

Generally, 15- to 24-year-olds are busy doing other things, and don't have time to watch TV, whereas cinema can attract this target group. Radio is popular with housewives and commuters. The national daily newspapers tend to target specific socio-economic groups and political sympathizers, while magazines reach targeted groups defined by their lifestyles, income levels, ages and sex. Posters can target commuters who travel by car, bus and train.

Audience state of mind

Audience state of mind or receptivity to messages varies across the media spectrum. TV audiences can be relaxed and passive, sometimes viewing in a trance-like manner (the 'couch-potato syndrome'). TV and its ads become a form of visual wallpaper, sometimes used as company and sometimes to 'warm up' a room. Radio can also be used in the background, but listeners do tend to work with the radio as they create visual images from verbal messages. The cinema delivers a captive audience that is happy to be involved in the suspension of disbelief, and will not leave the room to make a cup of tea. In fact, many viewers thoroughly enjoy the special cinema ads. The national press is deliberately read as information is sought. Some research reveals unconscious feelings of guilt (waste and/or inadequacy of knowledge) if a newspaper is left unfinished. Magazines are absorbed in a more relaxed mood.

Cost of production

The cost of producing a TV ad can range from £5,000 to £5,000,000, depending on the length, complexity and actors involved, whereas radio has a lower cost of production ranging from £500 to £20,000. Stationary pictures with a voice-over promoting the local Indian restaurant can cost just a few hundred pounds, while a more lavish 90-second full-production cinema advertisement could cost up to £1 million or more. Radio and the press sometimes provide free help with basic productions. Posters can be produced for as little as £125 for a 6-sheet (1.83- × 1.2-metre) poster or £11,000 for a backlit 96-sheet (12- × 3-metre) poster campaign for two weeks. Direct mail can be as cheap as the cost of a letter, but if a four-colour brochure is specially designed and produced, then the costs can be anywhere from several hundred to several thousand pounds for design and artwork alone.

Minimum cost of space

Advertising space is rarely bought in single units. A single ad is unlikely to achieve as much as a campaign or a series of ads would. Ads are generally scheduled and bought over a period of time rather than as one-offs. The cost of space is relatively high on TV compared to radio; a single off-peak 30-second spot on a regional radio station could be as little as £20, compared to £500 for TV. A national 30-second spot in the middle of *Coronation Street* could cost up to £100,000. A one-off, full-page, four-colour ad in the *Sun* or the *Financial Times* costs £45,386 and £50,151, respectively. Smaller space can be bought, right down to the square column centimetre (approximately £205 and £190 for the *Sun* and *Financial Times*, respectively).

Cost per thousand

Within a particular medium, say the press, there is a wide range of media vehicles available, from *Amateur Gardening* to *The Economist*. The CPT varies vastly across different media vehicles (eg from approximately £5 in the *Sun* to £70 in the *FT* – see Appendix 7.1 on page 202) and across different countries (eg 70 cents in Bulgaria to $19 in Norway for 30-second peak-time viewing – see Appendix 7.2 on page 203). Although CPT varies greatly, the actual selection of a particular medium (say, the press versus television) and a specific media vehicle (say, *Amateur Gardening* versus *The Economist*) is influenced by the quality of the media as well as the relative cost.

Message

TV has sight, sound, colour and movement, which makes it an ideal medium for product demonstrations and impulse purchases, but the time constraint and viewing mode make detailed messages almost impossible. It is time constrained (whereas a press ad is not). Ads are viewed serially, whereas press ads compete with other ads and editorial, often on the same page. Remote control channel zapping has made TV more vulnerable as an advertising medium. TV, radio and cinema are highly transitory, in that the viewer cannot refer back to an ad once it has been shown (unless it is taped). On the other hand, the audience can refer back to press ads, posters and direct mail. TV's fleeting messages leave no room for detail but can grab attention, create awareness and arouse interest. More and more ads across the media spectrum, including TV, are tying in with direct response mechanisms (0800 numbers, Web addresses or coupons to fill in) so that more detailed information can subsequently be delivered to the audience.

Ease of media buying

Some popular TV programmes (and magazines) require long lead times for booking space. Advertisements are still pre-emptable (they can be outbid and kicked off a particular spot on the day they were booked to be broadcast). Big agencies generally do not get pre-empted.

Different rates or prices can be bid; the top rate guarantees the spot, but agencies and clients want to avoid paying these extremely high rates, so they make bids at prices lower down the scales (giving various amounts of notice about pre-emption). Both script and final film require approval/clearance from the Broadcast Advertising Clearance Centre (BACC). This takes time. Cinema can have longer lead booking times but shorter clearance time from the Cinema Advertising Association. Radio is the most flexible of all, with same-day clearance and short lead booking times. The national dailies tend to have flexible position and size and short lead times, while magazines have longer lead times. Certain positions cannot be booked in the short term, ie one-year lead time. TV and radio can obviously offer a higher frequency since an advertisement could theoretically go out every half hour all day. The lack of national network coverage makes the regional press a tough task for media planners and buyers involved in national campaigns.

WHICH MEDIA AND WHICH VEHICLE?

Does the impact of a double-page spread (DPS) justify the cost? Would the reach be increased by placing two single-page advertisements in two different magazines instead? Should TV be supplemented by radio, by posters, or by both? Is a *personal media network* worth creating so that the target audience is hit with a brand's message first thing in the morning on the radio, on posters in the neighbourhood area, in the appropriate paper on the way to work, on TV that evening, in the cinema that night, and finally on the radio in the car coming home from the cinema?

Media buyers' computers churn out cost-ranking analyses which list the publications in order of their cost per thousand – with the lowest at the top. CPT offers a quantitative criterion, but does it reveal *heavy-user* information? Perhaps a high CPT conceals within it a large chunk of the heavy users, which may make the advertisement more effective? Qualitative criteria (audience size and how they use the media, targetability, message type, ease of booking, restrictions and competitive activity) all affect the choice. In the end experience, judgement, and a little bit of creative flair influence the decision to buy space. See the media decision tree in Appendix 7.1.

HOW MUCH SPACE, HOW OFTEN, AND WHEN?

Having selected the media type, and specific vehicles within each media type, the next question is how much space and/or airtime should be booked. What season, month, week, day or hour should the advertisement appear? How many times should the ad be seen?

Table 7.1 Summary of media characteristics

	TV	Radio	Cinema	Daily and Sunday press	Evening and regional press	Magazines	Posters	Direct mail	Internet
AUDIENCE Audience size	Some wastage, large and national, new niche opportunities	National coverage now available	National coverage	Large and mostly national	Small, no networks	Mostly national (and international)	National coverage can be difficult	Large national and international	Rapidly growing national and international audience
Audience type	Few 15–24 year olds, high 55+	Many housewives, commuters	Young, upmarket	Socio-economic	Geographic segments	Lifestyle/demographic	Commuters, car drivers, etc	Any target available	Targeted by site type – any target available
Audience state of mind	Moving towards active viewers with interactive potential	Often active audience – background/audio wallpaper	Captive audience, willing suspension of disbelief	Deliberately read	Deliberately read	Relaxed and involved with magazine			Active, inquisitive
COST Cost of production	High	Low	High	Low–med	Low	Low–med	Med	Low	10–30% of the cost of media
Minimum cost of space	High (for peak time national exposure)	Low	High	Med	Low	Low–med	Low–med	High but can experiment in small quantities	Generally no minimum. Large portals require £1,000 minimum spend
Average cost per thousand	Low (£7.30)	Very low (less than £2.50)	£45	Low–med (£8)	Med (£30)	Med (£12–70)		High (£500)	Banners = £15, pop-ups = £30, other rich = £35+

Table 7.1 *continued*

	TV	Radio	Cinema	Daily and Sunday press	Evening and regional press	Magazines	Posters	Direct mail	Internet
Extra advantages	Adds credibility to product or company, rapid, high coverage, interactive capability	Transportable medium	High impact and captive audience	Quick coverage build	Location specific	Quality and low wastage			Generates fully accountable direct response and dialogue with audience
MESSAGE Variable/sense	Sight, sound colour, movement time constraint	Sound and time constraint	Big impact, enhanced sight and sound	Now mostly colour with some black and white	Black and white with some colour	4-colour	4-colour, big impact	4-colour and 3-D possibility	Infinite colour, 3-D, sound, interactive
Serial ad sequence	Viewed serially, no competition from other ads or editorial but zapping prevalent	Serially, less zapping	Serially and no zapping	Must compete with other ads and editorial on same page Slow coverage build with monthly mags					Non-linear medium, can jump back and forward
Transitory	Highly transitory since you cannot refer back to ad to once shown (unless taped, or with interactive ads which can be bookmarked)			Can keep clippings or refer back if desired			Can refer back, walk back or drive past	Can refer back/keep coupon	Can refer until campaign ends
Demonstration	Idea for usage and impulse purchases	Difficult	Yes	Benefits or results can be shown but not product usage			Only short image benefit	Yes	Yes
Detail/technical	Viewer cannot absorb detail	Urgency and topical	Visual and audio	Yes	Yes	Yes	No	Yes	Yes
Urgency/topicality	Difficult to adapt ads to daily events, high level of recall	Unique immediacy, urgency and topicality	No	Yes	Yes	Magazine image spills on to ad	Cut image?		Yes

Table 7.1 *continued*

	TV	Radio	Cinema	Daily and Sunday press	Evening and regional press	Magazines	Posters	Direct mail	Internet
EASE OF MEDIA BUYING	Complicated	Inflexible	Flexible	Flexible	Flexible	Flexible	Inflexible	Flexible	Timing flexible, rates negotiable
Lead times	Long	Short/medium	Short	Short	Short	Medium Long	Long	Short Medium	3–10 days, depending on richness of media
Clearance	Script (1-week), finished film (1-week), BACC	Same day clearance BACC	One week clearance, CAA	Code of advertising practice (clearance is not compulsory)					Generally required for editorially driven content and where advertiser = potential competitor
Audience research*	BARB and TGI	RAJAR and TGI	CAVIAR, TGI & EDI	NRS, QRS, TGI and BMRC	JICREG and TGI	NRS (and ABC), QRS and TGI	POSTAR and TGI	TGI	MMXI, ABCE, Nielson Net Ratings
High-frequency facility	Yes	Yes	No	Yes	Daily and weekly	Weekly/monthly	Yes	Yes	Yes
National coverage	Expert's job but network exists and international cable/satellite	National network through NNR	Yes	Yes	No national network but all major conurbations covered	Yes	Yes	Yes	Nearly half all adult UK population covered. London/South-east bias

*Audience research: see 'Further contacts' on page 204
Source: Media Planning Group

How many times is too many times? Can the audience become irritated? Frequency? This last question becomes more difficult when a campaign uses several different advertisements, particularly when each new ad builds on the last one. The creative side of the campaign can sell itself to the client, but the media schedule often requires much more detailed justification. Once the media schedule has been agreed, it can be passed on to the media buyer to start booking the space (within booking deadlines).

Media schedule

The media strategy is then refined into the tactical details specifying exactly what space should be booked where. Figure 7.1 shows the proposed media schedule for the Orange campaign that is featured in the short case at the end of this chapter.

MEDIA BUYING

It pays to plan carefully. Plan first, then buy. A skilled media buyer can save enormous sums by playing one media owner off against another. After all, there are many different routes (or media vehicles) to the minds of the target audience.

There are series discounts (ten inserts or ads for the price of nine), and volume discounts if you spend over a certain amount. Many agencies pool their media buying together to gain the maximum discounts. Negotiating and discounting varies from country to country. Countries such as Austria and Denmark allow very little negotiation with media owners. Media buyers and media planners/schedulers need to work closely together. A global new-media planning resource was launched in early 2001. WORD (World Online Rate and Data) will provide media planners with a database that can be used to plan domestic and global online campaigns. It is available both in print and online (www.wordonline.net).

MEDIA RESEARCH

Media research basically tells the media buyer and scheduler which publications are read by what type of people, how many and what type of people are likely to watch a particular television programme, who listens to what on the radio, which kind of films attract what kind of audience, which poster sites are passed by most people, etc. The media buyer can then decide if the particular media vehicle's audience profile matches his or her target market,

MEDIA PLANNING

Press Schedule

Orange™

Client:	Orange	Period:	3rd July - 6th August 2000	Date:	23rd August 2000
Campaign:	Best Network	Status:	Booked / v10	Format:	Page / tablold page

Media (all 4clr)	Size	No. Ins.	Cost per Insertion	Total Gross Cost	Total Client Cost	10th	July 17th	24th
Page / tablold page equivalent.						All dailies on Wed / Fri option unless otherwise specified		
The Guardian	38x6	4				3 x Tabloid Page (Thu/Fri)		
The Times	37x6	5				3 x Tabloid Page (Thu/Fri)	Tabloid Page	Tabloid Page
Telegraph	38x6	3				Tabloid Page (Wed) 1/2 price	Tabloid Page	Tabloid Page
The Independent	38x6	2				Tabloid Page (Thu/Fri)	Tabloid Page	Tabloid Page
Financial Times	38x6	2				Tabloid Page (Thu/Fri)	Tabloid Page	
The Sun	page	3				Page (Thu/Fri)	Page	Page
Daily Mirror	page	3				Page (Thu/Fri)	Page	Page (Tues)
Daily Mail	page	3				Page (Mon - Fri)	Page (Mon - Fri)	Page (Mon - Fri)
Sunday Times	37x6	2						
Sunday Telegraph	38x6	4				3 x Tabloid Page	Tabloid Page	Tabloid Page
Independent on Sunday	38x6	4				3 x Tabloid Page	Tabloid Page	
Observer	38x6	2				Tabloid Page	Tabloid Page	
Sunday Business	38x6	2				Tabloid Page	Tabloid Page	
News of the World	page	2				Page	Page	Page
Sunday Mirror	page	2				Page	Page	Page
Sunday People	page	1				Page		
Mail on Sunday	page	4				3 x Page	Page	Page
Regional Titles								
Metro	page	2				Page (Thu/Fri)		Page
Evening Standard	38x6	3				Brand Page (Mon - Fri)	Page (Mon - Fri)	Page (Mon - Fri)
Belfast Telegraph	38x6	2				Tabloid Page (Thu/Fri)	Tabloid Page	
Irish News / Newsletter	page	2				Page (Thu/Fri)		Page
The Glasgow Herald	38x6	2				Tabloid Page (Thu/Fri)	Tabloid Page	Tabloid Page
Daily Record	page	2				Page (Thu/Fri)	Page	
Scotsman	38x6	2				Tabloid Page (Thu/Fri)	Tabloid Page	
Scotland on Sunday	38x6	1				Tabloid Page	Tabloid Page	
Sunday World	page	1				Page		
Sunday Mail	page	1				Page		
O Magazine	page	1					Page	

	Total Cost to Client	£
	Total Budget	£
	Difference	£

	Cov and Freq	Scotland Cov and Freq	N. Ireland Cov and Freq
ABC1 Adults	82% @ 4.1	92% @ 3.8	84% @ 4.0
All Orange	81% @ 4.1	96% @ 3.8	83% @ 4.0
Non-Orange	82% @ 4.3	93% @ 4.3	84% @ 4.1
AB Businessmen	90% @ 5.2	93% @ 5.1	91% @ 5.0
Decision Makers	93% @ 5.6	97% @ 7.3	94% @ 6.0

N.B. Performance figures are for national press and magazines.

Figure 7.1 Proposed media schedule for the Orange campaign

and if the audience size proves to be cost effective in terms of cost per thousand, coverage, frequency, OTSs, TVRs (see pages 183–84), etc.

How many people watch *Neighbours* or *News at Ten*? How many listen to Capital Radio's breakfast radio show? How many people read the *Sun*? Advertisers are even more interested in what type of people are in the audience and whether they are heavy, medium or light users of the product type or even the specific brand. Although the *Sun* is considered to be a working man's paper, 31 per cent of its readership are ABC1s. So some strange anomalies do exist, and media buyers must tread cautiously. Information concerning socio-economic groups, product usage types and lifestyle data all help to build a *profile* which the advertiser can then use to target the most relevant audience.

An initial search into the British Rate and Data (BRAD) directory reveals a limited amount of information regarding circulation and audience type (socio-economic groups). This can be cross-referenced (or cross-tabulated) with the Target Group Index (see page 132) to reveal, for example, types of audience according to lifestyles and typical product purchases, in addition to the usual demographic information.

The qualitative data explain how the media are used by target audiences – the role the media play in people's lives. Some advertising agencies use focus groups to research the obscure media used by a particular group of opinion leaders or to investigate how an audience uses the media.

The short case at the end of this chapter shows how careful quantitative and qualitative media research helped top media agency Media Planning Group to develop a media strategy which combined uniquely with the overall creative strategy to produce a highly effective advertising campaign for Orange.

THE CHANGING MEDIA SCENE

The control and regulation covering each type of media is discussed in Chapter 8. Here are some other changes that are occurring in the media world.

Print

Technology today allows low-cost entry into the world of publishing. This has reduced the publishing industry's traditional high investment barrier to entry. In effect, this means that we are seeing new magazines, journals and newsletters appearing alongside multi-edition, tailor-made magazines such as the *US Farmers' Journal* (which produces over 1,000 different editions of each month's publication targeted at over 1,000 different types of farmer). The result? More accurately targeted media that allow advertisers and PR people to target their messages more effectively.

Broadcasting/narrowcasting

Today there are around 200 channels in the UK. Television is moving slowly from broadcasting towards interactivity and 'narrowcasting', from broad/mass audiences to smaller and more distinct target audiences, eg dance music channels and home-shopping channels. The new, wider choice means that audiences are fragmenting into many smaller interest groups fed by sports channels, kitchen channels, children's channels, educational channels, etc. Different channels attract different audience profiles or different psychographic and demographic segments. This helps advertisers and PR people to have access to and communicate with more distinct and tighter target audiences.

The Internet

The Internet offers a whole gamut of communications opportunities, including two-way communications, ie listening as well as talking and collecting as well as sending information. Banner advertising (eg placing an approved advertisement on other Web sites) is just one form of advertising available on the Internet. Placing links with other sites is sometimes paid for and sometimes reciprocal. Registering with search engines is generally free and therefore not considered by some as advertising. There are many forms of online and offline advertising and promotion. See Chapter 20.

Ambient media

Beyond TV, radio, cinema, posters, the press and the Internet, there are many other advertising media, ranging from scented posters, mirrored posters, graffitied posters, to floor posters (see Schick razor opposite), from heated bus stops, painted train platforms, tunnel entrances, taxis, buses, trains and planes, to banners in space visible from earth, to aerial balloons, to the bottoms of beer glasses, to lottery balls, to screen savers, to the back of stamps (and around the front edge of stamps in the US), to cutting fields into patterns (crop circles), to free book marks at checkouts of bookstores. See orang-utans' 'scaffoldizing' in the Orange case study at the end of this chapter. Some of this overlaps with sales promotion, direct mail and PR, which are all dealt with separately in Chapters 13, 14 and 15 respectively. Here are some costs.

Aerial banner	Towing charge	from £260 net per hour
Balloon displays, tethered		£800 per balloon per day
Balloon releases	Release of 5,000 balloons	from £2,500 net
	Release of 1,000 balloons	from £1,250 net
Golf	Inside golf holes	£300 per quarter per three holes
	Tee signs	from £295 per hole pa
Hospital waiting rooms	A1 size	£888 per poster pa
Taxi cabs	Interior panel	from £24 per month
	Liveried taxi	£6,500 pa incl production
Teletext	National	£3,500 per full page per week

Look up, down and all around, as new media opportunities proliferate

MEDIA RESEARCH BUREAUX

TV audiences are measured by *BARB* (Broadcast Audience Research Bureau), which monitors a sample of 4,500 homes through their *people meter*. The meter records what stations are turned on and the hand-held remote control unit inputs data about who is watching the TV.

Radio audiences are measured by *RAJAR* (Radio Joint Audience Research). In 1992 RAJAR replaced JICRAR (Joint Industry Council for Radio Audience Research).

Cinema uses *CAVIAR* (Cinema and Advertising Association Video Industry Audience Research) to measure cinema and video audience size and profiles. Admissions are also measured by Gallup/EDI.

Newspaper and magazine readership is measured by National Readership Surveys, which carries out 28,000 in-home interviews each year. *ABC* (Audit Bureau of Circulation) audits the sales or circulation of over 2,000 different publications, including the nationals. ABC also audits and verifies Web site traffic.

Freesheets or local newspapers use the *VFD* (Verified Free Distribution system).

Posters use *POSJAR* (Poster Joint Audience Research) and *PAB* (Poster Audit Bureau).

BRAD (British Rate and Data) is the media buyer's reference book because it lists all the above circulation/audience figures as well as the costs (rate card costs). It also gives detailed information on deadlines, mechanical data and commissions on 2,718 newspapers, 3,160 consumer publications, 5,461 business publications, 1,334 new media, radio and TV networks, and much more. The monthly book, which contains over 1,200 pages, costs £265 for a single copy or £497 for an annual subscription. The information is also available online for the same price, or as part of planning version BRADnet for £1,950.

CASE STUDY 7.1

Orange 'covered' media campaign

Situation

When it comes to choosing a mobile phone, operators offering national coverage have an edge. So while Orange was seen as more customer-friendly than its key competitors, BT Cellnet and Vodafone, as a younger network it could not traditionally compete on coverage. In addition, BT Cellnet had spent over £56 million on their 'Netman' advertising campaign, giving them virtual ownership of the coverage issue. Orange had to overcome the issue of its own expansion. It was no longer the localized network of its launch (and of many people's perceptions), but a fully fledged national network with over 92 per cent coverage of the population. Overall, there was a need for a step change in communicating the coverage message.

Objectives

Media Planning Group and the creative agency, WCRS, were briefed to run a campaign informing customers that Orange had now achieved 92 per cent coverage. The marketing objective was to shift existing perceptions that Orange had poor coverage vs the other networks. This was particularly important among current Orange customers, as negative word of mouth would undoubtedly damage the brand's ability to recruit any new members.

Strategy

The creative message was a simple one – *'covered'*. But the media task was more complex: Media Planning Group had just two weeks to get the message across to as many people as possible.

The media strategy was threefold:

- to dominate the selected medium;
- to use the medium unconventionally;
- to generate free PR.

The natural medium to reach a mass audience quickly and impactfully would normally be television, but with a budget of £800,000 it would not be possible to dominate it.

Tactics/action

An unconventional solution of posters and press was therefore developed to reach a broad cross-section of the population in two weeks. Perhaps most importantly, these were media that could be used unconventionally to physically demonstrate the 'covered' campaign theme.

Using outdoor, the agency literally covered major conurbations by:

- using up to 16 consecutive 48-sheet panels – a media first;
- physically wrapping over 40 sites – another first;
- covering the floors of key railway stations.

Media Planning Group even managed to sabotage the famous Wonderbra poster campaign, with Playtex's cooperation, of course (see colour plates section).

The use of press was similarly unconventional, bringing the creative message to life by wrapping the Saturday and Sunday review sections of the national press. Most of these were again media firsts and involved moving advertisers off outside back cover sites. Other selected newspapers were dominated with strip sites on the front and back covers of every section – effectively covering the newspaper as well.

Tactical activity can take many forms, but among the most impactful have been those that exploit 'The future's bright, the future's Orange', running simple 'strip' executions of the end line in the national press on highly appropriate days.

The heavyweight 'Orange Internet' campaign in the first quarter of 2001 used TV, posters, the press and the Internet, and was enhanced by fractional press which linked product benefits to the editorial environment, combining creative input and the media in a highly effective way.

Another example of a media first within the Orange campaign was the example of 'scaffoldizing' that was used on the 'Orang-utans' campaign, a media idea developed specifically to enhance the creative execution (see page 197).

For the Orange 'in-bound roaming' campaign, targeting foreign travellers coming into the UK, bespoke media solutions were used at key entry points to the country. For instance, a media first was created at the Eurostar Gare du Nord terminal by placing ads on seat covers in the waiting area.

Control

The £800,000 campaign made Orange an estimated £2.73 million return on its investment by generating significant customer acquisition and retention. Orange accounted for 40 per cent of all new mobile phone subscribers during the period from February to May. Millward Brown research found that the number of Orange users agreeing that Orange offered wide coverage rose from 46 to 68 per cent across the campaign period.

The Orange Internet campaign also immediately entered *Marketing* magazine's Adwatch survey at No. 1, and registrations to the Web site reached 200,000 within a month.

Finally, the campaign was voted best multimedia campaign and overall campaign of the year at the *Media Week* awards.

Men and women

The teams of people dedicated to the Orange business at both Media Planning Group and WCRS are quite large, with over 25 people regularly involved in the business. The coordination and placement of the posters and press campaigns within the 'Covered' campaign involved over 75 additional people, so the total team involved in the production of the campaign was in excess of 100.

Money

The total budget for the 'Covered' campaign was £800,000, which was a small sum compared to the £56 million that had been spent by one of the key competitors. The budget was a key factor in determining the objectives of dominance within the chosen media.

Minutes

The planning and implementation of the 'Covered' campaign took over six months for the team at Media Planning Group. Millward Brown and other research companies monitored the period of the campaign and feedback on the progress and success of the campaign was reported to the Orange client on a regular basis.

Key points from Chapter 7:

1. The proliferation of new media vehicles (TV stations and magazines) creates more but also offers discrete communication channels to better-defined audiences.
2. More money is spent on buying space than on producing the ads themselves.
3. Media planning and buying is a highly skilled area.

Three examples of innovative media from the Orange 'covered' campaign

APPENDIX 7.1

Cost per thousand

CPT calculates the cost of reaching 1,000 of the population audience. The table below demonstrates the wide range of media vehicles available for amateur gardeners, golfers or car enthusiasts, etc. Note that the figures are calculated on rate card costs – substantial discounts are available, particularly during a recession, when it is a buyer's market.

Cost per thousand of selected media vehicles

Vehicle	Cost £	(Approximate 2001 prices) Audience size	CPT £
Press (full colour page)			
Mail on Sunday	54,357	6,061,000	8.97
Financial Times	51,150	715,000	71.50
Sun	45,386	9,508,000	4.77
Radio Times	18,500	3,545,000	5.22
Cosmopolitan	16,272	2,007,000	8.11
Hello	14,280	2,250,000	6.35
Economist	13,200	331,000	39.85
Sainsburys	13,100	2,854,000	4.59
Manchester Evening News	10,535	333,000	31.60
Autocar	8,020	559,000	14.35
Golf World	4,220	437,000	9.66
Horse and Hound	3,322	355,000	9.35
Amateur Gardening	2,825	326,000	8.67
Amateur Photographer	2,825	184,000	12.86
Radio	(30-sec spot)	Weekly reach	CPT
London Regional – Capital Radio	1,850	578,000	3.20
London Regional – Atlantic Radio	581	277,000	2.10
National Package – Atlantic Radio	2,938	1,130,000	2.60
TV			
Carlton area (*News at Ten* – London area)	15,000	990,000	15.15
ITV National	70,000	5,505,000	12.72

APPENDIX 7.2

Typical CPTs across European TV (adults 15+)

Viewing/rates

Country	Average minutes viewed per day Adults	Typical peak 30 sec CPT US $	
		Adults	Main shoppers
Austria	147	15.27	41.39
Belarus	210	0.12	–
Belgium	255	9.75	16.18
Bulgaria	152	0.70	–
Croatia	135	0.54	–
Czech Republic	197	3.99	7.47
Denmark	166	16.15	20.87
Finland	161	8.64	12.83
France	179	7.72	16.49
Germany	195	9.72	16.50
Greece	225	3.43	5.96
Hungary	–	3.66	6.85
Ireland	52	6.74	12.44
Italy	271	10.45	20.55
Latvia	–	2.57	4.81
Lithuania	210	2.31	3.76
Netherlands	157	6.29	10.84
Norway	154	18.95	–
Poland	252	3.12	6.53
Portugal	247	7.33	31.36
Romania	210	0.60	–
Slovenia	176	6.76	14.79
Spain	214	4.24	9.98
Sweden	140	16.52	–
Switzerland	155	26.16	47.63
Turkey	251	10.50	23.77
UK	215	13.44	21.65
Yugoslavia	266	0.71	1.40

FURTHER READING

The Account Planning Group (1987) *How to Plan Advertising* ed, D Cowley, Cassell, London
Advertising Association (1997) *The Marketing Pocket Book*, NTC, London
Campaign, Haymarket Marketing Publications Ltd, London
Davies, M (1992) *The Effective Use of Advertising Media*, 4th edn, Business Books, London
Douglas, T (1984) *The Complete Guide to Advertising*, Papermac, London
Engel, J, Warshaw, M and Kinnear, T (1991) *Promotional Strategy: Managing the Marketing Communications Process*, Irwin, Homewood, Illinois
Media International, Reed Publishing Services, London
Media Week, EMAP Business Publications, London
Zenith Media (1998) *European Market and Media Fact*, Zenith Media Worldwide, London

FURTHER CONTACTS

For trade associations and professional bodies, see page 178
Audit Bureau of Circulation (ABC), Saxon House, 211 High Street, Berkhamsted, Herts HP4 1AD (tel: 01442 870800; Web site: www.abc.org.uk)
British Audience Research Bureau (BARB), 18 Dering Street, London W1R 9AF (tel: 020 7529 5531; Web site: www.barb.co.uk
British Rate and Data (BRAD) – see page 178
Cinema and Advertising Association Video Industry Audience Research (CAVIAR), 12 Golden Square, London W1F 9JE (tel: 020 7534; Web site: www.carltonscreen.com)
Joint Industry for Regional Press Research (JICREG), Bloomsbury House, 74–77 Great Russell Street, London WC1B 3DA (tel: 020 7636 7014; Web site: www.jicreg.co.uk)
National Readership Surveys Ltd, 42 Drury Lane, London WC2B 5RT (tel: 020 7632 2915; Web site: www.nrs.co.uk)
Postar Ltd, Summit House, 27 Sale Place, London W2 1YR (tel: 020 7298 8035; Web site: www.postar.co.uk)
Radio Joint Audience Research (RAJAR), Gainsborough Business Centre, 81 Oxford Street, London W1D 2EU (tel: 020 7903 5350; Web site: www.rajar.co.uk)
Verified Free Distribution (VFD) – contact the Audit Bureau of Circulation (ABC), Saxon House, 211 High Street, Berkhamsted, Herts HP4 1AD (tel: 01442 870800; Web site: www.abc.org.uk)

8

The changing communications environment

INTRODUCTION

We are children of change. This chapter looks at how marketing communications are affected by the business environment and its many apparently uncontrollable factors.

Markets are pulled and pushed in different directions by forces that are outside an organization's immediate control. New laws; changing regulations; fluctuating economic cycles; demographic shifts; new social values, attitudes and cultural norms; fast-changing technology; and agile competitors are some of the key factors that constantly move markets away from the existing status quo. Today's marketing mix and marketing communications mix can soon become obsolete.

This means that the *MIIS* (marketing intelligence and information system) discussed on page 141 should constantly feed back information on patterns, trends or sudden changes in any of these uncontrollable forces. This requires, in turn, a constant alertness and preparedness to change products, services, advertisements, images, communications and even an organization's attitudes or culture.

The 'SW' part of a *SWOT* (strengths, weaknesses, opportunities and threats) analysis monitors the external opportunities and threats that emerge in the business environment. The *PEST* acronym provides a useful starting point to scan the business environment for any of these change factors that directly or indirectly affect a business and how it communicates:

- **P**olitical (including legal and regulatory);
- **E**conomic (global economic shifts and cycles of recession and boom);
- **S**ocial (new values, attitudes, lifestyles, ethics and demographics);
- **T**echnological (the Internet, database, digital TV and much more).

Competition could also be added as a key factor operating in an organization's environment. For the purposes of this chapter the focus will be on the PEST factors. Any of these change factors could ultimately push a business into extinction if the changes are constantly ignored. There is a tendency to resist change, perhaps because of the insecurities it heaps upon an individual. Some organizations wait until the last moment before changing. Others see an advantage in being proactive rather than reactive. We will now consider how these PEST factors affect the organization's marketing activities and its communications in particular.

POLITICS

Legislation and regulation

National and international laws and regulations change. This can affect the basic product or service and methods of communication.

Pan Am's downfall

It was claimed that *Pan Am* failed because 'it never got a handle on how deregulation of the 1970s would affect a powerful world airline'.

Fortune, 13 January 1992

UK legislation provides laws that essentially support the principles of being honest and truthful. The laws are bolstered by a host of self-regulatory professional codes that draw on the same set of basic business principles, eg marketing professionals should conduct their business in a *legal*, *decent*, *honest* and *truthful* manner.

Before looking at the laws, it is worth mentioning that short-term, dishonest deals ('rip-offs') that slip through the system generate short-term gains, but they tend not to generate long-term sales since repeat business does not come back. The *'everlasting customer'* or the *'lifetime customer'* concept is a long-term winning strategy since the marketing perspective is broadened towards selling 10 cars, 10 fridges, or thousands of cans of food or beer, or 50 years of office cleaning to one customer over a long period of time instead of grabbing a one-off, short-term sale. It *costs five times as much* to sell to a new customer as it does to an existing customer. Fooling a customer is myopic. You can *only cheat a customer once*. Flouting the law or regulations restricts a business to a short-term vision. Incidentally, Japanese management guru *Kenichi Ohmae* claims that the most fundamental difference between Eastern and Western business strategies is the *time horizon*. Japanese companies build long-term strategies, while Western companies plan short-term profits.

There are many laws that affect business, and marketing communications in particular. UK television advertising alone has at least 60 statutes and regulations that affect it. These include the 1987 Consumer Protection Act, the Sex Discrimination Acts 1975 and 1986, the Race Relations Act 1976, the Telecommunications Act 1984, the Copyright Designs and Patents Act 1988, and the Broadcasting Act 1996. Here is a brief description of some of the laws that directly affect marketing communications.

The *1968 Trade Descriptions Act* legally obliges companies and individuals to avoid making false or misleading statements about the goods or services being marketed.

The *1979 Sale of Goods Act* demands that goods sold match their description.

The *Control of Misleading Advertisements Regulations 1988* provides the safety net of the *Office of Fair Trading*, where complaints about marketing communications (advertising, shop-windows displays, etc) can be referred for scrutiny.

The *Data Protection Act 1984* requires any organization or individual to register if they hold names, addresses or data on individuals *on computer*.

The *Trade Marks Act 1994* adapted UK trade mark law to fit with European legislation. This means a wider range of products and service attributes can now be registered as trade marks. Subsequent unusual applications include the sound of a dog barking (Dulux paint), the musical jingle for Mr. Softee's ice cream, car tyres that smell of roses (Japanese company), Microsoft's catchphrase 'Where do you want to go today?' and 'Ooh ahh Cantona' (Eric Cantona).

There are, as mentioned, many other laws and regulations, both national and international, that affect a business and its marketing communications. For example, the EU Telecommunications Data Protection Directive (enforced by the Data Protection Registrar) makes it illegal for companies to fax homes or businesses that have opted out. See Fax

Preference Service details on page 232. Some of the legislation may not appear to affect the marketing communications directly, eg product liability laws, but caution, coupled with expert advice, is required, particularly in the international arena. *Product liability* puts an increasing onus of responsibility on both manufacturers, distributors and retailers to make sure that the products they market are safe and sound. It also affects marketing communications (and, in the sparkling wine case below, packaging communications). The *'borderless world'* knows few barriers when it comes to liability.

Sparkling wine shooting

The 20-year-old case of a US consumer suing a UK paint company (for alleged injurious effects of a lead-based paint) strikes fear into the heart of many potential exporters. According to Mickey Pohl, a growing awareness that a manufacturer carries a heavy and detailed obligation to warn potential users about any dangers that might lurk in the use of its products has prompted some sparkling wine manufacturers to print disclaimers on the packaging warning against possible risks involved in uncorking their products.

M Pohl

EU legislative process

On a local scale, centralized EU legislation is beginning to affect every European company in some way. The Single European Currency is a basic example. Many organizations are only now reluctantly accepting the new European environment. Many will react with some urgency, but how many have really seized the opportunity of selling in the world's most competitive market? And how many will get wiped out within 10, 20 or 50 years? More and more legislation will come from a centralized European state. The process of European legislation is shown in Figure 8.1. It is vital to make an organization's voice heard, so the advice from the DTI (Department of Trade and Industry) is to find out how proposed legislation could affect a particular organization, then get in early and have a say in the emerging EU regulations. Chapter 9 considers the effects of the EU on the communications mix and on client/agency relationships in more detail.

This legislative process is particularly relevant to regulations that affect *marketing communications*. Here some EU countries prefer central legislation over self-regulation and its voluntary codes of practice. For example, EU legislation aims to outlaw cigarette advertising across all promotional media (sponsorship is also in the European definition of promotion). Currently, in the UK, voluntary agreements specify the amount of space and

Scrambled thinking

Some time ago I stopped outside a bookshop in Wales and saw in the window a small card saying: 'There are 56 words in the Lord's Prayer, 297 in the ten commandments, 300 in the American Declaration of Independence and 29,911 in the EEC directive on the export of eggs.'

Lord Moran in the House of Lords debate on the European Communities (Amendment) Bill, 21 January 1997

precise wording of warnings on packs or on advertisements for cigarettes. These agreements also specify that no positive claims can be made about tobacco and that no tobacco advertising is permitted on television. It is this self-regulation that has moved the market, and its communications, in new directions as voluntary codes change. Once there was a time when cigarettes were promoted as being good for you. Today they are advertised as being bad for you (the mandatory health warnings).

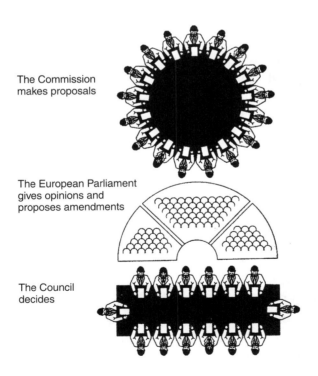

The Commission makes proposals

The European Parliament gives opinions and proposes amendments

The Council decides

Figure 8.1 The EU legislative process

The EU directive on cross-frontier broadcasting was adopted in 1989 and implemented in 1991. It basically covers television and can be summarized as follows:

- allows television channels to cross frontiers of member states;
- limits the total amount of advertising airtime to 15 per cent of daily transmission;
- sets guidelines for broadcast sponsorship (see page 446 for examples of programme sponsorship);
- bans tobacco advertising and prescription medicine advertising;
- sets guidelines for children's advertising.

European countries have no central set of detailed controls over marketing communications... yet. Table 8.1 shows the lack of agreement on advertising across Europe. Some types of advertising are permitted, restricted or banned by either legislation or voluntary codes (regulations). Appendix 8.1 shows the lack of European legislative and regulatory harmony in other advertising media, including newspapers, magazines, radio, posters and cinema. Sales promotions also suffer from a lack of harmony (see page 350).

Harmonious people?

As countries plug into the global economy, their political choices get narrower. The political choice used to be siding with the Soviet Union or the United States. That dynamic is gone. What are the choices when you look at the French, the US or the British elections in the past few years? There are not a lot of differences among those people.

Herbert Baume, Quaker Oats, CEO at AMA

Self-regulation – codes of practice

Various professional bodies draw up their own codes of practice to which their members must adhere. Failure to do so may result in expulsion and sometimes negative publicity, along with a form of blacklisting. A breach of a code can also result in the withdrawal of an advertisement or sales promotion, etc. This can be expensive as the development of any campaign costs money. The risks are arguably higher in television, where a 30-second advertisement can easily cost a million pounds. Most advertisers want to stand out from the crowd. To do this they sometimes have to be daring, bold and controversial. The

Table 8.1   Advertising restrictions across Europe

	Alcohol		Tobacco		Food		Cosmetics & personal hygiene products		Non-prescription medical products		Cleaning & household products		Children & advertising		Political advertising		Religious advertising	
	TV or Press	Radio	TV or Press	Radio	TV or Press	Radio	TV or Press	Radio	TV or Press	Radio	TV or Press	Radio	TV or Press	Radio	TV or Press	Radio	TV or Press	Radio
Austria	✗	✗	✗	✗	✗	✗	✓	✗	✗	✗	✓	✓	✗	✗	✓	✗	✗	✗
Belgium	✗	✗	✗	✗	✗	✗	✗	✗	✗	✓	✓	✓	✗	✗	✓	✗	✓	✗
Denmark	✗	✗	✗	✗	✗	✗	✓	✓	✗	✗	✓	✓	✗	✗	✓	✗	✓	✗
Finland	✗	✗	✗	✗	✓	✓	✓	✗	✗	✗	✓	✗	✓	✗	✗	✗	✗	✗
France	✗	✗	✗	✗	✗	✗	✗	✗	✗	✗	✗	✗	✗	✗	✗	✗	✗	✗
Germany	✗	✗	✗	✗	✗	✗	✓	✓	✗	✗	✓	✓	✗	✗	✓	✓	✓	✓
Greece*	✗	✗	✗	✗	✓	✓	✓	✗	✗	✗	✗	✗	✓	✗	✗	✗	✗	✗
Ireland	✗	✗	✗	✗	✗	✗	✗	✗	✗	✗	✓	✓	✗	✗	✗	✗	✗	✗
Italy	✗	✗	✗	✗	✗	✗	✗	✗	✗	✗	✓	✗	✗	✗	✗	✗	✗	✗
Luxembourg	✓	✗	✗	✗	✗	✗	✓	✗	✗	✗	✓	✓	✗	✗	✓	✓	✓	✓
Netherlands	✗	✗	✗	✗	✗	✗	✗	✗	✗	✗	✗	✗	✗	✗	✓	✗	✓	✗
Norway	✗	✗	✗	✗	✗	✗	✓	✓	✗	✗	✓	✓	✓	✗	✓	✓	✓	✓
Portugal	✓	✗	✗	✗	✓	✓	✓	✓	✗	✗	✓	✓	✗	✗	✗	✗	✗	✗
Spain	✗	✗	✗	✗	✗	✗	✗	✗	✗	✗	✓	✗	✗	✗	✗	✗	✗	✗
Sweden	✗	✗	✗	✗	✗	✗	✓	✓	✗	✗	✓	✓	✗	✗	✓	✗	✓	✗
Switzerland	✗	✗	✗	✗	✗	✗	✗	✗	✗	✗	✗	✗	✓	✓	✓	✗	✓	✗
Turkey	✓	✗	✗	✗	✓	✓	✓	✗	✗	✗	✓	✓	✗	✗	✗	✗	✗	✗
United Kingdom	✗	✗	✗	✗	✗	✗	✗	✗	✗	✗	✓	✗	✗	✗	✗	✗	✗	✗

✗ indicates that the advertising of the product is restricted in some way
✓ indicates that there are no advertising restrictions

Note: 'Press' refers to newspapers or magazines
* Greek 'Political or religious advertising' restrictions refer to religious restrictions only
Source: European Advertising & Media Yearbook, 2000

advertiser's dilemma here is whether to (a) be so controversial that the advertisement teeters on the brink of being pulled off the air or (b) play safe with a less controversial creative treatment.

Although marketing communications must adhere to the laws of the land (ie one cannot misrepresent or blatantly mislead), the voluntary codes are both *cheaper* and *quicker* to apply should any complaints or claims be made. The codes also offer useful guidance to the marketer, so that most problems are ironed out before an advertisement goes out on air or is published in the press. Essentially, advertisements should:

- be *legal, decent, honest* and *truthful*;
- show *responsibility to the customer and society*;
- follow the *basic business principles of fair competition*.

Professional bodies need to be vigilant in order to maintain the credibility of their profession. This is particularly true in advertising, where the consumer's scepticism and resistance to advertising is heightened or lowered according to the credibility of the advertising industry. This credibility is founded upon the industry's reputation and determination to maintain standards of legality, decency, honesty and truthfulness.

Press and print advertisements and the ASA/CAP

Press and print means all non-broadcast media, ie the press, posters, leaflets, direct mail, video cassette commercials, teletext and cinema advertising. In the UK, the Committee of Advertising Practice (*CAP*) is the custodian of the British code of advertising practice. They provide a rulebook for all advertising except radio, TV and cable (which is covered by the ITC). The code offers guidelines as to what is acceptable and what is not.

British Code of Advertising Practice

If any member of the public objects to a published advertisement they can contact the Advertising Standards Authority (ASA) and complain in writing. The ASA is the customer side of the CAP; the CAP deals with the trade or the advertisers directly. Complaints are analysed to determine whether they are worth further investigation. If the complaint is deemed to be reasonable, and the association consequently upholds the complaint, then the advertiser is asked to *withdraw* it immediately. The ASA is not a legal body and therefore has non-statutory powers. Some advertisers may choose to ignore a request to withdraw an advertisement. The ASA will then issue a *media warning* to all CAP member organizations (including media owners). This effectively blacklists the advertisement. The result is that the advertiser will find very few media owners prepared to sell them any advertising space. The media may implement their terms and conditions of business, which require adherence to the codes. Agencies who persistently breach the codes *jeopardize their membership* of professional and trade organizations. This means trading privileges and financial incentives may be forfeited, and potential new clients may exclude agencies who are not members of recognized professional bodies. If all else fails, the association can invoke the final legal backstop of the *Control of Misleading Advertisements Regulations 1988*. Although rarely needed, these empower the Director General of Fair Trading to obtain an injunction against the advertiser.

It is worth checking with the CAP before printing a mailshot or publishing an advertisement. Having said that, many campaigns are published without prior CAP approval and run the relevant risk.

It has been suggested that some of the more controversial short campaigns seek to gain free editorial coverage by being banned. There are, of course, risks associated with this kind of exposure (see 'Lack of control', page 426).

Television advertisements and the ITC

TV advertisements, on the other hand, must gain approval before broadcasting. The *ITC* (Independent Television Commission) and the Radio Authority publish free guidelines (the ITC Code of Advertising Standards and Practice – see below). The ITC and the Radio Authority replaced the IBA (Independent Broadcasting Authority) in 1991.

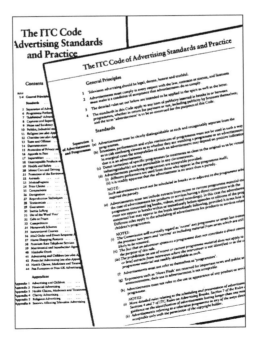

The ITC Code of Advertising Standards and Practice

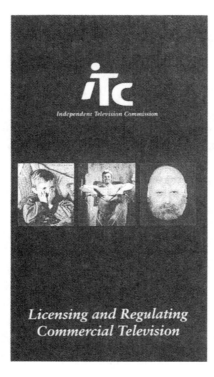

The ITC Code of Advertising Standards and Practice leaflet

Initial scripts are approved by the BACC (Broadcast Advertising Clearance Centre) and a *clearance certificate* is issued. However, this does not guarantee that the finished production will also be acceptable, as the film's treatment is sometimes difficult to envisage from a script or storyboard, and so it is also screened for final approval before broadcasting. Even after an advertisement is cleared for broadcasting, it can still be 'pulled' off the air if the ITC requests it. Their attention can be aroused by complaints from the public (see Persil's spotted dog advertisement on page 103). If, after they have examined the material and considered the complaint, they feel that the complaint should be upheld, they can then pull the advertisement off the air.

In addition to advertising, other marketing services have their own regulations and codes. For example, the *Code of Sales Promotion Practice* is also published by the CAP and basically provides guidelines for sales promotion activities. The *IPA* (Institute of Practitioners in Advertising, *IPR* (Institute of Public Relations), *PRCA* (Public Relations Consultants Association), *ISP* (Institute of Sales Promotion) and other professional bodies all have codes of practice to which their members must adhere. Any breach of the code can result in a member being warned or ultimately struck off the institute or association member list. This may have some short-term negative publicity plus, in the medium to longer term, exclusion of that member from pitch lists. Some clients refer to the appropriate institution/association when choosing a new agent/consultant.

Direct marketing

Since 1992 the ASA/CAP has had the responsibility of regulating the direct marketing industry. Essentially this is to ensure that consumers receive as much or as little direct mail as they want. The CAP's new rules require direct marketing campaigns to:

1. Give consumers a choice before transferring their names to other companies.
2. Remove names from lists on request.
3. Correct personal details immediately upon notification.

The direct marketing industry is currently under scrutiny from the EU. The *European Advertising Standards Alliance* (EASA) consists of the organizations in Europe that already operate self-regulatory codes of advertising practice. It hopes to coordinate the disparate activities and act as focal point for pan-European consultation. Whether voluntary codes of practice will be preferred to centralized legislation remains to be seen.

This will affect *all direct marketing* activities, including *telemarketing*. At present there is little EU harmony in either regulations or legislation, eg cold calling is banned in Germany and in some US states. Equally, sales promotions, incentives, premiums and free gifts are generally unacceptable in Germany and also cause problems in France (see page 351). The EASA may provide a platform for promoting self-regulation and harmony across Europe.

Macro-political effects on business and communications

We now move from national and international regulations and legislation, which affect marketing communications, to international political negotiations, which affect the world economy. It should be remembered that the larger international trading companies need to monitor the results of worldwide political agreements. Plans are prepared to meet a range of scenarios built around possible results from, say, the current major economic disputes. *Fortune* magazine describes two scenarios used by an oil company.

Scenario 1: Sustainable world and global mercantilism

This assumes that all the major international economic disputes are solved. There is European unity. The United States and Japan agree trading terms (and avoid a trade war).

Free trade prevails across the globe and stable growth is maintained. As a consequence, environmental issues receive more attention. The implications for Shell: new emission restrictions and a reconfiguration of the energy industry in which less oil and more natural gas is used.

Scenario 2: Global mercantilism

This assumes a gloomier world where regional conflicts basically destabilize the world.

Trade wars and recessions rage. Trading blocs form and consensus on environmental issues is never achieved. This scenario implies less regulation, a piecemeal approach to environmental issues and much more oil consumption.

Worldwide political agreements not only affect product portfolios (the range and types of products or services), they also affect the social agenda which determines what are considered to be the most important social issues in the minds of customers. This, in turn, affects the organization's social responsibility policies and subsequent communications programmes (see 'Marketing communications and publicity', and 'The PR mix', page 420). The social factors examined on page 218 also consider how the agenda can change over relatively short periods of time. First, we will consider how the national economy affects organizations and their marketing communications.

ECONOMICS

Effects on markets and communications

Industrial and consumer markets are directly and indirectly affected by the state of the economy. The global shift in economic power from west to east is affecting many markets. Closer to home, exchange rates, interest rates, unemployment, levels of disposable income, etc all affect how much money is around, how much will be spent and, in a sense, the size of many markets or industries.

During a recession almost everyone cuts back on spending. Consumers spend less. Companies spend less. Many organizations cut back on all types of spending, including marketing (although there are exceptions like Procter and Gamble who, according to Bill MacNamara, ex-ASDA divisional marketing director, 'automatically raise their marketing expenditure in a recession'). A classic fall in derived demand emerges: as primary consumer demand falls, the secondary demand (for the commercial products and services required to make and market the consumer products) also falls. This reduces growth in the marketing service industries like advertising and design. It becomes a buyer's market as prices tumble and better deals are demanded by clients. Several agencies and clients go into liquidation. There is therefore an increased need to check the financial stability of any agency/partner/supplier/customer.

Meanwhile, advertisers have to address the difficulty of encouraging people to buy during a serious recession. Appendix 8.2 explains how some American advertisers fight the enemy of recession by using its own images. During a recession many buyers search for better deals, which include price cuts, extended terms and value-for-money sales promotions. These promotions may not enhance brand loyalty (see Figure 12.4 on page 356). The scars of an economic recession may be permanently expressed in terms of buying patterns, attitudes, values and, ultimately, the advertising imagery, which reflects the changing norms, roles and values of a culture.

Recession-induced psychological change

Even a phenomenally strong economic recovery may not bring back the consumer-spending patterns of the 1980s. Values, attitudes and lifestyles may combine to create lower levels of consumption, new buying processes and an overall pattern of trading down (away from premium-price brands). The worldwide recession brought job cuts and quality-of-life worries out of the headlines and into millions of homes. Some feel that consumer markets have changed because of a recession-induced psychological change that moved people away from the self-indulgence and excess of the 'me, mine, more' mentality of the pre-Millennium to the 'learning to live with limitations' of the post-Millennium.

This could affect buying behaviour and the supporting advertising messages, for example a move away from images of personal achievement to images about personal relationships, or even a move away from advertising that is built around the user imagery (from where '*the user is the hero*' to where '*the product is hero*'). This suggests that advertising will have to provide more hard information as consumers buy more carefully, seeking out the best deal, and display a price consciousness that rejects premium-price brands for better-value products that provide relevant benefits and excellent performance.

A 1992 survey by the Grey International Advertising Agency appears to support this theory, at least in the United States, where many of the trends are often transferred across the Atlantic within a few years. Ninety-one per cent said that they themselves, or a relative or a friend, had been affected by the recession (this is further supported by a *Time*/CNN poll which found that 23 per cent of Americans were out of work because of the recession at some point during 1991). Other key findings in Grey's survey showed:

- 85 per cent had cut back on spending;
- 82 per cent said that they were learning to make do with less;
- 90 per cent said that the simple joys in life are what matter most;
- 87 per cent were more aware of the importance of the family;
- 81 per cent were yearning for more lasting values.

This compares with a 1987 survey by Grey which found that Americans in every social and economic stratum were involved in an all-out quest for ego gratification, as demonstrated by the top four goals: (1) making life the best it can be, (2) enjoying what I do, (3) being able to afford the things I enjoy, (4) staying physically fit.

SOCIAL CHANGE

Norms, roles and values change. Today, fathers change nappies, cook dinners and shop in supermarkets. Many women earn more than their male partners. Roles are becoming less clearly defined. It is no longer abnormal to have two working parents. Attitudes towards issues change. Once environmentalists were considered to be hippies, communists, anarchists or outcasts because of their lack of conformity with other people's beliefs, values and attitudes. Today, most political parties and major corporations recognize the importance of environmental groups.

A new interest in ethics

Social consciousness among buyers is increasing. Consumers want to know more about products and their producers. Do they damage the environment? What do they do in the community? Do they donate political funds? Do the organizations disclose information, and so on?

A classic UK publication called *Shopping for a Better World* (Adams *et al*, 1991) ranked household brands according to nine different ethical criteria (see Figure 8.2). Many buyers

SOFT DRINKS AND MIXERS

Brand	Co											Alert!
7 UP	PEP	x	?	?	xx	✓	x	x	y	n	
Apeel	PHM	x	?	?	xx	?	xx	x	y	n	AT
Aqua Libra	GRM	✓✓	✓	x	✓	✓	✓	x	Y	n	Atg
Britvic 55*	BAS	x	?	x	xx	✓	✓✓	x	y	n	AtG
Britvic Fruit Juices*	BAS	x	?	x	xx	✓	✓✓	x	y	n	AtG
Britvic Quencher*	BAS	x	?	x	xx	✓	✓	x	y	n	AtG
C-Drinks	NES	✓	?	x	✓	?	x	x	Y	n	a
C-Vit	SKB	x	?	?	✓	?	✓	?	Y	C	
Canada Dry*	BAS	x	?	x	xx	✓	✓✓	x	y	n	AtG
Capri-Sun	RHM	x	?	?	x	?	?	x	n	C	
Cherry 7 UP	PEP	x	?	?	xx	✓	x	x	y	n	
Cherry Coca-Cola	COC	✓	x	✓	✓✓	✓	x	x	y	n	
Cherry Pepsi	PEP	x	?	?	xx	✓	x	x	y	n	
Citrus Spring*	BAS	x	?	x	xx	✓	✓✓	x	y	n	AtG
Coca-Cola	COC	✓	x	✓	✓✓	✓	x	x	y	n	
Corona*	BAS	x	?	x	xx	✓	✓✓	x	y	n	AtG
Cottee's	CAD	✓✓	✓	✓	x	✓	✓✓	x	Y	n	
Crush	CAD	✓✓	✓	✓	x	✓	✓✓	x	Y	n	
De L'Ora	RHM	x	?	?	x	?	?	x	n	C	
Dexters	GRM	✓✓	✓	x	✓	✓	✓✓	x	Y	n	Atg
Diet 7 UP	PEP	x	?	?	xx	✓	x	x	y	n	
Diet Coca-Cola	COC	✓	x	✓	✓✓	✓	x	x	y	n	
Diet Fanta	COC	✓	x	✓	✓✓	✓	x	x	y	n	
Diet Lilt	COC	✓	x	✓	✓✓	✓	x	x	y	n	
Diet Pepsi	PEP	x	?	?	xx	✓	x	x	y	n	
Diet Sprite	COC	✓	x	✓	✓✓	✓	x	x	y	n	
ED Smith	CAD	✓✓	✓	✓	x	✓	✓✓	x	Y	n	

Brand	Co											Alert!
Fanta	COC	✓	x	✓	✓✓	✓	x	x	y	n	
Ferguzade	SKB	x	?	?	✓	?	✓	?	Y	C	
Five Alive	COC	✓	x	✓	✓✓	✓	x	x	y	n	
Five Alive Citrus	COC	✓	x	✓	✓✓	✓	x	x	y	n	
Five Alive Lite	COC	✓	x	✓	✓✓	✓	x	x	y	n	
Five Alive Tropical	COC	✓	x	✓	✓✓	✓	x	x	y	n	
Five Alive Tropical	COC	✓	x	✓	✓✓	✓	x	x	y	n	
Gini	CAD	✓✓	✓	✓	x	✓	✓✓	x	Y	n	
Groosome Joosome	RHM	x	?	?	x	?	?	x	n	C	
Hires	CAD	✓✓	✓	✓	x	✓	✓✓	x	Y	n	
Holland House	CAD	✓✓	✓	✓	x	✓	✓✓	x	Y	n	
Hycal	SKB	x	?	?	✓	?	✓	?	Y	C	
Idris*	BAS	x	?	x	xx	✓	✓✓	x	y	n	AtG
Just Juice	RHM	x	?	?	x	?	?	x	n	C	
Kia-Ora	CAD	✓✓	✓	✓	x	✓	✓✓	x	Y	n	
Libby	NES	✓	?	x	✓✓	?	x	x	Y	n	a
Lilt	COC	✓	x	✓	✓✓	✓	x	x	y	n	
Lucozade	SKB	x	?	?	✓	?	✓	?	Y	C	
Moonshine	NES	✓	?	x	✓	?	x	x	Y	n	a
Mott's	CAD	✓✓	✓	✓	x	✓	✓✓	x	Y	n	
Mr & Mrs 'T'	CAD	✓✓	✓	✓	x	✓	✓✓	x	Y	n	
Napolina	CPC	x	?	?	xx	?	✓✓	x	n	n	
Oasis	CAD	✓✓	✓	✓	x	✓	✓✓	x	Y	n	
Old Colony	CAD	✓✓	✓	✓	x	✓	✓✓	x	Y	n	
One-Cal	RHM	x	?	?	x	?	?	x	n	C	
PLJ	SKB	x	?	?	✓	?	✓	?	Y	C	
Pepsi Cola	PEP	x	?	?	xx	✓	x	x	y	n	
Quosh*	BAS	x	?	x	xx	✓	✓✓	x	y	n	AtG

Figure 8.2 An example of brands coming under increasing ethical scrutiny

are becoming aware that the supermarket is the economic ballot box of the future. And investors also are becoming increasingly interested in the corporate citizenship of organizations that they might consider funding. The relentless charge of change is demonstrated by the now redundant South African column in Figure 8.2.

Banks are becoming weary of lending funds to higher-risk, unenvironmental companies. Insurance premiums will also reflect the higher risk of non-green companies. The corporate responsibility record is now a criterion in joint ventures. For example, who wants to invest time and money in an organization that has a poor environmental record? To put it another way, who wants to inherit a *green time bomb*? Similarly, eastern European companies look towards the community record of potential Western partners.

Adams *et al*'s (1991) sister publication for investors and chairmen was called *Changing Corporate Values*. Basically it gives a three- or four-page profile of major organizations' corporate ethical record, as shown in Figure 8.3.

Some estimates suggest that a 'green screen', or false green claims by corporations, will only last approximately six months, since probing pressure groups, investigative journalists, scrutinizing financial analysts and information-hungry customers will eventually reveal a much bigger problem than that which was originally hidden. This implies that the marketing people have a vested interest in ensuring that an organization operates in a socially responsible manner. Corporate attitudes towards altruism and ethics are changing, as are personal religious beliefs.

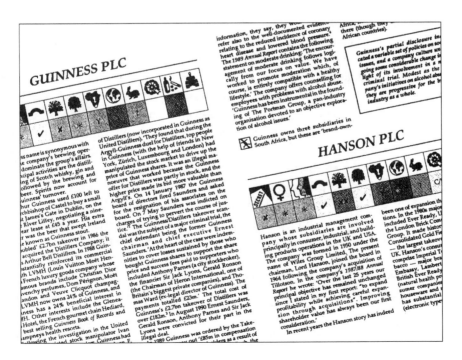

Figure 8.3 An example of corporations being subjected to ethical scrutiny

Finally, one extraneous factor that affects the business environment is the environment itself. If the world continues to heat up, northern European attitudes, emotions and feelings about different stimuli (particularly colour) may change. This would affect almost all forms of marketing communications, and possibly even radio.

Demographics

The statistical analysis (or division) of a population/audience by age, sex and social status helps marketers to segment and target markets (see the socio-economic data starting on page 60). This can be combined with location/geography – hence the term *geodemographics*. In addition, there are demographic cycles, trends and movements that can help an organization to learn about its market many years in advance. According to Matthew Gwyer (1992), we know that by *2030 the UK population will start to shrink* and deaths will exceed births. The period total fertility rate (PTFR) is now at 1.8 children per family, which is below the replacement level of 2.1. By 2030 the 80-year-old plus market will expand to 3.4 million (three-and-a-half times more than in 1961).

The demographic shift during the 1980s *pulled the market away from Guinness* as a disproportionately large number of younger drinkers (20 year olds) emerged after the 1960s baby boom. Guinness was positioned as an older, unfashionable drink. To chase the moving market, Guinness and the now extinct but then brilliant advertising agency Allen Brady and Marsh repositioned the product as a younger and more fashionable drink. The 1990s saw the demographic bulge move on to create a disproportionately large number of 30 year olds. Guinness chased this swell by using a maturing blond-haired man to help to position the drink appropriately. During the early 2010s Guinness may reposition itself as a 50-year-olds' drink. The *beer market will shrink* since volume customers are the younger session-drinkers who pour as many as a dozen pints down their necks on Friday and Saturday nights. Or perhaps the *ozone* layer will completely crumble and the weather will warm up, followed by increased liquid consumption, including beers. Or will there be *another baby boom* of the 1990s (as less women use the pill because of cancer scares), creating a vast 18–25-year-old market by the early 2010s? Or then again, perhaps an even bigger *health trend* will curtail all regular drinking behaviour. Or will the *EC ban* all alcohol advertising? Maybe real estate companies will force *pubs to increase their prices* and thereby push drinkers back into their homes to consume canned draught beers? Or perhaps the *decline of Western civilization* will follow the decline of the Roman and Greek empires with over-indulgence and decadent lifestyles, including heavy drinking, and thereby create a short- or medium-term boost in the beer market?

1998 saw more UK consumers over the age of 45 than under the age of 30. What are the implications of an *ageing UK population*? Bigger typefaces and print to help older eyes read commercial messages? Many products and services repositioned as the more mature person's choice? There will still be youth markets, but they may not be as attractive since they will shrink in size and competition may become quite ferocious. Then again, *AIDS* may yet wipe out a whole middle generation, leaving behind a polarized society of very old and very young.

The falling marriage rate, the increasing divorce rate and the increasing number of births outside marriage contribute towards the sad term '*disintegrating family*'. In addition, the single-person household is expected to increase. The traditional happy family advertising formula is becoming obsolete. Some years ago Oxo showed the husband cooking the family lunch while the wife was out at play. In the early 1990s, Persil cast comedian Robbie Coltrane as a friendly adult/grandchild who helps his grandmother to wash up by using a top brand of liquid. The traditional housewife/woman shopper is no longer the sole key decision maker. Just take a look around a local supermarket on a Saturday morning, where you will see male shoppers buying Fairy Liquid, Ariel and Palmolive soap.

Decision-making units (DMUs) are changing (see 'Segmentation and target marketing', page 35). Over 60 per cent of mothers in the UK work either part time or full time, compared with 10 per cent in the 1930s and 20 per cent in the 1950s. Incidentally, it has been suggested that *guilt-ridden working mothers* may ease their discomfort by buying the 'best' brands for their families instead of buying the store's less expensive own brand. A recent Gallup poll suggested that 90 per cent of working mothers suffer some psychological discomfort in combining the roles of mother and worker.

The effects of the changing structure of DMUs apply to a broad sweep of products and services and not just *FMCGs*. Insurance, health care and double glazing target both partners instead of just the head of the household or the main income earner. Most telesale phone calls only fix an appointment to visit when *both* partners/spouses are available for a sales presentation.

Futurologist Alvin Toffler forecast many years ago that technology could facilitate vast demographic shifts as populations migrate from the cities to work in their own electronic cottages (complete with phone, fax and computer). Although there has been some movement, the vast demographic shift has not yet occurred. Technology, meanwhile, has relentlessly marched on into new realms of marketing.

Everything changes

It wasn't so long ago that Eurovision Song Contest winners wearing dresses were women!

TECHNOLOGY

Technology keeps changing the face of marketing communications. You only have to think of taped customer care announcements, automatic bank dispensing tills, robot-manned compact disc stores, and outbound and inbound telesale voice machines to see how this is true. We are witnessing marriages between technologies such as geographic information systems, analytical modelling market analysis and data-mining. *Home computer shopping* in the US allows customers to move their home computer's mouse to scan aisles, pick up products, examine them in three dimensions and put them into an electronic basket. Payment is by credit card and delivery comes the next day. Bar codes and information-collecting technology have increased in diversity and accuracy. Interactive TV programmes and *interactive TV advertisements* are here. *Satellites* provide new programmes and new conference facilities for *sales meetings, press conferences, training programmes* and much more. It has been suggested by the European Association of Advertising Agencies that satellite communication will increase non-verbal commercial communications.

> What satellite broadcasting is going to mean for us, apart from reach, is greater emphasis on non-verbal communication: the big visual idea, and the use of visual symbols. Where the message transcends national frontiers, it will often transcend national languages. Remember, we have nine different national languages in the EC. This is going to put a premium on the visual and musical content of commercials, with less emphasis on verbal communication.
>
> Rijkens (1992)

Computers can even do a lot of a manager's *reading* by scanning journals, newspapers and trade magazines for relevant material and printing out headlines, summary abstracts or complete articles (see online research databases in the 'Marketing intelligence and information system' section on page 141). Database marketing is where a real technological opportunity lies for all types of organization, both large and small (see Chapter 13).

Print technology allows magazines to run liquid-filled ads, heat-sensitive ads, double-image ads (which create the effect of movement), 3-D ads, scratch 'n' sniff ads (in fact 3M used scratch 'n' sniff in their 1992 annual report), perfumed ads and, of course, singing and speaking press ads. According to *Marketing Breakthroughs* in October 1992, a

Moore's law

Every 18 months, processing power doubles while costs hold constant.

Gordon Moore, founder of Intel, observed that each new generation of computer chips (semi-conductors) doubled in power every 18 months. This has been valid for 30 years and is predicted to continue for the next 30 years... has held since the 1960s, and recent developments in so called 'molecular electronics' – arranging molecules in electronic circuits – suggest improvements are likely to continue for another 30 years.

Paul Krugman, Unleash after 100 years of trial and error, *Fortune*, 6 March 2000, pF12

This means that in just over 30 years computer chips will be 1 million times more powerful than today.

Canadian publisher was reported to have been worried about the declining presence of its daily newspaper on the breakfast table, so it had its logo printed on millions of fresh eggs.

Novelty marketing gadgets have been employed for many years now, ranging from robots to *light-sensitive supermarket displays* which react when triggered by a passing customer. Shopping carts can carry video screens promoting 'today's special offer' as the customer passes various sensors discreetly placed around the store.

Pepsi can now page groups of their customers with bleepers already supplied. In fact bleepers and other items with computer chips can be triggered by simply moving within a certain range of a pack or product. Today, location-based marketing means that mobile phones can alert you to special offers as you enter the vicinity of the retail outlet. MIT (the Massachusetts Institute of Technology) have developed hot badges that flash when two like-minded people come within range of each other at a party. Brand relationships and human relationships have many similar emotional responses. The Internet also provides virtual meeting places, virtual discussion groups, virtual greeting cards, virtual gifts and virtual exhibitions (see page 498). Invisible computers will be in everything that uses electricity.

Push technology means that specific relevant messages can be pushed out and delivered on a one-to-one basis through the Internet.

Packaging technology has, for many years now, provided self-heating tins and special Coca-Cola cans for use in American spaceships. And spaceships themselves are available for advertising purposes. In fact technology permeates every aspect of marketing and marketing communications.

The networked car can take care of it

Drivers and passengers can verbally request and listen to e-mail messages, locate a restaurant or hotel, ask for specific sports scores or music, and use voice-activated telephone services – all without interfering with the driving. The network car accesses the Internet via a satellite link using an antenna in the roof which tracks the satellite as the car moves. Safety features include a head-up display that projects onto the windscreen – drivers navigate and check vehicle functions without taking their eyes off the road. The car can include network theft deterrent measures. In an accident, when the airbag inflates, the car itself contacts the emergency services, reporting its exact location. Today's modern luxury car has more computer power than the first manned spacecraft that landed on the Moon.

IBM

This is only the start. Perhaps we will see Philips projecting their logo, through a laser beam, on to the moon, oxygen bars offering 'nutraceuticals' (staple foods packed with vitamins and minerals) and gas for the jet-set hyperactive executives and fun lovers? Memory drugs, male birth control pills and remote control surgery might all affect markets, their structure, the communications channels and communications tools. Without vision and a broad perspective it is easy to get it wrong. Here is what 'experts' said about the technological possibility of telephones, radio, talking films, computers and personal computers.

'This "telephone" has too many shortcomings to be seriously considered as a means of communication. The device is inherently of no value to us.' – Western Union, internal memo, 1876
'The wireless music box has no imaginable commercial value. Who would pay for a message sent to nobody in particular?' – David Sarnoff's associates in response to his urgings for investment in the radio in the 1920s.
'Who the hell wants to hear actors talk?' – Harry M Warner, Warner Bros, 1927
'I think there is a world market for maybe five computers.' – Thomas Watson, Chairman of IBM, 1943
'There is no reason for any individuals to have a computer in their home.' – Ken Olsen, President, Chairman and founder of Digital Equipment Corp, 1977

Figure 8.4 shows the ever-accelerating speed with which new ideas are adopted. An open mind helps to exploit trends and emerging opportunities earlier than a closed mind. Change is constant. It churns up new opportunities and threats in all markets. The only certainty is

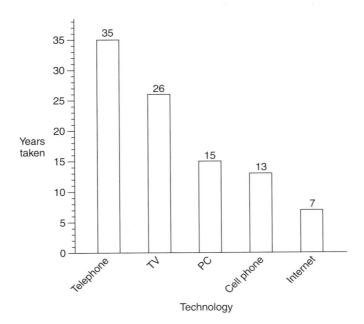

Figure 8.4 Years taken to achieve 25 per cent market penetration

that all markets constantly pull away from the status quo, fuelled by an ever-increasing array of variables easily categorized under the PEST factors. It is every marketer's responsibility to observe, analyse and anticipate future developments in the marketplace and, in particular, in the changing communications environment.

APPENDIX 8.1

Lack of European advertising harmony

NEWSPAPER ADVERTISING RESTRICTIONS

	Alcohol	Tobacco	Food	Cosmetics & Personal Hygiene Products	Non-Prescription Medicinal Products	Cleaning & Household Products	Children & Advertising	Political Advertising	Religious Advertising
Austria	®v	®v	®	✓	®v	✓	®v	✓	✗
Belgium	®v	®	®/®v	®v	®	®	®v	✓	✓
Denmark	®	®v	®	✓	®/®v	✓	®v	✓	✓
Finland	®	✗	✓	✓	®v	✓	✓	→ ®	®
France	®	®/✗	®	®	®/®v	®v	®v	®/®v	®
Germany	®v	®v	®	✓	®v	✓	®v	✓	✓
Greece	®	→	✓	✓	✗	®v	✓	®	®
Ireland	®v	®	®v	®v	®	✓	®v	®v	®v
Italy	®v	✗	®v	®v	®	✓	®v	®	®
Luxembourg	✓	®	®	✓	®	✓	®v	✓	✓
Netherlands	®v	®/®v	®v	®v	®v	®v	®v	✓	✓
Norway	✗	✗	®	✓	®/®v	✓	✓	✓	✓
Portugal	✓	✗	✓	✓	®	✓	®	®	®
Spain	®v/✗	®	®	®	®	✓	®v	®	®
Sweden	✗/®	✗	®v	✓	®v	✓	®v	✓	✓
Switzerland	®v	®v	®	®	✓	®	✓	✓	✓
Turkey	✓	®	✓	✓	®	✓	®	®	®
United Kingdom	®v	®v	®v	®v	®v	✓	®v	®v	®v

MAGAZINE ADVERTISING RESTRICTIONS

	Alcohol	Tobacco	Food	Cosmetics & Personal Hygiene Products	Non-Prescription Medicinal Products	Cleaning & Household Products	Children & Advertising	Political Advertising	Religious Advertising
Austria	®v	®v	®	✓	®v	✓	®v	✓	✗
Belgium	®v	®	®/®v	®v	®	®	®v	✓	✓
Denmark	®	®v	®	✓	®/®v	✓	®v	✓	✓
Finland	®	✗	✓	✓	®v	✓	✓	®	®
France	®/✗	®/✗	®	®	®/®v	®v	®v	®/®v	®
Germany	®v	®v	®	✓	®v	✓	®v	✓	✓
Greece	®	®/®v[1]	✓	✓	✗	®v	✓	®	®
Ireland	®v	®/✗[2]	®v	®v	®	✓	®v	®v	®v
Italy	®v	✗	®v	®v	®	✓	®v	®	®
Luxembourg	✓	®	®	✓	®	✓	®v	✓	✓
Netherlands	®v	®/®v	®v	®v	®v	®v	®v	✓	✓
Norway	✗	✗	®	✓	®/®v	✓	✓	✓	✓
Portugal	✓	✗	✓	✓	®	✓	®	®	®
Spain	®v/✗	®	®	®	®	✓	®v	®	®
Sweden	®/✗[3]	✗	®v	✓	®v	✓	®v	✓	✓
Switzerland	®v	®v	®	®	✓	®	✓	✓	✓
Turkey	✓	®/✗	✓	✓	®	✓	®	®	®
United Kingdom	®v	®v	®v	®v	®v	✓	®v	®v	®v

Notes: [1] Health warning 10% of surface. [2] Health warning 15% of surface. Banned in publications directed to people under 18. [3] Banned over 1.8% volume.

Key to all tables: ✗ : Banned by law   ® : Restricted by law   ✗v : Banned voluntarily   ®v : Restricted voluntarily   ✓ : Permitted

Source for all tables: *European Advertising & Media Yearbook, 2000*

TELEVISION ADVERTISING RESTRICTIONS

	Alcohol	Tobacco	Food	Cosmetics & Personal Hygiene Products	Non-Prescription Medicinal Products	Cleaning & Household Products	Children & Advertising	Political Advertising	Religious Advertising
Austria	®v/X	Xv	®	®	®v	✓	®v	®	X
Belgium	Ⓟ	X	®/®v	®v	✓	®	®v	X	X
Denmark	®	Xv	®	✓	X	✓	®	X	X
Finland	®	X	✓	®	®	®	®v	®	®
France	X	X	®	®	®/®v	®	®	®/®v	®
Germany	®v	X	®	✓	®v	✓	®v	✓	✓
Greece	®	X	✓	®v	X	®v	®/ X	®	®
Ireland	®/X¹	X	®	®	®	✓	Ⓟ	X	X
Italy	®v/X	X	®	®v	®	®v	®	®/X	®/X²
Luxembourg	®	X	®	®v	®	✓	®v	✓	✓
Netherlands	®v	X	®/®v	®v	®v	®v	®v	X	X
Norway	®/ X	X	®	✓	X	✓	®	✓	✓
Portugal	®/ X	X	✓	✓	®	✓	®	®	®
Spain	®v/X	X	®	®	®	®	®v	®	®
Sweden	®/ X	X	®v	✓	®v	✓	X	®v	®v
Switzerland	X	X	®	®	✓	®	✓	X	X
Turkey	✓/X	✓/X	✓	®	®	✓	®	®	®
United Kingdom	®/ Xv	®/X³	®	®	®	®	®	®/®v	®

Notes: ¹ Banned for spirits. Restricted for all other alcoholic beverages on content and on broadcast time.   ² Restricted to commercial channels. Must not offend moral, civil or religious convictions.   ³ Banned for cigarette and cigarette tobacco. Restricted for cigars, pipe tobacco, ancillary products and accessories.

RADIO ADVERTISING RESTRICTIONS

	Alcohol	Tobacco	Food	Cosmetics & Personal Hygiene Products	Non-Prescription Medicinal Products	Cleaning & Household Products	Children & Advertising	Political Advertising	Religious Advertising
Austria	®v/X	Xv	®	®	®v	✓	®v	®	X
Belgium	®v	X	®/®v	®v	X	®	®v	X	X
Denmark	®	Xv	®	✓	®	✓	®	✓	✓
Finland	®	X	✓	✓	®	✓	®v	®	®
France	X/ ®	X	®	®	®/®v	®v	®v	®/®v	®
Germany	®v	X	®	✓	®v	✓	®v	✓	✓
Greece	®	X	✓	✓	X	®v	®	®	®
Ireland	®/X¹	X	®	®	Ⓟ	✓	®	X	X
Italy	®v/X	X	®v	®v	®	✓	®v	®/X	®/X²
Luxembourg	®	X	®	®v	®	✓	®v	✓	✓
Netherlands	®v	X	®/®v	®v	®v	®v	®v	X	X
Norway	X/ ®	X	®	✓	X	✓	®	✓	✓
Portugal	®	X	✓	✓	®	✓	®	®	®
Spain	®v/X	®/X³	®	®	®	✓	®v	®	®
Sweden	X/ ®	X	®v	✓	®v	✓	®v	✓	✓
Switzerland	X	X	®	®	®/X	®	✓	X	X
Turkey	✓/X	X	✓	®	®	✓	®	®	®
United Kingdom	®v	®/X⁴	®	®	®	®	®	®/®v	®

Notes: ¹ See 'TV' note 1.   ² See 'TV' note 2.   ³ Only new, low-tar and low-nicotine brands for two-year period following launch.   ⁴ See 'TV' note 3.

Key to all tables: X : Banned by law   Xv : Banned voluntarily   ✓ : Permitted
                     ® : Restricted by law   ®v : Restricted voluntarily

CINEMA ADVERTISING RESTRICTIONS

	Alcohol	Tobacco	Food	Cosmetics & Personal Hygiene Products	Non-Prescription Medicinal Products	Cleaning & Household Products	Children & Advertising	Political Advertising	Religious Advertising
Austria	®v	®v	®	✓	®v	✓	®v	✓	X
Belgium	®v	X	®v/®v	®v	X	®	®v	✓	✓
Denmark	®	Xv	®	✓	X	✓	®v	✓	✓
Finland	®	X	✓	✓	®v	✓	✓	®	®
France	X	X	®	®	®v/®v	®v	®v	®v/®v	®
Germany	®v	®v	®	✓	®v	✓	®v	✓	✓
Greece	®	®	✓	✓	X	®v	✓	®	®
Ireland	®v/X¹	X	®v	®v	®	✓	®	®v	®v
Italy	®v	X	®v	®v	®	✓	®v	®	®
Luxembourg	✓	X	®	✓	®	✓	®v	✓	✓
Netherlands	®v	®v/®v	®v	®v	®v	®v	®v	✓	✓
Norway	®v/X	X	®	✓	X	✓	✓	✓	✓
Portugal	✓	X	✓	✓	®	✓	®	®	®
Spain	®v	®	®	®	®	✓	®v	®	®
Sweden	®v/X	X	®v	✓	®v	✓	®v	✓	✓
Switzerland	®v/X	®v	®	®	®	®	✓	✓	✓
Turkey	✓	✓	✓	✓	X	✓	®	®	®
United Kingdom	®v	®v/X²	®v	®v	®v	✓	®	®v	®v

Notes: ¹ Banned for spirits. Voluntarily restricted for other alcoholic beverages. ² See 'TV' note 3. Also health warning over 30% of screen for 4 seconds.

OUTDOOR ADVERTISING RESTRICTIONS

	Alcohol	Tobacco	Food	Cosmetics & Personal Hygiene Products	Non-Prescription Medicinal Products	Cleaning & Household Products	Children & Advertising	Political Advertising	Religious Advertising
Austria	®v	®v	®	✓	®v	✓	®v	✓	X
Belgium	®v	®	®v/®v	®v	X	®	®v	✓	✓
Denmark	®	Xv	®	✓	X	✓	®v	✓	✓
Finland	®	X	✓	✓	®v	✓	✓	®	®
France	✓	X	®	®	®v/®v	®v	®v	®v/®v	®
Germany	®v	®v	®	✓	®v	✓	®v	✓	✓
Greece	®	®	✓	✓	X	®v	✓	®	®
Ireland	®v	X	®v	®v	®	✓	®v	®v	®v
Italy	®v	X	®v	®v	®	✓	®v	®	®
Luxembourg	✓	®	®	✓	®	✓	®v	✓	✓
Netherlands	®v	®v/®v	®v	®v	®v	®v	®v	✓	✓
Norway	X	X	®	✓	X	✓	✓	✓	✓
Portugal	✓	®v/X	✓	✓	®	✓	®	®	®
Spain	®v/X	®v/X¹	®	®	®	✓	®v	®	®
Sweden	®v/X	X	®v	✓	®v	✓	®v	✓	✓
Switzerland	®v/X	®v/®v	®	®	✓	®	✓	✓	✓
Turkey	✓	®v/X	✓	✓	X	✓	®	®	®
United Kingdom	®v	®v	®v	®v	®v	✓	®v	®v	®v

Note: ¹ Banned in Cataluña and the Basque country.

Key to all tables:
X : Banned by law Xv : Banned voluntarily ✓ : Permitted
® : Restricted by law ®v : Restricted voluntarily

Source for all tables: EAAA – European Association of Advertising Agencies.

APPENDIX 8.2

Fighting the enemy of recession with its own images

Moods, aspirations and tones of communications also vary according to the state of the economy. This is how some US advertisers are reported to advertise during a recession.

During a recession everything out there repeatedly tells the consumer 'don't spend, don't spend'. People are irritated if tempted to buy things they think they cannot (or should not) afford. So some US recession-related campaigns use the recession as part of the 'reason to buy'. The advertisements give the consumer 'permission' to buy. This breaks down into three basic arguments:

1. *You need this* – advertisements like those for Armani go back to basics with copy which reads: 'Clothing. Basics. Period.' Professor Ralph Whitehead of the University of Massachusetts says that they are 'back to basics in content but very slick and stylish in form; in substance they recall the older practice of citing product features rather than lifestyles, but they achieve this with contemporary cinematic style.' The Gap clothing store has attempted the 'basic but best' with the 'no frills dressing, essentials not whims' approach.

2. *You deserve this* – arguably a more feminine and soothing approach to help to calm the bruising from the recession. Advertisements and images articulate how the recession-bruised consumers really feel inside. They conjure up feelings of sympathy and under-standing, followed by a suggestion that consumers should treat themselves. The permission can be reinforced by rationalizing with suggestions like 'if you don't give yourself a break or a treat, then you are likely to under-perform anyway.'

3. *It is your responsibility to buy this* – the ex-US president George Bush Snr. promoted spending during his last Christmas in office. Ellen Goodman of the *Boston Globe* reported: 'There is the implication that anyone who truly loves their country and wants it to recover from this recession will contribute this season to the hundreds of needy malls. We're all supposed to be buying not just for Aunt Evelyn but for Uncle Sam.'

APPENDIX 8.3

Sample of complaints against advertisements upheld by the ASA

ASSET WINDOWS LTD
Unit 16
Clifton Industrial Estate
Cherry Hinton Road
Cambridge CB1 4WT

Complaint: Objection to a drop leaflet for windows, featuring the written testimonial "My wife and I have never seen such dedicated craftsmanship. I am pleased that we chose Asset Windows." The complainants, whose names were printed below the testimonial, maintained that although their windows were installed by Asset, they did not make the statement, nor did they give their permission for the use of any such testimonial. (B.10.2/3/7; B.17.1.1)

Conclusion: Complaint upheld. The advertisers submitted a copy of the completion document relating to this particular job. It included a questionnaire and carried, in handwriting, the comments reproduced in the advertisement. On being sent a copy of this document by the Authority, the complainants said they had not seen it before, denied making the comments it contained and disowned the handwriting. The Authority was concerned that the advertisers had presented what appeared to be fictitious testimonial, and noted that this would have been apparent if the complainants had been asked to sign the statement and give express prior permission for its use in advertisements [both requirements of the Code]. The advertisers were requested to comply with the Code in future testimonial claims.

Complaint from: March, Cambridgeshire

Barclays Bank Plc
PO Box 120
Longwood Close
Westwood Business Park
Coventry CV4 8JN

Agency:
Dean Street Marketing

Leaflet

Complaint from:
West Midlands

Complaint: Objection to a leaflet to enter Barclays Bank Christmas Competition which included, under "Competition Rules", the condition that "The Bank may amend these rules or withdraw the competition altogether at any time without notice". The complainant objected that the condition was in breach of the Code. (BCSPP 4.2; 6.2.2)

Conclusion: Complaint upheld
The advertisers stated that the clause had been introduced in order to allow withdrawal in the event of unforeseen circumstances that might be detrimental to either the advertisers or the customer – eg. new legislation deeming the competition illegal, or where a promotion was considered politically insensitive. While the Authority concluded that such a clause would be acceptable if it were made clear that it related to circumstances outside the control of the advertisers, they were requested to amend future advertising material accordingly

---

British Airways
Heathrow Airport
Hounslow
Middlesex TW6 2JA
(Previous complaints upheld during last 12 months: 1)

Agency:
Saatchi & Saatchi Advertising Ltd

**Press
Complaints from:**
Middlesex, Warwickshire

Complaint: Objections to a national press advertisement headed "British Airways would like to offer you a flying start to 1992. An extra 500 Air Miles." The complainants objected that the advertisement, which gave details of when the offer applied, did not make clear that the offer was limited to one application per person. (BCSPP 4.5; 5.8).

Adjudication: Complaints upheld.
The advertisers acknowledged that there had been an oversight and apologised. The Authority noted that the advertisement would not appear again, but advised the advertisers to take greater care when devising advertising for future promotions and reminded them that sales promotions should be designed and conducted so as not to cause avoidable disappointment.

Benetton Spa
Villa Minelli
31050 Ponzano
Veneto Treviso
Italy
(Previous complaints upheld during last 12 months: 2)

Press

Complaints from:
London, Leicestershire

Complaint: Objections to an advertisement in The Face magazine captioned "United Colors of Benetton" featuring a man with wasted features apparently suffering from AIDS, prostrate on a bed, being comforted by two other men one of whom had his cheek pressed against the sufferer. The advertisement also featured a distressed woman at the bedside comforting a child. The complainants considered the advertisement extremely offensive and distressing. (B 3.1; B 15.2)

Conclusion: Complaints upheld.
The Authority considered the advertisement to be in breach of the Code. It was noted that, before publication, the Committee of Advertising Practice had advised both the advertisers and media that the advertisement was likely to cause offence and occasion distress. The Face magazine stated that, while they considered that the advertisement may cause offence to some readers, they had published it so that readers would be aware of Benetton's disregard for the sensitivities of the public. The Authority was concerned that the advice of the Committee of Advertising Practice had not been heeded. It deplored the advertisers' apparent willingness to provoke distress with their advertising approach and requested them to withdraw the advertisement.

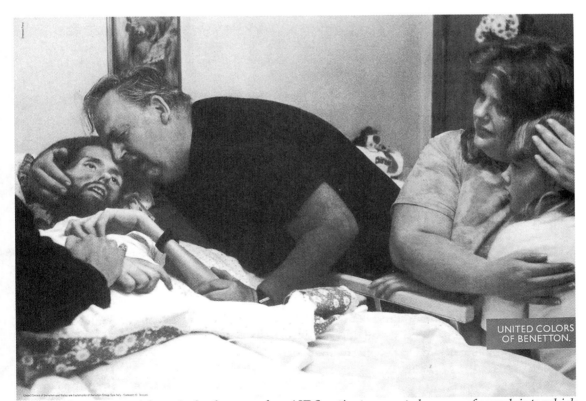

Benetton's controversial tragic death scene of an AIDS patient generated a wave of complaints which the ASA upheld

Key points from Chapter 8:

1. Markets constantly move away from products.
2. Monitoring and exploiting the changing PEST factors can create competitive advantage.

FURTHER READING

Adams, R, Carruthers, J and Hamil, S (1991) *Changing Corporate Values*, Kogan Page, London

Adams, R, Carruthers, J and Hamil, S (1991) *Shopping for a Better World*, Kogan Page, London

The Central Statistical Office, *Social Trends* (annual) gives demographic breakdowns and forecasts

Cetron, M and Davies, O (1992) *The Futurist* (World Future Society), summarized in *Crystal Globe: The Haves and Have Nots of the New World Order*, St Martin's Press, New York

Doyle, P (1992) What are excellent companies? *Journal of Marketing Management* **8**, pp 101–16

Grey International Advertising Inc (1992) *The Post-recession Marketplace: Life in the Slow Lane*

Gwyer, M (1992) Britain bracing for the age bomb, *Independent on Sunday*, 29 March

Knowlton, C (1991) Shell gets rich by beating risk, *Fortune*, 26 August, pp 51–53

MacNamara, W (1991) A New Discipline, *Marketing Week*, 6 December, pp 34–37

Ohmae, K (1983) *The Mind of the Strategist*, Penguin Business Library, London

Ohmae, K (1985) *Triad Power: The Coming Shape of Global Competition*, Free Press, New York

Ohmae, K (1990) *The Borderless World*, Collins, London

Pohl, M (1991) UK unaware of legal pitfalls in US, *Marketing Week*, 13 September

Rijkens, R (1992) *European Advertising Strategies*, Cassell, London

FURTHER CONTACTS

The Advertising Standards Authority (ASA), 2 Torrington Place, London WC1E 7HW (tel: 020 7580 5555; Web site: www.asa.org)

Broadcast Advertising Clearance Centre (BACC), 200 Grays Inn Road, London WC1X 8HF (tel: 020 7843 8000; Web site: www.bacc.org.uk)

The Department of Trade and Industry (DTI), Victoria Street, London SW1H 0ET (tel: 020 7200 1992; Web site: dti.gov.uk)

European Association of Communication Agencies (EACA), EACA Secretariat, 152 Boulevarde Brand Whitlock, B-1200 Brussels, Belgium (tel: 00 32 2 7400710; Web site: www.eaca.be)

European Marketing Confederation, Secretariat: Place des Chasseurs Ardennais 20, B-1030 Brussels, Belgium (tel: 00 32 2 7421780; Web site: www.emc.be)

Fax Preference Service, 5th Floor, Haymarket House, 1 Oxenden Street, London SW1Y 4EE (tel: 020 7766 4422; fax: 020 7976 1886; Web site: www.dma.org.uk)

The Independent Television Commission (ITC), 33 Foley Street, London W1P 7TL (tel: 020 7255 3000; Web site: www.itc.org.uk)

Independent Television Network Ltd (formerly ITVA), 200 Grays Inn Road, London WC1X 8HF (tel: 020 7843 8000; Web site: www.itv.co.uk)

Institute of Practitioners in Advertising (IPA), 44 Belgrave Square, London SW1X 8QS (tel: 020 7235 7020; Web site: www.ipa.co.uk)

Institute of Public Relations (IPR), The Old Trading House, 15 Northburgh Street, London EC1V 0JR (tel: 020 7253 5151; Web site: www.ipr.org.uk)

Institute of Sales Promotion (ISP), Arena House, 66–68 Pentonville Road, London N1 9HS (tel: 020 7837 5340; Web site: www.isp.org.uk)

Public Relations Consultants Association (PRCA), Willow House, Willow Place, London SW1P 1JH (tel: 020 7233 6026; Web site: www.prca.org.uk)

9

International marketing communications

Globalization of markets 236; *The global opportunity – is it really happening? 236; Respecting global complexity 236; Touching a global nerve 238; Forces driving globalization 239; The elite global players 240; Below-the-surface similarities 240;* Global difficulties 241; *Language 242; Literacy 243; Colour 243; Gestures 243; Culture 244; Original national identity 244; Media availability 244; Media overlap 245; Lack of media data 245; Lack of media credibility 245; Varying media characteristics 245; Different media usage 245; Different media standards 246; Different cost structures 246; Legal restrictions 246; Competition 246; Non-global names 246;* Global misses 247; *Wrong names 247; Wrong strapline 248; Wrong product 248;* Strategic global options 249; *Global marketing strategy 250; Global advertising strategy 251; Four global advertising strategies 252; Advantages of central strategy and central production 254; Disadvantages of central strategy and central production 255; Agencies in the international arena 256; Choosing an international agency or independent local agency 256; Advantages of using an international agency 257; Disadvantages of using an international agency 257; The key to successful central communications 257;* Case study 9.1: *American Express: Blue V2 258;* Appendix 9.1: *Is Europe united? 264;* Appendix 9.2: *Western weirdos 265;* Appendix 9.3: *Those weird working Brits 267;* Appendix 9.4: *Difficult to work with other European cultures? 267;* Appendix 9.5: *An international business dialogue gone wrong 268;* Appendix 9.6: *Translation tips 270;* Further reading 271

GLOBALIZATION OF MARKETS

This chapter examines opportunities and the difficulties, strategic options and actual implications for implementation of international marketing communications, in particular global communications.

The global opportunity – is it really happening?

Today yoghurt, pizza, spaghetti, rice, kebabs, Indian cuisine, Chinese meals, Mexican food and American burgers are both popular and easily available in many countries around the world. The Rolling Stones and Shakespeare also have a universal appeal. There are more people learning English in China than speak it in the USA. Back in 1985 approximately one billion people from different time zones across the world watched the Live Aid charity concert simultaneously. In 1998 almost two billion people watched football's World Cup final. Perhaps the global village is still growing? A European football league has emerged among Europe's best clubs. The London to Brussels train is quicker than that from London to Newcastle. Perhaps clichés like 'the world is getting smaller' are nothing more than oversimplified generalizations cast upon a culturally complex world? See Is 'Europe united?', Appendix 9.1, on page 264. Some say that human beings have more things that bind them together than separate them; others that market differences are greater than market similarities. There are, in fact, what Young and Rubicam advertising agency call cross-cultural consumer characteristics. These identify the common ground. The man or woman living in a smart apartment block in London's Knightsbridge probably has got more in common with his or her counterpart living in a smart apartment block off New York's Central Park than he or she has with someone living in a drab south London suburb. There are indeed some common denominators and some common sets of needs and aspirations that can be identified, particularly in similarities of lifestyle. Suffice it to say that the young and the rich have very similar tastes throughout the world.

Respecting global complexity

The total global concept suggests that the big global marketing players can accelerate the globalization process by transcending cultural boundaries and bringing their messages, goods, services and traditions to the markets they choose. Here are some seemingly bizarre cultural norms that suggest that the total global concept will not happen, at least not in the next few generations. Lailan Young (1985) reports that the Barusho bride in the Himalayas has a tough time on her wedding night as she has to share the bridal bed with her mother-in-law until the marriage is consummated.

Post-natal male exhaustion

On the other side of the world, in the southern Indian state of Kerala, Puyala women return to the fields to tend the crops after the birth of their babies, while the husband goes to bed. The rest of the family ministers to his needs until he recovers. In the Andaman Islands especially anxious husbands will stay in bed for anything up to six months.

Lailan Young (1985)

The lost kingdom of the Minaros was 'discovered' in a mountain hideaway 16,000 feet up in the Himalayas by a French explorer in 1984. The Amazon-like women totally dominate their men, marrying several at a time and keeping them in line by brute force. The former Kwakiutl of Vancouver Island demonstrate what is almost a parody of industrial civilization: the chief motive of this tribe was rivalry, which was not concerned with the usual concerns of providing for a family or owning goods, but rather the aim of outdoing and shaming neighbours and rivals by means of conspicuous consumption. At their potlatch ceremonies these people competed with each other in burning and destroying their valuable possessions and money. This is in contrast to the Dobu of north-west Melanesia. This culture is reported to encourage malignant hatred and animosity. Treacherous conduct unmitigated by any concept of mercy or kindness and directed against neighbours and friends is expected. The Zuni (a branch of the Pueblos of New Mexico) are a people whose life is centred on religious ceremonial, being prosperous but without interest in economic advancement. They admire most those men who are friendly, make no trouble and have no aspirations, detesting, on the other hand, those who wish to become leaders. Hence tribal leaders have to be compelled by threats to accept their position and are regarded with contempt and resentment once they have achieved it. Even cultures that are relatively better known have their own intricacies over something as simple as a handshake, eye contact and the use of colours. For example, brown/grey is disapproved of in Nicaragua; white, purple and black are the colours of death for Japan, Latin America and Britain, respectively.

Understanding other cultures – the oppressed male

The Kagba women of North Colombia not only practise free love but free rape, and few men are safe.

Lailan Young (1985)

If you think some of this is strange, see how strange other cultures view the seemingly bizarre behaviour patterns of the tea-drinking, nose-blowing, ballroom dancing and kissing population of Europe in Appendix 9.2, on page 265; or see how other Europeans view the British approach to business in Appendix 9.3, on page 267. See how Europeans view each other... believe it or not somewhere in Europe there is a belief that the Germans are messy and unpunctual (Appendix 9.4, page 267). Finally, in the context of being apparently normal, Geertz (1983) offers an insight:

> the world... does not divide into the pious and the superstitious... there are sculptures in jungles and paintings in deserts... political order is possible without centralized power and principled justice without codified rules; the norms of reason were not fixed in Greece, the evolution of morality not consummated in England... We have, with no little success, sought to keep the world off balance, pulling out rugs, upsetting tea tables, setting off fire crackers. It has been the office of others to reassure; ours to unsettle.

Touching a global nerve

Despite the complexities of cultural idiosyncrasies, there are many common needs that manifest themselves into common wants and purchasing patterns, particularly where there are similar levels of economic wealth. It follows that if a manufacturer, or service supplier, targets roughly the same socio-demographic groups in different countries and touches a common nerve within these target markets, then the same product or service can be packaged and promoted in a uniform manner. The pricing and distribution may vary but the branding, packaging and even the advertising can be the same. The manufacturers of world brands can therefore position their products in a similar manner in the minds of millions across many different cultures. This is the result of careful analysis and planning by expert marketing professionals rather than a trial-and-error approach to market extension. See how Rosabeth Moss Kanter described the effect global convergence had on her son on page 37.

The next challenge lies in moving the rest of the communications mix in a uniform manner so that not just advertising and packaging but also sales promotions, direct mail, sponsorship, etc, reap the benefits of a global approach. This globalization issue has revealed itself through the increased use of the Internet. Even local firms going on to the Net attract customers from all over the world. A Web presence equals a global presence, whether you like it or not. Pepsi have discovered Internet difficulties with their European blue can being seen by its US customers, who much prefer the traditional red can. Similarly, Tia Maria, although it is consumed around the world, has different age segments in different countries, eg in the UK Tia Maria is about girl power, targeted at 18- to 24-year-olds, while in The Netherlands it's drunk neat by pensioners. Now this 'common nerve' presents a

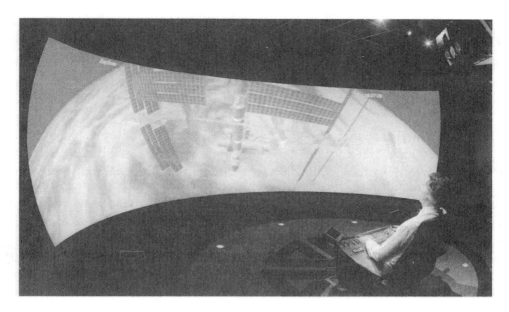

The world is getting smaller via TV, the Internet, and international buyers scouring the world, among many other driving forces. Photo courtesy of Trimension Ltd

positioning challenge. Despite these difficulties, Coke and computers have proved that large, lucrative global markets do exist.

Forces driving globalization

It is not just a product-orientated corporate push for growth but more of a market-orientated reaction to the emergence of common global lifestyles and needs. These are emerging as cheap travel combined with higher disposable incomes which allow travellers to leap across borders, visit other cultures and return home with a little bit of that culture's soul in their own. Television itself has brought into the sitting rooms of Europe's homes pictures and images of America's *Sopranos*, Australia's *Neighbours*, Africa's famines and atrocities, and Tiananmen Square's students. It has also brought stunning scenes from the depths of the oceans, the balmy beaches of the Caribbean, the rugged beauty of the bush and the once rich and fertile Amazon rainforest. This global awareness is exploited by the corporate push for growth, which has forced many suppliers from saturated local markets to venture into overseas markets. Improved production, distribution and marketing techniques have accelerated the movement of products and services from all around the world into local markets. Professional buyers now scour the world in pursuit of new suppliers. The Internet gives immediate access to literally a world of new sources. Political barriers are falling in China and the eastern bloc and, of course, Europe's own internal political barriers are being dismalted also. The doors of the world's markets are opening. The key, it seems, is to identify core benefits that are common to different cultures along with any relevant cultural idiosyncrasies.

The elite global players

The significant benefits derived from a global brand and a global communications strategy are currently reserved for a relatively small number of players. This elite brand of players recognize the right conditions and apply thorough research and planning to exploit the brand's assets on a global scale. Although Rein Rijkens (1991) has identified a 'trend towards greater internationalization and centralization', it should be remembered that a single communications strategy (incorporating everything from branding to the complete range of communications tools) rarely works for all the players operating in international markets. The desire to harness the global opportunity is natural because international markets offer huge rewards. They also present intricate problems. Careful cultural homework needs to be included in the detailed research and planning that goes below the surface.

Below-the-surface similarities

Similar buying behaviour and buying patterns do not necessarily mean a uniform market with uniform needs, uniform communications channels, uniform decision-making processes, uniform decision-making units, or even uniform reasons for buying. Take the case of buying premium priced water. In a Khartoum slum an impoverished family pay 20 times the price paid by families with water main connections, while half a world away a middle-class family buy bottles of mineral water. This demonstrates 'unreal similarities'. The buyers appear to behave similarly by purchasing expensive water. They are, however, very different; in fact they are from totally dissimilar groups with different aspirations, motivations, lifestyles and attitudes, not to mention disposable income. On the surface there is a market for private water in both countries, but the distribution channels, communications channels, advertising messages and levels of disposable income are poles apart.

   An analysis that goes below the surface (or below the sales results) will reveal a range of different motives, aspirations, lifestyles and attitudes to the same product. Surface information can create a false sense of simplicity. International markets can also suggest surface solutions that ignore the cultural complexities and intricacies of distant markets. As Sir John Harvey-Jones once warned (1988):

   Operating in this milieu requires much greater sensitivity to national differences than we are accustomed to having. The mere fact that one stays in the same sort of hotel almost anywhere in the world, that one arrives in the same sort of car, that it is now possible to call by telephone or telex directly from almost anywhere in the world, all gives a superficial feeling of sameness which is desperately misleading and must never be taken for granted.

Globalization, intertwined with cultural idiosyncrasies, appears to be emerging in many markets around the world. The marketing maxim 'think global, act local' remains valid. The challenge goes beyond communicating with new international customers and into working with international partners whose idiosyncrasies and languages pose many problems. Take nomenclature for a moment. The French normally refer to advertising as 'publicité', which can cause some confusion, while the Yugoslavian word for advertising is 'propaganda'. Other cultures have difficulty translating 'marketing', 'marketing communications' or 'advertising' as they have not yet created such words.

Despite all this, globalization is occurring and offering huge rewards.

Rudyard Kipling's advice to McDonald's

'Asia is not going to be civilised under the methods of the west. There is too much Asia and she is too old.'

Rudyard Kipling (1891)

McDonald's India now offers tailored products for the Indian market – mutton, chicken, fish and vegetable products, not beef, pork or their by-products. The Big Mac is called Maharaja Mac.

GLOBAL DIFFICULTIES

International markets are riddled with hidden cultural differences that make global advertising an intriguing challenge even for the most capable international marketing expert. Here are some of the intricacies that contribute towards the difficulty of global marketing:

- language;
- literacy;
- colour;
- gestures;
- culture;
- original national identity;

- media availability;
- media overlap;
- lack of media data;
- lack of media credibility;
- varying media characteristics;
- different media usage;
- different media standards;
- different cost structures;
- legal restrictions;
- competition;
- non-global names.

Language

Language obviously requires translating, although there are exceptions to the rule (where the language reflects beneficial cultural aspects of the product, eg Audi's *Vorsprung durch Technik* strapline). Some expressions simply do not translate (see 'Wrong strapline' on page 248). See also Majaro's translating tips in Appendix 9.6 (page 270).

Language barriers can be expensive

Trillion (after million):
The product of a million raised to a third power
(America and France.) Million million (1,(000,000),(000,000))

New English Dictionary, 1932

Britain and Germany, the nos. represented by 1 followed by 18 zeros, ie 1,(000,000), (000,000), (000,000)

Collins Pocket Dictionary, 1992

What is that as a percentage?

Billion:

In American and French, a thousand million 1,000(000,000); in English and German, a million million 1,(000,000), (000,000)

Literacy

In many developing countries literacy is low (Dudley, 1989). This limits the amount of explanation in advertising. Even with high literacy the reading of translated Western-style advertisements still causes problems, eg before and after toothpaste advertisements which are not adjusted for Arabs, who read from right to left.

Language, literacy and logic

Combine these three in the international arena and a new challenge emerges – writing instructions – a skill in one language, a complex skill in several. Try this set of instructions for 'knapsack'.

Directions for assembling:

1. Lead for hind leg in an opened position.
2. Lead the frame of the sack support up.
3. Insert the blushing for blocking in the proper split, push it deeply and wheel in an anti-time sense till it stops.

Colour

Colour has a direct access to our emotions. Watch how red is commonly used in advertising in the West. Colour, however, does not have uniform meaning across the world; for example, blue in Iran means immorality, white in Japan is death (hence McDonald's white-faced Ronald McDonald has problems). All Asians associate red with prosperity and good luck. If we take the example of a financial services Web site: if an Asian see *no* red, he or she will leave; if a Westerner sees red, he or she will leave.

Gestures

Humour is rarely globally appreciated, and even basic body gestures are not global. In some parts of India shaking the head from left to right means 'yes'. Touching the lower eyelid may be just an itch but it also suggests to a South American señorita that you are making a pass, or to a Saudi that he is stupid. Scratching an earlobe has five different meanings in five Mediterranean countries: 'You're a sponger' (Spaniard), 'You'd better watch it' (Greek),

'You're a sneaky little...' (Maltese), 'Get lost you pansy!' (Italian), while a Portuguese will feel really pleased. Even thumbs up is deemed to be a devastatingly obscene gesture to a Sardinian woman. Thrusting your palms towards someone's face may be meant to be endearing but to a Greek there is no greater insult, since this gesture is called a 'moutza' and comes from the Byzantine custom of smearing filth from the gutter in the face of condemned criminals. The A-OK gesture (thumb and index finger in a circle with the rest of the fingers open) means money to a Japanese, zero in France, 'OK' in America and 'I'll kill you' in Tunisia.

Culture

Culture creates a quagmire of marketing problems: religion, sex, eating, greeting, habits, lifestyles, the role of women, the list is endless. Ferraro (1990) points out nine critical dimensions that contrast the United States with the rest of the world's cultures. She says that US culture places a high value on (a) individualism, (b) a precise reckoning of time, (c) a future orientation, (d) work and achievement, (e) control over the natural environment, (f) youthfulness, (g) informality, (h) competition and (i) relative equality of the sexes.

As always, the Web complicates matters. For example, Scandinavians are reluctant to use credit cards, the currency of the Internet; the French dislike revealing personal information; the Germans prefer to pay with a cheque, after delivery of the goods.

Original national identity

National identity can be an asset or a liability. For example Dudley (1989) reports that Marathon Oil makes a point of stressing its US association in Italy, where American high technology is beneficial, but in Germany Marathon avoids the issue of its American parentage because of the German concern over US control in the German energy industry.

Media availability

Television is sometimes unavailable since (a) developing countries to not have a high penetration of televisions in domestic households, (b) some countries do not have commercial TV stations, and (c) others do but they restrict the amount of advertising time. Unilever and BAT make their own medium available in East Africa by running their own mobile cinemas.

TV helps

The further away from a TV screen, however, the more difficult many experts say it becomes to create and to deliver a pan-European message.

Financial Times, 1993

Media overlap

Television, radio and the Internet from one market can spill over into other markets, eg half the Canadian population has access to American television. Kahler and Kramer (1977) report that 'Belgium, with no commercial TV, can be reached through two Dutch, three French, three German, two English, and one Luxembourg channel.'

Lack of media data

Great Britain and Ireland have well-structured and categorized media analysis data (audited data). Without reliable media data the optimum cost and effectiveness of the overall campaign is unlikely to be achieved. Properly structured media markets are easier to work in.

Lack of media credibility

Unregulated or poorly regulated media in some countries may flaunt the principles of legality, decency, honesty and truth, which in turn may make these media untrustworthy or create audience scepticism about the particular source of information.

Varying media characteristics

Coverage, cost and reproduction qualities can and do vary from country to country.

Different media usage

Kahler and Kramer (1977) suggest that the British tend to see TV as a visual medium, while TV to the Americans is a visual accompaniment to words.

Different media standards

A lack of uniformity of standards means that different types of both film and artwork may be required for different markets, eg different page sizes may require different artwork, which increases cost.

Different cost structures

Different countries have different forms of negotiation and bartering. The Americans and the Japanese are poles apart. In less developed countries cash may not be available but barter, or counter trading, can offer an acceptable alternative.

Legal restrictions

Whether voluntary codes or actual law, there is as yet no harmonized set of laws or regulations. This presents the advertiser with different problems in different countries. As Majaro (1982) says, 'In Germany, superlatives are forbidden by law. In Sweden, misdemeanours by advertisers may be charged under the criminal law with severe penalties.' Table 8.1 on page 211 shows the range of varying television regulations just across Europe. The table in Appendix 8.1 on page 226 shows the varying press, print, cinema and radio restrictions applied in Europe alone. Web sites complicate things further. For example, Land's End's Web site in Germany cannot mention its unconditional refund policy because German retailers successfully sued in court. (They normally do not allow returns after 14 days.)

Competition

Different markets have different key players using different strengths. For example, Ford's position of 'safety engineering' worked in many countries but not in Sweden, where, of course, Volvo occupied the position. Competition may react in different ways in different markets.

Non-global names

Some brand names simply restrict themselves from seizing the global opportunity. The section on Global misses lists many unfortunate examples.

Central agency, local creative

The trend towards using the same creative work across Europe is developing more slowly than the tendency to use the same advertising agency network.

Rachel Kaplan

GLOBAL MISSES

Some marketers carefully choose names that work for their local domestic market. This insular perspective more than likely restricts any future growth opportunities into international markets and almost certainly restricts the brand from developing into a global brand.

Wrong names

Here are a few examples:

- Sic (French soft drink);
- Pschitt (French soft drink);
- Lillet (French soft drink);
- Creap (Japanese coffee creamer);
- Irish Mist (in Germany 'mist' means manure);
- Bum (Spanish potato crisp);
- Bonka (Spanish coffee);
- Trim Pecker Trouser (Japanese germ bread);
- Gorilla Balls (American protein supplement);
- My Dung (restaurant);
- Cul toothpaste (pronounced 'cue' in France, which means 'anus');
- Scratch (German non-abrasive bath cleaner);
- Super-Piss (Finnish car lock anti-freeze);
- Spunk (jelly-baby sweet from Iceland).

Even sophisticated marketers get it wrong. General Motors discovered that Nova meant 'it won't go' (no va) in South America. Ford launched the Pinto in Brazil and soon realized that it was slang for 'tiny male genitals'. Coca-Cola's phonetic translation in China meant 'Bite the wax tadpole'. After launching into English-speaking markets, Japan's second largest tourist agency was surprised to receive a steady influx of enquiries for sex tours. The Kinki Nippon Tourist Company soon changed its name.

These translation problems are not insurmountable. For example, Curtis shampoo changed its name from 'Everynight' to 'Everyday' for the Swedish market, since the Swedes wash their hair in the mornings. Mars changed their well-known 'Marathon Bar' to 'Snickers' to fit in with the worldwide brand name communications strategy.

Wrong strapline

The New York Tourist Board found 'I love New York' difficult to translate into Norwegian since there are only two Norwegian verbs that come close: one translation is 'I enjoy New York', which lacks something, and the other is 'I have a sexual relationship with New York'. Kentucky Fried Chicken's 'finger-lickin' good' came out in China as 'eat your fingers off'. Frank Perdu's slogan 'It takes a tough man to make a tender chicken' was misunderstood when translated as: 'It takes a sexually excited man to make a chick sensual'. Coors puts its 'Turn it loose' slogan into Spanish where it read 'suffer from diarrhoea'. Scandinavian vacuum cleaner manufacturer Electrolux used this in a US campaign: 'Nothing sucks like an Electrolux'. When Gerber first sold baby food in Africa it (1) put a Caucasian baby on the label and (2) didn't realize that in Africa companies routinely put pictures on the label to show what's inside, as there is a high rate of illiteracy. When Parker Pen marketed its ballpoint pen in Mexico, its advertisements were supposed to read: 'It won't leak in your pocket and embarrass you'. Unfortunately *embarazar* does not mean embarrass. It means 'impregnate', so the slogan had an entirely inappropriate meaning. Braniff ran advertisements on Spanish-language radio announcing leather seats: 'Fly Braniff *en cuero*'. *En cuero* means 'in leather' but sounds identical to *en cueros* when spoken quickly. *En Cueros* means 'naked'. Mitsubushi Pajero had problems since 'Pajero' in some parts of the Spanish-speaking world means a 'liar', in others a 'plumber' and in others something much much worse. Other expressions that are sometimes imprecisely translated include US cigarettes with low asphalt (tar), computer underwear (softwear) and wet sheep (hydraulic rams).

Wrong product

In the attempt to get the packaging, advertising and branding right, global marketers can sometimes forget the fundamental product and whether it is suitable for the market in the first place, leading to campaign failure. Here are some examples of international product failures arising from the basic product itself: Christmas puddings in Saudi Arabia (where the word 'Christmas' is illegal and 50,000 of the Anglo-Saxon population go on leave during

Christmas anyway); toothpaste to combat betelnut stains (where stained teeth implies wealth in some cultures, as does being overweight in others). Another example is Kellogg's 'Pop Tarts' in the UK since (unlike the US) too small a percentage of British homes have toasters. General Food's packaged cake mixes found the Japanese market too small for them (3 per cent of homes had ovens). Coca-Cola had to withdraw their two-litre bottle from Spain because few Spaniards owned refrigerators with large enough compartments. Tennent's Caledonian, a successful Scottish lager, flopped initially in the UK because it came in 24-packs rather than 6-packs. Phillips had to change the size of its coffee makers to fit into the smaller Japanese kitchens and its shavers to fit smaller Japanese hands. See the case study at the end of Chapter 5.

The global Web

Like it or not, once you're on the World Wide Web you're global. This presents great opportunities but also new challenges. Web positioning on a global scale is not easy. Apart from language, literacy, colour, gestures and culture, marketers now have to try to think how global audiences search for information – what words, what search engines, etc. Even if you do translate correctly, you probably have to redesign your Web pages, as many other languages require more words and more space to deliver the same message.

STRATEGIC GLOBAL OPTIONS

More and more businesses have to compete in the global arena. For many companies there is nowhere left to hide. Those that do not move into the global market will probably find that the global market will come to them, as new international competitors target their once-safe local market. There is a need to be proactive rather than reactive. Those that ignore this small part of the globalization process may not be around in 50 years.

A defensive strategy (eg consolidate existing customer base, stay native, and block competition from entering with, for example, a series of flexible distributor promotions) may safeguard the company, at least in the short term. Offensive strategies are required if a company is seeking entry into new markets, eg increasing promotional spend in key national markets, supported by a flexible operations system. Strategic alliances and joint ventures offer a lower-cost, lower-risk (and possibly lower-margin) method of entry into these new, large and increasingly competitive markets. Global competition has even prompted global cooperation in the marketing communications industries. Advertising and PR independent networks are popping up alongside the global agencies that have expanded to meet their clients' global requirements.

Global marketing strategy

Warren Keegan identified five marketing (product/communication) strategies for multinational marketing. These were determined by the state of the various international markets, analysed by (a) whether the need (or product function) was the same as in other markets, (b) whether the conditions of product use were the same as in other markets, and (c) whether the customer had the ability to buy the product.

1. Same product/same communications
   This applies to markets where the need and use are similar to the home market, eg Coca-Cola, with its centrally produced advertisements which incorporate local differences in language.
2. Same product/different communications
   This applies to markets where the need or function is different but the conditions of product use are the same, eg bicycles in Europe and bicycles in Africa (recreation and transport, respectively).
3. Different product/same communications
   This applies to markets with the same product function or need but with different conditions of product use, eg different petrol formulae but same advertising image – Esso's tiger.
4. Different product/different communications
   This applies to markets with different needs and different product use, eg greeting cards and clothes are held to be 'culture bound' but it should be noted that some clothing companies (like Levi's) use the same, centrally produced, wordless advertisements internationally.
5. New product (invention)/new communications
   This applies, for example, in the case of a hand-powered washing machine.

The question of whether the complete communications mix can be standardized by centrally controlling and producing everything from advertising to sales promotions to point-of-sale to PR to direct mail, etc, is highly unlikely because of, first, the differences in regulations and laws, which vary from country to country, and, second, the array of differences highlighted in the Global challenges section. There are of course exceptions to the rule. IBM's Aptiva ran a 'win tickets to the 1996 Olympics' across 12 European countries, while a new point-of-sale campaign rolled out to 15 European countries. Mars also developed a pack specifically for the Euro '96 football championships featuring a green colour base with white netting effect that appeared in shops in the UK, France and Germany.

Not totally pan-European approach

All promotional ideas for Snickers' sponsorship of Euro '96 were shared with each European office, and the individual brand managers then assessed the viability for their marketplace. Language barriers will often dictate the feasibility of an individual promotion. For example the 'Snickers – tackles your hunger in a BIG way' strapline was not utilized in any country other than the UK due to language interpretation difficulties.

Gordon Storey, Mars external relations manager

Global advertising strategy

The question of whether at least the advertising can be standardized (same communication) is a source of great discussion. Kahler and Kramer (1977) suggest that successful standardization is dependent on the similarity of the motivations for purchase and the similarity of use conditions. For culture-free products such as industrial goods and some consumer durables, the purchase motivations are similar enough to permit high degrees of standardization. Culture-bound products, in contrast, require adaptation. Customs, habits and tastes vary for these products and customer reaction depends on receiving information consonant with these factors. It has been argued that 'buying proposals' (the benefits proposed in the advertisement) has a good chance of being accepted across large geographical areas, whereas the 'creative presentation' (creative treatment) does not.

Essentially, if the international market had a similar set of needs and interests (to the established market), then a successful adaptation of the advertising message was more likely (as in the case of pattern advertisements – see page 253). Simon Majaro (1982) observed that the gap between the time a product reaches its decline stage in the most advanced market and the introduction stage in the slowest market is narrowing. If this trend continues, the point will be reached where the pattern of the life cycle in a domestic market will become identical with the pattern in the foreign markets. This will of course have tremendous impact on the communications strategy of firms operating internationally. It would mean that in time it would become possible for the communications objectives of such firms to become more and more homogeneous, thus allowing for a larger measure of standardization. In other words, if the trend continues, it should become possible for the same campaign, subject to the manipulation necessitated by linguistic and cultural variations, to be undertaken in all markets. This is indeed the kind of standardization that Coca-Cola has achieved in world markets. This strategy stems in the main from the fact that the product life cycle profit of Coca-Cola is pretty homogeneous throughout the world. Rein Rijkens (1991) confirmed the trend towards 'greater internationalization and centralization', where basic creative ideas are centrally produced for international use. Kahler and Kramer (1977) felt that transferability of advertising was dependent on the possibility of a more homogeneous consumer, who might, for example, evolve out of the ever-integrating European community. If the European consumer showed a willingness to accept the products of countries within the community, and if that consumer was motivated similarly to those in other countries, a common promotional approach would be practical; but if national identities prevailed, separate campaigns would be more likely to succeed.

Four global advertising strategies

The four basic strategies available for global marketing communications are:

1. Central strategy and production.
2. Decentralized strategy and production.
3. Central strategy and local production (pattern advertisements).
4. Central strategy with both central and local production.

Central strategy and production

Advertisements are controlled and produced by the head office (or its agency). This includes message modification, such as translations and tailor-made editions for various markets. Examples of centrally controlled and centrally produced advertisements include Coca-Cola's emotion-packed 'General Assembly' advertisement showing the world's children singing happily and harmoniously together, which was similar to their 1971 'I'd like to teach the world to sing' (McCann's) in that it was packed with emotion and carried a universal theme. The 21 language editions of this advertisement opened with 'I am the future of the world, the future of my nation' and ended with the tag line 'a message of hope from the people who make Coca-Cola'. Each country then edited in their own end shot of the appropriate child's face. Incidentally, the German edition was dubbed slightly out of synchronization since they associate quality films with dubbed (slightly out of sync) American and British films. Scottie's nappies save production costs by omitting any dialogue and just using a different voice-over for each country. Levi's do not bother with voice-overs, dubbings or translations as there is no dialogue – just music by Steve Miller. Their unified logo and brand image does away with the need for different pack shots (close-ups of the pack/label) for each country, so their commercials, produced by the London agency BBH, are used throughout Europe.

Decentralized strategy and production

Advertisements are controlled and produced by each local subsidiary and its agency specifically for the local market. This approach generates lots of different advertisements by the same company. Each division or subsidiary works with its own local agency to produce tailor-made advertisements for the local market. As well as being an expensive approach, it can destroy uniformity and a consistent global presence, but it does allow more creativity to suit the specific needs of the local market.

Central strategy and local production (pattern advertisements)

The pattern provides uniformity in direction but not in detail, which allows the advertisements to be locally produced but within the central strategic guidelines. This is where head office guides the strategic direction of the advertisements but allows local production. These advertisements work to a formula, or pattern. In the Blue Band margarine advertisements, whether in Scandinavia or Africa, the appropriate happy mother can be seen spreading margarine on bread with her happy family sitting around eating it. Impulse fragrance uses a 'boy chases girl' formula across Europe but still allows for cultural idiosyncrasies like eye contact, sex appeal and law-abiding citizens to be tailored into each country's different production. Renault's pan-European strategy was to 'endow the car with its own personality'. In France the car was shown with eyes. In Germany the car talked back. In the UK the end line was 'What's yours called?'

Central strategy with both central and local production

Centrally produced non-verbal commercials are used to build a unified identity, while local productions supplement this platform. This is demonstrated by the Levi's example, given below. Although 'standardized' generally refers to production, it can also include centrally controlled media strategies, planning and buying. The centralized/standardized global campaign problems are discussed later in this chapter. As Rein Rijkens (1991) says: 'As far as advertising is concerned, the company will continue its policy of central production of non-verbal commercials and cinema films, to be shown throughout Europe and intended to establish a uniform identity for Levi Strauss as a business and for its products. Advertising produced locally by the Levi Strauss subsidiaries will respond to local circumstances and to the local competitive scene.' This formula, also applied by other companies marketing a uniform product and using one advertising strategy on an international scale, has proved successful and may well be further developed once the single market really comes about.

Advantages of central strategy and central production

1. Consistent image
    A consistent image (and positioning) is presented around the world, allowing consumer awareness and familiarity to prosper.
2. Consolidated global position
    Leaves the brand in a stronger position to protect itself from any attack.
3. Exploits transnational opportunities
    Reduces message confusion arising when (a) advertising in one country spills over to another (eg boundary-bouncing satellite TV), or (b) when migrants and tourists physically travel to another geographical area (geographical segment).
4. Saves costs
    Economies are enjoyed by not having several different creative teams (and production teams if central production) working on the brand around the world (saves reinventing the wheel). Possibility of centrally produced (or at least centrally designed) point-of-sale material also. Levi's have found that they save £1.5m by shooting a single TV ad to span six European countries (at £300,000 production cost per each one-minute TV ad).
5. Releases management time
    And/or reduces the size of the marketing department, which might otherwise be tied up briefing creative teams, approving creative concepts, supervising productions, etc. It may even save time invested with packaging designers, sales promotion agencies, etc, if pack designs and promotions are run from central office.
6. Facilitates transfer of skills
    Within the company and around the world since, in theory, it is the same job anywhere around the world. It also stimulates cross-fertilization of company ideas if staff are moving around internationally.
7. Easier to manage
    Easier to manage centrally since there are, in total, a smaller number of decisions and projects to manage:
    (a) One creative decision facilitates harmonization of creative treatments, particularly in areas of media overlap.
    (b) Media policies – manage the media overlap between countries to maximize effectiveness and recommend preferred media choice in specific territories.
    (c) Budgets – determine local budgets for each product in each market so that the method of allocating resources is balanced.
    (d) Agree activity programme and a specific reporting system to facilitate easier management.

Disadvantages of central strategy and central production

1. Stifles creativity
   Stops local creative contributions from both company staff and local advertising agency (whether part of an international group or independent agency). The account may be considered by the local agency staff to be dull and boring, and the supposedly 'best brains' (from the creative department) may avoid being involved with it.
2. Frustrated local management
   Although the local office may be accountable for its performance, it does not have control over its own destiny, since advertisements are centrally produced or directed. This may lead to a sense of frustration.
3. Minimal effort from local agency (if using an international agency with its network of overseas branches)
   The high global advertising spend may put the brand high on the agency's head office list, but the local agencies may find it is uneconomic to spend too much time and top brains on it.
4. Lost opportunities
   The opportunity to react quickly to changes in the local market is lost.
5. Different product life cycles
   Different markets may be at different stages of their life cycle, which may make the standardized approach unsuitable. It may, however, still be possible to standardize each stage of the brand's development, eg Boot's launch of Nurofen in the UK and northern Europe.
6. Wrong idea
   Some central advertising concepts may simply not work as well as a locally created original idea. Sales therefore perform below their potential.
7. Difficult translation
   Some ideas just do not lend themselves to translation, eg Pepsi's 'Come alive' was translated in some countries as 'Come from the dead' or 'Come out of the grave'.
8. False savings
   Local language adaptation/modification costs may negate the cost savings generated by the centrally controlled creative work.
9. Market complexities
   The many other local market differences (eg variations in consumer protection regulations and media availability) may make a standardized message extremely difficult.
10. Inexperienced staff
    A lack of suitably qualified expert staff who can manage the coordination of transnational standardized campaigns may make the whole centrally controlled advertising concept too risky.

Agencies in the international arena

There are several different types of agency from which an international advertiser can choose:

- international agencies (multinationals);
- independent networks / associations / confederations of agencies;
- local independent agencies;
- house agencies.

In addition to deciding whether to centralize control over advertising (and effectively standardize it), another dilemma facing the international marketing manager is whether to put all international advertising in the hands of one international agency or hand it out to local independent agencies. Many local independent agencies have grouped themselves into networks or associations, which means that they have a ready network of contacts with the other network member agencies in the various international regions. A fourth and less common option is for the client to set up its own house agency specifically to handle its own worldwide advertising. The two extreme options will now be considered, ie whether to choose a single international agency or several independent local agencies.

Choosing an international agency or independent local agency

This question is linked to whether the communications should be controlled centrally or left to run autonomously. Should the marketing team at headquarters work with just one large multinational advertising agency or should they allow a range of independent agencies to use their unique skills on a local basis? A coordinated message can be developed in either situation. For example, centrally produced advertisements (with local modifications / translations, etc) and pattern advertisements (formula advertising) can work under either system. Although a centrally produced advertisement is more likely to be handled by a large international agency, there are exceptions where local independent agencies with local media buying and production skills (if pattern advertisements are required) may be preferred. It is possible to choose to work with a range of independent local agencies while adhering to centralized policies. These policies can help the client to manage the whole advertising process by giving specific guidance on creative directions, media strategies, budgets and activity programmes. As Majaro (1982) says: 'Obviously where the product profile justifies communications standardization, it may be advisable to use the services of an international agency with offices in all markets.' Majaro continues: 'Hoping to attain the same results by using a host of local agencies with no international expertise is a formula for waste in worldwide marketing.'

Advantages of using an international agency

Compared to local agencies, the international advertising agency claims the following advantages:

- Full service – because of the international agency's size, it can offer a full range of services, including research, planning and translation under one roof.
- Quality – some clients feel reassured by the quality feeling of a large international agency (as opposed to taking a chance with a smaller local agency). Quality and standards should, in theory, be universal.
- Broad base of experience – training and transferring personnel is common among the international agencies.
- Presence in major advertising centres – the agency branches are located at the centre of most major cities/marketing territories.
- Cost saving – less duplication in areas of communication, creative and production departments
- Easier to manage – a single central contact point combined with the points listed in 'Advantages of central strategy' on page 254.

Disadvantages of using an international agency

It is arguably easier for a single international agency to standardize the message. The disadvantages of standardization (see page 255) therefore apply where central control moves in. In addition, the overseas subsidiary may lack enthusiasm if the account was won elsewhere. It is as if, by necessity, various branches of the international agency are brought in. The lack of excitement may be compounded, particularly where all the creative work has been handled by head office. In a sense, the branch's job is relegated to media scheduling and planning.

The key to successful central communications

If Shakespeare and the Rolling Stones can do it, so can advertising.

Maurice Saatchi

Rather than engaging in high-risk, new product development many corporations prefer to consider the lower-risk, new market development approach. Harmonization of brand strategy across different markets has been on the agenda for years. Making it actually happen is another thing altogether. Take advertising: although more and more advertising is use in more than one country, only some of it works successfully.

Understanding the disadvantages in addition to the advantages is the first step towards implementing centralized communications. Identifying the barriers reveals the levels of resistance among distant marketing managers. It follows that internal marketing skills are also required. Before international communications are standardized (centralized) 'management thinking must first be harmonized internationally'. Diminishing local autonomy without diminishing local responsibility requires skilful management handling. Indeed, maintaining management motivation requires people skills, particularly when their responsibilities for advertising budgets are being slashed.

Many local managers will perceive the central advertising campaign to be dull and disappointing because it is based on the lowest global common denominator – those common cross-cultural characteristics that somehow find commonality across borders that can result in dull ideas.

Inspiring managers to continue to excel under a blanket of apparently bland advertising is a challenging job. It becomes more challenging the longer internal communications are delayed.

CASE STUDY 9.1

American Express: Blue V2

Situation

Ogilvy US originally proposed the idea of Blue back in 1996. The credit card industry in the United States was seen as a diseased and stagnant category in desperate need of redefinition. Previous AmEx efforts (the Optima Card) within the credit card territory had been successful but not on the magnitude of revenue – or with any distinct emotional identity – that was needed to be considered a success.

Objectives

The business goals were aggressive and the competition fierce. Ogilvy US were now playing directly against Visa and MasterCard, both of which aggressively outspent AmEx across all communications fronts. Adding to the challenge was a complacent consumer, largely immune to, and cynical towards, credit card communications.

Ogilvy were challenged by AmEx to jolt the competitive status quo and to register emotionally with an indifferent consumer within an extremely compacted schedule: nine months from product inception to launch on 15 September 1999.

Adding to the above challenge was the nature of the 360-degree collaboration itself. Ogilvy were charged not only with strategic leadership in creating the brand affinity and general advertising, but also with ensuring that the emotional affinity held constant – both strategically and executionally – across all the five partner agencies' communication efforts. And remember, as far as AmEx were concerned, this all had to appear seamless to the consumer. Executed by many different constituents but with one message, one voice, one look and one emotional appeal.

Strategy: challenging the conventions of the category

Creating the Blue Card brand identity
The Blue Card was also designed to be a distinctly different proposition to the Green Card franchise – both emotionally and functionally. The aim was to launch a credit card to a group of people who had previously not seen American Express as relevant to their needs. It was conceived both in terms of an emotional affinity that would embrace a younger, hipper and more modern prospect mindset, and as a product that would solidify American Express's venture into the lending business.

The Blue brand affinity was realized within the context of competitors' shortcomings:

The credit card market as defined by the competition:	*Desired Blue brand behaviour:*
<ul><li>selling a piece of plastic and miles;</li><li>dishonest and deceptive practices;</li><li>institutions that dictate terms;</li><li>credit cards – passive transactional devices;</li><li>**out of control.**</li></ul>	<ul><li>selling an experience;</li><li>honest, open disclosure;</li><li>people in control, managing their own lives;</li><li>credit cards – interactive and enabling tools via the Web;</li><li>**self-reliance.**</li></ul>

Target insight: The 'self-reliance' theme proved to resonate with consumer groups on an international scale. Blue was the right product positioned in the right place at the right time. A new consumer was emerging, defined less by demographics than by a mindset that is:

- motivated by a success that is not just financial;
- optimistic;
- entrepreneurial in spirit.

To be in control is the ultimate definition of success, and financial empowerment is seen as the key to attainment of this success. No competitor was seen as delivering on this critical dimension.

The Blue Card design

Creating the symbol of change: Credit cards are a constant presence in our lives and the cards a person chooses says as much about him or her as it does about the company from which it was issued. Yet card design continues to be one of the most neglected forms of brand advertising on the market. That opportunity – and the fact that a dramatic symbol of change was needed both for AmEx and for the category – begged for a card that was designed in a radically different way. Blue needed to be both sexy and an icon for a progressive way of thinking.

The Blue Card creative idea

Like Apple and Volkswagen before it, Ogilvy took a unique design and used it as the icon for a revitalized company.

The media strategy

Blue's aggressive acquisition targets dictated accomplishing a rapid brand reappraisal from a historically resistant target. This challenge required a move away from the traditional planning of high TV and press weight levels.

Consumer research provided the insight that life, not work, was the driving emotional factor for AmEx's target market. The goal was to surround the target group in relevant but surprising ways throughout their day and week. Three key lifestyle areas were identified for communication focus:

- technology;
- music/entertainment;
- active lifestyle.

Media opportunities were then selected or created to reflect these lifestyle interests. A communication framework was developed to link media with the message. As a result, various messages, from the emotional to the rational and from the information to the attitudinal were 'shuffled' simultaneously across all communications so that consumers would be surrounded by the 'Blue Story'.

The resulting media plan represented a dramatic shift from the typical AmEx approach: TV carried only 40 per cent of the overall weight, and print and radio 20 per cent, while non-traditional media carried an unprecedented 40 per cent.

Tactics: the Blue Card 360-degree launch

US launch: September 1999
Blue was launched across almost every conceivable medium:

- traditional:
  - TV;
  - print;
  - radio;
  - outdoor;
  - direct mail;
  - direct TV;
- non-traditional:
  - interactive;
  - cinema advertising;
- outside-the-box:
  - Blue Concert in New York's Central Park: 'trimulcast' of concert, simultaneous TV, radio broadcast and Internet cybercast;
  - Blue promotion event crew;
  - press event at New York music club – Lush introduced by Sheryl Crow;
  - advertising on water bottles, transit cards, popcorn bags;
  - advertising projections on buildings.

Blue was there at every turn to ensure that prospects were interacting with the brand.

International launch: 2000
Based on the success of the US effort, AmEx decided to take the Blue positioning, target audience mindset and benefits bundles as a platform to roll-out the campaign to the international market. During 2000 Blue V2 was launched in the following international markets: UK (July), Sweden (September), the Netherlands (September), Italy (October), Spain (October) and Japan (October).

International adaptation of US campaign
Example UK:

- focus of brief: online benefits with safety net of AmEx;
- adapted TV to local needs;
- local DRTV;
- mailing to existing AmEx Card members;
- Blue TV played on huge plasma screen in London's Leicester Square;

- Blue survival kit at V2 Music Festival;
- PR in *Time Out* magazine.

Planned roll-out of Blue in 2001
During 2001 Blue V2 is scheduled to be launched in the following international markets: France, Germany, Austria, Argentina, Mexico, Hong Kong and Australia.

Action: outline of media plan

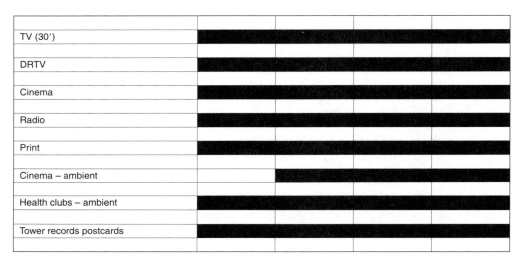

TV (30′)					
DRTV					
Cinema					
Radio					
Print					
Cinema – ambient					
Health clubs – ambient					
Tower records postcards					

Outline of 1999 American Express Blue launch plan

Control

Results at 1 March 2000:

- Cards distributed: 200 per cent over 2000 plan projections;
- Card spend: 358 per cent over 2000 plan projections;
- Communication tracking:
    - 48 per cent of Blue prospects viewed it as more modern, cool and innovative;
    - 33 per cent of Blue prospects said they were likely to apply within next 6 months.

Sources: AXP / CLT Research Associates, 2000

Men and women/Minutes

Over 150 people were involved from conception to launch across 6 markets and over a period of 18 months.

Money

Not available.

APPENDIX 9.1

Is Europe united?

Europe's single market

The single market has the potential to expand beyond the initial European Union (community) and into northern, central and eastern Europe. The EU's single market means freedom of goods, services, people and capital. The new single market is just what is says – one big new market with many more customers, more competitors, more suppliers, more choice and lower costs. This brings with it a web of cultural idiosyncrasies, language barriers and a reported sense of xenophobia that sometimes translates into a pattern of what the Henley Centre for Forecasting calls 'patriotic purchasing impulses' (though this does not stand in the way of getting good value for money, which proves that behaviour does not always follow attitudes and aspirations). Net result? Opportunities (and threats) galore.

Is it really single?

In practice, the single market is splintered by different levels of economic development (north and south), culture, attitudes and lifestyles, languages, retail trends, direct mail trends, sources of information, time taken to make a decision and so on. John Mole (1990) says that 'southern Europeans work to live and northern Europeans live to work.' The agency Ogilvy and Mather says that 'The national cultural, social and psychological differences will remain for so many years to come that the reality of a truly common market may never exist.' Some of the EU idiosyncrasies reported by Philip Kotler (1988) are that the average Frenchman uses twice as many cosmetics and beauty aids as his wife. The Germans and the French eat more packaged branded spaghetti than the Italians, while Italian children like to eat a bar of chocolate between two slices of bread as a snack.

Different mixes for different EU countries

Different marketing mixes and communication mixes are required for different European countries. In Holland, dentists derive 40 per cent of their turnover from the sale of products such as toothbrushes. In Germany, supermarkets are expected to sell only cheap, utilitarian brushes, while the pharmacies handle the premium brands. In Italy, a premium brush has to carry a fashionable, exclusive label. This makes any above-the-line campaigns difficult. The communications mix was built around direct mail to dentists supported by point-of-sale and product literature, packaging design and sales presenters.

EU effect on client–agency relationships

Advertising agencies may see a concentration of clients with bigger (and fewer) marketing communications budgets. It will be interesting to see if client head offices and advertising agency head offices will concentrate geographically. Arguably, this will lead to the big agencies getting bigger. Perhaps there will still be room for the small local agency, while the medium-sized agencies may be caught in no man's land and become extinct. This may lead to many more mergers and acquisitions, even stock market listings to raise more funds. Whether this will improve the quality of client service is debatable. Agency management may have to devote resources to their stockholders and focus on half-yearly profit figures rather than client service. In the short term these priorities can be mutually exclusive, with one being chosen at the expense of the other. Clients obviously do not like being treated as second-class citizens. The larger, less personal, listed corporation may lose the charm of having direct and immediate access to the agency's chairman. The inevitable staff changes may cause key teams to leave. Sometimes the clients go with them. At other times the client fires the new agency because it is now part of a group that holds competing accounts, or the agency resigns the account because the new corporation has acquired some competing accounts that create a conflict of interest.

APPENDIX 9.2

Western weirdos

Nose blowing

Where most North Americans are repulsed by an Indonesian who blows his nose on to the street, the Indonesian is repulsed by the North American who blows his nose in a handkerchief and then carries it around for the rest of the day in his pocket.
(Ferraro, 1990)

Ballroom dancing

It is common in such dancing for the front of the bodies to be in constant contact – and they do this in public. In spite of the close physical touching involved in this type of dancing (a form of bodily contact not unlike that assumed in sexual intercourse), our society has defined it as almost totally asexual. Although ballroom dancing can involve high levels of intimacy, it is equally possible that there is no sexual content whatsoever. Many adult men in the United States have danced in this fashion with their mothers, their sisters, the wives of the ministers at church socials without anyone raising an eyebrow. Yet many non-American cultures view this type of dancing as the height of promiscuity and bad taste. It is interesting to note that many of those non-Americans for whom our dancing is a source of embarrassment are the very people we consider to be promiscuous, sex-crazed savages because their women do not cover their breasts.

(Ferraro, 1990)

Kissing

What's so strange about a kiss? Surely kissing is one of the most natural things in the world, so natural indeed that we might almost ask what are lips for if not for kissing? But this is what we think, and a whole lot of people think differently. To them kissing is not at all natural. It is not something that everybody does, or would like to do. On the contrary, it is a deplorable habit, unnatural, unhygenic, bordering on the nasty and even definitely repulsive. When we come to look into the matter, we shall find that there is a geographical distribution of kissing; and if some enterprising ethnologist were to prepare a 'map of kissing' it would show a surprisingly large amount of blank space. Most of the so-called primitive races of mankind such as the New Zealanders (Maoris), the Australian Aborigines, the Pauans, Tahitians, and other South Sea islanders, and the Esquimaux of the frozen north, were ignorant of kissing until they were taught the technique by the white men... The Chinese have been wont to consider kissing as vulgar and all too suggestive of cannibalism... the Japanese have no word for it in their vocabulary.

(Pike, 1966)

Tea drinking

In England, tea breaks can take a half-hour per man, as each worker brews his own leaves to his particular taste and sips out of a large, pint-sized vessel with the indulgence of a wine taster... Management suggested to the union that perhaps it could use its good offices to speed up the 'sipping time': to ten minutes a break... The union agreed but failed... Then one Monday morning, the workers rioted. Windows were broken, epithets greeted the executives as they entered the plant and police had to be called to restore order. It seems the company went ahead and installed a tea-vending machine – just put a paper cup under the spigot and out pours the standard brew. The pint-sized container was replaced by a five-ounce cup imprinted – as they are in America – with morale-building messages imploring greater dedication to the job and loyalty to the company... The plant never did get back into production. Even after the tea-brewing machine was hauled out, workers boycotted the company and it finally closed down.

(Stressin, 1979)

APPENDIX 9.3

Those weird working Brits

When asked about planning, most British managers immediately think of financial forecasting and budgeting. The annual budget is the backbone of the organization and the major exception to the otherwise inconsistent approach to systems… the British aversion to working within a rational and systematic framework. They take pride in 'muddling through', in 'getting there in the end'. This should not necessarily be construed by outsiders as intellectual idleness. British thinking is interpretive rather than speculative. It prefers tradition and precedent and 'common sense', in other words the interpretation of experience untrammelled by theory or speculation. This usually involves finding the expedient rather than the innovative solution. There is a deep scepticism about great schemes and constructs on a macro or a micro economic level.

(Mole, 1990)

APPENDIX 9.4

Difficult to work with other European cultures?

The complexities of working within EU cultures

To some, overcoming local customers' idiosyncrasies may seem relatively easy compared to overcoming local partners' working practices. Whether they are suppliers, distributors, sales agents, advertising agents, strategic partners or just prospect contacts, understanding and overcoming each other's approach to business is essential. Here are some excerpts from John Mole's excellent book on other cultures, *Mind Your Manners* (1990), considering how various Europeans see each other:

Somewhere in the world there are people who think the Germans are messy and unpunctual. (The chances are they are in Switzerland.) There are countries where Greece is regarded as a model of efficiency. There are countries in which French bosses would seem absurdly egalitarian and others where Italian company life would seem oppressively regulated.

They are so inefficient. It is hard to get them to do things. At home I ask for something to be done, politely of course, and it gets done on time without any fuss. Here there are always reasons why it can't be done the way I want it. If it gets done at all. Sometimes they just ignore me. You have to follow up much more here. Set deadlines. They always want me to discuss things instead of doing them. Punctuality? Meetings never start on time. And they always drag on. You invite a customer to lunch at one o'clock and he arrives three-quarters of an hour late and thinks nothing of it. It is very frustrating. I get very irritated and I don't know how to handle it.

Was this said by a Danish manager about working with British employees or by a British manager working with Italians? The answer is yes to both parts of the question.
(Mole, 1990)

APPENDIX 9.5

An international business dialogue gone wrong

Bob: *How long are you here for, Renee?*
Renee: Since last night.
Bob: No, I mean when do you have to leave for the airport?
Renee: Oh. Twelve o'clock at the latest.
Bob: Well in that case, we'd better press on.
Renee: Sorry?
Bob: Let's resume, shall we, or would you like some more coffee?
Renee: *No, let's resume.* Would you like to?
Bob: What?
Renee: Resume.
Bob: Yes, suits me. Over to you then.
Renee: Oh. Well, perhaps we could turn to the new quality control system. You say you're not very happy about the effect on throughput.
Bob: That's right. It's slowing things down very badly. This week, for example, we're already two days late for one of our regular customers.
Renee: Uh-huh. What sort of an order is it?
Bob: XB-90s. Three thousand.
Renee: *Ah, not so important, then.*
Bob: Well, I think it is.
Renee: *Oh. What's your usual delivery delay?*
Bob: We don't usually have any delay at all, if I can help it.
Renee: But how much time do you need to turn an order round?
Bob: We quote 14 days.
Renee: *And how long does it actually take?*
Bob: Well, 14 days, of course! What sort of an operation do you think I'm running?
Renee: I don't see the problem then.

Bob: The problem is that the new system is causing delays.

Renee: *Look, I'm sure I mustn't tell you this,* but the board are very keen to see it in operation in all subsidiaries before the end of the year.

Bob: *That's hardly news.*

Renee: Oh, sorry, I thought they told you already.

Bob: Of course they have. I mean, we can all see benefits coming from a really effective control system, but...

Renee: *I think it's too early to talk about benefits.*

Bob: Oh I don't know. Look, do you think there's any chance the board will change their minds?

Renee: *Eventually, but...*

Bob: ... but it'll take a few more meetings?

Renee: No, I was going to say it's not very probable.

Bob: I see. Oh well. What's next?

Renee: Sorry?

Bob: *Have you got your agenda?*

Renee: Why? Do you want to fix our next meeting?

Bob: No, I just mean what other points...

Explanations

Renee is a composite European. Her 'language' refers sometimes to the Latin-based languages like French, Italian, Spanish, sometimes to Germanic ones.

The italics show where Renee and Bob are talking at cross-purposes. Here's why they misunderstand each other:

How long are you here for, Renee?
Renee responds to this question as if it meant 'How long have you been here?' because, translated word for word, that's what it means in her language.

Let's resume
Renee mistakes this for a similar word in her language meaning 'summarize'. She therefore thinks she's inviting Bob to sum up the meeting so far and is surprised when Bob doesn't do so.

Not so important
In her language, 'important' refers to size as well as status and priority. Renee is not necessarily dismissing Bob's orders as 'unimportant', just noting that it's not very big.

What's your delivery delay?
To Renee, 'delay' simply means a period of time, and doesn't necessarily carry any suggestion of lateness.

And how long does it actually take?
To Europeans, 'actually' means currently or at the moment. Also, many non-native speakers confuse 'I do it' with 'I'm doing it'. So Renee thinks she's saying 'How long is it taking you at the moment?' It's therefore no wonder that she doesn't see the problem!

I'm sure I must not tell you this
Non-native speakers often confuse 'mustn't' with 'don't have to'. Renee in fact thinks that Bob already knows the board's opinion. Bob's reply:

That's hardly news
compounds the misunderstanding, as Renee takes 'hardly' to mean 'hard' or 'tough'. So she not only misses the irony, but also thinks Bob is disappointed.

I think it's too early to talk about benefits
Renee thinks that 'benefits' carries the same meaning as in her language – 'profits'. This is clearly inappropriate here.

Eventually…
… in Renee's language, means 'conceivably' or 'possibly' and carries no idea of 'finally'. Hence the misunderstanding.

Have you got your agenda?
'Agenda' to Renee means diary.

(Reproduced by kind permission of Canning International Management Development from *The New International Manager*, 1993)

APPENDIX 9.6

Translation tips

Simon Majaro (1982) suggests the following tips for advertising copy that is going to be used in a foreign language.

1) Avoid idioms, jargon and buzz-words.
2) Leave space to expand foreign language text (Latin languages take 20 per cent more space and Arabic may need up to 50 per cent more space).
3) Check local legal requirements and codes of conduct.
4) Ensure that the translators speak the everyday language of the country in question. British English and American English differ, as does the Spanish spoken in Spain and Argentina.
5) Brief the translator thoroughly so that they get a feel for the product, its benefits, the customers and competition. Do not just hand over the copy and expect it to be translated.
6) Check the translation with distributors and customers in the particular market. This also gives local users the opportunity of being involved and raising any criticisms of the promotional materials before they are published for use. Having it translated back into English can be an additional safeguard.

FURTHER READING

Anholt, S (2001) *Another One Bites the Grass*, Wiley, Chichester

Dudley J (1989) *Strategies for the Single Market*, Kogan Page, London

Ferraro, G P (1990) *The Cultural Dimension of International Business*, Prentice-Hall, Englewood Cliffs, NJ

Geertz, C (1983) *The Interpretation of Cultures: Selected essays,* Hutchinson, London

Harvey-Jones, J (1988) *Making It Happen: Reflections on leadership,* Collins, London

Inskip, I (1997) Marketing international brands in Asia needs fresh thinking, *Marketing Business*, May

Kahler, R and Kramer, R (1977) *International Marketing*, South Western Publishing Company, Cincinnati

Kashani, K (1989) Pathways and Pitfalls of Global Marketing, *Marketing Business*, June

Keegan, W J and Schlegelmilch, B B (2001) *Global Marketing Management, A European Perspective,* Financial Times/Prentice-Hall, Englewood Cliffs, NJ

Kotler, P (1988) *Marketing Management: Analysis, planning, implementation and control,* 6th edn, Prentice-Hall, Englewood Cliffs, NJ

Majaro, S (1982) *International Marketing*, Allen and Unwin, London

Mazur, L (1997) Successfully managing cultural differences, *Marketing Business*, September

Mead, G (1993) A Universal Message, *Financial Times*, 2 May

Mole, J (1990) *When in Rome...: A business guide to cultures and customs in 12 European nations*

Morris, D (1988) Watch your body language, *Observer*, 23 October

Pike, K (1966) *Language in Relation to a Unified Theory of the Structure of Human Behavior,* Mouton, The Hague

Rijkens, R (1991) *European Advertising Strategies,* Cassell, London

Usunier, J C (2000) *Marketing Across Cultures*, Financial Times/Prentice-Hall, Englewood Cliffs, NJ

Winick, C (1961) Anthropology's Contribution to Marketing, *Journal of Marketing*, **25**

Young, L (1985) *Love Around the World*, Hodder and Stoughton, London

Three examples of innovative media placement from Media Planning's 'covered' campaign for orange (see page 198)

Lara Croft is the personification of the highly successful Lucozade Energy campaign (see page 315)

Images from the launch of the AmEx Blue

The Daewoo marketing communications campaign rewrote the rules of marketing cars in the UK (see page 319)

The HEA Drug Education campaign fought a battle against huge odds to turn the tide of drug use in the UK (see page 325)

The new Talisker packaging has been designed to convey its status as the only malt from the Isle of Skye (see page 532)

The Tango Megaphone campaign demonstrates how far reaching a truly creative sales promotion can be (see page 358)

Red, white and

We're flying the flag for wine buffs – earn free hotel stays with MOMENTS.COM and ItsWine.com

ItsWine.com is the latest partner with whom you can earn rewards as a MOMENTS.COM member. Make any purchase from the MOMENTS.COM online wine shop and earn MOMENTS points at the generous rate of 1 for every £2 spent.

You can redeem your MOMENTS points for free stays at Heritage Hotels, Le Méridien and Posthouse, as well as an ever-growing range of partner rewards.

If you're not yet a member of the world's most generous rewards programme you can join now by calling **0800 500 500** quoting reference ITS1, or by visiting **www.moments.com**

MOMENTS.COM

Le MERIDIEN   HERITAGE HOTELS   Posthouse

DIVISIONS OF THE FORTE HOTEL GROUP

Greedy?
Materialistic?
Freeloader?

You'll need this.

**Welcome to the new rewards and recognition programme from the Forte Hotel Group.
With MOMENTS.COM you'll earn free hotel stays. Faster.**

As a MOMENTS.COM member you'll be part of one of the most generous hotel rewards programmes available. Use your card worldwide at over 240 Le Méridien, Heritage Hotels and Posthouse, and look forward to free stays with no blackout dates, dining offers, free use of our health spas and much more.

Redemption is easy. Joining is free. To register, call MOMENTS Member Services on +44 870 242 62 62 quoting reference: xxxx, or visit our website at **www.moments.com**

MOMENTS.COM

*Le*MERIDIEN   HERITAGE HOTELS   Posthouse

DIVISIONS OF THE FORTE HOTEL GROUP

The creativity of the Moments.com campaign had to cut through all the clutter of other loyalty schemes (see page 397)

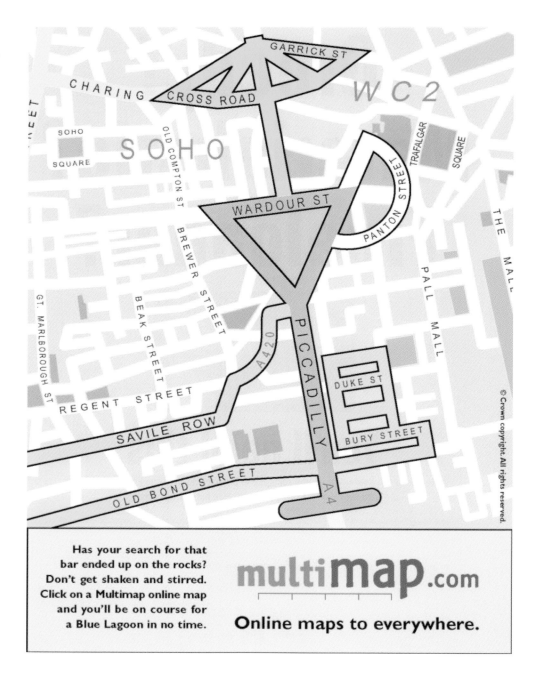

Has your search for that bar ended up on the rocks? Don't get shaken and stirred. Click on a Multimap online map and you'll be on course for a Blue Lagoon in no time.

multimap.com

Online maps to everywhere.

Three adverts from the first consumer campaign for Multimap.com demonstrate the 'campaignability' of the advertising idea (see page 596)

COLWYN BAY

CHESTER

WREXHAM

BETWS-Y-COED

LLANGOLLEN

BLAENAU
FFESTINIOG

SHREWSBURY

WELSHPOOL

LLANELLTYD
DOLGELLAU

MACHYNLLETH

ABERYSTWYTH

LLANDRINDOD WELLS

ABERAERON

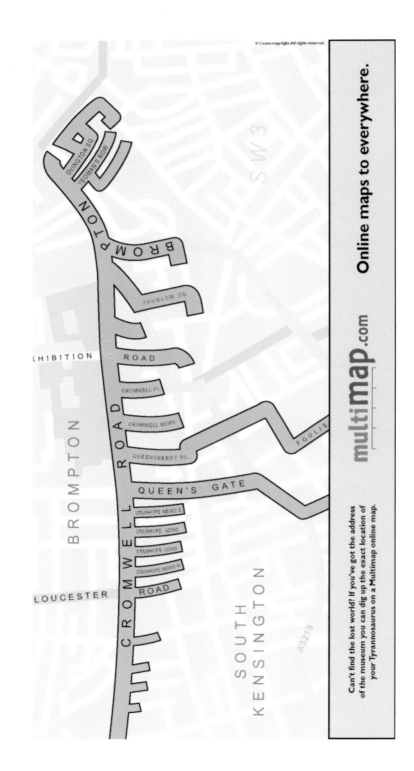

multimap.com

Online maps to everywhere.

Can't find the lost world? If you've got the address of the museum you can dig up the exact location of your Tyrannosaurus on a Multimap online map.

The new Kiss branding has been designed to give it greater standout and work across many environments (see page 619)

The delivery of the Gatwick Express 'Aero' proposition – the best of the train and the plane can be clearly seen through the design route that has been developed (see page 622)

Part 2

The marketing communication tools

10

Selling and sales management

INTRODUCTION

Twentieth-century salesman

I sold systems that people didn't want, didn't need and couldn't afford.

Bill Gardner, IBM veteran with 23 years' service, now retired

Twenty-first-century salesman

Forty-five per cent of the variable component of my paycheque depends on how Jon Gorney at National City Corporation rates me.

Don Parker, IBM salesman

There was an era when selling was all about short-term tactics, quick sales, in–out and on to the next unsuspecting prospect. This era is now over. It is probably best summarized by the well-known Heaven and Hell story.

A man dies and arrives at the Pearly Gates, where St Peter tells him he cannot enter until Hell has been given an equal opportunity. Although he knows he wants to go to Heaven, St Peter insists that the man checks out Hell first. To his amazement the man discovers that Hell was a party town, with free-flowing drink, good music, lots of friendly supermodel lookalikes everywhere, perfect weather, immaculate golf courses, football pitches, Internet connections and white sandy beaches. Best of all, everyone is friendly and concerned that the man feels comfortable in his new surroundings. St Peter appears and asks the man for a decision, upon which the man says, 'Hell's for me!' When he returns the next day all he sees are bodies, scorched, burning and screaming. 'But… this isn't the same place' he shouts at St Peter in the distance. 'Oh yes it is', St Peter replies. 'Yesterday you were a prospect, today you are a customer.'

Today selling has moved away from the short-term, quick-sale scenario. Combative salesmen are being transformed into 'customer servants'. Selling today is more about 'partnering' and relationship building – 'You don't sell to people, you partner with them.' This is particularly true with KAM (key account management), which requires a more strategic approach to selling. Today selling is about building durable relationships that are dependent on satisfying the customer constantly. IBM today are following a growing trend towards basing salesforce salaries partly on customer satisfaction. Salesman Don Parker says that '45 per cent of the variable component of my paycheck depends on how Jon Gorney at National City Corp rates me'. Many companies are now measuring success not just by units sold but also by the far more rigorous yardstick of customer satisfaction (see Chapter 19 for more details). And selling has moved beyond the marketing and sales departments as companies realize that in today's heated competitive markets the whole company must sell. As Keith Francis suggests in the Institute of Professional Sales' magazine, *Winning Business*, 'It is every employee's responsibility to sell the value of working with their company rather than the competition.'

Size and importance of the salesforce

The word 'sales' is conspicuous by its absence on business cards. 'New business development', 'Account manager' or 'Key account manager', even 'Relationship manager' and 'Marketing executive' are often preferred, yet selling's impact on most markets at some stage is vital. The 'selling' stigma is surprising, given the size and importance of selling. A study called *Balancing the Selling Equation* (Abberton Associates, 1997) indicates that there are approximately 470,000 professional salespeople in the UK alone. The London Business School's Associate Professor of Marketing, P J S Law, cites selling as a vital ingredient:

'I cannot think of a product or service which has not, at some stage on its journey from producer to customer, been the subject of face-to-face negotiations between buyer and seller.' The salesforce budget allocation varies according to industry type (see below), but average percentage of turnover spent on selling is estimated to be between 3 and 4 per cent. To put it another way, approximately £19 billion is spent on selling compared to some £12 billion spent on advertising or £3 billion spent on PR.

Industrial markets

Some markets, particularly industrial markets, depend on personal selling more than others – winning an order for, say, a heavy industrial machine cannot be done by advertising, direct mail or telesales (telephone selling). This kind of selling requires a top-level sales professional. Consumer goods, on the other hand, rarely use personal selling to the end-user or consumer because of the high cost per visit (ranging from £27 to £500, depending on the seniority of the salesperson, the frequency and length of the visit, etc). Having said that, there are always exceptions to the rule. Avon trained 3,000 new Avon ladies to sell their cosmetics in China in the mid-1990s only to be thwarted by a five-year government ban on direct selling as a result of concerns over the perils of pyramid-selling schemes. The ban will be reviewed in 2003. The ban was followed by a propaganda campaign showing the evils of the companies involved. Two other forms of salesforce, field marketing and multi-level marketing, are both growing in popularity. These are discussed later in this chapter.

Integrating with the communications mix

An organization's own salesforce, or a distributor's or agent's salesforce, all have to be kept abreast of any new advertising or sales promotion campaigns. Their product knowledge has to be kept up to scratch. Some advertisements are wasted when they succeed in pulling customers into stores only for the customers to find out that the sales staff behind the counter are not familiar with either the advertisement or the particular offer being made. Equally, salespeople may spend considerable time ensuring that wholesaler and retailer point-of-sale materials are professionally coordinated with a national advertising campaign (see Thomson's Tours case study, Chapter 18, page 550). The amount and type of personal selling required changes as a product or service moves through its life cycle (see 'Types of salespeople', below). Figure 1.3 on page 10 showed how more of the marketing budget was spent on personal selling in industrial markets than in consumer markets. Figure 1.2 on page 10 indicated that as a customer moved through the mental stages towards buying (AIDA), selling became more effective in the final stages. This suggests that selling needs to be integrated with other communication activities such as advertising, direct mail, telesales, etc.

SALESFORCES

Types of salespeople

Some sales reps (sales representatives) are excellent at winning new business ('order getters') and find the servicing of regular accounts to be dreadfully tedious compared to the exciting buzz of new business. Other reps are meticulous professionals who service an account ('order takers') with such professionalism, pride and affection that they create barriers for competition by building a 'wall of warmth' around their customers. In reality, most reps have to do a bit of both jobs. Shiv Mathur (1981) wrote an intriguing article about 'transactional shifts' which suggested that different types of marketing managers (and salespeople) were required as a product passes through its life cycle, since the product requires different levels of service support at various stages.

> I used to have a territory where I was a free agent... today the computer recommends which calls I should make... my sales aids remind me what to ask and say... my manager knows where I am and I spend half my time on training courses... but I do sell 30 per cent more per annum.
>
> A domestic appliance executive

In an increasingly impersonal world of faceless faxes and voicemail, face-to-face communications or personal selling can provide a reassuring, personal touch. In addition, the salesperson can respond immediately to a buyer's changing needs and moods. The salesperson can also provide instant feedback from the customer or marketplace (see 'The intelligent rep', page 142). On the other hand, a salesforce can be expensive in terms of cost per thousand contacts and sometimes it can prove to be uneconomical on a cost per order basis. This largely depends on the size and profitability of the order, the distance travelled to get it, the number of meetings required, etc.

Types of salesforce

The three key resources, the 3Ms (men – and women – money and minutes) are limited. Selling soaks up all three resources. There are various combinations of types of salesforce. An organization's field salesforce can be supported by an in-house telesales team who do the prospecting and appointment setting, thereby freeing the field salespeople to do what they are best at – selling. Resources can also be invested in agents, distributors, wholesalers, retailers and their reps so that they become an extension of the salesforce. Alternatively, a temporary sales team can be contracted in to screen and make appointments (telesales) or to go out and sell (see 'Field marketing', page 282). There is no single correct *salesforce mix*.

Within the commercial tyre market one company achieves 200 calls per executive per annum while its largest competitor achieves over 1,600. The former company has focused on large accounts and uses agents to service the independent trade. The latter sells direct to customers all of sizes. Both companies are highly profitable and both have highly efficient sales organizations.

Abberton Associates

The correct approach is, of course, to monitor constantly the effectiveness of each salesforce mix (sales, market share and profitability) and the efficiency (number of calls, cost per call, conversion rates of enquirers to customers, etc). There is always room for improvement.

Functions of selling

A ridiculous heading? The purpose of selling is to sell. However, research suggests that as little as 5 per cent of a salesman's time is in fact spent actually 'selling' (see 'Time – the scarce resource', page 287). In addition to prospecting, appointment setting, letter writing, travelling, training and administration, many salespeople are also responsible for some customer care, post-sales service, entertaining, intelligence gathering, forecasting, understanding customers, developing customized solutions, team selling, etc. Some managers say 'Customers seek longer-term relationships with fewer suppliers than formerly, and in return for security of business ask their suppliers to do more for them.' (See the McGregor Cory case study in Chapter 19 for an example of how longer-term relationships are built.) Forecasts suggest that there will be a concentration of key accounts (large customers) and they will need suppliers who work with them as *strategic partners* instead of adversaries (see Consultative selling, below). *Team selling* may become more popular as R and D, production, distribution, sales marketing and even legal and financial people are called into discussions with the customer. Everyone sells in some way or other.

Collecting feedback

The best salespeople are expert listeners. They ask intelligent questions and listen carefully. The best salespeople are masters at capturing data. Since the salesforce is in the front line of the market, it provides a fast and accurate *feedback* mechanism. Competitor activity, customer needs, and new opportunities and threats can and should be picked up by the salesforce and fed back, without delay, to the sales manager or marketing manager. Reasons why an old customer is lost or a new customer is won should also be fed back immediately.

> *Key questions*
>
> Master salesmen are masters at gathering information. They are equipped with 'must know', 'useful to know' and 'nice to know' questions before every meeting.

Consultative selling

Looking at customers as partners with whom a company wishes to develop a long-term, repeat-business relationship requires a shift in the business paradigm from 'selling *to* them' to 'working *with* them'.

Offering expert advice and consultancy demands an attitude shift where the customer is seen as a partner rather than just a sales target. The short-term 'win–lose' scenario (the seller gains at the customer's expense) is replaced by the longer-term *strategic partnership* 'win–win' scenario. This builds customer retention through enhanced customer satisfaction, which in turn creates a sustainable marketing advantage. These new partnerships may involve joint development programmes that might not bear fruit for five or more years. This may seem inefficient in the short term but highly effective in the medium to long term. If this approach is to work longer term even the board of directors must be consulted and brought into the loop. In the case of new product developments this approach may clash with *time-based competition as competitor catch-up periods* shorten. In the case of a low-technology product a well-trained contract field salesforce might accelerate the initial distribution penetration level by selling into the independent stores (thereby blocking some of the gaps inviting entry from a competitor).

EXTENDING THE SALESFORCE

Mindshare

In business-to-business or industrial markets, many manufacturers and importers sell into distributors, who, in turn, sell into wholesalers and/or end-users (ultimate customer).

Winning the battle for the distributor's *'mindshare'* (or share of mind) can be an important part of salesforce management. Mindshare means the amount of attention and effort that a distributor's salesforce gives to a particular manufacturer's product. A distributor often carries many different product lines supplied by several competing suppliers. The mindshare concept aims to develop the distributor's salesforce into a part-time extension of the supplier's salesforce.

All suppliers would obviously like to have the distributor's salesforce recommend, select, or push their particular brand to the end-user. Mindshare can be won by creating and maintaining a *partnership approach* that develops a mutually beneficial business relationship. This means the manufacturer must supply:

- a reasonable quality of product (and price and delivery);
- creative and frequent sales promotions* (eg a distributor sales rep club where the top distributor's reps are presented with awards, in front of the distributor's own management, once they attain a certain level of sales; there might be a silver, gold and platinum club for 50, 100 and 200 unit salespeople, respectively;
- product training;
- joint visits (manufacturer and distributor visit end-user together);
- cooperative advertising (where the manufacturer shares the cost of the distributor's advertising when it promotes both the parties);
- merchandizing and display services.

Mindshare requires a longer-term approach to selling, since the sales reps' efforts do not necessarily result in an immediate order. But mindshare will contribute to longer-term sales. It is therefore management's responsibility to develop a suitable time horizon and a mindshare strategy that works.

Mindshare benefits

An American marketing consultancy, the Richmark Group, claims that a mindshare strategy has been found to be more powerful than strategies based on product differentiation and other more traditional market strategies. Manufacturers who successfully implement this strategy can build a market position that is almost impossible for competitors to duplicate. The three examples below show how mindshare can make a competitor's marketing communications totally ineffective. Imagine the manufacturer makes electrical cable Z100,

---

* Many effective salesforce sales promotions are based around 'psychic income' (see 'Motivating', page 285), since recognition often packs more punch than money.

the distributor is an electrical wholesaler and the end-user is the electrical contractor who will buy and install the cable under the floorboards of a new house.

An end-user (electrical contractor) customer asks a distributor's rep (electrical wholesaler's rep) for a competing brand, say brand A1000. The distributor's rep recommends and offers the Z100 cable instead.

The end-user seeks advice in selecting a specific brand. The distributor's rep recommends the manufacturer's brand Z100.

The distributor's rep actively solicits orders for the Z100 brand.

Field marketing

It is possible to hire flexible salesforces for ad hoc tactical activities or regular repeat activities. Reduced cost, flexibility and direct measurability make a contract salesforce or field marketing team attractive compared to a full-time, in-house field sales team. Cost can be further reduced by using a syndicated or shared team as opposed to a dedicated team devoted to one particular product only. There are, of course, risks, particularly if they have a tendency for hard selling, misrepresentation or even rudeness. Careful scrutiny and supervision can usually identify these potential problems before they develop into a full-blown crisis. Field marketing tends to be used by FMCG or impulse goods manufacturers, but can be used by a wider range of organizations (see below).

Typical field marketing activities include:

1. Selling into independent retail outlets, eg field sales teams sold Christmas charity cards to almost 18,000 outlets during January, February and March.
2. Merchandising and display – arranging stocks and literature in retail stores and other outlets, eg 25,000 newsagents and doctors' surgeries had the Department of Social Security's Family Credit information point-of-sale material placed in them within 14 days.
3. Sampling/promotions – providing teams (eg the Pepsi Challenge) in shopping precincts, superstores and at national events and exhibitions.
4. Market research into shelf facings, stocking levels and positions in store (including number of shelf facings or number of units that can be seen).
5. Monitoring customer care/service – with mystery shoppers who are employed to observe service and report back details of the specific levels of in-store service and customer care.

The Thomson's Tours case study at the end of Chapter 18 has an example of how a field marketing team can operate flexibly and efficiently.

Multi-level marketing

Multi-level marketing is a system of selling goods directly to customers through a network of self-employed salespeople. The manufacturer recruits distributors, who in turn recruit (or sponsor) more distributors, who in turn recruit more distributors and so on. Each distributor is on a particular level of discounts (depending on the size of stock purchased). The distributor effectively earns income on his or her own direct sales to the distributors he or she has recruited. The distributor also earns a percentage of the earnings of all of the other distributors connected through his or her chain or line of distributors.

Multi-level marketing is sometimes called network selling, retail networking or pyramid selling. Several companies have proved that network selling can be a legal and successful method of marketing. Pyramid selling has a bad image because it was exploited unscrupulously, with new distributors being promised fortunes in return for large investments in stock which never sold. In addition, these selling systems tend to exploit personal contacts and networks, which can cause an individual to view all his or her friends and family (or anyone with whom he or she comes into contact) as sales prospects. This mercenary perspective is sometimes enveloped in a kind of corporate evangelism which gives this sales and distribution method a poor image, despite the several legitimate and successful systems that thrive in the United States.

The Trading Schemes Regulation 1997 allows a maximum initial fee of £200 (within the first seven days) to be charged for enrolment as a distributor. Goods are then purchased at a discounted wholesale price, which allows the newly enrolled distributor to add his or her own margin of profit when selling the goods to an end-user. Goods are returnable (and 90 per cent of the cost recoupable). Any training fees must be clearly stated in the written contract and training must not be compulsory.

MANAGING THE SALESFORCE

The primary responsibilities of the salesforce manager include *recruitment, training, motivating, controlling* and *collecting feedback*.

Recruiting

Determining the right size and structure of the salesforce is vital. What is the *optimum call frequency*? Who should service the account? As an organization changes or grows, so too the salesforce and its responsibilities must change. *Salesforce attrition* is a fact of life. Some salespeople move to new companies, some are promoted, others retire or are fired. This means that recruitment is a continual process that demands skills, cash and time. Recruiting the right salesperson is a resources-consuming management activity. Recruit the wrong people and sales can actually be reduced instead of increased. Keeping the right sales team together is largely determined by levels of training, motivation, control and feedback.

Training

Training is an ongoing affair, not a one-off activity. It is a continuous process. Like thinking, it requires practice (Tony Buzan's classic books emphasize that thinking is a skill that needs development and exercise). Basically the salesforce has to acquire and maintain three pieces of knowledge and one set of skills – selling skills. The three pieces of knowledge that the professional salesperson must have are:

1. Product (4Ps, features/benefits and USPs).
2. Market (customers and competitors).
3. Company (history, structure, etc).

Appendix 10.1 shows a list of questions salespeople can use to assess their level of knowledge. The arts of selling, salesmanship, sales techniques and selling skills require separate training.

The 7P approach to selling skills

There are several different stages involved in selling. The 7P sequential approach identifies areas for skill improvement. The seven states are:

1. Prospecting (looking for potential customers).
2. Preparation (objective setting, continual customer research, etc).
3. Presentation (demonstration, discussion).
4. Possible problems (handling objections).
5. 'Please give me the order' (closing the sale or getting the order).
6. Pen to paper (recording accurately all relevant details).
7. Post-sales service (developing the relationship).

Each stage requires a certain amount of training and practice. Training should also include non-selling activities (information-gathering techniques, time-management skills, personal expense control, etc). Preparation is continual and includes an initial analysis of the customer's business, issues and objectives, clarifying exactly what they want to achieve as well as identifying their compelling reason to act. Their financial position, access to funds and decision-making units are also carefully studied. Eventually a risk analysis will be completed, identifying potential problems, their sources and their likely impacts.

Using problems (objections) to close that sale

Julie says: 'I don't like the way you dress, I don't think you make enough money, and you drive like a maniac.'
Frank hears: 'I don't like the way you dress (BUYING SIGNAL), I don't think you make enough money (BUYING SIGNAL), and you drive like a maniac (BUYING SIGNAL).
Frank's response: 'If I let you pick my suits, if I double my income, and if I promise never to exceed the posted speed limits – will you marry me then?'

Frank Pacetta, Xerox sales manager

Motivating

Maintaining the salesforce's motivation is a vital part of sales management.

It can be as easy as publishing the monthly sales figures against targets for each sales rep and circulating the figures among the sales team. This can lead to competition among members, which may inhibit them from sharing ideas, contacts, leads and even closing techniques. On the other hand, it can keep everyone focused on targets, with peer pressure as a source of motivation. It is the sales manager's job to build a team feeling and get everyone working together, sharing ideas rather than hiding them from each other.

'Psychic income' is often a stronger motivator than financial income, yet it does not need to cost the company any more money than the traditional financial incentive. Psychic income offers rewards aimed at the higher levels of need, such as being valued, recognized, rewarded and challenged (see Maslow's hierarchy of needs on page 109).

This is how it works. A bonus cheque for £1,000 tends to get spent on dull and boring things like reducing the overdraft or paying the mortgage. On the other hand, the same £1,000 spent on a holiday for two or a spectacular piece of Waterford glass acts as a constant reminder of a job well done. Even a clap on the back, a thank-you note, a presentation ceremony or a photograph in the newsletter (or in the annual report) can arouse feelings that satisfy the higher levels of Maslow's hierarchy of needs. This contrasts with the £1,000, which is probably used to satisfy the dull, boring and soon forgotten lower levels of need. The reward itself is soon forgotten here, whereas the psychic income reward tends to linger longer and therefore offer better motivational potential.

> *Two holes of golf with Jack Nicklaus*
>
> The Maritz Corporation specialize in psychic income packages. They even give out pyramid-shaped paperweights that list Maslow's needs. They tailor their awards so that individuals are offered an appropriate range of stimulating options. Some of their choices have offered trips to the moon, ballooning across the wine fields of Burgundy or two holes of golf with Jack Nicklaus. As you approach the 18th green there is an 80-piece orchestra perched on scaffolding, playing the tune of your choice.

The *annual sales conference* should be a motivator and act as a forum for sharing ideas ('How I made a sale' contest), identifying and solving problems, improving techniques, and recognizing and rewarding achievements. The conference should also provide a pleasant environment that reinforces feelings of being glad to work with the company.

Controlling

Controlling the salesforce involves analysing sales:

- by product;
- by market/region;
- by salesperson.

Sales can also be analysed by profitability or the 'contribution' each order makes towards the overall profitability of the organization. This encourages the salesperson to sell higher-margin products/services rather than succumbing to the temptation of (a) giving discounts and (b) pushing easier, low-margin items.

The bottom line tends to be turnover or sales, number of new accounts (customers) won and old accounts lost, and the quality of those accounts (size and creditworthiness). Further analysis reveals number of orders (and average order size), calls to orders ratios, etc. Even miles driven gives some indication as to whether a rep is chasing his or her tail or leaving room for improvement. Good planning helps control.

Good sales forecasting provides targets and yardsticks for measurement. Sales forecasts can be drawn up by sales reps for each customer for each month and eventually put together to form an overall sales rep forecast. This can be modified to allow for low forecasts that reduce target sales figures, thereby reducing pressure on the reps and making it easier for them to attain their daily, weekly, monthly, quarterly and annual targets. There are, of course, more sophisticated forecasting models that take into account a host of factors including prices, competitors, state of the economy, etc.

Typical quantitative standards are as follows:

- sales volume as a percentage of sales potential;
- selling expense as a percentage of sales generated;
- number of customers as a percentage of the total number of potential customers in the territory;
- call frequency ratio, or total calls made divided by total number of customers and prospects who are called upon (or visited) by the salesperson.

Time – the scarce resource

The average salesman spends *less than 10 per cent* of his or her time actually engaged in face-to-face selling (Abberton Associates, 1997). The rest of the time is spent filling in report forms, travelling, setting up appointments, attending internal meetings, etc. Is this the optimum use of a key resource? Definitely not, so some companies use other communication tools (eg direct-response advertisement, or a mailshot) to generate enquiries, then categorize or qualify the quality of the enquiry or lead into 'hot, medium or cold' prospects. A telesales team can then further qualify the lead by determining how urgent, immediate or serious the enquiry is (see 'Hybrid marketing system' on page 374 for further examples). They can even set up appointments in a way that minimizes the travel between appointments. 'The extinguisher' on page 288 is an extreme example, where the salesman seizes the relatively rare face-to-face opportunity and makes a sale every time (although he may also soon be locked up!).

Reducing the call frequency

Servicing customers with a mixture of telephone calls and personal visits, instead of visits only, allows sales reps to become more efficient by reducing the frequency of their visits but maintaining the frequency of contact/service by phone. There is obviously a fine line between the less personal telephone call and the more personal visit. Some buyers may prefer to avoid the interruption of a sales visit and appreciate a courtesy call ('just checking to see if everything is all right or if there is anything you need'). This minimizes time wastage (for both parties) while maintaining the customer service facility. Getting the balance between calls and visits is vital since competition is also out there, every day, knocking on the same doors. Optimum call frequencies need to be carefully planned.

CREATIVE SELLING

There is always room for creativity in marketing, and particularly in selling. Whether it is a new form of presentation, a new way of prospecting or a new way of showing determination to win the business, the list is endless. The extinguisher's creative approach below is not to be recommended. The case study, Selling life assurance, at the end of this chapter shows how a small budget and a smart salesman can create an effective and integrated marketing activity.

The extinguisher

I recall a story of an interesting sales pitch that was written about in a marketing magazine many years ago.

Having recognized the weary tread of a door-to-door salesman coming up the stairs, the giggling office staff scrambled behind doors and under desks to avoid the approaching salesman's eye contact. I only realized that a salesman was looming when I noticed the sniggering bodies scattered behind the furniture. Too late. I turned around to see a shabby little man with a greasy raincoat and coffee-stained briefcase move towards me. Before I knew it he had opened his briefcase and poured a jar of petrol over himself. Out of his inside pocket he drew a lighter and set fire to himself. Then, while standing in the classic salesman pose (right arm holding out a spray can and left arm pointing to the label), he said 'And this, ladies and gentlemen, is the FlameZapper miniature fire extinguisher...' As he proceeded to spray himself, he continued, 'You can carry it anywhere...' He left several cans lighter and several pounds heavier.

CASE STUDY 10.1

Selling life assurance

This case study demonstrates how innovative salespeople can be when motivated to create new methods of prospecting and selling.

Situation

The traditional marketing methods of advertising, exhibitions, seminars, mailshots and cold calling are commonly used by many organizations in the fiercely competitive life assurance market.

Objective

To find a new, competition-free, low-cost way of getting in front of groups of prospective clients in a friendly (non-hard-selling) atmosphere.

Strategy

To develop good relations with independent NHS and private hospitals whereby the hospitals can benefit from some fund-raising, while the sales team gain access to new prospects in an informal, non-hard-selling environment.

Tactics

Life assurance and hospitals work in much the same way – both offer a service nobody really wants to use. The NHS and private hospitals in south Hertfordshire, Middlesex and north London were approached to establish which hospitals were having summer fetes. These were then offered assistance and support in return for permission to do some soft selling. A children's bouncy castle was provided and all the profits (castle admission fee) would go to the hospital. As the children bounced around, their parents were approached by asking if they would like to enter a free prize draw and simultaneously identify whether any of the financial services would be of interest to them. The sales team's dress was strictly casual (no suits).

Action

In addition to the fete's visitors, the hospital administrators/managers were approached with a view to extending the services on an ongoing basis to the hospital staff. This presented further opportunities to give seminars to junior doctors and to sponsor various activities, including a squash competition. One hospital agreed to distribute details of the company's AVC (additional voluntary contribution/pension scheme) with the staff's pay slips. Other hospitals, after careful consideration, allowed the assurance salespeople access to the internal phone directory.

Control

The results to date have been positive in terms of sales of new policies, associated services and recruitment of new salespeople.

Men and women

One manager
Three associate salespeople
Once castle supervisor

Money

One bouncy castle supervisor	£15.00
One bouncy castle	£30.00
Eighteen prizes	£63.00
Total	£108.00

The cost of the castle was paid out of the bouncy castle takings on the day and the balance or surplus was donated to the hospital. Life assurance branded mugs, T-shirts, golf balls and torches were used as prizes. Eighteen prizes ensured that each associated salesperson had another opportunity to get back in front of six prize-winning prospects to present them with their prize. This was in addition to the other prospects who actually requested an appointment. The cost to each salesperson was £26 (cost of the prizes + supervisor divided by three).

Minutes

It takes several months of visits and discussions to build up a certain level of trust in the relationship between hospital administrators and the assurance company. Once permission has been given to participate in the fete, it takes only a matter of days to book a castle and brief the associates. The real time-consuming activity is the follow-up. Unless all leads are meticulously followed up, the whole effort is wasted. Several hospitals have since invited the assurance company to participate in their Christmas fairs, etc.

APPENDIX 10.1

Salesman's self-assessment questions

The product

1. How does it work (what does it do?)? Can you demonstrate it with ease and professionalism?
2. Feature vs benefits.
3. What are its advantages to the consumer (benefits)?
4. What are the advantages and disadvantages over the competition?
5. How old is the design?
6. Where is it made?
7. What safety, health or environmental standards and regulations are relevant?
8. Does it meet those standards? (What do those standards mean in layman's terms?)
9. What materials are used?
10. What back-up service do you offer?
11. How is it packed, from where is it delivered, order lag/lead time, minimum order quantities?
12. Are there any back-up promotions (point of sale, literature, promotions, cooperative advertising, samples, etc)?
13. What is the price (FOB, CIF, Ex-works, Ex-VAT, £ sterling, cash discounts, trade discounts, bulk discounts, credit terms, validity)?

Your customers

	Know	Don't know
1. How many different customer types can you identify?		
2. Who are the major customers/prospects in your area?		
3. Why do they buy from you (benefits)?		
4. Why have they all not placed orders?		
5. Do they buy at particular times only?		
6. Who are the decision makers?		
7. Do different customers/prospects look for different benefits?		
8. What is the exact number of your customers?		
9. What is the exact number of your prospects?		
10. How much time do you need to cover them all?		

Major customers

	Know	Don't Know
11. What is their total buying power (how much do they buy)?		
12. What other suppliers do they use?		
13. What is the major customer's turnover/sales for the past three years?		
14. Who will be your most important customers this year?		
15. What are the key trade journals in your market?		
16. Do you know when each of your top six customers orders?		

How many Knows?

15–16 excellent;
11–14 very good but room for improvement;
9–10 very good;
7–8 room for improvement;
Below 7, clean up your act!

Questions for experienced salespeople

	Yes	No
1. Do you regularly check your records/file?		
2. Do you have all customers ranked in order of importance (usually business volume)?		
3. Do you allocate your selling efforts to customers in direct proportion to the customer's importance (ie spend a long time with major accounts and less time with minor accounts)?		
4. Do you control your sales appointments (ie have you mastered the art of keeping customer contacts to a practical time minimum without appearing brusque)?		
5. Do you avoid personal visits where a telephone call might suffice?		
6. Are you at all times contactable (answer machine, bleeper, ring in every morning/afternoon)?		
7. Do you send customers Christmas cards (and sometimes even holiday cards)?		
8. Have you got a system that picks up customers who have passed their normal ordering cycle without placing an order?		
9. After every sale, do you check to see if delivery was OK, etc?		
10. Do key (major) accounts have your home telephone number?		
11. After losing an account (customer) do you always find out the *real* reason why?		
12. Do you keep a file on lost accounts (reasons why)?		

How many Yes's?

11–12 excellent;
9–10 very good;
7–8 room for improvement;
Below 7, clean up your act!

Some general questions on the competition

1. Have you examined their product?
2. What are the advantages and disadvantages of their product?
3. How does their product compare with yours?
4. Why do your customers buy your product and not the competition's?
5. What about the competition's actual company (structure, history, staff, etc)?
6. Price, delivery, promotion, etc.
7.
8.
9.
10.
11.
12.
13.
14.

Add your own questions to test your sales team's knowledge.

Your company

1. Do you know the full (registered name) of your company?
2. Do you know who founded the company?
3. Do you know why it was founded?
4. Do you know who currently owns your company?
5. Do you know who sits on the board?
6. Do you know whether you have any environmental policies?
7. Do you know if you have any ethical policies?
8. Do you know what are the past three years':
   - turnover;
   - market share;
   - number of employees?
9. Do you know your company's:
   - strengths;
   - weaknesses?

Key point from Chapter 10:

Consider and evaluate different types of salesforces.

FURTHER READING

Abberton Associates (1997) *Balancing the Selling Equation*, CPM Field Marketing Ltd Thame, Oxfordshire

Buzan, T (1988) *Make the Most of Your Mind*, Pan Books, London

Buzan, T (1989) *Use Your Head*, revised edition, Pan Books, London

Constable, J and McCormack, R (1987) *The Making of British Managers*, CBI/BIM, London

Denny, R (2000) *Selling to Win*, Kogan Page, London

Francis, K (1998) What is KAM?, *Winning Business*, Jan–Mar

Jobber, D and Lancaster, G (2000) *Selling and Sales Management*, Financial Times/Prentice-Hall, Harlow, England

Mathur, S (1981) Strategic industrial marketing: transaction shifts and competitive response, City University Working Paper 33, City University, London

FURTHER CONTACTS

Institute of Professional Sales, Moor Hall, Cookham, Maidenhead, Berkshire SL6 9QH (tel: 01628 427370; Web site: www.iops.co.uk)

Institute of Sales and Marketing Management, Romeland House, Romeland Hill, St Albans, Herts AL3 4ET (tel: 01727 812500; Web site: www.ismm.co.uk)

Advertising

INTRODUCTION

The oblivion of advertising

We are witnessing the oblivion of advertising.

Regis McKenna

Some say advertising is dead. Others say it is a maturing industry. The fortunes of advertising have grown alongside the growth of mass media. Now that this growth has stopped, questions are being asked. Mass media is fragmenting continually (200 TV stations, millions of Web sites and an explosion of new magazines and radio stations). Martin Sorrell (WPP) says, 'Massive audiences become more and more difficult to buy.' It is therefore suggested that the current lavish levels of advertising production, which depend on mass audiences to make it cost-effective, will decline as well. Although advertising does have a unique ability to simplify and condense a complicated selling message into an emotionally charged 30-second piece of film, media proliferation has meant that the traditional 30-second TV advertisement is no longer the answer to everything. But brilliant advertising images for both broadcast and narrowcast, online and and offline, on pack and off pack are still required. More TV and radio stations, Web sites, posters, papers, point-of-sale and cinemas will still need advertisements to fill them. The different is that no marketer will want them on their own, in an unintegrated, free-standing manner.

The party's over

The party's over: advertising as we know it will no longer be up to the task on its own. It will need to learn new ways of increasing customer interaction and working outside the broadcast media.

HHCL

Perhaps the days of selling mass-produced goods to a mass market through mass media are largely over, but advertising per se is not. One thing is for sure, and that is that agencies and advertising are going through a period of exciting change. As Sorrell concedes, 'Brand advertising in the next 20 years is going to demand a great deal more than the ability to write, produce and place a 30-second spot on network television.' Advertising is changing. It is already moving into the world of infomercials, subverts, i-candy, interstitials, screen savers (see Appendix 11.1), sponsorship, direct mail and other interactive opportunities as it moves from a 'tell medium' to a dialogue medium; eg 75 per cent (in 2000) of all branded goods in the US carry a 1–800 number, encouraging a free-flowing dialogue with customers. Massive databases exist – in the United States, Procter and Gamble have 44 million names on theirs, Kraft 40 million, R J Reynolds 40 million. The advertiser's playing field is wide open to creativity and integration across other disciplines. Clients are ready for the move (see Chapter 6 for more on how irate clients feel about the old advertising practices). The days are over when clients politely smiled as Lord Leverhulme's legacy echoed, 'Half my advertising is wasted, trouble is I don't know which half.' Today, better disciplined clients demand more measurement, more integration, more dialogue from their communications, including their advertising. Having said all that, advertising is not dead. Its unique features will allow it to integrate seamlessly across the host of communications tools.

Advertisers have to think 'outside the box'. The days of the dynamic dialogue have arrived, when advertisers engage customers in a two-way flow of communication through direct mail, telesales, the Internet and more. There will be more links, more hooks, more 0800 number and Web site addresses attached to every communications tool, including advertising. The key to success, say HHCL, 'will be to understand customers' needs for interaction and involvement and developing strategies to maximize them'. They propose a change of advertising language from 'impact' to 'dialogue', from 'poster advertising' to 'street dialogue', from 'direct mail and radio' to 'kitchen dialogue', from 'customer base' to 'customer community', with more than a 30-second dialogue but a series of ongoing experiences. Many customers want more information than traditional advertising can provide (or at least the facility to have it should they need it). So again seamless links from advertising into other communications tools are required. Marketers will like it. Customers won't care. Consciously or unconsciously, customers want a relationship with a brand. Some will want a dialogue. Some will want to be left alone to get on with their busy lives which are packed with 'real' relationships.

Who is going to explore the Web to find out about frozen peas?

John Fanning

Although some passive, television viewing couch potatoes may be replaced by active, PC-loving couch mice, not everyone wants interaction all the time. As John Fanning says, 'It must also be said that just as a majority of the population in most countries are prepared to vote on election day, but only a small minority wish to become political activists, so too the majority of consumers exposed to most advertising have no desire to talk back.'

Customers might just want advertising to inform them, entertain them and challenge them… just as it always has. After all, advertising does inform, persuade and remind. It can still very quickly help to build brands, raise awareness and nurture brand relationships. And all in a relatively controlled environment (compared to the vagaries and uncontrollable nature of editorial exposure generated by PR and sponsorship campaigns – see the uncontrollable nature of PR on page 426). So, although it will not be the same as before, there is a future for integrated advertising. This means that managers will still have to be able to manage the development of an advertising campaign.

MANAGING AN ADVERTISING CAMPAIGN

This chapter focuses on how an advertising campaign is planned and managed. The first three elements of the SOSTAC® + 3Ms approach to planning (previously discussed in Chapter 2) are used here to give structure to the development of an advertising campaign:

- Where are you now? (situation – S)
- Where do you want to go? (objectives – O)
- How will you get there? (strategy – S)

The advertising campaign planning process incorporates an analysis of the current situation (research) and a clear definition of the overall communications objectives, as well as the specific advertising objectives. Only then can the advertising strategy be devised. The strategy summarizes broadly what to say (message), how to say it (execution, tone or creative strategy), who to say it to (target audience), where to say it (media choice or media strategy), when to say it (timing) and, sometimes, how much it will cost (budget). Strategy can also guide the integration or links between advertising and all of the other communications tools.

THE SITUATION

There is a lot of research to be done before any exciting creative work can be started. *What* are the current sales trend, market share trend and overall market trend? Are there any regions or segments that buy more than others? *How* big are the competition's sales (per region and per distribution channel)? What is the profile of the customer and of the non-customers who might be converted? *Who* is the target market now and in the future? Who are the heavy users? *When* do they buy? *Where* do they buy?

How is the brand positioned in the minds of various target markets? *Why* do people use/not use the brand? This can be the most difficult question to answer because real reasons are often deeply hidden beneath apparently rational buying behaviour. What are the current features and benefits of your product or service? A feature is translated into a benefit by using three words: '… which means that…' For example, 'This car has a crush loading of over five tons, which means that it can roll over without the roof caving in.' Many advertising campaigns can demonstrate benefits without having to use words (in fact wordless advertisements like Levi's may become more popular as satellite television grows – see Chapter 9), but it is the application of this three-word formula that helps to identify real benefits that can then be demonstrated. Spending time 'interrogating the product' is a good investment.

Product interrogation

In addition to the previous question, further questions, or product interrogation, can sometimes reveal hidden benefits which advertising can subsequently highlight. Is there anything unique about the product (USP – unique selling proposition)? Product (or service) interrogation explores and examines every angle, including product characteristics, user characteristics, ways of using, benefits of using, disadvantages of non-usage, competitor comparisons, product heritage, customer cases, newsworthiness and more. How does it compare against the competition's features and benefits in both people's imagination and in reality?

The cunning K Shoe lady

Some years ago shoe manufacturer K Shoes and their agency BBH discovered a hidden USP. This was that the quality of the leather in their shoes was such that their shoes did not creak or squeak. This subsequently opened up the opportunity of dramatizing the benefits of squeak-free shoes. One of the TV advertisement's showed a lady wearing K Shoes quietly entering an apartment in which her lover was dining with another woman. The K Shoes lady proceeded to dump a bowlful of slimy noodles on the head of the two-timing man. The K Shoe lady turned silently and walked confidently out of the apartment.

BBH

How does the product or service compare with competitors' products in the mind of customers (how is is positioned)? Or have they even heard of it? (What percentage are *spontaneously aware* of your product or service? Is it *top of the mind* or *front of mind*, ie do customers include it in the first three brands they think of when considering your product type?) What is important to the target customers? Or perhaps there is a high level of awareness but low level of preference, possibly because of a poor product or poor image? What do customers consider to be the most important factors (key buying criteria) when making a choice? What is their *ideal product*?

Trend identification

What new values, trends, attitudes or lifestyles/business styles are emerging that may affect the organization's product or service? Individualism, self-exploration, materialism, environmentalism, ageism, sexism, interaction… once the advertisers identify a relevant trend, they can then reflect it through advertising imagery.

Review of past advertisements

An analysis of competitor advertising campaigns can trigger ideas and, more importantly, provide some insights into competitor strategies, thereby helping the strategic thoughts of the advertising for the brand in question. Even the brand's past campaigns can give some guidance as to how they reflect the state of the market, what the objectives are, and what works and what does not.

Consumer research and trend identification

Another major exercise was embarked upon to understand the consumer environment that the new advertising executions would have to operate in.

The central thesis was quite simply that in the early and mid-1980s consumers felt most comfortable following the crowd and feeling a collective sense of involvement. In this context advertising that showed session-drinking in the pub (men making wisecracks) was quite appropriate. Brands in the main lager arena prospered. The role these brands occupied was to lubricate the session-drinking of the male-dominated pub. In the late 1980s this climate changed and the process of change continues. Now the consumer wishes to stand *out* from the crowd and express his *individuality* much more. He does this by demonstrating his discernment in the clothes he wears and the brands he chooses.

The implications for the advertising were fundamental: a more sophisticated audience, a change in the pub environment, less session-drinking orientation and a different attitude to premium brands. Indeed a significant opportunity if Draught Guinness, already moving in the more fashionable image arena, could catch the crest of this wave and exploit it fully. In order to do so, this social change needed to be confirmed and understood in some detail.

Ogilvy & Mather

Answers to all of the questions raised in the situation analysis/review are required before setting advertising/communications objectives. In a sense, researching the current situation reveals the objectives for the campaign. *Good research makes objective setting easier.*

Research, however, costs time and money (and people), so it needs to be budgeted for or, ideally, to be built into a *continual system of information gathering* (see 'Marketing intelligence and information system', page 141) to help both objective setting and subsequent measurement of the campaign's effectiveness.

OBJECTIVES

After analysing the situation through primary and secondary research sources (see Chapter 5) a clear picture of where you are emerges. The next step is to define exactly where you want to be. 'If you don't know where you're going, any road will take you there.' Ideally, *objectives should be quantified* in terms of success/failure and timescale. This makes control easier, since actual results can be measured against quantified objectives. The previous year's objectives, and corresponding results, help to make the planning job a little easier, as previous experience provides a better idea of what are realistic objectives for the future.

Objectives should be *SMART*:

- **S**pecific;
- **M**easurable;
- **A**ctionable;
- **R**ealistic;
- **T**ime specific.

A clear strategy (how to get there) is not possible without clearly defined objectives (where you want to go). Without a clear strategy, a loose set of tactics, lacking cohesion (and sometimes pulling in different directions) is likely to emerge.

Establishing clear objectives is necessary to give a focus to the organization. Clear objectives also given direction to the subsequent creative efforts. Some marketing managers and agencies break objectives into many different types. We focus on just two types here:

1. Marketing objectives.
2. Communications objectives.

Marketing objectives

Typical marketing objectives refer to sales, market share, distribution penetration, launching a number of new products and so on. See the objectives on page 41.

Communications objectives

You will find examples of communications objectives on page 42. As mentioned in Chapter 2, communications objectives typically refer to how the communication should affect the mind of the target audience, eg generate awareness, attitudes, interest or trial. The DAGMAR (defining advertising goals for measuring advertising results) and AIDA (awareness, interest, desire and action) hierarchical models reveal some of the mental stages many buyers have to move through before buying. Again, these objectives (eg 'to increase awareness') are more useful when quantified ('to increase awareness from 35 per cent to 45 per cent within a six-week period').

Another way of looking at communications objectives in a competitive market for, say, the purchase of a car would be as follows:

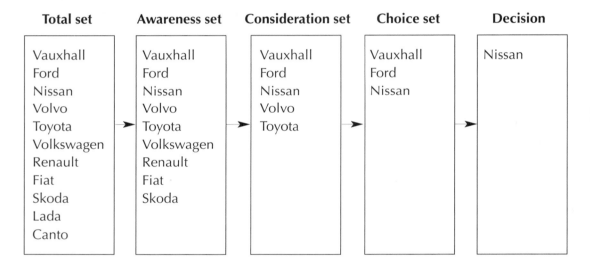

Total set	Awareness set	Consideration set	Choice set	Decision
Vauxhall	Vauxhall	Vauxhall	Vauxhall	Nissan
Ford	Ford	Ford	Ford	
Nissan	Nissan	Nissan	Nissan	
Volvo	Volvo	Volvo		
Toyota	Toyota	Toyota		
Volkswagen	Volkswagen			
Renault	Renault			
Fiat	Fiat			
Skoda	Skoda			
Lada				
Canto				

A particular campaign's objective may be to move a significant number of prospects from one set to the next. Some advertisements go further by seeking to reinforce/reassure existing buyers.

STRATEGY

With the situation fully researched and clear objectives identified, the campaign or advertising strategy can now be developed. It will include positioning, objectives, target audience, key benefits, secondary benefits and often a statement on what kind of media will be used. The strategy will not get bogged down in detailed tactics or any specific creative messages. It should offer strategic direction to the client and agency team. Some clients will work with the agencies to develop this key statement. Other agencies do all the work and present the campaign strategy to the client for approval.

The campaign strategy forms the foundation for the more detailed planning and development of the actual message (or the advertisement itself), and the selection of the media. Figure 11.1 (page 306) illustrates how the initial SOS forms the basis for the subsequent development of the message and media plan.

Strategy first and tactics later?

Quite apart from the fact that a good deal of post-rationalization goes on to justify in marketing terms what seems like a good idea, the advertising objectives and strategy can often be devised simultaneously.

Tony Douglas

THE MANY STAGES OF MESSAGE DEVELOPMENT

Creative briefs

With the review complete, objectives set and strategy agreed, the creative team can finally be called in and briefed. The creative brief is a key document. Each agency has its own style (see top advertising agency BMP DDB Needham's style in Figure 11.2, page 307). It is here where all the volumes of research findings and weeks of discussions have to be concentrated into a single-page creative brief that translates the details and research jargon into relatively simple layman's terms that explain exactly what the advertisement should do.

This is the brief that the planner or account manager gives to the creative team. It succinctly covers all the key information such as: the target audience and its perceptions, motivations and buying criteria; advertising objectives, proposition, tone and how the audience should feel after the advertisement; and constraints and choice of media. It is an important document and should be signed (or approved) by an account director before being passed to the creative team. Sometimes the client wants to approve it also.

Both the agency and the client need to have a clear focus on exactly what the advertising should say or what it should achieve. Many creative people don't want too much detail ('Just tell me exactly what you want!'). They will then set about delivering a creative idea or concept. Figure 11.2 (page 307) shows the summary creative brief which BMP DDB Needham used for the award-winning National Dairy Council. Note: at the suggestion of

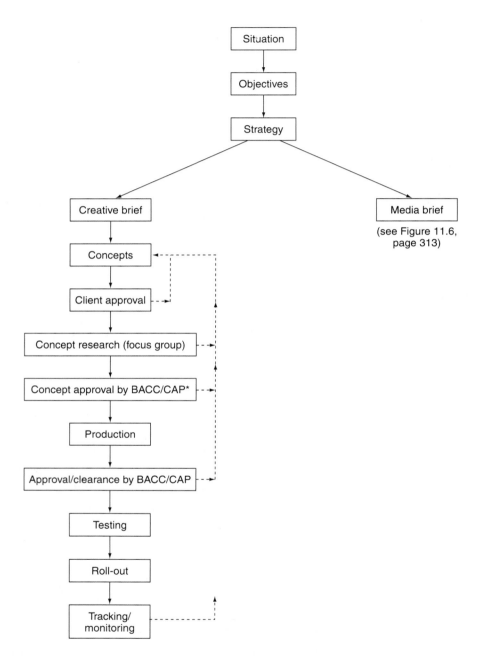

*Contact with the BACC / CAP (see Chapter 8) may occur earlier

Figure 11.1   The remaining stages of the campaign planning and execution

Why are we advertising at all?
Every pint of milk which is sold through a supermarket rather than a milkman loses the dairies 10p in profit. More and more people are moving some or all of their order to the supermarket. What is more, the tendency is to consume less milk when it is bought from the shops – because it is less 'on tap'. The fundamental benefits of having milk delivered have not been presented in advertising for a very long time and there is evidence that these benefits have become back of mind among the people who are drifting away. Rather like a big brand which has been unadvertised and allowed to drift, what we need is a big, impactful relaunch of the delivery service.

What is the advertising trying to do?
1. Represent the strongest rational and emotional arguments for having a milkman.
2. Add to the self-esteem of the milkmen.

Who are we talking to?
Busy mums, who have moved some or all of their order from the milkman to the supermarket.
Milkmen.

What do we know about them that will help us?
Busy mums are the people most in need of the convenience a milkman offers. They get through about ten pints a week and, on top of carrying it all home, it is yet another thing that they constantly have to bear in mind. Their needs for milk may vary wildly, eg at the weekend, people dropping in. If, as is common, they have whole milk for some of the family and low fat for others, they have even more to keep track of.

Lapsing users are the people who have most forgotten what benefits the milkman offers. Everyone agrees that the main advantages are 'don't have to go out' and 'don't have to carry home'. On a more emotional level the milkman brings a personal, human-scale service, making your house seem more of a home. These fundamental advantages have become progressively back of mind among those who are lapsing.
(We should also bear in mind that some of the people we are talking to still have a milkman at the moment.)

What is the main thought we need to put across?
The milkman delivers help to your doorstep.

What's the best way of achieving this?

1) The milkman delivers the benefit, personifies the service and is the secondary audience and should therefore be central to the advertising idea.
2) We need to make this benefit concrete.
   – he carries a full range of milks, including semi-skimmed milk.
   – he is flexible; he can juggle the most complicated orders and can deliver a bumper supply for the weekend.
   – he carries all that heavy milk for you.
3) If it is useful, we could also support the argument with the recycling of bottles (green).

Why do we think we are saying the right thing in the right way?

(Summarize the evidence)
The need for a comprehensive relaunch comes from NCD research which shows that, in particular, those who are lapsing have a lower awareness of the advantages of a milkman order.

The central thought of help from a milkman is universally recognized as the main reason for having a milkman – whereas the secondary points appeal to different sub-groups and support this main benefit by giving concrete examples rather than an empty promise.

Essential practical considerations?
– logo
– tel no.
– address, etc.
– budget discipline

Any other client expectations we must consider?

Tone of voice
The style of the commercial should be charming, friendly and witty because this is how people see and want to see that milkman.

End line
The end line for milk must be incorporated – (see separate brief).

Figure 11.2   BMP DDB Needham's creative brief for the National Dairy Council

the client, one extra task was added – targeting milkmen themselves (as a secondary audience) to improve morale.

CONCEPTS

Ideas or concepts are roughly designed into 'roughs' or 'scamps' which can be developed into a storyboard (like a comic version – see Figure 11.3). The idea can then be further developed into better-quality visuals known as key frames (see Figure 11.4). These, in turn, can be shot on video to create an animatic (moving cartoon of the advertisement complete with music, voice-over and sound effects). Any of these visual presentations of the advertising concept (concept board, storyboard, key frames, animatics) are discussed and/or *researched* before the idea is allowed to go on to the expensive production stages and eventually to the even more expensive media stage (buying space and actually advertising). If the concept 'researches well', ie gets good feedback from the focus groups, it can be taken forward for further refinement and eventual production (see the Hofmeister Bear concept research, page 130). Despite poor research findings (ie the focus groups do not like the concept), some clients and agencies sometimes pursue an idea regardless of the negative research. For example, Heineken's long-running 'refreshens the parts other beers cannot reach' campaign did not research well but was, nevertheless, produced. It eventually went on to become a successful campaign.

Advertising agency BMP DDB Needham's rough concept idea for the National Dairy Council (Figure 11.3) was developed from the initial creative brief (shown in Figure 11.2). This is the birth of an award-winning advertising campaign that generated over 250 per cent return on investment (see advertising budgets on page 22).

Client approval

Concepts have to be justified or explained to clients. Agencies support their concepts with a 'message rationale' which basically explains why the concept is brilliant and guaranteed to achieve outstanding results!

Meanwhile the previous milkman concept was developed into key frames. This was then presented along with the message rationale to the client. The key frames can also be shown during focus group research. Figure 11.4 (page 310) shows a selection of the National Dairy Council's key frames.

Figure 11.3 National Dairy Council storyboard

Production

The production of an advertisement requires time and careful attention to detail. It may involve overseas locations, casting, contracts, rehearsals, special effects, weeks or months of sophisticated computer graphics, studio shoots, editing and more.

Figure 11.4 National Dairy Council key frames

The finished milkman campaign took over 14 weeks from brief to completion. Figure 11.5 shows what the finished television advertisement looked like.

Clearance

The finished advertisements should be checked before publication or broadcasting by the regulatory bodies (the CAP for non-broadcast advertisements and the ITVA for broadcast advertisements – see Chapter 8 for a full explanation of how these bodies work). ITVA clearance is compulsory while CAP is voluntary.

"2 semi-skimmed, 1 silver
top, number 18 - mmm,
rice pudding tonight"

"Lads, lads, what are you
playing at, you know
they're away for a fort-
night. But next door want
2 extra. Go on then..."

VO. Whatever your order,
your milkman can
deliver all the fresh
milk you'll ever need.

Figure 11.5 Finished National Dairy Council advertisement

Testing

With the production stage completed, some clients or agencies *test* the finished advertisement in a hall test (see page 124). Others will test the advertisements in a geographical region (eg Anglia TV or Ulster TV region) before rolling out nationally or internationally. Other clients put their advertisements out without testing because of time constraints. The 'first to market' with a new product or idea can often steal the initiative.

Roll-out

If an advertisement has been produced and subsequently tested (successfully), then it can be released, or rolled out, across its whole market.

Tracking

The advertising campaign can and should be monitored, or tracked, to see how it is working, eg what level of awareness it is generating or whether it is affecting attitudes or even sales. This allows any problems to be corrected sooner rather than later.

While the advertising messages are being developed, the media planners are busy devising media strategies and plans to ensure that the advertisements get the optimum exposure.

THE STAGES OF MEDIA PLANNING

More money is spent on media than on the production of the advertisement itself (eg BT spend over £90 million on advertising in the UK, of which only a few million go on production; the rest is spent buying space in the media). It is here that large savings can be made. Media planning is becoming increasingly scientific as press and TV proliferate. Although media buying, some argue, is an art in itself, some media planners understand the qualitative side of the media as well as the quantitative side and can therefore use media in a creative manner. The media awards in *Media Week* give an insight into the creative use of media.

Expert media planning and buying can also save vast sums of money, which can either be redeployed to buy more advertising space or saved and used elsewhere in the communications mix. There is, of course, the temptation to keep the saving and add it on to the bottom-line profits (by taking it away from the bottom-line expenses). Figure 11.6 shows the process of media planning.

Media strategy

Media people should not be briefed to book space after the advertisement has been created. They need to be involved early on, as their creative media input can influence the finished creative message. Carat Research shows that placing advertisements in unexpected positions can boost the likelihood of seeing them. From ads appearing upside down, to perfume

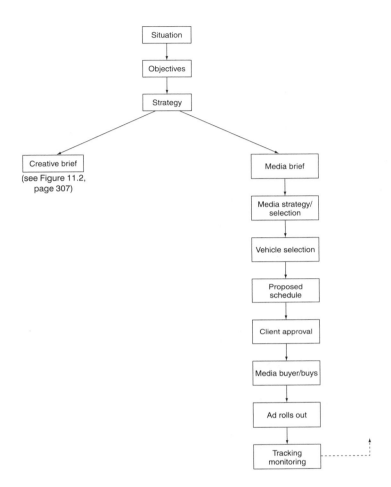

Figure 11.6 The media planning process

ads in finance pages, to a McDonald's ad in *Vogue* magazine, to buying all the back pages of specific colour supplements for a year (Boddingtons), to buying an entire newspaper for one day (Microsoft and *The Times*), to the entire three-and-a-half minute break in *News at Ten* (Peugeot 406), the media planners have plenty of creative scope (see the Money Channel's use of banners, pop-ups and interstitials in Appendix 11.3 on page 333). And they have plenty of new media to play with, from Video Vans (with large computer screens and mobile billboards) to interactivation, to floor posters, to laser-beamed buildings (see 'Ambient media' page 196), right through to 'new media' such as the Internet and its wonderful World Wide Web with its potential for interstitials, subverts, banner ads and much more (see Appendix 11.1 on page 331 for explanations and Appendix 11.2 on page 332 for typical CPMs for Web sites as well as Chapter 20). It is worth noting that Web sites can be bought

Description	Size	Cost per Insertion	no.	Jan	Feb	Mar	Apr	May	Jun	Jul	Aug	Sep	Oct	Nov	Dec	TOTAL COST
					Selfridges Launch	National Roll - Out						New Autumn Launches		Christmas Upweight		
Cosmopolitan	Page		4													
Elle	Page		3			M*	M* S	M* S*	S			M*	M	S*	S*	
Glamour	Page		4				M	M				M	M			
Marie Claire	Page		10			M	M S	M S	S			M	M	S	S	
Vogue	Page		8				M S	M S				M	M	S	S	
Good Housekeeping	Page		2										E	E		
You	Page		2			S (25)							S			
You	Inserts		1		M (11)											
Yellow	Page		1		M											
ES Magazine	Page		4		M (2)	M (2) S (23)							S			
Evening Standard	Page		3		M (9)								S S			
Metro	Page		3		M (2) M (9)	M (2)							S			
Metro	25x4		3			S (23) S (30)							S			
Sunday Times Style	Page		2			S (18)							S			
Manchester Evening News	Page		1		M (2)											
Routemaster buses	L-sides		1		M											
TOTAL																

TOTAL

Client Total

Budget

Reserve

M - Denotes Make-up activity
S - Denotes Skincare activity
E - Denotes Eye product activity

* Denotes activity booked by Tokyo

An example of a print media schedule for Shiseido Cosmetics

into for banner advertising (an ad at the top of a page), subverts, interstitials or sponsorship, games, competitions, direct retailing (where the host site handles the transactions) and e-mailings to registered members.

Chapter 7 also looks at media research, planning and scheduling. Appendix 11.3 shows the levels of media research and Appendix 11.4 shows the levels of media research and analytical tools available. Meanwhile here are some additional examples of how media strategy can work creatively and effectively. Haagen-Dazs ice cream used the weekend press to allow the advertisements to be savoured and enjoyed at leisure, while 'the intimacy of the experience could be hinted at better through the personal communication of the press'. Part of Guinness's media strategy was to use black-and-white 'fractionals' (ads within a small space) in newspapers which, as *Media Week* awards explain, meant that they 'effectively dominated the mono newspaper world with fresh and extensive copy rotations, so that no reader would see any one execution more than once over a period of seven months'.

Media schedules

In addition to the creative use of the media, careful analysis can identify the optimum media schedules. A media plan is then developed and presented to the client (eg Shiseido, opposite). This plan shows the types of places where the advertisement could be used. The space is then negotiated and bought. (See 'Media planning, scheduling and buying', Chapter 7.)

CASE STUDY 11.1

The continuing evolution of Lucozade Energy

Situation

Lucozade Original was launched in 1927 as the drink to aid convalescence. After several attempts to move the brand out of the sickroom through the 1970s and early 1980s, it was famously repositioned using Daley Thompson. There is now a range of products targeted against specific energy requirements for attitudinally discrete consumers.

Lucozade Energy still comprises about 75 per cent of total brand. It has a broad consumer franchise, being drunk across a huge range of occasions when some form of an energy boost is needed. However, most people still mainly associate the brand promise with occasions on which they need a 'large' energy boost. It does not form part of their repertoire for normal, everyday situations when an energy boost is required.

Objective

To increase frequency of consumption among occasional users of the brand.

Strategy

To drive the relevance of the 'Everyday Energy' promise in a contemporary and motivating manner. Creative target: 18- to 24-year-olds.

Tactics

Creative solution: Lara Croft campaign.

Lara Croft personifies Lucozade Energy: she oozes energy, has a feisty personality and is very appealing. Consumers see her as 'streetwise', 'fearless', 'sexy' and 'attractive'. She would imbue the brand with cool, hip, contemporary and dynamic values.

The objective was to develop a high-impact campaign using one creative platform or idea that would work across several different media. This would enable the brand to reach the target consumer at home (through TV), instore (through themed promotional activity and point-of-sale), on the street (through outdoor media) and also through the Internet. The utilization of multimedia was a departure from previous campaigns for Lucozade, where TV had been heavily relied upon as the key medium.

Action

- 360-degree solution that went right through the marketing mix: advertising, PR, promotional activity, packaging, point-of-sale.
- Multimedia advertising campaign: TV, posters, bus sides, interactive across 1999 and 2000.

The campaign was launched in June 1999 and continues into 2001.

Control

- 1983: £10m brand → 1998: £125m brand → 2000: £160m brand.

Since the Lara Croft campaign was launched the brand has grown at three times the rate of the total carbonated soft drinks market in the UK. Ex-factory sales increased by over 40 per cent in the six months following the launch of the campaign. Lucozade became the third largest soft-drink brand in the UK, despite a huge price premium.

The effectiveness of the advertising was also measured through a tracking study that was undertaken throughout the advertised period. Awareness of the total campaign reached 95 per cent among the target audience. The campaign was well branded and positively moved key brand imagery dimensions (eg 'Gets you energized, a drink for everyday').

The posters achieved one of the highest ever recognition scores on Poster Track and SignPost tracking studies. They also achieved the number 1 position for recall and popularity in *Marketing*'s Poster Watch. The Internet site achieved 5.7 million hits between June and October 1999: an increase of 32 per cent a month on average. The site was awarded the 1999 *The Grocer* award for Best New Media in the UK. Lucozade won the 1999 *The Grocer* award for Best Multimedia Campaign.

Men and women

In developing the campaign, over 50 people were involved both in the UK and in Australia, where the TV commercials were produced. However, teams that were involved throughout the process included those from the brand owner (GlaxoSmithKline), the advertising agency (Ogilvy & Mather) and the owner of Lara Croft (Eidos). Teams from other agents were involved at various times throughout, including the production company, animators and promotions, PR and design companies.

Money

Total advertising spend in UK:

- 1999: £5.1 million;
- 2000: £4.0 million.

Minutes

Activity	Timing
Strategy and creative brief agreed	August 1998
Concept presented	October 1998
Qualitative research	November 1998
Revisions to creative brief	December 1998
Qualitative research	January 1999
Production	February–May 1999
Quantitative pre-testing	May 1999
On air	June 1999

CASE STUDY 11.2

Daewoo car launch: exploding conventions in car marketing

This is a case that broke the mould for car marketing in the UK: one where client and advertising agency worked together, not just to rewrite the rules of advertising engagement, but also to redefine the way cars were bought and sold in the UK.

Situation

In 1994 Daewoo Motors approached a number of advertising agencies to help launch the Daewoo brand in the UK. Choosing to work with Duckworth Finn Grubb Waters (DFGW), Daewoo had to move quickly to overcome lack of awareness, inertia in an over-supplied market and a model range that was based on outdated 1980's Vauxhalls.

Objectives

Despite the difficulties detailed above, Daewoo had a very ambitious launch agenda and set of objectives: to achieve 1 per cent market share within 3 years. To put this into perspective, Hyundai had only managed to reach 0.64 per cent after 12 years and established contenders such as Saab and Mazda were both well below the 0.9 per cent mark. The objectives for Daewoo were therefore:

1. to launch the Daewoo brand into the UK car market;
2. to rapidly (within 3 years) build a 1 per cent market share;
3. to establish and maintain a presence as a mainstream (ie not niche) player in the UK car market.

Strategy

Challenging sales targets call for radical solutions. Fortunately Daewoo had no predetermined marketing strategy, but it did have Korean management, which encouraged innovation and was willing to think beyond the boundaries of traditional car marketing.

Research indicated that there was a fundamental unmet need in the UK car market, which represented a sizeable opportunity for Daewoo. Consumers felt that the process of buying a car was distinctly unpleasant, with:

- confrontational purchase experiences with pushy car salesmen;
- hidden costs (delivery charges, number plates);
- poor after-sales service and no focus on customer care.

A car company that could demonstrate commitment to a *relationship* with the customer that went beyond selling could capitalize on this unmet need. However, as an unknown company and indeed the fourth Korean entry into the market, owning this territory was by no means an easy task.

With analysis and planning, the barriers to achieving this task were also identified:

- Ignorance: Defined as 'Daewho?' As a brand with zero presence, Daewoo also had no car-building presence in the UK market.
- Scepticism: Consumers had serious doubts about the ability and indeed genuine desire of any car company to deliver this promise.
- Apathy: Why would customers bother to get involved?

DFGW and Daewoo developed a positioning of 'The most customer-focused car company in the UK'. This promise was underpinned by a unique set of pillars (see table opposite) that confronted the barriers and established tangible and credible ways to overcome them. Consumers' bad experiences of car-buying, for example, were contrasted with Daewoo's 'hassle-free' approach with free creches, etc.

The most customer-focused car company in the UK

Direct	Hassle-free	Peace of mind	Courtesy
Deals direct, so can afford to be generous with no compromise promise	Interactive in-store terminals Free café facilities Free crèches Fixed, no-haggle prices Extended test drives Location on retail parks No delivery charges No commissioned salesmen	3 years' comprehensive warranty 3 years' full AA cover 3 years' free servicing 6-year anti-corrosion warranty 30-day money back or exchange guarantee All safety features as standard: airbags, ABS, etc	Free collection and delivery for service Free courtesy cars

Tactics

Daewoo's launch had to do something special to have any chance of meeting the challenging objectives. The three phases of the launch campaign addressed each barrier, while building the foundations of the brand.

Phase One: Overcoming 'Daewho?'
It is unconventional, to say the least, to begin advertising in a market before the product is available. However, consumers are more receptive to brands they are already familiar with. With this in mind, a campaign launched in October 1994, six months before any cars arrived. This highlighted Daewoo's corporate credentials: the company's sheer size and its range of high-technology engineering products.

The biggest car company you've never heard of…

Phase Two: Overcoming scepticism

Car buyers are a cynical audience and Daewoo's advertising had to convince them that Daewoo really would be different. To this end, the 'Daewoo dialogue' campaign was launched. The advertising invited people to tell Daewoo what they wanted from a car company. Thus, not only was Daewoo able to glean useful data, but it was also able to be seen to be customer focused, which is clearly more credible than telling people you are.

We're looking for guinea pigs to test-drive 200 Daewoo cars for a year...

Phase Three: Overcoming apathy

As we have shown, the agency had developed an innovative role for advertising to act as consumer research, but developmental research had shown that many people would not necessarily bother responding. To boost response the customer-focused guinea pig commercial was developed, which offered customers the chance to become one of 200 drivers who would be given a free car for a year's extended test-drive.

Action

The Daewoo launch campaign ensured that each of the core brand values (direct and courtesy, hassle free and peace of mind) became the subject of a TV commercial. The look and feel of the campaign was distinctive, honest and down to earth. There were no glossy location shots.

The media strategy mirrored the attempt to overcome the established barriers. A large proportion of the spend was on TV advertising to overcome lack of familiarity and was spread throughout the year to demonstrate consistency and build trust; finally, to build fast awareness, CIA medianetwork bought a pattern of five spots over two ad breaks, disrupting the usual one spot per break wisdom. The press strategy ensured an enduring presence by owning key sites in the major titles throughout the year.

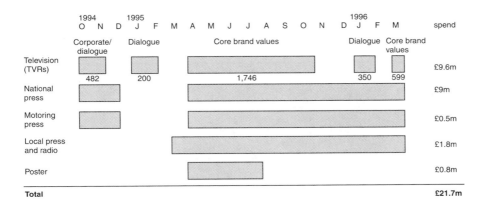

Control

Sales, brand and image measures all tell the same story. The Daewoo launch was the most successful car launch since SMMT records began.

Sales
Daewoo sold 18,005 cars in the first year, representing 0.92 per cent market share, and almost attaining the 3-year target of 1 per cent.

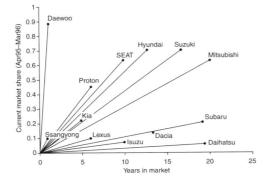

Brand
Awareness at over 90 per cent, was almost universal within the duration of the campaign.

Overcoming the barriers
Daewoo showrooms were visited by 400,000 people in the first 12 months. Quantitative research shows their reasons to be as follows:

Daewoo buyers' reasons for visiting a Daewoo showroom in the first place

	Daewoo buyers %
The cars are good value for money	88
There are no salesmen pestering you	75
I thought I would like the cars	68
I thought they would be better at looking after their customers than other car companies	56

Source: FDS, May 1996

Men and women

The Daewoo UK launch was unique in its combination of people involved. Instead of a cast of thousands, Daewoo UK consisted of just a managing director, a deputy managing director and a marketing director. On the agency side, a core team of agency partners, planner and account director ensured that the launch would run smoothly, and that decisions were quickly implemented. With key decisions in place, the implementation team widened, with key personnel in charge of each of the areas of TV and print production, media planning and buying, and ultimately tracking research.

Money

Daewoo's launch marketing spend was £22 million. However, in the context of the spend of other more established players this is not a great deal of money. For example, Vauxhall spent £94 million during the same period, Nissan £51 million and many others spent similarly large amounts. Significantly, Daewoo modelling is able to demonstrate a clear return on investment of up to £190 million.

Minutes

Daewoo approached DFGW in 1994. Unusually the Daewoo launch story spans three separate calendar years. As an entirely new entrant to the European car market, the initial awareness campaign broke in October 1994 to overcome ignorance of Daewoo as a brand. This was followed by a dialogue campaign in early 1995 to gather information and encourage trial, and finally by core brand value commercials in 1995 and 1996.

CASE STUDY 11.3

HEA Drug Education – how advertising turned the tide

Here is a case of how advertising fought a battle against huge odds to turn the tide of drug use in the United Kingdom. It is the story of a brave client building a strong campaign with an innovative advertising agency.

Situation

Britain during the 1990s faced an explosion of drug use among young people. In only five years the proportion of 14- to 15-year-olds in contact with drugs had doubled. Fifty-six per cent of 16- to 25-year-olds had tried drugs, nearly half of them (47 per cent) starting before they turned 15. In 1995, the government awarded the responsibility of educating the public about illegal drugs to the Health Education Authority (HEA). The HEA chose Duckworth Finn Grubb Waters to help them develop a three-year campaign to turn the tide.

Objectives

The client's brief was to reduce the demand for drugs among young people: a complicated task because it involved two important factors, firstly a large number of new users starting to take drugs, and secondly, only a small number of users stopping.

Given more time, the best solution would have been to tackle the adoption of drug use. Over the long term this would have reduced the number of new users, while the older users would gradually stop. However, both the need for clear results within three years and the

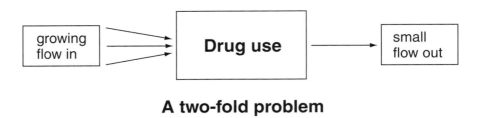

A two-fold problem

large numbers of young people already using drugs at the time meant that both problems needed to be tackled simultaneously.

Three key objectives regarding drug use were agreed:

- to stop people starting;
- to get current users to give up;
- to ensure that the inevitable number of people who did continue to use drugs harmed themselves as little as possible.

Tackling the problem on three fronts

Strategy

Research revealed that young people were not being pressured into taking drugs. Instead, they actively chose to take them, weighing up the pros and cons. The real problem was that within the enclosed world of youth culture, the pros outweighed the cons by an enormous and unrealistic margin. Millions of young people were ignorant of the health risks associated with recreational drugs.

The challenge therefore was to let young people have the information and conclude for themselves that drug taking was not a good idea. They already knew, and had dismissed, the fact that drugs were illegal, and their parents would disapprove. Research provided the key insight into how to persuade these young people away from drugs, which was, ironically, concern for their health. The strategy was clear: give them the facts, not the fear, and their own judgement should do the rest.

Tactics

In an ideal world, the campaign would have featured every drug available. Budget constraints meant that to educate the target market sufficiently for each drug would have been difficult. A selection criteria was therefore developed. Each drug featured must be one that:

- young people were likely to come across (ie be offered);
- they were likely to use, or consider using;
- carried health risks, about which they knew very little.

Therefore the campaigns focused on ecstasy, speed and LSD, and briefly featured magic mushrooms and mixing drugs.

Trying to persuade such a cynical audience was difficult enough, but if the government had been suspected as the source, the task would have been impossible. Gone were the 'just say no', and the 'drugs are bad' campaigns of the past. The audience was seen as capable of making their own decisions, and were to be treated as equals.

In order to maximize the effectiveness of the campaign, the advertising also promoted the National Drugs Helpline, so as to open up a dialogue and to educate further, on a one-to-one basis.

Infiltrating youth culture: actions

In order to maximize the budget of £6.8 million over three years, the agency worked closely with their media partner, New PHD. The 11- to 15-year-olds were tackled using teen magazines, while the 16- to 25-year-olds were reached through style press and dance radio. Crucially each burst of activity combined radio and press activity to create universal coverage.

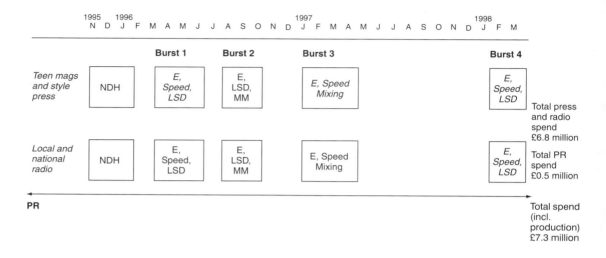

The creative work adopted an open, honest tone that allowed people to make up their own mind, and admitted that, in this untested market, doctors did not yet have all the facts. Bravely, the client (the government) agreed with the agency, allowing the creative work to acknowledge the positive effects of drugs. It was crucial in giving credibility to the campaign to admit that drugs could be fun.

The press ads featured young people in drug-taking situations, with a biological textbook 'cutaway' to reveal medical facts. The ads carried detailed information in an easily digestible form. On radio, scripted ads illustrated health risks, and vox pops revealed people talking about their drug experiences to a credible young man who delivered facts about drugs. These ads contributed to and mimicked the way people learn from their peers.

Control

The success of the campaign can be demonstrated both from direct response and advertising awareness, and from claimed drug use.

The advertising helped generate over a million calls to the National Drugs Helpline over the term of the campaign. Awareness levels nationally reached 62 per cent for radio executions, and 55 per cent for presswork. In a selected test region, awareness reached a staggering 90 per cent.

Three years after the launch of the campaign, drug use was on the decline:

- More people claimed to have stopped using drugs within 12 months of the campaign starting (from 1995 to 1996 the figure rose from 14 to 28 per cent).
- Fewer people considered using drugs – the proportion of 11- to 25-year-olds who claimed they would definitely or possible consider using drugs in the future went down by 14 per cent.

In addition to fulfilling the campaign's objectives, post-campaign analysis revealed that:

- With an annual £2.3 million ad spend, £28 million was diverted from the black market into the legal economy.
- The campaign saved British industry some £11 million per year in lost working days.
- The campaign added value to the field of drug education, saving organizations an estimated £3 million in potential development costs of materials.

Men and women

The HEA Drugs Education campaign demonstrated tight collaboration between several agencies, from the advertising agency and the youth PR company, to the below-the-line agency and an innovative media agency, and of course the client. Each used different levels of human resourcing in order to effectively plan and deliver the campaign. The advertising agency used a core team managing partners, an account planner and director, and an account manager, in order not only to manage internal process but also to effectively coordinate the work of the other agencies, and ensure that time was efficiently used. Once decisions were taken, a wider team of supporting departments began work, from the print and radio departments, to media planning and buying, as well as PR 'selling in' of stories.

Money

The HEA Drugs Education budget was £6.8 million over three years, to change a market that accounted for 8 per cent of world trade. In the UK this market was made up of £13 billion of drugs circulating every year. Duckworth Finn Grubb Waters were able to prove that over £28 million was diverted from the black market into the legal economy as a result of the campaign. British industry saved £11 million per year in lost working days.

Minutes

The HEA appointed Duckworth Finn Grubb Waters in July 1995. Much of the planning and creative work was developed during the pitch process – although there was still much to do when appointed to the business. The launch of the Drugs Helpline occurred in November 1995, just three months after the agency was appointed – an unusually fast turnaround time. However, for the three years of the campaign, there was continuous planning and evaluation for each burst, and constant tracking and refinement in order to reach the maximum effectiveness.

APPENDIX 11.1

New forms of advertising

Infomercials

They are simply long TV advertisements. Can last up to three minutes.

DHTML (dynamic HTML)

DHTML is an animated form of advertising that allows creative flexibility in terms of placement on a Web site. The creative can be tailored in terms of its shape to the needs of the advertiser, and can move freely around the screen of the Web site, in any direction (subject to site approval). The ad appears to hover above the content on the page, and in doing so achieves cut-through and generates a good response.

I-candy

I-candy conveys a brand message through animation and games. As Robert Dwek explains: 'Cheeky-chappy icons and banners, which when clicked unleash a burst of impressive audio and graphics on a quasi Web site that takes you straight back to the one you were on. A typical example of i-candy featured a bull charging with excellent sound effects, knocking a cartoon man across the screen.' Levi's attached its i-candy to 140 sites (that liked taking this kind of advertising because it also adds value to their sites by increasing the user's enjoyment).

Interstitial

An interstitial (or intermercial) is an intrusive, linear, usually full-screen size animated advert called up between content on a Web site that acts in a similar manner to a TV spot, but after playing allows users to visit and interact with the advert itself.

Subvert

A subvert is an advertisement (say 20 seconds long), accessed through the World Wide Web by clicking on a banner advertisement (an advertisement attached and flashing on someone else's Web site). By clicking on the banner ad, the user is taken to a 20-second experience that delivers a snappy brand message and then automatically reconnects the user back to the Web page from where he or she started.

Screen savers

Screen savers appear on most PCs. In a sense every terminal is a potential advertising site. So if a company gets customers to download a screensaver from the Internet or from a CD ROM on to their PC, then effectively they have created a new moving personal poster site. Tens of thousands of people regularly download Guinness's new screen savers, as they provide interesting variety; they also provide a powerful 'free medium' to the advertiser.

Narrowcasting

Television is moving from broadcasting to narrowcasting, from broad/mass audiences to smaller and more distinct target audiences, eg rock music channels and religious channels. The newer, wider choice means audiences are fragmenting into many smaller interest groups fed by sports channels, kitchen cooking channels, children's channels, educational channels, etc.

APPENDIX 11.2

Typical CPMs for Web site banner advertising

Web site	Target market	Traffic/audience size	CPM Same as CPT (cost per thousand)
Yahoo! UK & Ireland	General Internet users	20 million hits per month	£33
The Times and *Sunday Times*	73% ABC1, 54% 25–44, 27% over 45	11 million hits per month	Banners £28 on front page, £23 elsewhere
Electronic *Telegraph*	60% aged 25–44, 84% male, 35% are senior/middle managers or IT professionals	7.5 million hits per month	£35 on main index pages, £20 elsewhere
Guardian & *Observer*	Existing and target *Guardian* print readers; Interest groups served by specific sites	100,000 hits per day	£30 minimum (100,000)

Web site	Target market	Traffic/audience size	CPM Same as CPT (cost per thousand)
Capital FM	16- to 34-year-olds in London	3 million hits per month (audited by ABC)	£25 per thousand standard impressions, £35 per thousand for increased targeting
Sporting Life	Everyone who is interested in sport	3 million hits per month	£30 run of site, £35 targeted placement
Arsenal FC	Football fans, male, leisure	600,000+ hits per month	From £25 run of site
NME	17- to 25-year-old men avid music fans	75,000 hits per month approx	Home page £30, run of site £15
Uploaded	ABC1 men, aged 18 to 34	2 million hits per month approx; 140,000 individual users	Home page £35, run of site £20
Internet Movie Database	Film fans and anyone who wants to find out anything about the movies	24 million hits per month globally, 1.5 million UK (audited by BPA)	From £24
Internet Bookshop	ABC1 adults	1.5 million hits per month	From £26

APPENDIX 11.3

Advertising placement

A major consumer portal wished to promote the Money Channel service. They placed a range of creatives, including banners, pop-ups, and interstitials in sites where the audience were looking for advice and information on buying a house or car. The ads offered a simple message that encouraged the audience to utilize their Money Channel for help in these areas. People who clicked on an ad were then followed through the advertiser's site through the use of cookies placed on their machine. The portal was then able to look at how effective the campaign was in terms of activity on their site, and not just the amount of clicks generated.

APPENDIX 11.4

Media research – levels of media research

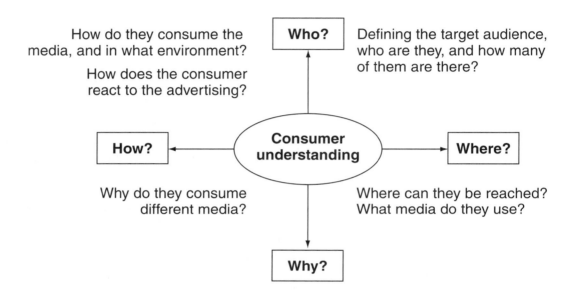

Source: Media Planning Group

APPENDIX 11.5

Media research – levels of media research and analytical tools

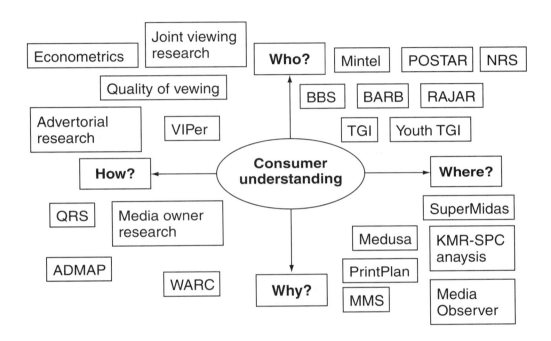

Source: Media Planning Group

Key points from Chapter 11:

1. Media planning can be creative.
2. Research can be used at all stages of the development of a campaign.

FURTHER READING

Aaker, D and Myers, J (1987) *Advertising Management*, third edition, Prentice-Hall International, Englewood Cliffs, NJ

Belch, G and Belch, M (2001) *Advertising and Promotion*, 5th edn, McGraw-Hill, London

Brannan, T (1995) *A Practical Guide to Integrated Marketing Communications*, Kogan Page, London

Broadbent, S (1992) *The Advertising Budget*, 2nd edn, McGraw-Hill, London

Cowley, D (ed) (1987) *How to Plan Advertising*, Cassell in association with The Account Planning Group, London

Douglas, T (1983) *The Complete Guide to Advertising*, PaperMac, London

Dwek, R (1997) Who's got the net by the eyeballs?, *Revolution*, October

Fanning, J (1997) Is the end of advertising really all that nigh?, *Irish Marketing Review*, The Marketing Institute, Ireland

Hart, A and O'Connor, J (1985) *The Practice of Advertising*, second edition, Heinemann, London

Howell Henry Chaldecott Lury & Partners (1997) *Marketing at a Point of Change*, HHCL, London

http://www.AdCritic.com (latest TV ads)

http://www.adforum.com

McKenna, R (1991), Marketing is everything, *Harvard Business Review*, Jan–Feb

Percy, L, Rossiter, J R and Elliott, R (2001) *Strategic Advertising Management*, Oxford University Press, Oxford

Smith, P R, Berry, C and Pulford, A (1996) *Strategic Marketing Communications*, Kogan Page, London

Sorrel, M (1996) *Beans and Pearls*, D&AD President's Lecture

Weinriech, L (2001) *11 Steps to Brand Heaven*, Kogan Page, London

FURTHER CONTACTS

Advertising Standards Authority (ASA), 2 Torrington Place, London WC1E 7HW (tel: 020 7580 5555; Web site: www.asa.org.uk)

Broadcasting Standards Commission (formerly known as Broadcasting Complaints Commission), 7 The Sanctuary, London SW1P 3JS (tel: 020 7808 1000; Web site: www.bsc.org.uk)

Committee of Advertising Practice (CAP) (as above)

Incorporated Society of British Advertisers (ISBA), 44 Hertford Street, London W1J 7AE (tel: 020 7499 7502; Web site: www.isba.org.uk)

Independent Television Commission (ITC), 33 Foley Street, London W1W 7TL (tel: 020 7255 3000; Web site: www.itc.org.uk)

Institute of Practitioners in Advertising (IPA), 44 Belgrave Square, London SW1X 8QS (tel: 020 7235 7020; Web site: www.ipa.co.uk)

12

Sales promotions

INTRODUCTION

Free Ladas boost sales by 36 per cent

After several seasons of declining gates, Russian football club Zenit have used a simple sales promotion to boost attendances up to 26,000. Entry costs 1.5 roubles and tickets for the Ladas lottery cost I rouble. Ladas cost 8,000 roubles (equivalent to three years' salary for the average industrial worker). The biggest roar of the evening comes not as the two teams run out on to the pitch but when the three cream-coloured Ladas are driven on to the running track. The opportunity of winning a Lada just pulls in the crowd.

Sales promotion is big business, in fact it is bigger than advertising in the UK (approximately £15 billion sales promotions and £12 billion advertising – see page 13). Its growth has been fuelled by several factors, including: (a) the movement towards relationship marketing (and rewarding loyal customers, eg club member benefits), (b) the growth of direct mail (and incentives), (c) the emergence of promotion-literate customers who expect promotions with certain product types, (d) during recessions, price-conscious customers search for value-for-money promotions, (e) powerful retailers favour suppliers whose products sell quickly (because of heavy advertising, exciting promotions, or both), (f) high television advertising costs force marketing managers to look for more cost-effective, below-the-line tools such as sales promotions.

Isolating and calculating the exact industry figures is difficult since, first, forfeited revenues from price promotions (discounts) are included in this figure and, second, some companies categorize some promotions as part of PR, ie some companies pay for a sales promotion such as free information booklets out of their sales promotion budget, while others see it as part of public relations. Whichever way it is looked at, sales promotion is a below-the-line activity that can be used externally with end-users (customers), and intermediaries (trade distributors), and also internally with an organization's own salesforce. Sales promotions, premiums, incentives and motivation schemes are used for both products and services in consumer, business-to-business and industrial markets There are three main categories:

1. Customer promotions (premiums, gifts, prizes and competitions, eg on the back of breakfast cereal boxes).
2. Trade promotions (special terms, point-of-sale materials and free pens, diaries, competition prizes, etc).
3. Salesforce promotions (incentive and motivation schemes, see page 285 for an explanation of how these become a form of psychic income).

Whether they take the form of competitions, price reductions, free gifts, coupons, samples, special demonstrations, displays or point-of-sale, consumer sales promotions tend to affect the latter stages of the communications/buying process (ie triggering action) such as a purchase or increased usage of a particular brand, whereas advertising tends to affect the earlier stages such as awareness, interest and desire (there are exceptions, particularly where direct response advertising is concerned). Promotions are action orientated, particularly as they often tempt the buyer to buy or at least try a product or service. These kinds of promotions often provide the final shove that moves a customer towards buying a particular product or service. In terms of learning about brands and learning to use them frequently, many sales promotions and the involvement they create (by filling in forms, collecting coupons, posting application forms, trying a free sample, etc) are considered by some to be a form of operant conditioning as demonstrated by Skinner's rats (see page 105).

Advertising, on the other hand, is thought by some to help buyers to learn and remember brands and their benefits by repeating the message and building associations between brands, logos, images and benefits – a form of classical conditioning as demonstrated by Pavlov's dog (see page 105). There are, of course, many exceptions to this today, as more advertising tries to involve the audience rather than just beat it over the head with a repeated message.

Ineffective sales promotions

Despite the phenomenal size of the sales promotions industry and the data available for analysis, there are a frightening number of sales promotions that are relatively ineffective, and some are actually damaging in terms of branding, sales and cash flow. Take price promotions such as discount vouchers, two for the price of one, free extra 10 per cent – they can help to boost sales in the short term, but what do they do to the brand in the long term? Discount the price and you discount the brand down to a point where it loses its brand values and competes solely on price (which is a not a protectable competitive advantage). So many sales promotions damage the core values, the image and the positioning of the brand. Other promotions attract only promiscuous consumers who switch back to another brand as soon as the promotion is over. Other promotions create temporary 'bumps' in sales, as shown in Figure 12.1.

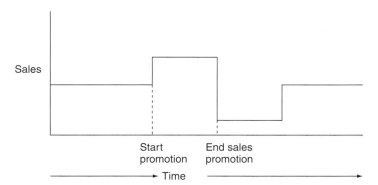

Figure 12.1 Some promotions boost sales temporarily as customers stock up but don't come back for twice as long

Some promotions create a temporary boost in sales followed by an immediate drop, as customers who initially bought more and stocked up then stop buying until they have used up their extra stock. Other promotions actually damage the brand image and even the holding company's corporate image, sales, profits and cash flow (eg Hoover's £48 million fiasco). The section 'Problem promotions' (page 350) includes many other unfortunate examples. The common error in consumer promotions is the lack of consumer franchise building (CFB) within many sales promotions.

Consumer franchise building (CFB)

Some promotions can enhance or add value to the image of the product or service. These types of promotions build 'consumer franchise'. This means that the gift is in some way related to the brand, its image or its properties. As Torin Douglas puts it, a brand property encapsulates 'the image of the product and ensures that extra mileage can be obtained out of the advertising over a period of several years' (eg Esso's tiger and Johnnie Walker's gentleman with top hat and tails). Franchise building promotions contrast with price/discount offers that dilute brand values and do not enhance brand loyalty, despite boosting short-term sales. The now classic Miss Pears competition reinforces the brand image of gentle, natural soap. Esso's tiger T-shirt was also franchise building. CFB promotions tend to have longer-term implications and are therefore more strategically driven, while non-CFB promotions can be driven by shorter-term tactical goals.

Freebies not required (always)

It is a popular misconception that loyalty schemes have to give things away, special service or treatment can work too.

Julie Bird

There is much room for more creative flair in sales promotions (see 'Creative promotions' on page 347). Effective sales promotions can creatively build the brand franchise while achieving many other objectives, such as increasing sales, cementing loyalty, building databases, generating publicity and more. Read on...

SALES PROMOTION OBJECTIVES

As the name suggests, a promotion is a limited period offer. It is therefore not surprising to find that sales promotions tend to have shorter-term tactical objectives (although, as previously explained, this need not be the case).

Some typical sales promotion goals might be:

1. Increase sales (although it may only be a temporary increase because customers can simply stock up with the goods or temporarily switch brands while the promotion is running) by:
   - rewarding loyal customers;
   - locking customers into loyalty programmes (where they have to keep buying the product or service over a period of time in order to collect the right number of coupons, vouchers, or items in a collection);
   - increasing repurchase rates of occasional users;
   - generating 'trial' among new customers (by triggering an impulse purchase);
   - demonstrating new features/modifications or introducing a new product/service;
   - developing new uses;
   - image development (awareness or repositioning);
   - deseasonalizing seasonal sales (eg skiing holidays in the summer).
2. Develop new sales leads.
3. Satisfy retailers with a complete package – gain trade acceptance.
4. Move excess stock.
5. Block a competitor (by offering incentives to customers to stock up).
6. Match a competitor (petrol tokens).
7. Build a database (some promotions also act as database builders: see how Rothman's offer of a free pack collected 750,000 customer names in the section on direct mail in Chapter 13).
8. Generate publicity.

Matching types of promotions with specific objectives

As shown below, some sales promotion techniques are more appropriate than others in achieving certain objectives.

Objective	Promotion tool
	Consumer
Trial	Sampling; couponing; free draw; price off; self-liquidator (send in some money which pays the costs of the promotion); premiums; in pack; on pack; near pack; reusable container; personality promotion
Retrial	Coupon for next purchase; price-off
Increase usage	Collections; games; competitions; extra quantity/bonus packs; price-off multiple purchase

Develop new uses   Companion brand promotions; publications; workshops
Image development   Publications; sponsorship; charity

Trade

Increase   Discount; extended credit; point-of-sale materials; tie-in with
distribution/shelf   advertising
facings/displays
In-store promo   Above + consumer offer + promotion allowance
Increase sales   Sales competitions and rebates (mostly independent stores/wholesalers)
Cement good   Gifts, holidays and awards
relations

Salesforce

Sales and   Psychic income and financial income
distribution

Some efforts have been made to rank the effectiveness of specific tools ('mechanics') against various objectives. Julian Cummins (1998) identified how certain sales promotion techniques match up with various objectives (Table 12.1).

Table 12.1   Linking the objective to the mechanics: how they match up

Objectives	Mechanics	Immediate free offers	Delayed free offers	Immediate price offers	Delayed price offers	Finance offers	Competitions	Games and draws	Charitable offers	Self-liquidators	Profit-making promotions
Increasing volume		9	7	9	7	5	1	3	5	2	1
Increasing trial		9	7	9	2	9	2	7	7	2	1
Increasing repeat purchase		2	9	2	9	5	3	2	7	3	3
Increasing loyalty		1	9	0	7	3	3	1	7	3	3
Widening usage		9	5	5	2	3	1	5	5	1	1
Creating interest		3	3	3	2	2	5	9	8	8	8
Creating awareness		3	3	3	1	1	5	9	8	8	8
Deflecting attention from price		9	7	0	7	7	3	5	5	2	2
Gaining intermediary support		9	5	9	5	9	3	7	5	1	1
Gaining display		9	5	9	5	9	3	7	5	1	1

Each square is filled with a rating from 0 (not well matched) to 10 (very well matched) Use it as a ready reckoner for linking your objective to the mechanics available

Source: J Cummins (1998)

STRATEGY OR TACTICS?

The short-term tactical approach

The general short-term, 'immediate action', tactical nature of sales promotion contrasts with the longer-term image and brand-building capability of advertising. This need not be the case, because sales promotions can be planned on a strategic level. But, first, why is there a tendency towards short-termism?

Perhaps the short-term focus is a result of:

1. Management pressure to boost quarterly sales. This therefore encourages the use of quick-response sales promotions.
2. This may be exacerbated by the shortening product life cycles which demand quick sales results.
3. Increased competition and increased new product introductions increase the need for tactical defensive sales promotions.
4. Sales promotions often lend themselves to the speedy response required to handle business problems when they arise.
5. Full-service agencies may try to sell the client additional services such as sales promotion on an ad hoc, 'add-on' tactical basis.

The strategic approach

All promotions should be part of a bigger and longer-term strategy. Longer-term strategies are about building and reinforcing brand image, strengthening user loyalty, and even inviting new users to join the club, as opposed to short-term tactical sales boosts. Whether planned on a one-off tactical basis or on a more structured strategic approach, the sales promotion can have an impact on the brand or organization's overall image (NB Hoover). Corporate image is central to the longer-term strategic communications of the organization. Tracking studies (or continual market research) can monitor changes in specific aspects or dimensions of an organization's corporate image. These changes can be caused by many different communications tools, including sales promotions.

Strategic impact of sales promotions

Years ago, Heinz used to say that they saw more far-reaching effects on image dimensions of their tracking studies from their sales promotion schemes than they ever saw resulting from advertising campaigns.

Jim Castling

Some organizations see promotions as only a short-term tactical tool to support what they call the more strategic communication tools such as advertising. Realistically, however, it is not always possible to achieve strategic goals if the client does not want them in the first place. Roger Hyslop, Chairman and Founder of the Triangle Group, gives an example of a retailer who says: 'I don't need this promotion to add to my brand image, otherwise I wouldn't be spending millions on television. What I need is to bring 50,000 people in to see my store opening.' The difficulty is compounded by the fact that strategic promotions may sometimes not generate maximum customer response in the immediate short term. Should the longer-term image-building capability of a sales promotion be forfeited for the shorter-term tactical 'trial sales' objective? Julian Cummins (1998) explains why a strategic approach is preferred:

1. It enables one offer to build on the previous one, and to establish a continuity of communication.
2. It makes it possible to communicate image and functional values, so promotions work harder.
3. It can produce considerable savings in time and money.
4. It enables offers to be fully integrated into the other activities in the marketing programme (eg linking with advertising and PR).
5. It facilitates a better approach to joint promotions (see below).

A strategic approach does not exclude the use of tactical promotions since it can provide a framework within which shorter-term tactics can be determined. In this way a sales promotion strategy makes the tactical planning easier and more productive.

How to develop a strategic approach

1. Identify what customers (and prospects) really want (in terms of promotions).
2. Identify the long-term strategic marketing and communications objectives (see Chapter 2 for examples of separate types of objectives).
3. Create guidelines for each product or service, showing the style of sales promotion that is most appropriate to the brand's long-term health. Ensure that this style contributes towards the strategic marketing goals (as opposed to sometimes going in the opposite direction).
4. Determine exactly how much of the total marketing communications budget is available for sales promotions.
5. Ensure that there is support and commitment from senior management (eg marketing director) so that sufficient management expertise and funds are available for the promotions to be professionally carried out.

6. Develop a method of evaluation so that longer-term performance can be measured against longer-term objectives. Ideally, this might then be compared to other types of marketing expenditure. Agencies and consultancies can review the effectiveness of their activities at the end of the year. Some agencies/consultancies are then asked 'Which communications tool is more effective and why?'
7. Develop a 'promotions file' which compiles ideas and costs throughout the year. These can then be reviewed closer to the time of planning.
8. Plan and forecast the sales promotions' results. This is obviously difficult to do, particularly the first time. Usually a best/worst/medium range of forecasts helps to build some kind of management control and criteria for success or failure.

PROMOTIONS WARS

Competitors compete with each other using different elements of the marketing mix, marketing communications mix, and sales promotion mix. In the 1960s petrol retailers competed against each other by using advertising to differentiate the products with claims such as more power (tiger in your tank), more mileage, more secure ('you can be sure with Shell'). Towards the end of the 1960s the competitive edge shifted away from product claims and into an increasingly popular sales promotion called Green Shield Stamps. Securing an exclusive Green Shield Stamp franchise was the key competitive tool as the stamps came to dominate the battle for market share right up to the first oil crisis in 1973.

Then competition became focused on basic supply and distribution of a scarce commodity. Spurred on by higher and higher prices, a price war eventually broke out in 1974 and marginal sales (brand switchers) shopped around for the best deal. This carried on until the second oil crisis in 1979. Price cutting meant lower margins, which required higher sales volumes, so developing new distribution networks of bigger and better-designed service stations became the key competitive tool at the beginning of the 1980s. Larger forecourts, free of queues, attracted drivers and distracted their attention from prices. Buying time (created with faster service) became more important than penny pinching. Bigger canopies, double-sided multiple pumps, space for passing lanes and self-service all quickened the speed of service, while the forecourt shops offered more than just spark plugs and fan belts.

The mid-1980s saw the battle move back on to the sales promotion plane with a variety of games offering a variety of prizes to lucky winners. These were soon replaced by guaranteed winners as collecting gifts or tokens delivered better rewards for both the petrol company and consumer. The late 1980s followed with a sales promotion war where different, better and more extensive ranges of guaranteed gifts became the key competitive weapon in the forecourt battleground. Large advertising budgets were used to support and promote various sales promotion campaigns.

Then one oil company spotted a chink in the armour of a competitor's sales promotions when research suggested that consumers were beginning to tire of the endless stream of cheap free wine glasses. The battle moved on to another plane. A new advertising campaign was launched, not to promote a 'better' range of free gifts but to attack the competition's 'inferior' range of free gifts. No inferior competitor product claims were made, only inferior competitor sales promotion claims. One advertisement showed a driver opening his glove compartment only to find a wave of free glasses pouring out on to the floor of his car. In addition to using advertising to promote a product or a sales promotion, or to criticize a competitor's sales promotion, in the early 1990s advertising was used to promote a sales promotion that promoted a sales promotion.

Esso launched the UK's biggest ever T-shirt promotion featuring a single design. It was designed to promote not only the Esso brand, but also Esso's main promotional medium – the Esso Collection (gifts for tokens promotional scheme). In less than two months over 800,000 T-shirts were given away through some 2,100 UK service stations. The subsequent 800,000 walking advertisements (people wearing the T-shirt with the striking design) helped to achieve the promotion's objective of stimulating additional consumer interest in the Esso Collection. Television advertising gave the promotion a high profile and stimulated high levels of redemption (number of responders claiming their gift). The T-shirt supplier immediately had to increase their daily T-shirt shipment from 10,000 to 40,000 units.

Since promotions can be expensive, the next battle for petrol market share may be fought with other elements of the marketing mix such as product (on-site shop, phones, service, windscreen washing and petrol filling), price (price wars), location (place) and corporate image (Shell's corporate image cost market share), as well as advertising and sales promotions. As Drayton Bird says, 'In the 1930s the national newspapers got into an incentive war that proved so crippling that finally all agreed to stop it.' In the 1980s the newspaper market suffered its own bingo war with million-pound prizes squeezing bottom-line profits.

What started as an exciting promotion for one paper was quickly copied by another. Success attracts imitators, copiers or 'me-toos' (similar products and similar ideas). If all the players offer similar incentives, then the competitive advantage is nullified. Some customers simply expect a sales promotion. Trading stamps swept the UK in the 1950s and 1960s, 'the problem being that almost everyone started offering them and the whole exercise became virtually pointless'. In this situation the promotion can become a 'dis-satisfier', ie the sales promotion does not motivate the customer towards a particular store or brand, but without the sales promotion the buyer will avoid the promotionless brand or the promotionless retailer. Today retail store loyalty cards clash for database building and lifetime purchases. The irony is that many customers hold more than one store loyalty card, which suggests the impossible – they are loyal to both competing stores.

Impossible loyalty

Two-thirds of British adults have loyalty cards. Half of these hold cards from more than one retailer.

Hollinger (1996)

CREATIVE PROMOTIONS

There is always room for creative innovation. Whether it's a trip to the moon or a party in an underground nuclear shelter, the only limitation to potential sales promotion creations is one's imagination. If it is stunningly successful, it is likely that the competition will follow, unless the innovative promotion relates uniquely to the brand in a creative way. This is demonstrated by the *Sunday Sport* tabloid newspaper.

Is your mother-in-law an alien?

The *Sunday Sport* offered a free test kit which helped readers to determine whether their mothers-in-law are in fact aliens.

This 'alien mother-in-law' type of promotion is arguably just a stunt designed to generate publicity that may, at least temporarily, increase levels of awareness, boost circulation and also reinforce reader loyalty by rewarding them with a gift that appeals to their mentality. Because the gift is relevant to both their target reader's sense of humour and the newspaper's image, it adds to the paper's branding. In a way it adds to the brand franchise or builds consumer franchise. One sales promotion that might have impressed mothers-in-law was for Cadbury. When it launched its white chocolate, Snowflake, agency Triangle achieved significant consumer trial by negotiating a covermount of a free bar on *OK!* magazine. When they discovered that the same issue was featuring Anthea Turner's wedding, they persuaded *OK!* to give free bars to all the celebrity guests. The additional brand exposure enabled Cadbury to hit the media headlines, gain an estimated £1 million worth of editorial coverage, and ensure a spectacular launch success as a result.

Creativity and originality can work well together, as where NatWest Bank's sales promotions and direct marketing were combined as a 'direct promotion' (most mailshots use an incentive of some description). NatWest moved away from the traditional clock/radio/calculator/travel bag type of incentive used by the banks from time to time. Instead they offered the choice of 1 of 10 limited-edition prints that were specially commissioned from five artists. They mailed to 65,000 names (who they thought had £25,000+ to invest) and received a 12.3 per cent response (instead of the targeted 5 per cent response level). Another highly creative and popular promotion was Guinness's inflatable armchair, which formed part of their campaign as sponsors of the 1999 Rugby World Cup. An application for the armchair was even received from Buckingham Palace!

Another highly effective yet high-risk sales promotion was created to support the Maxwell House relaunch. To provide a unique brand-related promotional campaign, agency Triangle persuaded TV personality Noel Edmonds to telephone people at random whilst floating across the country in the hot-air balloon featured in their advertising. Half-a-million pounds was given away, including a top prize of £100,000, and the brand recorded its highest market share ever during the promotional period. Highly creative sales promotions may involve an element of risk. Insurance (indemnity insurance, redemption insurance, etc) is advised with all sales promotions, but particularly highly creative and high-risk promotions. Incidentally, creative thinkers will spot the creative PR opportunity that can be exploited when a creative sales promotion is developed. The press are usually interested. One other dimension that creative thinkers can explore is the huge synergies and creative potential released by marketing marriages, or joint promotions.

Joint promotions

Joint promotions and cross-promotions offer economical routes to target the same customers with relevant offers. Cathy Bond (1991) gives this example: Coca-Cola led its army of soft drinks brands into a joint promotion with Cadbury in spring 1991. It was only a matter of time before arch rival Pepsi popped up with another mega-brand deal, in this case with Kellogg. When Deep Pan Pizza created a joint promotion with Lego, giving children free branded toys, sales of children's meals doubled. The choice of toys was changed every quarter to encourage repeat visits, and the cost was built into the price of the meal. Caution must be exercised when choosing a partner. Equal standing brands, budgets and branding details need to be clarified, with nothing left to chance. Stuart Hardy, managing director of WLK (who married Mothercare and Lever's Persil in a joint promotion) says: 'In any true relationship each side is going to have 50 per cent of the say. A lot of marketing people want 100 per cent of the say and only 50 per cent of the costs.' Although there are lots of opportunities, relatively few joint promotions seem to get off the ground. 'For every one joint promotion that gets off the ground, 10 never make it,' says Roger Hyslop (1989).

Integrated promotions

Sales promotions integrate with other marketing communications tools, particularly packaging ('on-pack' promotions), point-of-sale, merchandising, sponsorship, PR, advertising and selling. Media-supported promotions do better than ones that are not supported. There are, however, many occasions when media support cannot be afforded or where point-of-sale materials flagging the offer are considered to be more cost-effective than above-the-line support. The Tango megaphone case study at the end of this chapter demonstrates how a unique promotion combines with PR to maintain the brand's market share with minimal above-the-line or point-of-sale support. But even a great sales promotion fails if no one knows about it. Some support, whether advertising, point-of-sale or PR is therefore required. Creative promotional ideas command press coverage, so some budget should always be left for PR requirements (stocks of photos, transparencies, photo CDs, Web sites with downloadable images and news items, etc).

Coke auctions

Coke's innovative Coke Auction campaign combined sales promotions and packaging with the unique online facility of online auctions with offline radio and TV advertisements with online e-mail viral marketing. Online auctions harness some of the Internet's unique functions. With innovation at the helm, Coke have somehow converted the normally discarded ring pulls into online currency called unsurprisingly 'Coke credits'. These credits are then used to bid for items from sports tickets to becoming stars in Coke ads (having their faces on the Coke signs) in major advertising venues.

P R Smith and D Chaffey (2001) e*Marketing excellence*, Butterworth-Heinemann, London

PROBLEM PROMOTIONS

As with most marketing communications tools, sod's law runs rampant across sales promotions and destroys many excellent ideas that have apparently been meticulously planned. Whether the sample packs burst and destroy other goods, premiums are pilfered, misredemption (non-buyers acquire other buyers' coupons), malredemption (large-scale fraudulent coupon redemption), over-redemption (with millions claiming their prizes), or door-drop samples that the dog or child gets to before the adult, the possibilities of a mini-marketing disaster seem endless. In addition, the *Competitors' Companion*, a monthly subscription magazine, publishes news and views on which competitions are running, what prizes they offer, exactly where to get entry forms, which qualifiers are required (eg a label) and the closing dates. According to the magazine 'You receive advice on the answers to their questions plus a regular list of winning slogans and tie breakers... that way, you can read what's catching the judge's eye today and make them work for you tomorrow.' Here are a few cases of promotions that went wrong, even for the biggest and the best of marketing companies.

In 1984 syndicates cracked Typhoo Tea's Cash Pot promotion. Cadbury Typhoo was reported to have had to make cash payouts of more than £1 million. According to *Marketing Week* their insurers were reported to have issued a High Court writ against Cadbury Typhoo seeking a 'declaration that some claims made by Cash Pot competitors are outside the rules of the competition'. Nevertheless, the expensive promotion apparently increased its market share to its 'highest level since its relaunch in 1982', but at what cost?

In 1990 Coca-Cola's MagiCan US promotion was supported by a massive $100 million push. The MagiCan looked and felt (even when shaken) like a regular can, but when the tab was pulled a mechanism inside the can pushed real rolled-up dollar notes through the hole in the top of the can. Prizes ranged from $5 to $200. Inevitably there were a few duds. Most of them just didn't work, but in a few cases the seal that held the 'liquid that gives the can the feel of the real thing' had broken. Although it was not harmful, one small boy (who was not aware of the promotion) drank the liquid and public health officials were called in. Massive media attention followed; 750,000 cans were held back while each one was shaken to determine whether the seal was broken or not. An immediate TV and press campaign was put into action to explain the promotion and to warn customers not to drink the liquid if the seal was broken (*Marketing*, 31 May 1990).

Pepsi's Philippine subsidiary offered one million pesos (£26,000) to anyone finding a bottle top with the number 349. Pepsi paid out £8 million before they realized that thousands of winning bottle tops were appearing everywhere. When payment stopped there were public demonstrations; then Pepsi plants were attacked with grenades, Pepsi lorries burned (three people were killed). Pepsi executives hired bodyguards before fleeing the country (*Precision Marketing*, 26 May 1997).

Heinz printed a recipe book promotional offer on its Pickering Fruit Pie Fillings but forgot to print a reply address, so no one could participate in the promotion. KFC gave a free plastic figure in some of its meals as a promotion. Although they tested the plastic for proximity to hot food, they did not test it for children sucking off the plastic and poking their eyes with the remaining wire. Personal injury claims followed.

Macy's department store ran a talent promotion to find an 'Annie' for a new production of the Broadway show *Annie*. The lucky 12-year-old winner later made even bigger news when she sued Macy's after she was 'dumped from the production'.

Hoover offered free flights to New York when purchasing any Hoover over and above £100. Wrong comparisons with response rates from dissimilar 'two flights for the price of one' promotions prompted wildly inaccurate forecasted response rates. (They forecast 5,000 responses and received 600,000!) The fixed-fee limit of £500,000 was agreed with the relatively small travel agent. When the agency went bust Hoover were exposed to a massive response (insurance is essential). Meanwhile the trade increased prices of the cheaper Hoover models so that effectively any Hoover purchase qualified for free flights (Hoover should have restricted the offer to certain models). The promotion cost £48 million, careers and corporate image.

Kraft Foods 'Win a free camper van' promotion had a computer error that generated hundreds of winners. As the prize-winners' claims kept coming in, Kraft realized there was a problem. Some disappointed customers vowed never to buy the firm's food products again. Others sought legal action. According to *Marketing Breakthroughs*, half a million special free sample minipacks of Vidal Sassoon shampoo were distributed in 1991 throughout Poland. When news of the promotion spread, around 2,000 mailboxes (mostly at apartment blocks) were pillaged. The sample packs then started appearing in street markets and soon sold out. The extra costs incurred by the damage added a new dimension to the sales promotion review process.

Car hire company Alamo normally offer one free day's car hire with every 30-day hire. This was fine until they discovered that it is illegal in Germany to give anything free after just one transaction (*Precision Marketing*, 26 May 1997). The international arena further complicates the life of the sales promotion professional, as regulations vary enormously.

There is, arguably, a worse scenario. No one responds to the sales promotion. Large stocks of premiums are left in the warehouse, and teams of order fulfilment staff (who dispatch the prizes) sit around with nothing to do.

The moral of the story? Check all possible disaster scenarios. Take out promotional insurance – professional indemnity insurance covers an agency's duty of care to its clients; product recall insurance protects against the cost of a recall of products or promotional gifts; over-redemption insurance protects against an unexpectedly high response. Whether the client pays or the agency pays is an issue that needs to be clearly agreed long before any sales promotion campaign rolls out.

MANAGING A SALES PROMOTION

Choosing an agency

As with advertising campaigns, a sales promotion can be handled in-house or given to an external agency. If the work goes outside to an agency, the usual selection procedure applies (see Chapter 6), ie: develop a pool; list possible agencies; invite them to present credentials; check references; select a shortlist; brief them; pitch; evaluation; selection; written contract. Figure 12.2 features an advertisement placed in the trade magazine *Sales Promotion* by a

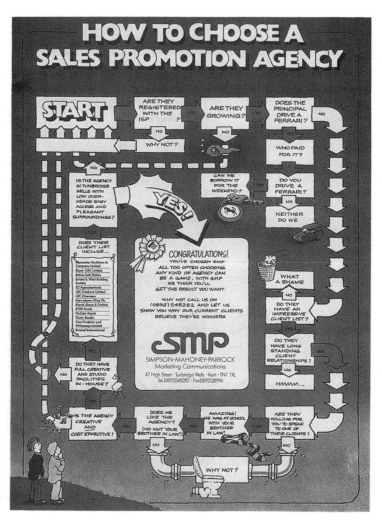

Figure 12.2   How to choose a sales promotion agency

marketing communications consultancy. It shows their interpretation of how to select an agency (while simultaneously doing all the selection work for the potential client).

Planning the campaign

The SOSTAC® + 3Ms checklist can be used to build a sales promotion plan (see Chapters 2 and 11 or the Tango case study at the end of this chapter for applications of the SOSTAC® planning checklist). The situation analysis requires research into past, present and possible future campaigns, combined with a clear analysis of the target market.

Research

Research is required at most stages of the development of the sales promotion. An initial review of previous promotions (including competitors') can be followed by further research into the target market.

In addition to the usual demographic and psychographic information (see page 35), further analysis may reveal what Philip Kotler identifies as three types of new triers who are attracted to (and respond to) sales promotion offers: (a) users of a competing brand in the same category, (b) users in other categories, and (c) frequent brand switchers. The 'deal-prone customer', the brand switcher, tends not to be loyal and is likely to switch away to the next low-price or free-gift offer that comes his or her way. In the UK, Peter Holloway, managing director of MS Surveys, calls this last group 'promiscuous nomads' who can be easily bought and lost the next day – but at what cost? The group at the other end of the target market loyalty spectrum is called 'the immovables', who are locked into brand loyalty. 'No amount of promotional effort will move them, so there is no point wasting money on them,' says Holloway. The real target group within the target market is called the 'loyal susceptibles' (see Figure 12.3, page 354). Holloway says that 'they are there to be won (or lost if they are your brand customers) and once their loyalty is broken, their new-found loyalties can be well worth having.'

Crossing the bridge

Crossing the bridge from your own island of subjective presumptions to the land of the real-life target consumer can be as revealing, remove as many uncertainties and avoid as many clangers as having a full medical check-up, or consulting a map before you go somewhere new. The first step towards making promotions, etc, work better for you is knowing who you really ought to be talking to.

Peter Holloway

Source: MS Surveys (1992)

Figure 12.3   Who is the *real* target for a sales promotion?

Knowing exactly who these people are and why they are more susceptible is the key to the sales promotions tapping into their susceptibilities, which in turn will increase market share beyond a short-term temporary boost.

After analysing the real target market, the sales promotion concept should be researched in focus groups or at least with customers, suppliers, friends and colleagues. When the idea or promotional tool is agreed, it is still worth testing it in a limited area or customer group to reveal any hidden problems or even opportunities before launching nationally or internationally.

Attention to detail

The choice of promotional tool can be directly affected by the availability of resources. The three key resources, men and women, money and minutes (the 3Ms), are tied up with a promotion. Careful contingency planning should cater for an unexpectedly large response. Insurance can help here because things do go wrong and costs can rapidly escalate (see 'Problem promotions', page 350). Although creating a promotion is exciting, finishing it is dull and boring, yet this is the mark of a true professional.

Cut-off dates, logistical arrangements (returning unused stocks), and even announcing the end of the promotion cost time and money. Shell wanted to avoid the flush of irritation that would undoubtedly rise up if their customers failed to cash in their carefully collected gift tokens before they expired and became worthless. So they advertised the end of the promotion.

Checklist

Here is a checklist covering some key sales promotions details:

1. Does the promotion exploit key strengths and USPs (unique selling propositions)?
2. Is it a franchise-building promotion? Does the gift, incentive or premium relate to or enhance your product/service or organization's image? Does it carry a selling message or at least a subtle reminder of some selling message? Unrelated premiums, contests, refunds or price discounts do not reinforce brand or enhance corporate values.
3. What can go wrong? Contingency planning, crisis management and insurance are worth considering (see 'Problem promotions' on page 350).
4. Has the promotion got legal clearance? Should it be checked with the Committee of Advertising Practice (CAP) sales promotions department?
5. Will the promotion only generate a temporary gain while customers stock up and do not repurchase for twice the normal period? (See Figure 12.1.) Will existing/old stocks (not carrying the promotion) waste?
6. Does the promotion need advertising and PR support? Is it newsworthy (ie can the PR people get some media coverage anyway)? With a consumer product, will the retail trade demand some above-the-line support? A great promotion will die on its feet if no one knows about it.
7. What other communications tools are required – new packaging, point-of-sale materials, new literature, contract field sales teams? Are these in the budget (time and money restrictions)?
8. Is there an administrative burden created by new order forms, coupons, judging, choosing winners, despatching gifts, etc? Or will this all be handled by an external agency?
9. Time: (a) cut-off date (clearly state when offer closes); (b) sell-off time (estimate how long it would take to use up the stock of incentives/gifts); (c) lead time (period required to set up the whole sales promotion through to launch date).
10. Is the sales promotion going to be costly? Does it fit the budget available? Is it cost effective? Can it be measured?

Control and measurement

Control, measurement and monitoring form the loop in the management system. How can the success or otherwise of the promotion be measured? The number of respondents, redemptions and increased sales are all relatively easy to calculate. But these are only the surface figures. They may be hiding the fact that many of the responders are the wrong people (promiscuous nomads), or existing customers who simply buy twice as much this week (stocking up) but do not buy next week. In fact, it may be that less than one-quarter of the respondents actually represent new business. Figure 12.4 considers this.

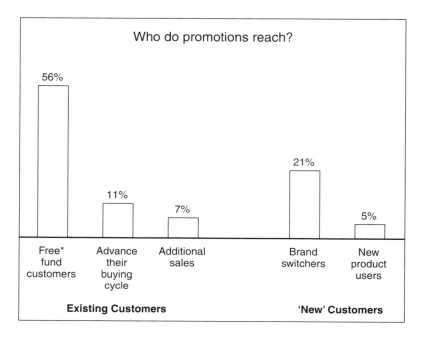

* 'Free fund' customers are those who are going to buy the brand anyway – just giving them a discount, ie funding them for no reason
Source: MS Surveys (1992)

Figure 12.4 A breakdown of who responds to sales promotions

The promotion may have worked well in one respect but failed in another. The purpose of measurement and monitoring is twofold:

1. To control current campaigns
2. To improve future campaigns by learning about what did and did not work with the current campaign. Each promotion has to work successfully across a number of communications stepping stones for it to succeed. As Holloway puts it:

It has to be: seen, interesting, understood, believed, relevant and compatible, persuasive, and produce the desired response among the right people... being seen questions the suitability of the vehicle of communication (in pack, on pack, off pack, POS, etc) and the design characteristics of the visual elements, eg many on-pack flashed offers are simply never seen by the target market. The middle criteria of communication effectiveness relate to the nature of the offer, the platform involved and the visual/copy elements of the promotion. Persuasion and response are dependent on the combination of the lot. There are few promotions we've come across in our pre- or post-testing which don't leave considerable room for improvement somewhere in the mix of essential ingredients.

Figure 12.5 indicates how the total sales promotion package (including advertising support, if any) has worked.

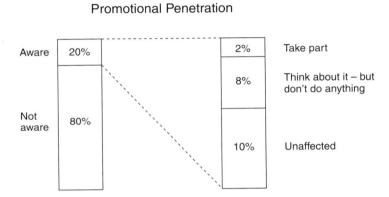

Source: MS Surveys (1992)

Figure 12.5 Promotional Penetration

To a haggis

Sales promotions come in all shapes and sizes. Here is a leaflet that was in a 'please take one' point-of-sale dispenser sitting on top of the counter in a butcher's shop in Edinburgh. Some would call this simply a free leaflet, others point-of-sale, others packaging, others sales promotion, others PR. Regardless of what budget it comes out of, it promotes the brand while reinforcing the brand properties in a simple, low-risk, cost-effective and friendly manner.

CASE STUDY 12.1

Tango Megaphone

The award-winning Tango Megaphone campaign is a classic example of how marketing communications work is evolving. Although the promotional technique is a traditional one, its application, using a range of media and communications devices, is highly contemporary. Tango Megaphone was voted Promotional Marketing Campaign of the Year in the SPCA Marketing Awards in March 2001.

Situation

Tango is one of the marketing successes of recent years. Its distinctive advertising has contributed to its emerging status as one of the few brands with real street cred. Nevertheless, it is still vulnerable to the trading power of megabrands like Coke and Pepsi, and to other would-be cult brands like Irn Bru. Competitive activity over the millennium period had a significant impact on Tango's market share and it was considered that promotional activity, in its broadest sense, was needed to redress the situation and to gain the high ground in the important pre-summer trading period.

Tango's brand resurgence has been fuelled by its new, irreverent, almost anarchic personality. Classically this has been developed through media advertising, so the role of promotion is not only to achieve short-term tactical objectives, but also to contribute actively to the development of the brand's personality.

Objectives

The first objective of the campaign was to raise awareness of Tango early in the year. The second aim was to increase penetration by reintroducing the brand to former Tango drinkers. There were also trading objectives to be met by increasing both volume and value share during the promotional period.

Strategy

Firstly, the strategy was to provide attractive incentives to the trade to encourage early stocking of a summer drink prior to the summer peak. However, the principal strategy was to create a compelling reason to purchase Tango rather than competitor brands, by appealing emotionally to the target audience.

Having achieved this, the strategy was then to find the most cost-effective and intrusive means of reaching the target audience – principally 16- to 24-year-old males. They are fun loving, streetwise and enjoy messing with the rules.

Tactics

'Not drinking Tango is wrong! It must be regarded as deeply suspicious. As a nation we must stand together and Out Non-Tango Drinkers!'

Working closely with ad agency HHCL, the multi-award winning marketing communications agency Triangle created this campaign at a time when the outing of public figures by the tabloid press had become fashionable. With tongue firmly in cheek, Tango invited the country's youth to call in for the Tango Megaphone, a specially produced premium which would help them in their quest to convert the nation to the orange elixir!

Action

The Tango Megaphone offer was communicated on over 40 million promotional packs. An interactive premium-rate telephone line was set up, with callers leaving their name and address in order to be sent the orange-coloured Megaphone.

The campaign was supported by special television advertising in order to achieve maximum exposure, together with four-sheet posters at street level. Both creative treatments reflected the culture and character of previous Tango advertising. Additionally, a major radio promotion was created and run on carefully targeted stations such as Kiss, Vibe and the Galaxy Group, thus maximizing media cost-effectiveness by minimizing wastage outside the core target market. This two-week campaign consisted not of conventional advertising slots but of arguably more credible pre-recorded trailers, live DJ reads and 'live' simulated calls. Consumers were invited to call in and nominate non-Tango Drinkers who deserved humiliation on radio, some of whom were then 'wound up' by DJs in pre-recorded sessions.

An extensive point-of-sale drive was undertaken in order to give the brand major visibility, particularly in the all-important 'impulse purchase' outlets. Special trade buying offers at wholesalers and in cash-and-carry depots encouraged retailers to raise normal stock levels.

A special section on the Tango Web site was devoted to the promotion. Megaphones were distributed free at 17 campus universities and distinctive sandwich-board men staged 'street protests' in key cities.

Control

Monitoring and control was achieved by the use of established research and audit techniques.

Advertising awareness increased from 35 to 57 per cent between March and May 2000 (source: Millward Brown). The radio campaign reached 45.3 per cent of all 15- to 19-year-olds (source: Rajar). Brand penetration increased from 3.6 to 5.3 per cent in the same period as the previous year (A C Nielsen). Value share increased from 9.9 to 12 per cent year on year, and volume share rose to 13.2 per cent (A C Nielsen).

Over 242,000 calls were received by the Tango Megaphone phone line, compared to a target of 200,000. The revenue generated by the premium calls covered the costs and mailing out of the premium, resulting in a fully self-liquidating offer.

Men and women

Triangle's Tango team is substantial, with both account-handling and creative executives working closely not only with the client-marketing team but with colleagues at advertising agency HHCL. The result is the best of both worlds – the excellence of specialist skills combined with the effectiveness of truly integrated campaigns.

Money

The promotional element (everything except paid-for media advertising) was developed and implemented for £80,000, by today's standards a relatively modest budget for a brand of this size. However, media spend and trade discounting will have added to this sum.

Minutes

The Shout Down Non-Tango Drinkers campaign was launched to the trade at the end of February 2000. Media advertising and in-store support was designed to peak at the end of March, in order to achieve the key objective of getting the summer sales peak off to an early start.

Key points from Chapter 12:

1. Sales promotions can be used strategically rather than simply as short-term tactical tools.
2. Sales promotions must integrate with other elements of the marketing mix.

FURTHER READING

Bird, D (1990) No mileage in frequency marketing, *Marketing*, 10 October, p 12

Bird, J (1997) How to keep them faithful the world over, *Precision Marketing* 26 May

Bond, C (1991) Marriages of some convenience, *Marketing*, 10 October, pp 23–26

Britt, B Coke's magic spells trouble, *Marketing*, 31 May

Castling, J (1989) Buying strategic sales promotion, *Sales Promotion*, July, p 11

Chapman, N (1985) Cadburys pays up in Typhoo game, *Marketing Week*, 17 May

Cummins, J (1998) *Sales Promotion: How to Create and Implement Campaigns that Really Work*, 2nd edn, Kogan Page, London

Douglas, T (1984) *The Complete Guide to Advertising*, PaperMac, London

Ehrenberg, A, Hammond, K and Godheart, G (1991) *The After-effects of Large Consumer Promotions*, London Business School, London

Farrell, J (1989) Which countries allow which promotions? *Marketing Week*, 16 June, pp 75–77

Hollinger, P (1996) Electronic age raises ghost of Green Shield Stamps, *Financial Times*, 9/10 November

Holloway, P (1989) Can research really help? *Sales Promotion*, July, pp 12 and 13

Holloway, P (1989) Getting it right in the 90s, *Sales Promotion*, February, pp 23 and 24

Hyslop, R (1989) Round table discussion, *Sales Promotion*, July, p 14

Kotler, P (2000) *Marketing Management: Analysis, Planning, Implementation and Control*, Millennium Edition, Prentice-Hall, Englewood Cliffs, NJ

Marketing Breakthroughs (1991) Polish give-aways struggle to reach target, *Marketing Breakthroughs*, December

FURTHER CONTACTS

British Promotional Merchandise Association (BPMA), Bank Chambers, 15 High Road, Byfleet, Surrey KT14 7QA (tel: 01932 355660; Web site: www.bpma.co.uk)

Institute of Sales Promotion (ISP), Arena House, 66–68 Pentonville Road, London N1 9HS (tel: 020 7837 5340; Web site: www.isp.org.uk)

Promota UK (formerly known as British Advertising Gift Distributors Association), Association House, 186 Beardall Street, Hucknall, Nottingham NG15 7JU (tel: 0115 956 2169; Web site: www.promota.co.uk)

Sales Promotion Consultants Association (SPCA), 47 Margaret Street, London W1W 8SD (tel: 020 7580 8225; Web site: www.spca.org.uk)

13

Direct marketing

WHAT IS DIRECT MARKETING?

Direct marketing brings the market directly into the home or office of an individual buyer instead of the buyer having to go to the market. This is why it is sometimes called *armchair shopping*. There are, however, occasions when an immediate sale is not appropriate, so direct-marketing techniques can be used here to move buyers through various stages of the buying process, eg to get buyers to visit an exhibition, call into a showroom for a test drive, establish contact, etc. The Direct Marketing Association in the UK defines direct marketing as:

> The distribution of information, products or services through any advertising medium that invites the individual to respond directly to the advertiser.

Direct marketing should not be used solely as a tactic, eg a one-off mailshot designed to win an initial sale. It can and should be used on a more *strategic* basis by integrating it with other marketing communications tools and in the longer term by developing a database (see page 376).

Direct marketing includes:

1. direct mail;
2. telemarketing;
3. door-to-door selling (pyramid, multi-level, network retailing and field sales forces (see Chapter 10));
4. direct response advertising (TV, radio, cinema, posters, Web and press advertisements that solicit an immediate response, eg 'phone now' or fill in the coupon'); see Appendix 13.1;

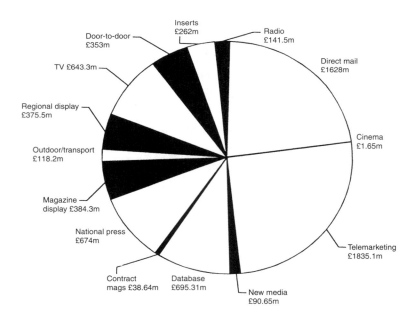

Figure 13.1   1998 UK direct marketing expenditure (£m), by medium

Source: The DMA Research Centre/Advertising Association

5. computerized home shopping (link home computer with a store so that one can browse around the aisles, pick up merchandise, inspect it by turning it around on screen, etc);
6. home shopping networks (which have turned millions of living rooms into shopping malls, eg Sky's Living channel and QVC are now carried into millions of homes worldwide);
7. miscellaneous (stuffers, inserts, leaflet drops/house-to-house distribution).

Note the figures show that:

- the two fastest-growing areas of the direct-marketing industry are new media and direct-response radio, with an increase in expenditure of 44 per cent for new media and 41 per cent for DR radio since 1997;
- direct mail is still growing, with a 10 per cent increase in expenditure, despite the disruption of postal strikes.

This chapter examines the growth of direct marketing and the development of database marketing and planning, while focusing on two popular types of direct-marketing techniques:

1. direct mail;
2. telemarketing.

As with all the marketing communications tools, the opportunity to integrate direct marketing is endless. Any marketing communications strategy should seek to link and *integrate* direct marketing techniques with other communications tools such as mainstream above-the-line TV advertising. For example, according to Ogilvy and Mather, research shows that awareness for a TV ad campaign can be increased by including a picture from the ad in a mailshot. This integration can work both ways, ie advertising images in mailshots boost response levels as well as advertisements linked to direct marketing (direct response advertisements). According to DP & A, estimates suggest that as much as 75 per cent of US advertising and 80 per cent of packaged goods now carry a direct-response mechanism (eg coupon or toll-free number).

Unintegrated communications activities can result in different messages being sent out through different media. This in turn dilutes the message impact, splinters the image and sometimes generates plain confusion in the buyer's mind.

A strategic decision to integrate the communications tools increases the communications' effectiveness. Similarly, a longer-term strategic decision to build a database for direct-marketing purposes can also create competitive advantage.

WHAT IS DATABASE MARKETING?

There is a major section devoted to database marketing (database building, data warehousing, data-mining, data manipulation, data maintenance) starting on page 376. Meanwhile here is a brief explanation.

A database is more than a list of names. A database is distinguished by the amount and quality of relevant marketing data held on each customer/prospect file. There are two types of information kept on a database that a simple mailing list does not provide: *historical data* and *predictive data*. Historical ('transactional data' or 'back data') includes name, address, recency and frequency of purchases, responses to offers and value of purchases. Predictive data identifies which groups or subgroups are more likely to respond to a specific offer. This is done through statistical scoring: customer attributes (eg lifestyle, house type, past behaviour, etc) are given scores that help to indicate the customers' future behaviour.

Database marketing is not a short-term, tactical, one-off marketing activity. It is a medium- to long-term commitment that facilitates the development of a *dialogue* and a *relationship* with each customer and prospect. It involves careful selection, collection and constant analysis of computerized customer records/data (and prospect customers' data also). Customers can then be telephoned or mailed with relevant offers at appropriate times in their buying cycles. The database can target, for example, 'customers who have bought three out of our four services and who are due this month to buy a service similar to our fourth service'. A mutually useful relationship can then blossom through properly managed database marketing.

Never sell to a stranger

Think of the old corner shop. If the shopkeeper ordered a new type of pickle, he wouldn't expect strangers to flock in and buy it. He'd recommend it to his regular pickle buyers and to people buying cheese and pork.

You wouldn't call that hard sell. You'd call it personal service, based on the shopkeeper remembering the preferences of individual customers and using this knowledge to anticipate their needs. No matter what the size and character of your marketplace, direct marketing now lets you offer that personal service to every customer.

Miles Young, Ogilvy & Mather Direct

A database gives an organization access to its own private marketplace. Organizations with properly managed databases enjoy a *competitive advantage* over competitors without databases. The value of this may result in a balance sheet valuation similar to brand assets. This is compounded by the fact that no one has an exclusive right on their customers. The customers are probably listed on several databases, which means that a competitor will probably talk to these same customers through their own database marketing activities sooner or later.

> *The diner*
>
> The diner whose ego is bolstered by the head waiter recalling his name is more likely to remain loyal than the diner whose repeat custom is incentivized by a voucher redeemable for a glass of house wine. Recognition of past custom is a powerful inducement to award future custom.
>
> Graeme McCorkell, the Direct Marketing Centre

ADVANTAGES OF DIRECT MARKETING

In addition to exploiting the power (and reduced costs) of computer technology, direct marketing can also open up a new distribution channel offering delivery from the supplier to the customer directly. This can save money by saving margins previously given to distributors or retailers, but it can also damage relations with distributors if they feel the direct marketing competes unfairly with them. It can, of course, work with them by referring enquiries to or generating leads for them, or simply expanding the market. Other advantages include:

1. *Targeting* – to isolate and talk to tight, well-defined, appropriate target markets, eg 'slimming pill buyers who read the *Sun*', and to exclude waste associated with promoting to a mass audience (see 'List selection', page 384).
2. *Cost-effective* – although initially a higher cost per thousand contacted, the cost per enquiry/order can be substantially lower, particularly with repeat sales.
3. *Control and accountability* – easy to measure results as the responses are directly attributable to the direct-marketing activity. This facilitates continuous improvement and clearer direction for future activities. It also helps subsequent forecasting and budgeting.
4. *Immediate and flexible* – this applies to telemarketing in particular as responses can be logged as soon as contact is made. Scripts can be rewritten overnight or discussion varied according to the contact's reactions.

5. *Opportunity to test* – and retest – any variable, eg prices, promotions, timing, lists and even the colour of a signature and/or the colour of the envelope (split mailings – 50 per cent blue and 50 per cent black).

6. *International* – can offer an alternative route for new market entry. Direct contact by mail or telephone may be cheaper and faster than a personal visit at the early stages of the buying cycle.

7. *Opportunity to build a database* – and win repeat sales by developing a personalized or individual dialogue and ultimately a continuous relationship with the customer base. A database also facilitates testing and researching the impact of, say, TV advertisements on different segments (see 'Building a database', page 376).

8. *Tailored messages* – customers with different needs or even different levels of loyalty can receive separate offers, eg brand-loyal customers can receive offers different from brand switchers.

9. *Long-term customers* – the opportunity of developing long-term active relationships with customers through the database.

10. *Multi-functional* – applies particularly to telemarketing since it can be used to 'profile' or segment existing customers into clusters, generate leads, qualify leads, sell, give customer service and collect information about reactions to advertisements, promotions, mailshots and even reasons for buying or not buying as the case may be.

Buying a loan?

A building society's telemarketing campaign included the revealing question: 'What factors did you consider/are you considering with regard to taking out a mortgage at another bank or building society apart from the name of the bank?' In order of priority the top four criteria were: (1) price or interest rate, (2) special deal/discount, (3) recommendation, and (4) convenience. This kind of feedback helps to determine the best sales and marketing strategy. The criteria, however, may change over time or as a recession lifts, etc.

DISADVANTAGES OF DIRECT MARKETING

In addition to sometimes upsetting the middleman (as mentioned previously), direct marketing has a problem with its image. Direct mail has connotations of 'junk mail' and is therefore vulnerable to criticism from environmental pressure groups. Although research shows that a large majority prefer to receive direct mail, there is a percentage who consider it to be an intrusion or invasion of their privacy. This is particularly true if they are telephoned in the evening or if a door-to-door salesperson knocks on their door after they have had a long and busy day. There is now both a Telephone Preference Service (TPS) and a Fax Preference Service (FPS). Both are free services for those people who do not welcome the intrusion of unsolicited interruptions. Telemarketing can be uniquely intrusive if a consumer has just come home and wants to be left alone to relax. Whether someone is watching a football match, listening to Beethoven or simply sleeping, a telephone call, even from a friend, can sometimes be considered a downright nuisance. On the Internet unsolicited direct e-mail is considered even more unacceptable – a breach of etiquette (Net etiquette). Any unsolicited direct e-mail on the Internet is called 'spam'. This invasion of privacy is worse because it costs the receiver both time and money – time to download the message and money charged when you are on line downloading. It is not surprising that 'spammers' get 'flamed' by angry Net citizens who send abusive messages back, sometimes repeatedly and sometimes with a mailbomb (a massive file) and often effectively close down the spammer's system. See Chapter 20 for more. This is an increasing problem as e-mail lists are offered at very cheap prices, eg $35 per million (compared to £200 per thousand 'snail mail' addresses).

Coming back to traditional 'snail mail' and direct marketing, the initial customer acquisition costs are high (subsequent transactions are much cheaper). Direct marketing has a high cost per thousand (people contacted) compared to above-the-line advertising. The very rough industry average response of 2 per cent suggests, by definition, that 98 per cent of mailings get chucked in the bin (albeit mostly after being read). Poorly targeted mailings might one day be considered a threat to trees and the environment. There can also be a heavy investment cost in developing a database. Direct marketing can prove to be expensive for a one-off sale. Used effectively, to develop repeat sales and 'lifetime value', it can prove extremely profitable, but used inefficiently, ie simply to make a single sale, direct marketing can be extremely costly. Finally there is, of course, the risk involved with any marketing communications activity. A bad mailing, for example, can not only lose money but reduce sales and damage the company's corporate image. In fact a spam mailing would be considered irresponsible by any well-known company.

For another insight into how some people resent junk mail vociferously (even in church), see Appendix 13.3 for Lindsay Allen's thoughts, which have been broadcast several times on BBC Radio 4.

THE GROWTH OF DIRECT MARKETING

Many years ago advertising guru David Ogilvy forecast that one day all advertising agencies would be direct-marketing agencies. The growth of direct marketing has been fuelled by:

- market fragmentation;
- tailor-made technology;
- the list explosion;
- sophisticated software;
- hybrid marketing systems;
- the constant search for cost-effectiveness.

Market fragmentation

In the 1960s we had mass marketing. The 1970s developed *segmentation*, while the 1980s moved into *target marketing* and *niching*. The 1990s and beyond are now in a new era – that of *one-to-one marketing* or direct marketing. Today, *mass markets*, by and large, are *dead*. They have fragmented into more discrete sectors or niches. This is clearly demonstrated by the plethora of product development and modification shown below.

Once there was one cola; today there is ordinary cola, sugar-free cola, caffeine-free cola, and so on. Once there were a dozen or so breakfast cereals; now the consumer can chose from over 100 different types. Once there was just a running shoe; now there are tennis, squash, basketball, indoor soccer, walking, running, jogging and aerobics shoes for both men and women. Once there was just coffee; then came instant coffee, powder, granules, freeze-dried granules, filter and percolator coffees, and *caffeine-free coffee*. Now we have 'politically correct' coffees from certain developing countries. Oxfam shops sell other 'ethical coffees' (coffees supplied by working cooperatives in developing countries) and there is even a brand of coffee sold in Amsterdam called 'Fair Wages For Coffee Pickers'.

The shampoo market has gone full circle. Initially it fragmented into dry, greasy and normal shampoos. Split ends, dandruff, sensitive scalp and blow-dry shampoos followed. Then TV audiences were informed that the shampoos didn't work very well and conditioners were needed. There are today shampoos targeted at the busy person, which have shampoo and conditioner all in one. These new, emerging, discrete needs, niches or mini-markets have a growing range of specialist magazines and new minority radio and television programmes that offer tightly targeted communications channels. The trend towards individualism, the increase in personalized products and the resulting bespoke solutions to buyers' needs are evidence of the continuing fragmentation of markets.

Tailor-made technology

Personalized products, eg inscribed silverware and handwritten letters, have been around for a long time. Technology today allows thousands or millions of personalized items

Reproduced from Marketing CD Rom Title 2: Segmentation, Positioning & the Marketing Mix. Kind permission from the Multimedia Marketing.com. Photograph: Steven Saunders

(eg personalized letters or maybe even personally labelled shampoo) to be produced economically in the course of a few days. This matches our increasing desire to be treated as individuals. Many years ago futurologist Alvin Toffler forecast that there would be a proliferation of personalized, tailor-made products. One of his many challenging books, *The Third Wave*, considered tailor-made remote *satellite* manufacturing systems that design individualized products on a computer screen in one country and are electronically linked to an automated factory in some less-developed country, where a laser could cut out the design as directed by the designer, on a screen, many thousands of miles away. A single product would then be produced to suit an individual's need. bhs are experimenting with such a system today.

Underwater and space manufacturing have not fully caught up with Toffler's predictions, but it seems as if America's *Farmer's Journal* is getting close. Its 825,000 circulation now receives a tailor-made magazine with a minimum of 2,000 and a maximum of 8,896 different editions per issue. Essentially, the pig farmer's edition will not carry features or advertisements about cereal farming, etc. The farmer prefers his magazine to carry relevant material. The advertisers like it because it offers better targeting. The magazine saves money on paper and post. The environmentalists might prefer it too. It has been suggested that one day everyone will have their own *personalized magazine. Personalized interactive TV programmes* are already running in Spain and France, while the Internet already provides personalized newspapers.

The list explosion

The third factor fuelling the growth of direct marketing is the proliferation of lists or databases available. The *only restriction is imagination*, or one's ability to define a target market or customer profile in a range of different ways. For example, home decorators could be redefined as 'home movers'. The million or so UK home movers could then be reduced to those moving into certain geographic locations or even neighbourhood areas, which might indicate their propensity to undertake the decorating themselves (as opposed to hiring someone to do it for them). A list, or a section of the list, can be hired or bought, and tested and/or refined by using certain software packages (see 'Sophisticated software', page 373). It is important to select and check lists carefully, since the quality of many of the UK's 'cold' lists has long been a problem for UK direct marketers, although data integrity is now much improved, especially with newer lifestyle databases run by people like Claritas.

The diversity of the lists available is intriguing and sometimes bewildering. The lists range from 'cynical humorous intellectuals' (18,000 *Punch* magazine subscribers) to 'slimming pill buyers who read the *Sun*' to 'young mothers' to 'fork-lift truck buyers'. Just about anything can be targeted. There was even a list of 'right-wing, money-orientated gamblers who are influenced by advertising, react to new ideas and have disposable income' (the list of 3 million British Gas shareholders is available from the British Investor Database). The Companies Act requires firms to hand over their registers to anyone for a minimal fee.

It is worth phoning list brokers and list owners to request a catalogue of lists (consumer or business to business) and spending an hour browsing through the range and types of lists available from just one particular source. A *compiled list* is collected from public records, directories, trade show registrations, etc. According to *World List News, a mail-responsive list* can produce a 300 per cent increase in response over a compiled list. The best list is an organization's own house list of customers, enquirers, visitors, employees, shareholders, etc. In the United States it is estimated that 80 per cent of all direct mail is targeted at existing customer lists.

Some examples of lists

Here is a small selection of lists that could be relevant for the three types of target customers shown below.

Prominent people: 25,000 Rolls-Royce, Lamborghini and Jaguar owners, 2,500 UK millionaires, 10,000 rich ladies, 7,000 tennis court owners, 13,000 private plane owners, racehorse owners, greyhound owners and even cat owners.

Entertainment seekers: 190,000 theatre goers, 27,000 Shaftesbury Theatre goers, 186,000 club goers.

Improvers: 47,000 named clergy, 25,000 buyers of self-improvement books, 106,000 house improvers, 1,000,000 house movers, and even a list of owners of Black 'n' Decker drills.

The diverse range of lists is, to the uninitiated, extraordinary. Here are some other odd lists of odd target groups.

100,000 aerial home photograph owners (people who have aerial photos of their homes), 15,000 personalized car number plate owners, 62,000 buyers of military prints and memorabilia, 49,000 tall ladies, 5,000 car phone enquirers, 160 prisons, borstals and detention centres, 21,000 women executives, 295,000 hypochondriacs, 4,100 management consultants, 43,700 librarians, 246,000 educational children's book buyers and so on. And, of course, the electoral roll is on a CD ROM.

These are just a selection from a few list catalogues. They do not represent the whole universe of people who fall into each category. They only represent those who have been trapped on to a list. The list can be bought or hired on disk, printed labels, envelopes and so on.

Sophisticated software

Basic technology today allows different mailing lists and databases to be added together and even superimposed on each other. Lists can be *merged* and any overlap or duplications can be '*deduped*' (deduplicated).

Geodemographics mix geographical location, type of neighbourhood and demographic data such as age, income and family life cycle. Everyone fits into a cluster. Key in an address and the database will identify the neighbourhood's cluster type or profile. This *geodemographic typecasting* uses shorthand names to identify cluster types. For example, in the United States one database company classifies people with mature families living in affluent suburbs as '*pools and patios*', whereas poorer rural areas are called '*shotguns and pickups*'. People living there may have aspirations to move towards '*golf clubs and Volvos*'.

They know you better than you do

An investigative journalist decided that he wanted to find out about himself as he was soon moving to south-east San Francisco. Having keyed in his new address, the database company told him that he was classified as a '*young influential*'. He was moving into a 'thirty-something childbearing neighbourhood'. They also told him that 'he may still be in a town house or a row house and may not have graduated to the detached single home but they were definitely starting to have children, making the transition from a couple-orientated lifestyle to a family-orientated lifestyle.' Furthermore, the 'young influentials' typically were aged 20–35, had a median income of $39,500, enjoyed jogging, travelling, new wave music and investing, read magazines like *Rudder, Scientific American* and *Town and Country*, and liked to eat yoghurt, wholemeal bread and Mexican food and drink low-fat milk.

This profile almost exactly matched the journalist's profile.

It is said that demographics say *'you are where you live'* (meaning your neighbourhood is a good indicator of your lifestyle and the kinds of products you are likely to buy) and psychographic databases say *'you are what you do'* (meaning your behaviour patterns and buying preferences can be estimated from collected data on your (or similar people's) lifestyle, eg whether you are likely to own a compact disc). In the UK, geodemographic packages such as *ACORN, PINPOINT, MOSAIC* and *SUPER PROFILES* are easily cross-referenced with media usage, product usage and lifestyle statements. Another system called MONICA classifies databases into age and social status by analysing the Christian or first name alone.

If you run up a bad debt…

… the computer will know about it, if you subscribe to a dubious magazine, forget to return library books or collect parking tickets, everyone with access to a computer will know about it!

This light-hearted suggestion was made in an article in *Marketing Week* (3 December 1982), but try to hire a TV if you have a county court judgment against you – the retailer will find out through their online database, United Protection of Traders Association.

Hybrid marketing systems

The addition and integration of new communications channels (eg telemarketing) to existing communications channels (eg advertising or the salesforce) can create a hybrid marketing system. Harvard professors Moriarty and Moran (1990) have said that 'a company that designs and manages its (hybrid) system strategically will achieve a powerful advantage over rivals that add channels and methods in an opportunistic and incremental manner'. A well-managed hybrid system allows an organization to achieve what Moriarty and Moran call *'a balance between its customers' buying behaviour and its own selling economics'*.

Direct marketing can, and should, integrate with other communications tools. It can link different direct-marketing tools to create a more cost-effective method of marketing communications. Depending on the quality of the lead, the lead can be followed up by mailing a brochure, or a hot prospect might be telephoned to set up an appointment or to invite the prospect to an event.

The *lead generation* might be created in the first place by a *direct-response advertisement* that invites readers/viewers/listeners to send in for a free gift. Research suggests that approximately 45 per cent of business enquirers will buy within 12 months. The challenge then lies in identifying the hottest prospects and directing the salesforce to the 1 out of every 2.2 enquirers who will buy within the 12 months.

Identifying the hottest prospects or 'screening' can be carried out by following up with an *outbound telephone* interview to determine the prospect's status. Alternatively, the analysis can be carried out directly from the coupon if it was designed to capture the required detailed information. The outbound phone call can screen and ultimately fix an appointment for the sales or progress to the next appropriate stage in the buying process. Alternatively, an *inbound* phone catering for an 0800 or free-phone number can accommodate enquiries generated from either a direct-response advertisement or a mailshot.

This is only the start. After the initial sale, *database marketing* can help to keep in touch with the customer as he or she moves towards a repeat purchase. Conservative estimates suggest that it is *five times easier to sell to an existing customer* than to a new one.

The constant search for cost-effectiveness

Falling computer costs have opened up computer database facilities to organizations large and small.

Ideally, costs should be measured against results, not simply outputs. The cost of testing* a telesales campaign (1,000 names at roughly £10 per call) might be, say, £10,000, but the result might be 2 per cent success or 20 new customers. The cost per order or cost per customer can then be calculated as £500. How does this compare with the current cost per new customer generated by other marketing techniques, such as exhibitions, advertising and field sales?†

The results, and costs, may vary if, for example, the telesales team is only focused on appointment setting and the field sales team handles the rest. This may result in, say, 15 per cent appointments (150); the sales team then convert, say, 30 per cent of these into 45 new customers. The telesales cost of £10,000 is added to the field sales cost of £8,550 (see note below). £18,550 divided by 45 gives a cost per new customer of £412. A recent Datapoint survey suggested that companies could increase their salesforce's productivity by at least one-third by providing in-house telesales marketing support.

The *lifetime value* of the customer can then be calculated by multiplying the average value of expected orders pa by the number of years the customer will exist. The cost per order of

---

* Since the set-up costs of a test remain fixed, it follows that a larger test run will reduce the cost per order by between £50 and £500.
† The real cost of a salesperson on a basic salary of £20,000 plus bonus, car (including depreciation), expenses, National Insurance and perks such as medical and life insurance is closer to £50,000. Five visits a day times four days a week (one day in the office per week) times 50 weeks = 1,000 sales visits a year. Each visit costs £50.00. Some customers could be serviced by a telesales call @ £10, while others need a sales representative to be there on the spot, face to face with the customer. The trick is to identify which ones need the extra attention. See Chapters 10 and 16 for further salesforce costs analysis.

subsequent orders will be significantly less than the cost of the initial order as, as already mentioned, estimates suggest that it is at least five times cheaper and easier to sell to an existing customer than to a prospect.

One last international question – what are the *marketing costs of entering a new market*? Could any of the marketing costs be reduced by telemarketing or direct mail?

Telesales can be used to *support a sales force* by servicing accounts over the phone instead of having a sales rep visit every month. Telesales can also be used to generate or even screen leads. At a cost of anywhere between £7 and £70 per appointment set up, a telesales campaign can release the salesperson from prospecting and even administration into doing what most reps are best at, face-to-face selling. Some estimates show that salespeople spend less than 20 per cent of their time actually selling; the rest is prospecting, travelling, form filling, etc. The average cost of a single sales visit of £150 (per call) can be reduced if salespeople are released from other duties and therefore make more visits. Some telesales campaigns link in with computer models that select the optimum call plan to minimize travel time. All of these activities, including order fulfilment, can be handled by an outside agency if needed.

Not surprisingly TV ads and mailshots can link together both activity-wise and image-wise. Drayton Bird's *Commonsense Direct Marketing* (1989) revealed that awareness for a particular airline's TV ad four months after screening was 50 per cent higher among those who had received a mailshot which featured a scene from the TV ad than among a similar panel who had not received the mailshot. The database can also be used to research the impact of, say, a TV advertisement or a sponsorship package among different types of audiences.

DATABASE MARKETING

This section looks at database building, data warehousing, data-mining, data manipulation and the importance of data maintenance/cleaning. Although all of this section applies to large databases like Procter and Gamble's US database of 50 million, it applies equally to smaller databases. The case study of the low-budget award-winning direct-mail campaign for St James Church (see Chapter 2) shows how the platform for success, the database, can be built creatively and inexpensively. The data were then stored, analysed and segmented to such an extent that 'the data were almost driving the creative'.

Building a database

A customer database is a list carrying customer information and can be an organization's most valuable asset. Databases can be bought, borrowed or built. Guarantee slips, subscription lists and sales promotions all trap names and addresses. Often the best source lies dormant, tucked in the bottom of a file somewhere in an organization. Every customer and his or her purchasing pattern, every enquiry and every complaint, comment or feedback can be logged into a database. The database then builds up a detailed picture of the customer's profile, which lets the company get to know its customers better. The database can identify which customers/prospects are in which stages of the buying cycle. This facilitates sequence selling, where attitudes are moulded and interest is aroused by a series of communications rather than going for an immediate straight sale. In a sense, prospects are moved up the 'ladder of loyalty' (see Figure 13.2), from suspects up to devoted loyal customers who advocate an organization's product or service. Considine and Murray's *The Great Brain Robbery* (1981) gives a full explanation.

Figure 13.2   The ladder of loyalty

Customer acquisition is the immediate goal. Selective retention of loyal and profitable customers is the long-term, financially rewarding relationship which, ultimately, the database aims to achieve. Welcome cycles (welcome letters, new member offers), up-selling (moving the customer on to higher-quality levels), cross-selling (other products/services) and reactivation (of previous customers) all help to nurture the relationship. The system should develop a dialogue or a two-way flow of information between the customer and the organization. Every time a customer responds, he or she can be encouraged to give information about their needs and situation (eg whether they want to stay on the database). Questionnaires are sometimes sent out to existing customers to gather even more specific data. The art lies in the retrieval of the data in an appropriate format, eg a list of 'all enquirers from the south-west in the past six months', a list of a particular category of business customer (SIC code), a list of 'customers who have bought all our products except product

X' and so on. Can the database identify the key characteristics of the customers on file? Careful thought and considerable advice is needed in setting up a database, since the system has to be told specifically what is expected of it. Information gathering is strategic, it has a long-term purpose and it costs time, money and expertise. Information is an investment.

In consumer markets, a database allows an individual to be targeted by overlaying lifestyle and geodemographic data that analyses our behaviour patterns. And this data is saleable. Why then are databases not included as assets on the balance sheet? Like fixed assets, databases can be realized or sold. They also deteriorate or depreciate (business lists deteriorate at 25 per cent or more pa). They need maintenance (need to be cleaned or adjusted/updated). Equally, an uncleaned or decayed list should be considered a liability to the extent that the data are so inaccurate that they generate much higher costs per order/response than orders generated from a properly maintained database or list. An inaccurate list can also damage the corporate image and even cause resentment, so it is always worth pre-screening data against a 'deceased file', which is publicly available.

Unaccounted assets?

Databases are an asset. Some say they are the most valuable asset a company has. Like other assets, they require investment for maintenance, otherwise they deteriorate – sometimes to the extent of becoming a liability (just as a dilapidated building becomes dangerous, a dilapidated database wastes money, causes insult and damages the corporate image – in other words, it is a liability). Assuming they are maintained, they then remain a realizable and valuable asset. So how come so few companies are showing them on their balance sheet?

Some years ago Rothmans used a sales promotion to build a database by offering their cigarette smokers a free pack of cigarettes when they had collected 10 coupons and returned them with a completed form. They generated 750,000 names within 18 months; 500,000 of the customer database were subsequently offered an FCF promotion ('friend get a friend', similar to MGM, 'member get member'). The database members received a free draw ticket after sending in their own name and address and a 'draw partner's' name and address. The draw partner had to be over 18 and a smoker of a competitive brand; 250,000 smokers of competitors' brands were named. Follow-up market research showed that 90 per cent were genuine. These names may provide an invaluable communications channel as fewer and fewer of these are available to cigarette companies. The lifetime value of a smoker may be around £29,000 (for an average 20-a-day smoker). This would represent over £7 billion worth of sales if all 250,000 converted permanently to this brand. Dunhill has also advertised a free product trial and gave a direct-response phone number that could be used to claim a free pack of cigarettes.

Address ....

....

.... Postcode ....

Signature .... Date ....

Prices may be subject to alteration without notice

☐ As a service to our readers we occasionally make our customer lists
available to companies whose products or services we feel may be of interest.
If you do not wish to receive such mailings, please tick the box.

TR   0 1 2 3 4 5 6 7 8 9   A B C D E   TM

There are, of course, other methods of compilation, some of which may cause concern. For
example, Manhattan psychotherapists Muriel Goldfarb and Daniel Ruinstein compile their
own lists of mild neurotics so that they can market counselling by mail. Lists of those
recently divorced and widowed, and previous patients, are added, together with those
named bereavement notices. These prospects are then offered a 10-session programme with
the first one free 'plus' a free tape recorder if he or she pays in advance.

In the UK it is now illegal to store any data about an individual on computer unless you or
your company are registered with the Data Protection Registrar (2000 cost was £150). The
Mailing Preference Service (MPS) is a free service for people who do not want to receive
unsolicited mail, or who only want to receive mail in certain categories. They can put their
names on an MPS application form (which they can get from the post office) and their names
are then entered on to a disk used by reputable list owners and mailers so that these are
cleaned from their lists. Reputable agencies subscribe to the MPS and therefore use MPS
clean lists. Any response mechanism (coupon, guarantee slip, order form, etc) should give
the respondent the opportunity to choose not to receive further mailings, or opt out by
ticking an opt-out box (see the example above). As mentioned earlier, there are now also a
Telephone Preference Service and Fax Preference Service. These forms of consumer
protection are strengthened by EU law (the Distance Selling Directive). It is essential for any
practitioners to take account of this when planning programmes.

Data warehousing and data-mining

Databases have to be stored securely. Large databases require large warehouses, metaphor-
ically speaking. This is where data warehouses come in. Successful database marketing is
all about data capture, storage, analysis, interpretation and application in a manner that
discovers patterns and relationships previously hidden in the data. It helps marketing to
become more refined and better targeted. The database analysis can be combined with

traditional market research to identify not just what customers do but why they do it. Applying advanced statistical analysis and modelling techniques to data to find 'useful patterns and relationships' is called data-mining. It can, for example, explore each and every transaction of 6 million customers and how they relate to each other.

Unexpected relationships?

Unexpected database connections revealed that:

- 82 per cent of motorcycle owners buy frozen seafood;
- 62 per cent of amateur cellists buy power tools.

Data-mining can find correlations that are beyond 'human conceptual capability' – see the seafood bikers and cellist DIYers in the box above. A range of statistical tools are used, including regression analysis, time-series forecasting, clustering, associations, logistic regression, discriminant analysis, neural nets and decision trees. These all have ready applications for the marketing manager. For example, a sequence-discovery function detects frequently occurring purchasing patterns over time. This information can then be layered with demographic data (from the main database) so that a company can tailor its mailings on each household's 'vulnerability or propensity to buy certain items at certain times'.

It can be mathematically interesting to see these techniques in action. However, it is also important that a manager knows roughly what the purpose and possible benefits are of any such data-mining analysis. The ability to ask a good question or write a good data-mining brief is a relatively new skill for today's marketing manager. Appendix 13.4 shows an excerpt from a data-mining brief.

Intelligent miner saves Safeway's top customer

An intelligent miner discovered that a particular cheese product, ranked 209th in sales, was frequently purchased by the top-spending 25 per cent of customers – the last clientele Safeway would want to disappoint. Under conventional analytical principles, the product would have been delisted; in actual fact, the item was quite important.

DB2, Spring 1997

Database manipulation

Database manipulation creates further opportunities for tighter targeting. For example, Grattan's ladies' fashion mail-order company decided to experiment with a new product, a grandfather clock. They guessed the likely target profile would be something like middle-aged, well-off ABs living in ACORN types J35 (villages with wealthy older commuters) and J36 (detached houses, exclusive suburbs). They then asked their computer to print out names and addresses that fitted this profile. The subsequent mailing produced 60 orders at £1,000. They then analysed those 60 orders with a view to identifying any hidden characteristic that could be added to the profile and fed into the database again to produce a different, more accurate target list. When they mailed this list they sold every one of the 1,000 limited-edition clocks.

In the absence of completely reliable data a less scientific analysis is sometimes used to separate or take out names that do not fit the target profile. For example, Rediffusion cable services felt that older home dwellers did not fit their hot-prospects' profile, so they took out older-generation Christian names commonly used by elderly relatives and office tea ladies, such as Albert, Alfred, Arthur, Bertram, Harold, Samuel, Victor, Winifred, Alice, Amelia, Constance, Grace, May, Mildred, Rose, Sabena and Violet.

Constant analysis not only seeks to identify the best prospects for various direct-marketing activities, it also provides guidance for future communications strategy, creative strategy, product strategy, and pricing and offer strategy. The responses are then fed back into the database so that a spiral of prosperity develops (see Bird, 1989). This is shown in Figure 13.3.

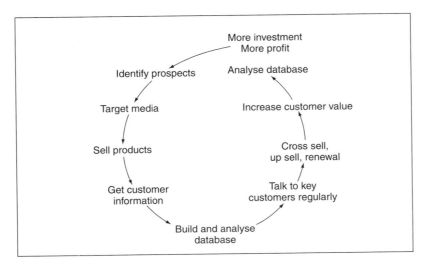

Figure 13.3 The spiral of prosperity

As responses come in it is important to monitor their source. Which promotion, insert, mailing, leaflet, editorial or direct-response ad generated the response? Accurate feedback of results by key code (which identifies which lists, media and tests were used) is absolutely essential so that next year resources can be channelled into the most successful response mechanisms. 'Constant improvement' is all part of the marketing mantra.

Database maintenance

Like any other asset, the database has to be maintained or 'cleaned'. It is estimated that business lists decay by 25 per cent pa because of constant career moves. During a recession redundancies can increase the 'gone aways' (obsolete addresses, positions or job titles) to give an increased decay rate of over 30 per cent. A company with a core list of 900,000 names can maintain the database with up to 40,000 calls a month. Other companies send their database names a reply-paid card asking them whether they wish to be kept on the mailing list. Non-respondents get wiped. This may seem costly but it can increase the accuracy of the list and ultimately improve the cost effectiveness of the responses. This, in turn, reduces wasted brochures, envelopes, handling costs and postage. It simultaneously maintains this asset's value.

PLANNING A DIRECT-MAIL CAMPAIGN

Whether an organization is planning an advertising campaign or a direct-mail campaign, a similarly disciplined approach should be taken, ie research in the situation, message development (creative mailing), media planning (list selection and timing), testing and monitoring, etc. In addition the SOSTAC® + 3Ms can be used as a checklist (see Chapter 2).

A direct-marketing campaign can be planned in the same way as an advertising campaign, ie by using SOSTAC® + 3Ms. However, the following six factors will now be examined in more detail:

1. Timing.
2. List selection.
3. Creative mailings.
4. Budgeting.
5. Operational implications.
6. Testing.

Timing

The mailing schedule illustrated in Figure 13.4 shows why a minimum of 12 weeks, preferably *6 months*, is needed to set up a direct marketing campaign that feeds into a database system from scratch. As Drayton Bird (1989) says: 'the faster you need something done the more likely there will be mistakes. The answer is either give more time, or pay a great deal more money.' Deciding whether the campaign should be multi-stage (generate enquiries, screening, follow-up phone calls and sales visits, etc) or single stage (straight order), multi-media or single media, and so on, is arguably less important than determining strategically how each mailing forms part of an overall campaign that develops a cumulative effect. *One-off large mailings should gradually be replaced by smaller, more frequent mailings* as the database identifies what is needed by whom and when. Many direct-mail agencies can develop a campaign in 4 to 6 weeks, but, ideally, the campaign should be researched and planned strategically, and with a greater emphasis on creativity, to achieve 'cut through'; the ideal lead time is 17 weeks.

Timing also refers to identifying when a target market buys and how often. Markets are constantly moving. Buyers drift in and out at different stages. Other markets are seasonal and others again have peaks and troughs on different days of the week. Are target respondents more receptive to a mailshot that lands on a Friday morning or a Monday morning?

The development and scheduling of the campaign is shown in Figure 13.4. Essentially it follows the normal advertising campaign development sequence: brief, concept development, research artwork, production, and roll-out (note that research can be supplemented by continual testing).

As in advertising, a *creative brief* is followed by *concepts* that are subsequently approved, amended, *researched* and eventually developed into *final copy and design*. This is turned into *artwork* that is checked / *proofed* and eventually turned into *final approved artwork* that goes to the *printer*. Prior to this (or sometimes simultaneously) a *list brief* is agreed. This defines the target market. Lists are carefully researched and checked.

A list proposal is subsequently approved for ordering (purchase or hire). *The letter shop* puts the required letter into the system ready for *laser printing* on to personalized letters. Proof letters are checked and approved while the lists are prepared, merged and purged (duplicate names withdrawn). The printer dispatches the brochure to the letter shop, which then presses the button. The letters are lasered, *folded, collated* and *inserted* with the brochure or mailing piece into lasered (or window) envelopes (sometimes preprinted with teaser messages or images) and *posted*. Then a dreadful quietness descends as the bags of mail are driven off into the sunset and the long wait begins. Pre-mailshot tension can run riot, with nightmares about postal strikes, redundant lists, a printing error, a wrong expiry date or, worse still, a nil response level.

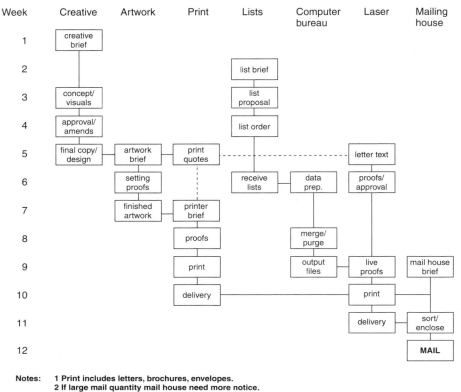

Figure 13.4 Example of a mailing schedule
Source: Institute of Direct Marketing

Good planning ensures that the best lists are used (perhaps based on test results), print, proofs, dates, etc are checked, and acceptable results projected. Even in a situation where a lot of variables are unknown, careful planning can reduce the chance of failure.

List selection

Five key planning questions

These are patently obvious questions that can be applied to any communications campaign, but, as Bird (1989) says, surprisingly few people do ask these questions:

1. Who are you trying to influence?
2. What are you selling?

3. Why should your prospect buy it?
4. Where will you find your prospect?
5. When should you speak to them?

Tips for selecting a list

List selection is the most important stage in the whole direct marketing process. Sixty per cent of any project's time should be spent on list selection. 'There's no point fishing in the pool if the pool ain't got any fish.' Here are some questions that should be asked before using a list:

1. Where do the names come from (eg compiled, previous mail responsive, subscription lists, etc)?
2. When was the list built?
3. How often is it cleaned (updated)? Is it MPS cleaned?
4. When was the list last used (and by whom) and what was the percentage of gone-aways (redundant names/addresses which the post office return to the sender)? Are there any known results or any references from past users?
5. What is the rebate per gone-away that is returned to the list owner for future cleaning?
6. What proportion of the target's total universe does the list represent, eg does the 1 million list of home movers represent all the home movers, or half, or what?
7. What selections are available (eg geographic split, job title, etc)? Are there any additional costs?
8. What 'net names' percentage is quoted (ie net usable names after deduping with other lists)?
9. Are there any rental restrictions (minimum quantities, competitive products subject to the list owner's approval, etc)?
10. Assuming the list has an appropriate profile (similar to your specified target market), clarify whether:
    – it has named individuals as opposed to job titles or 'the occupier';
    – it is in an appropriate format, ie labels, disk, etc; if disk, check that the disk format suits the letter shop's requirements;
    – it is postcoded (for post office Mailsort discounts).
11. How much does it cost? What is the lead time from order to delivery?

If the list is hired, permission is usually given for one use only. *Sleeper names* are planted in the list to ensure that it is not used more than once (the sleepers immediately notify the list owner if they receive two mailings). Hiring charges vary from £50 to £350 per thousand. Many lists are not available for purchase but those that are, are often priced at least four times higher than the rental price. Prices in the United States are cheaper. For example, every single residential phone number in the US is in 'Phone Disc USA', which is available on interactive compact disc (CDI) for $1,850 annual subscription.

Creative mailings

> *Growth will come through mastering the skills of creativity*
>
> The search for value has led companies to seek efficiency through downsizing, rationalizing and right sizing – approaches that eventually result in a diminishing level of return. But what will fuel growth in the future? Growth will come through mastering the skills of creativity – and making creativity actionable.
>
> John Kao, Harvard Business School

Creative mailing devices

Opportunities for creativity abound. Most mail competes with bills and statements. Many of the top creative people still feel television advertising is sexier, so perhaps most mailings are restrained either by the people that create them or by the managers who commission them. Here are some odd exceptions.

A plastic green cucumber was mailed by the Direct Mail Sales Bureau to all UK media buyers to raise awareness of the direct-mail option.

The Prince's Trust, when targeting company chairmen, mailed a box containing a *ceramic bowl* created by one of the very businesses the Trust had supported (the bowl provided a gift for the chairman's secretary, to encourage her to pass on the pack; it also brought the achievements of the Trust to life for the chairman).

A *briefcase* was mailed to car distributors. When opened, the briefcase resembled a car dashboard complete with audio cassette and car phone. Insert the tape and lift the phone to hear a sales pitch about why the particular car phone was outstanding. The briefcase further doubled as a point-of-sale item for the distributor.

The mailing piece and the incentive can affect the budget significantly. Not all creative mailings need anything other than a few clever words. A recent mailing simply said '*Good Morning*'. This generated a lot of interest, anticipation and eagerness to get the next mailing in the sequence.

Budgeting 'money'

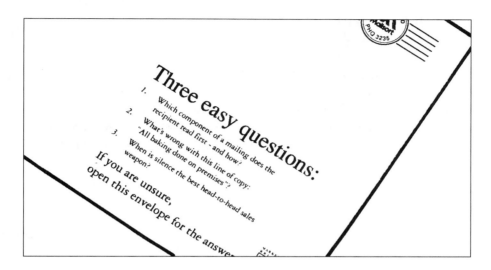

One way of budgeting is by asking: 'How much can the organization afford to spend to recruit a new customer? How much is a new customer worth or what is the allowable cost per customer? What is their *lifetime value*?' Then multiply this by the number of customers required and, bingo, a budget emerges. Another way to build a budget or at least a *ballpark cost figure* is to calculate 50p per shot. Thus if an organization is running a 20,000 mailshot, then ballpark costs to cover everything (design, artwork, print, list, letter shop, insertion or collation incentive, envelope and postage) would be £10,000; a 500,000 mailshot would obviously enjoy economies of scale and cost less than £250,000.

Cost per thousand

This translates into £500 per thousand contacts, compared with:

Telesales (at, say, £10)*	£10,000
Door-to-door drop	£250
Inserts (inc print)	£100
Magazine ads	£50
Web balance ads	£30
National press	£10
TV ads	£5

---

* The cost of a telesales call can vary between £5 and £20, depending on the type of phone line (see 'Telemarketing' on page 391).

Cost per response and cost per order give the bottom line of success or failure. Percentage response levels vary from 0.5 per cent to 5 per cent, although there are many examples now of much higher rates – as high as 60 per cent – especially when targeting existing customers with strong creative combined with highly relevant incentives. (Note, enquiries, as opposed to orders, are easier to get and therefore pull higher response levels.)

How much would you spend on winning a customer? What kind of incentive would you offer them to take action and place an order? Here are a few examples: $50 Amazon voucher; Alliance & Leicester (bank) £50 (to open an account); Virgin £400 (free laptop to selected customers); Fedex £1,000 (free PC); Streamline.com $1,000 (free fridge-freezer).

The direct-mail budgeting worksheet shown in Figure 13.5 helps to identify and control costs.

Operational implications/action required

A strain on your office?

Even if the response is fairly modest it can still be a strain on your office resources. Could your telephone system handle thousands of calls in an hour? Could your staff still treat customers with enthusiasm at the end of a whole day of frantic answering? Do you have space for sackfuls of mail? Do you have time to answer every reply quickly? If not, a specialist fulfilment company can help.

The *Royal Mail Guide to Successful Direct Mail*

If carefully thought out, *the operational requirements* clarify how the campaign will actually work. For example, what happens to the information that is collected during a telephone conversation? How do the sales representatives' diaries get updated and who monitors representatives' availability? Research by RSCG Direct found '*an irresponsible use of response-handling mechanisms*' with only a 70 per cent chance of respondents receiving information. The majority of this 70 per cent were never contacted again. Only 5 per cent ever received a follow-up telephone call. Is there a plan/system that ensures 'follow up'? Who controls and delivers stocks of goods or stocks of brochures? How and when are invoices generated?

Marketing is the last bastion of under-automation, whereas manufacturing and production have generally been automated to the point where labour costs account for only 8–12 per cent of production costs. Sales and marketing costs can account for between 15 and 35 per cent of costs. Automation can deliver both cost savings and increased effectiveness of marketing and sales follow-through. Hybrid systems help salespeople by

CAMPAIGN TITLE:
BUDGET:
TARGET:

Est   Actual

PROMOTION DATE:
MAIL QUANTITY

		Estimated Costs	Actual Costs	Invoice Y/N	Comments
1 ORIGINATION	- Copywriting/Design - Artwork Production				
2 DATABASE LIST PREPARATION	- List Rental - Data Preparation - Merge/Purge - Mailsort				
3 LASER PRINTING	- Text Setting - Printing				
4 PRINT PRODUCTION	- Letterhead - Continuation sheet - Brochure - Flyer - Order Form - Other				
5 ENVELOPES	- Outer - Reply				
6 LETTERSHOP	- Folding - Collating - Enclosing				
7 POSTAGE	- Postage - (Discount)				
8 MISC.	- couriers etc				
9 TOTAL COSTS					
10 COST PER 1000 MAILED = (Total Cost/Qty. mailed) × 1,000					
11 COST PER RESPONSE = Total Cost / No. of Responses					
12 COST PER SALE = Total Cost / No. of Sales					
13 TOTAL REVENUE					
14 REVENUE TO COST = Revenue / Total Cost					

Figure 13.5 Direct mail budgeting worksheet
Source: Institute of Direct Marketing

reminding them which customers need attention this month, next month and so on. Enquiries generated through an array of marketing efforts are all dealt with (brochure despatched along with letter; telesales follow up for an appointment; eventual appointment for the salesperson). Nothing slips through the system. No enquiries are lost. All are followed up. The system has to accommodate returned goods and cancelled orders also (see Appendix 13.2 for more information on new legislation in this area). Up-front investment in a hybrid system is falling as more and more sales-tracking software packages come on to the marketplace.

Test and control

Test, test and test

One of the advantages of direct marketing is the ability to test, retest, change, monitor and learn what works best. Everything can be tested, including the colour of the signature. A white envelope will do better than a manilla envelope and a brightly coloured envelope will do better than a white one (but will it damage the long-term corporate image?). If 10 per cent of a direct-marketing budget is allocated to continual testing, then response levels will be continually higher.

Drayton Bird tested 12 different 'appropriate' lists, three different prices, two different ways to pay, different times for the mailings, alternative ways of responding and several creative approaches. He found that the best combination of all these factors produced a result *58 times better than the worst combination*. By identifying the best and worst responses for each variable, the maximum response variation (difference between best and worst) was found. Table 13.1 shows the results.

Table 13.1 The impact of different direct-mail variables on response levels

Variable	Different response between worst and best
List	× 6.0
Offer	× 3.0
Timing	× 2.0
Creative	× 1.35
Response	× 1.2

Ideally, everything should be tested in isolation to give more realistic results. There are sometimes so many combinations that testing might appear endless. However, the big variables (those likely to have a *significant* impact on the bottom line) should be tested. Work down the list but stop when the cost of testing outweighs the benefits. As mentioned, direct mail lends itself to testing. It allows the marketing manager to become more scientific and more precise – basically a better manager. Testing the colour of a signature may only yield one-twentieth of 1 per cent difference in response, but even so it still generates increased revenues so it is worthwhile testing everything.

The Eskimo story

Two Eskimos break a hole in the ice and drop their fishing line in. After some time a deep voice booms out slowly: 'There ain't no fish down there.' The two shocked Eskimos quickly pull up their line and wander off further down the ice, break another hole and drop their line in. The same voice eventually booms out the same message, upon which the younger Eskimo braces himself and shouts back 'Who is it that speaks to us?' A deathly silence follows. Eventually, the voice booms out: 'The ice rink manager'.

Why fish in the wrong pond? If there ain't no fish in the pond, don't fish there. Spend time researching lists and databases.

TELEMARKETING

As Michael Stevens (1991) says:

The telephone is such a commonplace, everyday piece of business equipment that it is often treated as something more akin to the office photocopier than a powerful means of communication. It requires planning and skill to get the best from a telephone call, yet the majority of business communication over the telephone lacks both. In some areas this can have a seriously damaging effect on the company's image, marketing efforts and resulting profitability.

What is telemarketing?

Telemarketing, or telephone marketing, is used for many different purposes, including selling, lead generation, customer care and even shareholder communication. In contrast with advertising, telemarketing's two-way communication flow offers the opportunity of conversing with a customer. This interactive *dialogue* can constantly collect and give new information. In marketing, fast *feedback* is invaluable. It allows an early assessment of, say, a special offer, an advertisement, or even the telesales campaign itself. The *flexibility* of a telesales campaign is dependent on feedback. Depending on the previous day's results a telesales campaign can change on a daily basis if required. A telesales script can be rewritten overnight and *tested* the following day. This kind of flexibility increases an organization's ability to seize sudden opportunities. Ideally, telemarketing should be linked into a *database/hybrid marketing* system (see page 374). This is not exclusive to large companies. Relatively inexpensive software packages for databases are available for both large and small companies.

An *outbound* campaign requires telemarketing professionals to make the calls, as opposed to an *inbound* campaign, which receives calls generated from 0800, free-phone, local phone, standard phone, or premium-rate phone (which act as 'self-liquidating', ie generate revenues that pay for other costs) numbers listed in direct-response advertisements, mail-shots or Web sites.

The growth of telemarketing

The following factors are contributing to the growth of telemarketing:

- management's constant search for cost-effectiveness;
- new ways of competing;
- market fragmentation;
- the emergence of niches;
- falling costs;
- the increasing capacity of computer technology.

Running a telemarketing campaign

In-house telemarketing departments are still relatively rare in the UK. The decision to set up a telemarketing department is a long-term strategic decision that often requires approval at board level. Over 40 weeks are required to set up and train the department. An in-house unit with six callers could cost £400,000 pa to run and £150,000 to set up. On the other hand, a variety of telemarketing agencies are available. They can run projects and even assist in the development of an in-house department. Either way, the campaign process is as follows:

1. Brief.
2. Agree brief.
3. Research target audience.
4. Develop contact strategy.
5. Detailed objectives.
6. Campaign costing.

7. Action plan.
8. Script development.
9. Clarify operational requirements.
10. Team briefing/training.
11. Test calls.
12. Campaign roll-out.
13. Monitor and control.
14. Campaign completion, analysis and reporting.

The basic *brief* should cover the SOS + 3Ms checklist as outlined in 'The brief' on page 166. The objectives can include list building/cleaning, market research, appointment setting, selling, etc. The telesales agency or in-house manager needs to determine if the *objectives* are realistic and comprehensive (exploit all the opportunities available within the budget). Having agreed the objectives, there is usually some further *research* into the target audience to find out: where the potential contacts can be found (lists or old records); how to contact (mail, phone, etc); when to contact; how they buy (several-stage/sequential selling or simple straight sale?); profile – their potential lifetime value; existing levels of awareness and previous contact with the company; ideal marketing message; back-up information required; types of objections, etc.

Developing contact strategies involves establishing the sequence of stages required to achieve the objectives. For example, qualifying the prospect could be by telephone interviews. Stage two may involve entering all the data into a bespoke marketing database. Prospects with less immediate needs might then be mailed a brochure, while telemarketing contacts the more immediate buyers with a view to setting up an appointment. Another stage will emerge when the not-so-urgent prospects who received the brochure start to mature into the buying mode. The database can prompt some telesales action, and so on.

Detailed objectives for the campaign, such as total number of calls, number of calls per person per hour, conversion rates, minimum amount of information to be collected, etc, can be agreed.

Campaign costing and target setting can be refined once the research and contact strategy has been developed. The *action plan* coordinates who does what and when. For example, the telemarketing manager needs to know when the mailings go out or when the sales team are available for appointments. *Script development* draws on the features, benefits and unique selling propositions (USPs). It will also include open-question, presentation, objection-handling and closing techniques.

Finally, the telemarketing team is ready to be *briefed and trained*. Telemarketing lends itself to *testing* and this is relatively simple to carry out. Lists, scripts, incentives, prices and timing can all be tested. The results will be carefully monitored and used to develop the optimum combination for the full roll-out of the campaign. These results should be analysed to continually build on previous success.

CASE STUDY 13.1

Goldfish

Situation

Prior to the launch of Goldfish, the credit card market in the UK was dominated by bank-issued cards. Increasingly they were competing with each other purely on the basis of their (APR) interest rate. Despite the level of market activity – a new credit card was launched every second day during the year in which Goldfish was launched – the marketing strategies and tactics employed were highly formulaic.

Where credit cards were underpinned by points schemes, the rewards on offer were usually meaningless and quite remote – even minor rewards required a substantial level of card spend. Consequently the marketplace was extremely cluttered, with no brand achieving any real standout.

Objectives

- To support Centrica's diversification into non-gas-related markets.
- To enter the financial services arena with a new brand that would dispense with the monopolistic/state-supplier imagery that was residual in the British Gas brand.
- To generate incremental revenue to offset revenue eroded from Centrica's core (gas) business, following the deregulation of the UK gas market.

Strategy

The strategy was to launch an iconoclastic brand that would stand apart from all other competitor offerings. But importantly, the unusual, challenging branding would be under-pinned by a strong rational benefit to offset its potential quirkiness. The positioning for the brand would be 'the surprisingly practical credit card'.

Tactics

In entering the credit card market, Goldfish offered consumers:

- a stylish new credit card, highly distinct from the existing bank-issued cards;
- the chance to engage with a highly inclusive brand, which would have no tiers of membership, unlike the gold/silver/green/blue/etc mentality of competitors. Instead, consumers would be able to choose from a range of card designs the one that most appealed to them;

- a card that has no fee;
- a below-average APR;
- a valuable points/rewards scheme which would offer real savings on home essentials, including the chance to save up to £75 on the gas bill.

Redemption partners in the reward scheme included:

- British Gas;
- Asda;
- Boots;
- BT;
- BBC (TV licence);
- Marks & Spencer;
- Halfords;
- Dixons;
- John Lewis Partnership;
- AA.

Goldfish™

Action

The main elements of the launch campaign comprised:

- an initial two-week 'teaser' campaign on national TV, introducing the name Goldfish in an intriguing way without actually announcing that it was a credit card; followed by
- a major TV launch, using Billy Connelly as the spokesperson for the brand, introducing the fact that Goldfish was a new credit card product which was 'surprisingly practical';

- a major direct-mail campaign targeting 8 million prime prospects, delivering the key and rational benefits underpinning the product.

Control

The launch achieved 86 per cent prompted awareness for the brand. Forty-one per cent of the target audience said that they had read the mail solicitation and were predisposed to apply for the card. The brand accounted for 18 per cent market growth in its launch year. Over 1.2 million cards have been issued, making Goldfish a significant player in the credit card market.

Men and women

The whole launch was run by a virtual marketing department. This was made up of two project consultants from Ernst & Young, two people from the advertsing agency, two from DP&A, one person from the PR consultancy, two people from the brand designers Wolff Olins and two from the joint-venture partners HFC and Centrica.

Money

The launch budget was £15 million.

Minutes

The go-ahead to commence development was given in mid-June 1996. The whole infra-structure, brand and campaign development were ready for launch in the first week of

September 1996. A two-week teaser campaign introduced the brand name but did not say it was a credit card.

CASE STUDY 13.2

Moments.com

Situation

The hotels market is highly populated with frequent-stayer/loyalty schemes, which aim to encourage consumers to increase their number of stays at a particular brand's portfolio of hotels. The key target group for these offerings is the frequent travelling business man/ woman. These schemes generally offer:

- preferred guest status while in the hotel;
- free nights, dining offers and car rental.

However, it is very difficult to see any genuinely distinguishing features between the various schemes on offer. Additionally, the small print in these schemes typically allows the hotel chain to 'close out' certain popular destinations and times of year when demand is traditionally high, so that reward redeemers don't occupy rooms that might be occupied by full-rate paying guests. The resultant disappointment and brand damage that results when loyal customers are unable to redeem what they want must be significant. The frequent travelling business man/woman accounts for 65 per cent of average hotel revenue and 50 per cent of this target group say that their choice of hotel is heavily influenced by their participation in a reward scheme.

Not surprisingly, e-mail penetration among this group is in excess of 75 per cent, but despite this little was made of the opportunities to communicate via the Internet – the vast bulk of communications was undertaken via traditional offline media.

Objectives

- To increase the value derived from Forte Hotels existing customers both in terms of frequency of visit and value.
- To launch a highly differentiated scheme that would achieve a significant and sustainable advantage over competitors.
- To successfully migrate participants from six existing individual loyalty schemes across the Forte portfolio, restricting resultant attrition to a maximum of 20 per cent.

- To stimulate participants to become actively involved in the scheme as quickly as possible – both in terms of points earning and redemption.

Strategy

All six previous loyalty schemes were drawn together into a single reward programme under the 'Moments.com' branding. The brand name deliberately and overtly used a '.com' suffix, in recognition of the high levels of e-mail / Internet use among the target audience, as well as communicating unequivocally that the Internet would be a key element of the product's delivery strategy.

By creating a separate and unique brand, the scheme would be able to operate across all three of Forte's hotel divisions.

Tactics

To achieve a sustainable competitive advantage over competitors' schemes, Moments.com:

- provides a faster points-earning rate (ie points would accumulate more quickly than in competitor schemes);
- would not have any close-out periods – points could be used exactly as cash and redeemed at any time in any Forte hotel;
- communicates in an honest, open and concise manner – it is friendly in tone and avoids 'small print'.

Everyone who participates in the scheme is asked to complete a 'personal preferences' questionnaire, capturing individual hotel and lifestyle preferences, and this data is appended to the individual's data on the marketing database. This enables Forte to make sure that each time a guest stays at one of their hotels, their individual preferences will be met.

Forte have rightly recognized that brand loyalty is a complex affair and will not be achieved through a points scheme alone – individual recognition, personalization and delivering against known customer preferences are as important as the opportunity to earn and redeem loyalty points.

The core customer proposition is that Moments.com is 'The world's most generous hotel rewards and recognition programme'. Moments.com set out to be the most rewarding scheme for hotel guests. In addition to building up points quicker than any other scheme, the point's value (ie its purchasing power when redeemed) was higher than all the competitors' offerings.

In order to ensure that programme redeemers are welcomed and treated as valued guests, the individual hotels are credited with the full sales value of a redeeming Moments.com customer, whereas at competitors' hotels differential valuations mean that redeemers are of less value to the hotel. The operating unit generally receives a discounted sales value, and is often actively discouraged from redeeming at the more highly demanded locations.

The launch was accompanied by a worldwide training programme including all Forte staff in over 50 countries, thereby aiming to ensure that staff recognized programme members and responded to individual stay preferences.

The generosity of the Moments.com programme has been verified by independent research by customer-loyalty expert Professor Steve Worthington of Staffordshire University, who officially cited Moments.com as 'the most generous hotel rewards and recognition programme in the world'.

In addition to free hotel stays, Moments.com points can be redeemed against a variety of rewards:

Standard redemption	Tactical redemption offers
Room upgrades	Molton Brown cosmetics
Companion dining	itswine.com
Moments.com Wine Club	Dorling Kindersley Travel Guides
Health & fitness clubs in hotel (massage, facial, manicure, etc)	Great Escapes Activity Days
	Conde Nast magazine subscriptions

Redemption
Although hotel loyalty schemes encourage participation and points earning, in many ways they actively discourage redemption (by making it hard for participants to get anything of value) – it is fairly typical that less than 10 per cent of such loyalty scheme participants actually redeem their points. Moments.com actively set out to encourage redemption in recognition that it was rewarding its best customers and acknowledging the fact that high levels of participation, redemption and customer satisfaction would correlate with increased market share and profitability.

Internet
The Moments.com Web site is at the core of the marketing strategy. Participants can make bookings, check their points' status and redeem points on line. The Web site also provides a gateway for last-minute special offers, stimulating incremental revenue. Known customer preferences and lifestyles are analysed and used to drive personalized e-mails promoting specific activities and hotels, which match the customer's information.

Creative
Creative treatments were put through a phase of vigorous market research to ensure that they resonated appropriately with the target audience, both in the UK and internationally.

The Moments.com core brand values of simplicity, clarity and honesty are reflected in all communications, across all channels. The tone of voice used is straight-talking, enthusiastic and jargon free, in complete sympathy with the manner in which business is conducted. The imagery, typography and layout of materials emphasize the generosity of the scheme and the importance of personal recognition and choice, as well as highlighting its modernity.

Greedy? Materialistic? Freeloader?

You'll need this.

Welcome to the new rewards and recognition programme from the Forte Hotel Group. With MOMENTS.COM you'll earn free hotel stays. Faster.

As a MOMENTS.COM member you'll be part of one of the most generous hotel rewards programmes available. Use your card worldwide at over 240 Le Méridien, Heritage Hotels and Posthouse, and look forward to free stays with no blackout dates, dining offers, free use of our health spas and much more.

Redemption is easy. Joining is free. To register, call MOMENTS Member Services on +44 870 242 62 62 quoting reference: xxxx, or visit our website at **www.moments.com**

MOMENTS.COM

*Le*MERIDIEN   HERITAGE HOTELS   Posthouse

DIVISIONS OF THE FORTE HOTEL GROUP

Creative treatment for the press executions adopted a deliberately ironic/tongue-in-cheek tone of voice to engage the attention of the target audience and deliver a high degree of stand-out. Although its hotel estate and customer base (67 per cent UK resident) is concentrated into the UK, 33 per cent of its customers originate overseas – staying in UK, international and local domestic market hotels. Consequently, the creative treatment had to appear completely 'borderless'.

As English has now become fully embedded as the international business language, it could be used as the dominant language for communications. However, all communications targeting French residents were produced exclusively in French. Additionally other French speakers (eg Algerians, Caribbeans) could request that all their communications would be in French.

Action

Direct Mail
Participants in the six previous schemes were targeted via direct mail. Packs included a new Moments.com membership card. Lapsed participants and frequent guests who were not signed up to any of the six previous Forte schemes were also targeted for acquisition, using a temporary card.

Volume
Full welcome pack – 80,000
Temporary card acquisition pack – 150,000

National press (5-week campaign)	In-flight magazines (3-month campaign)
Daily Telegraph	American Airlines
The Times	Air France
Sunday Times	BA
Mail on Sunday	Lufthansa
	Delta
	British Midland*
	Alitalia
	Thai Airways
	Emirates
	JAL
	Quantas

* Tipped-on membership card

Press

The programme was promoted via UK national press and airline in-flight magazines, including the use of temporary 'tipped-on' membership cards which gave instant participation in the scheme while the full membership card and welcome pack were being produced.

In-hotel recruitment

In-hotel recruitment was undertaken via point-of-sale display and 'Take-One' leaflets in hotel public areas. Active face-to-face recruitment was also undertaken via reception staff who were used to target primary prospects (frequent and high-value guests) using a 'Give-One' pack, including temporary membership card.

Online

All promotional material featured the Web site, where new applicants could register. E-mail campaigns were used to promote online registration and tactical points promotions. An HTML format is currently under development.

Ongoing contact

A programme of continuous contact with participants is in place to ensure their continued involvement and to stimulate incremental revenue growth via tactical promotions. To date this has included:

- two quarterly statements;
- a summer 'Double Points' promotion, to increase occupancy levels during the traditionally weaker occupancy season;
- a winter promotion featuring half-price redemption offers during hotel tough periods and tactical partners to the UK base designed to 'burn' saved points;
- an Internet registration mailing to all Moments.com members incentivizing E-comms registration;
- specific tactical promotions for Heritage Hotels and Le Méridian brands;
- Winter-earning-offer monthly inserts in Moments.com MasterCard statements to encourage card usage.

Database

Whenever a member joins Moments.com he or she completes a personal preferences form which captures detailed information about specific hotel preferences and lifestyle data. This data can be provided both online and offline, and is used to populate the CRM database. When guests check into the hotel their Moments.com card is swiped through a POS terminal and they are automatically allocated a room, which matches their known preferences.

Control

- 87 per cent of the migrated base have activated their Moments.com card.
- Cold recruitment resulted in a 5.04 per cent response rate, with a 17.8 per cent conversion to activity, producing 2.4:1 ROI.
- In-hotel activity has contributed to 62 per cent recruitment since launch.
- The Internet mailing produced a 67 per cent uplift in Web site registrations, which means that over half the member base have given their e-mail address.
- The MasterCard usage campaign has increased spend activity by 59.6 per cent.

Recruitment
In the 10 months since launch 200,000 participants have been recruited, of which 72 per cent are active.

Transaction value
Average transaction value for Moments.com members is 74 per cent higher than the average transaction value for non-programme guests.

Redemptions
Although only 10 months old, Moments.com is already showing a 17 per cent increase in redemptions over the previous best-performing scheme, and has evened out tough periods in seasonal hotel occupancy.

Customer satisfaction
Follow-up consumer research has been conducted to determine guests' satisfaction with the programme:

- 75 per cent rated Moments.com as 'good' or 'very good';
- 80 per cent rated the direct-mail communication as 'clear' and easy to understand.

Prior to launch, it was anticipated that the migration to Moments.com would generate a 1 per cent level of complaint. The actual rate was a minimal 0.03 per cent.

APPENDIX 13.1

Direct response press ads

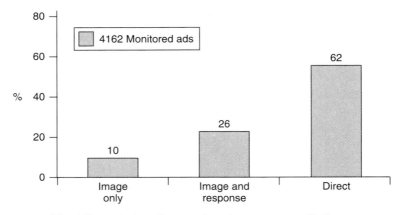

Note: The majority of press advertisements are still direct
Source: DMA

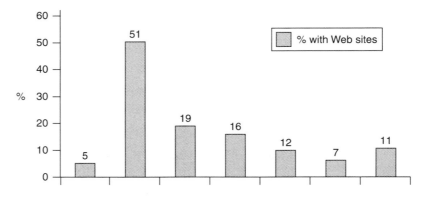

Note: 11 per cent of press advertising now features Web site addresses
Source: DMA

APPENDIX 13.2

The Consumer Protection (Distance Selling) Regulations 2000 – An overview

The Regulations came into force on 31 October 2000 and implement Directive 97/7/EC on the protection of consumers in respect of distance contracts.

All EU member states were required to implement the Directive by 4 June 2000. The Directive sets out a minimum standard. Member states may introduce more stringent provisions. This appendix summarizes the main provisions of the UK Regulations.

Scope of the Regulations

The scope of the Regulations is not limited to the Internet (or e-commerce) but includes other means of communications. Schedule 1 of the Regulations is an indicative list, including mailshots, catalogues, telephone and fax. This paper concentrates on the Regulations as applicable to the Internet.

The Regulations only apply to contracts with consumers. Business-to-business sales are not caught. A narrow definition of consumer is used – an average person acting outside his or her trade, business or profession.

In addition, the following types of contract are exempted, namely those: relating to financial services, an illustrative list of which is given at Schedule 2 to the Regulations (the distance selling of such services is the subject of a separate Directive); concluded by automatic vending machines or automated commercial premises; concluded with telecom operators through the use of public payphones; for the disposal of a freehold interest in land or a leasehold interest which is for less than three years; for the construction of buildings where the land on which the building is constructed is being disposed of (other than by a lease of less than three years); and auctions (Regulation 5).

Large parts of the Regulations (the obligation to give prior information, written confirmation and a right to cancel) do not apply to contracts with roundsmen making regular supplies of foods, beverages or other goods for everyday consumption. Contracts for accommodation, transport, catering and leisure services, where these services are to be provided for a specific date or within a specific period (for example theatre tickets), are also exempted from the relevant provisions (Regulation 6).

Information to be provided pre-contract (Regulation 7)

Before the contract is formed the consumer must be provided with:

(a) the identity of the supplier (and address if payment is required in advance);
(b) the main characteristics of the goods or services;
(c) the price, including all taxes;
(d) delivery costs, where appropriate;
(e) the arrangements for payment, delivery or performance;
(f) the existence of the right of cancellation (unless the contract is excepted from those provisions);
(g) if the distance communication is at a premium rate, the cost of using that means of communication;
(h) the period for which the price or offer remains valid; and
(i) the minimum duration of any contract for the supply of products or services performed permanently (ie continuously, for example a mobile phone, satellite TV or electricity contract) or recurrently (eg a book club).

In addition, if the supplier proposes, in the event of the goods or services ordered being unavailable, to provide substitute goods or services then the supplier must so inform the consumer. The substitute goods or services must be of equivalent quality and price and the supplier must also confirm that the costs of returning any such substitute goods will be met.

The Regulations require that the above information be provided in a clear and comprehensible manner appropriate to the means of distance communication used, with regard to the principles of good faith in commercial communications and those governing the protection of those unable to give their consent, such as minors. This wording is lifted straight from the Directive and the DTI has not provided any interpretation of it in its guidance on the Regulations. An earlier draft of the Regulations specified the prominence which had to be given to the information if included in a contract or other document, but these provisions have been dropped.

The supplier must also ensure that the commercial purpose behind the supply of the information is made clear to the consumer.

Written confirmation and additional information (Regulation 8)

Certain information must be confirmed in writing or 'another durable medium available and accessible to the consumer' either prior to the conclusion of the contract or, in the case of services, at an early stage during the performance thereof and, in the case of goods, at the time of delivery.

In its guidance the DTI has confirmed that e-mail will count as a 'durable medium available and accessible to the consumer'.

The information to be provided in writing or another durable medium is:

(i)   the information referred to at (a) to (f) above;
(ii)   information about the conditions and procedures for exercising the consumer's right of cancellation. In particular, if the supplier requires the consumer to return the goods in the event of cancellation the supplier must state this. The supplier must also state whether the consumer or supplier will be responsible for the costs of return;
(iii)   the geographical address of the supplier to which complaints may be addressed (the DTI guidance states that a post office box number is insufficient);
(iv)   information about any after-sales services or guarantees;
(v)   if the contract is of indefinite duration or of a duration of more than a year the conditions and procedure for terminating such contract; and
(vi)   if the contract is for the supply of services, the fact that the consumer will not be able to cancel the contract after provision of the services has begun with the consumer's agreement.

The right of cancellation – Regulations 10, 11 and 12

The consumer can cancel a distance contract without penalty and without giving any reason during a period of at least seven working days after:

(i)   *in the case of goods* – the day after the day of the consumer's receipt of the goods (Regulation 11); or
(ii)   *in the case of services* – the day after the day on which the contract was concluded (Regulation 12).

Except that:

(i)   if the written confirmation is not provided, the period is three months plus seven working days from the day after the day of receipt of the goods/conclusion of the contract for services (as applicable);
(ii)   if the information is provided late but within the three-month period, the cancellation period expires seven working days from the day after the day on which the information is supplied.

So, if, for example, a consumer orders goods which are delivered (with the written confirmation) on a Thursday the cancellation period will not expire until the end of the Monday in the second week following the week of sale.

The right of withdrawal or cancellation must be exercised in writing or another durable medium available and accessible to the supplier. A telephone call is insufficient. The notice must, however expressed, indicate the intention of the consumer to cancel the contract. A standard form cancellation notice can be downloaded by consumers from the DTI Web site.

The Regulations provide a non-exhaustive list of how notice of cancellation may be given which includes by hand, by post, by fax or by e-mail. The notice is effective when delivered, posted, transmitted or sent, as appropriate. It will be in the interest of suppliers to set out prominently the numbers or addresses to which notices of cancellation should be sent – so as to ensure that they can be dealt with appropriately and are not overlooked.

Exceptions to the right to cancel – Regulation 13

There are exceptions to the right to cancel in the following cases:

(a) if provision of the service has commenced, with the consumer's agreement, before the end of the cancellation period and the consumer has been informed, in accordance with Regulation 8(3) that negation of the right to cancel will be the result of such commencement;

(b) where the price of goods or services is dependent on fluctuations in the financial market outside the supplier's control (it is perhaps unclear how far the definition of 'financial market' goes);

(c) goods made to the consumer's specifications, or personalized. The DTI guidance indicates that this exception is not intended to apply to options which may be selected at the time of ordering, for example the upgrading of certain elements of a personal computer or the choosing of alloy wheels for a car;

(d) goods which by reason of their nature cannot be returned or are liable to deteriorate or expire rapidly (perishable goods);

(e) the supply of audio or video recordings or software which were unsealed by the consumer;

(f) supply of newspapers, periodicals and magazines;

(g) gaming and lottery services.

Return to consumer of sums paid and return of security

If the consumer cancels the contract he or she must be reimbursed as soon as possible and in any case within 30 days beginning with the day on which notice of cancellation was given.

The amount to be reimbursed will be the full purchase price plus any delivery costs (unless delivery was the subject of a separate contract).

If the supplier has placed a contractual obligation on the consumer to return the goods and the consumer fails to do so, the supplier may charge the consumer the supplier's direct costs of recovering the goods. The DTI guidance interprets 'direct costs' as the cost of return postage or, for larger items, the cost of a van making a routine trip to the consumer's home.

A supplier cannot charge for the recovery of items delivered in substitution for those ordered. On cancellation any related credit agreement is also cancelled (Regulation 15).

Obligation on the consumer to restore goods after cancellation (Regulation 17)

If a consumer cancels a contract for goods he or she must 'restore' the goods to the supplier.

'Restoration' only entails making the goods available for collection by the supplier from the consumer's home. However, the consumer's obligation will also be discharged by delivering or sending the goods to the supplier. If the goods are sent the consumer must take reasonable care to ensure that they are received by the supplier and not damaged in transit. This might extend to properly packaging the goods.

While the supplier is free to place a contractual obligation on the consumer to return the goods, the only penalty which the supplier can impose on a consumer who fails to return goods is an obligation to pay the cost of recovering the goods.

In addition to the obligation to 'restore' the goods, the consumer must retain possession and take reasonable care of them. This obligation continues for 21 days beginning with the day on which the consumer gave notice of cancellation. After 21 days the obligation to 'restore' continues, in theory, to subsist but the obligation to retain possession and take reasonable care ceases.

The supplier can extend the consumer's obligation to retain possession and take reasonable care of the goods by serving, within 21 days from the date of cancellation, a written request to make the goods available for collection. If the consumer unreasonably refuses or fails to comply with such request then the obligation to retain possession and take care shall continue until the consumer does 'restore' the goods.

If the supplier has imposed a contractual obligation on to the consumer to return the goods then the supplier has six months within which to serve the notice requesting that the consumer make the goods available for collection – and thus extend the consumer's duty to retain possession and take reasonable care of them.

A supplier can sue a consumer for breach of the consumer's obligation to retain possession and take reasonable care of the goods and to 'restore' them to the supplier.

In view of the above provisions, suppliers should take the following steps:

(a) impose a contractual obligation on consumers to return goods on cancellation and (if not commercially undesirable) pay for the costs of such return. It would be advisable to specify a method of return – post where practicable and otherwise by courier. A reasonable time limit for return should also be set – for example within five working days of exercise of the right of cancellation;

(b) ensure that the obligation to return and any obligation to pay for the costs of return are set out in the written confirmation to be supplied to the consumer under Regulation 8;

(c) following receipt of notice of cancellation send the consumer a letter or e-mail which (i) confirms the consumer's duty to return the goods in an 'as new' condition within a set timescale; (ii) states that if the consumer does not so return the goods within the specified timescale the supplier's costs of recovery will be charged to the consumer; and (iii) states that the letter or e-mail should be treated as a formal request to deliver the goods to the supplier in accordance with The Consumer Protection (Distance Selling) Regulations 2000. Having imposed a contractual obligation to return the goods on the consumer the supplier has six months in which to serve this notice. However, the consumer may argue that the obligation to return was not successfully incorporated in the contract for sale – in which case the supplier would have only 21 days from cancellation to serve the notice requesting delivery. Accordingly, for maximum protection the supplier's system should automatically issue a letter or e-mail of this nature on receipt of a notice of cancellation.

Performance – Regulation 19

The contract must be performed within 30 days from the day after the day on which the consumer sent his or her order to the supplier or within such other period as the parties may have agreed (the 'performance period'). If the goods or services are unavailable for supply within the performance period, the supplier must notify the consumer and refund the purchase price. Notification and refunding must be carried out as soon as possible and in any event within 30 days after the day on which the performance period expired.

The supplier may deliver substitute goods of an equivalent quality and price provided that the supplier, in its pre-contract notification to the consumer, reserved the right to do so and notified the consumer that the supplier would bear the costs of return of such substitute goods in the event of cancellation.

A supplier can contract out of the obligation to refund the price of attendance at outdoor leisure events which are cancelled and which, by their nature, cannot be rescheduled.

Fraudulent credit card use – Regulation 21

If a third party has made fraudulent use of a consumer's payment card in connection with a distance contract, then the consumer may cancel the relevant payment and have it refunded to their card by the card issuer.

The third party fraudulently using the card must not have been acting, or to be treated as acting, as the agent of the consumer. If the consumer alleges that he did not authorize use of his or her card it is for the card issuer to prove that use was so authorized.

The Regulations amend the Consumer Credit Act to remove the right of the card issuer to charge consumers the first £50 of loss arising from fraudulent use in connection with a distance contract.

Inertia selling – Regulations 22, 23 and 24

The rights of consumer recipients of unsolicited goods and services which were previously set out in the Unsolicited Goods and Services Act 1971 are now incorporated into the Regulations.

The recipient of unsolicited goods or services may treat them as an unconditional gift. The precondition that the consumer must have made the goods available for collection by the sender for a certain period (as per the Unsolicited Goods and Services Act) has been removed.

Demanding payment for unsolicited goods and services remains a criminal offence.

No contracting out – Regulation 25

Contractual terms are void insofar as they:

(i)   are inconsistent with any provision in the Regulations for the protection of consumers; and/or

(ii)   impose on a consumer, in circumstances where the Regulations impose a duty or liability on the consumer, an additional duty or liability. The exception is that a supplier may require a consumer to return goods following cancellation (provided that the only penalty for non-return will be that the consumer has to bear the costs of recovery by the supplier).

Choice of the law of a country which is not an EU member state will not be effective if the contract has a close connection with the territory of an EU member state.

Enforcement – Regulations 25, 26, 27 and 28

The OFT and Local Authority Trading Standards Departments are designated enforcement authorities under the Regulations. Enforcement authorities are under a duty to investigate complaints (unless they consider them frivolous or vexatious) and may apply for injunctions to prevent continued breaches of the Regulations.

Breach of the Regulations is not an offence in itself (save in respect of the inertia selling provisions).

Unsolicited direct marketing

Article 10 of the Directive states that direct marketing to consumers may only be carried out where there is no clear objection from the consumer. In addition, direct marketing by automated calling systems or fax may only be carried out with the consumer's prior consent.

Anti-spamming provisions were considered during consultation on the implementation of the Directive. However, in the Regulations as enacted Article 10 is not implemented. Instead, the DTI issued a press release on 4 September 2000, stating that it considered that the self-regulatory regimes in place for mail and e-mail provide the necessary protection required by the Directive in respect of mail and e-mail.

Other EU member states have taken different approaches. To date Austria, Denmark, Finland, Italy and Germany have adopted a legislative requirement that spam e-mails can only be sent to consumers who opt in to receiving them. On the other hand, France, the Netherlands and Spain appear to favour an approach whereby consumers must opt out in order not to receive spam.

A new Directive (Com (2000) 385) concerning the processing of personal data and the protection of privacy in the electronic communications sector) will, if adopted, harmonize the position by introducing a mandatory 'opt-in' for unsolicited commercial e-mails throughout the EU.

Source: Bristows (2000) (www.bristows.com)

The above appendix is an overview of The Consumer Protection (Distance Selling) Regulations 2000 as at July 2001. It does not purport to provide comprehensive legal advice and reliance should not be placed upon it.

APPENDIX 13.3

Opinion formers in the communications channel – junk mail (by Lindsay Allen)

This junk mail's getting worse, isn't it? It's wild this time of year. I don't know about you, but there isn't a day passes in our house but it gets stuffed through the letterbox. Home-printed leaflets from window cleaners, full-colour glossy booklets from supermarkets, free newspapers, special offers, vouchers – there's no end to the stuff! It isn't helped by the fact that many of these outfits now sell their mailing lists to each other. So if, for example, you buy a jotter made from recycled paper somewhere, you discover within about six months you're on the Ecology list and you're getting junk mail about everything from saving whales to stopping the DOE building a road somewhere!

The worst is the junk that comes disguised as real letters in proper business envelopes. Sometimes you have to read the first couple of paragraphs before you discover that it's not a letter at all – just more junk mail dressed up to look important.

The frustration with all of this is not just the wastage of paper (I could probably save a rainforest somewhere if whoever was trying to save it took me off their mailing list!). But the fact is you can easily lose valuable stuff among the rubbish. Sometimes I've had to search the waste bin for an important letter that's accidentally got dumped with the junk.

Life's like that. Full of junk! Seriously!

Most of what takes up our time is of little or no importance, but we fill our lives with it; banal TV programmes, pointless committee meetings, fruitless arguments, petty ambitions.

Many of us manage to get our day in, get our life in even, just wading through this junk. And the real danger, of course, is that the important message gets lost in the middle of it.

Maybe over the years you have been ignoring important stuff because you couldn't see it buried among the junk. Or maybe it's even worse than that. You know the important stuff you need to do something about, but you haven't time to handle it properly because all your time's taken up with junk!

Your marriage is maybe going down the tubes because of the amount of time you spend entertaining potential clients in the evening. Somebody else is raising your kids. Perhaps you're too busy pursuing some ambition that isn't worth a fraction of what your kids are worth.

The Bible says that we should be wary of falling into that trap. Handle life in the same way as your mail. Sort through it. Deal with the important stuff first and ignore the junk.

Or as Jesus put it in the Sermon on the Mount, 'Seek first the Kingdom of God'.

The important message is the one from God. Don't lose it among all the junk mail that life throws at you.

Source: First broadcast on BBC Radio 4. Reproduced with kind permission

APPENDIX 13.4

An excerpt from a data-mining brief

Data-mining brief

Find meaningful patterns in our data, target potential consumers, retain existing consumers more effectively, predict who would buy certain products, anticipate the volume of high sales of specific high-margin products and discover and capitalize on opportunities for cross-couponing.

DB2, Spring 97

Key points from Chapter 13:

1. Databases can and should be developed for all types of organizations.
2. Organizations that ignore direct marketing and database techniques will suffer a competitive disadvantage.

FURTHER READING

Bird, D (1989) *Commonsense Direct Marketing*, 2nd edn, Kogan Page, London

Brann, C (1984) *Cost-effective Direct Marketing: By mail, telephone and direct response advertising*, Collectors' Books, Cirencester

Considine, R and Murray, R (1981) *The Great Brain Robbery*, The Great Brain Robbery, 521 South Madison Avenue, Pasadena, California 91101

Direct Marketing Centre (1992) *The Practitioner Guide to Direct Marketing*, Direct Marketing Centre, London

Exhibition Venues Association (2000) *UK Exhibition Facts*, Vol. 12

Howard, M (1989) *Telephone Marketing vs Direct Sales Force Costs*, commissioned by Datapoint (UK) Ltd, London

McCorkell, G (1997) *Direct and Database Marketing*, Kogan Page, London

Moriarty, R and Moran, U (1990) Managing hybrid systems, *Harvard Business Review*, November–December

Moriarty, R and Shwartz, G (1989) Automation to boost sales and marketing, *Harvard Business Review*, January–February

Royal Mail (1991) *The Royal Mail Guide to Successful Direct Mail*, Royal Mail, London

Stevens, M (1991) *The Handbook of Telemarketing*, Kogan Page, London

Tapp, A (2001) *Principles of Direct and Database Marketing*, 2nd edn, Financial Times/Prentice-Hall, Englewood Cliffs, NJ

Toffler, A (1980) *The Third Wave*, Collins, London

Watson, J (1989) The direct marketing guide, *Marketing Magazine*, 9 February

FURTHER CONTACTS

Direct Marketing Association, Haymarket House, 1 Oxendon Street, London SW1Y 4EE (tel: 020 7321 2525; Web site: www.dma.org.uk)

Federation of European Direct Marketing (FEDMA), Avenue de Tervuren 439, B-1150 Brussels, Belgium (tel: 00 32 2 7794268; Web site: www.fedma.org)

The Institute of Direct Marketing, 1 Park Road, Teddington, Middlesex TW11 0AR (tel: 020 8977 5705 Web site: www.theidm.com)

Mailing Preference Service, 5th Floor, Haymarket House, 1 Oxendon Street, London SW1Y 4EE (tel: 020 7766 4410; Web site: www.mpsonline.org.uk (under construction))

The Office of the Data Protection Registrar, Wycliffe House, Water Lane, Wilmslow, Cheshire SK9 5AF (tel: 01625 545700; Web site: www.dataprotection.gov.uk)

Publicity and public relations

INTRODUCTION

Positive publicity is dependent primarily on good relationships with the media (media relations). This is only one of the responsibilities of public relations. There is some overlap between public relations, public affairs, corporate affairs and community affairs, community relations, corporate relations, and corporate communications. Many organizations have different structures with separate departments serving specific requirements. Public relations integrates with most aspects of an organization's activities. The first part of this chapter considers public relations in its entirety and the importance of establishing a solid platform of credibility. The second half of the chapter focuses on raising visibility and one particular aspect of public relations – publicity.

WHAT IS PUBLIC RELATIONS?

Public relations is regularly, and sometimes worryingly, referred to as 'PR', which is often confused with 'press releases' or 'press relations'. These are, in fact, only a part of real public relations. A simple definition of public relations is: 'the development of and maintenance of good relationships with different publics'. The publics are the range of different groups on which an organization is dependent. These include employees, investors, suppliers, customers, distributors, legislators/regulators/governments, pressure groups, the community, the media and even competition. Most of these groups have different (sometimes conflicting) interests in any particular organization. The UK's Institute of Public Relations (IPR) uses the following public relations definition: 'the planned and sustained effort to establish and maintain goodwill and mutual understanding between an organization and its publics'. The 1978 World Assembly of PR Associations in Mexico agreed what is now known as the 'Mexican statement': PR practice is the art and science of analysing trends, predicting their consequences, counselling organization leaders and implementing planned programmes of action that will serve both the organization's and the public interest.

While marketing traditionally focuses on markets or just three of the publics, ie customers, distributors (the 'trade') and competition, public relations is concerned with many more publics. Add in the emergence of globalism (eg Web sites can be viewed around the world), increased media interest in business, new investor criteria (eg ethical policies), more effective pressure groups, information-hungry customers and the constant search for cost-effective communications tools and you can soon see why PR has grown in importance. The new understanding of powerful PR was clearly demonstrated when the *Financial Times* suggested that: 'perhaps both management and unions, before embarking on a dispute, must learn to ask: "How will this play in the media?"'

The Power of PR

Other than point-of-sale materials in Dixons Store, PR was the sole vehicle for the launch of Freeserve. Five months after launch it announced their one millionth customer. Six months later it was floated on the Stock Exchange.

Marketing Business, June 2000

Product PR and corporate PR

The previous definitions give an indication of the diverse nature and far-reaching effects of public relations. We need to separate product PR (product/brand publicity) and corporate PR (corporate image enhancement). Product PR (sometimes called 'marketing PR') is the responsibility of the marketing manager, while corporate PR is the responsibility of the corporate communications director. A manager responsible for product PR would ultimately report to the marketing manager, whereas a manager responsible for corporate PR would probably report to a board director or the board itself. Both types of PR do, however, integrate with each other. Dr Jon White, in *How to Manage and Understand Public Relations* (1991), suggests that:

> public relations is a complement and a corrective to the marketing approach… it creates an environment in which it is easier to market… public relations can raise questions which the marketing approach, with its focus on the market, products, distribution channels and customers, and its orientation towards growth and consumption, cannot. Public relations concerns are with relations of one group to another, and with the interplay of conflicting and competing interests in social relationships.

Publicity objectives can vary from promoting a product (product PR) to promoting a company (corporate PR) among employees, customers, investors, the community, local government, etc. Marketing will tend to be sales/market-share orientated, while public relations can, but not always, be sales/market share-orientated; eg a PR objective may be to recruit the best employees, to win permission to build a new factory, to influence government (see the Wind Power study case on page 437).

Norman Hart (1992) gave an interesting interpretation in an article entitled 'Is there a new role for PR in marketing?' Taking the IPR definition, which talks about relationships between an organization and its publics, he made the point that the definition says nothing about products and nothing about the media. PR can be interpreted as more of a corporate activity, such as corporate communications, than a product activity, such as product publicity (product PR):

> The fact is that advertising is just one of a number of channels of communication available to promote a product (and thus a subset of marketing) or to promote an organization (and thus a subset of public relations). Equally, editorial can contribute powerfully to product promotion (marketing) or corporate promotion (public relations). The simplest way of expressing the difference is to discriminate between brand or product image and corporate or company image.

The influence of public relations stretches far beyond product marketing and into corporate strategy, particularly where long-term decisions affecting choice of markets, products, factory locations, production processes, etc, are concerned. External groups are becoming more demanding and organizations are beginning to have to demonstrate their social responsibility on a global basis. Ethics and social responsibility have traditionally been the bastion of public relations. Today all managers need to develop their awareness and understanding of at least the PR implications of both board room and marketing department decisions, strategies, policies and actions (or the lack of these).

PR is more than communications

Publicity and visibility should not be raised before a solid platform of credibility has been developed through decent, safe products, friendly customer service, caring ethics and socially responsible policies. The PR mix (see Figure 14.1) gives an indication of the diverse nature and far-reaching effects of public relations. It is more than just communications; it is part of the broader business disciplines such as corporate planning, finance, personnel, production and marketing. It cannot work effectively unless it is integrated into these areas and unless it also links with product quality, customer care and design management (corporate identity). These are the credibility elements that build a platform for subsequent publicity, which, as can be seen from Figure 14.1, is just one of the many visibility tools. A 1996 MORI poll revealed that 66 per cent of the general public felt that industry and commerce don't pay enough attention to their social responsibilities. Even more (86 per cent) felt that a company that supports the community is a good one to work for. In the United States, a *Business Week* poll revealed that 90 per cent of Americans believe that companies have responsibilities to their employees and communities that go beyond making profits. Today ethical issues are highlighted by new pressure group techniques (see Appendix 14.5 for some excerpts from Naomi Klein's best-selling and shocking *No Logo*). It is not surprising to find the *Chicago Tribune* reporting that Sears Roebuck had hundreds of elderly protesters picketing their store as a result of a decision to reduce pensioners' life insurance benefits. Any amount of press releases, or even advertising, announcing Sears' caring ethics will have a negative effect until this basic credibility problem is sorted out.

Organizations need to engage in, and provide evidence of, solid ethical policies. One way is by joining a per cent club (by promising to donate 1 per cent or half of 1 per cent of profits to the local community). There are even 2 per cent and 5 per cent clubs. Another way is by ensuring regular ethical and/or environmental audits and, of course, taking appropriate action.

Imagine your funeral

I went on this training course (at Procter and Gamble) where you had to imagine what the minister might say about you at your funeral. When I realized that mine would say I was the leading expert on housewives' toilet cleaning products, I realized it was time for a change.

Hamish Taylor, Managing Director, Eurostar

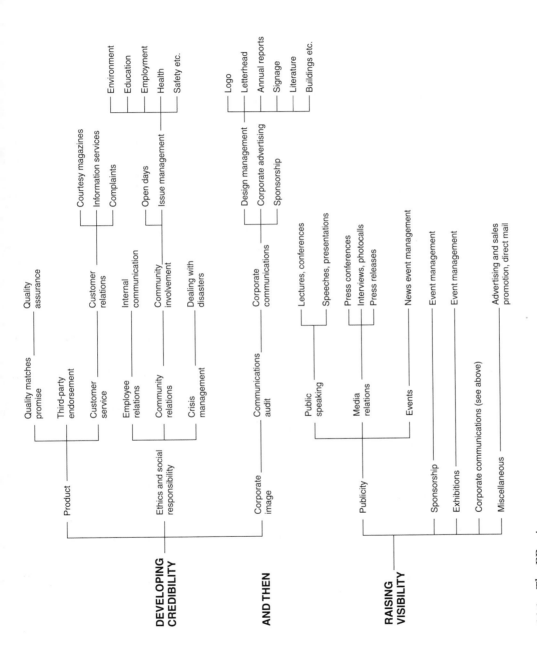

Figure 14.1 The PR mix

Source: Adapted from the video notes from the award-winning PR video *Actions Speak Louder Than Words*, with kind permission from PRTV (London) Ltd

As well as making good business sense, marketing, PR and corporate communications professionals are in the exciting position of being able to help improve their local communities, support valid causes, improve the environment, and much more. The bottom line is that it makes long-term business sense to be ethical as it creates a platform of credibility that enriches all subsequent communications. As Bob Leaf, Burson Marsteller, succinctly says in the PR film *Actions Speak Louder Than Words*: 'Ethics is good for business.'

Marketing communications and publicity

Some organizations insist on public relations people and sales promotion people sitting in together on various advertising/direct-marketing meetings so that they cross-fertilize ideas and create synergy through integrating the marketing communications at an early stage. Chapter 1 mentioned the British Airways free-flights promotion, which PR exploited to the point where massive awareness was generated from carefully orchestrated and integrated below-the-line activities. Here is another example of how product PR and advertising can work together.

The PR mix

Figure 14.1 also shows how the 'visibility' or publicity-generating activities such as news releases, news conferences, publicity stunts, conferences, events, exhibitions, sponsorship and sales promotions can all integrate. Before looking at publicity in more detail, it is worth mentioning again that the key to long-term success is to develop credibility before raising visibility. Credibility is created by a proper product and/or quality of service. This means that the product must match the promise made by the marketing communications, ie do not sell a Rolls-Royce and deliver a Ford Ka. False expectations only lead to disappointment, frustration and extremely high post-purchase dissonance. This kills off any long-term repeat business. Good customer service makes doing business a pleasurable experience for all parties. Having the right sort of people or institutions associated by their using or endorsing a product improves credibility. So too ethics, social responsibility (see Chapter 8) and corporate image (see Chapter 21) all contribute towards building a credible image.

There is no point waving a flag, shouting, leaping, roaring, advertising or raising an organization's visibility if it does not have a solid platform of credibility supporting it. The days when the two aspects were held separately are gone. Spending thousands or millions on raising a profile is not just wasteful but actually damaging if a lack of credibility is exposed. So today, more than ever before, it is worthwhile investing men (and women), money and minutes in getting the credibility right before raising visibility.

Media relations and publicity

Take a look at the local and national newspapers, trade journals, radio programmes and television. Spot the commercial news items or features that have made news. Although they appear to be written by an editor or journalist, *many of the news items and features have been written by skilled PR professionals.* Like advertising, editorial publicity can achieve many similar communication goals, such as increasing awareness or repositioning. News and feature editors do not have time to scout around for all the items they run. They depend on a constant feed of professionally presented news items and news releases from organizations. Despite this over 126 million press releases (out of 130 million sent out) get thrown into editors' bins every year in the UK alone. Many of them are badly written and inaccurately targeted (sometimes even addressed to people who have long left the newspaper).

Publicity can be generated through written press releases and feature articles for the press, video news releases for television programmes, syndicated radio tapes for radio programmes and digital press packs for all and sundry (see Appendices 14.1, 14.2 and 14.3 respectively). Publicity is also generated by press conferences, press receptions and media events (what the media less reverently call 'stunts'), and public speaking at conferences, lectures, seminars, dinners, chat shows, etc. (The Hewlett-Packard case study on page 493 shows how carefully planned conferences are a potent PR tool that also directly affect lead generation and sales.)

Legendary stunts

The most celebrated was by a New Yorker called Jim Moran, who once contrived a bar-room brawl between a fairly well-known band leader and a bystander. When the judge asked what they were fighting about, the band leader told him it was over the recipe for Pimms Cup. Pimms had hired Mr Moran because they were having trouble establishing the brand name in the United States. The 'brawl' received so much publicity that he solved the problem with a single blow.

The *Independent on Sunday*, 1 April 1990

The other visibility tools such as sponsorship, exhibitions, corporate identity, advertising, sales promotions and direct mail are all dealt with as separate chapters elsewhere in this book. Positive editorial is usually the result of carefully managed media relations. Organizations and/or individuals must take time to understand what the journalist or editor wants, the news angle, the relevance of the piece, the appropriate time to deliver it to a news organization, the correct format or layout of the press release and so on. One point to bear in mind is that PR campaigns, and particularly media relations campaigns seeking editorial exposure, do not have to be short-term, one-off news events. See how Adidas maintained a six-year media relations campaign for its Predator Boot in Appendix 14.4 on page 446.

As mentioned, editorial coverage can achieve many objectives similar to advertising, but there are three important points that differentiate editorial coverage from advertising:

1. There is no media cost.
2. The message has higher credibility.
3. There is no control over the message.

Creative photographs catch the eye of both editors and audiences

No media cost

There is no media cost since, unlike advertising, the space is not bought. There are, however, other costs, since news releases have to be written, carefully targeted and distributed to the right editor at the right time in the right format. This can be done by an in-house press officer or public relations department or it can be handled by an external public relations agent or consultancy. There are news release distribution companies that specialize in getting releases physically or electronically to news editors' desks at the right time. The 'TSB sponsorship of Roy of the Rovers' press release and montage of press clippings on page 423 shows the kind of free publicity that a well-written, carefully targeted and properly timed

Media clippings (bottom) generated from the news release (top)

news release can generate. (For a full explanation of how the sponsorship worked see the study case on page 465.) This kind of editorial coverage creates valuable positive publicity. The editorial coverage has higher credibility than advertising copy. No space was bought and therefore no media costs were incurred. However, whether it is in-house PR people or an external consultancy (in this case, QBO Consultancy), it does cost someone's time and expertise to:

- select the right target media (appropriate press and editors) at the right time;
- write the news releases;
- print, address, pack and post the news releases;
- handle any press enquiries. (There are, of course, other minor costs, some of which are hidden: photographs, stationery, stamps, phone calls, wear and tear of the word processor, laser printer and so on.)

Editorial coverage is used increasingly to stretch the above-the-line advertising campaigns. Good press officers push the knock-on PR potential of advertising. The Lucozade and Daewoo advertising campaigns featured as case studies in Chapter 11 enjoyed in excess of £1 million worth of additional free editorial coverage. Bruno Magli shoes enjoyed an uncontrolled estimated $100 million worth of free exposure during O J Simpson's trial (see page 427). The calculation is simple: add up the column inches of coverage, time the amount of broadcast coverage and find the equivalent cost for the same amount of advertising space. There are more sophisticated methods of evaluation, which include: positive/negative comments; the position on the page; whether a picture is shown; the number of times a brand name is used, etc. Forte Hotels' constant quantitative report on editorial coverage is outlined on page 429.

Higher credibility

Editorial coverage has higher credibility than advertising because it is perceived as being written by an editor or journalist and not by an advertiser trying to sell something. There is arguably less resistance to the message. Some estimates suggest that a message carried in a piece of editorial has three times more credibility than a similar message carried in an advertisement. Despite the attraction of the message credibility factor, editorial coverage is risky because there is no control over the message. An editor can take a news release and criticize the sender for sending it. Advertisers, on the other hand, can control the message since they buy the space and publish exactly what they want to say (within the law and advertising regulations). Despite this, editorial clippings and their associated levels of credibility are often compiled and used as endorsements in direct mailshots, sales literature, advertisements and exhibition stands. You can even see them above theatres promoting a show,

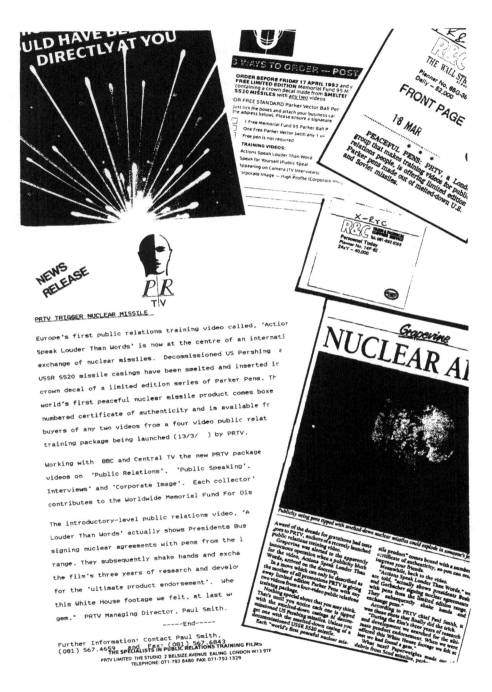

The same news release and brochure can generate totally different types of editorial coverage, as indicated by the press clippings

where extracted comments from the press are highlighted in bright lights outside the front door. The third-party editorial coverage adds credibility to the claim that this is a good show. Equally, a reviewer can severely criticize a show and therefore damage the credibility (and viability) of a show, product or service.

Lack of control

The uncontrollable element of media relations is demonstrated by the montage of press clippings (editorial coverage) generated by PRTV's 'Nuclear Missile' news release (see page 425). This shows how the same news release gets totally different editorial coverage from two different editors. On the one hand the *Wall Street Journal* gives it brief but positive front-page exposure, while *Personnel Today* treats the same news release with a lot of cynicism and, arguably, negative editorial coverage, despite a lot more detail about the promotion. It can be argued, in the case of PRTV, that 'any publicity is good publicity', but this is certainly not the case with Ratners, IBM and McDonald's. These examples demonstrate the dangers of uncontrolled publicity (see the next section). Even carefully controlled media events such as annual general meetings can go wrong (see box below). Every media event has an element of risk attached to it, since if things do go wrong, the press are waiting – with cameras perched and pens ready.

Fat cat pig

The production of a pig at the British Gas annual general meeting helped give the bandwagon against 'fat cats' (overpaid directors) a memorable push.

Andrew Bolger, *FT*

Any publicity is good publicity?

The adage 'any publicity is good publicity' is not always true. Although PRTV's negative editorial coverage shown on page 425 is, arguably, useful publicity, this is not always the case. Retail jewellery giant Ratners discovered this when they fell foul of the power of negative publicity. Their chairman, Gerald Ratner, told the press that his jewellery was 'crap'. It gained national coverage but it also kept customers away from his shops and lowered morale among his employees. He relinquished his joint position of chairman/managing director and the Ratners shops have since disappeared. On the other hand, unexpected editorial coverage can sometimes help, as shoemakers Bruno Magli observed when their sales jumped 50 per cent because of references to their shoes during the trial of O J Simpson (US media experts estimated the publicity was worth $100 million). Uncontrolled editorial exposure, and particularly negative publicity, can somersault out of control, as IBM discovered during the 1996 Olympics when one of its official Olympic computers started churning out incorrect information. 'The press reported the story ad nauseum, even blaming IBM for things it had nothing to do with. In the aftermath of the tragic bombing in Centennial Park, for example, the *Philadelphia Inquirer* erroneously reported that an IBM system may have contributed to security lapses.' (*Fortune* magazine, 9 September 1996). How a company handles the spotlight is a test for its company values. When 21 customers were shot dead in California in 1984, McDonald's knocked the restaurant down within days and eventually donated the land to a local community college. Continued publicity and association with such a tragedy is certainly not 'good publicity'.

Reducing the lack of control

Red faces can be avoided by checking to see if any events clash with a particular news release or event (like launching a new hamburger bar on national vegetarian day). There are directories available (such as *Foresight*) that list events and categorize them by type, region, date, etc. There are other directories that list editors' names, addresses and numbers (again categorized by type of magazine or programme). This is, of course, available on disc also. The publication *Advance* helps to ensure better targeting of news releases by identifying editorial topics that will be covered by particular media in the future. Editorial risk can be further reduced with the help of companies (such as Echo Research) that compile lists of journalists who have written articles on a particular organization or on its products, or on any particular issue, together with a favourable or unfavourable rating for each article. A further analysis compares the incidence of solicited and unsolicited press coverage, which can be cross-referenced with the ratings to identify any apparent bias in specific journalists' relationships with organizations. Sandra Macleod of Echo Research says 'Once a journalist calls, by punching in a few key words on his or her desk terminal, the PR manager is able to call up the profile of the caller on the screen even before the preliminary hellos.' So the pressurized PR manager is briefed automatically.

Despite the best preparation and briefing, things still go wrong. In advertising, the organization gets a chance to approve the final copy (or wording), but with editorial coverage deadlines are too tight even for the friendliest of editors to allow the PR manager sight of the copy and layout before it is published. Hence Mr Pimlott had a bad day.

Bad day for Mr Edward Pimlott

whose letter to the *Grantham Journal* led to this apology: 'In a letter printed in our July 25 issue, Mr Pimlott apparently described himself as a pillock of the community. This was our error. Mr Pimlott described himself as a pillar of the community.'

Independent, 28 August 1997

Controlled integration of publicity

Publicity should be integrated with other elements of the marketing communications mix. Chapter 1 explained how many major advertising campaigns are now supported by press launches and followed up with a press and publicity campaign to maintain the visibility generated by the public relations people. The example on page 425 shows how PR, sales promotion and direct mail work together in the case of a nuclear missile pen promotion. The TSB sponsorship campaign (see page 423) was totally integrated with the media relations (editorial) campaign. The Tango case study (see page 357) demonstrates how an integrated packaging, PR and sales promotion campaign maintains the brand's share without any traditional above-the-line support. In other cases, blown-up press cuttings can look effective at trade fairs and exhibitions. Third-party endorsements can be used in advertising, news releases, sales literature, packaging design, sales promotion and so on. A single photographic shoot can produce a range of material suitable for advertising, packaging, exhibitions, direct mail, press packs, etc. Strategically, the marketing communications tools should all work together (eg consistent positioning) rather than pull in different directions. Ideally, each activity should be planned for maximum integration.

Unforeseen opportunities and threats invariably emerge that make it difficult to plan for everything. For example, editorial is difficult to forecast (even if an editor promises to use a news release, it often gets 'spiked' or replaced by some other news item at the last moment; at other times the news release gets used later than expected). Successful positive publicity can trigger all sorts of ideas for mailings, promotions and further press coverage. Crises and negative publicity are equally difficult to forecast and plan, although many top companies today invest in crisis management programmes before crises occur. This allows them to respond in the most effective manner. A well-handled crisis can actually leave an organization in a stronger position, eg Johnson & Johnson's excellent handling of the 1982 Tylenol poisoning crisis (when seven people died of cyanide poisoning that had been inserted in their headache tablets) in Chicago.

Measuring media relations

Free publicity, news coverage or editorial can be monitored, measured and analysed. The most basic approach is 'column inches', how many columns of press coverage refer to a particular organization, its product or purpose. News clippings can be compiled in-house, by an agency or by a specialist news clipping company that monitors, cuts out, pastes up and delivers the clippings daily, weekly or however regularly the client wants. Similar media monitoring services are available for television, radio and the Internet (scanning newsgroups, online editions and search engines, such as www.ewatch.com). The size of file, number of references, and quantity of space or time devoted to a chosen product, organization or issue is, again, a simple method of measurement. More detailed analyses give a breakdown of: front-page mentions; exclusive mentions; size of mention/cutting; number of beneficial credits; neutral credits; adverse credits; and opportunities to enquire (includes reach of article, circulation, and whether a contact address and/or phone number, enquiry card, coupon, etc, was included). Various formulae attempt to calculate the quality of the coverage rather than the quantity. These can include photographs/diagrams, position on the page, etc.

A quantified report

When we have a story about a new hotel or product we identify five key messages we want to put across – it's never more than five – and we're lucky if we get two across in print. We then identify the key target audiences and the most appropriate publications to reach them. This establishes a matrix which ensures the maximum efficiency for our efforts.

Richard Power, Director of Corporate Communications, Forte Hotels

All stories are then monitored on a scale of one to five, according to how favourable they are and how many of the key messages are included. This enables Power to give Rocco Forte and other executive directors a quantified report on just how well they are communicating.

David Churchill, *PR Week*

These forms of analysis measure what gets into the press; they do not measure what gets into the minds of the target audience, ie whether the editorial has changed or reinforced the target audience's attitudes and intentions, or voting patterns, shared values, sales levels, etc. This has to be measured separately by researching attitudes and behaviour patterns. Sales can be measured but it can be difficult to isolate PR from other communications activities when attempting to gauge the effect of any aspect of public relations. The Hewlett-Packard case study in Chapter 16 shows how an integrated public relations activity works. The ongoing PR campaign for the Adidas Predator Boot (Appendix 14.4, page 446) proved the selling power of PR. The Wind Power case study, on page 437, shows how a PR campaign can also deliver against other (non-sales) measurable objectives.

CASE STUDY 14.1

Monster.com's $40 million pan-European campaign

Situation

Monster.com is one of the top career management services across the globe and currently has sites in 13 countries. The Monster Career Network is a lifelong career service job seekers can use to expand their careers, providing continuous access to some of the most progressive companies, as well as interactive, personalized tools to make the process effective and convenient.

Miller/Shandwick Technologies (MST) was charged with organizing PR for a pan-European integrated campaign for Monster Europe, the leading global career management portal, who were investing $40 million in their first, highly creative multimedia and TV advertising campaign across Europe, entitled 'Listen to the Voices'. Developed by advertising agency Saatchi & Saatchi, the campaign was to support the growth of Monster's network of national career management sites across Europe through the adoption of an integrated pan-European communications approach and strategy.

The challenge was to create pan-European interest in Monster's ad campaign, making it relevant across borders and languages. MST had to leverage a massively ambitious ad campaign for PR and press interest in order to make the most of Monster's marketing spend.

Objectives

The entire integrated campaign focused the whole of Monster's European management and staff on the success of the brand, and with the ad campaign breaking across Europe reinforced the energy and dynamism that Monster stands for.

The objective was to position Monster as the number one online recruitment organization through its integrated marketing communications strategies, underpinning its meteoric rise in Europe – growth of 190 per cent – using a traditional business model. The solution was to organize a high-profile press preview event for pan-European media in Monster's eight major markets once the commercials were finished and translated into the requisite

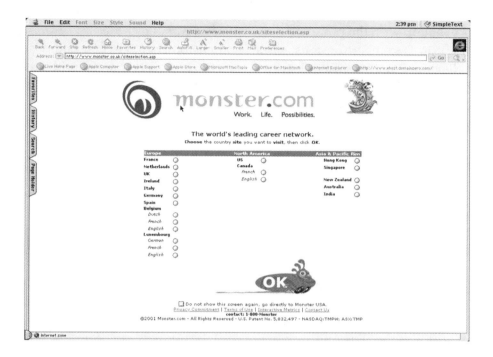

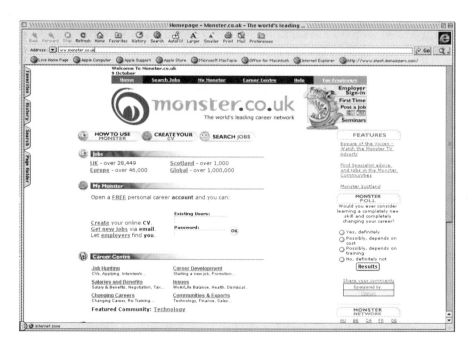

Screenshots taken from the Monster Web sites

languages, with merchandising for the campaign for the press launch. Next MST were to follow this event up with the production of a Monster company video, to be presented at a global summit in December to Monster staff and customers alike, that demonstrated the success of the brand and its meteoric growth. Finally, MST was charged with creating and designing laminated desktop Monster brand messaging cribsheets in order to keep staff on message during the campaign.

Strategy

MST conceived and organized the high-profile press preview event in Soho, London, which is the hub of the film and media industry in the UK, at Soho House, a favourite haunt of the stars and frequented by the likes of Madonna, Guy Ritchie, Sting and Trudi Styler. MST also coordinated the press materials and invitations to key press targets across Europe and organized one-to-one interviews with several Monster senior management people from Europe and the United States.

MST then created a brief for the company video, and selected the production company, Steam TV, to film it in Glasgow at a European management summit and at their London HQ offices. The corporate video was to feature the enormous success of Monster in each of its markets in Europe as the 'new millennium brand of the future', to reinforce the brand values to Monster management and so that it could be used as a promotional tool by the sales and marketing division.

The aims of the video were to also acknowledge the people who contributed to Monster's growth and to reinforce the 'feel good' factor of being part of the Monster phenomenon and the cohesiveness of all European sites engineering it together. The pacey storyline depicted a Monster employee wearing a specially made Monster 'suit', as she careered through her day, running around London and finally ending up back at the office the next morning. Meanwhile, the video shot all the pan-European management citing the reasons why Monster was the success it is, with a backdrop of monster logos, colours and whizzy guided tours of their offices.

Finally, MST designed and created desktop messaging cribsheets for Monster staff to be kept on message during the campaign.

Tactics

Implementation of the above three elements of the pan-European press event, the company video and the desktop cribsheets required considerable focus on detail and maintaining delivery at every level. From liaising with the advertising company to deliver different language versions of the ads for the preview, to liaising with Monster marketing management on the merchandise, MST had to be in the driving seat on all fronts and on schedule.

For the pan-European press preview event, the press packs were developed and releases drafted in five languages, together with other collateral, biographies of the internationally known creative team, visuals, CD shots and videos. Pan-European coordination of the required localization for eight markets was also paramount, requiring endless handholding and quality control. Interfacing with the most senior Monster management, MST identified media opportunities and gave them their schedules for press interviews and briefed them on the journalists' needs in terms of topics and issues to be discussed.

Action

In addition, MST was responsible for UK media pitching, securing broadcast opportunities with CNN, CNBC, Bloomberg and Sky, as well as key marketing publications and target media. Finally, the event management and staffing of one-to-one interviews went without a hitch, and follow-up reporting was conducted at every level across Europe and to US management.

MST monitored the roll-out and presentation of the video too, in Dublin in December. It has since been used extensively in sales and marketing situations.

Control

This was a truly pan-European rollout, the 'event' for European media, for which MST provided an all-inclusive package – from strategy to canapés. Twenty top-tier media were flown in from Germany, France, Spain, Belgium and The Netherlands. Press interviews, totalling 18 on the day, were arranged along with a press conference for an exclusive preview screening of the ad campaign in several language versions. Pan-European broadcast opportunities were also secured, including CNN, CNBC, Bloomberg and Sky News. Coverage secured throughout Europe numbered 26 quality media articles in top-tier media in each market. Follow-on press interest was secured in 2001 at the Campaign Advertising Awards, when the Monster campaign won a top award.

The client, from the VP of Europe based in Boston, to the CEO of Europe in the UK, were all visibly and vocally delighted with the event, with its inherent and cohesive nature for Monster. The client was even more thrilled with the company video, which again reinforced Monster's brand messaging, so much so that they used it for several global rendezvous meetings to ensure the Monster 'feelgood' factor was present among all the delegates.

Finally, they were so impressed with MST's design for a brand-messaging desktop crib-sheet, to ensure that all staff were totally on message in the eventuality that they were called by the press, that they asked for it to be translated into every European market language.

Men and women

The agency team comprised a director, an account manager, an account executive and a group assistant who all worked with the client team from planning to implementation.

Money

Budgets were not available, but a figure in excess of the 'normal' was recommended, as the campaign was so exciting and unusual – delivering PR on a new state-of-the-art advertising campaign. The team had to be very aware that no such budget existed and deliver against very strict budgets.

Minutes

The timetable was very tight, with the agency given only a few weeks to develop and launch the PR campaign, as it had to take place before the TV launch across Europe. The key milestone for the campaign was therefore to get the mindshare and involvement of all eight European countries to buy in to the idea of the launch and to get organized to achieve it within the restricted time frame.

Frames taken from the award-winning $40 million 2000 Monster.com pan-European advertising campaign entitled 'Listen to the Voices'.

CASE STUDY 14.2

European Press Network's world 'first' with EPNworld

Situation

With its headquarters in Paris, European Press Network's EPNworld was the world's first interactive press agency dedicated to the distribution of freelance correspondents' contributions. Operating as an online marketplace, EPN facilitates contacts between member corespondents and editors, while journalists retain the right to set their own price and to negotiate copyright.

The challenge that faced Miller/Shandwick Technologies (MST) was to launch EPNworld, a portal for the trading of pictures, copy, features and news articles from high-calibre professional journalists around the world to publishers and news groups. Billed as a 'new system of news distribution', EPNworld's Web site works within a unique Internet-based framework by giving access to editors and publishers to articles filed by a worldwide network of journalists. This was particularly challenging, as media traditionally do not like reporting on other media. There were also credibility issues through launching anything new 'online' without being associated with the much publicised 'dot com' market.

Objectives

The ultimate challenge was to convey with clarity what the new service would bring to the world of publishing, given that the founder was Duncan Barclay, son of one of the Barclay Brothers media moguls.

Strategy

MST convinced the client not to launch the service in its then current format, but to take the technology to the next stage of development and do some 'futurecasting'. In partnership with Microsoft, another MST client, EPN created the 'wireless workstation' and demonstrated how in the future journalists would submit their work through the EPN site in the middle of the assignment, be it in a war zone, or even the scene of a crime. The launch event was appropriately held at the prestigious Foreign Press Association headquarters and MST organized a range of knowledgeable guest speakers such as BBC TV Foreign Affairs Editor John Simpson, who covered the history of journalism from before the fax or the Internet.

Tactics

The MST team ensured that the whole building was branded through the use of good spot-lights projecting an animated logo on to the walls and newstand-style boards outside the building. Posters were designed by the MST team as a backdrop to the entrance, depicting salient industry facts and figures, such as 800 million TVs, 500,000 publishers, 3 global news agencies. Plasma screens were also positioned outside the main launch area to ensure that any overspill of attendees and late arrivals could see and hear the speakers for the evening. Microsoft's mobility division gave demonstrations of the latest pocket PC and an insight into devices that could be used by journalists in the future. These all served to keep up the momentum throughout the evening and to top it all EPN gave away prizes including a trip to Paris on Eurostar, a Compaq iPAQ pocket PC and signed copies of John Simpson's book *The World My Master*.

Action

MST conceived the launch event. The team was relatively small, just three people, including an account director. The event needed to be given shape and the essential media guests for the launch were identified and diary-dated, so the attendance level was high.

Through MST's work on Microsoft's mobility division, they had developed both a thorough understanding of the technology involved and excellent contacts with leading pan-European and trade and technical media. Using this experience MST developed new pitching angles in order to deliver the requisite results. By the time of the event, the confirmed attendee list of target media had reached 85 and was still rising. Word had got around and journalists were calling MST to find out what was happening and if they could be a part of it.

For the client, journalists were not just an audience there to write about EPN, they were also one of the key target audiences for the service itself. MST worked the media list for the launch to incorporate a broad range of titles and contacts in this space and thus brought together a large range of journalists to make the event vibrant from the outset.

MST made effective recommendations regarding the look and feel of the event based on the client's requirements and eccentricities, and also on the media and audience that would be attending. MST felt that the overall contribution to the successful launch of EPN was predicated upon support and contributions from each member of the team.

Control

The client was very pleased with the results. Not only was the event extremely well attended, but the diversity of the international journalists attending left nothing to be desired. Press coverage included articles in The *International Herald Tribune*, *Wired*, *Sky*, the *Guardian*, *The Times*, Silicon.com, BBC Online and *UK Press Gazette*. More importantly for the client, the hit rate on the EPN Web site increased by 200 per cent post-launch and the journalist sign-up rate from the evening was 70 per cent. Riding high on the kudos of the event, EPN was also about to sign partnership deals with News Corporation and The American Writers Guild. In addition, the MST team drafted copy for subsequent advertisements to appear in *The Guardian* on 22 and 23 November 1998 with the theme of 'Getting a fresh perspective on global news agencies'.

Men and women

The agency team included a director, an account director, an account executive and an assistant account executive. They worked with the client team throughout the planning and implementation of the campaign.

Money

The budgets were secured for the event specifically to pay for the 'window dressing' of the venue and the multimedia assault at the launch, as well as for the launch itself.

Minutes

Timings were critical as the team had so much to organize for the launch, so a very strict project management matrix was put in place to deliver all that was needed.

CASE STUDY 14.3

Wind power

Situation

The British wind industry, led by its trade body, the British Wind Energy Association (BWEA), was encountering fierce opposition from some pressure groups and a hostile media. Despite enjoying high levels of public support (up to 80 per cent) and a planning predisposition to approve suitable wind farm applications, planning approvals had declined dramatically. Since January 1995, 77 per cent of all applications had been rejected.

The commercial viability of this still fledgling industry was under threat, particularly as the Non-fossil Fuel Obligation (NFFO), a government initiative to kick-start the industry

and help the government meet its renewable energy targets, was due to be withdrawn. In communications terms, the wind industry had been too reactive, allowing myths to develop and misunderstandings and inaccuracies to go unchecked. Wind power had much to commend it, in both environmental and business terms. The industry also had the support of influential groups such as Friends of the Earth, the Country Landowners Association and the National Farmers Union. But its positive messages were not getting across. The time had come for concerted action.

Objectives

1. To reverse the balance of negative coverage across all target media groups (previously at 47 per cent negative, 29 per cent positive and 24 per cent neutral).
2. To highlight the untapped potential of wind power to UK electricity supply at a time of declining fossil-fuel reserves.
3. To achieve a favourable allocation of forthcoming NFFO contracts (which are shared out among other renewables such as hydro, solar, biomass, etc).
4. To communicate the environmental and business benefits of wind farming.
5. To encourage the government to set a specific target for wind power growth, rather than its more general target for renewables as a whole.

Strategy

To develop a short-term campaign to grab media interest and recommend a sustained programme of follow-up activity.

A number of communications channels were considered. To ensure maximum effectiveness within tight budgetary constraints a media-led, issues-based campaign was developed. The media relations programme had to dovetail with a parallel public affairs programme. This involved a presentation to the Environment Secretary, wind farm visits by MPs, briefings with all political parties during conference season, and liaison with researchers and civil servants.

The media campaign was tailored to include regional and national variations and special interests (eg Cornwall, Wales and Scotland). Some direct-mail activity was included. The strategy considered how to say what to whom and when. It was factually based to counter the emotional subjectivity of whether wind farms are ugly or not.

Tactics

- Media relations, supported by:
  - lobbying;
  - direct mail (of press packs and policy report);
  - promotional materials (campaign identity).

Owing to budgetary constraints there was no advertising activity.
Media relations included:

- devising industry-standard responses to critical issues and preparing positive key messages;
- press office support;
- media attitudinal research;
- campaign research to devise news angle;
- press releases and supporting material;
- rigorous media training, including Q&A document;
- media invitations;
- collation and commissioning of photography;
- strategic alliances with PR teams in supporting groups, eg Friends of the Earth;
- proactive and reactive letter writing;
- drafting feature articles in key titles;
- tracking features;
- arranging broadcast-standard footage of wind farms.

Action/production

- Campaign proposition devised following detailed desktop research – briefly, that despite being Europe's windiest country (40 per cent of the total wind resource), the UK was in danger of being the poor relation in wind power generation compared to more progressive EU countries like Germany, Holland and Denmark, which produce considerably more electricity from wind but have a fraction of the UK's resource.

- Agree small number of key messages for constant reiteration – clean, cheap, popular and natural.
- Choose and media train BWEA spokespeople.
- Establish letter-writing team to respond to anticipated 'backlash'.
- Campaign name chosen – Switch on to Wind Power.
- News value enhanced by timing launch to coincide with publication of new BWEA policy report, week of BWEA annual conference and publication of US-based WorldWatch report on wind as the world's fastest-growing source of energy.
- Launch event at Royal Geographical Society, London, with Charles Secrett, from Friends of the Earth, and environmental campaigner Jonathan Porritt.
- Obtained third-party written support from the City, farmers, planners, environmental groups, councillors, celebrities and businesses (including Anita Roddick).
- Dedicated press office handled numerous media inquiries, coordinated mass mail out of comprehensive press packs and drafted detailed Q&A sheets for client.
- Momentum maintained by handling media relations for subsequent opening of Europe's largest wind farm in mid-Wales.

Follow-up activity

- targeted at specific groups;
- not always media led;
- included research followed by presentations to tourist boards, council and planning/development bodies;
- crisis management plan developed.

Switch on to wind power launch

	July	Aug	Sept	Oct	Nov	Who?
Brief	X					Client
Planning	X	X				Harrison Cowley
European/local authority research		X				Client
Press pack content		X				Harrison Cowley
Industry-standard messages		X				All
Media training			X			All
Book venue		X				Harrison Cowley
Agree 3rd party support		X				Harrison Cowley
Invitations issued		X				Harrison Cowley
Media sell-in			X			Harrison Cowley
Scriptwriting			X			Client
Report published			X			Harrison Cowley
Launch, London			X			Harrison Cowley
Welsh press pack				X		Harrison Cowley
Media 'warm up'				X		Harrison Cowley
Carno opening				X		All
Media follow-up					X	Harrison Cowley

Control/evaluation

- Contingency planning anticipated potential problems and ensured effective news management.
- Detailed evaluation and media analysis showed high penetration levels in *all* target media for industry's positive messages.
- Marked turnaround in positive coverage – 69.3 per cent positive, 19.2 per cent negative and 11.5 per cent neutral.
- In excess of 50 million opportunities to see or hear (excludes substantial TV and radio coverage).
- Planning concerns helped to get government to announce record number of NFFO contracts for wind power.
- Local opinion survey after Welsh wind farm opening showed 92.5 per cent support for wind farming.

Men and women

Handled by Alan Hyde of Harrison Cowley (Bristol) PR Consultants.

Money

Total Budget – £15,000 in fees, plus £5,000 production (included launch costs).

Minutes

Six months.

Reproduced by kind permission, National Wind Power

APPENDIX 14.1

Video news releases

A video news release (VNR) is conceptually the same as a written press release, except that it is produced on broadcast-quality video (BETACAM or BETACAM SP). VNRs keep broadcasters up to date with news items (which they might otherwise have missed). VNRs also save broadcasters from having to send their own busy camera crews out to cover a story.

The VNR consists of two sections: a 90-second 'A' roll which carries a commentary designed to show the editor and/or journalist how the story could run 'on air', and a three- to five-minute 'B' roll which is a selection of loosely cut shots ('rushes') designed to be re-edited by broadcasters into their own style, ie the broadcasters use their own commentary, graphics and captions so that as far as the viewers are concerned the story has been originated by the broadcaster. As with a press release, a VNR is paid for by the organization that is looking for some positive publicity. The TV stations receive VNRs free of charge. Again, as with press releases, there is no guarantee that the material will be used, since a bigger story can break at any time. Equally, a VNR can be used negatively, since, unlike advertising, there is no control over the message.

A VNR can stretch the impact of communications activities such as sponsored events. For example, a British PLC sponsoring an air show display team commissioned VISNEWS to produce and distribute a VNR package to run throughout UK air shows during the summer. As the air show moved from region to region, the local TV broadcasters were offered the VNR as a preview story to be included in the 'things to see at the weekend' section. The VNR was subsequently used (broadcast) on 10 different regional television stations reaching a total audience of 4.2 million at a cost of approximately £5,000, giving a cost per thousand of £1.20 (the £5,000 excludes production costs, but these were minimal since the VNR was made mostly from existing corporate library footage).

A VNR can stretch the exposure of advertising campaigns if some behind-the-scenes shots and/or other previously unseen footage are edited creatively into a newsworthy story. In this way, the OTSs (opportunities to see) of a brand can be increased substantially without any above-the-line media costs (ie no television advertising space has to be bought). Instead of advertising on television, pop bands use VNRs to get their album publicized on national breakfast television, the early evening news and the mid-evening news.

The TV revolution

The television revolution and its proliferation of 200 stations means there is a huge demand for programmes but less money available for each programme. Here lies the opportunity for organizations to help the programme makers by supplying relevant footage in the form of a timely VNR.

Costs

Costs over production, distribution (to the TV programmes) and evaluation (monitoring actual usage) can range from £10,000 to £15,000 for a UK TV campaign, £25,000–£40,000 for a pan-European campaign and £60,000–£75,000 for a worldwide campaign. Some costs can be saved if VNRs are included in the planning of, say, the production of other film footage, eg advertising or corporate videos.

APPENDIX 14.2

Syndicated radio tapes

A syndicated radio tape is, on average, a three-minute recorded interview about an event, a company, a product or service. The tape and script are copied and mailed out (or syndicated) to approximately 35 radio stations in the UK (out of approximately 200). The same principles as apply to VNRs apply here, ie it should be newsworthy and not a blatant plug.

For around £1,000 the companies that offer a syndicated tape service have a basic package that usually includes:

- preliminary discussion;
- interviewer – selecting, booking and briefing;
- structuring the interview;
- studio session (one hour);
- recording (three minutes);
- editing master tape;
- two spare copies for client;
- cue sheet preparation (written introduction to the taped interview);
- selecting 30 relevant radio stations (only one per area where stations overlap);
- producing and distributing a boxed, labelled copy to each individual radio station's presenter or producer;
- monitoring – three to four weeks after dispatch a written report is produced, giving details of which stations broadcast the information; this is sometimes followed up with a more detailed report;
- a 40 per cent take-up of a professionally produced, newsworthy, accurately targeted syndicated radio tape is considered to be an 'average success rate'. There is usually a range of optional extras (eg localized cue sheets or overseas distribution).

Case
Thompsons Solicitors' syndicated tape interview on industrial injuries was broadcast by 12 radio stations, reaching an audience of 993,000, at a total cost of £750.

Down-the-line interviews

Syndicated tape producers usually offer an alternative service – 'down-the-line interviews'. This is where the interviewee is brought into the studio, linked up live to local radio stations one at a time, and interviewed on a one-to-one basis. On average the interviewee does about 10 separate interviews per day. Some interviewees have been known to do up to 15 separate interviews in one day. This is exhausting and sometimes the later interviews are not as good, as the interviewee cannot remember if he/she said something before or not. Ballpark costs are £150 per interview.

Case
SAGE Software's down-the-line interview on the Millennium Bug was taken by eight stations, reaching an audience of 1.5 million at a total cost of £792.

APPENDIX 14.3

Digital press kit

Buena Vista International's film *Starship Troopers* had an innovative 'digital press kit' available to support its launch.

The kit comprised a ready-made mini-site packed with material related to the film. It was designed in such a way that it could be incorporated into other media sites. This makes a convenient package for media partners, distributorships, agents and promoters to link the mini-site to their own Web site.

APPENDIX 14.4

Selling power of sustained PR – the Adidas Predator

 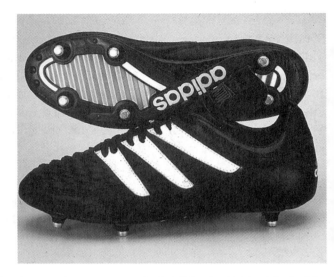

Ex-Liverpool hero and Australian footballer Craig Johnson approached Adidas in 1991 with the idea of creating a rubber boot that creates friction between boot and ball, giving greater power and swerve

Stage 1 FIFA approval June '92	FIFA endorsed the legality of the boot and the advantage it creates (but did not announce it publicly). In addition FIFA released a statement, at Adidas's request, stating that they were unsure whether the boot would be passed as legal. Hold back publicity until launch. Huge media interest started to build.
Stage 2 Maintain momentum Early Dec '93	Keep the media excited. Leak information about key players testing the mystery boot, while purposely keeping the boot under wraps. AllSport picture agency commissioned to shoot some paparazzi-type photographs of stars caught in the act of testing. Long-lens shots reveal Adidas logo but not boot design. 'Leaked photos' circulated to sports and picture editors in the nationals, apparently without the knowledge/permission of Adidas. Meanwhile Jamie Rednapp and Adidas add to the intrigue by refusing to comment. Within two days a full page in the *Sun* using the actual paparazzi-type shot.
Stage 3 Launch End Dec '93	Launch at the 1994 World Cup draw held in Las Vegas. Endorsed by top World Cup personalities suitable for each market, eg Franz Beckenbauer, Glen Hoddle, Paul Ince and many more.
Stage 4 Media testing Feb '94	Picking off key journalists and key TV shows. Media tour – kids' shows, offering Craig and opportunity for journalists. Heightening curiosity.

Stage 5 Heighten curiosity	Commission TV documentary on 'Craig's Boot' (approximate cost £500,000). BBC's *QED* broadcasts to its biggest audience for years as 'Craig's Boot' is seen by 5 million viewers.
Stage 6 April '94 Local retailer launch	Point-of-sale material positioned in stores to increase curiosity. One month before stock arrives empty cages are positioned on walls of hundreds of retailers with message 'Predator arriving on…' Retailers take deposits for boot sales one month before boot arrives.
Stage 7 Stock delivery mid-May '94	Point-of-sale changed. Cage with bent bars positioned on retailers' walls.
Stage 8 Pre-ad campaign publicity drive mid-May '94	VNR about the production of the boot. Re-edited with different players for different markets. A roll 2 minutes, B roll 12 minutes (£20,000 production and distribution). In UK alone 15 TV features on national and local TV, plus *QED* showed the 70-minute airtime programme, 'Craig's Boot'.
Stage 9 Retail sales mid-May '94	Boots sell out.
Stage 10 Ad breaks end of May '94	Ad campaign launched as already committed to schedule, plus World Cup image/profile had to be maintained.
Euro '96	New Predator launched via new stars Beckham, Gazza.
New Predator launch June '98	Launch New Predator Accelerator at World Cup '98 with new stars, plus Adidas official sponsor of World Cup '98, the first sports brand to have this status.

£80,000* PR spend in UK market in 1994 through Hill and Knowlton.

APPENDIX 14.5

Pressure groups make ethics an issue (excerpts from Naomi Klein's No Logo *(2000))*

Nike

'According to Campaign for Labor Rights, the largest ever anti-Nike event so far took place on October 18, 1997: eighty five cities in thirteen countries participated. Not all the protests have attracted large crowds, but since the movement is so decentralized, the sheer number of individual anti-Nike events has left the company's public relations department scrambling to get its spin onto dozens of local newscasts. Though you never know it from its branding ubiquity, even Nike can't be everywhere at once.'

---

*   Excludes cost of 'Craig's Boot', which eventually more than paid for itself. Return on spend 15:1, which means that £1.2 million worth of quantified media exposure was generated. More importantly, the boot sold out before the TV advertising broke, thereby proving the selling power of good PR.

Shell

'There was an explosion of protest and activity targeting Shell oil after the shocking hanging of Nigerian author and anti-Shell activist Ken Saro-Wiwa.

But the most significant landmark in the growth of anti-corporate activism also came in 1995, when the world lost Ken Saro-Wiwa. The revered Nigerian writer and environmental leader was imprisoned by his country's oppressive regime for spearheading the Ogoni people's campaign against the devastating human and ecological effects of Royal Dutch/Shell's oil drilling in the Niger Delta. Human rights groups rallied their governments to interfere, and some economic sanctions were imposed, but they had little effect. In November 1995, Saro-Wiwa and eight other Ogoni activists were executed by a military government who had enriched themselves with Shell's oil money and through their own people's repression.'

Amnesty Ethics

'Amnesty International, in a departure from its focus on prisoners persecuted for either their religious or political beliefs, is also beginning to treat multinational corporations as major players in the denial of human rights worldwide.'

Key points from Chapter 14:

1. PR and marketing are not subsets of each other, although they do integrate.
2. Editorial coverage has lower costs, higher message creditability and high risks because of lack of control over the message.
3. Integrated PR contributes to marketing communications synergy.

FURTHER READING

Bernays, E (1923) *Crystallizing Public Opinion*, Boni & Liveright Inc, New York

Bernays, E (1955) *The Engineering of Consent*, University of Oklahoma Press, Norman, OK

Bland, M (1987) *Be Your Own PR Man*, Kogan Page, London

Churchill, D (1992) The power behind the image, *PR Week*, 15 October

Cutlip, S, Centre, H and Broom M (1985) *Effective Public Relations*, 6th edn, Prentice-Hall International, Englewood Cliffs, NJ

Hart, N (1992) Is there a new role for PR in marketing?, *Public Relations*, **11**, 1 September

Haywood, R (1990) *All about PR*, 2nd edn, McGraw-Hill, London

Jefkins, F (1988) *Public Relations*, 3rd edn, M & E Handbooks, Pitman, London

Klein, N (2000) *No Logo*, Flamingo, London

Murphy, D (1992) Don't forget the hype, *Creative Review*, October, p 16

PRTV (1991) *Actions Speak Louder Than Words* (PR training video), Chartered Institute of Marketing/Institute of Public Relations, London

Ross, D (1990) *Surviving the Media Jungle*, Mercury Books, London

White, J (1991) *How to Understand and Manage Public Relations*, Business Books, London

FURTHER CONTACTS

Communications Advertising and Marketing Education Foundation (CAM Foundation), Moor Hall, Cookham, Maidenhead, Berkshire SL6 9QH (tel: 01628 427192; Web site: www.camfoundation.com)

Institute of Public Relations, The Old Trading House, 15 Northburgh Street, London EC1V OJR tel: 020 7253 5151; Web site: www.ipr.org.uk)

Public Relations Consultants Association, Willow House, Willow Place, London SW1P 1JH tel: 020 7233 6026; Web site: www.prca.org.uk)

15

Sponsorship

INTRODUCTION

Mixed feelings?

We do not sponsor sports. It's a very cluttered market where you can spend millions without getting much return.

David Goldesgeyne, Head of sponsorship for Lloyds Bank

Each World Cup has proven even more rewarding than the last, in terms of global name exposure, premium positioning, sales promotion results cementing relationships with trade customers.

Gillette World Cup News

So what should be sponsored? How does one choose what to sponsor and what to reject? Maybe arts are good for computers and sports are bad for banks? If sports sponsorship is so good for Gillette, why do they bother to advertise at all? Or perhaps their advertising doesn't work, which means any meagre improvement would be deemed to be a success? Do sponsorship funds come out of the above-the-line budget, ie does it always mean reducing the advertising budgets, or can they come out of some corporate fund? How much should be spent? How much is too much? When does it become less value for money? How is it measured? Finally, what exactly does sponsorship mean? These are some of the questions this chapter answers. We will start with the last question.

WHAT IS SPONSORSHIP?

Sponsorship is more than patronage, altruism or benefaction. It can indeed help others while simultaneously achieving specifically defined communications objectives (see page 454). Some sponsors see sponsorship as a form of *enlightened self-interest*, where a worthy activity is supported with cash and/or consideration in return for satisfying specific marketing or corporate objectives. As sponsorship matures, its diverse range of programmes, objectives, advantages and disadvantages require a relatively sophisticated level of management understanding.

Target audience must be researched in detail, crystal-clear qualitative and quantitative objectives must be set, appropriate types of sponsorship vehicles must be agreed, considered and selected. A programme of integrated communications has to be planned with precision and sufficient budgets have to be allocated to allow for 'leveraging', stretching or maximizing the overall sponsorship impact.

Range and types of sponsorship

All sectors of society can be targeted and reached through sponsorship. Just about anyone or anything can be sponsored. You can even sponsor *the possibility of an event* – Granada TV once sponsored Manchester's bid to host the 2000 Olympics. The range of sponsorship opportunities is limited only by one's imagination. The obvious areas are *sport, arts, education, community* and *broadcast*.

Whether the events are large or small (eg blind golf and blind cricket), sport offers an effective route into the mind of various target markets. Even within a particular *sport* there is a range of different sponsorship opportunities. Take soccer for example. It is possible to sponsor a *title*, eg the Worthington Cup or the Barclaycard Premier League, or a *stadium*, eg the Reebok Stadium. Perhaps a more interesting example is where Maxwell House Coffee's

Taste of Chicago sponsorship *maximized the off-site potential* by buying all 37,000 tickets and then giving them away free in return for two empty MH jars. It is also possible to sponsor: a *club*, eg JVC and Arsenal, Blackdeath Vodka and Scarborough FC (incidentally, since the 1980s, five of Japan's baseball teams have been owned by railway companies, four by beverage companies, two by newspapers and one by an auto company); a *match day* (eg York City gave 12 stand tickets, free buffet, free bar, free ads in the programme, hoardings in the car park and the opportunity to present the man of the match award and join players in the bar after the game – all for approximately £1,000); a *kick-off* (in the United States, Anheuser Busch sponsor NFL kick-offs and they are referred to as 'Bud Kick-offs'); a *ball*, eg Crystal Palace FC match ball sponsorship costs £250; a *fair play award*, often tied in with another sponsorship package; a *player* (players receive individual sponsorship and in return they open stores, meet employees and acknowledge the sponsor in the programme); a *pass*, a *tackle*, a *goal*, a *save* or a *miss* – the Pizza Hut and American Express examples below show US baseball creating such exciting opportunities. It is even possible to sponsor a fictitious team (see the study case on page 465).

Sponsoring a catch – fan catches 33,000 pizzas

Pittsburgh Pirates fan Ted Bianucci was picked at random out of a crowd at Three Rivers Stadium to take the field to try to catch three pop-ups (balls shot out of a gun used to help catchers practise defence). Sponsors Pizza Hut promised every spectator in the park a free soda at Pizza Hut (just show the ticket stub), a pitcher of soda or a small pizza if the fan caught one, two or three of the pop-ups. No one had ever previously caught all three. Bianucci, to the cheers of 33,789 people, caught all three balls – and $150,000 worth of pizza generates a lot of good feeling and probably extra business as 33,000 customers enter Pizza Hut's premises.

Sponsoring a miss

American Express and Best West International Hotels jointly sponsored a programme that donated $300 to children's baseball league every time top baseball pitcher Nolan Ryan bowled or pitched an opposition player out. If Ryan pitched a 'no-hitter' (bowled the whole team out for nought), then a whopping $1.25 million would be donated by the sponsors to the league. AmEx and Best West also donated three cents every time an AmEx card was used to pay for a Best West hotel. In addition, $2 was contributed for every newly approved AmEx card member application which came from a 'take-one' box at each Best West hotel.

Arts sponsorship can be even more diverse – from sponsoring the opening of EuroDisney, to a film premiere, to a particularly obscure type of play to gain access to an otherwise difficult target market. *Education* is a sensitive area and sponsorship can come in cash or in kind, eg a computer company donating computers to schools. *Community sponsorship* is becoming increasingly important as businesses recognize the importance of their community and their corporate responsibility. The corporate citizen is alive and well within the 'per cent club' (in the UK, corporate members of the per cent club promise to spend one-half of 1 per cent of their profits on community programmes. In the United States there are also 2 per cent and 5 per cent clubs). In the UK, it is possible to sponsor the police, the fire brigade and the coast guard. Off-licence chain Thresher has sponsored a van for Avon and Somerset police force, while Newcastle Breweries has sponsored a mobile police station.

Other types of sponsorship

Here are some other forms of sponsorship, which give an indication of the variety and potential available. An organization can sponsor *an expedition* (Mercury have sponsored a walk to the North Pole). British Aerospace, Memorex and Interflora signed as sponsors for *a voyage into space* (the package was subsequently cancelled). An organization can also sponsor *a species* (Systematics Association, a scientific group involved in classifying organisms, recently named seven wasps after the directors of Salomon Brothers after they waived a $300,000 debt arrangement). The *'Ugly Bartender'* contest sponsored by the Multiple Sclerosis Society is its second biggest revenue generator. Some years ago *cows* wearing Vladivar Vodka jackets in a field near the London to Brighton railway line were sponsored during the Brighton festival. Akai sponsored *bullfights* at £10,000 a fight. BP sponsored Eugene Ionesco's play, *Journeys Among the Dead*. Sponsoring *a war*? It is possible to sponsor sections of the US Army (eg the Medical Corps). On the other hand, sponsoring *peace* initiatives is also possible. For example, during the height of the cold war the *Irish Times* sponsored an official televised arms debate between Soviet and US diplomats. It is even possible to sponsor an Amnesty International Tour.

Sponsoring bad sex

It is possible to sponsor bad sex – Hamlet Cigars are sponsoring the *Literary Review*'s Annual Bad Sex Grand Booby Prize. The award is given to the writer whose novel contains the worst description of the sex act.

Broadcast sponsorship offers possibilities ranging from sponsoring other people's advertisements (Midland Bank's £50,000 and Cancer Research), to *the weather*, specific *programmes* and *themed weeks on cable television* (see the ITC sponsorship code on page 469).

Advantages of sponsorship

Sponsorship can be *cost-effective* (compared to advertising) in terms of reaching a particular audience. It does allow access to very specific types of audience that otherwise might be difficult to reach. Sponsorship can achieve many different objectives (see 'Objectives', pages 457–58), including: increased awareness; image enhancement; improved relationships with many different 'publics'; increased sales, sampling and database building; creating a platform for new promotional material; beating advertising bans, etc. It also offers creative opportunities, including the engagement of an audience in a relaxed atmosphere of goodwill. Hospitality events open doors and create a dialogue that conventional media simply cannot match. As Alan Mitchell says, 'sponsorship reaches the parts conventional advertising cannot'. Sponsorship lends itself to integrated communications and the cost-effectiveness of integrated activities. Finally, the effects of a sponsorship programme are measurable.

Disadvantages of sponsorship

Some say that sponsorship is insidious and that it undermines artistic integrity. In areas such as health and education, some feel that the issues involved are too important to be left to the whim of a corporation. Although sponsorship can deliver extremely cost-effective benefits, it can be misunderstood as an excessive indulgence by employees if they are kept in the dark about it and if there are redundancies occurring at the same time. In both cases sponsorship, particularly high-profile sponsorship, needs to be presented to the employees as a cost-effective business tool that can help the business to survive and thrive in the future. Sponsorship of a competitive activity, such as a football club, can alienate the company or product from the opposition fans, eg a national audience if the teams are involved in an international competition, or an even larger audience if the team or player behaves badly. Today's footballers are arguably the modern-day sandwich-man (person carrying two advertising boards up and down a street). TSB got around this potential problem with an innovative sponsorship programme which is explained in the case study on page 465.

Insider sponsorship

As sponsors of Middlesbrough, Cellnet has emblazened its name on the inside of top goalscorer Ravanelli's jersey since his trademark after scoring is to lift his shirt inside-out over his head.

Global media coverage may not be a good thing if what is being sponsored in one country is unacceptable in another country, eg bull fighting, camel wrestling, dwarf throwing, etc. If the medium is the message (ie the choice of sponsorship reflects the values of the sponsor), the message can become tarnished through its association with a socially unacceptable event. Some sponsorship deals can alienate a whole nation, particularly if the sponsor is perceived to have negotiated too good a deal for itself (see Appendix 15.2, page 470). The uncontrollability of so many variables from weather to fans to strikes to riots makes sponsorship more risky than advertising. Even pop concerts are risky, as Naomi Klein points out: 'Celine Dion's concert tour was picketed by human rights activists in Boston, Philadelphia and Washington, DC. Although she was unaware of it, her tour sponsor – Ericsson cellular – was among Burma's most intransigent foreign investors, refusing to cease its dealings with the junta despite the campaign for an international boycott.' Finally, ambush marketing allows non-sponsoring competitors to soak up some benefits without paying full sponsorship fees (see 'Ambush marketing', page 463).

Not the Salvation Army

This is not the Salvation Army, this is business. Our programme is focused and we are able to quantify what has happened. When I am criticised for paying the wages of dancers while staff are losing their jobs I say that, by supporting dancers, I am supporting more jobs at Digital.

Geoff Shingles, Chairman, Digital

RUNNING A SPONSORSHIP PROGRAMME

The SOSTAC® + 3Ms acronym (see Chapter 2) can be used to develop and manage a sponsorship programme.
SOSTAC® + 3Ms involves:

1. Analysing and summarizing the current sponsorship situation (including competitive review, previous sponsorship experiences, sponsorship strategies, etc).
2. Defining sponsorship objectives.
3. Clarifying strategy (how the sponsorship programme contributes towards the overall corporate mission, marketing objectives, communication objectives, and how it can be leveraged or stretched, exploited and supported by other communications tools).
4. Developing the tactical details of how it all fits together.
5. Defining target audiences.

6. Considering men (and women), money and minutes (the resources required to run a programme).
7. Building in some form of measurement or evaluation to see whether the programme is worth repeating.

SOSTAC® + 3Ms is not, strictly speaking, a sequence of activities, more a checklist that should be incorporated into a programme or plan.

A more sequential approach for a sponsorship programme could be along the following lines:

1. Define objectives.
2. Define and analyse target audience/s.
3. Sponsorship policy and programme selection.
4. Fix budgets.
5. Sponsorship strategy.
6. Detailed plan of tactics.
7. Test or run a pilot scheme.
8. Implement the (modified) programme.
9. Monitor and measure.

Objectives

Clear objectives help to focus both the spin-off activities (eg sales promotions linked with the core sponsorship programme) and the marketing support activities (eg advertising and publicity that announces the sponsorship programme). A sponsorship programme can satisfy many objectives simultaneously. The range of objectives is varied:

1. Increase *awareness* – eg Canon used the Football League partly to create a presence, become a familiar household name and generally raise awareness of a previously relatively unknown company in the UK marketplace.
2. Build an *image* – can help to reposition or strengthen a brand or corporate image through association with particular types of sponsorship activities, eg a caring image through community programmes.
3. Improve or maintain *relations* – with customers, the trade, employees, and even investors through hospitality and entertainment at a sponsored event. Rumbelows department store sponsored English soccer's League Cup. Part of the agreement allowed the sponsor to appoint their own employee of the year to meet the teams and present the cup to the winning captain. Community relations can also be enhanced by supporting appropriate local activities.

4. *Increase sales and open closed markets* – Coca-Cola was banned in Arab markets because it built an Israeli bottling plant. Sponsorship of the 1989 Arab Youth Football Competition in Riyadh helped to open the door again.

5. *Increase sales (sampling and direct sales)* – action-orientated sampling opportunities abound in a captive market where the buyer is in a relaxed frame of mind, eg buying and drinking Victoria beer at a touch-rugby competition sponsored by Victoria beer. Some market research can also be carried out. Sponsorship can create a dialogue, whereas a lot of advertising is a monologue (although there are some campaigns that engage the customer in more than just a monologue).

6. *Attract distributors/agents* – ECON are sponsoring a radio station's weather forecasts to build awareness and attract enquiries from agents in other markets.

7. *Create promotional material* – some events offer wonderful photo opportunities with scenes, sights and stars. One climbing equipment company sponsors climbs primarily to secure stunning photographs with branded climbing gear featuring prominently.

8. *Circumventing advertising bans* – sponsorship, particularly of televised events, allows sponsors a way around mainstream above-the-line advertising bans, eg tobacco companies sponsoring sports events such as snooker. Incidentally, the famous Steve Davis vs Dennis Taylor snooker final kept one-third of the British population glued to their TV sets until 3.00 am.

9. *Miscellaneous* – ranging from, for example, the generation of new product ideas (new product educational competitions) to graduate recruitment.

Target audience/s

There are two different audiences. The first is the one immediately involved with the programme, the second the one that can be reached through advertising and media coverage. Although there are many spin-off objectives that offer benefits to different target groups (as in the previous Rumbelows Cup example), the primary objective should be linked clearly with the primary audience. This involves some *research* into the lifestyles, attitudes, behaviour patterns, leisure activities, issues and demographics relevant to the primary target group. Previous research should have identified the current situation, ie how the sponsor is positioned in the target audience's mind. This will reveal the kinds of specific communications objectives that need to be set.

Sponsorship policy and programme selection

A sponsorship policy helps the programme selection process by defining sponsorship parameters such as the preferred types of sponsorship that fit with the overall *mission statement*, the marketing and communication objectives. Questions to ask include the following. Is there any relevance between sponsor and subject, eg do a chess competition and a computer company share values of intelligence? Is there a consistent *message* or objective behind all the organization's chosen sponsorship programmes? Does the association add value to the company or product? Is the association *internationally acceptable*? Think global, act local (sponsoring bull fighting or camel wrestling is globally unacceptable). Are there certain types or areas of sponsorship that are preferred? It is often felt that it is better to concentrate in certain areas. What is the *ideal time* in terms of seasonality and length of commitment, eg three-year minimum? When should a sponsorship programme be dropped, changed or simply reviewed? Are both *solus* or *shared*/joint sponsorship programmes acceptable? Can *staff involvement* be incorporated? Does the sponsorship lend itself to *leverage* by offering potential for spin-off promotions and publicity? Does it lend itself to sales promotions, etc? Is it *unique*? Is it *protectable* from ambush marketing (see page 463)? What is the *competition* doing? Are 'me-too' sponsorship packages (competition follows with a similar sponsorship programme) preferred to unique (and uncopiable) sponsorship programmes? What kind of *budget* is required? What is defined as *value for money*?

The sponsoree's promise

In the search for funding, sponsorees may promise the world to potential sponsors. The potential sponsor needs to exercise some caution. Here are two points worth considering:

1. Have the contract checked by an expert. In particular, check the exit clause and exit arrangements since *it may be harder to get out of sponsorship than get into it*. For example, it is easy to start supporting a local theatre, but when the sponsor wants to switch into a different type of sponsorship the eventual withdrawal of funds may prompt the local paper to print a headline that might read 'Company X Pulls Plug On Theatre' or 'Company X Leaves Theatre In The Dark'.
2. Can they deliver their promises? Can they provide proof? Have they done it before? Have they any references? Are they financially secure?

Budgets

Budget allocation may in fact determine programme choice rather than the other way around. The formulae for determining the sponsorship budget vary but a rough rule of thumb suggests that the basic sponsorship fee should be at least *doubled* to get maximum leverage from the programme (see point 5 on page 464). This then leaves a budget for supporting marketing activities such as advertising and publicity, and maybe even some direct marketing. It also allocates some money for other spin-off activities. For example, sponsors of the Olympics will tend to milk the sponsorship to the maximum by running sales promotions offering Olympic prizes and donations in addition to simply carrying the 'official Olympic sponsors' logo. Payment can be *in cash* or *in kind*. A sponsor's services or facilities are likely to have a much greater value than cost, eg a newspaper sponsoring a boxing match can offer the fight promoter free advertising space in return for exclusive sponsorship rights. The cost may be minimal if the newspaper is not selling all its advertising space, while the value to the promoter is, of course, much greater.

There are also various government sponsorship grant programmes that contribute significantly towards the cost (see 'Further contacts', page 471).

If the 3Ms (men and women, money and minutes) are the three key resources, then they each need to be built into plans or to be budgeted for. Who is responsible for what, eg the supporting advertising, the spin-off sales promotions, the hospitality tent, the invitations, the publicity, etc? Is it all handled by an agency or controlled and administered by the in-house team? Time can be the greatest constraint to leveraging a sponsorship programme fully, since there may be lots of great ideas for exploiting the opportunities to the full, but each one takes time to plan and ultimately put into action. Some estimates suggest *a minimum of nine months* is needed to develop a proper sponsorship strategy and programme plan.

Sponsorship strategy

The strategy statement briefly explains which types of sponsorship programmes are preferred, why a particular sponsorship programme is selected, how it will be exploited and integrated, and at what cost. To maximize the effect, sponsorship must be *integrated* with other elements of the communications mix, eg advertising, sales promotion, direct mail and public relations. It should also be explained internally and sometimes used internally as part of *psychic income* (see page 285) as a means of improving employee relations.

Tactical plans

Squeeze as many benefits as possible into the programme. Sponsorship does not involve just adding the organization's name to an event, team or situation and waiting to see if awareness takes off overnight. A well-planned sponsorship programme involves attracting media coverage, corporate entertainment, new client recruitment, miscellaneous spin-off promotions and staff motivation schemes. (See 'Tactics', page 47, to (a) help develop a whole communications plan around the sponsorship package or (b) integrate the sponsorship programme into the rest of the marketing communications activities.)

The launch is the easy bit. The real work starts then, as years one, two and three need constant attention to detail. A series of checklists and detailed plans (including contingency plans) have to be developed.

Pilot scheme

In an ideal marketing world all risks are reduced by testing and researching everything. Extra research costs resources, primarily time and money. Sometimes the nature of a sponsorship programme does not lend itself to testing, eg sponsoring the English Football League, but customers can be asked what they would think of it (before signing on the dotted line). Alternatively, a local league can be sponsored to allow management to move up the learning curve. Heinz was reported to have jointly sponsored the 1991 rugby World Cup so that they could learn about how sponsorship worked. The cautious or delayed approach arising from testing can also cause opportunities to be lost, since the competition may snap up the best sponsorship programmes.

Roll-out

This is the exciting side that everyone sees without fully realizing the amount of work that goes on beforehand. Nevertheless, it is deceptively hard work since, even though the sponsors are enjoying entertaining their clients, it is still work. In smaller sponsorship programmes the sponsor has constantly to think on his or her feet while entertaining, as minute problems inevitably crop up from time to time. In larger sponsorship programmes the constant alertness, attention to detail and readiness to react can be delegated to other members of staff (or a consultancy).

Monitor, measure and evaluate

This is where the clearly defined sponsorship objectives make life easy, since results can be compared with predetermined targets. Having measured the result, further analysis as to why a programme was particularly successful or unsuccessful will help future sponsorship programmes. The first three objectives listed on page 457, awareness, image and relations, would normally require some formal market research activity such as a survey. There is, in addition, an interim method of evaluating sponsorship – by the amount of media coverage or name mentions. There are many monitoring companies that provide such services.

25 days' continuous monitoring

In 2000 cricket sponsors Cornhill Insurance received:

280 hours of TV coverage (Channel 4 and Sky)
11,250 banner sightings
450 references in the national press.

Cost: £14 million over three years.
Result: Spontaneous awareness up to 35 per cent.

Although cricket is on TV for long periods, its audience is often quite small. Sponsorship research company AGB divide broadcast time by audience size to give cricket a ranking of 67, less than half that of ice skating. There are other, sometimes simpler, approaches to measuring the effectiveness of sponsorship. For example, Volvo calculated that its $3 million tennis sponsorship generated 1.4 billion impressions (number of mentions/sightings × audience size), worth about $18 million in advertising. It is worth noting that this only measures the amount of media coverage or output. It does not measure the ultimate objectives of, say, increasing awareness, changing attitudes or improving relations with different groups. This is where money may have to be spent on commissioning a piece of research that looks inside, instead of outside, the minds of the target audience.

The other objectives can be relatively easily measured if a system of measurement is set up in the first place, eg everyone is briefed to log or identify the source of any enquiries from customers, agents or distributors. Then again, a common-sense approach may help to identify results, eg new distributors or increased sales emerge, without changing any of the other elements of either the marketing or communications mix (and assuming the competition has not had a strike or a factory fire).

Waffles or lager?

In 1979 Belgium was 'better known for its waffles than its lager'. When TV ads were beyond budget, sponsorship of the Queen's tennis tournament beckoned. TV exposure and tennis's 'aspirational and achievement' image matched Stella's objectives. Stella rose to no 1 in Britain's premium lager sector. Sales increased by 400 per cent.

The Observer, 1 April 1988

Canon got good value for their money when they sponsored the Football League for a limited period only. As Frank Jefkins observed: 'Hardly an office in Britain is without a *Canon* machine. It only took £3 million and three years – peanuts in that sort of business when you think what the sales are valued at.'

AMBUSH MARKETING

Ambush marketers attack official event sponsors by running competing promotions, events and advertisements close to the official sponsors'. This way they create an aura of being an official sponsor without paying the official sponsor fees. For example, Nike managed to 'ruin the 1996 Olympics for the official sponsors by ruthless advertising and by exploiting its star names' (Alison Boshoff). The IOC stepped in next time round by ordering that all poster sites in Athens be bought up and fairly distributed. For the 1998 World Cup, Adidas paid £20 million to be an official sponsor and, among other things, built a football village under the Eiffel Tower, while Nike responded with a site on the outskirts of Paris. Adidas signed up Paul Gascoigne, Paul Ince and David Beckham, as well as sponsoring the kit of nine teams, including Germany, France and Spain, while Nike sponsored six squads, including the favourites, Brazil (which cost £250 million over 10 years). The *Daily Telegraph* reported that 'rumours have it that Nike is willing to spend £20 million to hijack its arch-rivals Adidas during the competition in France'. Adidas planned a series of 'counter-stunts' and intended to 'ambush their ambush by having our own stunts and tricks'. Both companies supposedly had £20 million to spend on the five months up to and including the competition (on top of Adidas's sponsorship fee).

There is nothing really new in this as ambush marketing has been around almost as long as sponsorship itself. Measurement of the 1991 rugby World Cup broadcast sponsorship demonstrated its ability to influence consumers and override the main event sponsors. Spontaneous brand awareness of Sony rose among rugby World Cup watchers by 8 points to 61 per cent (between September and November). According to ITVA, despite the recession, 'the company went on to record sales in December… Sony was also invariably the first name mentioned as sponsor of the rugby World Cup and overwhelmingly seen as the main sponsor. However, Sony was not a sponsor of the event itself; it sponsored only the ITV coverage.'

Shani and Sandler's 1989 study of ambush marketing revealed that it works. For example, Wendy's got what it wanted for about $20 million or so less than McDonald's spend. McDonald's didn't leverage its sponsorship well at all, advertising its super-value meals and Double Big Macs instead of its Olympic sponsorship.

Unpredictable sponsorship results from an ambushed knee

When US skater Tonya Harding's associates hammered her main competitor Nancy Kerrigan's knee, they performed a dastardly deed – which happened to boost Kerrigan's sponsors, Campbell Soup's, fortunes for the first time in a decade. Campbell was also a sponsor of the US Figure Skating Association. After the incident Campbell placed ads everywhere, and when Kerrigan recovered and came back to win silver Campbell's sales skyrocketed. Which just goes to show that no amount of planning could have produced the publicity it received from the wounded-knee incident and the sales bump that accompanied it. Campbell was even mistakenly perceived by the general public as a full-fledged Olympic sponsor in 1994, even though it wasn't.

Howard Schlossberg

MISCELLANEOUS TIPS

1. Choose sponsorship programmes carefully, separate the initial excitement from the numerical analysis.
2. Think global but act local (today's satellite communications may highlight a sponsorship programme that is acceptable overseas but unacceptable at home and vice versa).
3. Consider exit strategies (how difficult or easy is it to switch into another programme 1, 3 or 10 years down the road?).
4. Remember, it is not like advertising. There is no total control over the message. Have contingency plans in case things go wrong.
5. Budgets should be developed to allow for maximum exploitation through other communications tools. Some organizations double the budget to allow for leverage opportunities; other companies, such as Coca-Cola, allow 16 times the sponsor fee to generate maximum leverage.
6. Check for any government subsidies. For example, Business Sponsorship of the Arts shares costs 50:50 for first-time sponsors and 33:66 thereafter.
7. Keep employees informed. Sometimes getting them involved increases the leverage. For example, Marks & Spencer sponsor projects that attract staff involvement.
8. Run a small pilot scheme to iron out any teething problems.
9. Beware of ambush marketing.

> *No war during World Cup*
>
> There will never be another war while the World Cup is being played because there would be no media coverage.
>
> Jeff Bliss, World Cup USA Licensing Executive

CASE STUDY 15.1

TSB's Roy of the Rovers

This case study demonstrates how careful audience and media research identified a previously untapped sponsorship opportunity that was integrated with PR to gain access to a traditionally difficult target market.

Situation

TSB research identified sport, particularly athletics and soccer, as a key active interest of its young customers. Success in sport demands discipline and control. Young people, research demonstrates, demand control of their money. TSB's youth products offer a mechanism to help control spending (eg an instantly updated account that prevents young customers from the nightmare of an unwanted and unauthorized overdraft). The overall marketing strategy for the youth market was therefore founded on sport and financial control, and linked TSB as the bank for, and in touch with, young people. In an Olympic year the bank became a £5.2 million sponsor of major British athletics meetings.

Account opening incentives, supported by TV and press coverage, focused on money-off anything from Nike trainers to Head tennis rackets at Olympus Stores. The media relations campaign focused on money control issues like 'buying a banger', 'getting a holiday job' or 'setting up a home of your own'.

The athletics opportunity had been seized but the soccer opportunity presented a somewhat more difficult challenge. The glamour of football is sometimes tainted by uncontrollable risks such as injuries, foul play, sendings off, disciplinary committees, board-room coups, protesting fans, rotten results, on- and off-the-pitch violence, and, of course, the weather. What marketing directors, with top brands in their custody, want logos in full colour in a national paper if it is on the shirt of a player just sent off for a vicious and cynical foul, or if it is being worn by a mass of rioting fans?

Real sponsorship of a fictitious team

Having said all that, football does attract audiences – intense, loyal, largely young, male, with leisure time and money to spend and save. Boys aged 7–12 are all targets for the bank's 'FirstSave' account. Banks want to recruit young customers since they normally stay with the same bank for life and because at least 50 per cent of these accounts are opened before the age of 16. Whether this is lethargy or loyalty is unclear, but it does reinforce lifetime value.

The dilemma

TSB faced the soccer dilemma at the launch of the Premier League's first season. The bank, a big institution, was ready to act quickly and it set aside a budget to take advantage of any creative media opportunities.

Objective

To reinforce the link between TSB and one of its youth markets.

Strategy

The strategy was sponsorship of Melchester Rovers supported by a media relations campaign. Melchester Rovers are the 'perfect' soccer team that pulls 125,000 schoolboy spectators week in, week out regardless of the weather. Its captain is not only best mates with ex-England captain Gary Lineker, but even more saintly. There are no riots, no drink driving, no smashed-up hotel bars, no spurned love children. The results can even be found out months ahead, and they usually win. The star player of this model team, Roy of the Rovers, and his squad are, of course, mythical. Roy has been Britain's best-loved footballer since his debut, in 1954, on the pages of the boys' comic *Tiger* (since 1976 he has had a comic named after him).

Tactics

In the comic, TSB logos feature on Melchester's red and yellow strip and on perimeter boards around the ground. Storylines around banking and young people are written into the comic. Competitions give away Olympus kit. There are covermounts (sales promotions attached to the comic itself).

Action

The media relations campaign involved a clear strategy.

- The race to sign up a legendary team was leaked to and covered by national TV and newspapers on a quiet Monday in the dog-days of August.

- Roy and his agent, Dave Hunt (in reality his editor), were 'snatched' leaving secret talks at the Tower Hotel.
- The leak served two purposes: it put the comic back on the map with the aim of widening the audience for TSB's sponsorship, and it ensured a packed turnout for the press conference/launch.
- The press conference to announce the sponsorship was held at the Tower Hotel and was hosted by sports broadcaster Danny Baker.

Control

The sponsorship programme launch gained media coverage on national and local TV, and in the national and regional press. New account openings jumped ahead of target. Some of the phenomenal press coverage generated can be seen in the montage on page 423 in Chapter 14, 'Publicity and public relations'.

Men and women

PR consultancy the Quentin Bell Organization (QBO) worked closely and intensively with the TSB marketing team.

Money

£20,000 sponsorship fee with an additional £12,000 media relations budget.

Minutes

TSB and QBO moved at breakneck speed from concept to launch within three weeks.

APPENDIX 15.1

ITC sponsorship guidelines

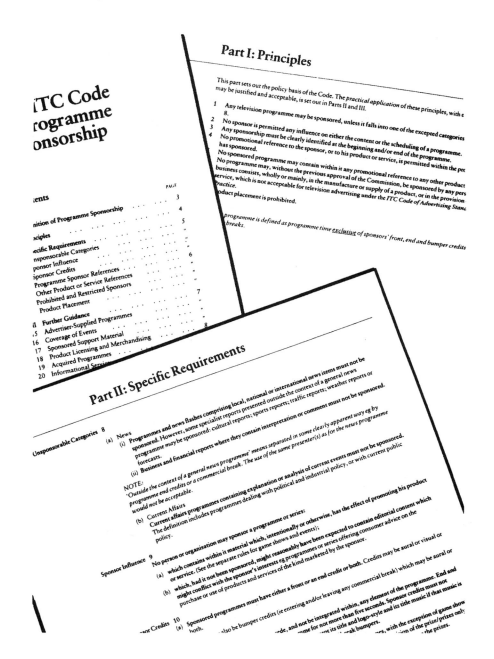

ITC Code Programme Sponsorship

Contents

Part I: Principles

This part sets out the policy basis of the Code. The *practical application of these principles*, with e may be justified and acceptable, is set out in Parts II and III.

1 Any television programme may be sponsored, unless it falls into one of the excepted categories 8.

2 No sponsor is permitted any influence on either the content or the scheduling of a programme.

3 Any sponsorship must be clearly identified at the beginning and/or end of the programme.

4 No promotional reference to the sponsor, or to his product or service, is permitted within the pro has sponsored.

No sponsored programme may contain within it any promotional reference to any other product

No programme may, without the previous approval of the Commission, be sponsored by any pers business consists, wholly or mainly, in the manufacture or supply of a product, or in the provision service, which is not acceptable for television advertising under the ITC Code of Advertising Stand practice.

Product placement is prohibited.

programme is defined as programme time *exclusive* of sponsors' front, end and bumper credits breaks.

Part II: Specific Requirements

Unsponsorable Categories 8

(a) News

(i) Programmes and news flashes comprising local, national or international news items must not be sponsored. However, some specialist reports presented outside the context of a general news programme may be sponsored: cultural reports; sports reports; traffic reports; weather reports or forecasts.

(ii) Business and financial reports where they contain interpretation or comment must not be sponsored.

NOTE:
'Outside the context of a general news programme' means separated in some clearly apparent way eg by programme end credits or a commercial break. The use of the same presenter(s) as for the news programme would not be acceptable.

(b) Current Affairs
Current affairs programmes containing explanation or analysis of current events must not be sponsored. The definition includes programmes dealing with political and industrial policy, or with current public policy.

Sponsor Influence 9 No person or organisation may sponsor a programme or series:

(a) which contains within it material which, intentionally or otherwise, has the effect of promoting his product or service. (See the separate rules for game shows and events);

(b) which, had it not been sponsored, might reasonably have been expected to contain editorial content which might conflict with the sponsor's interests eg programmes or series offering consumer advice on the purchase or use of products and services of the kind marketed by the sponsor.

Sponsor Credits 10 (a) Sponsored programmes must have either a front or an end credit or both. Credits may be aural or visual or both. ...also be bumper credits (ie entering and/or leaving any commercial break) which may be aural or ...de, and not be integrated within, any element of the programme. End and ...me for not more than five seconds. Sponsor credits must not ...t its title and logo-style and its title music if that music is ...ak bumpers, ...res, with the exception of game show ...tion of the prize/prizes only ...the prizes.

APPENDIX 15.2

Sponsorship gone wrong?

Legislative inquiry into Nike's 10-year kit sponsorship deal with Brazilian football team. (Nike negotiated a $400 million, 10-year kit sponsorship deal with the Brazilian Football Federation.)

> A sense that Nike had too much control over the country's affairs was magnified by original provisions in the contract allowing the company to promote 50 Nike branded Brazil friendly matches involving eight first team players... With World Cup qualifiers and other friendlies to organise, it became clear that the original number of Nike friendlies was too large. In November 1999 Brazil found itself double booked to play two matches. This [sic] led to a second-string Brazil team playing in Australia, while most of the country's top stars featured in a game against Spain. Consequently last April Nike reduced the contractual number of games it would promote to two a year.
>
> Also under the initial contract – since changed – legal disputes with the CBF were to be settled outside of Brazil. 'The CFB transferred part of its autonomy as a public entity to Nike,' said Aldo Rebelo (head of the 25 member committee of Brazil's Lower House of Congress investigating Nike's sponsorship deal.

R Collit and M Garrahan (2001) Nike finds Brazil deal a bad fit, *Financial Times*, 12 January, p 19

Key points from Chapter 15:

1. Almost any target audience can be reached through sponsorship.
2. Almost anything can be sponsored.
3. Sponsorship can provide a cost-effective marketing communications tool, satisfying a range of different objectives.
4. Maximum leverage is generated through integrating sponsorship with other communications tools.

FURTHER READING

Boshoff, A (1997) World Cup's battle of the boots, *Daily Telegraph*, 4 December

Giles, C (1991) *Business Sponsorship*, Butterworth-Heinemann, Oxford

Head, V (1981) *Sponsorship: The Newest Marketing Skill*, Woodhead-Faulkner, Cambridge

Jefkins, F (1990) *Modern Marketing Communications*, Blackie & Sons, London

Klein, N (2000) *No Logo*, Flamingo, London

Mitchell, A (1997) Sponsorship works, *Marketing Business*, September

Shani, D and Sandler, D (1989) Olympic sponsorship versus ambush marketing, *Journal of Advertising Research*, Aug/Sep

Schlossberg, H (1996) *Sports Marketing*, Blackwell, Oxford

Shank, M (1999) *Sports Marketing: A Strategic Perspective*, Prentice-Hall, Englewood Cliffs, NJ

Turner, S (1987) *Practical Sponsorship*, Kogan Page, London

FURTHER CONTACTS

Association for Business Sponsorship of the Arts (ABSA), Nutmeg House, 60 Gainsford Street, London SE1 2NY (tel: 020 7378 8143; Web site: www.aandb.org.uk)

Business in the Community, 137 Shepherdess Walk, London N1 7RQ (tel: 0870 600 2482; Web sites: www.bitc.org.uk, www.business-impact.org)

European Sponsorship Consultants Association (ESCA), Marash House, 2–5 Brook Street, Tring, Herts HP23 5ED (tel: 01442 826826; Web site: www.sponsorship.org)

The Independent Television Commission (ITC), 3 Foley Street, London W1W 7TL (tel: 020 7255 3000; Web site: www.itc.org.uk)

The Institute of Sports Sponsorship, 4th Floor, Warwick House, 25–27 Buckingham Palace Road, London SW1W 0PP (tel: 020 7233 7747; Web sites: www.sportsmatch.co.uk, www.sports-sponsorship.co.uk)

Sponsorship News, CharterHouse Business Publications, PO Box 66, Wokingham, Berkshire RG41 5FS (tel: 0118 977 2770; Web site: www.sponsorshipnews.com)

16

Exhibitions

INTRODUCTION

Imagine bringing a whole market together, under one roof, for a few days. An exciting idea? An explosive concept? It happens all the time. Exhibitions are unique in that they are the only medium that brings the whole market together – buyers, sellers and competitors – all under one roof for a few days. Products and services can be seen, demonstrated or tested, and face-to-face contact can be made with a large number of relevant decision makers in a short period of time. Relationships can be strengthened and opportunities seized if planned carefully.

British companies spend £1.7 billion a year on exhibitions (Exhibitions Venues Association, 2000). European organizations appear to place greater emphasis on exhibitions, since they spend a larger proportion of their advertising budget on them – 30 per cent compared to UK organizations' 9 per cent (National Association of Exhibition Hall Owners). In some UK business-to-business markets and industrial markets exhibitions can take up to 40 per cent of the marketing budget (Exhibition Industry Federation). Over 10 million visitors attended more than 800 major exhibitions in the UK alone in 1999 (Exhibitors Venues Association, 2000).

Thinking outside the box also opens up the possibility of creating your own exhibition, road show, conference, workshop, seminar or event, or even your own virtual exhibition (see page 498). This chapter, however, focuses on real exhibitions per se, although an event such as running a successful conference is covered in the case study on page 489 and virtual exhibitions are costed and discussed on page 500).

Exhibitions bring a whole market together under one roof

EXHIBITION PLANNING

Exhibitions offer an array of opportunities, problems and challenges to the keen marketing manager. They can be leveraged to the maximum effect by integrating them with other communications tools and developing a longer-term perspective incorporating an overall exhibition strategy. Detailed exhibition planning skills require the manager to:

1. prioritize exhibition objectives;
2. develop an exhibition strategy;

3. select the right shows;
4. agree a design strategy;
5. determine pre-show promotional tactics;
6. train exhibition staff;
7. finalize exhibition operational (daily action) plan;
8. ensure follow-up;
9. evaluate – post-show.

Exhibitions are a powerful marketing communications tool but they require detailed planning and coordination of resources. Much research and analysis has to be conducted, and many decisions have to be made.

Exhibitions require detailed advance planning

Prioritize exhibition objectives

If you don't know where you are going, how do you know when you have arrived? How do you know if it is a good show or a waste of time and money? How do you know if you have had a good day or a bad day? How can you achieve if you don't know what you are trying to achieve? Clearly defined objectives are required to focus the effort. Typically, enquiries and orders can be easily quantified and broken into daily (or even hourly) objectives. A sweepstake among staff (guessing the numbers of enquiries and orders) can help to focus everyone's attention. Although exhibitions are hard work, they are dynamic in the variety of objectives they provide:

- Sell – generate sales and enquiries from new and existing customers, agents and distributors.
- Launch new products.
- Maintain a presence – in the market.
- Press coverage – internal (newsletter) and external PR opportunity (see IBM exhibition press coverage in post-show evaluation on page 484).
- Reinforce relationships – with customers, distributors and agents through hospitality and introductions to senior managers and directors.
- Support local distributors / agents – by exhibiting.
- Market research – customers, non-customers and distributors.
- Test new ideas – product testing and informal creative discussions.
- Competitor analysis and intelligence gathering.
- Staff motivation – some exhibitions can be the focal point of the year. They allow staff to come to the show (exhibition) and feel a certain amount of pride in their organization.
- Meet new staff or potential recruits.

Develop an exhibition strategy

Ideally, exhibitions should not be used as a one-off, ad hoc activity. They can be used more effectively when (a) they are viewed as a possible series of exhibitions; (b) they are integrated carefully with other communications tools; (c) they are selected and planned well in advance; and (d) their effectiveness is constantly measured. An exhibition strategy summarizes the frequency and types of show selected (eg national, international, real or virtual – see page 477). Perhaps different segments of the market are served by different exhibitions, different product / service sectors, different geographical regions, different buying cycles (eg Christmas products have exhibitions in January for the coming Christmas season). Considering the bigger picture requires a knowledge of what exhibitions are available, suitable and affordable. This means continually collecting exhibition brochures and keeping them safely in an exhibition file for regular review.

An exhibition strategy can also give guidance about the kind of integrated marketing support provided and the total level of spending. Remember the cost of hiring space at an exhibition is often only a small proportion of the total exhibition costs (between 20 and 25 per cent, see p 485).

Select the right shows

As with advertising or any marketing activity, exhibitions need careful targeting. There is an increasing number of exhibitions available, usually more than an organization can attend.

Some are better than others. All of them have sales staff dedicated to promoting and selling their exhibition space. The exhibitor must choose carefully. The skill in selection is somewhat similar to that of the media planner (who must choose which media and specific media vehicles, except that media planners have access to considerably more audited information (see Media selection, in Chapter 7). There are various listings giving a diary of exhibitions and events for up to two years in advance.

The big investment in exhibitions requires careful selection of specific exhibitions

Selection checklist

1. Type of exhibition:
    local, national or international; vertical (tight focus of interest for buyers or sellers) or horizontal (wide range of interest for buyers or sellers); general public; trade events; private events; symposia or conferences, where a limited amount of exhibiting facilities are available.
2. Target audience:
    type and number of visitors; audited figures should be made available, eg ABC (Audit Bureau Circulation) figures are approved by the Association of Exhibition Organisers (the use of ABC figures is also a compulsory requirement of membership of the AEO, largely because ABC's figures are reproducible again for checking and testing).
3. Timing:
    does it meet buyers' purchasing patterns and can the organization prepare for it in time? For example, foreign shows may need to be planned 18 months in advance.

4. Facilities:

any limitations or constraints; how the organizers intend to promote the event; supporting contact events, eg dinners, award ceremonies, seminars, breakfast receptions, etc.

5. Costs:

comparing 'cost of space' and 'size of audience' ratios between different exhibitions. The space cost is useful for comparison but it represents only a small proportion of the total cost of exhibiting. Various estimates suggest that the cost of space rental is only 25 per cent of the total cost of exhibiting. The cost of the stand design is generally excluded if the exhibitor already owns a mobile stand unit, but miscellaneous items (see 'Daily checklist' on page 482) rapidly escalate costs. See the budgeting checklist on page 501.

6. Previous success:

How long has the show been running? Has it been a success previously? Is it enjoying year-on-year growth? Are there any customer (exhibitor) testimonials or references available?

7. Endorsements:

What official bodies are supporting it? There are independent surveys that list visitor numbers, visitor quality, sales enquiries and a summary of exhibitors' results (see 'Evaluate – post-show', page 484).

Agree a design strategy

The stand design is a key factor in the overall exhibition strategy. It should present the right corporate image (see Chapters 14 and 21), announce the product or service, visualize benefits (arising from the product or service), attract interest and look aesthetically pleasing while providing for other functions such as display, demonstration, discussion, hospitality and storage (of spare samples, literature, coats, etc). Identifying measurable exhibition success criteria such as sales or orders, number of enquiries, cost per enquiry, cost per order, qualified contact names for a database, visitors' recall or level of awareness of the particular organization's stand, key messages intended by the stand, etc, all help to guide the overall design of the exhibition stand.

A visitor may have less than five seconds to scan and decide whether to enter a particular stand instead of the many others competing for that same visitor's attention. Buyers have only a limited amount of time to visit a limited number of stands (US Center for Exhibition Research suggests that the average visitor attending a show barely calls on 13 stands, regardless of the size of the exhibition). Buyers have to choose quickly whether to enter or not. Many exhibitions provide a computer printout of the exhibitors that fall into a particular category of suppliers of interest to a particular visitor. The printout usually includes a map identifying the location of the specific organizations listed in the category.

An exhibition stand has to attract interest, look aesthetically pleasing as well as fulfil a range of other functions

This means that a buyer can pause and decide what route he or she will take, and which stands to visit, before entering the main exhibition hall. Despite a preplanned schedule of visits, an excellent stand design or promotional stunt can still attract an unplanned visit from a busy buyer. A stunt can also attract time-wasting, stand-congesting, non-target market visitors. Some stunts have been found to deter senior decision makers who feel that stunts are aimed at lower-level visitors.

The 'three-second' test

When you next visit an exhibition look around you and see how many (if any) stands clearly tell you what they offer. How many exhibition stands actually explain what business the exhibitor is in? Do any of them explain benefits? How many stand designs actually help you within three to five seconds before you pass by?

It is surprising to observe the number of organizations that promote their name first and foremost, perhaps followed by a product name and somewhere, almost hidden, the product and product features are displayed. Product benefits (what buyers really seek) cannot be seen easily. Most buyers have to make the psychological leap and commit themselves by walking on to a stand to engage in discussion that may eventually reveal the hidden product benefits. Larger organizations may feel that they have too many products to highlight any one individually, or that their name is associated with the product area so strongly that all visitors (including those from overseas?) actually look for the company name since they already know the exhibitor's business. Perhaps some exhibitors do not want to reveal their benefits to the competition too readily? Perhaps others simply don't ask their stand designers to consider this issue?

The design should be consistent with the organization's corporate identity guidelines (the design manual specifies the logo style, typefaces, primary and secondary colours). The stand design should attract visitors and facilitate a simple selling sequence of attracting a visitor, providing a comfortable space and facilities to demonstrate products, and fostering an environment for detailed discussion and negotiations if appropriate.

The design brief for an exhibition stand can use the basic SOSTAC® + 3Ms discussed in Chapters 2 and 6. Essentially the designer needs to know: Who is the target audience? In what kinds of exhibitions might the stand appear, their locations and preferred stand locations (within the exhibition), stand size and function (display, demonstration, hospitality area, access and service facilities required), and is the stand to be reusable. Information on competitors and their stands is also useful. Additional information such as the design manual and the dimensions of any display items is also important. The success criteria must be listed and objectives prioritized, eg presenting an image, attracting new business, meeting old customers, launching a new product, etc. The designer also needs to know the overall exhibition strategy discussed earlier. Tactical information is sometimes included. This includes any promotional ideas, specific numbers of staff and visitors on the stand at any one time, whether any promotional off-stand activities will be attracting visitors on to the stand, whether the stand will be used for photo opportunities, and what kind of electronic gadgetry (videos, interactive compact discs), products and sales literature need to be displayed. The designer also needs to know about the 3Ms, the three key resources of men and women, money (budget) and minutes (time).

The whole exhibition design should focus on key, measurable objectives (are all the elements linked up to and consistent with the overall exhibition strategy, etc?). Sound, sight, space and even smell can be used creatively by a designer (there are, however, likely to be some constraints imposed by the organizers). Good designers exploit both two-dimensional design (eg graphics) and three-dimensional design (eg the use of space).

Determine pre-show promotional tactics

To maximize effectiveness, exhibitors do not depend on stand design alone to attract visitors. Careful pre-show promotions can ensure a steady flow of visitors on to a stand. Direct mail, linked with an incentive or sales promotion, free tickets, inserts, advertising, publicity, etc, all basically attempt to get visitors to decide to visit a particular stand before they arrive at the exhibition in the first place. Given that the average visitor only visits 13 stands, it is important to get on to the appropriate target visitor's 'must visit' list. Pre-show marketing helps to identify who to expect and who to chase up. It also provides a fresh opportunity to talk to customers and prospects on the back of the urgency and excitement created by the show.

Given that exhibiting is a resource-consuming activity, pre-show activity aims to maximize the effectiveness of the investment. Some types of show, such as conferences and seminars, are almost totally dependent on pre-event activity, as attendees will not walk in off the street (see the Hewlett-Packard case study on page 493). Advertising and editorial opportunities range from the usual trade, professional and domestic press, local and regional media, transport (taxis, trains, buses, stations to the exhibition) through to the exhibition catalogue itself. Sponsorship of guides, maps, promotions, teaser promotions, free gifts and competitions can all be offered to the target visitor through advertising, editorial, inserts, mailings and even telemarketing. Interestingly, over 30 per cent of UK exhibitors in 1999 used e-marketing (compared to virtually none in 1997) and there were corresponding falls in the use of trade press advertising, sales representatives and direct mail (Exhibitors Venues Association, 2000). Good exhibition planning can integrate with other communication activities at an early stage. This means that the costs of sales promotions and incentives can be reduced significantly by increasing the organization's buying power when sourcing many different sales promotion gifts simultaneously. Delivery and invoicing can also be staggered or delayed so that cash-flow bottlenecks do not occur. It might also be possible to run a joint promotion with a non-competing exhibitor so that your product or service (or even just the incentive) is combined with someone else's to promote both sites as 'must see' sites.

In summary, pre-show promotional activity can involve:

- direct mail invitations (c/w incentive?)
- e-marketing;
- telesales key customers/prospects;
- press activities;
- sales force briefing (to invite their customers);
- company calendars, diaries, etc, can include dates of key exhibitions;
- sponsored activities;
- perimeter advertising (around the venue);
- press advertising (trade magazines);
- joint promotions.

Train exhibition staff

Having done all the hard pre-show work, created a stunning stand, hyped up the promotion and generated a good flow of traffic on to the stand, what a shame it is to lose business through staff who don't know exactly how to deal with people. Manning an exhibition stand is hard work. The day becomes even longer when staff have no goals, no targets and no exhibition training. The team needs to be briefed about why the organization is exhibiting (including specific objectives broken down into daily objectives). Exhibition training helps staff to know: how to physically stand (importance of body language); approach a visitor (never with a closed question such as 'May I help you?' – try open-ended questions like 'What caught your eye?'); what kind of information should be gleaned from visitors (how to qualify a prospect – see Appendix 16.4); when a senior manager should be called over; how to demonstrate (product knowledge and skills); how to close a sale; and how to present records. It is possible to practise before the show starts each day (or during quiet moments).

Finalize exhibition action plan

Everything, from staffing to samples and sales promotions, has to be meticulously planned. Never underestimate the importance of attention to detail. Even contingencies should be allowed for. Exhibitions are hard work. A staffing roster schedules staff so that they can have a break and a chance to look around the exhibition (and report back on their observations). More importantly, the roster ensures that the stand is never undermanned or overmanned with inexperienced staff. How many visitors are expected? How many staff will be required? How many junior and senior staff? Who mans the stand and when? Comfortable shoes, regular breaks and solid rest between exhibition days are also essential. Individual performance on the stand can also be measured against preset criteria (number and quality of enquiries, etc).

Sod's law – 'what can go wrong will go wrong' – runs rampant in exhibitions. Contingency planning reduces risks, but inevitably something unforeseen still occurs. The author has had two such experiences, both of which happened at international shows: the first in Birmingham, where a new electrical product set itself on fire while being exhibited; the second in New York, where the freight company lost all the samples and display units. Sam Black's *Exhibitions and Conferences* (1989) highlights a stunning array of errors in exhibitions, ranging from a stand that was built upside down (because the architect read the plans upside down) to neighbouring stands encroaching on each other's area (sometimes by accident).

Daily checklist

The checklist opposite needs to be gone through at the end of each day so that everything is in place for the next day.

Small budget – big creativity

NCH Action For Children Charity had to break through the clutter with a small 2 × 2 metre stand. Their stunning backlit graphic of children's faces, supporting the 'All Children Dream' theme did the trick.

The stand staff were fully trained in exhibition techniques and fully briefed to communicate key messages and collect key information. They fulfilled their 'key contacts hit list', snapped publicity photos with visiting MPs and shone out from the heaving masses.

Ensure follow-up strategy

The exhibition is not an end in itself, although by the end of the show the exhausted staff probably feel like it is. Careful follow-up work must start almost immediately. This is where the organization can earn its return from the exhibition. Leads, enquiries, quotations, sales and after-sales discussions need to be followed up in a professional manner. This requires a follow-up meeting where all the staff go through the cards they collected, the people they talked to and the projects or jobs that were discussed. This prevents the

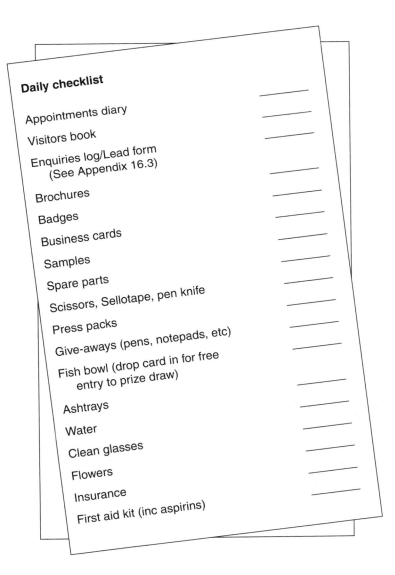

Daily checklist

Appointments diary

Visitors book

Enquiries log/Lead form
(See Appendix 16.3)

Brochures

Badges

Business cards

Samples

Spare parts

Scissors, Sellotape, pen knife

Press packs

Give-aways (pens, notepads, etc)

Fish bowl (drop card in for free
entry to prize draw)

Ashtrays

Water

Clean glasses

Flowers

Insurance

First aid kit (inc aspirins)

duplication, contradiction and conflict that can arise where two people from the same prospect organization have asked two different members of staff for a quotation for the same job. Or two different enquiries have emerged for the same job from two different prospects. Worse still are unfulfilled enquiries. How many times have you left an enquiry with an exhibitor only never to hear from them again? Lack of post-show follow-up makes all the previous exhibition efforts a waste of time.

The manager can determine who follows up what, with a report-back meeting date set to see what sales are actually generated. More detailed evaluation of the true exhibition results can be carried out so that future efforts are improved. It is worth formalizing the evaluation process so that the trend, individual performance, and competitor performance can all be measured.

Eighty per cent make the same old mistakes

Every four or five years 80 per cent of companies exhibiting make the same old mistakes, because a new man has been appointed.

Harry McDermott, Exhibition Surveys

Evaluate – post-show

Post-show evaluation measures performance against the preset objectives. It also examines whether the objectives were realistic, whether the show was the right show, and what was good and what was bad about the organization's performance. A competitor's performance can also be evaluated to a certain degree. How can the performance be improved? Should the exhibition be run again next year? Was it value for money?

Some post-show questions

1. What percentage of the potential number of visitors to the whole exhibition (that fit the target market profile) visited our stand?
2. What percentage stopped but did not visit our stand?
3. What percentage saw but did not stop at our stand?
4. How many leads/enquiries were created?
5. What was the cost per contact/visitor?
6. What percentage of contacts/visitors plan to buy the product or service?

7. What was the cost per 'serious' visitor?
8. What was the cost per order?
9. How effective was each staff member's performance? (According to Harry McDermott of Exhibition Surveys, 'Stand staff should indoctrinate every visitor they meet on a stand. When those visitors think of the types of product shown they should think of the exhibitor. Research can get visitors to rate individual staff because the visitors' comments can be linked back to the stand record of contacts.')
10. Did we overspend or underspend (too large or too small a stand / too many or too few staff)?

Exhibition value analysis

Exhibition value analysis is a type of survey that includes both a multi-client survey and a confidential private survey so that comparisons can be made between the client company and its competitors' performance. The survey covers visitor potential, the percentage that saw, stopped or visited a particular stand, visitors' perceptions, intentions to buy, and the stand's strengths and weaknesses based on a sample of known visitors to it (supplied by the company). See Appendices 16.5 and 16.6 at the end of this chapter. Some research findings suggest that companies do not attend trade exhibitions to sell, but rather to build corporate and brand awareness.

Costs

Exhibition costs need to be looked at carefully. Various sources suggest that the cost of hiring the exhibition space represents as little as one-fifth of the total costs of exhibiting. This obviously depends on whether the cost of the stand design is included, whether there is much integrated promotional activity and whether the opportunity cost of taking members of the sales team 'off the road' are included. The most important thing is to be consistent, so that year-on-year comparisons can be made. Cost per enquiry, cost per order, percentage of sales, return on investment (ROI) and experimental non-attendance are now considered. Note that in the ROI calculation costs are treated as an investment (as opposed to an expenditure), which, technically speaking, is not correct.

Cost per enquiry

Cost per enquiry averages at £20 and £30 for UK and overseas exhibitions respectively (Exhibition Industry Federation, 2000). However, the bottom line for many organizations is still 'How much business did it generate?'

$$\frac{\text{Total exhibition costs}}{\text{Number of serious enquiries}} = \text{Cost per enquiry}$$

Cost per order

Total exhibition costs can be divided by the number of orders taken to find the cost per order. There are some difficulties here, however. First, there is the timescale (some orders instigated by contact at a trade show/exhibition can take several months or longer to be finally confirmed). Second, the regular orders (which would have been brought in by the normal salesforce visits anyway) should, ideally, be separated from those incremental orders generated solely by attending the show. Third, there is a school of thought that suggests that exhibitions do not generate sales; they only allow the exhibitor to meet a useful target market, but whether they buy depends on a number of factors totally divorced from the show (eg the product, competitors' products, prices). An average of averages shows a cost per order in UK and overseas exhibitions of £70 and £113 respectively (EIF, 2000). The UK range appears to be anywhere from £60 (tourism), £215 (engineering) to £323 (marketing services). This, of course, ignores both the size of the orders and their profitability. The size of the orders could be expressed as a percentage figure in the same way as a marketing communications budget is sometimes expressed, ie marketing expenses as a percentage of sales. In this case, exhibition costs as a percentage of sales generated can be calculated as:

$$\frac{\text{Total exhibition costs}}{\text{Number of orders}} = \text{Cost per order}$$

Percentage of sales

As we have said, the difficulty here lies in isolating the sales generated exclusively through the exhibition, ie ignoring sales that would have been taken by the salesforce regardless of the exhibition. Nevertheless, the cost of taking the same number of enquiries or sales by routine sales visits should be compared to the costs of enquiries or sales taken during the exhibition.

Return on investment (ROI)

The long-term profitability of the sales is probably the most important of all the criteria. This is difficult to calculate because the lifetime value of a customer (see Chapter 13) is often difficult to calculate, particularly in industrial markets. However, the short-term ROI can be calculated by dividing the profit or contribution made from the orders by the total cost of the exhibition.

For example, if the orders taken during a show amounted to £200,000 and the total cost of or investment in the exhibition was £20,000, the calculation would be as follows:

Sales	£200,000
Less cost of sales (say 50%)	£100,000
Contribution =	£100,000
Less cost/investment in the exhibition	£20,000
Return or profit on the investment	£80,000

This can then be expressed in percentage terms:

$$= \quad \frac{£80,000}{£20,000} \quad = \quad 400 \text{ per cent}$$

The real ROI should in fact only be calculated from additional or new sales that were generated by the exhibition. Say it only generated five new customers, who, in total, bought £50,000 worth. The real ROI (on new business) would be 25 per cent. The word investment is a bit misleading, since if the exhibition stand cannot be used again it is not an investment but an expense. If the exhibition only produced one new customer, who bought £10,000 worth, then the ROI would be negative.

Press coverage

One simple gauge is to collect the press clippings from the show. How important publicity and press coverage are as exhibition objectives determines how important is this criterion. See more on evaluating press clippings on page 429.

Good pre-show planning helps generate publicity

Experimental non-attendance

Some organizations decide to stop exhibiting and use the opportunity to measure the impact of non-attendance on their sales and on their competitors' exhibition results.

The many other functions exhibitions provide are not included in the costs or revenues used in the previous calculations. Other, non-selling exhibition activities such as maintaining a presence, projecting an image, entertaining customers, marketing research, competitor analysis and product testing all, in a sense, save costs that would have been incurred if they were commissioned outside the exhibition. Arguably these 'saved costs' could be subtracted from the other costs in these calculations. Real costs can certainly be saved by careful coordination throughout the whole exhibition planning cycle (see pages 474–82).

TWELVE REASONS FOR POOR PERFORMANCE

Back in 1990 James Dudley highlighted research findings indicating the 12 main reasons for poor performance. How much has changed?

1. Inadequate statements of purpose and objectives – nobody quite knows what they are supposed to do.
2. Poor-quality visitors.
3. Bad location of the stand.
4. Ineffective quality and design of the stand.
5. Undistinguished performance of personnel running the stand, because of poor selection, training, motivation or management.
6. Lack of follow-up of leads and enquiries.
7. Ignoring the competition and letting them steal your prospective visitors.
8. Poor recognition of company by buyers.
9. Poor corporate identity, leading to low recall of your stand by visitors.
10. Breakdown in organization and control, leading to last-minute panics such as an unfinished stand on the opening day of the show or late arrival of literature, giveaways and so on.
11. Inadequate arrangements made for staff working on the stand, such as locating their accommodation too far from the event, failing to obtain car park permits or not organizing meal vouchers.
12. Inadequate control of costs and budgets, leading to over-expenditure and consequently a poor return on investment.

CASE STUDY 16.1

Sedgwick at RIMS Monte Carlo

This case study demonstrates the kind of detailed and integrated planning required to run a successful exhibition.

Situation

With 60 European offices Sedgwick is the largest European-based insurance broker and risk-management consultancy (and ranked third in the world). Although Sedgwick is well respected, the similarity of competitor products and services makes professionalism, quality and expertise vital in adding value to the 'invisible' service. The credibility of the whole company is largely dependent on the credibility of the sales and support staff. Exhibitions literally provide a platform for staff visibility and customer contact. RIMS (Risk and Insurance Management Society) Monte Carlo is a focal point for the European risk and insurance market. It takes place every two years and comprises a three-day, high-level conference and exhibition that attracts all major companies and buyers in the sector. It is therefore essential for Sedgwick to be there.

Target audience

The target audience is risk managers of medium-sized to large companies and managers responsible for buying insurance (finance directors, company secretaries and heads of administration) across Europe.

Objectives

Marketing objectives:

- To introduce the new European client service network.
- To introduce several pan-European products (including the multilingual service and the eastern Europe network).
- To create an opportunity for cross-selling (new products to existing customers).
- To attract 100 visitors to the stand per day.

Communications objectives:

- To reinforce Sedgwick's position as the foremost European-based broker with the best European network (including eastern Europe).
- To demonstrate true pan-European expertise (eg multilingual).
- To project a visibly European image (and not UK dominated).
- To create a totally cohesive 'one company' (single European company) in a clear visual statement.
- To improve internal communications by creating a focal point for the meeting of staff from across the continent to break down barriers between divisions/trading companies.

Strategy

The above objectives would be achieved in a cost-competitive manner by developing an outstanding pan-European exhibition involving: a press conference and a press lunch; senior speakers at the main conference dinner; hosting a major dinner; and an innovative exhibition crowd-pulling concept, all integrated into the creative theme 'One Europe, 1st in Europe'.

Stand design

The nature of the industry and the economic environment were such that lavishly designed stands could create a worry in the minds of clients that 'we are paying for all this'. For these reasons the stand looked smart, professional and European but was not a luxurious extravaganza. Visually, the stand took its style from the *ERA* magazine to create a cohesive look. All graphics were in French and English.

Tactics

Given that most of the RIMS exhibition visitors fell into the target group, it was essential to create a hub of activity around the Sedgwick stand. A new product demonstration was placed alongside a crowd-pulling cartoonist who sketched visitors on pre-printed, branded paper, giving full service and address details on the back. This allowed both client and prospect visitors to take away something that was personal to them but was also Sedgwick branded. The same artist drew European cameos of many countries for a competition. The production of Sedgwick's European magazine, *ERA 2* (published in six languages), was carefully planned so that it was available for the exhibition. The first article in *ERA* focused on Sedgwick's eastern European operations.

Action

The stand was manned by an international team at all times.

Control

A post-exhibition meeting was held to arrange a follow-up schedule for all enquiries and to evaluate the overall exhibition performance. The new products and services helped to develop existing clients and attract new clients. One indicator of the stand's success was the front-page coverage of the stand and Sedgwick's keynote conference speaker in a magazine sponsored by a direct competitor. All stand members felt that the exhibition was a morale booster and it helped them to feel more confident with their clients. The staff began to feel part of one European company. In fact, a subsequent pan-European slogan competition received 400 entries from company staff (nearly 20 per cent of the European workforce). Arguably, the winning slogan was born out of the new post-exhibition mood: 'One Europe, one broker. Sedgwick.'

Men and women

The entire project was planned by an in-house team with both international and exhibition expertise. Senior management support and commitment to the exhibition were evidenced by the constant presence and involvement of the managing director of the French operation (the local host). The UK-based European PR manager controlled the overall plan and execution.

Money

A basic 3-metre × 3-metre unit of exhibition floorspace costs between £3,000 and £9,000 depending, on the exhibition. At RIMS the 3-metre × 6-metre (two units) cost £6,500. An additional £5,000 was budgeted for all other items, such as the cartoonist, contractor, transport, graphics, and telephone lines. The high-quality, lightweight, flexible, reusable exhibition kit was tailored for the RIMS exhibition and subsequently built into the 18 square metres of rented space. The standard shell scheme option was rejected ('too bland'), as was the purpose-built stand option ('too expensive' – cost anywhere from £10,000 to £30,000).

The budget did not cover travel and accommodation which, as is customary in a large organization, was paid for by each individual trading company.

Minutes

RIMS is a biennial event. Sedgwick's planning started 18 months in advance. Early commitment and good relationships with the exhibition organizers helped to secure the best stand location (and choice of halls), speaker opportunities and details of attendees, especially the press. Quarterly meetings were held with French colleagues. Planning meetings immediately before the exhibition were held on site. Daily planning meetings for all staff members (around 70) were held early each morning to agree the day's strategy before the exhibition doors were opened to the public.

CASE STUDY 16.2

Hewlett-Packard's conference

Situation

Hewlett-Packard has been a long-time player in the minicomputer systems market. The emergence of the UNIX operating system as an industry standard, coupled with increasing demands by customers to protect their huge investments in computer systems, produced a paradigm shift, which, many feel, will eventually force all IT (information technology) companies to offer 'open systems', ie hardware, software and systems compatible with other manufacturers' systems. This means suppliers may have to offer service and partnership (see Chapter 10) as a significant USP (unique selling proposition or the supplier's unique advantage).

Problem

Although HP was the first major player to migrate its products to the UNIX platform, it did so long before the paradigm shift occurred and was therefore not immediately recognized as an open systems supplier.

Target

Executive directors responsible for long-term investments and for management of change:

1. Directors and board-level managers in companies with £10–50 million turnover.
2. Directors and board-level management, IT management and financial management in companies with over £50 million turnover.

Objective

As other major IT companies joined the open systems market, HP realized that it was imperative to establish itself not just as a player, but as the only credible IT company that could truly be the customer's systems partner. A secondary objective was to generate immediate business opportunities for both direct and indirect sales.

Strategy

A two-pronged communications strategy was developed to position HP as 'the knowledgeable partner' and 'agent of change' for implementing IT solutions, while using a creative theme 'think again' (about computer systems) to help undermine a competitor's current advertising approach through a series of top-level conferences.

Tactics

A series of open-systems conferences were designed, using guest speakers from within and outside the IT industry, in conjunction with a widespread communications campaign themed 'think again'. For each one-day conference, personal invitations were direct-mailed to up to 60,000 targets from a number of list sources, and follow-up letters were sent to non-responders in a select target group of 5,000 'key contacts'. Press releases announcing the events and highlighting the prestigious speakers received editorial coverage in key IT journals. National advertisements were also placed in the *Financial Times*. Using a TV personality to compere, HP purposely limited itself to a short 'wrap up' (summary conclusion) by HP's UK managing director. Business and management luminaries were invited to address the conference on such topics as the dynamics of organizational change, competitiveness and speed to market, and protecting IT investments. The speakers were completely at liberty to address their own subjects in their own way and were not instructed to sell HP.

Action

The conferences (with morning and afternoon sessions at a central, desirable venue) included small exhibition areas where HP software partners displayed their solutions. In addition, a major management consultancy and HP offered qualified attendees free consultancy time to evaluate systems needs. A prize draw for HP computers valued at several thousand pounds was conducted at each conference session.

Control

Measuring the response was based on the number of applicants registering for the conference, as well as the number of qualified attendees who registered for the free consultancy on the day. In addition, follow-up research was conducted that surveyed attendees

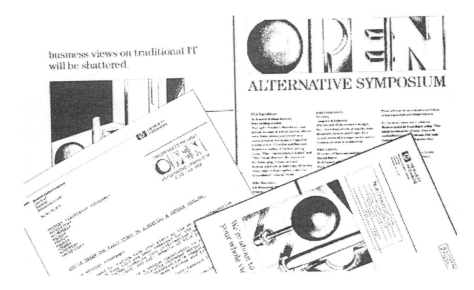

and people who were invited and/or confirmed but who did not attend. The objective of this research was to measure perceptions of HP overall and as an open-systems supplier. The overall response to the marketing campaigns in terms of attendance at the conference sessions averaged 2 per cent, which HP regarded as an above-average response. The follow-up research showed 96 per cent indicating a likeliness to consider purchasing HP in the future. Response to a personalized survey (see the questionnaire on page 497) was 56 per cent for attendees and 20 per cent for non-attendees.

Men and women

The open-systems conferences were managed by HP's marketing communications team, working with a number of external agencies responsible for PR, direct marketing, advertising, telesales, event coordination and stage/audio-visual production.

Money

The overall budget per conference day, excluding keynote speakers' fees and media advertising, but including mailing, PR, stage set, etc, was approximately £140,000. Keynote speakers' fees ranged from £2,500 to £25,000 plus expenses. The media spend (advertising costs) brought the average total cost per conference close to one-quarter of a million pounds.

Minutes

The whole project took 16 weeks to plan and three conferences were undertaken in the first year.

HEWLETT PACKARD

"The Open Alternative"
Your Final Chance to Win an HP Palmtop

If you name is incorrect or incomplete, please correct it below:

Mr/Mrs/Miss: _____

Position: _____

Company: _____

Address: _____

_____

_____ Postcode: _____

Telephone: _____

Thank you for attending our recent "Open Alternative" Symposium.

Now we would like to know what **you** think of Open Systems, and, by telling us you could win an HP Palmtop computer.

Complete and return this short questionnaire – it shouldn't take more than five minutes of your time and your completed card will be entered into the prize draw to take place on 17th July

Which conference session did you find most useful?

- [ ] Dr Rosabeth Moss Kanter
- [ ] Mike Harrison - UK MD of Oracle
- [ ] Tony Fisher - UK MD of Hoskyns
- [ ] John Pendlebury - Partner, Coopers & Lybrand
- [ ] Mick Linsell - Director of Systems and Quality, Parcelforce
- [ ] John Golding - UK MD of Hewlett-Packard Limited

Why? _____

How do you rate the symposium organisation, both beforehand and on the day?

- [ ] Excellent
- [ ] Good
- [ ] Average
- [ ] Poor

CSF 71

What are your views of Open Systems based IT after the symposium?

- [ ] Open IT is now first choice for my business
- [ ] I am prepared to consider a move to Open Systems
- [ ] Open IT is inappropriate for my business

Other: _____

If you are not considering Open Systems IT, why not?

_____

_____

Which computer systems do you use at present?

- [ ] DEC
- [ ] HP
- [ ] IBM
- [ ] ICL

Other: _____

Do you have any UNIX systems installed?

- [ ] Yes
- [ ] No

Which supplier do you perceive as the leading Open Systems IT company? _____

Why? _____

In the left hand column please rank (1 is the most important, 7 the least) the qualities you perceive to be the most important in the Open Systems market place. In the right hand column give HP marks out of 10 for its capability in each area.

'Qualities'		HP 'Score'
	Range of hardware	
	Price	
	Performance	
	Software availability	
	Support capabilities	
	Market profile	
	Standards commitment	

Other: _____

_____

Will you consider HP as a supplier for future IT procurements?

- [ ] Yes
- [ ] No

If not, why not? _____

Thank you for your time, now fold and seal by moistening the edges. Once we receive your card it will be entered into the draw, with the winners notified by post during late July.

APPENDIX 16.1

Virtual exhibitions

The atrium

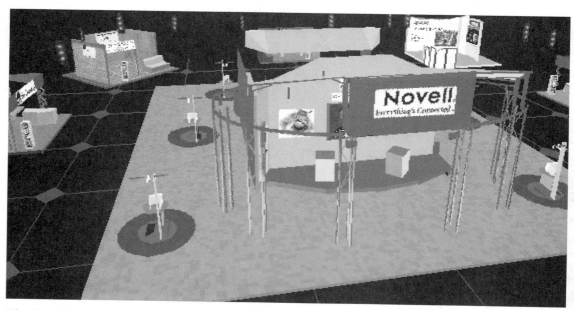

The Novell networking hall

The Java Forum pavilion

The conference centre

Today we have virtual exhibitions with real visitors exploring real companies and their virtual exhibitions in cyberland. It is entirely built in cyberspace. The show can last for a set period of time (24 hours a day, seven days a week, for 52 weeks, without the costs of physically manning the stand). The number of virtual visitors can vary from 2,500 to 25,000 per day. The cost of a stand depends on what is required. Some stands can be designed with original creations (ranging from £10,000 to £20,000) as opposed to off-the-shelf stands that begin at £3,000. An entire virtual exhibition can be provided for other show organizers. A basic show with approximately 50 basic shell schemes can be produced for as little as £25,000 and they can then sell the booths on to their customers.

VIRTEX '97 League table report – Unique visitors/institutions on stands

Superscape	2,074	Siemens GEC Communications Systems	725
Novell	2,057	Conference centre	701
IBM	1,548	Computer associates	630
International Thomson Publishing	1,006	Lexmark	599
Frontier	887	Axent technology	504
Kasten Chase(s)	783	Bay networks	479

Generating site traffic

Advertisements (in the *Telegraph* 'Connected' supplement and *Network Computing*) supplemented by frequent press releases to generate editorial coverage – including BBC *Midlands Today, The Midlands at Westminster, Southern Counties*, Kent and Shropshire Radio, Radio 5 Live and a live television piece for the new BBC World Service station. Editorial coverage was in *Internet* magazine and *Net Connections*, the cover of *Multi-media* magazine, industry press and the *Guardian*, plus a supplement for *The Economist*. More conventional promotional methods were also used, including two press facilities, banners on the home pages of Virtex's larger exhibitors (including Oracle and Siemens Nixdorf) and also a banner on the Netscape UK home page for a month. Search engines are currently increasing traffic through high listing because of the size of the site and CD ROM distribution also promotes the site.

APPENDIX 16.2

Budgeting checklist

	Estimated cost	Actual cost
1. Space		
☐ Exhibit	_____	_____
☐ Hotel suite	_____	_____
2. Display		
☐ Design & construction	_____	_____
☐ Graphics	_____	_____
☐ Refurbishing	_____	_____
☐ Products for display	_____	_____
☐ Rental fee	_____	_____
☐ Used display purchase	_____	_____
☐ Literature holders	_____	_____
☐ Tool kit	_____	_____
☐ Lighting fixtures	_____	_____
3. Furnishing the display		
☐ Tables	_____	_____
☐ Chairs	_____	_____
☐ Ashtrays/trash cans/rubbish bins	_____	_____
☐ Floral arrangements	_____	_____
☐ Lead printer rental	_____	_____
☐ Audio-visual equipment rental	_____	_____
4. Show services		
☐ Set up/take down	_____	_____
☐ Electricity	_____	_____
☐ Water, gas, air	_____	_____
☐ Telephone, fax	_____	_____
☐ Cleaning	_____	_____
☐ Photography	_____	_____
☐ Security	_____	_____
☐ Overnight services	_____	_____
5. Shipping and storage		
☐ Shipping	_____	_____
☐ Drayage	_____	_____

☐ Storage   _____   _____
☐ Insurance   _____   _____

6. Advertising and Promotion

☐ Pre-show promotion   _____   _____
☐ On-site promotion   _____   _____
☐ Post-show promotion   _____   _____
☐ Direct mail   _____   _____
☐ Public relations activities   _____   _____
☐ Premium incentives   _____   _____
☐ Special show literature   _____   _____
☐ Telemarketing activity   _____   _____

7. Personnel

☐ Travel expenses   _____   _____
☐ Hotel accommodation   _____   _____
☐ Show registrations   _____   _____
☐ Meals   _____   _____
☐ Out-of-pocket expenses   _____   _____
☐ Special uniforms   _____   _____

8. Special activities

☐ Guest entertainment   _____   _____
☐ Receptions   _____   _____
☐ Sales meetings   _____   _____
☐ Speaker expenses   _____   _____
☐ Presenters / live talent   _____   _____
☐ Training expenses   _____   _____

9. Hospitality

☐ Meeting room   _____   _____
☐ Food / drink   _____   _____
☐ Gifts   _____   _____
☐ Audio-visual equipment rental   _____   _____

10. Other

☐ ———————   _____   _____
☐ ———————   _____   _____
☐ ———————   _____   _____
☐ ———————   _____   _____
☐ ———————   _____   _____

Total Budget

Reproduced by kind permission of Nomadic Display

APPENDIX 16.3

Lead forms

Nomadic▨Display®

Show: _____

Name: _____

Title: _____

Company: _____

Address: _____

City/Town: _____

State/Country: _____ Postal/Zip: _____

Phone: _____ Fax: _____

QUALIFICATION SUMMARY:

Owner Club Member:　　Yes　or　No

Industry: _____

Product Interests: (Circle One)

Tabletop	Backwall	Island
SpaceStrut	Classic	Modular
Graphics	Plus	Other

Currently Uses: _____

Next event is: _____

Circle Interests:　　Wants to visit a showroom

　　　　　　　　　　　EC call requested

　　　　　　　　　　　Renting

　　　　　　　　　　　Instaship

　　　　　　　　　　　Being a distributor

　　　　　　　　　　　No immediate requirement

Purchase Time Frame is: (Circle One)

Less than 30 days	1-3 mos	6-9mos
One Year plus	3-6mos	9-12mos

Received pre-show mailer? Yes　or　No

Fulfillment Type: (Circle One)

NA	Euro	French	German
UK	Italian	Spanish	

Notes: _____

_____

_____

Lead Taken By: _____

(Full Name and Date)

4/96

Reproduced by kind permission of Nomadic Display

APPENDIX 16.4

How to qualify a prospect

Here is an excerpt from Don Engebretson's *Exhibiting at USA Trade Shows* video:

The six essential qualifying questions

1. Thanks for stopping, how are you familiar with...? *or*... what attracted you to our display? *or*... what do you see that you like? (gives history of the prospective buyer, tells you where to start selling);
2. What's your situation now? (tells you if the prospective buyer actually has a real live need);
3. What would you like to achieve/change? (further defines prospective buyer's application of your product);
4. What are your concerns as to budget? (tells you if the prospective buyer has the money);
5. How does your timetable look like on all of this? (gives you the prospective buyer's timetable for buying or acting);
6. How would you like to proceed from here? (lets the prospective buyer take over).

APPENDIX 16.5

Exhibition value analysis

The synopsis shown below indicates the type of information the evaluation should include.

EXHIBITION EVALUATION

Synopsis of

CONFIDENTIAL PRIVATE CLIENT REPORT

CONTENTS		USES
PERFORMANCE SUMMARY	Compares performance with objectives, with exhibition potential, and to your competitors. A factual measurement of achievement	Use as a synopsis for debriefing, in structuring the next exhibition presence.
COMMENTS ON PERFORMANCE	Conclusions and advice	Use the recommendations for consideration, implementation and discussions with staff or with Exhibition Surveys
ACTION RECOMMENDATIONS	For future developments, changes or corrections	
YOUR POTENTIAL AUDIENCE	The number of exhibition visitors interested in your company's products	Use to set budgets, allocate resources, measure results. Factual independent data of your company's exhibition potential
STAND ATTRACTION RATING	Your stand's success in being seen by your target audience	Measure your designer's performance in creating an attention-getter for your market
STAND EFFICIENCY RATING	Your sales staff's success in contacting your target audience	Measure your stand and your staff's performance in processing visitors
COST PERFORMANCE	Your achieved cost per interested visitor	Use to evaluate and improve cost-effective competitive performance and to compare with your normal cost per sales call.

YOUR VISITORS, THEIR REACTIONS AND OPINIONS

Visitor quality, product interest and plans to buy	] Specific] evaluations	Use to evaluate performance and make future decisions in the context of exhibition potential
Recall of visiting your stand	] against potential	
Impact of your presentation on visitors	] of your company's	
Performance of stand personnel	] achievements in	
Marketing communications (Association Question)	] these critical areas	

PERFORMANCE COMPARISON WITH COMPETITORS

Number of visitors to specific named stands	] Tabular presenta-] tions of performance	Use to evaluate performance and make future decisions in competitive context
Most memorable stands	] across the show,	
Most impressive demonstrations/ presentations	] including client] companies and] competitors	

APPENDIX

The questionnaire

Exhibition Surveys Ltd,
22 Digby Drive, Melton Mowbray, LE13 ORQ

Exhibition Surveys

APPENDIX 16.6

Exhibition survey's questionnaire

Exhibition Surveys

CADCAM EXHIBITION SURVEY

1. Please tick all previous years you have visited the Exhibition.

    1-1( )1991   -2( )1990   -3( )1989   -4( )1988   -5( )First time this year

2. Why did you visit the exhibition this year?

    2-1( )To see new products & developments   3-1( )General interest
    -2( )To see a specific company or product   -2( )To make business contacts
    -3( )To buy   -3( )To evaluate the show before exhibiting
    -4( )To obtain technical or product information   -4( )Other...................
    -5( )To help select future suppliers   (specify)

3. Please name any other computer exhibitions that you have visited in the past 2 years....................
.... 4-1( )I visit no other exhibitions

4. How many hours did you actually spend at the exhibition? ....hours spread over ....day(s)
                                                     5   6

5. How did you learn that the exhibition was to take place?

    7-1( )Organisers' direct mail -2( )Exhibitors' direct mail -3( )My company
    -4( )Trade/technical press -5( )Exhibitors' representative -6( )Friend/associate   -7( )Other...................(state)

6. Try to name three companies whose stands attracted your attention the most.

Company name	Saw demon-stration	Interested in products	Obtained literature	Design of stand	Other reasons (please specify)
....	( )	( )	( )	( )	....
....	( )	( )	( )	( )	....
....	( )	( )	( )	( )	....

7. Tick the products and services that you found of interest at the exhibition. Also tick those that you plan to buy or recommend to buy **as a result of what you saw at the Show. (Tick all appropriate boxes).**

Interested	Recommend/Plan to buy		Interested	Recommend/Plan to buy	
8-1( )	8-1( )	2D Drafting & Design	10-1( )	10-1( )	Manufacturing Control Systems
-2( )	-2( )	3D Solid Modelling	-2( )	-2( )	Networking
-3( )	-3( )	3D Surface Modelling	-3( )	-3( )	Numerical Control
-4( )	-4( )	Architectural CAD	-4( )	-4( )	PC CAD
-5( )	-5( )	Business Software	-5( )	-5( )	Plastics
-6( )	-6( )	Civil Engineering Design	-6( )	-6( )	Plotters
-7( )	-7( )	Computer-Aided Manufacturing	-7( )	-7( )	Printers
-8( )	-8( )	Drawing Office Equipment	-8( )	-8( )	Process Planning Systems
9-1( )	9-1( )	Electrical CAD	11-1( )	11-1( )	Scanning Systems
-2( )	-2( )	Electronic CAD	-2( )	-2( )	Structural Analysis
-3( )	-3( )	Finite Elements Analysis	-3( )	-3( )	Technical Documentation
			-4( )	-4( )	Workstation CAD

8. What role(s) do you play in the purchase of the following?

Product Category	Final Say -1	Specify -2	Recommend -3	No-Role -4	Product Category	Final Say -1	Specify -2	Recommend -3	No-Role -4
Personal Computers	12(}	{ }	{ }	{ }	Plotters	14(}	{ }	{ }	{ }
Networking Products	13(}	{ }	{ }	{ }	Printers	15(}	{ }	{ }	{ }

9A. Are you a user (or a manager of users) of **Plotters**? 16-1( )Yes -2( )No (Goto Q10)

9B. Which company **first** comes to mind when you think of **plotter** manufacturers? (Please enter below)

9C. Which other manufacturers of **plotters** can you think of? (Please enter below).

	Manufacturers' names	Number of plotters
FIRST CHOICE	....	( )
OTHER CHOICES	....	( )
. .	....	( )
. .	....	( )
. .	....	( )
. .	....	( )
. .	....	( )
	TOTAL	10

9D. Thinking about all these brands, imagine a hypothetical purchase situation: if you had a budget of 10 units, how would you allocate these 10 units amongst each brand? (Enter above in right-hand column).

        ...continued

10. How useful was this year's exhibition?

17-1( )Very useful -2( )Useful -3( )Moderately useful -4( )Hardly useful at all -5( )Not useful

What features of the Show did you particularly like? ....

What was negative, disappointing or missing? ....

....

11. Of all the exhibitors seen at the exhibition, which **one** impressed you the most? and Why?

....( )None was impressive

Company .... Reason ....

12. Were you employed on your company's stand during the Show?   ( )YES   ( )NO

13. Did you stop to look at, or talk to, or to acquire literature from any of these companies at the Show? (Tick all appropriate boxes). If you talked to any of these companies, please indicate the degree of helpfulness of the person you talked to by placing the following code in the 'Helpfulness of personnel' column below: (4) If Good; (5) If Fair; (6) If Poor and (7) If Stand too crowded - no one to talk to. If a sales person from any of these Companies has called on you in the past year, please tick 'Sales Person Called' column.

	Looked -1	Talked -2	Literature -3	Helpfulness of personnel	Sales Person called -5		Looked -1	Talked -2	Literature -3	Helpfulness of personnel	Sales Person called -5
Calcomp	18( )	{ }	{ }	{ }	{ }	Oce	22( )	{ }	{ }	{ }	{ }
Canon	19( )	{ }	{ }	{ }	{ }	Roland	23( )	{ }	{ }	{ }	{ }
Graphtec	20( )	{ }	{ }	{ }	{ }	Tektronix	24( )	{ }	{ }	{ }	{ }
Hewlett-Packard	21( )	{ }	{ }	{ }	{ }	Versatec	25( )	{ }	{ }	{ }	{ }

14. Altogether, at approximately how many stands did you stop for a discussion or to obtain literature? ....

15A. Did you visit any of the following companies' stands? Please tick column A.

15B. May we have your views about those companies that you visited?
(Please rate Columns B, C, D, E in terms of: 1 very good, 2 good, 3 satisfactory, 4 not very satisfactory, and 5 unsatisfactory)

Visited		Stand Quality	Presentation of Products	Overall professionalism of staff on duty	Demonstrations seen
A		B	C	D	E
26( )	Calcomp	35( )	44( )	53( )	62( )
27( )	Canon	36( )	45( )	54( )	63( )
28( )	Graphtec	37( )	46( )	55( )	64( )
29( )	Hewlett-Packard	38( )	47( )	56( )	65( )
30( )	Oce	39( )	48( )	57( )	66( )
31( )	Roland	40( )	49( )	58( )	67( )
32( )	Tektronix	41( )	50( )	59( )	68( )
33( )	Versatec	42( )	51( )	60( )	69( )
34( )	Others.................	43( )	52( )	61( )	70( )
	(please state)				

16. Which 3 companies **new** products or developments did you see at the exhibition?

Companies   1. ....   2. ....   3. ....

New Product   1. ....   2. ....   3. ....

To help classify your answers, may we have some information about yourself?

17. What is your job title? ....

18. What is your job function? ....71-1( )Trainee

-2( )Full-time student

19. What are the major products or services of the organisation with which you are employed?

....

....

20. What is the approximate number of employees in your organisation (at your location)?

72-1( )1-9 -2( )10-49 -3( )50-99 -4( )100-249 -5( )250-499 -6( )500-999 -7( )1,000 and over

21. Please name three computer magazines that you read regularly ....

....

....

May we have your name to validate our survey? ....

THANK YOU FOR YOUR HELP

Key points from Chapter 16:

1. Exhibitions are hard work. Exhibitions can work well for the exhibitor if they are planned and integrated with other marketing tools.
2. Every element of exhibition performance can be monitored and measured with a view to making improvements in the next exhibition.

FURTHER READING

Black, S (1989) *Exhibitions and Conferences from A to Z*, Modino Press, London

Cotterell, P (1992) *Exhibitions: An Exhibitor's Guide*, Hodder & Stoughton, London

Dudley, J W (1990) *Successful Exhibiting*, Kogan Page, London

Engebretson, D (2000) *Exhibiting in the USA* (video), Trade Partners UK, Department of Trade and Industry, produced in association with Multimedia Marketing.com, London

Exhibition Industry Federation (2000) *The UK Exhibition Industry: The Facts & How to Exhibit*, EIF, London

Seekings, D (1996) *How to Organise Effective Conferences and Meetings*, Kogan Page, London

Talbot, J (1989) *How to Make Exhibitions Work for Your Business*, Daily Telegraph/Kogan Page, London

FURTHER CONTACTS

Association of Exhibition Organisers, 113 High Street, Berkhamsted, Herts HP4 2DJ (tel: 01442 873331; Web site: www.aeo.org.uk)

British Exhibition Contractors Association, 36 The Broadway, London SW19 1RQ (tel: 020 8543 3888; Web site: www.beca.org.uk)

Exhibitors Venues Association, (formerly Exhibition Industry Federation), 15 Keeble Court, Fairmeadows, North Seaton, Northumberland NE63 9SF (tel: 0845 601 4192; Web site: www. exhibitionvenues.com)

Society of Events Organisers, 29A Market Square, Biggleswade, Bedfordshire SG18 8AQ (tel: 01767 316255; Web site: www.seoevent.co.uk)

17

Packaging

THE IMPORTANCE OF PACKAGING

Since many sales assistants have been replaced by self-service systems, packaging today often has to act as a *silent salesperson*, helping customers by bringing a particular brand to their attention, highlighting USPs (unique selling propositions/unique benefits), giving friendly tips on usage and, ultimately, helping them to break through the *misery of choice* created by the increasingly vast range of seemingly similar brands. The plethora of 'me toos' (similar products and brands) and the relentless fragmentation of markets means that pack designs have to work very hard in these highly competitive, shorter life cycle markets of today.

The design of the pack can create *competitive advantage* by adding value, improving the product (eg improving the freshness or making it easier to pour, etc), developing stronger shelf presence, positioning a brand in a particular way, and creating or strengthening the brand's relationship with the buyer. The pack should be what top designer Michael Peters calls 'a visual magnet' that entices the customer to purchase and, eventually, become loyal to a particular brand. Packaging can also be an *extraordinarily effective advertising medium*, particularly in terms of cost and penetration, and reach or cover of a target audience. On the shelf and in the home it continues to work day in, day out, for 52 weeks of the year. It is also a *free medium*. The Talisker case study on page 532 demonstrates how pack design can create a sustainable competitive advantage.

No single element of the communications mix comes under as much *environmental* scrutiny as packaging. In a sense, we will see less and less packaging as oversized cartons and unnecessary layers of packaging are stripped away by environmental pressures. Good pack design also pleases the distributor/retailer by helping to make distribution, warehousing and use of shelf space more efficient. In fact, many warehouses are becoming fully automated distribution centres, demanding packs of a size that suits the warehouse handling equipment. Good pack design also *saves manufacturing costs*.

Falling in love with a pack

Packaging *facilitates choice*. Choice is rarely made on a rational basis. In fact the consumer is faced with several thousand packs screaming 'buy me'. A well-designed pack offers *relief from the misery of choice*. Ernest Dichter (1964) suggested that 'this relief may be derived through being permitted to like a product, almost to *love it indiscriminately and irrationally*'. A well-designed pack can offer this permission and so assist in the choice.

THE THREE BASIC FUNCTIONS OF PACKAGING

The three basic functions of packaging are to:

1. protect (and contain);
2. offer convenience;
3. communicate.

First and foremost, a pack must *protect* its contents during storage, transport and usage. Some packs have to protect the user from the contents (as in the case of children with weed killers, medicine, chemicals, etc). Sadly, some packaging today must also protect the contents from tampering. Six people died in Chicago when Johnson & Johnson's Tylenol pain relievers were laced with cyanide. There is a relatively new market for tamper-proof packaging and tamper-evident packaging.

Second, the pack must offer *convenience* in pouring, squeezing, storing, stacking and consuming (in cars, the garden, the beach, the home and, one day, in space). Sugar and milk have yet to be mastered in terms of truly convenient packaging. Even a minute improvement in convenience can create competitive advantage, as demonstrated by Schlitz beer's Pop-Top can which helped to boost sales from 5.7 million in 1961 to 15.1 million way back in 1970. On the other hand, some pack designs are so poor that they cause their own problems. In 1985 the Norwegian company Elopack used TV advertising to try to explain how to open Elopak cartons.

Third, the pack must *communicate*. Before concentrating on the communications aspects of packaging, it is worth mentioning that all three packaging functions are interdependent. The first two, protection and convenience, both communicate indirectly. For example, if the product is damaged, tarnished or stale, then a negative image is what remains, despite advertising, publicity and sales promotions that claim otherwise. Equally, if the instructions for storage or pouring are not communicated clearly, then the pack loses its protective and convenience capabilities.

Some products prioritize some functions over others. Some design solutions (or redesigned packs) cannot optimize all three functions simultaneously because of constraints such as cost or overall pack size limitations. *Trade-offs*, or compromises, between functions will then occur. Surprisingly, some optimum functions can be forfeited for other reasons.

OVERPROTECTIVE PACKAGING

There is a balance between protective packaging, sales, returns and overall costs incurred. Here are three examples from James Pilditch's outstanding book on packaging design, *The Silent Salesman* (1973). They demonstrate how overpackaging can be identified, reduced and subsequently used to boost sales and/or profits.

An electric light bulb company had a breakage rate so low that it prompted the question – were the bulbs overpackaged and too well protected? It subsequently reduced the grade of cardboard and returns (of damaged bulbs) went up. The overall saving in packaging costs was greater than the increased costs of breakage/returns.

A detergent company used stronger boxes than its competitors. The distributors were aware of this and liked the better boxes because they were able to put them on the bottom of the pile without their collapsing. The product was hidden at the bottom instead of being at eye level, which is the optimum 'buy level'. So the box weight was reduced. The boxes started to collapse and the detergent was soon freed from the bottom of the pile. Sales soon increased.

A London discount house was concerned over the lack of stealing. They thought: 'Maybe we make our goods too hard for people to get at.' So the packs were redesigned.

THE LONG-TERM COMMITMENT

The pack design needs to develop and change as markets constantly move away from existing products (and their packs). The pack may have to reflect changes in the customers' aspirations, incorporate demographic shifts such as an ageing population, exploit new technologically driven opportunities (such as microwaves, which require new food packaging), or simply highlight a new improvement in the product itself. There needs to be a constant review of customers, their perceptions, motivations and aspirations, and, of course, a constant review also of competitive packs. Sometimes customers simply get tired of a design.

One of the problems with packaging design is that it never shows up in a normal media budget. A major redesign involving a change of shape as well as a change in graphics can cost anywhere from £25,000 to £250,000 for the design stages. The tooling cost (the machine part/s that the production line needs to produce the new pack shape) will probably double the cost. Packaging design is an *evolutionary rather than revolutionary process*. But not all designs involve three-dimensional changes; often it is simply a two-dimensional change of

Spot the difference: subtle design tweaks increase shelf presence

graphics. Sometimes this is so subtle (a design tweak') that the consumer is not even aware of the change, yet the new design will be working harder for the manufacturer. Look at the Heinz beans cans and the subtle 'design tweak'. Packaging design often does not sit comfortably in the marketing budget at all, but failure to get a pack right is tantamount to possibly wasting millions of pounds' worth of above-the-line advertising.

A constant design analysis looks at ways in which design can help to strengthen a brand's position. Heinz had maintained market share, but only at the expense of margin. Pack design gave it a lift. Turquoise is rarely associated with food except for Heinz. Subtle alterations have been made to make the product 'more appealing' and give it a 'stronger image for the future'. The Heinz lettering was changed from a 'thin typeface to a fuller, more generous style; the keystone was broadened and a white in-line used to sharpen its impact; the lettering of "oven" and "with tomato sauce" was changed from turquoise to gold and the tone of the turquoise background was enriched to create added warmth'.

Packs cannot afford to stay static, because markets and moods change. Nestlé's successful After Eight mint chocolate was becoming tired and beginning to look dated. The current pack probably doesn't appear to have changed much. It is the fruit of 18 months of detailed research and development. Five hundred design concepts and 50 dummy packs were considered before agreeing on the new look for the 1990s.

It is possible, as Dichter (1964) suggests, to fall in love with a pack. It is also possible to form extremely strong trusting relationships with a pack, even when it comes to babies.

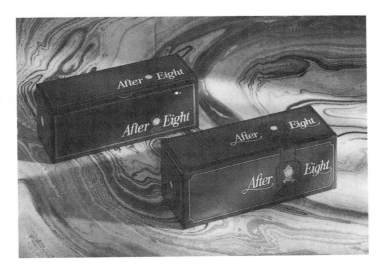

The result of 500 design concepts

> *Would you pour a pile of white powder over your new baby?*
>
> Would you have the confidence to pour an unknown pile of white powder over your new baby?
>
> Put the powder inside the pack called Johnson's, and emotions are immediately evoked of the caring mother–child relationship. You would certainly trust the product with your baby. You would not be willing to pay much, if anything, for the powder alone. You would be willing to pay a premium for a brand you trust and believe in.
>
> Mary Lewis (1991)

The relationship-enhancing pack can also help to strengthen branding and even the corporate profile of the manufacturer or distributor that controls it. The next section of this chapter suggests how.

BRANDS, PACKS AND CORPORATE IDENTITIES

Some brands, and their packs, are inextricably linked with the corporation that owns or makes the brands (eg Heinz, Honda or BP). Others keep a lower profile with a more subtle form of corporate endorsement (like ICI's Crown Paints). Others still prefer to keep the free-standing brand/pack identity very separate from the corporation, which remains anonymously behind the scenes (eg After Eight chocolates and Nestlé). There are advantages and disadvantages to all three approaches.

The *corporate culture* and *diversity of products and markets* can determine the specific approach. For example, a few years ago Allied Lyons was reported not to see the need for corporate advertising which linked the company to the brand. Financial analysts were not necessarily aware that the much-loved brands that were seen to be successful (and which they or their families bought every day) came from the same company that was under threat from a takeover bid. Somehow the success of the brand management was divorced from the image of the company's management. The shareholders had to decide whether they had faith in the ability of the existing management (and therefore retain it by not selling or swapping their shares) or allow new management (new owners) to take over and run the company. The corporate advertising established the link between the brands and the company and, arguably, saved the company. Today, Allied advertises its brands along with a corporate endorsement. Packs can work in exactly the same way – linking the brand to the parent company. However, this may be restricted by the diversity of products and markets. For example, think of Esso ice cream, Lada Airlines and Beecham's Beer. If any of these products existed, the corporate link would not support the brand proposition; it would, arguably, detract from it.

The strengthening of the link between a company and its brands/packs can help the company by facilitating new product launches and brand stretching or brand extension (eg Heinz Weight Watchers). It can also reinforce corporate presence and, in turn, reassure different audiences, eg existing customers, new customers, investors and even employees (see 'Advantages of a good corporate image' on page 616). On the other hand, the link can create a design straitjacket which, as Mary Lewis (1991) pointed out, 'inhibits the active development of sub-brands aimed at different target markets'. Since different target markets often require radically different images, these images may pull in different directions, thereby detracting from the consistency of the overall corporate identity and image. In addition, if a particular brand has a problem (such as product tampering or a faulty production batch), it is immediately associated with the parent company. This negative reflection can, if the link between brand and parent company is clearly established, affect all the other brands operating under the same corporate umbrella. As James Pilditch (1973) said: 'The pack can contribute to instant consumer recognition of the company or the brand.' Now let us consider the other communication functions of the pack.

THE COMMUNICATION FUNCTIONS OF THE PACK

The communication function breaks down into several different mini-functions:

1. *Grab the attention* of the passing shopper.
2. *Persuade* and convince the viewer that the contents match the promise made by advertising or the pack itself. The pack should say 'buy me'.
3. *Build brand personality* and forge links with the buyer.
4. *Build loyalty* with a pack that:
   - looks nicer on the table;
   - is easy to find in the garden shed or in the warehouse;
   - is distinctive and easily recognizable in a shop carrying 9,000 separate items;
   - is easier to use than the competition's.
5. *Instruct* the user about how to use the product to optimum benefit.
6. *Inform* the user of mandatory requirements such as warnings, source of manufacture and/or ingredients. Buyers tend to want more information today.

THE SILENT SALESMAN

The pack is the last and sometimes the only opportunity to communicate with and sell to a customer. All the other elements of the communications mix can get lost in the competitive and noisy jungle of commercial messages where each appeals for your attention. The pack is the *silent salesman*. Initially it has to shout boldly to grab attention and then fade into the background and let the product benefits come forward. A well-designed pack can stop customers dead in their tracks, invite them to have a look, pick it up, and pause for a few valuable moments while they are engaged at the point-of-sale. It is here that the pack can *develop a dialogue* by attracting, intriguing, arousing unconscious aspirations, informing, reminding, involving, entertaining and, above all, persuading.

The pack can arouse, or trigger stored images from a television advertisement that have been lying dormant in the memory bank if either the advertisement includes a 'pack shot' (close-up of the pack) or the pack includes some of the images from the advertisement. The brand can reflect images and aspirations. The pack can help the customer to recall those aspirations and develop associations between the aspirations and the brand. The hand lifts the pack off the shelf, allowing the customer, his or her other aspirations and the brand to move closer together.

Packs like Heinz are sometimes called '*trigger packs*' because there is little dialogue other than the announcement of a strong, confident tone. The pack design concentrates on being recognized through its unique visual identifiers, the colours, keystone, name and lettering, while heavy advertising communicates the brand values and aspirations. It is interesting to see Campbell's Soups dispense with Andy Warhol's legendary red and white livery and replace it with another aspirational soup setting. The Campbell's graphics portray product values that are arguably less protectable from the inevitable 'me toos' sometimes produced by the retail stores' own labels. The Heinz pack and image are unique and therefore more protectable.

THE DESIGNER'S TOOLS

The six variables or tools a designer can use are:

1. shape;
2. size;
3. colour;
4. graphics;
5. materials;
6. smell.

Shape

Some brands have such distinctive pack shapes that the brand is recognizable from the shape alone (eg Baileys, Mateus Rosé, Perrier and Cif (formerly Jif) Lemon). Other pack shapes communicate conscious and unconscious meanings.

Ask a group to draw the first image, abstract or otherwise, that comes into their minds when the word 'love' is mentioned. If they struggle with this, ask them to imagine they are a design consultancy whose job is to design a logo for a new political party called 'The Love Party'. After a minute ask them to do the same for 'hate'. (Close your eyes or make a doodle yourself before reading on.) Over 95 per cent of the drawings tend to conform to the same perceptions about shape. The love image usually has softer edges, curves and maybe heart shapes, while the hate image tends to have jagged edges and sharper shapes like swastikas and daggers. We may not consciously associate these meanings with shapes but they are there. During the Second World War US *paratroopers* were tested to find whether they were *shape orientated* or *colour orientated* by being shown a film of abstract shapes and patterns. The shapes moved from right to left and the colours moved from left to right. The para-troopers were then asked which way the design was moving. Shape-orientated men are supposed to be more intelligent, stable and less emotional. The *Thurstone test* can be used for packaging design also. It has revealed that younger children respond to colour more than form, while adults, and men in particular, react more to form.

Pilditch (1973) suggested that a *rectangular box* created images of sharpness, neatness and cleanliness, while a *round box* had associations of security, plentifulness and generosity. Go into a chemist's shop and observe the different packaging shapes used for adult and children's bubble baths. Some shapes give the product a value much greater than its contents. Shapes can also be *masculine or feminine*. Whisky bottles tend to be masculine in shape, while some perfume bottles are feminine.

Shape affects the protection and convenience functions in *holding*, *pouring* and *storing*. How a pack fits into the hand is part of the study of *ergonomics*. A well-designed pack fits the hand more comfortably and creates what Coca-Cola proudly call '*in-hand embellishment*' (it feels good in the hand). Back in 1910 part of the packaging design brief for the now famous Coca-Cola bottle read:

> We need a new bottle – a distinctive package that will help us fight substitution… we need a bottle which a person will recognize as a Coca-Cola bottle *even when he feels it in the dark*. The Coca-Cola bottle should be so shaped that, even if broken, a person could tell what it was.

False ergonomics communicate unreal values to customers. For example, dimples (for fingers to grip) are sometimes placed down the side of a bottle when in fact the bottle is rarely held by the two dimpled sides; instead, it is held by the two flat front and back sides

Can recognize the brand even by feeling it in the dark

of the pack. The subtle impression created by these false ergonomics is one of 'this pack looks slightly better or friendlier'. Customers do not consciously choose one brand instead of another. Ergonomics can help to express that one brand is nicer to use than another. Real ergonomics help the user to have a more pleasant experience with the pack and therefore encourage repeat purchasing.

Some shapes *reinforce product values* by designing product features into the pack, as with the honeycomb effect on the base of a honey jar of the dimpled plastic two-litre beer bottles associating the product with a dimpled beer mug. Other shapes *reinforce brand values*, eg the unique Monk's Liqueur bottle designed in the shape of a monk. The ultimate *brand shape* is arguably Cif Lemon's lemon-shaped pack. The Law Lords granted Reckitt & Colman exclusive rights to this shape, ie only Cif can use this unique get-up or shape to package lemon juice.

An immediately recognizable shape

Can manufacturers own monopoly rights to a pack shape? The test, it seems, is 'whether the shape serves mainly to distinguish a product from its rivals and whether a competitor using the shape is seeking to mislead purchasers' (Warden, 1990). There are an infinite *number* of shapes. Pack shape can form a valuable property of the brand. It can become part of the brand or become part of the brand equity. The shape of Sheridan's double liqueur bottle certainly helps it to stand out from the crowd.

A pack shape that stands out from the crowd

Size

Size communicates. Would you give your loved one a *perfume packed in a two-litre bottle?* The corollary, ie large pack communicates better quality, is also true in other product sectors such as breakfast cereals. Consumer perceptions about cornflakes have been found to change according to size of pack. Large cereal packs build feelings of plentiful, expansive, energy-giving food whereas a smaller pack may make the cornflakes seem heavy, solid and no good. Size can be used to communicate in different ways. For example, a 33-centilitre bottle of premium beer cannot be fully poured into a half-pint glass. This forces the drinker, after filling a glass, to carry the bottle away from the bar and over to the table where the unemptied bottle continues to work both as a badge and an advertisement.

Different sizes are aimed at different segments, eg the family pack. Pack *size can determine target markets*, or is it that target markets can determine pack size? This may be similar to Ehrenberg's philosophy of marketing which states that marketing means excluding many customers from a particular product (target marketing excludes the mass). Certain segments exclude certain sizes, as Coca-Cola discovered when it had to withdraw its two-litre bottle from the Spanish market after discovering that few Spaniards owned large fridges. If the colour were changed, would the pack then fit the fridge? Warm colours like red and yellow seem to advance or make the pack appear larger, while cold colours like blue recede and make the pack appear smaller. Although a change of colour would not have saved Coca-Cola's large bottle in Spain, colour does communicate in many different ways.

Colour

Colour communicates. Albert Kner, former design chief of the Container Corporation of America said 'Colour is the *quickest path to the emotions.*' Words have to be translated into images in the mind. These images, in turn, have to be assembled, organized and categorized to give them meaning. This may be followed by an emotional response, which may subsequently trigger a physical response. Colour skips all this and goes straight into the emotions, often creating a physiological response. *Colour is physical.* Russia's Pedagogical Institute has found that most people can *feel colours.* Eyeless sight or 'bio-introscopy' suggests that all one's skin has seeing power. Red, green and dark blue have been found to be sticky. This may have something to do with electromagnetic fields. There have been claims that the Chinese can teach children to see with their elbows. Forgive the digression. Many years ago the US Color Research Institute found that the colour of walls in an office could make people feel sleepy, excited or healthy. More recently, a British police force has experimented with pink cells for prisoners. Red increased blood pressure and pulse, while blue had the opposite effect.

The Luscher colour test uses colour cards to analyse the reader's psychological, and specifically emotional, state. The choice of green suggests a 'desire of the ego, and… self-assertion and a certain degree of self-sufficiency'. Green today has another international meaning – environmentalism.

Colour codes

Some product sectors, particularly food, appear to have colour codes. For example, within the carbonated drinks sector, red is cola and yellow is tonic. Freezer meat is red, fish is blue and anything low calorie/diet is white. Pilditch (1973) has suggested that in the wake of health scares many of the world's cigarette packs now emphasize white: 'They hope white is associated with cleanliness and purity.'

Colours have meaning for people. Many people associate colours with images, eg 'garden fresh', 'mountain cool' or 'rugged manliness'. There was a group of people for whom 7-UP's green bottle had almost medicinal links and therapeutic overtones: 'the thing to take when you had the flu and the doctor told you to take a lot of liquid'. Whether it is an annual report, a reception area, some sales literature or a piece of packaging, colour communicates. This applies to products and services in both consumer and industrial markets.

Colour affects perception. This is probably best demonstrated by Ernest Dichter's research (1964) into how packaging colour affects people's perceptions of taste. Unknown to the respondent, the same coffee was put into four cups. One of four different coloured coffee cans was placed beside each cup. Respondents were then asked to match the statements below with each cup tasted. The research revealed strong perceptions linked with specific colours.

- Dark brown can: 73% 'Too strong aroma or flavour';
- Red can: 84% 'Richer flavour or aroma';
- Blue can: 79% 'Milder flavour or aroma';
- Yellow can: 87% 'Too weak flavour or aroma'.

More recent research into packaging colour and perceptions of washing machine powder provided even stranger results. The same powder was put into three different coloured packs. The housewives tried them on delicate clothing for a few weeks and were then asked which was best for delicate clothing. Respondents thought the performance (of the same powder) was vastly different. Statements below demonstrate the striking finding:

- Largely yellow pack: 'too strong… ruined their clothes';
- Largely blue pack   'did not work… clothes were dirty looking';
- Blue and yellow pack   'fine' and 'wonderful'.

This differs from previous US research reported by Terrell Williams (1982) that tested identical washing powders in three different coloured boxes, yellow, blue and red. The yellow detergent was 'mild, too mild really'. The blue detergent was 'a good all-round laundry product'. The red detergent was 'good for stains and the like'.

Colours may not be international, since different colours have different meanings in different cultures. For example, white is life, purity and diet here in the UK but it means death in Japan. Softer pastel colours and brighter colours are perceived differently around the world. In China bright colours symbolize quality. Scott entered the Taiwan market with their American blend of pastel-coloured toilet tissues; the launch flopped. Sales took off when they changed the colours to bright red, yellow and gold. Can you imagine UK toilets with bright red toilet paper? Pilditch (1973) remarked that: 'Not only do simpler folk like stronger colours, but people who live under bright sun have different values from those whose outlook is dimmed, say, by England's "leaden" skies. Think of this when designing packs to sell to Italian winegrowers, or Glaswegian dockers.' This is important, because cross-border packaging may become more common than cross-border advertising.

The cost of colour

Four colours obviously cost more to print than two colours. Can one be economic with the use of colour, the number of colours and the kind of inks? Is single colour too downmarket? Are four colours really needed? Has anyone tested a change in colours?

Graphics

Graphics communicate on different levels. The two-dimensional design on a label can help to *create and protect individuality/uniqueness, reinforce a brand name or image*, help to reposition, increase shelf presence, etc. The use of graphics is arguably the easiest of the designer's tools to analyse, as marketing managers are reasonably design literate as far as graphics are concerned. A naked body on the label of a bottle of beer will attract attention. However, not every brand manager wants this kind of attention. Graphics can use other images to make a pack stand out from the crowd. In terms of branding, the visual image should be distinctive and should make the pack *immediately and easily recognizable*. Even an ordinary tin box can become a valued item once some attractive graphics have been applied. Graphics *add value* by adding *aesthetic quality*. This creates *'stay after value'*, which allows the branding to keep working inside the home for many years, sometimes generations. Graphics are sometimes used as a kind of *sales promotion* by becoming *a limited edition/collector's item*, as in the case of the Guinness centenary Christmas label. Graphics can add value by offering, for example: additional features such as games (eg a box of matches with matchstick puzzles); intrigue (eg the label positions the ancient drink mead as a bottle of history rather than just a bottle of alcohol); a room-enhancing, stimulating plaything rather than just a dull necessity (baby lotion with colourful children's toys); or simply creating quality associations with images of far-off places (coffee with palm trees).

Repositioned as a bottle of history rather than just a bottle of alcohol

Good graphics can create a mood or trigger *lifestyle aspirations* that reflect the often latent desires of the target market, eg a shampoo label showing an English country scene for one target market and a rugged desert for another aspiring lifestyle segment.

Attention to detail combined with an understanding of the cues and symbols that are relevant to a particular target market allow the designer to *play with the unconscious meaning of symbols and images*. In the case of a cooking fat, according to the psychologists, the positioning of a *wooden spoon* made it 'possible for the housewife to rehearse the use of the product while it was still on the shelf.' Pilditch (1973) explained that 'the spoon also served to inject the product with some of the reliability of grandmother's honest-to-goodness, my doesn't that smell good, old-fashioned kitchen'. In a separate piece of research the analysts turned to the number and layout of *biscuits* on a package. A picture showing biscuits scattered all over created psychological discomfort, or dissonance, because it suggested gaiety, disorganization, permissiveness and irresponsibility ('never know how many were eaten by the kids'). A different picture showing the biscuits in a neat line triggered associations with orderliness, parsimony, and fear of disrupting the line by taking a biscuit, which again resulted in unconscious psychological tension or discomfort. The third image of just a few biscuits on a plate cut out the chaos and the irresponsibility and invited the viewer to feel free to take a biscuit. The number of biscuits was, however, limited to demonstrate authority and control.

Graphics affect taste

In the same way as colour, graphics also affect taste perceptions. In fact, packaging designers can test different label graphics by asking focus groups or consumer panels to give their opinions on the taste of (unknown to them) the same product. The more elegant bottle will tend to have a refined taste, the macho label might have a stronger flavour, etc.

Typography creating a tactile experience

Graphics integrate with other packaging variables to create effective communications. Mary Lewis (1991) suggested that 'if the form (shape and size of the pack) makes the statement then the graphics should step back'. The Lewis Moberly consultancy worked on Yves Rocher aromatherapy oils and created a *tactile experience* prompted by graphics 'by running the typography (letters) right round the bottle to encourage the viewer to turn it, touch it and begin to experience the product through the pack'.

Many years ago Coca-Cola discovered that their dynamic white contour curve (the flowing white ribbon underlining the Coca-Cola and Coke logo) 'reminded observers of the famous profile of the hobble-skirted contour bottle'.

The graphics should be developed only after some other key questions have been asked. These include: Does the pack use the *logo* effectively? Can the graphics make space for future *on-pack promotions*? Do the graphics leave space for international copy translation (usually requires more space than English)? Will the graphics lend themselves or at least link with point-of-sale *materials*? Are the graphic images unique and *protectable* or can someone else design something similar, leaving customers confused and unaware of their own brand-switching decision?

The other pack functions are also helped by good graphics, eg a blend of visual and verbal instructions can make a product and pack much easier to use and store (*convenience and protection*).

Spreadable graphics that add value

A new spreadable butter was reportedly the same as the old butter except that the graphic instructions read 'do not put in fridge'.

Graphics can also indicate production processes or corporate caring values such as 'recycled' or 'free from animal testing'. There is some confusion currently because of the lack of central agreement on appropriate logos.

Packaging that expresses caring corporate values

Finally, *bar codes* linked with *EPOS* (electronic point-of-sale) scanners at retail store checkouts help internal communications between the retailer and supplier by updating stock levels, reorder information and other sales analysis (eg by product, by store, by day, etc).

Bar codes provide useful marketing information

Materials

Materials communicate. Certain materials, like glass or metal, have an intrinsic value. Glass still seems to be associated with higher quality. Many wine drinkers would be suspicious of a supposedly top-quality wine if it was presented to them in a plastic bottle. Having said that, the packaging of wine has gone through the most radical of shake-ups. Twenty years ago, if someone had forecast that an individual would be drinking wine out of cardboard boxes within 20 years it is likely that the comment would have been taken as an insult – with hints of socially unacceptable behaviour. Yet today the wine box is arguably packaging's greatest innovation, with a nation happily drinking from cardboard boxes.

The materials used in packaging *affect perceptions of product quality*. A good example of this was discovered in the United States, where, ironically, the better product was perceived to be in the more difficult to open package. Crisps of equal freshness were packaged in wax paper bags and polyvinyl bags. The crisps in the polyvinyl bag were perceived (by 87 per cent) to be 'superior in taste and freshness' despite being more difficult to open.

Guinness found that packaging materials, and tins in particular, affected taste perceptions. There were comments like 'too gassy, it taints the flavour and its tastes of tin' (Nicholas, 1991). Prelaunch research of the *Guinness draught can* showed that in blind taste tests equal numbers preferred the pure draught Guinness and canned draught Guinness. Subsequent sight tests (showing the source, ie can or tap) revealed the hidden associations of tin cans: there was a 70:30 split in favour of the draught Guinness. Pretty Polly used tin as an innovative piece of packaging for its nylon tights.

Certain overseas markets have different packaging material expectations from what is considered to be the norm in the UK. For example, in *Europe*, meats, fruit, vegetables, pet

Materials can be used innovatively to create extra 'shelf presence'

foods and fruit juices are packed in glass. This means that if UK manufacturers want to enter these markets they will have to work with a new packaging medium, which may well be glass. In the UK tin has an emotional quality. It can become even more emotional when mixed with shape and colour, eg a red, heart-shaped, tin box of chocolates for St Valentine's Day. Today tin box packs are used for boxer shorts and children's clothes as well as food.

Technological developments allow relatively sophisticated printing techniques to be used on almost any kind of surface, as demonstrated by the attractive graphics used on today's cardboard wine boxes and tin boxes.

Some packaging materials have to work very hard. For example, microwave packs have to be able to protect and store the food at temperatures below zero and then have to offer convenience cooking by being able to be put into a microwave at very high temperatures. Some packs are then used to eat out of. *Self-heating* and *self-cooling* cans offer new levels of convenience. Apart from the *convenience and communications* implications of packaging materials, the final materials choice is integrated with a host of other factors such as optimum size, weight, strength, cost and filling speed, overlaying with other features such as colour, closure, secondary packaging, shelf life, barrier properties, tactile characteristics and shelf impact.

Finally, material is the variable that is affected directly by *environmental pressure groups*. New legislation is putting pressure on manufacturers and retailers to use more environmentally friendly packaging. The US *garbologist* now probes landfill sites to determine the state of decay of various materials. In Europe, Germany leads the way in environmental legislation. A company's overseas growth may be stifled by packaging and materials that do not meet legislative criteria. Despite the *logistical nightmare*, the refillable pack is here to stay. The environmental factor has a direct impact on packaging and, in particular, on packaging materials. Warner-Lambert is developing a new *disposable plastic* made almost entirely out of biodegradable starch derived from potatoes, corn, rice and wheat.

Smell

Smells can change shopping behaviour. In a Philadelphia jewellery store some years ago, casual shoppers lingered longer than usual because, claims the Monell Chemical Sense Center, scents change shoppers' moods. In this particular case it was a fruity floral scent. Mood-changing odours change people's brain patterns. The *Chicago Tribune* reported Alan Hursch, neurological director of the Smell and Taste Treatment and Research Foundation in Chicago, as saying, 'Eventually we will be able to influence in a much more powerful way. By making people more relaxed or more trusting you could sell them more.' Scented packaging is becoming more popular.

WHAT IS A BRAND?

As Mary Lewis (1991) said, 'The brand is the aura of beliefs and expectations about a product (or service) which make it relevant and distinctive. It stretches beyond the physical and into the psychological and is extremely powerful.'

WHY REDESIGN?

'If it ain't broke, don't fix it.' Perhaps, but some pack designs can become tired, dated or the market simply moves away, making the pack's current position a liability. On the other hand, valuable brand equities or properties such as names and logos are assets worth maintaining. They may need 'tweaking' from time to time, but rarely need to be disposed of. Perhaps a creative brand manager and a professional printer can produce an updated or even new graphic design for a pack. Jan Hall, formerly of Coley Porter Bell, says this would be like 'putting together the *Pope and a paint company* to paint the Sistine Chapel'. Alan Topalian (1984) suggested that the designer's interest (or input) into the pack increases progressively during the course of the product's life cycle (see Figure 17.1). In other words, the pack design has an increasingly important role as competition becomes more intense.

A PACKAGING DESIGN BRIEF

The SOS + 3Ms can be used as a checklist when writing a design brief. See how it is modified for a packaging designer brief (page 539), a corporate identity design brief (page 610) and an advertising brief (page 166).

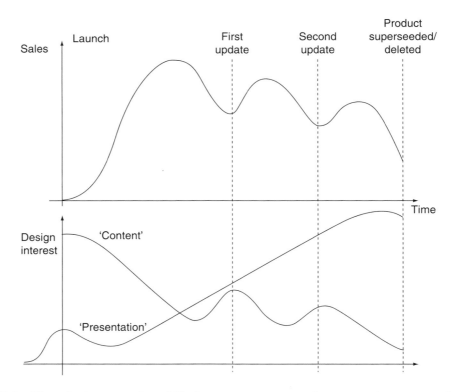

Figure 17.1 How design attention shifts between content and presentation as a product progresses through its life cycle

Situation/background

- company (history, production facilities);
- product (range, features and benefits, material properties, eg liquids, gases, chemicals);
- market (size, growth, competitive structure, positioning, specific requirements such as pallet configuration);
- target markets: segments, targets, decision-making units – particularly tricky with gift products, eg at whom do you target the design, the giver or receiver?;
- reason for design (eg pressure from retailers' own labels);
- brand factors and personality, key design elements;
- merchandising display opportunities.

Objectives

What packaging functions are prioritized (protection, convenience, communication)? If communication, state specifically, eg repositioning from what to what? Or is the new pack design primarily aimed at shouting louder or creating a stronger shelf presence, etc?

Strategy

How does the pack fit in with the rest of the communications mix (the communications objectives and communications mix)? See Pretty Polly design brief on page 539 to see how PR and merchandising are built into the brief. The brief may also state whether the pack design is a low-risk design project (new unit load, new material, temporary sales promotion, secondary panel changes, new ingredients, etc) or a high-risk design project (new name, new colour, new image, new logo, new shape, etc).

Tactics

Details are not always required here.

Men and women

These are contact names for technical discussions (eg production manager) and for marketing discussions. Clarify who makes the key decisions, (who 'signs off' or approves artwork, etc) and who can provide answers to miscellaneous questions. Names of any other agencies that may be working on other marketing communications aspects, such as advertising and sales promotion.

Money

Money means the design fee, rejection fee (some designers charge a rejection fee for presenting ideas or concepts, even during a pitch), changeover costs (this may incur capital expenditure if a change of shape requires a new machine tool) and, ideally, an indication of the maximum unit cost of the new pack (the designer will need to know size of production runs, etc).

Minutes

The timescale. What are the launch deadlines? When must concepts be presented, agreed, researched, refined and approved? When must the final artwork be delivered? How long has been allowed for tooling (can take up to 50 per cent of the total design time, eg three months).

Measurement

What kind of research will be carried out to monitor the effectiveness of the new pack design?

Miscellaneous

Design constraints, eg size, shapes, colours, images or materials to be used or avoided because of technical, legislative and corporate restrictions on materials, warnings/warranties, and logos respectively.

THE PACKAGING DESIGN PROCESS

The brief may emerge after an initial review of the pack design. The designer/s (whether in-house or an external consultancy) often take the brief away, interpret it and rewrite it. Then they present this to the marketing team to ensure that everyone agrees with each other before embarking on any further creative work or research. This may be followed by further research and eventually a range of concepts (two-dimensional labels and three-dimensional pack shapes, sizes and mechanisms) are developed for further research. This guides the selection of a concept for ultimate development into the new pack. Figure 17.2 shows the standard stages of a design project (this was the process used in the Talisker case study at the end of this chapter).

INDUSTRIAL PACKAGING

The design resource is not exclusively reserved for FMCG goods. There is always room for design, creativity and innovation in industrial markets. Electric cable manufacturer BICC used pack design to stand out from the competition in the commodity cable market and to offer USPs to a traditionally conservative market. They moved from the traditional reel of cable to a newly designed box of cable. This helped the electrical wholesaler by making stacking, storage and identifying (holes in the pack allowed the different colours of cable to be seen) a lot easier. The pack, however, was not allowed to look too up-market as the conservative buyers assumed it would be more expensive. Before phasing out the old cable packs (reels), they were used to advertise the imminent arrival of the new packs – the box of cable.

THE PACKAGING OPPORTUNITY

Packaging is an area of opportunity, since consumers have revealed high levels of dissatisfaction with packaging in general. Impenetrable packs, inadequate labelling, messy packets

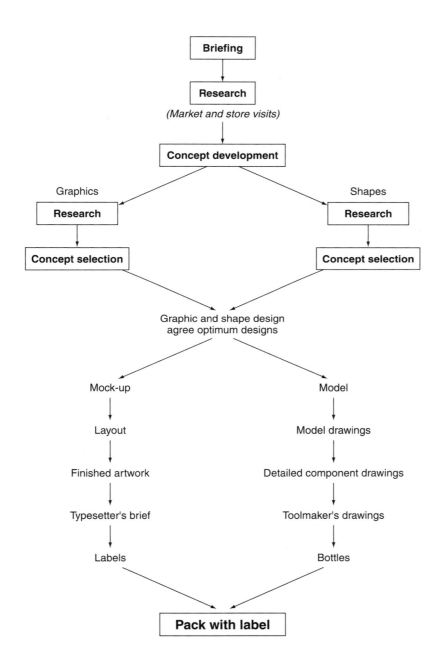

Figure 17.2   Packaging design process
Source: Adapted from the pack design management video *From Dream to Reality*

and overpackaging are common complaints. In short, packaging, by and large, is not user-friendly. Boxes of tea leak leaf dust, sugar packs spill everywhere, bottles dribble after pouring and so on. In a market where pack design is weak, a new design can steal the advantage. It is worth remembering that although pack design, at worst, is just a recognition symbol, at best it can offer so much more. As the cost of advertising rises, product life cycles shorten and competition becomes fiercer, marketers need to get more from their packaging. Creative packaging can create competitive advantage. Even dull and seemingly staid pack designs can be redesigned to create a competitive, cost-effective edge.

There is a whole lifestyle wrapped up in a package. The combination of the size, shape, name, graphics, colours, materials, contents and the supporting communications, ie advertising, point-of-sale, PR and promotions, all create the brand.

Will milk eventually be delivered in easy to open, biodegradable, pan-European, udder-shaped cartons?

CASE STUDY 17.1

Talisker

Situation

Talisker is a brand owned and marketed by Guinness UDV and is the only single malt produced on the Isle of Skye. As a premium malt whisky, it is one of the leading brands in UDV's Classic Malt portfolio.

Objectives

The first objective was to reappraise the brand in light of consumer trends and consumer insight around the brand's taste experience. The second was to raise awareness of the brand as the only malt from the Isle of Skye and to improve standout and distinction against the competitive set.

Strategy

Assessment of the brand's visual equity was carried out by Tutssels Enterprise IG and the client against its personality and emerging values. The market needs were assessed globally and within different groups of consumers. Single malts are experiencing growth within younger drinkers. How could the rugged appeal of the Talisker brand be accentuated?

Tactics

Using lateral thinking techniques, a redesign was developed and evaluated to clarify its unique emotional and visual attributes. A detailed visual equity study was carried out by Tutssels, which included workshops using tools developed from Edward de Bono's techniques. There was no further consumer research. Clients from the core (and most diverse) markets – the United Kingdom, France and the United States – assessed the designs against the existing research findings, current market activity and their in-depth knowledge of the brand. Throughout development design mock-ups were assessed on shelf to address impact and differentiation. It was found that France had a very specific language category that needed to be addressed, and specific visual cues associated with luxury brands. Therefore two designs were implemented: one for all international markets, and the other for France only.

Action

Tutssels created a range of concepts stretching the defined visual equities to meet the new communication elements. Ongoing developments in two- and three-dimensional mock-ups were produced, along with bottle glass colour options and those of labels and carton designs.

The following were the stages involved:

1. Visual audit, market/research assessment.
2. Visual audit conclusions and design brief, concepts against the brief (in two dimensions).
3. Shortlisted routes – three-dimensional mock-ups, assessment of bottle colour.
4. Two alternative routes presented to core markets forum for discussion.
5. One route developed from the forum, further three-dimensional mock-ups, liaison with production department.
6. Fine-tuning of design, copywriting, etc.
7. Artwork – creation of image (model/photography).
8. Handover of artwork to printer, and overview of proofs.
9. Trade launch of the international design.
10. Ongoing development for the French design.

Control

Reviews were held of the competitive activity within the lead (and most diverse) markets.

Talisker cartons before and after the reappraisal

Men and women

The project team comprised Tutssels Enterprise IG (creative director, account director, creative team and project manager) and the client: international brand director marketing managers from lead markets – the United Kingdom, France and the United States – and production managers), a total team of between 15 and 20.

Minutes

The design programme undertaken from January to October 2000. The trade launch was in November 2000. The French route is still under development.

Timelines
Situation and objectives — 4 weeks
Strategy — 3 weeks
Action — 4 months, ongoing
Control — 3 months

Money

No details available.

CASE STUDY 17.2

JET's new oil pack

Situation

Conoco distributes petrol and oil throughout the UK under the JET brand name. Research showed that, as an oil brand, JET was perceived to be of a lower quality and performance than the major brands such as Castrol and Duckhams, despite having a comparable specification. Consumers were seven times more likely to reject JET for a major competitor. The JET brand was clearly underperforming but had substantial potential if the communication to the consumer could be corrected.

Objectives

1. To reposition JET oil as a quality, 'good-value' product with a unique identity.
2. To increase sales by 15 per cent from a base of 1.5 million litres per annum within 12 months of launch.
3. To increase margin by 10 per cent.

Strategy

The unique identity and product repositioning would be achieved through a new structural pack design, in addition to the national programme of petrol station redesign that was being undertaken during the same period and without the aid of extensive advertising support.

The design brief

Part of the brief explained that the key criterion for the repositioning was defined as the JET brand personality. This personality profile was developed as a whole and used to steer the development of all aspects of the brand. The specific objective given to the design consultancy was to define the personality as the new direction for the JET oil brand through and beyond the 1990s via the use of packaging design. The personality details were made up of the target consumer, target consumer needs, brand personality, and consumer take-out.

1. Target consumer: 52 per cent of petrol/oil buyers are price conscious inasmuch as they rank price as the first or second requirement when choosing to buy petrol.
2. Target consumer needs: a brand of petrol/oil that is a legitimate alternative to the other full petrol brands of oil.

3. Brand personality: a smart buy for the savvy motorist.
4. Consumer take-out (or how the consumer feels about the new JET oil before, during and after buying it): 'Choosing JET makes me a smart buyer.'

The pack had to offer clarity of communication through the pack form (shape and function), and a substantial simplification of product use (eg opening, closing, pouring, carrying). The marketing and commercial targets had to be achieved without the aid of extensive advertising.

The brief required the packaging design consultancy, PI Design Consultants, to design and develop the packaging to the prototype stage, including any tooling development, and also to provide a solution that contained intellectual property, ie something new and unique so that it was protectable (through design registration and patents), and that would allow Conoco to gain long-term advantage from the design work.

The design solution

The design solution was a pack that communicates clearly while making product usage easier through the unique swivelling closure that transforms the shape from an oil pack into a pouring jug. The pack has a series of ergonomically refined details to support ease of use, eg the extended handle that allows optimum hand position for carrying and pouring, including two-handed use for women. The handle curve ensures that at any holding angle the weight of the pack is below the holding point, maximizing comfort and control, a feature unique to this design. The pack also has a unique single piece cap that provides an exceptional degree of control when pouring. This feature was critical to the design. Most devices of this type are two-piece components, which are costly to manufacture and inferior ergonomically.

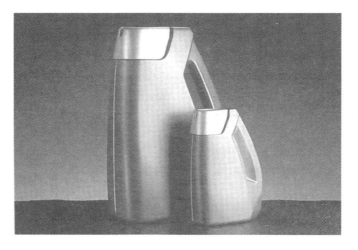

JET's award-winning new pack design

JET schedule

Activity	Month
Briefing	0
↓	
Concepts	1
↓	
Visit to filling plant	2
↓	
Feasibility study	3
↓	
JET weekend (including clients, sales and marketing, advertising agency and packaging consultants)	6
↓	
Liaison with market research agency	↓
↓	
Design development and presentation	14
↓	
Detailing and refining pack	15
↓	
Market research	15
↓	
Qualitative research results	15
↓	
Decision to proceed with design	16
↓	
Visit to production site	17
↓	
Detailed component drawings	18
↓	
Tooling and component progression	19
↓	
Tool trials – prototypes produced for evaluation	21
↓	
Production tooling and patent progression	23
↓	
Project signed off	23
↓	
Product launch	29

Results

It took almost two-and-a-half years from brief to launch. Within six months distribution to independent dealers (under the JET brand) was improved by 50 per cent. Sales volume for the first 12 months was 2.1 million litres, representing a 33 per cent year-on-year increase. The increased margins were sustained and overall profit increased by 43 per cent. The design cost of the project, including tooling costs, was around £120,000 and payback has been achieved. Current sales data indicate that repeat sales are achieving a satisfactory level and a long-term change in the consumers' perception of the JET brand is reported. The pack design also won an Institute of Packaging's Gold Star Pack Award.

APPENDIX 17.1

Pretty Polly: Italia Hosiery Collection design brief

1. The brand identity had to establish Pretty Polly's presence in the higher-priced market sector.
2. Targeted at younger, discerning, style-conscious and knowledgeable hosiery consumers, the designs had to appeal to the emotions. They were to offer Italian style, glamour and sophisticated sensuality.
3. The overall look of the packs had to be recognizably Pretty Polly, with the logo endorsing the sub-brand Italia. The imagery had to reflect the unique selling points of Italia.
4. At the same time the packs had to function well: providing a large window through which the product could be seen and giving product information with clarity and simplicity, thus making selection easy.
5. When merchandising on shelf, only the top third of the pack is visible to the consumer. This alone had to make a big impact, enticing consumers to pull out the pack and take a closer look.
6. The packaging had to add value to the brand and communicate its superiority over the competition.
7. The packaging imagery also had to be adaptable, so it could be extended to public relations and point-of-sale material.

Packaging imagery provides opportunities for publicity and point-of-sale

Key points from Chapter 17

1. Packaging has three functions, one of which is to communicate.
2. Packaging design can create competitive advantage.

FURTHER READING

Bayley, S (1986) *Coke! Coca-Cola 1886–1986: Designing a Megabrand*, Conran Foundation Boilerhouse Project, London

Dichter, E (1964) *Handbook of Consumer Motivations: The Psychology of the World of Objects*, McGraw-Hill, New York

Lewis, M (1991) in *Understanding Brands*, ed D Cowley, Kogan Page, London

Milton, H (1991) *Packaging Design*, The Design Council, London

Nicholas, R (1991) Come home to a real beer, *Marketing Week*, 15 February

Opie, R (1987) *The Art of the Label*, Quarto Publishing, London

Pilditch, J (1973) *The Silent Salesman*, 2nd edn, Business Books, London

Smith, P R (1991) *From Dream to Reality* (video), Media Services, London Guildhall University, London

Southgate, P (1994) *Total Branding by Design*, Kogan Page, London

Topalian, A (1984) *Management of Design Projects*, Alto Design, London

Warden, J (1990) White Paper gives shade to trademarks, *Marketing*, 27 September

Williams, T G (1982) *Consumer Behavior*, research report, West Publishing, St Paul, MN

FURTHER CONTACTS

The Chartered Society of Designers (CSD), 5 Bermondsey Exchange, 179–181 Bermondsey Road, London SE1 3UW (tel: 020 7357 8088; Web site: www.csd.org.uk (under construction))

The Design Business Association (DBA), 35–39 Old Street, London EC1V 9HX (tel. 020 7251 9229; Web site: www.dba.org.uk)

The Institute of Packaging, Sysonby Lodge, Nottingham Road, Melton Mowbray, Leicestershire LE13 0NU (tel: 01664 500055; Web site: www.iop.co.uk)

18

Merchandising

INTRODUCTION

There was a time when below-the-line point-of-sale (POS) materials were considered relevant only to cosmetics, perfumery, confectionery and other impulse purchases. Today merchandising techniques apply to a broader spectrum of markets, from consumer to industrial. Although vast budgets can be spent above the line on advertising to gain the customer's attention or change an attitude, fewer resources are sometimes allocated to the crucial moment in the buying process – the point in the buying cycle where the customer is physically in front of the product or service and is about to make a decision as to whether to buy or pass by – the point-of-sale.

Shopping for happiness

Going shopping is claimed to be Britain's second most popular leisure activity after watching TV. This is also evident in the United States, where retailers almost double as leisure centres. *'Mall walking'* is now a significant activity. In the north of England customers are transported by the coachload to spend a day at one of Europe's largest retail centres, Gateshead's Metro Centre.

In many consumer markets the consumer's *final decision to buy is often made inside*, and not outside, the store. In the United States, almost three-quarters of purchase decisions are made inside the store. Merchandising techniques such as display and store design are therefore vital communications tools that can guide a buyer towards making a purchase. They are often the last chance to communicate with the buyer. Merchandising does not just apply to the traditional retail outlets of supermarkets, garages and department stores, but also to DIY stores, brown-goods retailers (stereos and TVs), corner shops, office-equipment showrooms and cash-and-carry wholesalers.

The merchandising opportunity lies relatively untapped in industrial wholesale outlets such as electrical wholesalers and builders' suppliers, where a lot of merchandising tends to look dusty, dirty and uninteresting. There is room here for creative, intelligent and effective merchandising. It does require a delicate balance, since a hard-working electrician in search of some 2-core 3-millimetre cable might assume a distributor to be too expensive if it looked too glitzy and comfortable. On the other hand, merchandising here can provide customers with useful information, eg reminding the buyer about other relevant products and any special offers.

TOMORROW'S MERCHANDISING TECHNIQUES TODAY

Over 10 years ago, Brian Oliver wrote in *Marketing* magazine:

Imagine walking into a high street department store and being greeted by a three-dimensional lifelike copy of John McEnroe's head. As you walk past, it starts to move and even speaks to you… pointing out the features of a tennis racket suspended in mid-air in front of you with no apparent means of support. Then a giant pair of moving lips mounted on a glass display suddenly start talking to you, inviting you to try on the store's winter fashions without even undressing. All you have to do, say the lips, is stand in front of a 'magic mirror', select an item of clothing and, before you can say 'Bruce Oldfield', your reflection is wearing it.

> *Bumping into 3D images*
>
> Today Reebok have developed 3D images which can be projected through a shop window and into the street. By means of 'mirror technology' the 3D image literally hangs in space in front of pedestrians. More and more pedestrians will bump into 3D images like this as production costs fall.
>
> *Marketing Business*

Lenticular displays present more than one image, which changes and catches the customer's eye as he or she walks by. Power sneakers and smart shoes are capable of uploading advertisements to our shoes as we walk by a store (like a sort of digital chewing). Mobile phone systems can link with satellites and know not just who we are but where we are, so that as you walk through a shopping mall the mobile rings and mentions a relevant special offer in a store that you are physically passing at that precise moment. Pepsi already give their customers mobile pagers (see Chapter 13). In-store LCD screens and video terminals positioned at checkouts can transmit special relevant offers (based on previous purchase data) to customers as their store card is 'swiped' through the checkout. And finally, virtual reality can allow all of this (walking, browsing, examining, buying and prompting) without having to leaving the home or the safe confines of your local secure virtual hall or mall. And if you get bored you can nip over to the Louvre or to the cinema for a break without ever leaving your seat.

The virtual world has arrived. Photograph reproduced by kind permission of Trimension

MERCHANDISING TOOLS

In addition to store design, layout, and merchandise ranges and policies, there are a number of in-store merchandising tools:

1. leaflets and dispensers ('take on' boxes);
2. stickers;
3. posters;
4. showcards and cardboard cutouts;
5. branded racks or display units;
6. dump bins;
7. three-dimensional:
   - injection moulded characters (note: the toolmaking process required takes too long for some campaigns);
   - holograms;
   - free-standing floor displays;
8. electronic gadgetry:
   - spotlighting systems;
   - video walls;
   - illuminated display systems with fibre optics;
   - lenticular technology;
   - magic mirrors;
   - interactive POS systems, eg product advice systems, personal consultation systems, smart card POS suggested items;
9. shelf space (number of facings, colour blocking – see page 547, integrated pack design – how all the packs look beside each other on the shelf);
10. shelf positioning (premium locations, cross-merchandising, etc);
11. in-store sampling;
12. window displays.

These systems have been available for many years. One possible problem with high-tech POS is that customers end up admiring the POS material instead of buying the product. On the other hand, products can benefit from POS support, as many products can get lost, eg among the 16,000 items of food that a superstore displays. An innovative POS attracts attention – a key stage in the AIDA communication model on page 97. Although it is important to present fresh images to repeat-visit customers to maintain their interest and loyalty, many retailers' obsession with product density and profit per square foot means that they instantly dismiss most of a supplier's branded merchandising tools. In fact the majority of stores do not have the flexibility or the luxury of space to dedicate to one-off 'stunts' with in-built novelty obsolescence.

DISTRIBUTOR EMPATHY

Skilful supplier merchandising requires an ability to empathize with both the customer and the retailer/wholesaler (distributor). Understanding customers is one thing. Understanding distributors and their perspectives, goals, strategies and tactics is another. It is easy to grasp the importance of maintaining the theme of an advertising campaign inside a store with carefully designed point-of-sale displays. It is not so easy to understand when, why and how a retailer will allow its space to be used for such in-store promotions and display, ie what its merchandising policies are and how to operate within that framework.

This 'distributor empathy' helps a supplier to make his or her product or service (and the relevant marketing communications) fit in with the retailer's plans. The retailer relationship is even more important in today's UK retail market since market power has moved from the manufacturer into the hands of a few major retail chains. It is therefore necessary to understand the various distributor strategies and their approach to merchandising techniques.

Many UK retailers do not enter into any merchandising arrangements with suppliers as they (the retailers) prefer to control all aspects of product presentation centrally to ensure commonality and consistency in all their stores. This is managed by carefully supervised store personnel and/or a roving display management and merchandising team. This does not mean that the supplier can have no involvement in the merchandising. Many stores encourage proactive contributions from their suppliers. Some suppliers gain permission to use their own display teams to ensure that their particular products or services have optimum display on their allocated shelf at all times (see the Thomson Tour Operators case study at the end of this chapter).

RETAIL STRATEGIES

Every retailer has its *own marketing mix*. This fits in with its retailing strategy, which should, in turn, exploit its source of *competitive advantage* (eg exclusive products, lower prices, location or image). A department store exploits location, its quality of service and its quality range of products. A small independent grocery cannot compete on product range or price but can compete on its convenient location, opening hours and friendly relationship/ rapport. A takeaway restaurant may promote its unique home-delivery service. Competitive advantage is relative to competitors' USPs (unique selling propositions) and customer needs. A constant monitoring of the uncontrollable variables that affect markets reveals how competitive advantage can emerge or erode over relatively short periods of time (see Chapter 8). Merchandising strategies are also affected by corporate cultures. For example, some distributors/retailers are more profit orientated than turnover orientated.

This, in turn, affects their pricing policies, promotion policies, merchandising policies and, in general, their merchandising strategies. The more common low-tech merchandising tools are now summarized and discussed under six key headings:

1. store image (external and internal);
2. store layout (customer traffic flows);
3. merchandise ranges;
4. colour blocking;
5. point-of-sale displays / retail sales promotions;
6. miscellaneous.

Store image

The human eye is more sensitive than is sometimes imagined. Clues about a shop are absorbed, often sometimes without our knowing it. Psychologists call these *'cue patterns'*. They help shoppers to decide what kind of a shop it is before actually entering (if entering at all). The store's exterior offers an opportunity to communicate with customers, eg to invite them into the store or to reinforce a desired corporate image. Inside the shop the concept of the *'retail theatre'* becomes evident. It has been suggested that a retail design concept lasts only three to five years, hence the need for the adaptable retail theatre which allows the store's interior layout and design to be changed easily. It is worth remembering that *products, service and store design* all contribute towards the overall store image, but if a customer has no prior experience of a particular store, nor any word-of-mouth reference from peers, then the decision to enter or not to enter may be made solely from the store's visual image (or simply the way it looks). The store's exterior is a bundle of cues. Even the psychological barrier or obstacle, the door, is removed or minimized wherever possible, thereby facilitating an even easier store entry.

Store layout

Customer traffic flow can be directed around a store through detailed attention to layout. For example, 9 out of 10 people are right-handed and naturally prefer turning to the right, so most supermarkets have the primary doors on the left-hand side so the shopping is done to the right in a sort of clockwise manner. *Flow-modelling time-lapse photos* analyse which people go where in the store (and at what times, days, weeks or months). Further analysis reveals where the *high-density areas* are and whether they match the high-turnover areas. Customer movements can be predicted by model questions like 'If a customer were here (in the store), where would he/she go next?' This is important because, as a general rule, if the goods are in the wrong place, they won't sell: 'Out of sight, out of mind'. *Primary and secondary visual points* (as opposed to clutter) are used to pull the customer around the store or to 'shop the full shop' (visit every part of the store). Lighting, signage, photographs, software packages and even popular products like KVIs (known value items) in a food supermarket help the customer to shop the full shop ('the more you see, the more you buy'). It is estimated that out of the 16,000 food items on display in a superstore only approximately 200 are essentials (KVIs) such as tea, coffee, bread, etc.

Merchandise ranges

Once inside the store the customer is faced with a bundle of retail cues that are never neutral. Fruit or perfume are positioned at the front of a store (supermarket and department store respectively). This helps to create images and feelings of freshness and luxury respectively. Impulse products are placed at key positions. Cross-merchandising reminds the customer of related end-use products, which are carefully positioned beside each other, eg shirts and ties together, pasta and pasta sauce. The maxim *'full shelves sell best'* is valid for FMCG retailers but not necessarily for some clothes boutiques. Although *eye level is buy level*, shelf positioning can reflect the current *product life cycle* stage. The larger retail chains use *merchandising display software* packages to determine the right allocation of space to a particular product or brand. An 'optimum shelf layout' print-out (see Figure 18.1) shows what mix and quantities of packs on a shelf maximize a store's objectives (eg maximize sales, minimize over- and under-stocking, maximize profitability). It even gives a colour print-out of what the recommended shelf layout would look like. Some retailers like to have their own brands placed alongside the main brands, often on the left-hand side (since the Western eye reads from left to right and therefore spots the own brand first).

Colour blocking

A supermarket customer scans shelves at the rate of four feet per second from a distance of eight feet away. Packaging, therefore, has to work very hard to attract the customer's eye. Retailers and packaging designers sometimes use colour blocking to attract attention by placing similarly coloured items close to each other to create a stronger shelf presence by means of a block of colour. Colour blocking can also link colours to product use associations, eg blue, green and white can be associated with stimulating and refreshing surf. This in turn might be built into the shower gel section.

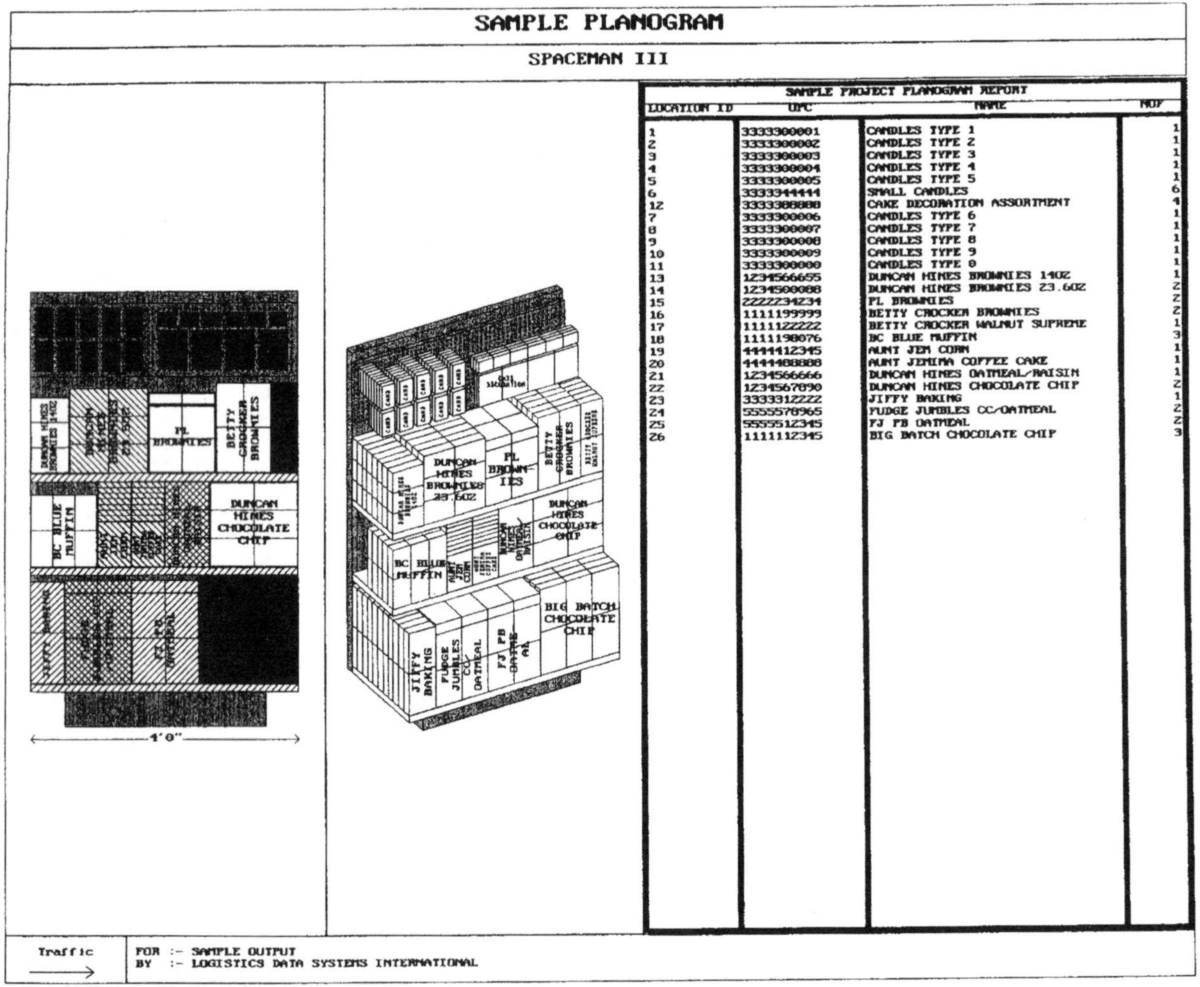

SAMPLE PLANOGRAM

SPACEMAN III

SAMPLE PROJECT PLANOGRAM REPORT

LOCATION ID	UPC	NAME	NUM
1	3333900001	CANDLES TYPE 1	1
2	3333900002	CANDLES TYPE 2	1
3	3333900003	CANDLES TYPE 3	1
4	3333900004	CANDLES TYPE 4	6
5	3333900005	CANDLES TYPE 5	4
6	3333344444	SMALL CANDLES	1
12	3333900006	CAKE DECORATION ASSORTMENT	1
7	3333900007	CANDLES TYPE 6	1
8	3333900008	CANDLES TYPE 7	1
9	3333900009	CANDLES TYPE 8	1
10	3333900009	CANDLES TYPE 9	1
11	1234566655	DUNCAN HINES BROWNIES 14OZ	2
13	1234566666	DUNCAN HINES BROWNIES 23.6OZ	2
14	2222223634	PL BROWNIES	2
15	1111199999	BETTY CROCKER BROWNIES	3
16	1111122222	BETTY CROCKER WALNUT SUPREME	1
17	1111198876	BC BLUE MUFFIN	1
18	4444412345	AUNT JEN CORN	1
19	4444488888	DUNCAN HINES OATMEAL-RAISIN	1
20	1234567890	DUNCAN HINES CHOCOLATE CHIP	2
21	3333378965	JIFFY BAKING	1
22	3333378965	FUDGE JUBBLES CC-OATMEAL	1
25	5555512345	FJ PB OATMEAL	2
26	1111112345	BIG BATCH CHOCOLATE CHIP	3

Traffic →

FOR :- SAMPLE OUTPUT
BY :- LOGISTICS DATA SYSTEMS INTERNATIONAL

Figure 18.1 Optimum shelf print-out shown from two angles

Point-of-sale displays/retail sales promotions

This includes displays, sampling points, dump displays and so on. Many retailers will not allow suppliers this free space, since every square foot of retail generates a certain amount of revenue. Engel, Warshaw and Kinnear (1991) suggest that the manufacturer's response to a store's non-use of its POS materials is to double the quantity made available. This demonstrates the supplier's lack of empathy with the retailer's merchandising policies, which is a waste of time and money as well as being a nuisance. On occasions, and in the appropriate store space, a retailer may allow the supplier the privilege of using extra space. Prime selling space can be bought by suppliers. A product's sales can be boosted depending on its location and shelf positioning. In-store *sales promotion* can *tie in with advertising, cooperative advertising, publicity* and perhaps even trade discounts and rebates. It should be designed to boost sales without creating any conflict with overall store image. Balance, proportion, lighting, colour and display units should be used to create the optimum impact on a consistent basis (perhaps across many hundreds of stores). Once the store grants permission, field marketing agencies can then provide merchandising teams to maintain proper POS displays or shelf facings (see the Thomson case study at the end of this chapter).

Miscellaneous

In-store *sound* effects can be used to make announcements (eg to direct shoppers' attention to a special offer), to add atmosphere (crowd applause in sports shop video walls), to relax the buyer or to stimulate the buyer to move faster (eg varying the types of music) and so on. Some POS tools engage customers in a dialogue by asking questions.

Scents are also used inside a store to change shoppers' moods and buying behaviour. The Monell Chemical Sense Center in Philadelphia has found its pilot projects highlight how the use of smell affects sales. For example, certain scents (in this case, a fruity floral scent) caused casual shoppers at a jewellery store to linger longer. An individual's brainwaves and moods (eg relaxed and trusting) can be changed by extremely low levels of certain scents. In the UK one home furnishings retailer uses a bakery/café to entice customers into the store to buy non-food-related products, eg clothing and lighting.

In supermarkets it is interesting to note how the smell from the fish counter is not as strong as the wafting smell of freshly baked bread at the bread counter.

London-based Digiscents offer to create 'a particular atmosphere in a retail store, relax patients in a waiting room, perk up your sales team, or evoke associations in your customers' minds' through a variety of dispersion techniques 'from central ventilation systems to hand-held sprays, in liquids, granules, gels or powder. Even pressure-sensitive micro-encapsulated strips. These produce specific moods, neutralising unpleasant odours, impregnating product or corporate literature, endorsing a company's corporate identity – an aromatic logo.'

Finally, '*mindshare*' (discussed in Chapter 10) combined with merchandising techniques provide an extremely potent communications package as the store's sales staff, space and display promote a particular supplier's goods.

MEASURING MERCHANDISING EFFECTIVENESS

The bar code scanner at the checkout records what is being sold instantaneously. It can record the sales effect of allowing a product more shelf space, different shelf location, special displays and so on. EPOS (electronic point-of-sale) scanners also measure sales responses to new advertising campaigns and price changes, as well as providing operational stock control data to central warehouses. As suppliers and distributors work more closely together and become strategic partners, some suppliers are given access to a selection of EPOS data which measures sales results, store by store around the country, on a daily, weekly or even hourly basis.

CASE STUDY 18.1

Thomson Tours

This case study demonstrates how vital merchandising is and how a field marketing agency manages the whole operation.

Racking is crucial to tour operators

Situation

Major travel operator Thomson Tours enjoys a dominant market share and offers a wide range of long- and short-haul holidays to prospective customers via the travel agent in the competitive, and currently economically vulnerable, travel sector. 'Racking' (the display of a brochure in travel agents) is crucial to the success of all tour operators. Holidays are rarely booked without a comparison of the product offering from several competitors. Over 75 per cent of holidays are booked from a brochure that has been picked up and read. Few consumers ask counter staff for a brochure. It is therefore essential to ensure that the 30 different types of Thomson brochures are positioned in the right store, on the right shelf at the right time of year. Stock of replacement supplies has to be ready so that the appropriate brochure is available at the point-of-sale at the right time. The several thousand travel agents mean that this is too big a requirement to be handled by Thomson's in-house marketing and sales team. Three thousand nominated UK travel agencies were targeted.

Objective

To ensure that the right brochures are available to the 3,000 nominated travel agents at all times.

Strategy

A comprehensive brochure management and merchandising support programme was developed and contracted out to the field marketing agency.

Tactics

- Stamping, racking and ordering brochures as required and where stocks allow. This includes use of BOBCAT – a computerized brochure-ordering system based on Psion technology developed by Thomson with CPM Field Marketing. The system allows the merchandiser to transmit daily via a hand-held computer to the brochure distribution house, thereby ensuring a speedy, accurate and effective stock control and delivery system.
- Carrying out short sales presentations, highlighting key selling points to counter staff.
- Supporting brochure launches with additional tactical activity during key periods. Blitz operations such as these involve the team making 3,000 calls in two days, with the final results presented to Thomson three weeks later.
- Three thousand agents are visited, normally every two weeks.

Control

Thomson previously sent off batches of brochures to travel agents without really knowing which agents were running out, which agents placed them on which shelves and which agents had them thrown in a pile in the store room. The new merchandising system gives them online data, which reduces wastage as the team ensures the right brochures are on the right shelf at the right time. This has helped to increase sales by ensuring that the brochures are available at all the targeted agents. At the same time it has helped to reduce costs incurred by inappropriate print runs, unnecessary deliveries, etc.

Men and women

The field marketing agency, CPM, allocated a team of 65 field staff, 8 supervisors and 1 account manager to the ongoing field marketing activity. This team is increased to 150 merchandisers and 8 supervisors to support blitz operations at key times such as brochure launches. Both teams are headed by a national field manager who reports to Thomson's marketing department.

Money

Comprehensive field marketing activities range from £50,000 to £1,000,000 annually, depending on the size and scope of the operation.

Minutes

All field marketing staff attend a fortnightly half-day briefing. This is supplemented by six-monthly one-day sales conferences where major briefing and reviews are presented. The normal call cycle, which covers every one of the 3,000 travel agents, is two weeks. This means that every targeted travel agent gets visited and updated once a fortnight. Alternatively, a faster blitz can be completed within two days by using an extra 150 merchandisers.

Key points from Chapter 18:

1. Merchandising techniques offer a last chance to communicate with the buyer.
2. Manufacturers need to empathize with their distributors' strategies and merchandising policies.

FURTHER READING

Danger, P (1968) *Using Colour to Sell*, Gower, Aldershot

Engel, J, Warshaw, M and Kinnear, T (1991) *Promotional Strategy: Managing the Marketing Communications Process*, 7th edn, Irwin, Homewood, IL

Erlichman, J (1992) How hidden persuasion makes shoppers spend, *The Guardian*, 11 August

FURTHER CONTACTS

British Promotional Merchandise Association (BPMA), Bank Chambers, 15 High Road, Byfleet, Surrey KT14 7QA (tel: 01932 355660; Web site: www.bpma.co.uk)

Institute of Sales Promotion, Arena House, 66–68 Pentonville Road, London N1 9HS (tel: 020 7837 5340; Web site: www.isp.org.uk)

POPAI (Point of Purchasing Advertising Institute), Devonshire House, Bank Street, Lutterworth, Leicester LE17 4AG (tel: 01455 554848; Web site: www.popai.co.uk)

Sales Promotion Consultants Association (SPCA), Arena House, 66–68 Pentonville Road, London N1 9HS (tel: 020 7580 8225; Web site: www.spca.org.uk)

19

Word of mouth

INTRODUCTION

People talk about organizations, their products, their services and their staff. Whether it is a complaint, admiration or an endorsement, products and services are often a source of conversation. Today it is not just the products themselves but their marketing communications, including advertising campaigns, editorial stories, publicity stunts and special offers, that are discussed. The multi-step communications model on page 77 shows how word of mouth (WOM) can work for both advertisements and products.

Of all the elements of the communications mix, WOM is by far the most potent on a one-to-one basis. No amount of advertising or expert selling could compete with a colleague or friend recommending or criticizing a particular product or service. Similarly, it is unlikely that a teaser advertisement could motivate a viewer actively to watch out for the next advertisement in a campaign in the way that WOM could. For example, a previous discussion about a particular advertisement among friends can arouse interest in and increase observation of subsequent television advertisements.

Communications tools themselves can be used to generate WOM. Publicity stunts, clever mailings, creative promotions and challenging advertising campaigns stimulate conversation among buyers and potential buyers, either because of their shock, humour and entertainment, or because of their abstract ideas. There are other devices and techniques that encourage and accelerate the WOM process, such as postcards, digital postcards (eg Carlsberg), T-shirts, photographs, awards and certificates (issued to visitors, customers and enquirers). NGN ('neighbour get neighbour') promotions (discussed in Chapter 3), referrals and networking all create opportunities for some form of dialogue about a particular product, service or organization. The Internet can accelerate word of mouth with its networks of news groups, chat rooms, discussion forums and viral marketing. In addition, the Internet has increased communications among customers, as demonstrated by the P2P and C2C models discussed in Chapter 3.

Spoof word of mouth

An e-mail that appears to systematically delete files on a PC when opened was nothing more than a spoof virus which, when opened, appears to attack the recipient's PC, deleting files on screen. It reveals the contents of the hard drive, appears to delete everything and leaves a message: 'Windows has detected no system software and is shutting down.' The screen goes black momentarily followed by a message. 'Good job this is only a game', followed by some advertisements for the game called Virus. It is intended that recipients will play the spoof on others and thereby spread the word.

Revolution

The personal WOM medium can be budgeted for, planned and integrated into the marketing communications mix. This requires an understanding of opinion leaders and opinion formers and the overall audience/target market (as explained in Chapter 3).

Marketing managers obviously want to ensure that, first, people always say nice things about their products and, second, people never say bad things about their products. The most influential and controllable aspect of WOM communication is, of course, an individual's own direct experience of an organization's products or services. This chapter therefore focuses on the two key factors that affect this experience: the level of quality and customer care. But first consider why and how WOM occurs.

Why and how word of mouth occurs

Why do people bother to talk about products and services in the first place? What exactly do they talk about? Do some people talk more than others? Are some people listened to more than others? Who are these opinion leaders and opinion formers? Opinion formers such as journalists are relatively easy to identify. So too are opinion leaders (influential individuals and organizations) in industrial markets, but in consumer markets careful research is usually required to identify the opinion leaders, their aspirations, lifestyles, media usage, etc. See how style leaders are fed specific messages on pages 75–77.

Research suggests that *dissatisfied customers* talk about their bad experience to two or three times more people than *satisfied customers* talk to about their good experience. A dissatisfied customer can tell up to 11 other people about the bad experience they suffered with a particular product or service. Often the company never gets to hear about the complaint, but the complaint is allowed to continue rampaging through a market. Bad news travels fast. As Philip Kotler said: 'Bad word of mouth travels further and faster than good word of mouth and can easily poison opinion about the company.' Satisfied customers tend not to tell so many other people. They are, however, more likely to be retained as loyal customers, since they enjoyed the experience in the first place.

Higher standards and higher levels of expectation among buyers are partly responsible for today's more vociferous customers. They are better informed and are less willing to make do with shoddy service or a faulty product. The consumer magazine *Which?* publishes a leaflet called 'How to complain'. Despite the higher standards and levels of expectancy, and greater customer confidence and knowledge about complaining, few dissatisfied customers actually bother to complain. Many organizations today try to get their customers to talk to them and tell them what is wrong (and also what is right) by asking them to fill in questionnaires (see Appendices 19.2 and 19.3 at the end of this chapter, pages 575 and 576) or by inviting them to phone a freephone (0800) number. Those who do phone in are generally invaluable to the company's future. Some organizations are so keen on developing a dialogue with their customers that they will operate outbound telemarketing campaigns as well as inbound (0800 numbers).

Welcome complaints

Only 1 in every 24 dissatisfied customers bothers to complain according to TARP (now known as E-Satisfy Ltd). Rather than facing an unknown enemy of bitter, disappointed and dissatisfied customers, a complaint offers a chance to sort out the previously unknown problem. It gives the organization the opportunity to find the enemy within (internal problems such as quality control or demotivated staff). One company chairman takes time to listen to the taped telephone complaints while driving home in his car. Many services companies actually ask their customers to fill in a form about levels of satisfaction or dissatisfaction.

Solutions are relatively easy. Identifying the problem is the difficult part. Complaints are generally helpful. Philip Kotler suggested that companies should 'set up suggestion and other systems *to maximise the customer's opportunity to complain'*. He pointed out that the 3M company claims that 'over two-thirds of its innovation ideas come from listening to customer complaints'. Listening is just the beginning. It is vital to have a system that enables a constructive response.

Stopping complaints before they happen

Telemarketing provides a low-cost method of keeping in touch with customers. Some customers may occasionally have the odd question that does not merit them making a telephone call, but nevertheless they would like it answered. If left unanswered the question can fester into a source of dissatisfaction. Frequent outbound telephone contact (where the company calls the customer) in the form of after-sales service (eg simply checking to see if everything is all right or whether any stocks need replenishing) can be used to support the field salesforce schedule of personal visits. Inbound (0800 and freephone) customer service lines can also reassure customers if they are made aware of the facility. ICL computer company has a team of *telephone diagnosticians* who handle fault reports from customers. Linked to a sophisticated computerized diagnostic kit, they can identify whether the fault really exists or not. Many problems arise from the user's lack of knowledge, which means many potential problems or frustrations can be sorted out over the phone. If a fault is identified, the diagnosis informs the engineer in advance so that he or she arrives with the right spare part.

The 1–10–100 rule

In *Customer Care* Sarah Cook (1992) points out it has been proven that, by actively listening to customers (and their complaints), companies can save, rather than spend, money. Federal Express's 1–10–100 rule illustrates the point. This says:

> For every pound your company might spend on preventing a quality problem, it will spend 10 to inspect and correct the mistake after it occurs. In the worst case, the quality failure goes unanswered or unnoticed until after your customer has taken delivery. To fix the problem at this stage, you probably pay about 100 times what you could have paid to prevent it from happening at all.

Influencing word of mouth

In addition to the other WOM tools discussed at the beginning of this chapter, WOM is, as already mentioned, directly affected by levels of customer satisfaction. This experience is, in turn, directly affected by two key controllable factors:

1. quality;
2. customer care.

The new importance of quality and customer care

Quality and customer care have become an important element in differentiating one company from another. Managed properly, they can create competitive advantage. Talking about quality and customer service, Tom Peters said that they were 'very commonplace words that had slipped out of the business lexicon in favour of a whole bunch of jargony words which 10 or 15 years ago were dominating America and coming to dominate the thinking patterns in Great Britain'. He continued: 'at the time everyone was involved in their portfolio strategy models, and their optimization and their regression analysis and their linear programmes and so on'. These are useful, but the message is clear – do not forget about customers, who are ultimately the centre of the universe for the corporation. Peters added: 'Ten years ago you would not have had a conference with that title ("Conference on Customers") in Manhattan, London, Milan or Frankfurt. Ten years ago we would have had "marketing strategies for the 90s" or something like that, that would have gotten out the next 10 obscure theories.'

QUALITY

During the 1950s Dr Joseph Juran's 'managerial breakthrough' programmes in Japan helped to create and consolidate quality systems in Japanese business through his 'breakthrough and prevention' versus 'control and inspection' approach. The design profession has developed a similar approach to product and manufacturing design. The design maxim 'design quality in, instead of inspecting faults out' speaks for itself.

Forty years later Tom Peters spoke to top British managers about quality and said 'Quality – one of the better-kept secrets – secrets well known to people such as the Germans and the Japanese – not so well known, unfortunately, to the Americans and British! Quality has always paid.'

Quality guru John Humble reasserted the importance of quality by highlighting its impact on financial performance when he said that 'research demonstrates that sustained financial performance is determined by the relative perceived quality of an organization's products and services' (Euromonitor Conference on Quality, London, May 1989).

Total quality management

Today total quality management (TQM) is becoming better understood. ISO (International Standards Organization) 9001:2000 gives companies an opportunity to set targets and formally measure quality standards throughout the organization. TQM has three elements:

1. A documented system that defines quality standards.
2. Organizational processes to ensure quality is focused on customers.
3. A system of measurement that helps to monitor and control.

TQM is not a bureaucratic quagmire creating mini-empires, but rather a visionary management system of improving both customer and employee levels of satisfaction, communication and motivation. There are many methods of measuring whether TQM is worthwhile or not. One simple criterion is the level of *customer retention* (how many existing customers come back again). Rank Xerox had a customer retention value of 52 (52 per cent came back and 48 per cent went elsewhere). They then launched their TQM programme. Six years later customer retention was up to 92, while return on investment had just about doubled. Today they measure (a) new customer satisfaction within 48 hours of installation, (b) all customers and their levels of satisfaction every month (see Appendix 19.3 on page 576), (c) levels of customer satisfaction compared against the competition (called 'benchmarking'), once a year, and (d) employee satisfaction.

The McGregor Cory case study at the end of this chapter demonstrates the improvements in customer communications that can come about through innovative TQM.

Partnership sourcing

Partnership sourcing encourages open communications and close cooperation between customer and supplier. In a sense it is the *ultimate in marketing communications*.

When John Egan became chairman of Jaguar he systematically questioned Jaguar owners, analysed warranty claims, etc, and found 150 recurring faults. Sixty per cent originated with bought-in components, so Egan raised the suppliers' standards by initiating joint studies and quality audits. Suppliers had to sign an agreement accepting responsibility for warranty costs caused by failure of their part/s. Partnership sourcing creates even closer involvement between suppliers and buyers by encouraging both parties to work together more closely on everything from specifying manufacturing systems, investment in machinery, delivery schedules and repeat orders to exclusivity. Price is only one element in the total cost negotiations. These can cover many other aspects that ultimately affect costs and sales (eg delivery size and frequency of deliveries, quality levels, materials and design specifications).

The case study at the end of this chapter demonstrates how partnership sourcing and customer care integrate successfully.

CUSTOMER CARE

A gentle mind and a Disney smile

The motto of one department store in the Ginza district of Tokyo reads: 'leading store in courtesy and kindness'. Employees make a written commitment to increase customer service called a 'kindness declaration'. The president's own proclamation is to 'treat customers with gentle eyes, gentle face, gentle words, gentle behaviour and a gentle mind'. Two examples from the employees' declarations read: 'I will never get upset' and 'I will keep a Disney smile'.

Open University

Customer care is more than an isolated 'smile campaign'. In fact it has to be sustainable and *internally marketed* or promoted so that all staff believe in, and are happy about, the customer care programme. The Mariott Hotel chief, Mr Mariott, once summarized the issue when he said 'How can we make customers happy with unhappy staff?' So staff have to be happy and trained in customer care. Involvement, reward and recognition can create forms of psychic income (see page 285) which motivate staff. Research findings from the Harvard Business School suggest that organizations should now refocus equally on their employees, their customers and their investors (as opposed to investors first, customers second and employees last). The idea is that happy employees generate happy customers, who generate repeat business plus positive WOM references which, in turn, boosts sales, profits and ROI.

Tom Peters said that managers need to be trained to 'allow people to use their heads as well as their arm muscles'. It has been suggested that 85 per cent of problems are created by managers. Empowerment is a great motivator, eg ideas or solutions generated by staff are more likely to be implemented. Some supervision is, of course, needed. Everyone cannot implement their own idea. Even cost-saving/revenue-generating suggestions need resources to manage them. In one year alone Matsuschita Electric had 6,446,935 suggestions or 79.6 suggestions per employee (Japanese Human Relations Association). It requires resources to deal with and respond to suggestions. A suggestion scheme without feedback defeats the purpose since it can create disillusionment, demotivation and even distrust. Feedback in customer care terms is also vital. A measurable customer care programme that is communicated to the staff helps them to understand the direct effect of their input.

> Promptitude in small matters is a source of great content.

The first generation

The first-generation customer care programme dealt with the customer interface. This can be difficult enough. Dealing with customers who have had a bad experience, or who are sometimes irritable, tired, confused, ripped off, lonely, greedy, demanding and occasionally

The 'have a nice day' syndrome may eventually make staff and customers even more weary

downright dishonest is, in itself, demanding. Nevertheless, a plastic smile supported by the 'have a nice day' syndrome may eventually make both staff and customers even more weary, as the Ed McLachlan cartoon opposite demonstrates.

The ability not just to be sympathetic but to solve problems is worth developing. *The second-generation* customer care programme goes beyond simply trying constantly to improve the first-generation results. The second-phase programme goes behind the customer interface and into the back room where organization structures, operational systems and management styles exist. The steps in the process from customer enquiry or complaint through to customer satisfaction have to be analysed for duplication and inefficiencies.

> *Arthur Daley*
>
> Customer care is the antithesis of the Arthur Daley school of used car salesmen, who, after making a sale, fall on their knees and pray that they never see the customer again.

Perhaps chairmen and directors are as guilty of the Arthur Daley syndrome as anyone. After all, how many of them actually spend time with customers instead of just spending time with shareholders, bankers, other directors and staff? David Jackson of Digital (1992) suggested that it is worth checking the director's diary to see what, if any, time is reserved for customers. He went on to ask these potentially embarrassing questions:

Do reports about customer satisfaction regularly appear on the agenda of senior managers' meetings?
Is impact on customer satisfaction considered when new investments are being appraised?
How many policies and rules introduced last year relate directly to improving life for the customer?

NCR make every corporate officer, including the chief executive officer, personally responsible for a couple of big customers.

> *Uncaring call centres*
>
> Thirty per cent of the £3 billion spent annually on call centre operations is wasted through inefficiency, poor equipment and poor staffing. Call centres that fail to match people's expectations and standards... will only succeed in alienating the customer and losing business to the competition.
>
> Brian Marshall

Ten stages of developing a customer care programme

Sarah Cook identified 10 stages of developing a customer care programme:

1. gain management commitment;
2. develop TQM;
3. listen to customers;
4. establish a customer care programme;
5. engender ownership;
6. understand internal customers (employees);
7. train;
8. communicate;
9. recognize and reward good service;
10. sustain a customer focus.

Listening to customers is a basic requirement of marketing. Yet how many organizations really listen to customers, let alone prospects? Effective listening is action orientated, ie feedback is not an end in itself. It facilitates improvement through better behaviour and actions.

> *Customer care – over-commitment*
>
> Roy Hill reported that some years ago, when Japan Airlines' passengers on a flight to Europe suffered severe food poisoning, the gentleman in charge of catering in Japan committed suicide.

Eight ways to lose a customer

Sarah Cook's list could be expanded to 100 ways, but here are just a few classics:

1. poor quality product or service;
2. making it difficult to buy (complex order or enquiry forms);
3. poor internal communications (playing 'pass the customer' until somebody eventually decides to deal with the customer);
4. slow response to enquiries, orders, problems or complaints;
5. slow phone answering;
6. inadequate information (no brochures, no prices, unknowledgeable salespeople, etc);

7. rash promises (the product/service doesn't match the promise);
8. arrogance.

Customer kindness

Philanthropists might see customer kindness simply as a nice way to work and live with other people. Some companies see it as a means of developing a competitive advantage. As mentioned previously, the Open University highlights a leading department store that sees courtesy and kindness as tools that sharpen its competitive edge. A store where the employees sign a 'kindness declaration' and the store's president makes 'gentleness policies' ('with gentle eyes, gentle face, gentle words, gentle behaviour and a gentle mind') may seem dreamlike, a land where shops aim to be 'kind and courteous, smiling, careful, friendly, gentle and warm'; a land where employees repeat 'I will never get upset. I will keep a Disney smile.'

> *Service while you queue*
>
> A Japanese store minimizes queuing as an obstacle to happy shopping by handing out towels (hot in winter and cold in summer) to motorists queuing for parking.

MANAGING QUALITY AND CUSTOMER CARE

Many organizations realize that their future survival lies in their customers' current levels of satisfaction. New customers can be won but at a much higher cost (five times) than that of retaining old ones. The everlasting customer can come back again and again if satisfied ('marketing is the selling of goods that don't come back to those who *do*'). Quality programmes and customer care programmes require resources, including the 3Ms. Some argue that certain markets, depending on the stage in their life cycle, require less service than others. How expensive are the trappings of service? What is the cost of TQM? Does it have a direct effect on return on investment? Can it be sustained? Is customer care a gigantic task? The final section of this chapter attempts to answer some of these questions, and finishes with a look at the manager of the future.

The trappings of service

Managers are constantly facing the question 'can costs be significantly cut by reducing the trappings of extra service?' This, of course, can affect the rest of the marketing mix, since reduced cost can allow prices to be cut or the savings enjoyed (from the reduced cost) to be spent on extra promotion, extra product improvements, or kept in reserve for short-term profits. On the other hand, would a lack of service create a competitive disadvantage? Or perhaps there is a segment of customers who don't want the frills but would welcome a more cost-effective basic product or service? Can extra service create competitive advantage, and for how long? Shiv Mathur (1981) has written some interesting papers addressing what he calls 'transaction costs'. He suggests that there are at least four different ways of making transactions and competing, by mixing different levels of customer service with different types of products in different markets. Some transactional mixes are more appropriate than others at various stages in the product life cycle.

The cost of total quality management

Companies like Rank Xerox consider the cost of quality to consist of three components: (1) cost of conformance, (2) cost of non-conformance, and (3) cost of lost opportunity. The cost of conformance means the cost of conforming exactly to a customer's specific requirements. In other words, what it costs to get it right first time every time so that the customer gets exactly what he or she wants every time instead of most of the time. If conformance does not occur (or it is not right first time), then the mistake, or non-conformance, has to be fixed. This second component costs money, time and efforts. Since the money spent on fixing the problem is no longer available for investment in the market, an additional forfeited opportunity or 'cost of lost opportunity' arises. This is the third component. They estimate that the cost of non-conformance plus the cost of lost opportunities is typically 20–25 per cent of the revenue of a company. For some companies that means one out of every four or five employees goes to work every day to fix yesterday's mistakes.

Federal Express's 1–10–100 rule on page 558 might calculate the cost as even higher. If the customer is lost, the cost could perhaps be boosted by the lifetime value or forfeited repeat sales.

Return on investment

Customer kindness and efficient service can help to retain customers by building customer satisfaction and, ultimately, customer loyalty. The cost of retaining customers is conservatively estimated at one-fifth of the cost of acquiring a new customer. Existing customers generate bigger margins and profits (per customer) than new ones. A customer retention level of 94 per cent yields profitability of just 50 per cent of what it would be at 98 per cent retention level (American Management Center, Europe). Customer satisfaction makes the difference between short-term success and long-term growth and prosperity. Higher customer retention generates higher ROI (as we saw in the Rank Xerox example on page 560).

If profits increase while customer satisfaction is falling, then poor financial results are on the horizon. Kotler makes the point:

> Profits could go up or down in a particular year for many reasons, including rising costs, falling prices, major investments, and so on, but the ultimate sign of a healthy company is that its customer satisfaction index is high and keeps rising. *Customer satisfaction is the best indicator of the company's future profits.*

Having said that, the company has to understand that customer care may incur immediate or short-term costs, while some of the financial benefits may sometimes only emerge in the medium to long term. Japan's world-class management guru Kenichi Ohmae sees management time horizons as a fundamental difference between Eastern and Western strategies. Western companies plan for short-term profits, while Japanese companies plan for long-term profits.

However, some Western companies are waking up to the value of investing in customer satisfaction, customer care and overall quality of product. Quantified objectives can be set that can translate directly into turnover or bottom-line profits.

Fortune magazine reports that there is an apparent correlation between the level of customer satisfaction scores and the organization's stock market performance. Top companies such as Campbell Soups, Heinz and Procter & Gamble were among the top scorers in customer satisfaction. They were also stock performance stars (*Fortune*, 16 February 1998). And even the act of measuring customer satisfaction has a correlation with successful commercial performance. Ninety per cent of companies showing 15 per cent interest in turnover measure satisfaction and 92 per cent with a turnover increase of 20 per cent (*Marketing Business*, March 1997).

One per cent customer satisfaction = $500 million

IBM calculate that each percentage point improvement in customer service satisfaction translates into $500 million more revenue over five years.

Sustained performance

After the initial enthusiasm dies down, the real management task begins – sustaining and even improving the levels of customer care, satisfaction and retention. Competitive advantage may erode as other companies develop their own TQM systems. In the long term, customer service is not just about customer care or product quality. According to Professor John Murray of Trinity College, Dublin (1990), it is about 'serving customers by creating and leveraging distinctive company capabilities in a manner that outperforms competing companies in a sustainable form'. In a sense this also requires clear communications with the customers so that they are fully aware, at all times, of just how good the company is, how much it tries and succeeds, and how much it cares. See Appendix 19.4 for an example of excellence in quality and customer service from Irish supermarket hero, Feargel Quinn.

Customer care – a gigantic task

Customer care is considered by some to be difficult to manage, as staff often encounter customers in an unsupervised situation. Large organizations can find the customer care concept difficult to spread throughout the organization. It seems sometimes that everyone loves to hate someone some of the time. Iain Murray of *Marketing Week* once commented:

> Few things can be more foolish than British Rail's continuing attempts to inculcate some small measure of charm in its employees. Even if it could be achieved, which, given the raw material to hand, it could not, it would never work in practice since railway staff have no vested interest in the satisfaction of customers and therefore see not the slightest need to be nice to them.

Nevertheless, there lies the challenge. Before the late King Hassan of Morocco made a visit to Britain the *Independent* newspaper reported that:

> the king has been known to close airports and entire cities when visiting. The king is accustomed to high standards of personal service. At home, he walks in his eight palaces preceded by his chamberlain carrying a mace while the courtiers cry 'May Allah preserve our Lord and Master'. It is hoped that British Rail staff will meet the challenge.

Despite the growing evidence of the importance of customer care, less than half (44 per cent) actually use a care programme.

Caring for customers, employees and stockholders

The challenges of customer care, product quality and employee satisfaction are worth meeting, as Harvard Business School professors John Kotter and James Heskett (1992) point out. Their 11-year study examined the effects of prioritizing three stakeholders: customers, employees and stockholders. They found that highly profitable companies serve the interests of all three stakeholders, while less profitable companies only satisfy one or two of these stakeholders (eg good customer care scores but low employee satisfaction). Over 200 major US companies were extensively surveyed. Those that successfully satisfied the three interests increased sales (over the 11-year period) by an average of 682 per cent, compared with 166 per cent for those companies that only satisfied one or two of these stakeholders. Differences in stock performance were even more extreme: up 901 per cent and 74 per cent, respectively.

Tomorrow's manager

Tomorrow's successful companies will be learner, flatter (less hierarchical) and more flexible. This means that tomorrow's marketing manager will have to be multi-skilled and fully understand people management, programme management, customer care programmes and quality management programmes.

CASE STUDY 19.1

McGregor Cory's partners

This case study demonstrates how customer care and product quality come together to create the ultimate communications tool.

Situation

Increasingly, manufacturers and retailers are realizing the benefits of contracting their distribution requirements to a professional third-party operator whose sole business is distribution. In this way valuable resources such as capital, labour and time can be released for reinvestment. The company can focus fully on its core activities.

McGregor Cory is a contract distribution services company operating in the UK and mainland Europe. With an annual turnover rapidly approaching £100 million, they are one of the top five UK players in a highly competitive market where word of mouth is sovereign.

Objective

To become an outstanding player in European contract distribution.

Strategy

To establish and develop long-term strategic partnerships with customers, through the provision of a total quality service.

Tactics

In the autumn of 1990 the total quality management (TQM) system was formally set up. It required a company commitment to staff and the customers. By the winter of 1990 things were already beginning to change – for the better. The TQM programme was designed to improve the quality of employment, the quality of product (actual delivery service) and the quality of customer care. It encompassed the following key areas:

1. staff motivation, training and consultation;
2. customer awareness and responsiveness programmes;
3. partnership documents (including multi-level channels of communication/man-for-man marketing);
4. a system of measuring effectiveness.

Action: staff motivation, training and consultation

Since the winter of 1990 staff have been invited to *team briefing sessions* that allow a regular, two-way, direct dialogue with management. There is no restriction on the subject matter during these discussions and, rather than providing a forum for mutual verbal abuse and accusation, they have proved invaluable in identifying new ways of improving McGregor Cory's service to its customers. Through group discussion and evaluation of operational systems a genuine sense of ownership is generated in individual employees. This, in turn, encourages greater employee commitment, especially when employees know that their suggestions will not go unheeded and, where valid, will be 'actioned'. Through the team briefing system, individual concerns are initially addressed to management, and if the matter cannot be resolved at this stage, it will be referred upwards, if necessary to the chief executive.

Personal recognition is also important in terms of motivation. Certificates of Merit are awarded for long service, or for an outstanding idea that measurably improves efficiency. Both the achievement and the presentation ceremony are reported extensively in the company newsletter – one of many invaluable uses of this popular communications tool. As well as increasing self-esteem and a sense of pride in one's work, the awards also tend to bring out the natural competitive spirit in the workforce, thereby promoting staff morale and improved service levels on a wider scale.

Exchange visits to and from the customer's workplace and open days for employees' families are ongoing activities aimed at developing the potential of the individual, while at the same time optimizing employee commitment to the corporate aim of outstanding customer service. The customers also appreciate it, as both parties are able to put faces to names. They also get to understand how the other works and, in particular, what the customer really needs.

Action: customer awareness and responsiveness programme

Here the importance of the customer is explained in a way that clearly shares the responsibility of all staff towards customers, the company, their jobs and their future. The concept goes beyond 'the customer is king' to 'the customer is a partner', where their business is part of McGregor Cory's business and McGregor Cory's business is considered to be an extension of the customer's operations. The continued importance of addressing customer needs swiftly and efficiently is reinforced by ensuring that key customer messages permeate every level of the organization. Specially commissioned posters, calenders, pens, mugs, coasters, notice boards, quality bulletins and the in-house newsletter constantly carry messages such as the cartoon calendar below.

The cartoon calendar format was originally suggested by a member of the UK staff. The 1993 concept came from staff in Holland.

Customer responsiveness is measured across a range of preset objectives (eg maximum number of rings of the telephone is three). Individual targets are set for each customer, as explained in the partnership document.

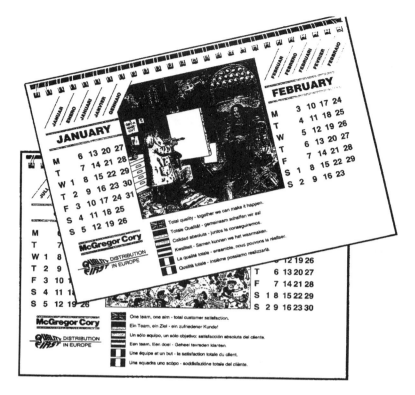

The partnership document

This non-legally binding document operates alongside the main contract of service and seeks to quantify the key aspects critical to establishing a long and successful partnership. The document includes (a) mutual responsibilities and expectations, (b) clearly defined performance criteria and their measurement, and (c) agreed multi-level channels of communication. This 'man-for-man marketing' ensures that each individual, from managing director to contract manager, at both companies, is appropriately matched to discuss relevant aspects of the operation. For each management level, regular opportunities to meet, review and forward plan for future needs are mutually agreed in advance, thereby ensuring a regular dialogue between both parties. It also helps to take any doubt out of the relationship.

Written and signed by both parties, key sections of the document are then placed on permanent display at the distribution centre concerned. In this way all those involved in the business are made constantly aware of their responsibilities and how their performance will be judged. The document remains subject to regular review and adaptation to meet the evolving nature of the operation.

A system of measurement and control

Without measurement and feedback the whole TQM system falls apart.

Customer satisfaction is measured at least twice annually, using critical success factors (CSFs) decided by the customer. These CSFs cover aspects such as handling, accuracy, delivery and housekeeping. Surveys may be conducted by post, telephone or face to face, whichever method is preferred by the customer. The surveys consist of a series of prompted and unprompted questions. The results enable McGregor Cory to measure with reasonable accuracy the company's progress in raising customer service levels, as well as to pinpoint any further areas for improvement.

In this way customer trust is gained at the outset, and customer satisfaction and loyalty are generated, which generally manifest themselves in repeat or extended business. The new TQM system has already boosted customer retention, while employee turnover and absenteeism are down.

A detailed survey of the Institute of Transport Management's 17,500 members – drawn from all areas of transport and distribution – asked respondents to identify one company they would entrust their distribution requirements to, taking account of key service considerations such as quality and reliability. McGregor Cory proved to be first choice. In the same year they won the *Motor Transport* award for customer care.

In an industry where word of mouth is sovereign, the ultimate accolade comes from the customers themselves: 'We cannot speak too highly of the full cooperation and identification of McGregor Cory with our aims and objectives' (taken from a letter to McGregor Cory from one of its major customers).

APPENDIX 19.1

Spreading the electronic word of mouth

Software company ICQ has improved the nature of 'chat' on the Internet. Traditionally Internet users go to chat rooms set up for people who have never met but with common interests. ICQ use the technology to help people who know each other to chat to each other. It sets up a closed list of colleagues, family or friends and allows them to chat to each other by telling members (when they are on line) which other members are on line at the same time.

ICQ encourages friends and colleagues to sign up by asking members to type in the email address of someone they would like to join. ICQ then emails them with the first member's recommendation. A facility called Future Users Watch then lets the member know when any of the user's recommendations actually get around to joining.

ICQ software was launched to 100 users in a beta test in November 1996. By August 1997 2.2 million registered users were being bolstered by 20,000 new signings every day. ICQ call it 'strategic word of mouth'.

Tony Williams, System seeks to unite friends, *Financial Times*, 11 August 1997

APPENDIX 19.2

Nissan customer questionnaire

PLEASE TELL US WHAT YOU THINK

1. Which ONE of the following statements BEST describes the way you feel about the action taken by our Customer Care Department and dealer network to respond to your request for assistance?

☐ I was completely satisfied.

☐ I was not completely satisfied but the action taken was acceptable.

☐ I was not completely satisfied but some action was taken.

☐ I was dissatisfied with the action taken.

☐ I was very dissatisfied – I don't consider any action was taken at all.

2. How satisfied were you with our Customer Care Department in *each* of the following areas?

	Very Satisfied	Quite Satisfied	Neither Satisfied nor Dissatisfied	Quite Dissatisfied	Very Dissatisfied
RESPONSE:					
Promptness	☐	☐	☐	☐	☐
Clarity	☐	☐	☐	☐	☐
Helpfulness	☐	☐	☐	☐	☐
Follow-through on promised action	☐	☐	☐	☐	☐

Please answer the rest of the items in Question 2 only if you PHONED our Customer Care Department:

	Very Satisfied	Quite Satisfied	Neither Satisfied nor Dissatisfied	Quite Dissatisfied	Very Dissatisfied
EASE OF CONTACT:					
Ability to get through on the first call	☐	☐	☐	☐	☐
Length of time on hold	☐	☐	☐	☐	☐
PERSONNEL:					
Courtesy	☐	☐	☐	☐	☐
Professionalism	☐	☐	☐	☐	☐
Knowledge	☐	☐	☐	☐	☐

3. How many times did you have to contact our Customer Care Department before your question/problem was answered?

1	2	3	4	5+	Final Action Still Not Taken
☐	☐	☐	☐	☐	☐

4. Please rate your overall satisfaction with our Customer Care Department.

Very Satisfied	Quite Satisfied	Neither Satisfied nor Dissatisfied	Quite Dissatisfied	Very Dissatisfied
☐	☐	☐	☐	☐

5. How likely is it that you would recommend Nissan vehicles to a friend or colleague?

I definitely will	I probably will	I might or might not	I probably will not	I definitely will not
☐	☐	☐	☐	☐

APPENDIX 19.3

Rank Xerox customer questionnaire

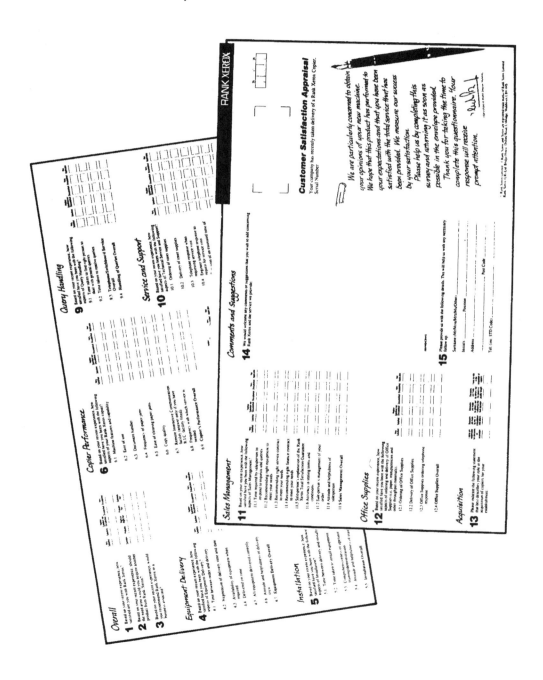

APPENDIX 19.4

Feargal's 15 goofs

In 1994 Irish supermarket Superquinn issued a list of 15 goofs and invited customers to catch them out. Anyone doing so received a bonus 200 points on their SuperClub loyalty card. Here, for the record, is what they said:

1. If we give you a wobbly trolley.
2. If we run out of plastic bags to place your firelighters in.
3. If we don't have bananas suitable for eating today and tomorrow.
4. If we run out of labels in the fruit and vegetable scales.
5. If any part of a customer aisle is less than 6ft (1.83m) wide.
6. If we have a burst sausage on display.
7. If there are no free bones for your dog available.
8. If you feel Tendercut Beef isn't tender enough.
9. If we have fresh food on display that you wouldn't put on your table.
10. If we are 15 minutes late doing our temperature watch.
11. If you find any product out of date.
12. If there are more than three customers in a queue for 60 seconds and any checkout not open.
13. If you find that we've charged you more than our sign says.
14. If an Irish product is not identified as such on your receipt.
15. If we ever have on display a baker's Kitchen Stick that's more than four hours old.

Superquinn has since thrown away the list and offered customers something bolder... find anything unsatisfactory in the store and the customer wins points. The customers are now the quality control inspectors. Even if customers over-exploit the offer, Feargal Quinn believes it all nurtures customer loyalty anyway.

Key points from Chapter 19:

1. Customer experiences of product/service quality and customer service have a bigger impact on individual customers than any other communications tool.
2. Customer retention boosts sales, profits and return on investment.

FURTHER READING

Barwick, S (1987) King Hassan's bed and breakfast in Brighton, The *Independent*, 11 July

Christopher, M, Payne, A and Ballantyne, D (1991) *Relationship Marketing*, Butterworth-Heinemann, Oxford

Clutterbuck, D (1989) Counsel of care, *Marketing Magazine*, 18 May

Cook, S (1992) *Customer Care*, Kogan Page, London

Crosby, P (1984) *Quality Without Tears*, McGraw-Hill, New York

Jackson, D (1992) The art and science of service, *Marketing Business*, July/August, p 32

Kotler, P (1997) *Marketing Management Analysis: Planning, Implementation and Control*, 9th edn, Prentice-Hall, Englewood Cliffs, NJ

Kotter, J and Heskett, J (1992) *Corporate Culture and Performance*, Free Press, New York

The Marketing Institute News (1991) Competitive advantages versus customer care, Marketing Institute of Ireland, **4**, 9, December

Mathur, S (1981) Strategic industrial marketing: transaction shifts and competitive response, City University, Working Paper No 33

Murray, J (1990) Civil servant without a smile, *Marketing Week*, 21 September

Ohmae, K (1982) *The Mind of the Strategist*, McGraw-Hill, London

Open University (1990) *Retail Management: Policy and Merchandising*, Open University Press, Buckingham

Peters, T (1992) *In Conversation With*, BBC Training Videos, London

Stevens, M (1992) *The Handbook of Telemarketing*, Kogan Page, London

Williams, T (1997) System seeks to unite friends, *Financial Times*, 11 August

Wilson, J (1991) *Word of Mouth Marketing*, John Wiley & Sons, Chichester

FURTHER CONTACTS

The British Quality Foundation, 32–34 Great Peter Street, London SW1P 2QX (tel: 020 7654 5000; Web site: www.quality-foundation.co.uk)

British Standards Institute, 389 Chiswick High Road, London W4 4AL (tel: 020 8996 9000; Web address: www.bsi-global.com)

e-Satisfy Ltd (formerly Technical Assistance Research Programme, TARP), 6 Spring Gardens, Citadel Place, Tinwort Street, London SE11 5EH (tel: 020 7840 6600: Web site: www.e-satisfy.co.uk)

Institute of Customer Care, St John's House, Chapel Lane, Wescott, Surrey RH4 3PJ (tel: 01306 876210)

20

E-marketing

WHAT IS E-MARKETING?

Building an e-business is one thing, building a marketing driven e-business is another. That's why e-marketing should be at the heart of e-business. E-marketing is simply marketing online – keeping very close to customers, forming relationships with them and keeping them happy online. E-marketing involves a dynamic dialogue, constant feedback (including watching chat rooms) and an array of new e-tools such as the Web, WAP, i-TV and much more – all connected seamlessly into a single database allowing excellent e-CRM (customer relationship management), which nurtures lifetime customers and increases your 'share of wallet' by continually adding extra added value online. Like a traditional business, marketing and, in this case, e-business is a part, albeit the central part of the business. e-commerce, on the other hand, is just a small part of the business – it is the sales side, or the transactional side. Isolated e-commerce falls over if an order is taken but not fulfilled because non-integrated systems (or incomplete e-business systems) do not alert dispatch, stock control or procurement.

On top of this many Web sites exacerbate the brand damage with their broken links, dead ends, cumbersome downloads, out-of-date content, impossible navigation and unanswered e-mails. Haven't Web masters ever heard of marketing – customer service, test marketing or even customer feedback? Many sites skip the cardinal rule of asking customers what they would like on a Web site. Then, having created the site, they forget to check whether they have got it right. Regular reviews should not be devoted to reviewing the latest technology but rather, they should be focused on customer reviews.

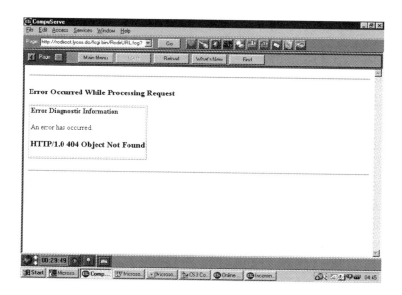

Many Web sites damage brands with broken links

The world's most popular Web sites have four common factors: high-quality content; ease of use; quick download; updated frequently (Forrestor Research, 1999). They're not packed with flash animations, big pictures and video clips that take the average customer too long to download. Ask how your Web site can help your customers.

The same applies to other online tools such as a WAP site, a DLS (dedicated landing site, ie – micro-site linked to an i-TV advertisement), or any kind of site accessed via a mobile device – whether phone, watch or car window. How can it help my customers? How can I improve their overall online experience? How can I add value to their experience? Eventually, we'll have to think in another dimension when voice portals become more popular and customers browse around without pictures or text – purely by sound. Ask a question and the voice portal will try to find the answer and make suggestions, from which some customers will drill down with more questions or keywords before finding what they want.

Before looking at some of the exciting e-tools, remember having great online areas is of absolutely no use if no one uses them. It's a bit like having a 'better mousetrap'. You know the story 'show me a better mousetrap and the world will beat a path to my door'. Not true. Sadly it's not the best products that succeed but rather reasonably good ones that everyone (a) knows about and (b) can easily find when they need them. The same is true of Web sites. Traffic-generating techniques, search engine optimization, Web rings, affiliation, and viral marketing (clever online word-of-mouth ideas) are obviously keys to success. E-strategy addresses how to split budgets between Web site development, Web site service and traffic generation. Many companies get this balance wrong.

> 95–98 per cent of dot com companies will fail within the next two years.
>
> Michael Fleischer, Gartner Group

Despite all the hype, the hopes and the many dot com disasters, it is finally happening. Online business is growing. E-marketing is becoming an integral part of e-business. Interestingly, it's B2B that is leading the way, with sophisticated state-of-the-art integrated or 'connected' Web sites.

It is really weird when you think of the billions of dollars, euros and yen slushing around the world's wires. It gets a little weirder when you consider that most of it is untouched and unseen by humans, and an increasing amount will be wireless – just floating through the air. That's when wireless technology – mobile phones, hand-held devices and maybe even 'bluetooth' wireless technology – connects wired and wireless devices together. And it gets even weirder when you consider that much of the cash slushing around will be directed and controlled by robots, virtual robots – automated systems, interconnected systems, wired Web sites automatically connecting credit card transactions, credit checks and shopping bots (online intelligent agents constantly seeking the best deal). Of course not all of it is human-less, but a surprising amount will be – even customer care, or at least parts of it, eg auto responders, FAQs, search engines within sites, and virtual assistants, in addition to real customer care staff, some of whom are online and others offline.

Today's marketers must embrace continual change and the online opportunities and challenges that constantly come with it. The digital impact affects every element of both the overall marketing mix and the communications mix. A host of new e-tools have been added to the marketer's armoury including Web sites, micro-sites, i-TV, i-radio, i-kiosks, hand-held devices, in fact just about anything (including Barbie dolls and clothes) can be connected. The customer doesn't care about the challenges this poses to the marketer, he or she just wants to be recognized, remembered and dealt with quickly, pleasantly and personally. This requires a seamless database regardless of which medium the customer uses, from shopping mall to Web site to telephone to i-TV to real telephone – it's got to be seamless. Now there's a challenge, tying the old legacy databases to the new Web databases. Another integration challenge is linking the front office (say Web site) with the back office (say fulfilment) together.

Integrating old wired 'legacy' databases with new wireless databases presents a new challenge

The business world is changing faster than ever before. Old approaches and models are being turned on their head. The white heat of change causes many business people to wake up sweating in the middle of the night and check the locks on their old business models. To no avail. The wired and unwired world has moved on through the night, turning old models over and paving the way for a host of new models. The old value chain is being replaced with non-linear value networks that extend enterprise ('the extended enterprise') into partners who fulfil any aspect of the old value chain. Plug-and-play companies pick off specific processes in today's value networks and target weak elements in old value chains. As more and more processes are subcontracted externally, the business becomes a 'box of contracts' (eg 70 per cent of what Cisco produce is never seen by Cisco). The extended enterprise constantly asks itself what is its core business and increasingly who are its competitors, as today's markets are immersed in a boundary-less world with category-less competitors (eg Yahoo! sell electricity).

Today's marketers have to have many people skills, not just to ensure that grand strategies and exciting tactics are properly executed by suitably motivated and trained teams, but also because new partnership skills are required to develop partners for an array of marketing marriages – whether co-branding exercises, cross-promotions, shared data-bases, co-sponsorships, alliance and affiliate marketing, Web rings, or simply managing strategic partners in the extended enterprise. New skills are required. Today's marketing communications professionals also enjoy an intriguing array of new tools – e-tools. This is where the online world begins to get really interesting.

Once we move beyond the PC and into the wireless world a whole new vision appears

Once we move beyond the PC and into the wireless world of pervasive deep computing, a whole new vision appears. Always on, everywhere, easy to use, integrated e-marketing can exploit these new tools. First, consider why they should be used. Why bother? How can they help? What marketing objectives can they fulfil?

HOW CAN E-MARKETING HELP MARKETERS?

E-marketing can help marketers to achieve many objectives, from increasing sales and enquiries, to getting closer to customers and listening to them, to adding extra service and added value; to gaining efficiencies and saving money; to strengthening the brand as it moves from visually orientated to an interactive and experiential orientation. These five objectives or benefits can be summarized as the 5Ss – Sell, Serve (added value), Save, Speak (listening to customers), and Sizzle (exciting branding):

1. *Sell* – Just about anything can be sold online from cars to kidneys, to 'alien implant removal services' to jumpsuits and jet engines. Some major B2B companies only buy online, so online selling is compulsory for their suppliers. Many companies have found whole new revenue streams from global customers previously out of reach. Other companies, like IBM and Dell, sell millions of dollars worth of kit and software every day. US car companies are finding over 50 per cent of shoppers browse online and shop offline. Soon more and more people will shop in a mixed mode like this, while others will complete most, if not all of the purchase online.

2. *Serve* – How can I help my customer? What information is of use to them? Are there any integrated services that they would like. For example, GE has a wonderful 'turbine optimizer' on one of their sites which allows customers to check their own turbine's operational efficiency. If they score poorly, they are asked whether they would like to know the saving that would be generated from improved performance. The cost, payback period and ROI generated from the savings created by an engineer's visit are all calculated and presented. A single click then allows the customer to book an engineer at a suitably convenient time. The engineer's routing plan is adjusted automatically and the visit is scheduled seamlessly in.

3. *Save* – Web sites can save vast overheads of physical presence. Fully integrated Web sites save a lot more. When the 'sell side' (customer-facing Web site) is seamlessly linked to both the 'inside' (production, order processing and finance) as well as the 'buy side' (raw material procurement and supply chain management), then huge efficiency gains are enjoyed as an incoming order updates sales records, production records, supply records and suppliers simultaneously. This way customers are given accurate delivery schedules. This differs from US toy companies, which lacked integration, couldn't, and didn't, tell customers about late deliveries, and were subsequently sued for late deliveries at Christmas time.

4. *Speak* – For too long marketers have been separated from customers by middlemen – distributors, retailers, ad agencies and market researchers. At last marketers can speak, listen and watch customers in a new way. In addition to engaging in a dynamic (database-driven) one-to-one dialogue with customers, marketers can watch discussion rooms, chat rooms and bulletin boards' customers swap tips, ideas, suggestions and criticisms of the brand. It's a marketer's dream. MTV refer to it as 'year-long focus groups'. Some marketers excel here and they build communities of common interest around the brand.

Markets are conversations.

Seth Goden (2000)

5. *Sizzle* – Web sites provide a wonderful opportunity to re-evaluate and sometimes rein-
    vigorate the brand. The 'sizzle' is the Web site magic that adds to the brand. It's the
    overall impression delivered by the Web site. The scintillating experience, dynamic
    engagement or plain old warm feeling left after a visit. Sadly many sites don't do this.
    Instead they damage the brand with slow responses, slow downloading and out-of-date
    content. Web sites require resources to service the site, update content and answer
    e-mails, as well as to create engaging online interactions.

*Excellent Web sites deliver all 5Ss and have good content, are regularly updated, quick to download
and easy to navigate*

E-STRATEGY

Web sites or WAP sites or both? Interactive TV, interactive kiosks or mobile marketing?
Build a brochure-ware Web site, a two-way communications Web site or a fully integrated
e-business Web site? These are just some of the questions that an e-strategy can answer.
What are the components of an e-strategy? We used STOP and SIT as acronyms for a
marketing communications strategy back in Chapter 2. STOP and SIT can also be applied to
an e-strategy.

The foundations of any kind of marketing strategy are built upon clearly identified target
markets and crystal-clear positionings and propositions. S stands for Segments, T for the
selected segments or Target markets and P for Positioning. Remember, strategies are created
for one reason and one reason only – to fulfil objectives. So when creating strategies look
over your shoulder and check that the strategy being considered actually fulfils your

original objectives. O stands for objectives – there is no point in rowing harder if you're rowing in the wrong direction. It is important not to get distracted. Make sure that the strategy fits the original goal or objective.

Assuming it all fits the overall objectives, then the remaining components of strategy are SIT – Sequence or Stages (S), Integration (I) and Tools (T). Sequence and Stages embrace a couple of strategic e-issues. Sequence means should there be a sequence of tools, eg a Web site before interactive TV before mobile? More importantly, should the business have a series of online stages of evolution? The first stage could be a static Web site (brochureware), the second stage a two-way site that accommodates two-way communications, such as orders, enquiries, e-mails, etc, and the third stage integration of the front office processes (sell side) with the back office processes (fulfilment, production, payment) so that the online business becomes a fully fledged, automated and integrated e-business. Any one of the stages is fine as long as the marketer knows where they are in the evolutionary stages and is aware of the implications, limitations and resources required by each of the three stages. For example, two-way communications requires resources to respond to enquiries, complaints and orders, whether automated or individualized and tailored by humans. Supporting services are essential for integration into a seamless database as well as for integration among the business processes, whether you call them front office and back office or 'buy side', 'inside' and 'sell side'. These are strategic questions for the online marketer.

Implicit in all this are resources. The strategy may in the end be determined by the resources available and their allocation. For example, when trying to allocate resources between Web site design, Web site service and Web site traffic generation, it has been suggested that UK companies tend to adopt a ratio of 5:2:1 (design, service and traffic), whereas US companies tend to use a 1:2:5 ratio – which makes sense, as there's no point having a wonderful (expensive) Web site if no customers or prospects bother to visit it. In addition, as mentioned earlier, popular sites are the ones that are frequently updated (serviced) and quick to download (having not too many lavish graphics or animations).

STOP and SIT combined with resource allocation present at least some of the components worth considering in an e-strategy selected from, hopefully, a *range* of e-marketing strategic options (the first strategy that comes to mind is not necessarily the best one). The strategy will guide the choice of e-tools, whether Web, WAP, , i-TV or i-kiosks, and other miscellaneous devices. Let us consider some of these tactical e-tools – we'll explore their advantages or how they can help to fulfil the five objectives or benefits of e-marketing. We'll also explore briefly some of their limitations or disadvantages.

TACTICAL E-TOOLS

Web sites

We've already explored the advantages, or 5Ss, of e-marketing. A well-designed Web site can deliver all of these. Equally, we've already mentioned the disadvantages and damage done by Web sites that are poorly designed, poorly resourced and not integrated into either offline business systems or online e-business systems. Here are a few other aspects worth considering.

Web sites should have a clear Internet value proposition (IVP), which suggests a reason, or reasons, for visiting, or better still, revisiting a particular Web site. Why should customers revisit your Web site? What's in it for them? What does your site propose? Can you summarize it? If you don't know what it is, then it is highly unlikely that your customers will know it. Ideally, you need an IVP that is different to your competitors' and that is not available in the offline world.

Effective Web sites are also carefully designed in terms of both form and function. Form means the way a site looks – aesthetics, which includes layout, graphics, colour and typography. Function means interaction, integration, navigation and structure. Going back to aesthetics, how would you describe the personality of your site? Is it formal or fun, professional and serious or engaging and enlightening? How would you describe your site? Does it match your overall desired 'positioning' in the marketplace? Aesthetics also combines content with structure to deliver personality, which must be agreed before anything is designed. Remember, heavy graphics (photographs) and animations (cartoons) may look aesthetically pleasing but take a long time to download and therefore can destroy the Web experience and damage the brand. As they say – 'remove graphic, increase traffic'. Some designers have the technical know-how to treat graphics to reduce downloading time (anti-aliasing, dithering and browser safe pallets). Having said that, it's best to design for the lowest common denominator, ie to allow for a wide range of constraints, including different browsers, modems, screen resolutions, colour displays and people (patience thresholds).

Page layout and navigation require expert advice and careful attention. Different customers search for items or content in different ways using different keywords, headings and links. The sales page should never be more than three clicks away. Telephone numbers and contact details should always be readily accessible. Site structure should be simple, consistent and well signposted in order to create flow. Then comes the content. This depends on copywriting skills. Copywriting for the Web requires different skills from other forms of writing. Think CRAB (chunky, relevant, accurate and brief) when writing copy for the Web. Write for scannability. On top of this comes functionality, interactivity and integration with the database and the other business processes. Service, and therefore systems, are important.

Also important is traffic generation. Having a beautiful Web site, WAP site, dedicated landing site or any other site is of no use unless you get the traffic. Should you put more effort into designing a Web site, servicing it or generating traffic to visit it in the first place? This is a strategic issue – a typical resourcing issue – how much should you spend on traffic? Equipped with a budget, then the next question is how do you generate the traffic?

You can increase traffic by improving search engine listings through regular registration of your site with the search engines and ensuring that the right words are inserted in the hidden titles and meta-tags, as well as ensuring that keywords are used frequently (but not overused, as some engines penalize overuse); and links help, as some engines count the number of links with other sites to determine a ranking or listing. Having a presence in relevant portals (or gateways), links and reciprocal links (with relevant non-competitive sites), Web rings (linking parallel non-competitive suppliers with each other, so they refer customers to each other), affiliate programmes (where commissions are paid to other referrers), banner ads, opt-in e-mail (cannot be uninvited spam), viral marketing (where word of mouth spreads online courtesy of a creative message, picture, animation, game, etc) and of course, offline promotion can generate traffic also. Many offline (TV) advertising campaigns for the early dot coms were dedicated to generating traffic. All the other nine offline communications tools (including packaging, mailshots, etc) should carry the Web address.

Now consider some other tactical e-tools such as mobiles, i-TV, i-radio, kiosks and miscellaneous items.

Mobiles

With 2 billion telephones currently in the world and an estimated 1 billion mobiles coming by 2003, marketers cannot ignore this potentially powerful new tool. We've moved from the big, bulky analogue mobile of the 1980s to smaller 2G (second-generation) phones with phenomenal SMS and text-messaging facilities to 2.5G WAP phones (I-Mode; GPRS and EDGE) and to 3G (third-generation) phones which are 100 times faster than 2G phones and have global standard UMTS. They can also show video. Smart phones come equipped with a computer and are sometimes described as 'TV on speed'. Mix in some Bluetooth technology (short-range wireless technology) and the phone becomes a powerful device interacting with vending machines, electronic gates, cars, homes and printers. We are finally moving beyond the hype, hysteria and disappointment of early m-commerce and woeful WAP into a new level of mobile 'interconnectedness'.

Advantages

Sell

It is, in theory, possible to sell anything that can be sold on a Web site on a WAP site. In reality, it's more difficult because of the limited number of really good sites, the lack of colour and the limited pictures. However, this will improve. Location-based marketing has emerged as customers step into range of particular cell locations – their phone rings and alerts them to physically nearby offers. Some companies, such as Guinness, are using text messaging to direct physical traffic to, say, pubs and clubs where Guinness offers are available.

Serve

Many useful added-value services are emerging through the mobile phone. British Airways offer a check-in service that allows passengers to check themselves in and choose their own seats. Voice portals will offer a similar service to browsing except that no visuals are required – just talk to it. See how the National Blood Service have used it in an integrated campaign in Appendix 20.1 at the end of this chapter.

Save

Mobiles and hand-held devices can be used as direct-marketing tools, thereby skipping the middleman and saving the margins. In addition, some companies find that phones and hand-held devices generate efficiency gains for salespeople, engineers and other staff who are out on the road and need to be updated with key information while on the move. Also, salespeople can update records and place orders more quickly and efficiently using a mobile device.

Speak

Faster, easier feedback is generated by WAP site visitors, as marketers can watch their reactions to campaigns in real time if they so choose.

Sizzle

Location-based marketing (see Appendix 20.1) is still relatively new and therefore has some intrigue and excitement about it, particularly when delivering interesting incentives and mesmerizing messages that tend to get talked about offline. Remember, customer permission should be gained before engaging in any location-based marketing efforts.

In Finland...

... customers buy flowers, buy CDs, bid in auctions, buy Coke from vending machines and pay for a car wash all with their mobiles.

Smith and Chaffey (2001)

Disadvantages

In addition to the obvious limitations of small black-and-white screens, there are a limited number of WAP sites (and even fewer really well-designed ones), and there is also the issue of poor coverage. Being cut off while in the middle of a transaction is at best infuriating, and at worst frightening, particularly when any personal or credit card details have been given.

When phones become instant postcards (text messaging) and other phones (3G) become TVs that stream video it is clear that media convergence will be here. Maybe this will herald the end of the term 'telephone' as an archaic single-purpose device?

I-TV

Interactive TV (i-TV) opens up the online world to a vast population, as the world's 1 billion TVs slowly upgrade to interactive digital TVs. This means more channels, better pictures (usually), and more interaction, including shopping, browsing, banking, gambling, voting and e-mailing. TV has traditionally been a 'lean back' medium, while the PC is a 'lean forward' medium. I-TV is a mixture of both – it uniquely combines television's emotional intensity with the Web's interactivity.

Advantages

Sell
The advantages to sales are through (1) better targeting and (2) instant gratification. Better targeting is provided by the wide range of new niche programmes and stations, eg MUTV (Manchester United TV). Instant gratification is achieved because i-TV allows aroused buyers to take action and try or buy both products and services immediately. Combine this with new home-delivery services that deliver such things as pizzas and videos to your door and the sales opportunities grow and grow.

Serve
I-TV can deliver extra information whenever and wherever the customer requires. The days of combining TV for brand building and press for detail may be coming to an end, as i-TV can deliver both of these to the customer whenever he or she wants them.

Save
I-TV can be used as a direct-marketing medium, which saves middlemen's margins by selling directly to end-users, although there are some online malls, which charge hosting costs, margins and/or commissions.

Speak

Every interaction gathers data, from which customer profiles that help marketers to get a better picture of their various customer segments can be built up. Programmes can also be community builders, encouraging customers to speak both to each other and to the company itself. It is worth noting that some stations may argue that they own the click data and customer profiling and that as this data is therefore not automatically owned by the advertiser, it has to be purchased from the i-TV station.

Sizzle

I-TV is exciting and has a lot of emotional impact. It is the most compelling content channel of all. It also has a lot of credibility ('as seen on TV'). For many of those companies that want to be seen as innovative or at the cutting edge, i-TV reinforces this position.

Disadvantages

I-TV is not the Web – it is a different experience. TV is viewed from eight feet away, a PC screen is not. TV is 'lean back'. PC is 'lean forward'. So Web-based materials cannot be simply dumped on to an interactive TV screen. They require repurposing (see Appendix 20.2). In addition, i-TV currently has many technological teething problems, including slow performance, lack of production skills and sloppy landing sites generated by 'mad couch disease' (bad design), which creates nausea among the viewing audience. Impatient customers don't want to wait for sluggish interaction. The lack of production skills reflects the fact that agencies and production companies require extra training to produce within the tighter technical confines of *interactive* TV. This problem is compounded by the lack of common standards across different i-TV platforms, which means that in addition to repurposing Web content to i-TV content, ads have to be repurposed for each i-TV platform. This should change eventually.

Production of i-TV materials from scratch, whether ads or programmes, requires new skills and new demands of working with a tighter production brief, which may limit some production styles – no fast edits, no jump cuts, no fast moves, no busy backgrounds, etc. Repurposing means recreating, or recoding content. Remember, PCs are usually used for close-up solus viewing, while TVs are often used for group viewing from a distance (maybe eight feet away, instead of two feet for PC viewing). This means small icons, buttons and text won't work in i-TV. Also, TV has a lower screen resolution of 720×576 (as opposed to today's typical PC with 800×600). On top of this, the further repurposing required between different i-TV platforms has caused some big-spending advertisers to pull out of i-TV until such time as costs come down and common standards emerge.

One relatively inexpensive route to i-TV advertising is simply to add some peripheral buttons onscreen that link to a DAL (dedicated landing site or micro-site). In addition to the usual production ad media costs, another £50,000 could pay for the micro-site development and another, say, £60,000 should pay for four weeks of hosting the micro-site (remember ownership needs to be clarified). It is interesting to note that all BBC programme bids now need to include a community-building element, whether online chat rooms, e-mail facilities or community voting facilities.

I-radio

It's over 100 year since Marconi made the first radio broadcast. Not much changed until recently. Now interactive radio is here. There are two types: Web radio and digital radio. Web radio is used by 'streamies', who listen to radio online through their PCs while surfing elsewhere and while multitasking. They can interact through the usual Web site interactivities should they so desire. Digital radio, on the other hand, has been described as 'radio with a buy button'. Usually accompanied by a big liquid crystal display (LCD) it offers more interaction and more opportunities to purchase items such as concert tickets, CDs and more.

Advantages

Again, the 5Ss can be used to demonstrate the benefits or advantages to the marketer.

Sell
Digital radio ('radio with a buy button') provides a means of making tailored offers to discrete and sometimes niche audiences.

Serve
Digital radio offers the customer more information on such things as bands, tours and concerts, as well as more convenience and other services such voting.

Save
Similar to i-TV, i-radio is a direct-marketing tool which can save middlemen's margins.

Speak
Radio has already established itself as a 'medium with dialogue', where presenters talk, respond to letters and e-mails and host phone-ins. In fact, talk shows (with audience participation) have been popular for many years. Radio can also provide instant feedback (more easily than the Web).

Sizzle

I-radio is good at building brands fast. The reach increases to 'glocal', where communities of interest listen in from anywhere around the world. It can build communities of interest. It also offers very 'sticky' stations (sites where audiences stay for long periods).

Radio is changing, as media convergence accelerates, with digital displays, phones with videos and radio streaming, and more. Perhaps they won't be called radios even five years from now.

Disadvantages

Compared to television, radio suffers the usual disadvantages – no visuals, no emotional impact, no product demonstrations. Bandwidth also costs money and the cost of streaming increases in line with the number of listeners.

Kiosks

Interactive kiosks (i-kiosks) come in all shapes and sizes. Compact and robust, they can be placed virtually anywhere that attracts passing footfall of target customers. Thus kiosks are ideal not only for sales and marketing, but also for public information purposes and corporate communications.

Advantages

Sell

Kiosks (include vending machines, ATMs and other devices) can widen distribution and ultimately boost sales by extending the reach to passing footfall of customers. From music kiosks (that create tailored CDs) to in-store kiosks (that extend the range of stock) to bus stop mini-kiosks (that sell theatre tickets) to micro kiosks, or touch pads attached to vending machines (that create virtual outlets), the kiosk is here.

Serve

An interactive kiosk with full multimedia facilities can do everything a Web site can do but better and faster, as the media may already be downloaded. Kiosks can provide information, ideas and suggestions, e-mail facilities, ordering facilities and service facilities (eg in airports kiosks help passengers to skip check-in queues by printing boarding passes).

Save

Kiosks provide physical presence without the associated costs of staff and buildings. Kiosks also provide information and service 24 hours a day, 7 days a week, without the enormous overtime costs of staff. Kiosks can be free-standing and unattended. So, although initially considered expensive, they can offer cost savings, particularly if they're used to their full potential.

Speak

Kiosks can trigger a dialogue with customers by answering FAQs, engaging in interactions and collecting data from them, which, in turn, can be integrated through the Internet into their own office network. Installed in the right place, kiosks can grab attention, attract interest and generate data from the ideal customer. But remember, if the dialogue is going to continue, the marketer must first ask for permission.

Sizzle

Shape of brand. Although branding can be visual as well as experiential (interactive), kiosks can physically represent the brand's aesthetics through shape and graphics. Kiosk design ranges from stunning design-led units (where the casing or outside cover is physically designed in the shape or colour of the brand) that are almost impossible to ignore, to more practical, engineered units. Without any interaction, the brand can stand out if the kiosk shape is used as a form of 'permanent media'.

Disadvantages

At £5,000 a kiosk, you can see why kiosks are deemed to be expensive. Setting up 500 kiosks can be seen to be very expensive. They also take some time to produce, particularly if the outer casing requires a shape that is unique to the brand. Installation of telephone and electricity cables in public places requires permission, which takes time. In addition, vandalism can destroy the branding as well as the functionality of the kiosk.

Miscellaneous tools

'A million businesses, a billion people and a trillion devices all interconnected...' You've heard it all before? Well it's happening. Keep your eye on Moore's Law. Pervasive computing is combining with deep computing to bring a new meaning to 'interconnectedness' – a wired world or, in fact, a wireless interconnected world. Some time ago IBM's Lou Gerstner said that he dreamed of 'a world made up of a trillion interconnected intelligent devices, intersecting with data-mining capability – where pervasive computing meets deep computing'.

In addition to 'wired-up Barbie dolls', we'll have computers in jackets and phones in our ties (and floating miniature submarines in our blood checking and reporting our bodies functionality). Ear rings and eye glasses embedded with instantaneous language translation, speech recognition and speech synthesis, not to mention thought-operated computers, are all here. Wearable technology has been around for some time. Today, the US Army and Military Police see wearable computers as an important part in a soldier's arsenal. And it's already happening in industry. NorthWest Airlines, Nabisco and General Dynamics are using wearable computers (connected to intranets) across different functions from customer service, distribution centres and inspection and maintenance.

Chips, implants – has the cyborg arrived wearing different (wired) clothes?

We are witnessing the emergence of a multi-channel culture, where customers access online information from a broad range of devices, from voice portals to kiosks to PCs, mobiles and TVs. Each time they interact they have a brand experience, a brand moment based on a moment of interactivity. A single click or interaction can wreck a relationship if it doesn't lead to what the customer is looking for, regardless of which tool used to connect.

Ideally, everything should be linked, or integrated, into a common database, so that customers are recognized and remembered whenever they log on, wherever they are and whichever tool is used. One integrated database test is to check whether you can return offline (in a real store) a product that has been purchased online. In addition to the database integration challenge, there are other challenges to having a multi-channel or multi-e-tool approach – namely, budgets and repurposing.

In an ideal world (with unlimited budgets) a business would have a presence in kiosks, on TV, in WAP, in i-mode and more. Even if a media budget were available, there is still the complication of repurposing, as unfortunately there are no perfect content management systems that seamlessly repurpose content for each tool (see below). Sometimes it may be easier to start again and create new content than to try to repurpose.

A single selling proposition must somehow be maintained across both all e-tools and all offline communications tools.

There are a host of new challenges that did not exist a few years ago. Equally, the online world presents new opportunities to those marketers who are willing to change, to learn new techniques, new tools and new ways of doing business.

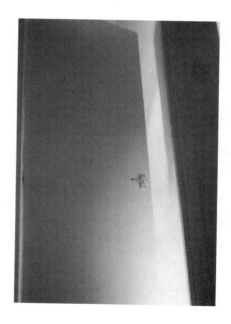

The online world presents today's marketer with a host of new opportunities and challenges

CASE STUDY 20.1

Multimap.com (multimedia mapping)

Situation

Multimap.com is an Internet mapping company based in London. It provides maps, travel directions, aerial images and local information through its public Web site, and it offers businesses location-based services to support their presence on the Internet. Multimap was established in 1995, and received funding from Flextech, now part of Telewest, in 1999.

Although Multimap.com had established itself as a respected online mapping business by early 2000, it wished to:

- expand its services rapidly, both in the UK and worldwide;
- increase awareness in line with its 'most visited site' status; and
- develop and build the reputation of the Multimap brand as category leader of Internet-based maps among the Internet-using public, and among business customers.

Multimap had a good, strong name but low brand awareness: the company participated in market research in early 2000 that revealed that only 6.2 per cent of UK Internet users were aware that they could access maps online.

Objectives

Overall, the marketing objectives were to establish Multimap.com as the first and preferred port of call for individuals who want online maps and directions, as well as for companies aiming to build and improve their e-business with location information.

Specifically, as the first stage in the development of the brand, the objectives were:

- to increase awareness among the Internet audience of Multimap.com as the first port of call for mapping services and location information; and
- to identify Multimap.com with excellence in and the benefits of online mapping services.

Strategy

Multimap decided to embark on a marketing campaign, which was put into practice in August 2000. Until that time there had been no serious investment in external marketing to the public. However, it should be noted that Multimap's investment in this campaign was actually quite modest, especially when compared with the marketing outlays of some of its dot com brethren.

The company decided to begin by targeting 25- to 35-year-olds living in the London area. Multimap.com had run a user questionnaire on the site for quite a while. This provided data on the typical age and location of the site's users, and how the site was used. There was a very great emphasis on people using the site during the working week. By pulling together a number of pieces of consumer data, Multimap was able to create a profile of the kind of person the campaign should reach – sociable, 25- to 35-years-old, independent, working.

There was also an expectation that although the campaign would not be aimed at business customers, the Multimap message would be 'overheard' by this audience, since many of the leads for Multimap's business services were generated by its public site.

Tactics/action

The first part of the strategy was offline and involved poster advertising on the London underground, along with a print campaign targeting the going out/entertainment sections of the London-based titles *Metro London*, *Evening Standard* and *Time Out*.

Given that the purpose of the campaign was to educate an Internet audience about Multimap and the services it offers, offline advertising may seem like a strange way to go about things. However, to Multimap, it was an entirely logical approach. The company was very clear that it wanted to reach Internet users, but felt that online advertising wasn't the best way of creating a brand. The company wanted to communicate with people in a reasonably sophisticated way and to reach them in the context in which they might find the map useful, rather than just when they were going online. The location and character of the poster campaign was very carefully planned. Not only did the team at Multimap spend a good deal of time working out what sort of images would be most appealing to their potential customer base, they also thought about the best way to place the images.

Multimap wanted to appeal to a sophisticated, advertising-literate audience in a way that didn't over-promise, that was warm and slightly humorous; and that avoided the kind of spiky gimmickry that many Internet companies were beginning to be known for. A poster campaign on transport was chosen to reflect Multimap's A to B strategy, which was targeting people on the move, from home to work and work to home, and from work to their social life, because that's when the use of maps would be most logical.

Following on from the offline advertising, Multimap ran an online campaign from October to December 2000. Crucially, the online creative executions built upon the images that were used in the offline work. The company believed that the more it could integrate the various elements of its marketing strategy, the more likely it would yield a positive result. For Multimap, this integrated approach was one of the most important elements of the campaign. However, it may not be fully understood by some other businesses working on a marketing strategy. For some, there is still a sense that integration isn't anything more than having everything happen at the same time, or everyone knowing what everyone else is doing, or even worse than that, everyone doing everything in the same way. Integration is ultimately about being very single-minded about what you're trying to communicate to whom, and then using the different marketing disciplines to do that in the way that they do best.

Control/results

Although the campaign did result in a ramp-up in growth of traffic on the Multimap site, the most important effect was on the awareness of Multimap, the perception of its brand and the growth of its business overall. The company was also able to achieve real consistency of message, whether talking to consumers, business customers or journalists.

Multimap.com continues to be the UK's favorite mapping Web site; in mid-2001 it was attracting about 3 million unique users every month, against just over 1 million at the launch of the campaign. It is also one of the top 10 most popular Web sites in the UK, and according to Jupiter Media Metrix, it is now the number one directory in the UK.

Equally importantly, Multimap.com has strengthened its position as the most significant provider of Internet mapping services to UK businesses: the company is now the mapping supplier to four out of the top five retailers with an online presence. The number of business customers has grown to almost 10 times that when the campaign began. Businesses that have chosen to partner with Multimap.com include Tesco, Marks & Spencer, Lloyds TSB, Upmystreet, Sony, Waterstone's, National Car Parks and Lycos.

Multimap is on track to maintain growth of its business and consumer services, both in the UK and abroad.

Men and women

Multimap had a small internal team of a marketing director, marketing manager and the close involvement of the principal partners, and they worked with an external team made up of marketing consultants and advertising and PR agencies.

Minutes

The preparatory work on developing the strategy for the marketing communications plan commenced in early 2000, with research being undertaken among key opinion formers. The external agencies were brought into the team in the spring of 2000 and detailed campaign planning took place between May and July. The offline campaign was launched in August 2000 and the online campaign followed in the autumn.

Money

Budgets were limited owing to the early-stage development of the brand, so all agencies knew that a key requirement was to create a significant impact in whatever media were selected.

APPENDIX 20.1

National Blood Service integrated mobile campaign

Phones are more than a communications tool, they are a device for gathering vital information as well as being a lifestyle accessory ('it's my identity'). Student mobile numbers were registered at five university fresher fairs. A series of catchy messages inviting students to book a blood donor appointment by phone. Appointments were spread so no bottlenecks occurred. A mobile message was later sent confirming the appointment.

P R Smith and D Chaffey (2001) *eMarketing eXcellence*, Butterworth-Heinemann, London

APPENDIX 20.2

Repurposing Web site content for i-TV

Here are 10 tips on repurposing Web content for i-TV:

1. Best-practice Web design is not best-practice i-TV design.
2. Avoid poor visual display (creates viewer vertigo – disorientation and nausea derived from straining to see i-TV).
3. Create new HTML content or clean up existing pages.
4. Increase font sizes (i-TV is further away than a PC screen).
5. Use sans serif fonts (not, for example, the serif font you are currently reading).
6. Review line thickness and colours.
7. Stay within the screen space available (different to PC).
8. Seek technical advice (on buttons, icons, interactions, templates, applications, gateways, personalization, etc).
9. Use retail store design (maps, floor layout, clearly labelled aisles, product descriptions, returns information, etc).
10. Navigation – should be logical, intuitive and simple (and provide multiple paths to content).

P R Smith (2001) *eMarketing eXcellence – the heart of eBusiness* (online courses), Multimedia Marketing.com, London

FURTHER READING

Bickerton, P and Bickerton M (2000) *Cybermarketing – How to use the Internet to market your goods and services*, 2nd edn, Butterworth-Heinemann, Oxford

Bickerton, P, Bickerton M and Simpson-Holley K (2000) *Cyberstrategy – Business strategy for extranets, intranets and the internet*, 2nd edn, Butterworth-Heinemann, Oxford

Chaffey, D, Mayer, R, Johnston K and Ellis-Chadwick, F (2000) Internet Marketing, Strategy and Implication and Practice, Financial Times Prentice-Hall, Harlow

Corporate Intelligence Group (2000) *Retail Intelligence, Mobile Commerce in Retail*

Forrester Research (1999) *Strong Content Means A Loyal Audience,* Forester Research, London

Godin, S (1999) *Permission Marketing*, Simon & Schuster, New York

Levine, R *et al* (2000) *The Cluetrain Manifesto*, Perseus Books, New York

Levison, J (1996) *Guerrilla Marketing Online Attack*, Piatkus, London

McGovern, G (1999) *The Caring Economy*, Oaktree Press, Dublin

Moore, G (1999) *Crossing the Chasm*, 2nd edn, Capstone, Oxford

Parker, R (2000) *Relationship Marketing on the Internet*, Adams Streetwise, Holbrook, MA

Siegel, D (1999) *Futurize Your Enterprise – Business strategies in the age of e-customer*, Wiley, New York

Silverstein, B (1999) *Business-to-Business Internet Marketing*, Maximum Press, Gulf Breeze, FL

Smith, P R (2001) *eMarketing eXcellence – the heart of eBusiness* (online courses), Multimedia Marketing.com, London

Smith, P R and Chaffey, D (2001) *eMarketing eXcellence*, Butterworth-Heinemann, London

Sterne, J (1999*) World Wide Web Marketing – Integrating the Web into your marketing strategy*, 2nd edn, Wiley , New York

Timmers, P (1999) *Electronic Commerce – Strategies and Models for B2B Trading*, Wiley, New York

21

Corporate identity

WHAT IS CORPORATE IDENTITY?

Corporate identity is how a corporation, company or organization expresses itself visually. It is important because it is the prime interface between an organization and its key audiences. The first contact people have with an organization – whether they are looking at an advertisement, buying a product or going for a job interview – will usually bring them into contact with its corporate identity.

Used effectively, identity can help a company to put across clear messages about who it is, what it does and how it does it. It can help to set expectations and to deliver against those expectations. On the other hand, a badly managed identity can make a company appear poorly managed, confused, cluttered and unprofessional.

Corporate identity is therefore an important strategic asset which can be used to achieve long-term communications goals. It cannot be used as a short-term tactical tool like advertising or PR, which can change from day to day if required.

Successful companies have a clear identity. A quick look at easyJet tells you immediately what kind of company they are: modern, good value, convenient, accessible and, of course, an airline.

In smaller businesses, including start-ups, the identity ethos will often come from one or more powerful individuals whose influence permeates the whole organization and results in a consistent approach. In larger organizations, corporate identities are professionally managed using proven processes and structures to make sure that they come across clearly and powerfully. Either way, to be effective, a corporate identity must be informed and driven by a clear vision and set of values. As Philip Kotler says 'designers identify *the essence of the company* and turn it into a concept backed by strong visuals symbols and logos'.

Logos

Logos, by the force of ubiquity, have become the closest thing we have to an international language, recognized and understood in many more places than English.

N Klein (2000) *No Logo*, Flamingo, London

As products and services become more and more similar, influenced by technology and communications, commercial entities and other organizations find it more and more difficult to come up with ways to build differentiation. Financial services are a prime example of this: life insurance from Axa is not really any different from life insurance from Prudential. What influences consumer choice is more likely to lie in the identity of the provider than in the product itself. Corporate identity has therefore become an important weapon in the fight to stay ahead.

The term 'corporate identity' has been in common use for 40 years or so, although in reality the principles of identity have been used by companies – consciously or unconsciously – since organizations began. More recently the term has been overtaken by new nomenclature – that of 'corporate branding'. This has happened as the skills and techniques that brand managers use to develop and market products and services have spread into the board room. The CEO is often cited at the 'corporate brand manager'. However, whether they call it identity or branding, most communications professionals are trying to do the same thing: help an organization to increase its value by managing the way it expresses itself.

See how expert designers achieved this for Kiss (Case study on page 619), for the Gatwick Express (page 622) and for the Natural History Museum below.

The Natural History Museum, London

More than a logo

Although when many people use the term 'corporate identity' they are referring to a logo, in reality corporate identity is much broader than this. As corporate identity specialist John Sorrell says, the logo is 'the tip of the iceberg'.

A corporate identity scheme may have a logo at its heart, but it will generally include a whole array of other elements, often referred to as 'visual language'. This may include one or more typefaces, a colour palette, the use of photography and illustrations, a layout style for using these items and even a particular style of written language.

As Figure 21.1 shows, the impact of a corporate identity programme does far beyond a logo or a lick of paint. It influences almost every manifestation of an organization, even its corporate headquarters – see Appendix 21.1.

A new letterhead and a new logo is no substitute for a new board of directors.
Rodney Fitch

Painting the lavatory door won't cure the plumbing.
David Bernstein

If you take a lousy low-profile company and give it a major corporate revamp, you end up with a lousy high-profile company.
Wally Olins

You can put on an Arsenal shirt but if you don't perform like an Arsenal player you have not accomplished very much.
Nick Chaloner

Even if you paint out a skunk's stripes it will still smell extremely nasty.
Source: unknown

The corporate identity mix

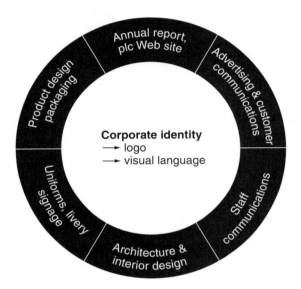

Figure 21.1 The corporate identity mix – corporate identity is the prime interface between an organization and its key audiences

Another key trend in corporate identity over the past 10 years has been the increased emphasis placed on communicating with staff. It is generally recognized that a company or other type of organization can only put across a strong and consistent identity if its staff understand what it stands for and their behaviour supports other key messages. Although there was a lot of talk about the importance of staff communications during the 1970s and 1980s, it is only in the 1990s that this aspect of identity management was developed in depth.

Logos

The crucifix, the hammer and sickle, the swastika, the red cross or a national flag immediately arouse emotions, feelings, images or interpretations of some kind. Logos are a language (sometimes international) of emotional response. Symbols, shapes and colour all have conscious and unconscious meanings (see Chapter 17). Visual symbols or devices can also be powerful as a means of increasing awareness by facilitating easy recognition. On the other hand, a logo cannot read like a graphic sign, eg 'Ladies'. A logo can act as a focal point to summarize or encapsulate an organization, although it should not be too complex. Many corporate identity professionals feel that if an identity needs too much explaining, then it isn't working.

A logo should be *distinctive, easily recognizable, memorable and reducible* (can work when reduced on to a business card or postage stamp). It should also *work in black and white* as well as colour, since many corporate images appear in black and white in the press. Ideally, the logo should also be *symbolic*, but this is rarely the case. With the growth of the Internet it is increasingly important that it works well on screen, as well as in its more traditional applications.

At first a logo has little or no value because it has no franchise. First it must be associated with the right kind of images and then its recognition levels can be developed (eg, Lloyds Bank's black horse and McDonald's yellow arches). This takes time, since initial reaction to change or anything new is often quite negative. Sometimes the initial reaction is one of upset, dislike or disgust, as the new logo does not fit in with the previous set of cognitions (and thereby creates 'cognitive dissonance' and possibly tension). The value of the logo eventually starts to increase as the years roll by and it becomes better understood.

Logo designs as visual devices

In the 1970s corporate images hardened. The 1980s saw them becoming soft and decorative. Some cynics say that if you wanted to make an abstract organization look purposeful in the late 1980s, you quite literally gave it a face – preferably a neo-classical one. The Woolworths group, on the other hand, changed its name, logo and total identity to Kingfisher, which was certainly distinctive, easily recognizable, memorable, and symbolic of its progressive leadership expansion and growth potential (although some argued that the bird has a life expectancy of only one year and that robins and blue tits are more popular anyway). Bovis construction company chose a humming bird, which again fitted the above criteria. Others suggest that there was a trend towards *humanizing* logos since organizations are all about people (eg the Prudential – see below).

More recently, there has been a trend towards purely graphic devices (in other words, away from figurative symbols). This has been driven by a number of factors. On the one hand, it is part of a general trend towards more direct communications which has resulted in a stripping out of superfluous elements. On the other, the Internet has become a more important channel of communication for many organizations. As Mark Wilson, of identity specialists Bamber Forsyth, says, 'The lower resolution of the Internet and digital television have driven us towards simpler, highly graphic identity elements that are seen smaller, and in more places, than ever before.'

Shanks & McEwan, a waste management business, updated their identity in 1999, simplifying their name and adopting a straightforward graphic logo.

shanks. waste solutions.

When introducing the new identity to staff, the company said:

> We're linking the phrase 'waste solutions' to our name in order to emphasize that we are a problem-solving company. We're also using the 's' as our symbol to make the new identity more distinctive and memorable. The full stops within the logotype and after the 's' symbol are important. This is our way of saying that we're the last word in waste management.

Don King's hair

World boxing promoter Don King's elevated hair style (brushed up six inches or more into the sky) makes him stand out in a crowded post-fight boxing ring. His 'unique visual symbol' helps to ensure that he is easily recognized and seen to be involved with the big fights.

The logo can be literal (eg Shell), logo types (stylized treatments of the company name with no additional symbol, eg Kelloggs), wordmarks that integrate a graphic element into the name (eg BHS), company initials (eg IBM) or purely abstract. Whichever type of logo is chosen, it is essential to research the choice carefully, particularly in global markets where symbols, colours and words can have very different meanings.

One UK design consultancy presented a new logo for Saudi Arabian Airlines that looked, to the uninitiated, distinctive, unique and easily recognizable. It received mixed reactions. Golden palm trees, crossed Arabian swords and crescent moon certainly appeared to the Western eye to be suitably upmarket and regal, but a detailed objection from another source criticized it as follows:

Wrong type of palm tree

(Saudi is the number two producer of dates but the palm tree shown is not a date palm)

Wrong type of sword

(the traditional Saudi sword is a fighting sword; the sword shown looks weak, old and ceremonial)

Wrong moon

(the crescent of the new moon used by Saudi Arabia represents a new beginning; the proposed crescent is that of an old moon, suggesting 'the end')

Wrong colour

(the old green colour was replaced by cream which represents hot, barren sand in the desert when Saudi is trying to irrigate the kingdom and make it green).

All of the above confirms the need for designers to invest in detailed research before attempting to develop any design concepts. Designers who neither budget nor plan for research (or several stages of research) vastly increase the likelihood of problems. Worse still, if problems occur after implementation of a new design, the costs immediately spin out of control, along with the highly embarrassed management team.

Whether the logo trend is towards simplicity, swooshes or sharp-edged internationally understood symbols, the corporate identity demands careful management across all the points of public contact. The next part of this chapter looks at how to manage the corporate identity.

MANAGING THE CORPORATE IDENTITY

Whether a £2 million global design or £15,000 local design, the management process is essentially the same. There are a number of stages in the management of corporate identity:

1. Gain board-level support.
2. Assess current situation and determine ideal image.
3. Brief and select a designer.
4. Develop design concepts.
5. Select, research and test concepts.
6. Explain internally.
7. Implement launch and maintain.
8. Review and update.

Gain board-level support

Ideally, the commitment must start at the top. An effective corporate identity programme needs support and commitment from the board of directors.

Assess the current situation

The key areas for design should be identified, eg for a bank it would be the retail environment design and for a car manufacturer it would be the product design. A *communications audit* examines how the organization is perceived internally by its own employees and externally by a host of different audiences. As soon as the ideal image is determined, the gap between the ideal and existing image can be addressed. This paves the way for a brief to improve, modify or design a new corporate identity and, in addition, to address other non-visual areas that affect the corporate image (eg product quality, customer care and employee care – see 'Total quality management', page 560).

Brief and select a designer

The brief should incorporate at least SOS + 3Ms (see Chapter 2 for a full explanation of the formula). Essentially, it must include basic information, ie the situation, objectives, strategy, targets and the resources of men and women, money and minutes. The strategy can give an outline of the range of communications tools that use the corporate identity. The design consultancy selection process is similar to the agency selection process described in Chapter 6.

Develop design concepts

The next step is the development of rough design concepts that match the brief. It is possible to score the concepts according to specific criteria in the brief. At the end of the day it also comes down to judgement or gut feelings about the early concepts. Having said that, many articulate and confident design agencies can justify an array of different concepts in a persuasive manner. Rejection fees (payment for rejected or unused concepts) should be clarified in advance of any concepts being presented. The number of concepts presented will depend on the size of the client, the nature of the brief and the approach of the design team; it may be two or three or several hundred, as was the case with the new global branding for BP.

Select, research and test

The role of research is generally to find out what associations a particular design sparks in the minds of the target audience. It can also be an effective 'disaster check' to identify any particular problems or concerns. People tend to prefer the familiar, and so the researchers need to probe beneath an initial response of 'I like it' or 'I don't like it' to discover whether a particular solution is appropriate or not. Mould-breaking identities such as Orange are often difficult to assess at the research stage because they can evoke a negative response simply because they are different from what people are used to. Often very detailed visuals are worked up, to help consumers understand exactly what a new design could mean for them. This can go as far as building complete mock-ups of major items such as petrol stations, or painting vehicles in a range of different liveries.

Explain internally

As mentioned previously, there is an inherent resistance to change. A new identity can create conflict, particularly if it is not understood. So any new identity will be resented if it is not presented and explained to the employees as 'their' new identity. They need to be fully briefed, first, so that they will not be embarrassed by others if asked what the new design represents and, second, so that they can use the new design in a careful and consistent manner.

BP wanted to make the colour green an integral part of the brand equity. They wanted to own the colour green in the same way that Coca-Cola 'own' red. Green's environmental connotations suited BP's commitment to improving its environmental performance. In order to convince BP managers that green was good for BP and to help them 'fall in love with green', they showed managers pictures of fresh green peas bursting from their pods, fresh mint, green apples and green fields. After winning over this level of managers, the next level could be educated through newsletters, manuals and meetings to ensure that all employees felt part of, and understood, the corporate identity change.

Implement, launch and maintain

The identity now needs to be placed at all the visual points of public contact. Although it is difficult, it can be done overnight, or on a gradual replacement basis. The implementation stage is usually the most expensive and time consuming. BP was reported to have spent under £1 million on design and research and £171 million on implementation. By specifying exactly the Pantone colours, typeface, positioning of symbols, etc, the *design manual* allows managers in different divisions or in different countries to commission their own marketing communications tools, such as brochures, exhibition stands and even advertisements, while adhering to strict corporate identity specifications. This maintains the consistency of the identity wherever it is used. There are other problems, often outside the scope of the design manual, that affect corporate identity, eg the purchasing department may clash with the design manager when buying the cheapest light bulbs or the cheapest stationery.

Ensuring that the identity is protected through constant policing indicates the survival of Drucker's first law: 'Everything degenerates into work.' It is possible to work with the personnel director to develop a reward system that can be built into salaries so that those who maintain the design standards benefit.

The need for cohesion

If an organization's identity is not coordinated or managed precisely, confusing signals about the organization go out to different audiences around the world. A splintered identity fragments the corporate image, which, in turn, dilutes the corporate presence among key audiences. The potential corporate asset (the identity) depreciates to the point where it becomes a liability – the organization not only has no presence but it also has an uncoordinated image. This sends out disorganized messages that weaken the initial or final impression left by the organization.

Air travel worries?

Attention to detailed design management can unconsciously influence air travellers. The same logo, typeface, primary and secondary colours and trim on all visual points of contact help to reassure the traveller, while reinforcing the airline's identity. The check-in desk logo, signs, colours and trims should be coordinated with the uniform (and badge), ticket holder, baggage tag, departure lounge carpets, right through to the plane's exterior graphics, interior carpet and even the trim on the china and linen. Without this coordinated corporate identity cognitive dissonance can set in. There is an unconscious unease or discomfort created by the inconsistent messages. A coordinated identity reduces this often unconscious tension, which in turn creates a more satisfied passenger. The cohesive identity does not make the traveller leap off the plane and scream for joy when arriving after a pleasant and soothing flight. But it might make the unconscious difference next time around when choosing between two mutually exclusive airline companies.

Detailed consistency

A logo displayed prominently in an office or on a letterhead makes a good strong statement, but it is the consistent 'echoing' of the logo, its exact primary and secondary colours, the specific typeface and overall design style on the 'secondary format' of products, packages, business forms and employee uniforms that provides the all-important, if subtle consistent reinforcement.

There is a need to think it through in detail and then to police the usage of all visual points of contact. This is where a design manual guides managers in different buildings and in different countries to specify, in a consistent manner, the *exact* graphic requirement for *every* point of visual contact.

In corporate identity terms, attention to detail needs to spread beyond just graphics. The *1990 US Hall of Shame* reported the following:

> To upgrade its image in 1982 AT&T told its repair people to wear dress shirts and ties, gave them attaché cases for their tools, and renamed them 'system technicians'. But Ma Bell didn't install air conditioning in its cars. So during the summer the technicians arrived on the job looking like they had just stepped out of a sauna. Said a union official, 'It's hard to have corporate appeal if your shirt is wringing wet.'

The importance of consistency applies right across the communications spectrum. In John Murphy's book on branding (1987) Klaus Morwind Henkel points to consumer research that 'has indicated that a lack of consistency between the brand name, the packaging and the advertising is subconsciously recognized by the consumer and leads to a feeling of detachment, ultimately resulting in brandswitching'.

So it is important to be consistent and to reinforce identity through all the appropriate points of public contact. Many feel that this should include advertising. Several years ago the UK advertising trade magazine *Campaign* (3 September 1988) suggested that advertising that isn't integrated into an identity programme 'is like a rogue elephant'.

Review and update

When does a corporate identity become out of date? Can the business environment change and move away from the organization and its values, leaving behind the obsolete, irrelevant and even damaging corporate identity? When do the staff and other audiences get tired of it? Mergers and acquisitions sometimes necessitate a new corporate identity. Occasionally, legal reasons force a change. Sometimes overseas ambitions are restricted by the use of a home-grown logo (eg BT's old logo clashed with overseas companies). Alternatively new identities are developed simply because old management wants to say something new or new management wants to announce its arrival. As Olins (1989) says: 'In a complex and changing company the corporate identity bears a great strain, twisting and turning to fit every new requirement. But a good corporate identity should last a generation.'

Hand-held torch of learning

The National Union of Teachers' 25-year-old 'hand-held torch of learning' was considered to have become 'too strident, aggressive and uncaring, with none too desirable connotations of the Conservative party and the Greek fascist party'. Although it was designed in the 1960s, it had a 1930s' look. It appeared that the time was right to move the logo on but keep it relevant and maintain the link with the union's heritage. The updated design shows an outstretched hand embraced by the spelt-out words of the NUT, tying the symbol together as one cohesive form, either male/female or adult/child to avoid alienation.

Global markets are constantly moving and changing, so much so that some organizations fear they are being left behind by the 'global update'. A review and redesign helps to keep abreast of trends and avoids being left isolated by a redundant identity.

Approximately every 12 years Shell reviews and updates its corporate identity. The shell device has served them well despite its being a petrol company with a 'high explosive' name.

The Shell logo moving with the times

Having examined corporate identity, now consider corporate image. What is the difference? Is one part of the other? The second part of this chapter looks at how corporate identity is a part of overall corporate image, which every organization has (whether it wants it or not).

WHAT IS CORPORATE IMAGE?

Every company has an image. Whether it is messy, muddled, fragmented and confused, or clear, strong, positive and unique depends on management's ability to harness this often under-utilized resource.

Corporate image is perception. Corporate identity is the reality of the tangible points of public contact, eg the buildings, the vehicles, the uniforms, the business forms and so on. Corporate image, on the other hand, is the sum of people's perceptions of an organization. Images and perceptions are created through all the senses: sight, sound, smell, touch, taste and feelings experienced through product usage, customer service, the commercial environment and corporate communications.

Corporate image embraces everything from the visual impression of a corporate logo, letterhead, uniform, livery, leaflet or advertisement, the aroma in the shop, reception, canteen or offices, to the pleasant feeling of a soft carpet, attractive wallpaper and air-conditioned rooms, and the atmosphere created by both the interior and exterior design of a building, to the experiences enjoyed or suffered with product quality and customer service. Corporate image is a result of everything a company does (or does not do).

Corporate image is formed from four areas:

1. Products/services (including product quality and customer care – see Chapter 19).
2. Behaviours and attitudes (social responsibility, corporate citizenship, ethical behaviour and community affairs).
3. Environments (offices, showrooms, factories).
4. Communications (advertising, PR, personal communications, brochures and corporate identity programmes – see Figure 21.2).

The corporate image mix

Figure 21.2 on page 616 shows the corporate image mix.

Figure 21.2 The corporate image mix – corporate image is the result of everything an organization does (or does not) do.

Advantages of a good corporate image

Corporate image (including the corporate identity) can create competitive advantage, particularly when there is little or no difference between competitors. It can help to:

- improve sales;
- support new product development;
- strengthen financial relations;
- harmonize employee relations;
- boost recruitment;
- manage crises.

Improve sales

A unique and easily recognizable identity projects or *raises corporate profile* above the mass of other corporations. Many customers will not buy from a company they have never heard of because they can have no confidence without knowledge and awareness. A well-known company usually has an advantage over an unknown company.

A well-managed corporate identity unconsciously *reassures customers*. Their confidence and trust can be increased by designing an identity that has a tone of planned cohesiveness that subtly presents a reassuring sense of order. As Wally Olins says: 'A coordinated design policy across product, environment and communication makes company products seem more desirable.' (See the airline example in the box on page 612.)

A strong corporate identity tied to the right corporate image *adds value* to a product or brand. In a sense it is a corporate endorsement.

Corporate identity can *reposition, reinforce* or *sharpen the position* (or perceived image) of the organization and its products or services. 'Younger', 'friendlier', 'high tech', 'traditional' or 'family firm' positions can be expressed through an identity. Some identities can persuade customers to make 'emotional rather than rational decisions', particularly in the 'indistinguishable financial services sector'.

A strong identity can give an emotional edge that allows an organization to reach deeper into relations with customers and staff.

Support new product development

The image can help new product development by providing a positive corporate platform for launching new products. For example, it is easier for Heinz to launch a new food product than it would be for an unidentified/unknown company. A strong corporate identity tied in with a positive corporate image makes it easier to introduce new products to the marketplace.

Strengthen financial relations

Carefully coordinated corporate identity helps to raise the corporate profile and to make the organization's *presence known* to influential players within financial circles. In this way it increases awareness, understanding and support. A well-managed corporate identity also increases confidence, suggests a sense of order (good management) and reinforces a desired image. In addition, corporate design can create a strong visual platform for corporate communications, press releases, annual reports, television interviews, etc.

During a *takeover* organizations that have ignored the potential of their identity asset often recognize too late their lack of visibility among key audiences such as shareholders, financial analysts, employees, customers and the business community. Corporate identity cannot, on its own, solve these problems, but over time and together with other resources, such as communications tools like corporate advertising and PR, it can work to close the vulnerability gap created by a lack of identity.

A strong, cohesive, unified identity can also *strengthen* a company during a takeover. Woolworths' new Kingfisher identity was designed partly to end the confusion between the holding company and the Woolworths retail chain. This was considered to be significant during the Woolworths vs Dixon's takeover bid. Dixon's was reported to have skilfully concentrated attention on Woolworths, which made it difficult to shift attention away from the relatively weak image of the Woolworths retail chain division. The new logo did, however, make a statement: Woolworths is changing, Woolworths' futuristic and progressive management is moving with the times.

Harmonize employee relations

Employees can become lost in an organization as it grows, diversifies or develops. A properly managed corporate identity can enhance employee harmony by creating a *sense of common purpose* that brings everyone on board the same corporate ship, moving in the same corporate direction. A good identity programme clarifies divisional and subsidiary participation. The identity should, if managed properly, boost morale among the employees. This new sense of purpose can contribute towards improvement in everyone's performance. PIMS (Profit Impact of Marketing Strategy, see Appendix 1.3, page 22) has found that high investment in corporate image correlates with a high ROI (return on investment). Caution needs to be exercised because of the inherent dislike of change. A new corporate identity needs to be communicated and managed carefully from within (rather than insulting staff by letting them find out second-hand).

Boost recruitment

An identity presents a company's image to many different audiences. Corporate identity helps recruitment by strengthening an organization's ability to attract (and keep) the best people. Who wants to be associated with an organization that has a tatty, run-down, worn-out image? A clear, strong and cohesive identity communicates positive messages to potential employees.

Manage crises

Corporate identity contributes towards the corporate image. In times of crisis, a company with a good corporate image enjoys a presumption of innocence.

To sum up, a corporate identity programme or any corporate communications programme provides an opportunity for an analysis of the organization's corporate strategy and its corporate culture. This, in turn, provides a forum for review, analysis and change if necessary. A new corporate identity programme must be *supported by real changes* in the organization, including the cultural and physical environment, the quality of products and the level of customer services. A new corporate identity can have the effect of raising everyone's expectations. A corporate identity programme cannot paper over the cracks in an organization. An attempt to do so can rebound negatively after a period of time. This can be partly explained by the theory of raised expectations.

Beware: The theory of raised expectations

This theory is derived from the field of political science and is usually applied to the area of popular revolutions. The basic tenet of the theory is that, contrary to intuition, the most likely time for a revolution to occur is not when economic and social conditions are at their worst, but when the situation has improved following a depressed period. The amelioration of conditions induces a greatly heightened sense of expectation... so when launching a campaign to improve and match a new image, they will be much more critical than before, anticipating improvements in standards that the company may not be able to deliver. 'Truth' makes the difference.

S Hooker (1991)

CASE STUDY 21.1

Kiss 100

Situation

Radio plays a part in the life of its audiences not reached or matched by other media such as the TV or the Internet. For many people it is there in the background all day – and sometimes all night. As a consequence, radio stations and programmes create unusually strong and loyal communities.

Launched in 1990, Kiss was the first commercial station to reach 1 million listeners. Irreverent, sexy and in tune with London's young scene, it established an exclusive club that it was cool to belong to. But 10 years later the youth market had changed. Kiss found its product falling behind the evolving tastes of a new young audience, and that it had become better known for its brand extensions, such as club nights and CD compilations, than for the station itself. The challenge was to reach out to new audiences without losing loyal older listeners.

Objectives

The objectives were threefold:

1. To give the Kiss brand more standout while building recognition and awareness among its key target audience of 15- to 24-year-olds.
2. To communicate the Kiss proposition – the promise of friends and sex.
3. To work across many different environments.

Strategy

Kiss made big changes to refresh the radio station, hiring new DJs and improving play lists. To reflect these changes to its product, it decided to invest in its identity. The challenge was to determine how much of the existing identity needed to change – whether it could be updated while retaining existing features, or whether it was time for a complete overhaul. Kiss needed to explore how far they could take the existing identity and at the same time ensure that it would still be relevant and meaningful in the future.

Tactics

The underlying brand proposition for Kiss – 'the promise of friends and the promise of sex' – still encapsulated what the station stood for. In close collaboration with the client, Bambe. Forsyth made the decision that it was time to say goodbye to the lips logo and the freestyle typeface, which had clearly had their day. They developed a new typeface that is strong and bold but with soft edges. The symbolism of the lips was translated into a heart, formed between the two Ss in the name. They also decided to drop the 'FM' from the name; giving the identity a more confident and modern feeling, but to retain the '100' to signpost the station to its new listeners.

While developing the new identity, they had to ensure that the visual language that accompanies it works across very diverse applications – from CDs, posters, flyers, ads and merchandise to environments and different formats on screen. The very strong, simple lines of the new identity ensure that it maintains its integrity across the many different environments in which it is used.

The palette of colours is very broad, to allow for many different moods, events and seasons.

Action

To attract attention and raise expectations for the new brand, Bamber Forsyth created a special launch Web site to tease and excite. Livesexy.com used flash animation and was updated daily. Listeners were encouraged to visit each morning for new tips and advice on how to 'live sexy' wherever they were, whatever they were doing. In just two weeks livesexy.com had attracted half a million new and existing listeners and helped Kiss build a database of loyal fans.

Working closely with the ad agency throughout the project ensured that the advertising was borne of the same thinking as other aspects of the brand and helped build a single coherent image.

Poster campaigns across the capital, press advertising and promotional items all helped establish new Kiss in people's hearts and minds.

Control

Kiss was relaunched in spring 1999, and by the end of the year there was a 17 per cent rise in listener figures, and an increase in market share from 12.1 to 16.2 per cent among the key target audience of 15–24 year olds. Kiss also achieved its highest ever share of the total adult audience. Over the same period, advertising revenue increased by 89 per cent, and major blue-chip advertisers added the station to their media list for the first time.

Kiss won Best Branding and Station of the Year awards at each of the major national and international radio awards ceremonies in 2000.

Men and women

Bamber Forsyth collaborated closely with staff at EMAP and at Kiss's advertising agencies, to ensure the implementation of a seamless and cohesive launch strategy.

Money

The design fee was £25,000. As many of the applications on which the Kiss identity appears are short-term campaign-based items, such as CDs, merchandise and poster advertising, the costs for implementation were relatively low.

Minutes

Bamber Forsyth had already established a relationship with EMAP while working with them to create their corporate identity. This meant that there was no need for a competitive pitch for the Kiss rebranding project. It also resulted in an extremely streamlined process – the project took nine weeks from start to finish.

CASE STUDY 21.2

Gatwick Express's new identity

Situation

Gatwick Express was one of the first train services to be privatized in the UK. Running a dedicated service between Victoria and Gatwick, the service had an excellent service record and positive reputation with customers. To improve the service further, the company decided to replace its entire fleet.

In the past the rail industry had tended to think in terms of passengers rather than customers. The look and feel of trains, both inside and out, were dictated by issues of practicality and cost rather than brand building. This began to change with privatization, but the desire of many rail operators to establish better relationships with their customers has been severely constrained by old rolling stock. Gatwick Express's decision to buy new trains changed all that. As the first rail company to replace its entire fleet, they had a unique opportunity to build an effective brand from the bottom up.

With passengers using Gatwick due to increase by 22 per cent by 2005, investing in retaining the lion's share of the airport transfer market made strong commercial sense.

Objective

At the time of ordering the new trains, 60 per cent of journeys between Gatwick and London were with Gatwick Express. The objective was to create a brand that would build on this strong position and automatically be the first choice to and from the airport. This meant appealing not just to air travellers but also to all the other people who use the link, including airport workers and commuters.

Strategy

The strategy was to create an identity appropriate to a leading transport operator with a strong customer focus and commercial outlook.

Gatwick Express decided to bring in a team of specialists to collaborate on the project and ensure that every aspect was carried out to a high standard. Bamber Forsyth were assigned as brand guardians and identity specialists; Alstrom, the train manufacturers behind the TGV and Eurostar, the engineers on the team; and Jones Garrard, the industrial design specialists in train form and structure.

Tactics

The first task was to define what the Gatwick Express brand should stand for and how these ideas should be communicated throughout the service.

The proposition 'Aero – the best of the train and the plane' was successfully developed and researched. This is not just a promotional soundbite, but a philosophy that then guided the development of the identity, from train interiors to signage, and livery to uniform.

Alstrom and Jones Garrard, using a flexible modular design, created a specification unique to Gatwick Express, featuring a striking extended front end that is immediately identifiable from a distance. In keeping with the new design, a modern comfortable environment was designed, reflecting the streamlined style of an aeroplane, and exploiting the pace and mobility possible in a train. The combination of colour and fabric designs are unique to Gatwick Express, and were inspired by airport runways and airport departure boards.

Every detail of the train was addressed, ensuring that moving through the train was easy and fast, while sitting down was comfortable and relaxing. The train exterior, in vibrant red and silver grey, carries the new visual identity, in a specially designed typeface, along the sides, windows and on the roof – hard not to notice as you are flying in to the airport. Clear and simple signage inside and outside the train draws on the international symbols familiar to airport visitors worldwide.

Action

It takes a long time to build new trains and a project like this starts several years before the results are to be released into the public domain. Bamber Forsyth helped design a programme of communication to inform and inspire staff and suppliers during the development process. The agency was also on hand at a series of presentations at Alstrom to show off the new train and excite the airlines, airport and trade about what was in store.

Control

Each stage of the process was thoroughly researched with customers, potential customers, the travel trade and staff using qualitative research techniques.

Independent market research was undertaken in October 2000 to gauge awareness of different transport methods between London and Gatwick, and also of Gatwick Express itself among train users. In both categories new Gatwick Express demonstrated that

awareness of its service had increased. It also increased its overall share of all journeys between London and Gatwick to almost 70 per cent.

Men and women

The issues that needed to be tackled were complex, involving designers, engineers, project managers, materials suppliers and other experts from a wide range of specialists. More than a dozen companies collaborated to help ensure seamless delivery of the brand proposition.

Money

The fee for developing the proposition and concept development was £120,000. The implementation costs, which would have been substantial had Gatwick Express not been ordering new trains, was absorbed as part of the investment in new rolling stock.

Minutes

April 1997	New trains ordered. Decision taken at Gatwick Express to develop new identity.
Summer 1997	Meetings with design agencies to discuss project and establish 'chemistry'.
August 1997	Bamber Forsyth retained to develop identity.
October 1997	Proposition 'best of the train and the plane' signed off.

December 1997 Design developed and researched.

March 1998   Detailed design and application to all non-train items.

April 1998   Identity signed off by Board.

December 1999 New trains delivered.

July 2000   First trains in service.

APPENDIX 21.1

Office personalities

You can tell a lot from a company's headquarters. Intel's blue fortress in San Jose is about power and control. Oracle's shining towers on Redwood Shore are brash testimony to the showmanship of its founder, Larry Ellison. The scattered low-rise blocks at Microsoft's Redmond campus imply a laid-back informality, but the intense figures trotting along ordered paths suggest a restless insecurity.

IBM's new headquarters at Armonk in New York state is so discretely tucked into a valley that it cannot be seen until you are almost upon it. It politely curves in an S-shape around the trees and rocks that could have easily been blasted away. For a company that employs 270,000 people and earned revenues of nearly $80 billion last year, it is implausibly tiny. Inside, it is light, open-plan, discreetly high tech, and very, very calm. It is a stealth headquarters, the antithesis of the swaggering IBM buildings from before 'The Fall'.

The rebirth of IBM – Blue is the colour, *The Economist*, 6 June 1998

APPENDIX 21.2

O – What?

As the people behind Accenture and Consignia could tell you, branding a new company is never easy. But when the name has to have pan-European appeal, it's trickier still.

Enter Opodo, the newly unveiled moniker for the European travel portal set up by nine leading airlines, including British Airways. The brand was yesterday described in fluent Madison Avenue speak as 'personal, wise, refreshing, surprising...'

But the surprise came when the company's marketing director, Nicholas de Santis, declared with transparent pride that it 'doesn't mean anything in any language'. Observer's researches, however, uncovered the tragic tale of Ja Ja Opodo who set up a monopoly of trade in the small African kingdom he ruled towards the end of the nineteenth century.

King Ja Ja was deported by the British for failing to comply with the Empire's rules on free trade.

A sobering lesson for the newly launched travel portal which is under investigation by the European Commission to ensure that its airline owners are not in breach of Brussels' own conception of what constitutes free trade.

Financial Times Observer Column, 27 June 2001

Key points from Chapter 21:

1. Corporate identity can create competitive advantage.
2. Credibility has to be developed before raising visibility.
3. The corporate identity can raise visibility.
4. Attention to detail and research are vital.

FURTHER READING

Bernstein, D (1984) *Company Image and Reality: A Critique of Corporate Communications*, Holt, Rinehart & Winston, London

Hooker, S (1991) Applying psychology to market research: the theory of raised expectations, *Market Research Society Newsletter*, January

Jenkins, N (1991) *The Business of Image*, Kogan Page, London

Murphy, J (ed) (1987) *Branding: A Key Marketing Tool*, Macmillan, London

Nash and Zull Products Inc (1989) *1990 US Hall of Shame*, Universal Press Syndicate Co, Kansas City, KA

Olins, W (1989) *Corporate Identity: Making Business Strategy Visible Through Design*, Thames & Hudson, London

PRTV (1993) *Corporate Image Video*, PRTV Ltd, London

Valentine, V (1988) *Signs and Symbols* (survey), Market Research Society, London

Index